DUKE

Duke Ellington, London, 1958

DUKE

A Life of Duke Ellington

TERRY TEACHOUT

GOTHAM BOOKS

GOTHAM BOOKS
Published by the Penguin Group
Penguin Group (USA) Inc., 375 Hudson Street,
New York, New York 10014, USA

USA | Canada | UK | Ireland | Australia | New Zealand | India | South Africa | China
Penguin Books Ltd, Registered Offices: 80 Strand, London WC2R 0RL, England
For more information about the Penguin Group visit penguin.com.

LIBRARY OF CONGRESS CATALOGING-IN-PUBLICATION DATA
Teachout, Terry.
  Duke : a life of Duke Ellington / Terry Teachout.
  pages cm
  ISBN 978-1-592-40749-1
 1. Ellington, Duke, 1899-1974. 2. Jazz musicians—United States—Biography. I. Title.
  ML410.E44T38 2013
  781.65092–dc23
  [B]
  2013011138

Printed in the United States of America
10 9 8 7 6 5 4 3 2 1

Set in ITC Galliard   •   Designed by Elke Sigal

To Mrs. T, who was never in doubt

There is one very good thing to be said of posterity,
and this is that it turns a blind eye on the defects of greatness.

W. Somerset Maugham

—————————

We wear the mask that grins and lies.

Paul Laurence Dunbar

CONTENTS

"I WANT TO TELL AMERICA"

H E WAS THE most chronic of procrastinators, a man who never did today what he could put off until next month, or next year. He left letters unanswered, contracts unsigned, watches unworn, and longtime companions unwed, and the only thing harder than getting him out of bed in the afternoon was getting him to finish writing a new piece of music in time for the premiere. "I don't need time," he liked to say. "What I need is a deadline!" Nothing but an immovable deadline could spur Duke Ellington to decisive action, though once he set to work in earnest, it was with a speed and self-assurance that amazed all who beheld it. At the end of his life, he left behind some seventeen hundred–odd compositions, a number that is hard to square with the memories of his collaborators, who rarely failed at one time or another to be frustrated by his dilatory ways. That was fine with him. He knew what he needed in order to create, and as far as he was concerned, nothing and no one else mattered. "As long as something is unfinished," he told Louis Armstrong, "there's always that little feeling of insecurity. And a feeling of insecurity is absolutely necessary unless you're so rich that it doesn't matter." Few of his pronouncements can be taken at face value—he was never in the habit of telling anyone, even those who supposed themselves to be his friends, what he really thought—but this one has the ring of truth. "He wants life and music to be in a state of becoming," said the trumpeter Clark Terry, one of the many stars of the band that Ellington led from 1924 until his death a half century later. "He doesn't even like to write definitive endings to a piece."

Whether it was true or merely one of his rationalizations for doing whatever he wanted to do whenever he wanted to do it, Ellington lived by those words. Time and again he found himself bumping up against deadlines because of his reluctance to finish what he had started. More often than not his talent got him out of the holes he dug for himself, and when it didn't, he counted on his charm to see him through. "Duke drew people to him like flies to sugar," said Sonny Greer, one of his oldest friends and his drummer for three decades. He was well aware of how charismatic he was, and used his powers without scruple whenever he thought it necessary. Once in a while, though, he cut it too close for comfort, and in the frantic days and nights leading up to his Carnegie Hall debut on January 23, 1943, some of his colleagues began to wonder whether Harlem's Aristocrat of Jazz (as his publicists dubbed him) had finally outsmarted himself.

As early as 1930 Ellington was telling reporters of his plans to compose a piece of program music about the black experience. "My *African Suite*," he called it. "It will be in five parts, starting in Africa and ending with the history of the American Negro." Sometimes he described it as a multimovement instrumental work, sometimes as an opera, but either way he made it sound as if the ink were wet on the page, and his serpentine way with words never failed to hypnotize even the most suspicious of interviewers into assuming that the curtain was about to go up. In 1933 Hannen Swaffer, an English columnist, published an interview in which Ellington spoke of the unwritten work so evocatively that you could all but hear it playing in the background:

> *I am expressing in sound the old days in the jungle, the cruel journey across the sea and the despair of the landing, and then the days of slavery. I trace the growth of a new spiritual quality and then the days in Harlem and the cities of the [United] States. Then I try to go forward a thousand years. I seek to express the future when, emancipated and transformed, the Negro takes his place, a free being, among the peoples of the world.*

Swaffer was no friend of jazz, or of blacks—he had once compared Louis Armstrong to a gorilla—but he bought Ellington's story hook, line, and sinker. "All this was said with a quietness of dignity," he assured his readers. "I heard, almost, a whisper of prophecy."

Many more journalists would prove as willing to take Ellington at his oft-repeated word. That same year *Fortune* told its readers that he was writing "a suite in five parts . . . With this suite in his repertoire, Ellington may some day make his Carnegie Hall debut." In 1938 *Down Beat* reported that he had finished work on a full-length opera about "the history of the American Negro." The truth was less impressive. Not only had he written none of his *African Suite,* but he completed only three extended works of any kind prior to 1943, and the longest of them, *Reminiscing in Tempo,* ran for just twelve minutes, the length of the first movement of a symphony. Constant Lambert, the most perceptive of all the classically trained music critics to write about Ellington in the thirties, praised him as "the first jazz composer of distinction" and compared him to Ravel and Stravinsky, but he also acknowledged that Ellington was a "petit maître" whose best works were "written in what may be called ten-inch record form . . . Into this three and a half minutes he compresses the utmost, but beyond its limits he is inclined to fumble." Even if his *African Suite* was anything more than a fantasy, how could a petit-maître manage to pull such a work out of his hat? Instead he kept on carving one three-and-a-half-minute cameo after another, and the only sign that he wanted to do something grander was his insistence on telling credulous reporters that he had either done so or was about to.

That was Ellington's way. He talked not to explain himself but to conceal himself. Even Ruth, his adoring younger sister, said that he "definitely wasn't direct. He wasn't direct with anybody about anything." Yet he talked so fluently and impressively that nearly everyone believed him, save for those who had reason to know better. In one of his most frequently cited verbal arabesques, he claimed that "Harlem Air-Shaft," which he recorded in 1940, was a musical depiction of the sounds of black apartment life: "You hear fights, you smell dinner, you hear people making love. You hear intimate gossip floating down. You hear the radio. An air shaft is one great big loudspeaker." It's a splendidly quotable tale, so much so that one hates to point out that the composition now known as "Harlem Air-Shaft" started life as "Once Over Lightly," a title that has nothing to do with life in a Harlem apartment house. Ellington talked with similarly seductive fluency when luring women into bed, drawing on an endless supply of the come-on lines that a friend of his dubbed "crotch warmers," most of which appear on paper to be eye-rollingly florid ("I knew you were here because the whole studio was suddenly aglow with a turquoise radiance") but which carried the force of iron conviction when spoken in his fine-grained bass-baritone voice.

Ellington kept on talking about his soon-to-be-completed tone poem–opera–symphony–suite for as long as he could get away with it. Then, in December of 1942, he stopped talking and started writing, announcing that the centerpiece of his Carnegie Hall program would be the premiere of what he now called *Black, Brown and Beige: A Tone Parallel to the History of the American Negro.* The concert, which took place six weeks later, was a celebration of his twentieth anniversary as a bandleader, and there were those, Ellington among them, who thought it far past time for him to appear at the best-known concert hall in America. Benny Goodman, after all, had played Carnegie Hall in 1938, and though three of Ellington's top sidemen, Harry Carney, Johnny Hodges, and Cootie Williams, were featured at that concert, the humiliating fact was that the King of Swing had beaten Harlem's Aristocrat of Jazz to the punch. Ellington, who was invited to sit in on piano with his own men and Goodman's rhythm section, declined with thanks but came to the concert. "He was furious," said a friend who saw him there. "He was just livid."

The event brought Goodman reams of free publicity, not to mention vast amounts of highbrow réclame, a commodity that Ellington coveted fiercely. Irving Mills, the manager who was chiefly responsible for making him a celebrity, had gone to enormous trouble to promote him not merely as the leader of a black dance band but as a musical giant. The publicity manuals that Mills Artists Inc. sent out to the managers of the theaters and ballrooms that booked Duke Ellington and His Famous Orchestra explained that he was no ordinary jazzman:

> *Sell Ellington as a great artist, a musical genius whose unique style and individual theories of harmony have created a new music. . . . Ellington's genius as a composer, arranger and musician has won him the respect and admiration of such authorities as Percy Grainger, head of the department of music at the New York University; Basil Cameron, conductor of the Seattle Symphony Orchestra; Leopold Stokowski, famed conductor of the celebrated Philadelphia Orchestra; Paul Whiteman, whose name is synonymous with jazz, and many others.*

It was bold talk for a publicist, and it had the advantage of being true. No matter what Constant Lambert may have thought, Ellington was not the first jazz composer of distinction, but he was the first to write music that used the still-new medium of the big band with the same coloristic imagination brought by classical composers to their symphonic works. "You know, Stan Kenton can stand in front of a thousand fiddles and a thousand brass and make a dramatic gesture and every studio arranger can nod his head and say, 'Oh, yes, that's done like this,' " said André Previn, one of his best-informed admirers. "But Duke merely lifts his finger, three horns make a sound, and I don't know what it is!" Nor were his innovations limited to the field of timbre. What set him apart was not his virtuoso command of instrumental timbre, but *how* he used it. Mere arrangers took pop songs and dressed them up in new colors and harmonies, but Ellington, though he recorded his share of catchy hits, was better known for the works in which he used the language of jazz to say things that it had never said before. Previn compared him to Stravinsky and Prokofiev, Percy Grainger to Bach and Delius, Ralph Ellison to Ernest Hemingway. Within the tight confines of a single 78 side, he spun "tone parallels" (a phrase that he coined) to every imaginable human emotion. He and the nine hundred musicians who passed through his band sang of joy and loneliness, passion and despair, faith and hope. His compositions included musical portraits of pretty women, tap-dancing comedians, express trains, Shakespearean characters, and the unsung heroes of his long-despised race, and he made it sound as if writing them were simple: "I just watch people and observe life, and then I write about them."

It stood to reason that he should play Carnegie Hall, but Ellington claimed that Irving Mills had passed up an opportunity to book the band there in 1937, believing that the appearance wouldn't bring in enough revenue to justify its expense. It had rankled ever since that Mills let such an opportunity to sell him as a great artist slip through his fingers. While the band had since given full-evening concerts at UCLA, the City College of New York, and Colgate University, all were too far off the beaten path of publicity to attract the attention of the press. The time had come to even the score, and William Morris Jr., Ellington's new manager, meant to do the job right. "I want you to write a long work," he told his client, "and let's do it in Carnegie Hall."

～

The program that Ellington drew up opened with a new version of "Black and Tan Fantasy," the 1927 composition in which he blended together the growling gutbucket trumpet of Bubber Miley, a Victorian religious ballad, and the funeral march from Chopin's B-Flat Minor Piano Sonata, an exotic-sounding brew that put him on the map of early jazz. But most of the other numbers were written in or after 1940, the year in which the Ellington band reached the height of its collective creativity. "Ko-Ko," "Cotton Tail," "Jack the Bear," "A Portrait of Bert Williams": These were some of the now-classic pieces that he presented at Carnegie Hall, together with a half dozen others written by Mercer Ellington, his son, and Billy Strayhorn, a young composer-lyricist who joined the Ellington organization in 1939 and soon became his closest musical collaborator. The only tunes not by Ellington, Strayhorn, or Mercer were "The Star-Spangled Banner" and "Rose of the Rio Grande," a specialty number long identified with the trombonist Lawrence Brown, one of Ellington's most admired soloists. The band's other stars all took turns in the spotlight as well, with the creamy-sounding alto-saxophone playing of Johnny Hodges making an especially fetching impression in Strayhorn's "Day Dream." Still, there was no question about who was standing at center stage. Everyone knew that it was Duke Ellington's night to shine, and he knew it, too. Yet he had put off writing what was to be his crowning achievement until the last possible minute. He started work on *Black, Brown and Beige* in mid-December, and he was applying finishing touches to the forty-five-minute score on the day of the premiere.

Ellington began writing *Black, Brown and Beige* backstage at the State Theater in Hartford, Connecticut, where the band was sharing a bill with Frank Sinatra. Next came a string of dates in Connecticut, Rhode Island, Pennsylvania, Ohio, Michigan, Canada, and upstate New York, with Ellington working on the score along the way. The band returned to Harlem on January 15, then started to go over the still-incomplete piece at Manhattan's Nola Rehearsal Studio, then as now a popular midtown rehearsal space for jazz musicians. Howard Taubman, the music editor of *The New York Times* and a longtime fan, looked in on Ellington that week:

> *On the day of my visit to his apartment in Harlem he was still asleep at 1 P.M. He had worked all the previous night, knocking off at 9 A.M. Since the band had had a night off, Duke had spent it writing music for the Carnegie Hall concert. The piano was still in the corridor where it had been pushed so as not to disturb members of his family. Sheets of freshly written music were on the piano, under the telephone, in the living room. As we chatted, members of Ellington's band drifted in, and from the kitchen they could be heard humming parts of the new score and arguing over how to do it.*

On January 22, the night before the concert, the band gave a preview performance of the complete program at a high school in Rye, a suburb north of the city. Ellington's friend Edmund Anderson, who had come to the dress rehearsal the previous day, saw Johnny Hodges running through "Come Sunday," his solo spot in *Black, Brown and Beige,* "practically before the ink on the music sheets was dry." While Anderson was thrilled by what he heard, others were doubtful. According to Barry Ulanov, Ellington's first biographer, the consensus was that the new piece was "choppy" and hard to follow, perhaps in part because Ellington, who had yet to finish the score, was forced to rehearse it "piecemeal, section by section, sometimes in sequence, more often out of it." Only Don Redman, the composer-arranger who had been Ellington's opposite number in Fletcher Henderson's band of the twenties, begged to differ. "You're so wrong," he told the doubters. But Ellington himself was unhappy enough with "Beige," the last movement, to make a cut after the preview, dropping a win-the-war lyric ("We're black, brown and beige / But we're red, white and blue") that was to have been sung at Carnegie Hall.

The three thousand ticketholders who packed the sold-out hall the next night applauded as Ellington was presented with a plaque citing his "twenty years of laudable contribution to music." It bore thirty-two engraved signatures, including those of Stokowski, Marian Anderson, Count Basie, Cab Calloway, Aaron Copland, Benny Goodman, Earl Hines, Jerome Kern, Fritz Reiner, Paul Robeson, Artie Shaw, Max Steiner, Lawrence Tibbett, Kurt Weill, and Paul Whiteman, a veritable who's who of American music in 1943. The audience responded no less enthusiastically to *Black, Brown and Beige,* clapping after every solo. But a recording of the concert reveals Ellington to have been audibly nervous, introducing the piece without his customary sangfroid. Small wonder: He had never in his life attempted anything as challenging as *Black, Brown and Beige,* and he had not given himself enough time for second thoughts, much less a second draft.

Despite the haste in which it was written, the score was littered with his fingerprints. *Black, Brown and Beige* was a compendium of Ellington's musical language at its most advanced—now suavely lyrical, now earthily plainspoken, on occasion as dissonant as anything by Schoenberg or Bartók—as well as the embodiment of his feelings about what it meant to be black. At every stage in his career, he had written pieces illustrative of his belief that the black experience was a fit subject for a serious composer. Their titles chart the course of his racial pride: "Black Beauty," "Creole Rhapsody," "Echoes of the Jungle," "Harlem Speaks," "Sepia Panorama." In 1939 he told the readers of *Down Beat,* "Our aim has always been the development of an authentic Negro music . . . Our music is always intended to be definitely and purely racial." He felt the same way in 1943. "The Negro is not merely a singing and dancing wizard but a loyal American in spite of his social position," he said to Howard Taubman. "I want to tell America how the Negro feels about it."

What he had to say was more specific than was immediately evident to the audience, for he had chosen not to publish the scenario, much of it written in verse, on which *Black, Brown and Beige* was based. In it he declared his theme to be the untold story of a suffering people: "Buried in the dark, uneasy conscience of Man / Lies the bright and glorious Truth / About your heritage." At the end he made an even more suggestive proclamation about the nature of his own art:

> *And so, your song has stirred the souls*
> *Of men in strange and distant places*
> *The picture drawn by many hands*
> *For many eyes of many races.*
> *But did it ever speak to them*
> *Of what you really are?*

In Carnegie Hall he opted instead for mellifluous generalities, preferring to let the music speak for itself. It did so compellingly, if at times haltingly. *Black, Brown and Beige* was a patchwork, a not-quite-unified composition in which stretches of sustained musical argument were linked by transitional passages that sounded as though they'd been lifted from the score of a Broadway musical. It was clear that the last movement had been written too hurriedly, for its sections barely hung together. (One of them was a 1942 composition by Strayhorn called "Symphonette-Rhythmique" that Ellington renamed "Sugar Hill Penthouse" and shoehorned into the middle of "Beige" without bothering to give credit to his silent partner, a fact that did not become known until six decades later.) Yet *Black, Brown and Beige* was still an astonishing advance on the dance-oriented music of the other big bands of the Swing Era, so much so that Ellington's own musicians found it hard to grasp. To take it in at a single hearing, much less to render fair judgment on what its composer had tried to do, was impossible, but every critic in town did his best, with results that ranged from reasonably perceptive to impenetrably dense.

The most favorable notice appeared in *Time*, which described *Black, Brown and Beige* as "one of the longest (45 minutes) and most ambitious pieces of tone painting ever attempted in jazz. Flavored with everything from Stravinskian dissonance to three-four time, it often seemed too ambitious.

But there were stages of the emulsion that might appeal to any musician." *The New York Times* praised the band but was evasive about the piece: "It had many exciting passages, but it was in the shorter works like 'Rockin' in Rhythm' and the familiar 'Mood Indigo' that the leader seemed most completely himself." The other reviews, written by critics who normally covered classical music rather than jazz—the newspapers of New York had yet to start hiring jazz critics in 1943—were rougher. "It hardly ever succeeds . . . because such a form of composition is entirely out of Ellington's ken," Douglas Watt wrote in the *Daily News.* "There is almost no continuity to the piece, filled with false climaxes." Robert Bagar, who covered the concert for the *World-Telegram,* said that *Black, Brown and Beige* was not "an in toto symphonic creation" but "a series of brief, air-tight compositions, all prettily tied together by modulatory bridges . . . Mr. Ellington can make some two dozen brief, air-tight compositions out of *Black, Brown and Beige.* He should." Henry Simon of *PM* criticized "Black" along similar lines, saying that it "all but falls apart into so many separate pieces," though he admitted to being impressed with "Brown" and felt that the work as a whole "showed . . . how well and how far Mr. Ellington has emancipated himself from the straight-jacket [*sic*] of jazz formulas."

Paul Bowles's review in the *New York Herald Tribune* was unsparing, and his attack stung all the more because he was, unlike his colleagues, a classical composer of note:

> It was formless and meaningless. In spite of Mr. Ellington's ideological comments before each "movement," nothing emerged but a gaudy potpourri of tutti dance passages and solo virtuoso work. (The dance parts used some pretty corny riffs, too.) There were countless unprovoked modulations, a passage in 5/4, paraphrases on well-known tunes that were as trite as the tunes themselves, and recurrent climaxes that impeded the piece's progress.

Most of the jazz press put a happier face on the occasion. "Duke Kills Carnegie Cats! 'Tone Parallel,' Famed Soloists Slick, Click; Carnegie Kicked," read the *Variety*-style headline over *Metronome*'s story about the concert, which was accompanied by a testy editorial called "Reactionary Reviewers" that dismissed the classical critics as "condescending" and "stupid." Mike Levin of *Down Beat* struck a similar note in his review, but the headline hinted at his own reservations: "Duke Fuses Classical and Jazz! Stuff Is There . . . Needing Development to Attain New Art Form." And there were plenty of dissenters, the most prominent of whom was John Hammond, a record producer–critic and a well-known skeptic when it came to the music of Duke Ellington, with whom he had had a public falling-out four years earlier. Now Hammond wrote a piece called "Is the Duke Deserting Jazz?" in which he claimed that Ellington had "alienated a good part of his dancing public . . . by becoming more complex he has robbed jazz of most of its basic virtues and lost contact with his audience." He had said much the same thing about *Reminiscing in Tempo*, claiming in addition that Ellington's biggest work prior to *Black, Brown and Beige* was "formless and shallow."

Ellington's public reaction to the reviews was unforthcoming: "Well, I guess they didn't dig it." Three decades later he described the Carnegie Hall concert as an "overwhelming success" in *Music Is My Mistress,* the autobiography in which he and Stanley Dance, his amanuensis, recounted his life and triumphs in language so circumlocutory that even his admirers found it hard to swallow. But at the time he had been worried about the likely response to *Black, Brown and Beige,* confessing his qualms to Helen Oakley in a preview of the concert that ran in *Down Beat.* He told her that he would have preferred to debut the work in Europe, believing as he did that European jazz fans were more receptive to "what [he was] attempting to do," adding that it would be "a great disappointment to him and, he considers, a deterrent to the ambition of all progressing American composers" if "a sincere interest and an intellectual discernment are not notably factors of the New York audience reaction."

To have unbent so far as to say such things to a journalist—even one who, like Oakley, was a friend—was both uncharacteristic of Ellington and indicative of his anxieties. Still more revealing was what happened next. The band repeated the Carnegie Hall program five days later at Boston's Symphony Hall, and again the following month in Cleveland. The latter performance was the last time that Ellington played *Black, Brown and Beige* in its entirety. In 1945 he recorded eighteen minutes of excerpts for Victor, and until his death he performed snippets from the complete work, even recording a revised version of "Black" for Columbia in 1958. But never again did he permit the critics to hear his magnum opus from beginning to end. Too proud to expose himself a second time to their wrath, he preferred to leave it on the shelf.

∾

If *Black, Brown and Beige* mattered so much to Ellington, then why did he wait so long to start writing it? Because he had always worked that way, and always would. At times his disregard of the clock crossed the line into irresponsibility, as Norman Granz learned in 1957 when he recorded an album that teamed the composer and his band with Ella Fitzgerald. Ellington had agreed to write new arrangements of his best-remembered tunes, but he strolled into the studio all but empty-handed, forcing Granz to cobble together an album out of existing charts that were altered on the spot to accommodate Fitzgerald's vocals:

> *We planned far in advance, but in the end Duke failed to do a single arrangement. Ella had to use the band's regular arrangements. She'd do a vocal where an instrumental chorus would normally go. . . . Duke would ask Ella what key she was in and he would have to transpose and there would be a lot of furious writing to change the key. Then Ella would try and fit in and the band would get swept along by its own memories of just how it ought to play . . . Really, at one point she became so nervous, almost hysterical, that she began to cry. Duke went over to her and said, "Now, baby," in his most gentle tones. "Don't worry, it'll all turn out fine."*

While *Ella Fitzgerald Sings the Duke Ellington Song Book* was an extreme case, it was far from atypical. Ellington composed as he lived, on the road and on the fly. He wrote his pieces in hotel rooms, Pullman cars, and chartered buses, then rehearsed them in the recording studio the next afternoon or on the bandstand the same night. He had little choice but to do so, for he was a professional wanderer who traveled directly from gig to gig, returning to his New York apartment, he said, only to pick up his mail. It would no more have occurred to him to take time off to polish a composition than to go on a monthlong vacation. Even if he had wanted to take a sabbatical to work on *Black, Brown and Beige,* the band's touring schedule would have precluded it.

"I work and I write. And that's it," Ellington said. "My reward is hearing what I've done, and unlike most composers, I can hear it immediately. That's why I keep these expensive gentlemen with me." But maintaining a touring orchestra was for him not a luxury but a necessity. The band was his musical laboratory, the great good place where he experimented with new ideas, and he was incapable of functioning as a composer without its constant presence. A largely self-taught musician, he had never acquired the conservatory-bred facility that would have allowed him to write out a piece in his studio, bring it to rehearsal, and have his sidemen read it down note for note. He was himself a poor sight reader, as were some of his best-known soloists. "You couldn't give him a piano part and say, 'Play this piano part,'" recalled Juan Tizol, his valve trombonist. "He was not that type of player. He couldn't play it." Throughout his career he relied on staff copyists (of whom Tizol was the first) who could decode his quirky musical shorthand, transforming it into playable instrumental parts that were then performed by the "expensive gentlemen" for whom they had been handcrafted, a motley gaggle of ever-feuding trouble-makers whose antics he viewed with wry resignation and a touch of pride: "There's no attitude, no discipline, nothing. . . . Outrageous things happen, and then they come back and blow their ass off, play like angels, and I forget about it." Even the music on their stands bore the nicknames by which they were known (Cootie, Rab, Tricky) rather than the names of the instruments that they played.

What Ellington sought and got from his "accumulation of personalities" was a loose, festive ensemble sound far removed from the clean precision of Benny Goodman's band. He had no interest in the smoothly blended play-ing that leaders like Goodman, Jimmie Lunceford, and Artie Shaw de-manded from their groups. He preferred to hire musicians with homemade techniques that were different to the point of apparent incompatibility, then juxtapose their idiosyncratic sounds as a pointillist painter might place dots of red and green side by side on his canvas, finding inspiration in their tech-nical limitations ("With a musician who plays the full compass of his instru-ment as fast or as slow as possible, there seems, paradoxically, less opportunity to create"). That is why his charts never sound quite right when performed by other groups, however accomplished the individual players may be. It is also why a keen-eared virtuoso like Jack Teagarden, the greatest jazz trom-bonist of his generation, found it impossible to enjoy the Ellington band. "I never did like anything Ellington ever did," he said. "He never had a band all in tune, always had a bad tone quality and bad blend." What Teagarden meant, whether he knew it or not, was that the band had an *unconventional* tone quality, one that had little in common with received ideas about how a big band ought to sound. Asked why he hired Al Hibbler when he already had a singer on the payroll, Ellington replied, "My ear makes my decision." To him, no other ear mattered.

Billy Strayhorn, who saw Ellington's working methods up close and un-derstood them best, gave them a name in a 1952 article about his mentor: "Ellington plays the piano, but his real instrument is the band. Each member of his band is to him a distinctive tone color and set of emotions, which he mixes with others equally distinctive to produce a third thing, which I call the Ellington Effect." Sometimes he worked "on" his players as a choreographer makes a ballet "on" his dancers, passing out or dictating scraps of music, then shaping and reshaping them on the spot into a piece that would later be reduced to written form. Even a work that had already been notated was subject in the heat of the moment to total transformation motivated solely by the whim of the composer. The goal, he explained, was "to mold the music around the man," and the men around whom his music was so tightly molded rarely sounded more themselves than when they were playing it.

The cornetist Rex Stewart, who spent eleven years with Ellington, never forgot the experience of seeing the Ellington Effect in full flower at a rehearsal in the forties:

> *I recall one occasion when he'd jotted some notes for the saxophones (Toby [Otto] Hardwick, Harry Carney, Ben Webster, and Barney Bigard) and each was given a part, but there was nothing for Johnny Hodges. Duke had the saxes run the sequence down twice, while Johnny sat nonchalantly smoking. Then, Duke called to Hodges, "Hey, Rabbit, give me a long slow glissando against that progression. Yeah! That's it!" Next he said to Cootie Williams, "Hey, Coots, you come in on the second bar, in a subtle manner growling softly like a hungry little lion cub that wants his dinner but can't find his mother. Try that, okay?" Following that, he'd say, "Deacon," (how Lawrence Brown hated that nickname) "you are cast in the role of the sun beating down on the scene. What kind of a sound do you feel that could be? You don't know? Well, try a high B-flat in a felt hat, play it legato and sustain it for eight bars. Come on, let's all hit this together," and that's the way things went—sometimes.*

Not only was Ellington inspired by the sounds and styles of his musicians, but he plucked bits and pieces from their solos and wove them into his compositions. Some of his most popular songs were spun out of melodic fragments that he gleaned from his close listening on the bandstand each night. "He could hear a guy play something and take a pencil and scribble a little thing," the pianist Jimmy Rowles said. "The next night there would be an arrangement of that thing the guy played. And nobody knew where it came from." This symbiotic relationship was important to Ellington's success as a popular songwriter, since his prodigal gifts did not include the lucrative ability to casually toss off easily hummable tunes. He had to work at it, and sometimes he needed a little help. "More than once," Rex Stewart recalled, "a lick which started out as a rhythmic background for a solo or a response to another lick eventually became a hit record, once Duke's fertile imagination took over and provided the proper framework." He took it for granted that such joint creations were his sole property, but if payment was unavoidable, he tried when possible to dole out modest flat fees rather than share with his musicians the publishing rights to (and royalties from) the pieces that he based on their "licks." It was as much a matter of vanity as money, for Ellington preferred for the public to think that he did it all by himself. "It wasn't *our* thing any longer," Hardwick said when he returned to the band in 1932 after a four-year absence. "It had become Ellington's alone. . . . Ten years ago it was '*We* do it this way,' and '*We* wrote that.' Now the we was *royal.*"

Could he have composed in a more traditional manner? Undoubtedly, if he'd applied himself to learning how to do so—and *Black, Brown and Beige* might well have been architecturally stronger had he tried. But Ellington knew little of the symphonic literature when he wrote *Black, Brown and Beige*, nor was he inclined to press his talent into other men's molds, instructive though the experience might have been. He insisted that *Black, Brown and Beige* was not an attempt to write a "jazz symphony": "To attempt to elevate the status of the jazz musician by forcing the level of his best work into comparisons with classical music is to deny him his rightful share of originality. . . . Ninety-nine per cent of the jazz people aren't interested in symphony techniques at all." In his case this was almost certainly true, though it fails to explain why he felt the need to write a forty-five-minute piece and perform it in Carnegie Hall, or to devote much of the second half of his career to composing a long series of jazz suites and other extended works, some scored for symphony orchestra (albeit by other hands). Most of the critics found them pretentious, but Ellington continued to turn out suites on a near-annual basis, and his unshakable devotion to the form caused some cynics to wonder whether he was trying to impress the classical musicians whose techniques he disdained.

If that was what he hoped to do, then he had little choice but to do it his way. Ellington's unorthodox methods evolved bit by bit and year by year, and by the time that he discovered their limitations, he had traveled too far down his own road to change course without a struggle. It was well within his power to familiarize himself with the structural techniques of the great classical composers, to learn how to write for string sections instead of hiring orchestrators, even to figure out how to write songs that drove the plot of a musical comedy rather than sounding as though they'd been written without prior knowledge of the script. (It was one of his biggest disappointments that he never succeeded in bringing a hit show to Broadway.) But accomplishing any of these goals would have taken more time than he cared to spare, and to do so he would have had to dismantle, either temporarily or permanently, the jury-rigged system that allowed him to keep his handpicked band on the road all the year round, playing his music as soon as he wrote it and pleasing paying audiences throughout the world.

So he chose to keep on being Duke Ellington, racing from town to town and sleeping with woman after woman, shoveling his songwriting royalties into the till in order to pay his expensive gentlemen salaries big enough to keep them riding on the band bus, cranking out shapeless suites whose inspiration varied widely, even randomly, from movement to movement, and passing the work of others off as his own. And—always—being a genius, a titan of modern music who to the end of his life could conjure high art out of thin air.

Though he carried himself like a prince of the realm, he was the son of a butler and the grandson of a slave. Washington, where Edward Kennedy Ellington was born in 1899, was one of America's most segregated cities, but it also had a black middle class that was proud and self-aware. Ellington's parents belonged to it, and their only son, a high school dropout whose regal demeanor belied his poor grades and seeming lack of interest in music, went out of his way to acquire its manners. For all his polish, it was his artistry, not his personality, that was the source of his enduring appeal. But it was the personality that made white people who might not otherwise have done so give him a second glance, and in time it opened doors of opportunity through which few other blacks had been allowed to pass.

Ellington's surface qualities were exploited to the hilt by Irving Mills. "We wanted Duke to be recognized as someone more important," Mills told an interviewer in 1984. By this he meant that the best way to position his client in a market full of talented black bandleaders was to present him to the world as a different kind of black man, fine-spoken and expensively tailored, a fellow whom broad-minded white folks could imagine introducing to their friends, even if they might not care to bring him home to meet their wives. Accordingly, Mills's advertising manual stressed Ellington's presentability as much as his talent: "He is as genial as he is intelligent, always creates a good impression upon newspaper people with whom he comes in contact and invariably supplies them with good copy for their stories." Ellington himself was happy to play the game, for he saw his public image as a contribution to the welfare of his people. "Every time you walk out [on] the street and you're exposed to a white citizen, you know," he said, "you're acting in behalf of the race." That was why he never let his guard down: He knew that there would always be somebody looking.

A different kind of black man: With Rex Stewart and the band, Philadelphia, 1939. Ellington's immaculately polished onstage appearance was one of countless manifestations of his lifelong resolve to "act in behalf of the race"

Over time Mills's strategy paid off beyond either man's wildest dreams. Long before Ellington died in 1974, he had become, after Louis Armstrong, jazz's biggest celebrity, as well as the first jazz musician to be widely hailed as an artist of consequence—and not just by his fellow jazzmen, but also by such distinguished classical musicians as Constant Lambert, Aaron Copland, and Percy Grainger. Their praise gave his work a cultural legitimacy at which no posterity-conscious black artist would have been inclined to turn up his nose. Yet he was, like Armstrong, a popular entertainer whose music was meant to please a mass audience. Long before the Swing Era, his band was seen in films and heard on network radio, and long after most of the other bandleaders who followed him into the limelight faded into obscurity, Ellington continued to perform on network TV and girdle the globe, playing "Sophisticated Lady," "Mood Indigo," "Solitude," "I Let a Song Go Out of My Heart," and the other hits that had made him famous (if never rich). Twelve thousand people came to his funeral at the Cathedral Church of St.

John the Divine in New York City, his adopted hometown and the place that he loved best. By then his baggy eyes and sardonic flattery were almost as familiar to the mourners as his music.

Underneath his soigné exterior, Ellington was a self-centered hedonist who lived a nomadic existence in which everything was subordinated to his art—and, insofar as possible, his pleasure. John Houseman, who worked with him on *Beggar's Holiday*, his first Broadway show, was fascinated by his way of life, though he mistook it for passivity:

> *At the time I worked with him the Duke had abandoned all attempts to organize his own life. Between late-night engagements with his band, concerts, recordings, interviews, composing and other activities he had turned over the scheduling of his days and nights to his wife, his manager and other associates. They woke him up when it was time, fed him, laid out the right clothes for him, transported and delivered him on time for whatever engagement he was committed to, picked him up, changed his clothes, delivered him once more, fed him again and finally put him to bed. In this way, he explained, by ceasing to concern himself with time and space, he was able to preserve his energy and his sanity.*

What Houseman did not see was that Ellington sought to exert the maximum possible amount of control over everyone in his life—by stealth. "What you need to do is wake up after two o'clock, make phone calls, but don't move an inch," he told Mercer Ellington. "Just lie flat on your back and phone, and tell everybody everything that has to be done, and lay all your plans without going out anywhere. . . . When you come downstairs you'll have prepared your day, and you'll be The Greatest!" After he died, Mercer found a handwritten note among his father's papers in which Ellington summed himself up in three lapidary sentences: "No problem. I'm easy to please. I just want to have everybody in the palm of my hand."

His selfishness was unswerving, though it did not exclude benevolence, if only on his own terms. "Ellington is the most complex and paradoxical individual that I've ever known . . . a combination of Sir Galahad, Scrooge, Don Quixote, and God knows what other saints and sinners that were apt to pop out of his ever-changing personality," said Rex Stewart. He was at once deeply (if superstitiously) religious and a tireless philanderer who, in the words of an admiring friend, had the sexual appetite of "a romping, stomping alley cat." He pretended to be a devoted family man for the benefit of the ever-vigilant press, he deserted Edna, his first and only wife, later settling into a long-term relationship with a Cotton Club showgirl whom he chose not to marry (he never divorced Edna) and on whom he cheated as often as he liked.

He was careful to keep his love life out of the papers, just as he tried never to show his vulnerability to anyone who might take advantage of it—but vulnerable he was, and would always be. While he believed that his music was (to use the phrase with which he described his favorite artists) "beyond category," he was painfully conscious of the racial slights that beset him throughout his life, even after he became a star. He was enraged when he learned that he had been passed over for a Pulitzer Prize in 1965. "That night I saw him, he was furious, he was so angry," Nat Hentoff recalled. "He said, 'That's another example of what it's like to be black. They think European music, classical music is the only criterion for art.'" It says much about Ellington that though he knew better than to take to heart the opinion of a board of musically uninformed newspapermen, he still longed for a Pulitzer, the ultimate token of establishment approval, and was devastated when he failed to get it.

None of it showed. The rage, the humiliation, the unbridled sensuality: All were kept far from prying eyes. His fans saw only what he wished them to see, and nothing more. So did his colleagues. "I think all the musicians should get together one certain day and get down on their knees and thank Duke," said Miles Davis. Yet to Ellington's own musicians, he was a riddle without an answer, an unknowable man who hid behind a high wall of ornate utterances and flowery compliments that grew higher as he grew older. And while most of his sidemen admired his artistry without reservation, many of them also believed him to be unscrupulous and manipulative. On occasion one of them would chafe at his high-handedness and give notice. Even Johnny Hodges and Billy Strayhorn, the band's two seemingly indispensable members, lost patience with him in the fifties and chose to wander for a time in the wilderness. But the wanderers (Hodges and Strayhorn included) usually returned to the fold sooner or later, knowing that the preternaturally sensitive settings that he created for his players made them sound better than they could ever have dreamed of sounding on their own. They were stuck with him and he with them, no matter how badly they behaved—and a few of them behaved badly enough to land in jail.

Yet Ellington almost never fired anyone, having discovered the secret of making unwanted players depart of their own accord before he was forced to cut them loose. A rare exception was the bassist Charles Mingus, who claimed to have goaded Juan Tizol into pulling a knife and chasing him off the bandstand, thus triggering his own dismissal. Mingus set down Ellington's

Behind closed doors: Composing at the Dorchester, his favorite London hotel, in 1963. Unposed offstage photos of Ellington are comparatively rare. He went out of his way to shape his public image to his liking—and to keep his private life out of the papers

farewell speech in his autobiography, and even if he embroidered it, as he surely did, you can hear the voice of the master in every petit-point sentence:

> *"Now, Charles," he says, looking amused, putting Cartier links into the cuffs of his beautiful handmade shirt, "you could have forewarned me—you left me out of the act entirely! At least you could have let me cue in a few chords as you ran through that Nijinsky routine. . . . When you exited after that I thought, 'That man's really afraid of Juan's knife and at the speed he's going he's probably home in bed by now.' But no, back you came through the same door with your bass still intact. For a moment I was hopeful you'd decided to sit down and play but instead you slashed Juan's chair in two with a fire axe! Really, Charles, that's destructive. Everybody knows Juan has a knife but nobody ever took it seriously—he likes to pull it out and show it to people, you understand. So I'm afraid, Charles—I've never fired anybody—you'll have to quit*

my band. I don't need any new problems. Juan's an old problem, I can cope with that, but you seem to have a whole bag of new tricks. I must ask you to be kind enough to give me your notice, Mingus."

The charming way he says it, it's like he's paying you a compliment. Feeling honored, you shake hands and resign.

If it wasn't true, it should have been. With Ellington, though, the truth was usually more than good enough, and the fact that so little of it can be found in *Music Is My Mistress* is frustrating. He of all people should have left behind a frank memoir, one in which he told the story of how a somewhat better-than-average stride pianist largely devoid of formal musical training managed to turn himself into a great composer—for that is what he was, and why he matters to us today.

In 1944 a journalist dubbed Ellington "the hot Bach," a comparison that is likely to have vexed him. A decade earlier he had claimed that "you can't stay in the European conservatory and play the negro music." He insisted that his own achievement was unique unto itself, so much so that he refused to call his music jazz. "I don't write jazz," he said. "I write Negro folk music." He was wrong: His music is one of the cornerstones of jazz. But he was right about the singularity of his music, just as he himself was as singular as a human being can be, an improbably gaudy bird of paradise who spoke at least one undeniable truth in the self-interview that ends his autobiography:

Q. Can you keep from writing music? Do you write in spite of yourself?

A. I don't know how strong the chains, cells, and bars are. I've never tried to escape.

1

"I JUST COULDN'T BE SHACKLED"

Fortunate Son, 1899–1917

WASHINGTON IS A theme park of power, a city to which fifteen million American tourists travel each year, there to gaze upon the marble monuments that enshrine their past and foreshadow their future. Few go looking for art, though no American city has more museums, and fewer still think of the nation's capital as a center of jazz, though it's said that before 1920 Washington was home to more nightclubs than Harlem. But even if that boast smacks of boosterism, it suggests the vitality to which there is ample testimony from those who saw it for themselves. And while only a handful of jazz greats grew up in Washington, one of them was Duke Ellington, who was born in a neighborhood whose name now evokes the black history that he would study in its schools as a boy and make for himself as an adult.

Robert Gould Shaw was the white colonel who commanded the otherwise all-black Fifty-Fourth Regiment at whose head he fell in 1863. Though a century went by before the creation of the Shaw urban renewal area in Washington's northwest quadrant gave a new name to its principal black neighborhood, the exploits of the Fifty-Fourth and its martyred leader (which would be memorialized by Augustus Saint-Gaudens and Stanford White in Boston's Shaw Memorial and, later, in the film *Glory*) would have been known to Ellington in his youth. The all-black schools that he attended made a point of teaching their charges such things. Late in life Ellington spoke of how R. A. Boston, his eighth-grade English teacher, had "spent as much time in preaching race pride as she did in teaching English," explaining to her students that "everywhere you go . . . your responsibility is to command respect for the race."

By 1900 Washington was home to eighty-seven thousand blacks, a third of the city's population. While the poorest of them lived on the southwest side of town, most of Washington's other blacks clustered in the vicinity of U Street, which runs through the center of Shaw. Some were professionals— doctors, nurses, lawyers, teachers, preachers—and a fair number worked for the federal government. A handful taught at nearby Howard University, America's most prestigious black college, and others at the Preparatory High School for Colored Youth, the country's first public high school for blacks, which was later renamed after Paul Laurence Dunbar, the black poet who worked for a time at the Library of Congress. Together they comprised the core of the city's black middle class, a group of Washingtonians as proud of their respectability as they were of their shared history. While they flocked to the fifteen-hundred-seat Howard Theatre, the city's first black-only theater, to see traveling productions of Broadway shows like *Shuffle Along* and musical groups like James Reese Europe's Clef Club Orchestra and Will Marion Cook's Southern Syncopated Orchestra, many preferred *The Evolution of the Negro in Picture, Song, and Story* and the other race-oriented community pageants that were also mounted there. The churchgoers among them regarded ragtime and jazz as disreputable to the point of criminality, preferring to partake of the more decorous fare that was readily available. Glee clubs and choral societies, small orchestras and chamber ensembles, even a short-lived opera company: All could be found in the neighborhood at one time or another.

The goal of these men and women was to lift up their race through economic and cultural self-improvement to the point where whites could no longer ignore their achievements. Booker T. Washington would have approved of their plan wholeheartedly, and most of those who write about black life in turn-of-the-century Washington make a point of mentioning what he said about the city in *Up from Slavery:*

> *During the time I was a student at Washington the city was crowded with coloured people, many of whom had recently come from the South. A large proportion of these people had been drawn to Washington be-*

cause they felt that they could lead a life of ease there. Others had se-
cured minor government positions, and still another large class was
there in the hope of securing Federal positions. A number of coloured
men—some of them very strong and brilliant—were in the House of
Representatives at that time . . . Then, too, they knew that at all times
they could have the protection of the law in the District of Columbia.
The public schools in Washington for coloured people were better then
than they were elsewhere.

But that was in 1878, a year after the close of the era of Reconstruction that had come in the wake of the Civil War. Soon the yoke of domination was set in place once more. George White, the last black congressman of the post-Reconstruction era, went back home to North Carolina in 1901, shortly after the Southern states disenfranchised their black citizens, and not until 1972 would a state that had once been part of the Confederacy send another black to Congress. Those were the days when books with titles like *The Negro a Beast* and *The Passing of the Great Race* were snapped up by white readers who learned from them that blacks were not only genetically inferior to whites but were breeding so rapidly that Western civilization was at risk. In 1913 Woodrow Wilson, the first Southern-born politician to be elected president since Reconstruction, segregated the federal bureaucracy by administrative fiat, thereby delivering a brutal blow to the fortunes of the city's middle-class blacks. "I have recently spent several days in Washington," Booker T. Washington wrote to a colleague shortly afterward, "and I have never seen the colored people so discouraged and bitter as they are at the present time."

The blacks of U Street, demoralized though they were by Wilson's actions, kept on striving, but their white neighbors took little note of their efforts. A historian of race relations in Washington later described the ghetto in which they lived as "a secret city all but unknown to the white world round about . . . white citizens of the District of Columbia manifestly were acquainted with only the most obvious facts about how free Negroes lived and knew almost nothing about what they thought." Neither the well-to-do professionals who owned Victorian row houses nor the laborers who rented tumbledown shacks in the alleys and side streets were thought worthy of coverage by the city's newspapers, which ignored anything that happened there short of actual violence.

Today that section of town, transformed almost beyond recognition by gentrification, is an integrated neighborhood where condos and renovated row houses change hands for six-figure sums—and where many aging black residents who grew up there can no longer afford to live. A *New York Times* reporter who visited U Street in 2006 described it as "the newest and hottest place in town for getting out on weekends after dark."* But when Duke Ellington was a boy and for long afterward, it was the only place in town where blacks could buy a house, see a movie, eat in a restaurant, rent a hotel room, attend a public school, or shop in a department store. Even the pet cemeteries maintained a color bar. In a 1948 report on racial segregation in Washington, the owner of a dog cemetery explained that "he assumed the dogs would not object, but he was afraid his white customers would."

Behind the invisible walls that separated them from the rest of Washington, better-off blacks salved their pride by erecting their own walls of disdain. They could never escape the daily shame of segregation, but they held their heads as high as they could, high enough to look down their noses at their less successful neighbors. "I could play the dances," Sonny Greer said, "but I couldn't mingle with all the highfalutin doctors and lawyers and all the fancy chicks from the university." Langston Hughes, who lived in Washington in the twenties, was disgusted by their snobbery: "So many pompous gentlemen never before did I meet. Nor so many ladies with chests swelled like pouter-pigeons whose mouths uttered formal sentences in frightfully correct English." He was disgusted, too, by the way that the city's light-skinned blacks treated "the usually darker (although not always poorer) people who work with their hands," taking scathing note of how "several of the light young ladies [he] knew were not above passing a dark classmate or acquaintance with only the coolest of nods" and "apologies were made by the young men for the less than coffee-and-cream ladies they happened to know." Such intraracial prejudice was (and is) the dirty little secret of America's black middle class, and jazzmen of Ellington's generation were well aware of its existence. The New Orleans bassist Pops Foster minced no words about it: "The worst Jim Crow around New Orleans was what the colored did to themselves. . . . The lighter you were the better they thought you were."

But there was no way for Washington's middle-class blacks to ignore their dark-skinned neighbors, try though they might, since both classes were packed into one and a half square miles of crowded city streets. The lives of college professors and (in Hughes's words) "the ordinary Negroes . . . folks with practically no family tree at all, folks who draw no color line between

---

* One of the neighborhood's landmarks is a slickly designed eight-story luxury apartment house called the Ellington whose website offers potential occupants "a level of living in sync with the vitality of U."

mulattoes and deep dark-browns" were inescapably intertwined, and an educated black who, like Hughes, felt more at ease among the "ordinary Negroes" who "played the blues, ate watermelon, barbecue, and fish sandwiches,
shot pool, told tall tales, looked at the dome of the Capitol and laughed out
loud" was never more than a stone's throw from the buzzing street life of
black Washington.

Nowadays it's harder to see that both sides of this cultural coin have a like
claim on our attention, since the popular culture of Hughes's "ordinary Negroes" long ago prevailed over the genteel culture of U Street's citizens. To
listen to the first recording of "Swing Low, Sweet Chariot," made in 1909 by
the Fisk Jubilee Quartet, whose members hailed from Nashville's all-black
Fisk University, is to be startled by its staidness. You might almost be hearing
four gentlemen in high-button shoes warbling close-harmony hymns in the
parlor. How to explain their near-Victorian tone? The answer is that the quartet consisted of university men, aspiring members of the middle class. Indeed,
the mere fact that they were singing spirituals (instead of, say, part-songs by
Brahms) was enough to make some of their fellow students look askance at
them. In 1909 spirituals were still widely viewed in the black community, and
in Fisk's own all-classical music department, as quaint relics of the bad old
days of slavery. The Jubilee Quartet's singing of "Swing Low, Sweet Chariot"
is polished to a degree that sounds "wrong" to postmodern ears—but does
that make it less authentic? In 1983 a surviving member of the quartet told an
interviewer that the group "interpreted [spirituals] as the slaves did . . . we
were closer to slavery and we got a deeper, an in-depth feeling of that music."

All of which is another way of saying that black life in turn-of-the-
century America was far more complicated than it looks from a distance, and
that the politer black musical styles of the period were as "authentic" as the
dance-based working-class music that today's listeners esteem. So, too, do
the ambitions of the middle-class blacks of U Street (if not their childish bigotry) deserve to be taken seriously. Even at their most affected, they were
trying to live decent lives and make a better world for their children and
grandchildren, some of whom, Duke Ellington among them, would go on
to do things of which they could only dream.

∾

What did Ellington think of the city of his childhood and youth? In old age
he wrote of it with dewy-eyed affection. Washington, he said, was good to
him—but he left it as soon as he could, never again to look back save through
the comforting haze of nostalgia.

Here as always, one must read between the lines of *Music Is My Mistress* to get anything useful out of it. On occasion Ellington let slip a few indiscreet words about the realities of life in Washington, admitting that the black community there was divided into "castes" and that "if you decided to mix carelessly with another you would be told that one just did not do that sort of thing." What he took greater care not to say was that his own parents belonged to the in-between caste that came to be known as the black bourgeoisie. It's impossible to understand the man whom Ellington became without understanding this fact and its implications, yet he did his best to keep anyone from knowing the whole truth about his young years. Throughout his life he spoke warmly of James Edward Ellington (always known as "J.E." or "Uncle Ed") and Daisy Kennedy Ellington, and his praise was fulsome to a fault. What he said has mostly been taken as gospel truth, but there was more—and less—to J.E. and Daisy than their loyal son admitted. While he was more inclined to prettify than lie outright, the result was the same: The Ellingtons of *Music Is My Mistress* are candy-coated caricatures whose goodness beggars belief. The first step in understanding their son is to scrub away the sugar and see his parents as they were.

J.E. was born in North Carolina in 1879 and moved to Washington around 1890. He entered the service of Dr. Middleton F. Cuthbert, whom Ellington described as "rather prominent socially," at some point between 1894 and 1898, eventually becoming Dr. Cuthbert's butler. The two men seem to have been on friendly terms: Barry Ulanov, who interviewed Ellington at length for his 1946 biography, described J.E. as the doctor's "confidant and very close friend." Not having gotten beyond grade school, he educated himself further by reading the books in the doctor's private library and acquired hand-me-down dishes and cutlery from other families whose parties he catered. "The way [J.E.'s] table was set," Duke's son said, "was just like those at which my grandfather had butlered."

It would appear that he also picked up Dr. Cuthbert's high-society manners. Whatever its source, J.E.'s suavity impressed all who met him, starting with his children. Ruth Ellington called him "a Chesterfieldian gentleman who wore gloves and spats." Her brother's memories were more specific—and worldly. He was particularly impressed by his father's fancy turns of phrase, which made their way into his own speech:

I have always wanted to be able to be and talk like my pappy. He was a party man, a great dancer (ballroom, that is), a connoisseur of vintages, and unsurpassed in creating an aura of conviviality. . . . He was

Beautiful and handsome: Family portraits of Daisy Kennedy Ellington and James Edward (J.E.) Ellington. These paintings, which hung in the living room of Duke Ellington's Manhattan apartment, were seen on national television when he was interviewed by Edward R. Murrow on *Person to Person* in 1957

also a wonderful wit, and he knew exactly what to say to a lady—hightoned or honey-homey. I wrote a song later with a title suggested by one of those sayings he would address to a lady worth telling she was pretty. "Gee, you make that hat look pretty," he would say.

Daisy was born in Washington in 1879. Her father was a police captain, one of only forty black officers in the District of Columbia, and her grandparents included a white senator and a Cherokee Indian. In black Washington that constituted a good family, far better than that of the man she married. She was a regular churchgoer, and she also seems to have been a prude: Ulanov, possibly following her son's lead, described her as "stiff-lipped" and "prim of mien and manner." Her pince-nez and light-colored skin made Daisy's gentility evident to all who saw her, as did her musical tastes. A competent pianist, she favored salon ballads like Ethelbert Nevin's "The Rosary," a favorite of Fritz Kreisler and John McCormack, which made her four-year-old son weep when she played it for him one day.*

---

* J.E. played piano, too, accompanying himself by ear in homespun versions of operatic arias and turn-of-the-century popular songs like "Sweet Adeline."

Ulanov believed that "the violently crossed influences of his father and mother" gave the mature Ellington a "startlingly ambivalent" personality that was at once "introspective" and "exhibitionist." True or not, Daisy and J.E. were an ill-sorted pair—they even went to different churches—and one wonders what her parents made of their decision to marry in 1898. They also appear to have been sexually incompatible: Mercer Ellington said that they "slept apart" after Daisy found out that her husband was having an affair with another woman. Though Ellington says nothing disparaging about either of them in his autobiography, he devotes far more space to Daisy, going so far as to claim, "No one else but my sister Ruth had a mother as great and as beautiful as mine." What he found most admirable about his father, by contrast, was his smooth-talking savoir faire, which he would endeavor to emulate. J.E., he said, "spent and lived like a man who had money, and he raised his family as though he were a millionaire." But he wasn't: J.E. was in service to a white man, and it was only much later that he struck out on his own, first becoming a full-time caterer during World War I and then, in 1920, taking a job as a maker of blueprints at the Navy Yard.

Might Ellington have been embarrassed by his father's pretensions? If so, he never let on. But a later generation was to take a dimmer view of ballroom-dancing black men who exalted appearance over reality. E. Franklin Frazier, the chairman of Howard University's sociology department, gave a name to such folk when he published *Black Bourgeoisie*, the still-controversial 1957 study in which he anatomized the "world of make-believe" in which they sought "to escape the disdain of whites and fulfill [their] wish for status in American life." Malcolm X, born a quarter century after Ellington, wrote with biting contempt in his own autobiography of the lower-tier bourgeoisie of Roxbury, the Boston suburb where he had lived as a boy:

> *I'd guess that eight out of ten of the Hill Negroes of Roxbury, despite the impressive-sounding job titles they affected, actually worked as menials and servants. "He's in banking," or "He's in securities." It sounded as though they were discussing a Rockefeller or a Mellon—and not some gray-headed, dignity-posturing bank janitor, or bond-house messenger.*

Was that how J.E. looked to the fortunate son who spent a lifetime putting the flesh of achievement on the bare bones of his father's hand-me-down manners? Or did Ellington prefer to think of him not as a make-believe gentleman in spats but as a dead-earnest striver who played his cards as well as he could? The only clue to be found in the pages of *Music Is My Mistress* is this sibylline sentence: "My mother, as I said before, was beautiful, but my father was only handsome." It's tempting to hear in those last two words the judgment of a son on the failings of a parent, but if Ellington ever said anything else to anyone else about J.E.'s failings, it went unrecorded.

෴

Duke Ellington was a spoiled child, and proud of it. The very first thing that he tells us about himself in *Music Is My Mistress* is that his parents pampered him:

> *Once upon a time a beautiful young lady and a very handsome young man fell in love and got married. They were a wonderful, compatible couple, and God blessed their marriage with a fine baby boy (eight pounds, eight ounces). They loved their little boy very much. They raised him, nurtured him, coddled him, and spoiled him. They raised him in the palm of the hand and gave him everything they thought he wanted. Finally, when he was about seven or eight, they let his feet touch the ground.*

It may seem an odd point for him to make so emphatically, but for once his memoiristic instincts played him true. Not only was he "spoiled rotten," but the child was father to the man: He arranged his adult life in such a way as to reproduce as closely as possible the way that his parents had treated him as a boy. Born in the home of his maternal grandparents on April 29, 1899, Edward Kennedy Ellington was named after J.E. and Daisy, who thereupon gave him whatever he wanted, as did Daisy's many female relations. While the fact that their first child had died in infancy helps to explain the favor with which the second was treated, the unremitting intensity of his mother's love, along with her certainty that he was destined to do well in the world, were a thing unto themselves. Daisy instilled in her son an attitude that might be described as "Ellingtonian exceptionalism," a doctrine to which he would subscribe forever after. "Edward, you are blessed," Daisy told him. "You don't have anything to worry about." Such love can be smothering, but he was inspired by it. When he descended from his upstairs bedroom to go to school, he would deliver a little speech to his mother and aunt: "This is the great, the grand, the magnificent Duke Ellington. Now applaud, applaud." He offered multiple explanations of how he acquired his lifelong nickname, but most of them point to his having been dubbed "Duke" by a childhood friend, partly because of his princely manner (the Duke of Wellington's name would have been known to his playmates) and partly because his mother dressed him so stylishly. Whatever the reason, it fit him well, and the schools that he attended, which taught "proper speech and good manners," improved the fit still further.

In addition to pampering him, Daisy and J.E., whose own father was a mulatto, gave him the medium-light brown skin that was one of his most recognizable features. In 1944 a reporter for *The New Yorker,* whose editors were sticklers for exactitude, described his color as that of "coffee with a strong dash of cream," the same shade favored by the hoity-toity Washingtonians of Langston Hughes's acquaintance. Ellington insisted that there was never "any talk about red people, brown people, black people, or yellow people, or about the differences that existed between them," in the family home. Such things, however, need not be discussed openly to be understood tacitly. Ellington's wife and the other women with whom he had long-term romantic relationships were all, like his mother, light-skinned or white, a circumstance unlikely to have been coincidental, any more than it was a coincidence that his closest black friends in later life (as well as most of the few musicians in his band with whom he socialized) tended to be members of his own class.*

Ellington spoke of the "wonderful feeling of security" that he drew from his childhood churchgoing, specifically mentioning it in connection with the way in which Daisy's praise had caused him to see himself as "very, very special." He went so far as to say that her belief in his uniqueness had made him fearless, which is absurd: He was a quivering mass of arbitrary, sometimes bizarre superstitions. Mercer believed that they stemmed from his having been overprotected as a boy, which makes sense. Yet it's just as plain to see that the confident carriage of his maturity was the result of Daisy's belief that he was born to higher things, and it probably also had something to do with the extent to which his parents had shielded him from life outside the invisible walls of U Street. The Ellingtons, Ruth said, did not discuss "hostile [racial] incidents" in front of their children. "I guess," she added, "that was their way of protecting us." Duke's small world may have been less secure than he admitted—Washington city directories show that his family lived at fourteen different addresses between 1898 and 1921, an indication that J.E.'s fortunes fluctuated erratically—but he does not seem to have

---

* The low-born, dark-skinned Louis Armstrong had so pronounced a preference in the opposite direction that he once wrote a piece for *Ebony* called "Why I Like Dark Women."

learned until later on what less privileged black children knew from the start of their young lives, which was that the color of their skin was enough in and of itself to get them killed, mutilated, or thrown in jail.

Instead of worrying about getting lynched, Duke played with his friends, read Sherlock Holmes and Horatio Alger, sang hymns in church every Sunday morning, and started taking piano lessons at the age of seven from a neighborhood teacher with the splendidly Trollopian name of Marietta Clinkscales. Within a few months, though, he lost interest in music and stopped playing altogether, later telling Barry Ulanov that what little he had learned "slipped away" from him. He was more interested in sports. For a brief time he sold refreshments at the city ballpark in order to watch the Washington Senators play, though he also cultivated a different aptitude: "All through grade school, I had a genuine interest in drawing and painting, and I realized I had a sort of talent for them. My mother and father both encouraged me, and the piano was allowed to fade into the background."

The piano stayed in the background until the summer of 1913, when Duke went to New Jersey "to get out and try my wings." He assumed that it would be easy for him to find work, but it wasn't, and he spent the whole summer washing dishes in a hotel. Though he hated the job, he loved the money he made: "I went back home, not as a penitent, prodigal son, but as a young man on his own with a supply of good clothes and some money saved up." It was there, too, that he first heard ragtime piano, in the form of a piano-roll version of Luckey Roberts's "Junk Man Rag" cut by a Philadelphia-based musician named Harvey Brooks. As much as Duke loved money and clothes, he loved "Junk Man Rag" more. "I cannot tell you what that music did to me," he said. "It was different from the average piano selection. The individuality of the man showed itself in the composition as he played it. I said right then, '[T]hat's how I would like to play a piano, so without being told, everybody would know I was playing.' "

Duke stopped off in Philadelphia on the way home and tracked down Brooks, who shared a few of his "short cuts . . . to successful playing." Then the awestruck boy returned to Washington, opened up the family piano for the first time in seven years, and started trying to play what he had heard. All at once the passion that Mrs. Clinkscales had been unable to rouse burst into full flower. "I hadn't been able to get off the ground before," he wrote long afterward, "but after hearing [Brooks] I said to myself, 'Man, you're just going to *have* to do it.' " Soon he started hanging out at Frank Holliday's poolroom, located next door to the Howard Theatre on T Street, a few short blocks from Ellington's home. Washington's ragtime pianists gathered there, and Duke spent hours standing next to the house piano, listening to their varied styles and trying to learn from their example. "It wasn't very long," he remembered, "before I could hear a tune and after a few moments I could reproduce it, often adding different variations. Soon I began to play for small dances and house parties."

Why had Mrs. Clinkscales's lessons failed to pique the interest of a child who was so sensitive to music that hearing it made him weep? "There was no connection between me and music, until I started fiddling with it myself," he explained. "As far as anyone teaching me, there was too many rules and regulations, and I just couldn't be shackled into that. As long as I could sit down and figure it out for myself, then that was all right." Very likely it was as simple as that: Then and thereafter, Daisy Ellington's spoiled child would try to do things his way or not at all.

By 1913 the ragtime craze that had swept across the country for a decade and a half was starting to die down, but it had already left its mark on American music. Raglike songs were first published in 1895, and the popularity of Scott Joplin's "Maple Leaf Rag," which followed in 1899, triggered worldwide interest in the music on which they were based. Even classical composers like Claude Debussy and Igor Stravinsky turned out pieces that incorporated the heavy melodic syncopation and marchlike "oompah" beat of ragtime. It was a fad, but one with lasting effects: Orchestrated versions of Joplin's rags soon made their way to New Orleans, where they were taken up by dance bands whose players loosened up their off-center rhythms and seasoned them with the blues, an amalgam that evolved into the music that by 1913 was starting to be called "jazz" (if not in New Orleans, whose musicians stuck to the word *ragtime* for some years to come). Meanwhile, Irving Berlin had written "Alexander's Ragtime Band" in 1911, and the song's phenomenal popularity helped spread the gospel of ragtime to whites who, following the lead of Vernon and Irene Castle, started one-stepping their way across America's dance floors. "In 1912 grandmothers of forty tossed away their crutches and took lessons in Tango and the Castle-Walk," F. Scott Fitzgerald recalled two decades later in "Echoes of the Jazz Age." The music to which they danced was much the same kind that had sent young Duke Ellington running to the parlor piano.

Much the same—but not exactly. In 1913 a group of East Coast pianists, the best known of whom were Eubie Blake, James P. Johnson, Luckey Roberts, and Willie "the Lion" Smith, was transforming classic ragtime into a more virtuosic style, one that replaced the evenly divided eighth and sixteenth notes of Joplin and his contemporaries with the fluid, tripletized rhythms that would soon be recognized as the trademark of jazz. The fast-moving, wider-ranging accompanying patterns that these men played with their left hands, in which fat midrange chords alternated metronomically with bass notes that dug deeply into the bottom half of the keyboard, caused their style to be dubbed "stride piano." Some were classically trained, while others were self-taught "ear men" who, unable to read music, worked out their styles by ear. None of them was familiar with New Orleans jazz, which had yet to make its way to the East Coast, and so their playing, heard on record today, has a slight rhythmic stiffness reminiscent of the classic ragtime on which it is based. But it was still different from anything else that the fourteen-year-old Ellington had heard, and he was so transfixed by it that he composed a rag of his own in the spring of 1914, piecing it together note by note at the keyboard. He had a part-time job jerking sodas at a place called the Poodle Dog Café, so he called it "Soda Fountain Rag."

Not until later did Ellington learn the rudiments of musical notation, and he never wrote down "Soda Fountain Rag" as an adult.* He did, however, play it in public on several occasions, and a few of these performances were recorded, giving us some sense of what the piece may have sounded like when it was new. It's a pastiche of the musical devices heard in the rags then being released on player-piano rolls, unoriginal but assembled with surprising competence, though the left-hand stride patterns often go askew (Ellington's right hand was more exact than his left). If the recorded versions of "Soda Fountain Rag" that have come down to us are representative of the piece that he wrote in 1914, less than a year after he first heard Harvey Brooks, then it is impressive how rapidly he assimilated the fundamentals of ragtime piano.

In those days it was common for middle-class black parents to react with horror if their children took an interest in ragtime. Not J.E. As Ellington recalled, "My father said something about playing that old ragtime music, or something like that, but I never had no real resistance against what I was doing." The difference, however, may have been that Duke—or his parents—saw music as a hobby, not a vocation. Instead of enrolling in Dunbar High School, which had a good music department, he went instead to Samuel H. Armstrong Technical High School, a vocational school for blacks that had opened in 1902, where he studied to become a commercial artist. Armstrong

---

* Ellington also left unnotated his second "composition," a mildly bawdy song called "What You Gonna Do When the Bed Breaks Down?" that he later described in *Music Is My Mistress* as "a pretty good 'hug-and-rubbin'' crawl."

was several notches lower than Dunbar on black Washington's totem pole of caste, and its students, according to Mercer Ellington, were "practically regarded as incorrigible." But Duke had talent as an artist, enough to win an NAACP-sponsored scholarship to New York's Pratt Institute. "What I was getting out of music then seemed like a gift or a bonus," he said, "and I didn't realize that that was where my future lay." At that point, though, it was the present that mattered more. In 1916 he played his first professional gig, and soon he was getting enough work to make him think twice about becoming a full-time artist. He decided that it made more sense to divide his time between playing music and painting signs, with the emphasis increasingly going to music.

That left no time for homework, and Duke's grades at Armstrong were fair to poor (average in English, history, and math, much worse in the sciences and—interestingly—music). Somewhere along the way his sense of destiny became so strong that he decided to stop wasting his time on formal studies of any kind. Bernice Wiggins, his first cousin, later spoke of a visit to the Ellington home during which he unveiled his rosy vision of the future to his mother:

> *I never will forget . . . he came in one evening and he said, "Mother, dear," and she turned around and looked at him and he always would come in and kiss her on both side of the cheeks and she says, "What have you been up to today?" as a mother would. He said, "Mother, your son is going to be one of the great musicians in the world." He says, "Someday . . . I'm gonna be bowin' before the kings and queens." And Aunt Daisy used to say, "The boy's talking foolish."*

But Daisy was probably too busy caring for Ruth, her second child, who was born in 1915, to worry overmuch about Duke's future, and in any case she seems never to have swerved at any time from the iron conviction that her precious little son, being blessed, would succeed at whatever he put his mind to doing. So he was left to his own devices, and in February of 1917 he dropped out of school, never to return.

The patterns of Ellington's life and personality were now set, and they bore a family resemblance to the shape of life on U Street. The hours that he had spent rubbing shoulders with ragtime pianists, Pullman porters, petty thieves, and card sharps in Frank Holliday's poolroom had introduced him to a way of living far removed from the middle-class world into which he had been born. To the end of his life he recalled with relish the lessons he learned there: "Interns used to come in, who could cure colds. And handwriting experts who would enjoy copying somebody's signature on a check, go out and *cash* it, and bring back the money to show the cats in the poolroom what *artists* they were. They didn't need the money. They did it for the kicks. . . . At heart, they were all great artists."

Yet Ellington never turned his back on the other lessons that he learned from J.E., Daisy, and their neighbors. He regarded them as identically valid, just as he learned as much from listening to "the schooled musicians who had been to the conservatory" as he did from the untrained pianists whose methods he emulated: "Everybody seemed to get something out of the other's playing—the ear cats loved what the schooled guys did, and the schooled guys, with fascination, would try what the ear cats were doing." It did not occur to him that his own elegant carriage was inconsistent with his racial identity, any more than that the authenticity of his music might somehow be compromised by its urbanity. That, he knew, bespoke a constrictingly narrow notion of "blackness." He took seriously the code of bourgeois manners to which his parents had introduced him, and though he shook off its tenets in adulthood, there was never a time when he failed to maintain the appearance of respectability. Throughout his life he pointed out that Harlem "has always had more churches than cabarets." Moreover, the composer of *Black, Brown and Beige* needed no one to remind him that his people came in all shades. "Once I asked him what he considered a typical Negro piece among his compositions," a white friend recalled. "He paused a moment before he came up with 'In a Sentimental Mood.' I protested a bit and said I thought that was a very sophisticated white kind of song and people were usually surprised when they learned it was by him. 'Ah,' he said, 'that's because you don't *know* what it's like to be a Negro.'" At no time did he question his own knowledge of what it was like, or his ability to turn that knowledge into music that gave voice to his people's anguish—and aspiration.

2

"SOFT AND GUT-BUCKET"

Becoming a Professional, 1917–1926

ONE OF DUKE Ellington's favorite sayings was that luck amounts to "being at the right place at the right time, doing the right thing before the right people. If all four 'rights' are in good order, you may count yourself lucky." He was unusually lucky, then, to have launched his musical career in the same month that the Original Dixieland Jazz Band made its New York debut. Until then New Orleans jazz was essentially unknown outside of the city of its birth and Chicago, where the five players who comprised the ODJB had caused a stir the preceding March. It was, however, nothing compared to the one that greeted their opening at Reisenweber's 400 Club Room on January 27, 1917. Within hours the word was out that something very new and very hot had come to town, and the quintet's first Victor recordings, cut on February 26 and rushed into print nine days later, introduced a generation of listeners—and musicians—to the raucous music that would give a name to the coming decade. Other jazzlike music had previously been recorded, but "Livery Stable Blues" and "Dixie Jass Band One-Step" were among the first 78 sides to be cut by jazz musicians from New Orleans, as well as the first whose label described them as jazz (or, rather, "jass"). Newspaper ads in New Orleans called the combined results "positively the greatest dance record ever issued," and purchasers throughout the country agreed: Victor 18255 is believed to have been one of the earliest popular records to sell a million copies. Its success put an end to what was left of the ragtime craze, for other bands rushed to record in a similar style, and their music became the gold standard in dance halls across America. The Jazz Age had arrived.

Two and a half years later, a promising young bandleader who had served his apprenticeship as a sideman placed an ad in the Washington phone book:

IRRESISTIBLE JASS

FURNISHED TO OUR SELECT PATRONS

The Duke's Serenaders

COLORED SYNCOPATERS

E.K. ELLINGTON, Mgr.

"Irresistible jass": The Duke's Serenaders, c. 1920. Sonny Greer is the drummer, Sterling Conaway the banjo player. The fledgling bandleader specialized in "under-conversation music," not full-fledged jazz, but few Washingtonians knew the difference, and Ellington profited handsomely from their ignorance

Not that E.K. Ellington, Mgr., was anything like a fully grown jazzman in 1919. Few East Coast musicians were—even the best of the stride pianists were still feeling their way into the new rhythmic language of jazz—and it was not until 1923 that Louis Armstrong and Sidney Bechet started making the records that taught their contemporaries how to swing. Ellington was a mere purveyor of jazz-scented dance music that was played at parties, some black and others white, by bands that he led or booked. He later described what they played as "under-conversation music," which sounds about right. Nor were his early clients discriminating about the songs to which they chatted and danced:

> All the embassies and big shots in Washington were hiring small bands to play for parties. It didn't seem to make much difference what band— they just hired a band. . . . I went down to the telephone office and arranged for a Music-for-All-Occasions ad in the telephone book. It was during the war, and there were a lot of people from out of town, war workers, who didn't know Meyer Davis and Louis Thomas from Duke Ellington. My ad looked just like theirs, and I began to get work. And give it. It got so that I would sometimes send out four or five bands a night, and work in them, too.

Meyer Davis, Ellington's chief competitor, had just launched his own long career as a society bandleader specializing in "music for exclusive and smart parties." Like Davis, Ellington made a handsome living dishing out the unexceptionably bland commodity that was (and is) society-band music. In 1966 he told an interviewer that he had brought in $10,000 a year, the equivalent of $123,000 today. "Well, he picked up the piano by ear and now he's making more money than I am," J.E. boasted. His son may have been stretching the truth, and part of that sum came from the sign-painting business that he had launched around the time that he became a professional musician: "When customers came for posters to advertise a dance, I would ask them what they were doing about their music. When they wanted to hire a band, I would ask them who's painting their signs." But he was still doing well for himself—and for his wife and son.

We know little about Edna Thompson, whom Duke married in 1918 and from whom he parted a decade later. She was interviewed only once, for a profile published in *Ebony* seven years before her death in 1966 in which she spoke tactfully but, it appears, truthfully about their life together. They fell in love, she said, in high school, at a time when he had "just learned the

"I'm still hooked": Edna Thompson, taken around the time that she married Duke Ellington in 1918. Though he left her for good a decade later, the unhappy couple remained legally married for the rest of Edna's life

difference between girls and boys." She played piano herself and wanted to become a music teacher, and she claimed to have taught her dashing boyfriend "how to read music." Judging by her pictures, Edna was both fair-skinned and pretty. According to Mercer Ellington, "My mother's folks were from a higher station of black society than my father's. They were schoolteachers and principals, and they considered all musicians, including Duke Ellington, low-life." Mercer thought that they would not have married had she not become pregnant. But the children of U Street were taught to do the right thing, so Edna and Edward were wed on July 2, 1918, with the birth of Mercer Kennedy Ellington following eight months later. In 1959 Edna spoke of the early months of their marriage as "hard days." In addition to painting signs and playing piano with other men's bands, her new husband was moonlighting as a messenger for the Treasury Department. But like many another teenage father, he was brought up short by what he later called the "tremendous responsibilities" of parenthood. He placed his first ad three months after Mercer was born, and soon he was making enough money to buy a house and a car.

Ellington never spoke about Edna to reporters, nor did he publicly acknowledge that they did not divorce after separating. It was not until the *Ebony* interview that most of his later fans became aware of his wife's existence, and all that she said at the time about their decision to remain legally married was, "I'm still hooked on Ellington. . . . I don't want a divorce and neither does he." He must have found it handy to use her existence as an excuse not to marry any of his later girlfriends, though it seems at least as likely that his philandering started early in their marriage. He claimed to have lost his virginity at the age of twelve, and his interest in women grew stronger as he grew older. "I think that what put him into show business in the first place, more than anything else, was that it was a good way to get a girl to sit beside you and admire you as you played the piano," Mercer wrote in 1978.* But Ellington's marriage was a closed book that he chose not to open: Edna, like all the rest of his women, goes unmentioned, even in passing, in *Music Is My Mistress*. In 1955, however, he wrote an unpublished play called *Man with Four Sides* whose protagonists, the Lanes, are a middle-class black couple of a kind familiar on U Street. The wife, Mrs. Martha Washington Penoctbottom Lane, speaks with "proper-type stiltedness" and "governs her little home with all the pomp and grandeur of an empress." Otho, her husband, is a secret drinker who longs desperately to "escape from the atmosphere / Of this house—which my wife / Dominates completely." Though Ellington never said as much, it may be that he meant the play as a withering critique of the life from which he extracted himself by leaving Edna.

Had he ever loved her? Or was their marriage an empty vessel of necessity and, later, of convenience? Fanny Holmes, the wife of Justice Oliver Wendell Holmes Jr., said that Washington is "full of famous men and the women they married when they were young." Perhaps the Ellingtons were that kind of couple—but we can never know.

The professional relationships that Ellington formed in the years after World War I lasted longer than most marriages. Sonny Greer, Otto Hardwick, and

---

* Ellington agreed. "I started out playing for pussy, not money," he told a journalist in 1964.

Arthur Whetsel, all of whom played in the Duke's Serenaders, spent most of the rest of their professional careers working with Ellington and were playing with him long after he left Edna. They admired him both as a man and as an artist. Greer described him as "sharp as a Gillette blade . . . I've never seen another man like him. When he walks into a room, the whole place lights up." Hardwick thought him "brilliant," though he spoke with amusement about Ellington's character: "Another remarkable thing about him is his passion for people. He's warm-hearted, of course, but that's not what I mean. *He likes to manipulate.* It's not like using someone, it's more like a game. Besides, what he does for you is beneficial. What he tries to get you to do—it's good for you, if you do it." All three men did what he wanted, and profited from it. They were the first in the long line of musical individualists who hitched their wagons to his star.

Hardwick and Whetsel were U Streeters, and both of them had gone to Dunbar High, where they acquired the same patina of good manners that served their future boss so well, just as their playing had a surface sheen that became a valued part of his musical palette. Hardwick, born in 1904 and always called "Toby" by his friends, started out as a bassist but took up C-melody saxophone at Ellington's urging, later switching to alto saxophone. His slick, slightly oily tone and smooth lip slurs are among the most memorable instrumental colors to be heard on "Black and Tan Fantasy" and "Sophisticated Lady," and though Johnny Hodges, who had a more up-to-date style, was to replace him as the band's star saxophone soloist, Hardwick's playing in the reed section was always instantly identifiable. As for Whetsel, Ellington appreciated his self-discipline and loved the gentle muted trumpet tone and "aural charisma" that light up "Mood Indigo" and can be heard to lovely effect on any number of other Ellington recordings of the twenties and thirties: "When he played the funeral march in 'Black and Tan Fantasy,' I used to see great, big ole tears running down people's faces . . . his tonal character has never been duplicated, it was such a fragile thing, nobody has really had his gentility, fragility."

Of the three, Greer was closest to Ellington, so much so that Mercer "thought of him as a member of the family." Greer felt the same way: "Duke Ellington was like my brother, and I was like his." Born in New Jersey sometime around 1895, he was a pencil-thin dandy who had worked in vaudeville as a teenager and thereafter played the drums with a stick-twirling flash rooted in his early stage experience. He hustled in poolrooms when jobs were scarce, but his musicianship was sufficiently honed to keep him busy. Greer moved to Washington in 1919 and started playing as a relief man in the pit band of the Howard Theatre the following year. Ellington, who met him around that time, was impressed that he had worked in New York: "Anybody who had been to New York had the edge on us." The two men started playing together not long afterward, and before long the association became permanent. Ellington's loyalty outlived Greer's ability, and though he finally nudged the drummer out of the band in 1951, he kept his old friend on the payroll for years afterward.

For all his crowd-conscious flamboyance, Greer's main goal was to make his fellow musicians look good. "I always strove for delicacy," he said. "I always tried to shade and make everything sound beautiful. It was my job to keep the band in level time, to keep slow tempos from going down and fast tempos from going up. Those things meant more to me than solos, which I rarely took." A time came when his methods sounded outmoded to younger ears. Gene Lees called his playing "slushy," while Johnny Mandel compared him invidiously to the drummers who followed him into the Ellington band: "We used to say that nobody but Sonny Greer, who had strange time, could play with that band. We did not foresee how good it would sound when Sam Woodyard or Louis Bellson was with it." But they heard him in middle age, after years of drinking had gnawed away at his skill. "Greer was not the world's best reader of music," said Ellington, "but he was the world's best percussionist reactor. When he heard a ping he responded with the most apropos pong." Whitney Balliett's description of his style has never been bettered:

> *He used timpani and tomtoms a lot, filling cracks and cheering the soloists. He used deceptive, easy arrays of afterbeat rimshots that drove the band while remaining signals of cool. He flicked cowbells to launch a soloist, and he showered everyone with cymbals. He sparkled and exploded, but his taste never faltered.*

None of these men was known for his hot solos, yet another indication that the "jass" played by the Duke's Serenaders was fairly innocuous sounding. Ellington says nothing in *Music Is My Mistress* about having listened to early jazz recordings, and except for a single encounter with James P. Johnson, he did not hear any of the foremost jazz instrumentalists of the day in person prior to 1923. What he knew about jazz was what he heard around him, and it's unlikely that anyone who lived in Washington knew much more about it than he did. But if he was a one-eared prince in a kingdom of the deaf, he was also wise enough to know his limitations, and to do something about them. Having "built up so much of a reputation that [he] had to study music seriously to protect it," he began studying harmony with one of the most accomplished classical musicians on U Street. Henry Grant was a pianist, conductor, and composer who taught at Dunbar (Hardwick and Whetsel played in his school bands) and led church choirs and neighborhood glee clubs. He helped found the National Association of Negro Musicians in 1919 and edited its journal, *The Negro Musician,* in whose pages he praised Eubie Blake, another of his pupils: "I marvelled at his natural technique and got my first lesson—an insight into the soul of an exponent of 'Ragtime.'"

While Ellington could not have found a more suitable teacher, he was too impatient with book learning to take more than "half a dozen" lessons from Grant. During that time, he said, "I discovered that F-sharp is not a G-flat. That was the end of my lessons . . . because I found out what I wanted to know." If this is true, then he stopped short of grappling with anything beyond the basics of elementary harmony, and he is not known to have listened to classical music other than occasionally at any time in the first half of his life. Barry Ulanov states flatly in his 1946 biography, written with Ellington's cooperation, that "Duke had little direct contact with the main stream of traditional music," and Ellington himself said repeatedly that he was not influenced by classical music: "If *serious* means European music, I'm not interested in that. . . . I am not writing classical music, and the musical devices that have been handed down by serious composers have little bearing on modern swing." To be sure, he also said that Grant "lighted the direction to more highly developed composition." But he never learned from Henry Grant or anyone else how classical composers use harmony to articulate and propel large-scale musical structures, and the day would come when his lack of that knowledge served him ill.

Ellington learned a more immediately useful kind of lesson when a friend played him a new piano roll by James P. Johnson. "Carolina Shout" was Johnson's *cheval de bataille,* the showpiece with which he vanquished all comers at "cutting sessions" in Harlem. The version that he cut for QRS in the summer of 1921 allowed other pianists to copy it note by note by slowing down to a crawl the playback mechanisms of their player pianos. That was how Ellington learned the piece, and he learned it so well that he soon felt confident enough to play the piece for the master himself. The occasion was a Washington concert called "The 20th Century Jazz Revue" at which he and other local artists appeared alongside Johnson. Ellington's fans insisted that he play "Carolina Shout" for the composer, who was sufficiently impressed to go club-hopping with his young admirer. It was a night that Ellington never forgot: "What I absorbed on that occasion might, I think, have constituted a whole semester in a conservatory." From then on he studied Johnson's playing so closely that Garvin Bushell, a saxophonist who heard him two years later, testified that "he was playing like James P.," though there were other pianists to whose tricks he paid close attention: "I also tried to copy the spectacular manner in which Luckey Roberts lifted his hands high above the keyboard as he played." Films of Ellington shot in the twenties and thirties show that he learned that lesson, too, though he never overdid it. In his showboating as in all other things, he took care to be tasteful.

He was, if anything, more impressed when he heard Sidney Bechet, who appeared at the Howard Theatre in January of 1923. It was, he said, his "first real encounter" with New Orleans jazz, and Ellington never forgot the "power and imagination" of the older man's clarinet playing: "Bechet to me was the very epitome of jazz. He represented and executed everything that had to do with the beauty of it all, and everything he played in his whole life was completely original." Bechet was the most advanced of all the early jazz soloists who made recordings by which we can gauge their prowess today. His performances of "Wild Cat Blues" and "Kansas City Man Blues," cut for OKeh later that year, were not only as fluent and rhythmically secure as anything that Louis Armstrong recorded with King Oliver's Creole Jazz Band, but were also formally coherent to a degree that Armstrong, for all his prodigious gifts, had yet to attain.

Hearing Bechet and Johnson must have persuaded Ellington that he would have to leave Washington to develop further as an artist. He knew that his hometown was no paradise. In 1919 Washington had been put to the torch by a four-day-long race riot in which white mobs, inflamed by rumors that a black man had raped the wife of a white navy man, came to U Street with murder on their minds. Carter G. Woodson, a dean at Howard University, recalled their coming: "They had caught a Negro and deliberately held him as one would a beef for slaughter, and when they had conveniently adjusted him for lynching, they shot him. I heard him groaning in his struggle as I hurried away as fast as I could without running, expecting every moment to be lynched myself." Ellington is not known to have spoken of the riot—he never discussed such things—but no black man who lived through those four nights could ever again doubt that he, too, was at risk. Perhaps that was when he first considered the possibility of moving to New York, for by 1923 he was sure that he wanted to live there: "Harlem, to our minds, did indeed have the world's most glamorous atmosphere. We had to go there . . . it was New York that filled our imagination."

Opportunity knocked when the clarinetist Wilbur Sweatman, who had played in Washington the preceding year, sent Sonny Greer a telegram inviting the drummer to come to New York and join his band. Today Sweatman is remembered as a novelty artist who was famous for playing three clarinets simultaneously, but he was a genuinely talented instrumentalist whose 1916 recording of his own "Down Home Rag," made two months before the Original Dixieland Jazz Band cut "Livery Stable Blues," comes close to breaking free from the rhythmic constraints of ragtime. Greer was interested in the offer but told Sweatman that he would only come if Ellington and Otto Hardwick could accompany him, and the clarinetist agreed to hire them as well. The three men went to New York in February, and a few days later they were playing at Harlem's Lafayette Theatre with Sweatman, who was billed as the "MUCH IMITATED RAGTIME AND JAZZ CLARIO-NETIST." It was Ellington's first trip to New York, as well as the first time that he had played on a vaudeville bill: "It was another world to us, and we'd sit on the stage and keep a straight face. . . . [Sweatman] was a good musician, and he was in vaudeville because that was where the money was then, but I think things were beginning to cool off for him, and soon we were not doing so well."

Sweatman went back to the road, and Ellington and his friends stayed behind in Harlem. Unable to find jobs, they hung out with other musicians, foremost among them Willie "the Lion" Smith, a cigar-chewing braggart who ranked just below James P. Johnson in the pantheon of Harlem pianists. Artie Shaw, who got to know Smith in the thirties, described him as having a "kind of nice, almost arrogant manner . . . he just knew who he was, he knew what he was about." Smith in turn remembered Ellington as a "good-looking, well-mannered fellow; one of those guys you see him, you like him right away . . . I took a liking to him and he took a liking to me." Ellington responded by listening attentively to his new friend's compositions, which were unlike anything being played by his contemporaries. Smith was one of the first stride pianists to dispense with the rigid left-hand accompaniment patterns that he and his colleagues had taken from ragtime, replacing them with melodic figures and classical-style ostinati that made his salonlike pieces, which bore such titles as "Echoes of Spring" and "Morning Air," sound like a blend of late ragtime and the light classics. Ellington was more open than most of his fellow pianists to Smith's approach. In 1939 he recorded a gracefully swinging evocation of Smith's musical language called "Portrait of the Lion," and a quarter century later he said that the older pianist had been his "strongest influence."

As much as Ellington and his friends loved New York and its artists, they could not live there without work, so they reluctantly returned to Washington. But they had seen the promised land, and the next time that Duke Ellington went there, it would be for keeps.

∾

By 1923 Harlem had replaced Washington as the unofficial capital of black America. It was a boiling cauldron of imaginative energy, and even its white neighbors were taking note of what would soon be dubbed the "Harlem Renaissance." The flourishing of the black middle class had everything to do with the emergence of this movement, which throughout its decade-long existence was mainly literary. Black poets, novelists, scholars, and intellectuals like James Weldon Johnson, Alain Locke, Claude McKay, and (later) Langston Hughes and Zora Neale Hurston published articles and books in which they proclaimed the emergence of what Locke, the head of Howard University's philosophy department, called a "new Negro" who had broken "the vital inner grip of prejudice" and was becoming "a collaborator and participant in American civilization."

Locke and his colleagues knew that blacks had made "substantial contributions" to American civilization through their music, but they paid little attention to jazz and the blues. Most of them seem to have felt that what black America *really* needed was a big-league classical composer of its own. Harlem's jazzmen, some of whom were broadly aware of what was going on among the intellectuals, sensed in turn that the New Negroes had no great interest in them. "The two worlds, literature and entertainment, rarely crossed," Cab Calloway said in his autobiography. "We were working hard on our thing and they were working hard on theirs." No one then suspected that it was the jazzmen of Harlem whose contribution to American culture would turn out to have been more enduring than any of the books published by the writers of the Harlem Renaissance, much less that an obscure twenty-four-year-old society pianist from Washington would soon move to the front of their ranks.

In the summer of 1923, Sonny Greer, Otto Hardwick, and Arthur Whetsel returned to New York in the company of the banjo player Elmer Snowden, who had been offered a job there that failed to pan out. Ellington followed them, and after a few weeks of scuffling, the cabaret singer Ada "Bricktop" Smith engaged the five men to serve as the house band at Barron Wilkins's Exclusive Club, the Harlem nightspot where she was headlining, with Snowden serving as their nominal leader. The club catered to wealthy whites but also admitted light-skinned blacks who could pay the tab, which

"This colored band is plenty torrid": The Washingtonians in early 1924. From left: Sonny Greer, Charlie Irvis, Bubber Miley (seated), Elmer Snowden, Otto Hardwick, and Duke Ellington. This six-piece combo was the seed from which Ellington's later bands grew, and in Miley it had a major soloist whose plunger-mute playing became an indispensable element of Ellington's orchestral style

was stiff enough for each member of the band to make thirty dollars a week plus twenty dollars a night in tips. The music they played, Ellington said, was "sweet and straight," which was what the club's patrons wanted to hear: "As a result of playing all those society dances in Washington, we had learned to play softly . . . we had arrangements for everything and it was what we've now named conversation music, kind of soft and gut-bucket."

Such fare may have satisfied the high-rolling whites who came uptown to drink at the Exclusive Club, but it failed to pass muster with the executives of Victor Records, for whom the band cut a test record on July 26, 1923. Like most other record companies, Victor assumed that it was impossible to market sweet dance music to black record buyers, who were thought to favor blues and jazz exclusively. As Snowden told Stanley Dance:

We had been playing like most of the [white] boys downtown before, only doing it with five pieces, and we didn't do any "jungle style." When we first recorded for Victor—Elmer Snowden's Novelty Orchestra—Whetsol [sic] wasn't doing any of that stuff. He used to use a cup [mute] under a hat, and his horn would sound like a saxophone . . . our music wasn't the kind of Negro music they wanted, so Victor didn't issue it.

No doubt Ellington would have liked to sign a contract with the label that employed Enrico Caruso and the Original Dixieland Jazz Band, but there is no reason to think that he was displeased with the quintet's playing. As he explained with every sign of satisfaction, he and his colleagues "were different in several ways." "We paid quite a lot of attention to our appearance," he said, "and if any one of us came in dressed improperly Whetsol [*sic*] would flick his cigarette ash in a certain way, or pull down the lower lid of his right eye with his forefinger and stare at the offending party." They were, at least for the moment, content to play sweet and straight and be paid generously for doing so, enough so to allow Ellington to bring Edna up from Washington. He began working on the side as a rehearsal pianist at the newly opened Connie's Inn, an even swankier whites-only Harlem club, where he got a close-up look at the process of putting together a cabaret floor show.

Around the same time, Ellington started going to Tin Pan Alley, the neighborhood in lower Manhattan where sheet-music publishers were clustered, to sell songs that he wrote with Jo. Trent, a black lyricist. None of them became a hit, but the flat fees that he accepted for writing such forgotten ditties as "Blind Man's Buff" helped to sweeten the family pot still further. On one of Ellington's first visits to Tin Pan Alley, Fred Fisher, the composer of "Chicago," offered to buy a song from him and asked the fledgling composer for a "lead sheet," a single-staff sheet of music containing the tune and lyrics. "I had never made a lead sheet before, nor tried to write music of any kind," he later said. Snowden claimed that Ellington "couldn't really read then," by which he meant that the young pianist was not yet able to read written-out music at sight. While he had made considerable progress since the days of "Soda Fountain Rag," he still had a long way to go before he could call himself a true professional.

In September he took a giant step toward that goal. Snowden's band, which was now known as the Washingtonians, signed a six-month contract to accompany a floor show and play for dancing at a newly opened club called the Hollywood, located on West Forty-Ninth Street near Broadway. Though the basement cabaret was seedy to the point of sordidness and its owners seem on occasion to have resorted to arson to pay their bills, it had one in-contestable advantage over the Exclusive Club: The Hollywood was located not in Harlem but in Manhattan's midtown theater district, meaning that it was covered by white journalists. In November the Washingtonians got their first high-profile review, a rave in the *New York Clipper,* a trade paper:

> *This colored band is plenty torrid and includes a trumpet player who never need doff his chapeau to any cornetist in the business. He exacts the eeriest sort of modulations and "singing" notes heard. . . . The boys look neat in dress suits and labor hard but not in vain at their music. They disclose painstaking rehearsal, playing without music.*

The " 'hot' cornetist" who caught the ear of Abel Green, an entertainment reporter who later became the editor of *Variety,* was not Arthur Whetsel, who had gone back to Washington. It was James "Bubber" Miley, who had joined the band when it started playing at the Hollywood and expanded from five to seven pieces, taking on a trombone player and a second saxophonist. Unlike John Anderson and Roland Smith, about whom next to nothing is known beyond their names, Miley was, as Green's review indicates, a find, the first jazz soloist of significance with whom Ellington had worked to date and the one whose contribution to his style was greater than that of anyone else with whom he played in the twenties.

Born in South Carolina in 1903, Miley was an experienced jazzman who had toured with Mamie Smith, a vaudeville performer who in 1920 became the first black singer to record blues songs. While on tour with Smith in 1921, he heard King Oliver's band in Chicago and was staggered by the New Orleans cornetist's muted "wah-wah" solos. Such playing had yet to be heard in New York—Oliver did not cut his first records until two years later—and Garvin Bushell, another of Smith's sidemen, recalled in his 1988 memoir the overwhelming impression that it made on him and Miley: "Bubber and I sat there with our mouths open. . . . The trumpets and clarinets in the East had a better 'legitimate' quality, but the sound of Oliver's band touched you more. It was less cultivated but more expressive of how the people felt." Miley taught himself how to use a "plunger" mute (the rubber suction cup better known to laymen as the business end of a plumber's helper) in order to mimic Oliver's raspy, growling sound, and by 1923, when he signed on with the Washingtonians, he had mastered the technique.

Ellington was as excited by Miley's playing as Miley had been by Oliver's. "Our band changed its character when Bubber Miley came in," he wrote in

1940. "He used to growl all night long, playing gut-bucket on his horn. That's when we decided to forget all about sweet music." Snowden was reluctant to make so drastic a change in the band's style, but the Washingtonians, Ellington said, were "a sort of cooperative organization, nobody was really the leader," and the group decided to go along with Miley. Their decision was cemented by the hiring in December of Charlie Irvis, a trombonist with a similar style. According to Ellington, Irvis "got a great, big, fat sound at the bottom of the trombone—melodic, masculine, full of tremendous authority." With the two plunger-wielding brassmen in place, the Washingtonians started to take advantage of the stability afforded by their contract with the Hollywood, where they would perform for much of the next four years. Such long-term employment is crucial to the growth of a working jazz band, for it allows the members to get to know one another's playing intimately and work out a collective style in relative tranquility. In addition, bands with regular gigs also find it easier to attract players of better quality, and by 1925 the Washingtonians were starting to acquire new members who, like Greer and Hardwick before them, would stick with Ellington for years to come.

Not, however, Elmer Snowden, whose departure from the band was both imminent and involuntary. When his colleagues found out that he was pocketing their share of a raise, they gave him the boot and persuaded a reluctant Ellington to take his place at the helm.* "It didn't take long before we thrust leadership on Duke," said Sonny Greer. "He didn't want it, but his disposition was better balanced than ours. He could keep us in line without doing much. We were a pretty wild bunch in those days, myself in particular."

Greer may have been wild, but he was also proud:

> *There were no small bands so well rehearsed as ours was then. Most of them played stocks, which we never did. Duke wasn't writing so much, but he would take the popular tunes and twist them, and Toby was doubling on C-melody and baritone, so we would sound like a big band, but soft and beautiful. . . . We worked as one man. Duke was the brains, always prodding us to do better, showing kindness and understanding.*

---

* Fred Guy, who replaced Snowden on banjo, stayed with the band until 1949. He started playing guitar in 1931, around the same time that other jazz banjo players were switching to the less percussive-sounding six-stringed instrument, thereafter becoming the unobtrusive but rock-steady linchpin of the rhythm section. "He was rather a serious type of fellow, and was always giving us advice," Ellington said, "but his guitar was a metronome and the beat was always where it was supposed to be."

The fact that the Washingtonians did not normally play from published "stock arrangements" of popular tunes of the day (they sometimes used them, but not often) may have had more to do with Ellington's limited sight-reading skills than the band's ingenuity. But it was also a matter of principle. As one of his sidemen explained, "Duke worked largely from head arrangements and he insisted everyone memorize their parts. He thought you couldn't get inside a piece of music if you were busy keeping up with the charts."* And his method of developing those arrangements was, or purported to be, thoroughly democratic: "We would just sit down at the piano and we'd say you take this and you take that." It is, however, notable that Ellington used the royal *we*, one of his favored turns of phrase, in the 1964 interview in which he explained how the Washingtonians arranged the tunes that they played. At that point Greer was at least as well known as Ellington: Not only did he double as the band's vocalist, but his expansive personality made him popular with the club's regular customers. But Ellington was already, as Greer put it, the "brains" of the group, and before long he was its leader in every sense.

In *Music Is My Mistress* Ellington spoke of the "new colors and characteristics" of the music that the Washingtonians were playing. They came not just from Miley and Irvis but from everything that he heard around him. He was as willing to learn from the quasi-symphonic sounds of the movie-house orchestras of New York as from the playing of Fletcher Henderson's big band, the group that impressed him most. He even learned from Paul Whiteman, the plump bandleader with the toothbrush mustache whose dance orchestra had accompanied George Gershwin in the world premiere of *Rhapsody in Blue* on February 12, 1924. Whiteman was a regular visitor to the Hollywood, where he left behind fifty-dollar tips, and Ellington, who throughout his life would speak admiringly of his musical achievements, understood the landmark importance of Gershwin's first "classical" composition. Two years later he wrote a short piece for solo piano called "Rhapsody Jr." whose whole-tone tunes are as much a nod to Gershwin's musical language—and ambitions—as is the piece's title.

Ellington also studied informally with Will Marion Cook, whose story epitomizes the disadvantages under which turn-of-the-century black artists worked. Born in 1869, Cook was a U Streeter, the son of a Howard University

---

* In jazz parlance, a "head arrangement" is a musical routine that is collectively worked out by the members of a band in rehearsal or on the bandstand. Such improvised "charts" are only written down, if at all, after the fact.

law professor. His musical talent was so outstanding that he studied violin at the Oberlin Conservatory of Music and Joseph Joachim's Hochschule für Musik in Berlin, and later on he also studied "a bit of composition" (as he put it) at New York's National Conservatory of Music with Antonín Dvořák, who was fascinated by spirituals and incorporated their melodic shapes into his *New World Symphony*. Unable to establish himself as a concert soloist because of his race, Cook chose instead to become a composer of popular music, collaborating in 1898 with Paul Laurence Dunbar on *Clorindy: Origin of the Cakewalk*, one of the first all-black shows to play on Broadway. Five years later his *In Dahomey* made Bert Williams, the black vaudeville singer-comedian, a Broadway star.

"Dad" Cook, as his protégés called him, believed in the promise of what he called "developed Negro music" whose creators, putting aside "puerile imitation of the white man," chose instead to draw on the untapped heritage of their own race. To this end he served as mentor to many younger men, including Sidney Bechet, James P. Johnson, and Ellington, who told of how

> *I got most of my instruction [from Cook] riding around Central Park in a taxi . . . he and I would get in a taxi and ride around Central Park and he'd give me lectures in music. I'd sing a melody in its simplest form and he'd stop me and say, "Reverse your figures." He was a brief but a strong influence. His language had to be pretty straight for me to know what he was talking about. Some of the things he used to tell me I never got a chance to use until years later, when I wrote the tone poem "Black, Brown and Beige."*

It's hard to imagine that Cook managed under such circumstances to do much more than offer him basic tips on composition and arranging, but Ellington was fond of quoting a piece of advice from the older man. "Dad, I don't want to go to the conservatory because they're not teaching what I want to learn," he said. "You know you should go to the conservatory," Cook replied. "But since you won't, I'll tell you. First you find the logical way, and when you find it, avoid it, and let your inner self break through and guide you. Don't try to be anybody but yourself."

Ellington was still trying to establish himself as a songwriter, and in the spring of 1925 he and Jo. Trent were invited to write several numbers for an all-black stage revue to be called *Chocolate Kiddies*. They were forced to work on the tightest of deadlines: "One day Joe [*sic*] Trent came running up to me on Broadway. He had a big proposition and there was urgency in his voice. 'Tonight we've got to write a show,' he said. '*Tonight!*'" Ellington knocked out five undistinguished tunes, only one of which, "Jig Walk," outlived the show. *Chocolate Kiddies* was never seen in the United States—it was written for a troupe of black performers who toured Europe in the midtwenties—and seems to have done little to advance its composer's career.

The Washingtonians, on the other hand, continued to receive favorable press notices for their performances at the Hollywood, which was renamed Club Kentucky in 1925 and transformed into what one contemporary columnist described as "a glorified interior of a southern negro cabin. Oil lamps flickered around the imitation stones and log walls, a mud-beamed ceiling crossed by rafters. Flower boxes along the small amber lighted windows." *Variety* called them "the 'hottest' band this side of the equator" in April, and *Billboard* praised the band even more fervently eight months later: "Possessing a sense of rhythm that is almost uncanny, the boys in this dusky organization dispense a type of melody that stamps the outfit as the most torrid in town." The following summer they left the club to tour New England, and a reporter for *The Boston Post* hauled out the biggest gun of all, referring to the group as "the Paul Whiteman of Colored Orchestras."

How good were the Washingtonians? Good enough to entice no less a giant of jazz than Sidney Bechet to play with them, though the irascible and sometimes unreliable clarinetist was too hard even for Duke Ellington to handle. After Bechet went missing for three days, Ellington demanded an explanation. "Where the hell have you been?" he asked. "I jumped in a cab and we got lost, and I just now finally found out where I was," Bechet replied. That put an end to his stint with the Washingtonians, but his willingness to work with them at all means that they must have been more accomplished than the average jazz band of the day.

They were good enough to make records, too, for the Washingtonians cut ten 78 sides, the first recordings by the Ellington band to be released commercially, between November of 1924 and June of 1926. These sides are old-fashioned "acoustic" recordings that the group made by playing into a megaphone-like horn, and they are technically primitive by comparison to the up-to-date electrical recordings that other jazz musicians started cutting in the spring of 1925. To hear them now is to wonder what all the fuss in *Variety* and *Billboard* was about, since the Washingtonians sound like any number of other sprightly but rhythmically stiff-jointed dance bands of the midtwenties. "If one searches for embryonic Ellington elements," says Gunther Schuller, "the pickings are very lean indeed." Only two of the

Washingtonians' records are of songs written in whole or part by Ellington, and several of the charts appear to be based on stock arrangements. Even Bubber Miley's growl-trumpet solos on "Li'l Farina" (named after a character from the popular *Our Gang* movie shorts) and Ellington's own "Choo Choo (I Gotta Hurry Home)," the first of the band's records to be issued, are only modestly interesting when heard in tandem with the playing that he would put on wax a few months later.

It may be, as some scholars contend, that the shortcomings of these records can be traced to the second- and third-rate songs that the Washingtonians recorded, and to the fact that several of their performances are based on written arrangements that the band may well have been sight-reading in the studio. "If the Washingtonians had been better readers, like Fletcher Henderson's musicians, the results might have been more impressive," Mark Tucker, an authority on Ellington's early years, has written. Very possibly, but it is also true that Bechet, Louis Armstrong, James P. Johnson, King Oliver, Jelly Roll Morton, and Fletcher Henderson's band had all managed by that time to make recordings of permanent interest that showed them at or near the peak of their abilities. Not so Duke Ellington. He was a reasonably seasoned twenty-seven-year-old professional when he recorded "Li'l Farina," the last and best of the Washingtonians' acoustic sides, in the summer of 1926, but had he been hit by a car on the way home from the recording studio, his name would be forgotten today. It took something more—and someone else—to propel him from the legion of faceless professionals into the ranks of the jazz immortals.

3

"ONLY MY OWN MUSIC"

With Irving Mills, 1926–1927

T HE NINETEENTH AND twentieth centuries butted up hard against one another on January 16, 1920, the day that the Volstead Act took effect
and the sale, manufacture, and transportation of alcohol became illegal
in America. Nobody knew it yet, but Prohibition was the last gasp of the
shaky reign of the genteel tradition in middle-class American life. In many
places that "tradition" was already more a matter of appearances than anything else—the number of saloons in America had tripled between 1870 and
1900—and the weary doughboys of the American Expeditionary Forces had
put a further dent in what was left of it when they sailed home from Europe
at the end of World War I and found themselves dissatisfied with the lives
they'd left behind. Those who had once hewed steadfastly to the old ways
now knew that they could never resume them, and everybody else seemed to
know it as well, starting with the men who wrote one of the hit songs of
1919:

> *How 'ya gonna keep 'em down on the farm,*
> *After they've seen Pa-ree?*
> *How 'ya gonna keep 'em away from Broad-way;*
> *Jazzin' a-'round,*

And paintin' the town?
How 'ya gonna keep 'em away from harm?

The answer was that you couldn't. That didn't stop the teetotalers from trying, but by 1926 everyone with eyes and ears knew that they had failed. It was in the Roaring Twenties that America slammed the door on the sedate ways of the Victorian era and embraced the brash new world of ballyhoo. Not only were men drinking, but so were women—and they were doing it in public. Speakeasies, unlike old-fashioned saloons, welcomed their custom and hired dance bands to encourage them to return. Edmund Wilson, one of the keenest observers of the period, wrote with nostalgia of the social freedom of that crazy decade: "In the twenties [people] could love, they could travel, they could stay up late at night as extravagantly as they pleased; they could think or say or write whatever seemed to them amusing or interesting." They could also go to cabarets and dance all night, and because enforcement of the Volstead Act was so lax, they could get drunk, go home with a stranger, and laugh about it, or try to, the next day.

The burgeoning popularity of jazz and jazz-influenced styles of music, which suited the high-stepping new styles of social dancing, was a natural outgrowth of this freedom. So was the rise of the advertising business. In *H.M. Pulham, Esquire,* published in 1941, John P. Marquand tells the story of a Harvard man who comes home from the war shaken to the core by the sights and sounds of trench combat, stops off in New York, and takes a job on Madison Avenue, where he plunges into an affair with a bright young career girl who is happy to sleep with him without benefit of clergy. It was that kind of time. Americans had more money to spend and longed to be told how and where to spend it, and other Americans obliged them. Not only did Harry Pulham, Jay Gatsby, and George Babbitt need music to dance to, but they needed someone to sell it to them—and that was where Irving Mills came in.

Born on Manhattan's Lower East Side in 1894 to a family of Russian Jews, Mills was the kind of man for whom the word *go-getter* might have been coined. Spike Hughes, a British composer-critic who worked briefly with him in the thirties, called Mills a "small, squat, hard-headed business man . . . with the naïve enthusiasm—and lack of humour—of the born, successful impresario." He got into the music business by working as a song-plugger, a singing salesman who pitched newly published tunes to music storekeepers and potential performers. In his 1930 study of Tin Pan Alley, Isaac Goldberg spoke of "the arts of persuasion, intrigue, bribery, mayhem, malfeasance, cajolery, entreaty, threat, insinuation, persistence and whatever else he has" that were employed by the song-pluggers of the day. It also helped if they had loud voices, and Mills's nasal baritone, which sounded as though he had a megaphone built into his throat, qualified with room to spare.

In due course Mills became a publisher in his own right, teaming up with his brother Jack in 1919 to start Jack Mills Inc. (later renamed Mills Music Inc.). Their first hit was "They Needed a Song Bird in Heaven, So God Took Caruso Away," a lachrymose tribute to the recently deceased tenor. A year earlier Mamie Smith had recorded "Crazy Blues," whose success triggered a nationwide passion for blues and blueslike songs, which the Mills brothers started buying by the carload. They had little choice, for the established songwriters whose output they longed to publish had already signed with other houses, leaving Irving and Jack with no alternative but to develop new talent. It was their willingness to work with black artists that eventually opened the door to lasting success. Another consequence of this willingness, Irving recalled, was that other publishers "looked down on me. They said, 'Geez, he fools around with niggers.' " But whatever his private feelings about blacks—and he appears never to have said anything offensive about them as a group—he knew that there was money to be made from their music, explaining, "I figured I might as well corral something so that I could have control of something . . . a dollar don't care where it's from, whether it's black [or] green."

Mills soon acquired a reputation for treating black songwriters decently, though he and his brother were as guilty of the usual sharp practices of the trade as were their colleagues. Regardless of their color, he always offered novice tunesmiths flat fees for their efforts. If they declined to accept cash on the barrelhead, he or a member of his staff would "suggest" improvements to their songs, then take a cowriting credit, thereby cutting the firm in for a bigger slice of the resulting royalties. Mills, who was musically illiterate, nevertheless insisted that his contributions to the songs for which he took partial credit had been substantial, and there may have been something to his claim. Duke Ellington thought so, or at least said so: "He could feel a song. He'd take a good lyricist, tell him, 'Now this song needs something right here,' and the cat would go over it, and it would come out perfect." Late in life (he died in 1985) Mills said that he "title[d] all the tunes" that he published, specifically mentioning Ellington's "Mood Indigo." He also claimed to have come up with the title of "It Don't Mean a Thing (If It Ain't Got That Swing)." In addition, his staffers supplied lyrics for instrumental numbers, thus entitling the firm to an even larger cut. But there were times when his contributions to the songs that appeared under his name were notional at best. According to Henry "Red" Allen, the New Orleans–born trumpeter who worked with him in the thirties, "A guy would record his own tune [for Mills], then, when the record came out he'd look at the label and find out that he had a co-composer, maybe even two, who hadn't added or altered a single note, yet they all took even shares. It was all part of the music business in those days."*

It was, for Mills, an immensely profitable business. He became a natty dresser whose Brooklyn home was decorated in an assortment of incompatible period styles. His hospitality was ostentatious, and one of his verbal tics was to offer his guests not a cigar, but a *good* cigar ("Have a good cigar, Spike"). In the twenties and thirties he looked like a well-groomed fireplug, in old age like a wealthy gnome, but at no time could he have been mistaken for anything other than a second-generation immigrant, for he was branded on the tongue with the accent of the big-city hustler, which he acquired on the streets of lower Manhattan and retained until his death. Even Bob, his loyal son, spoke of his "limited vocabulary," and a strong scent of snobbery hangs over what some of his acquaintances had to say about him. What Ellington made of so rough-hewn a character can only be imagined, but he is not known to have uttered a disagreeable word about Mills, and most of those who knew the man believed his contribution to black music to be largely positive. Not all: John Hammond worked for Mills in 1934 and later claimed to have seen at the time "how tremendously Duke was being exploited." In 1936 he wrote an article for the *New Masses* in which he declared that Mills's way of doing business with songwriters was "as ingenious as it [was] unfair to the author and composer." But he also praised Mills years later as "a man who saved black talent in the 1930's, when there was no one else who cared whether it worked or not."

It is unclear when Mills and Ellington first crossed paths. In 1973 Ellington said that they met "during [his] first six months in New York" and that he sold an unspecified number of blues songs to the Mills brothers for "fifteen or twenty dollars" apiece. In 1940 he remembered it differently: "The band had

---

* In addition to some sixty-odd songs written with Ellington and his musicians, Mills is also credited with having cowritten "If Dreams Come True," "Lovesick Blues," "Minnie the Moocher," "Moonglow," "Straighten Up and Fly Right," "Washboard Blues," and "When My Sugar Walks Down the Street."

been at the Kentucky Club about three and a half years [i.e., late in 1926] when I first met Irving Mills. We were playing the *St. Louis Blues,* and he asked what it was. When I told him, he said it sure sounded nothing like it. So maybe that gave him ideas." Mills recalled the song that he heard as Ellington's "Black and Tan Fantasy," and in 1937 he told a reporter for *Time* that as soon as he heard the Washingtonians, he "signed the Negro pianist to a contract on the back of a menu."

This much is certain: Duke Ellington and His Kentucky Club Orchestra, as the band was billed by Vocalion, its new record company, reported to Room 1 of Brunswick Studios in midtown Manhattan on November 29, 1926, to cut two issued instrumental sides, "East St. Louis Toodle-O"* and "Birmingham Breakdown." Not long after that, Ellington signed a personal management contract with Mills, and for the next thirteen years their fates would be entwined.

In later years Mills was crystal clear about what he had seen in Ellington in 1926. He had already figured out that one of the most effective ways to plug the songs that he published was to arrange for them to be recorded by suitable singers, and since a growing number of those songs were being written by and for blacks, he also needed a black band with a suitable leader. At first he tried Fletcher Henderson, but Henderson was insufficiently reliable:

> *He never had the same men twice, or he didn't have the arrangements ready, or there were always some little things that didn't make the date perfect. It was not good for the band, not good for the singer. So much for Fletcher Henderson. When I heard Duke play, I heard not only Duke, but I fell in love with every individual man as a soloist. . . . I left the club and was so intrigued with the possibilities of the band that to make sure that I'd get them to record, I went back to the club. I dated up Duke to come to the office and arrange the recording.*

---

* Ellington always pronounced the last word of the title "*TOAD*-lo," a reference to the "todalo," a black dance step. He may have meant for it to be spelled "Toddle-O" on the label of the original recording, but the word was spelled "Toodle-O" in 1926 and "Toddle-Oo" or "Toodle-Oo" on many (though not all) subsequent versions. Though Ellington copyrighted the song as "East St. Louis Toodle-O" and continued to spell it in that manner, "East St. Louis Toodle-Oo" became the "official" title by default after 1927. The song is usually known by the latter name today.

"A great creative artist": Irving Mills, Percy Grainger, and Ellington at New York University, 1932. Throughout his thirteen-year association with Duke Ellington, Mills promoted the bandleader as "a great musician who was making a lasting contribution to American music," emphasizing the fact that his jazz compositions were admired by noted classical musicians like Grainger

The "possibilities" of which Mills spoke a half century later centered on Ellington's compositions. From the outset of their association, Mills promoted Ellington both as a bandleader and as a composer, something that had never before been done in jazz. "Every now and then the record companies wanted me to make outside tunes," Mills later explained, "so occasionally I would make a 'Twelfth Street Rag' or some old, old tune. Otherwise I stuck to 100 percent Duke Ellington." That wasn't quite true—Ellington recorded many Mills-published songs by other hands—but in the main he stuck to his own work, a policy that was to make him unique among his fellow leaders. In a crowd of soon-to-be-familiar faces, he stood out as the only one, black or white, who wrote or cowrote most of the songs that his musicians played. Nobody had to tell him what that meant and would continue to mean, both as a musical opportunity and as a source of income. *Music Is My Mistress* contains a half-page list of the things that Irving Mills claimed to have done for

Ellington, and the first item on it was his insistence that Ellington "make and record only [his] own music."

Mills said that he immediately recognized Ellington to be "a great creative artist—and the first American composer to catch in his music the true jazz spirit." He also understood what it would mean to have under exclusive contract a popular bandleader who, like Ellington, wrote his own material. Whenever the Washingtonians performed, whether in person or on record, they would be promoting a catalog of songs that were written by their leader and published by Mills Music Inc., which reaped the lion's share of their sheet-music sales and performance royalties. In addition, Mills grasped early on that Ellington's soloists were part and parcel of his composing method and that their ability to generate tunes that their leader turned into full-length songs could also be profitably exploited: "We gave every man in the band an opportunity to write. . . . They came in with ideas, and Duke helped to develop it and give it the style."

If the Washingtonians had sounded the same way in November of 1926 that they did on the records they cut earlier in the year, then Mills's ability as a talent scout would have bordered on the prophetic. But the hiring of a new trombonist had made a big difference: Joseph Nanton, always known as "Tricky" to the members of the band and "Tricky Sam" to the public, replaced Charlie Irvis, and by November he was, after Miley, the band's principal solo horn. Born in New York of West Indian parents in 1904, Nanton was intellectually curious to a degree unusual among jazz musicians of the period. Rex Stewart, who got to know him in the thirties, described the trombonist as a "thinking, knowledgeable man" with the melancholy face of a basset hound and an unquenchable taste for liquor, which he quietly sipped on the bandstand: "He was well acquainted with such erudite and diverse subjects as astronomy, how to make home brew, and how to use a slide rule. He could recite poetry by ancient poets that most of us never knew existed, and he knew Shakespeare." He also knew what to do with a plunger: His muted solos had a raw, vocalized quality that bore a startlingly close resemblance to human speech. (Unlike Miley and most other plunger-mute players, his preferred sound was not "wah-wah" but "yah-yah.") Nanton spent the next two decades in Ellington's trombone section, and in time his playing became the most recognizable color on the composer's palette.

It mattered, too, that Ellington was now working with a bigger band. The Club Kentucky bandstand was so small that it would hold only seven musicians, so he took the opportunity to add three new men when the

Washingtonians toured New England in the summer of 1926. Working with this group had taught Ellington how to use the expanded tonal resources of a ten-piece band to the best advantage, and when Irving Mills and Vocalion Records invited him to show what he could do, Ellington brought all ten players into the studio and led with the strongest card in his hand. "East St. Louis Toodle-O," the Washingtonians' first electrical recording, had been written for the larger band the preceding summer, and it makes arresting use of the wider range of tone colors available to a ten-piece ensemble.

"East St. Louis Toodle-O" gets under way with eight bars of moaning low-register saxophone-section chords (the bass line is played by a tuba, darkening the sound still further) that serve as an ear-catching minor-key introduction. The introduction is promptly repeated, this time as the opening section of a thirty-two-bar AABA-song-form chorus, with Bubber Miley playing a raspy, blues-drenched plunger solo that floats freely atop the arc of rising and falling chords. What would normally follow is a string of additional choruses constructed along similar lines, but Ellington surprises us by introducing a contrasting sixteen-bar strain with a two-bar tag. The major-key harmonies of this strain are first used to accompany a solo by Tricky Sam Nanton, then heard underneath an ensemble theme whose polkalike rhythms bear a definite resemblance to the tune of "I Wish I Could Shimmy Like My Sister Kate." The two strains alternate unpredictably, with Miley returning at the end to round out what is not a mere repeating-chorus song but a full-fledged instrumental composition. The form of "East St. Louis Toodle-O" is simple but satisfying, and though Miley's solo is the best part, it is the dark-hued saxophone-and-tuba accompaniment that helps to make it so—a sign that Ellington may already have been starting to think of orchestral color as his musical signature.

He was also, as would be the case for the rest of his career, collaborating closely with his star sidemen. Although Ellington receives sole credit on the label of Vocalion 1064 as the composer of "East St. Louis Toodle-O," later recordings of the piece credit Bubber Miley as co-composer. What did Miley contribute? The chantlike four-bar melodic motif heard at the beginning of his solo was definitely his own creation. Miley told a friend that "the inspiration for the 'East St. Louis Toodle-O' came one night in Boston [on the band's 1926 tour of New England] as he was returning home from work. He kept noticing the electric sign of the dry-cleaning store Lewandos. The name struck him as exceedingly funny and it ran through his head." Miley started singing an improvised tune that fit the name of the store: "Oh, Le-wan-*dos!* Oh, Le-*wa*-ah-an-dos!" Out of that fragmentary idea came the rest of his solo, a set piece that he repeated with minor variations each time the band played "East St. Louis Toodle-O."

Ellington said that Miley had conceived of the song as a musical portrait. As he explained in *Music Is My Mistress*, the trumpeter "always had a story for his music, such as: 'This is an old man, tired from working in the field since sunup, coming up the road in the sunset on his way home to dinner. He's tired but strong, and humming in time with his broken gait—or vice versa.' That was how he pictured 'East St. Louis Toodle-oo [*sic*].'" Ellington loved to trot out such tales, some of which were attached after the fact to the compositions that they were alleged to have inspired. Miley himself seems to have said no such thing, nor did he claim to have contributed more to the piece than his trumpet solo. But the solo was a defining contribution in and of itself, and Tricky Sam Nanton, speaking with specific reference to "East St. Louis Toodle-O" and "Black and Tan Fantasy," called Miley "an idea man. . . . His ideas were more or less the backbone of the band. His ideas and the tunes he wrote set the band's style."

The question of what constitutes a "tune" is central to grasping the nature of Ellington's achievement as a composer. Miley made one statement that may touch on the matter: "When I get off [i.e., play an inspired solo] the Duke is always there." What did he mean? Perhaps he was saying that Ellington used his best improvised solos as the raw material for finished compositions that showed off Miley's playing to even more advantageous effect, as he would do with other players later on. We can only speculate, since no manuscript materials for the original version of "East St. Louis Toodle-O" survive, and it's safe to assume that the piece, like the rest of Ellington's early compositions, was worked out on the bandstand and in the studio long before anyone thought to write it down. But most scholars now believe that Ellington supplied and scored the chordal backdrop for Miley's solo, composed the second strain, and established the overall running order.

In doing so—if that is what he did—he established a pattern for many other pieces that he would write in years to come. One of his favorite gambits, for instance, was to launch his records not with an ensemble chorus but with an instrumental solo accompanied by the band. At times, as in "East St. Louis Toodle-O," these solos took the place of written-out themes, for Ellington made a point of hiring players whose styles were so characterful (and melodically appealing) that he could get away with giving them nothing more than a cushion of interestingly scored chords over which they would then improvise. When he wrote a melody of his own, it was often, like the second strain of "East St. Louis Toodle-O," both unsingable and unmemorable. Most of the themes that he is known to have written himself, as opposed to the ones that he derived from his bandstand listening, typically arise from and adumbrate their underlying harmonies rather than having a fully independent life of their own.

His approach to form was just as unconventional. Instead of putting together close-knit multistrain miniatures in the manner of the ragtime pianists from whom he learned his craft, Ellington treated the sections of his compositions as if they were separate pieces in a mosaic that could be rearranged at will. The Ellington band recorded "East St. Louis Toodle-O" several more times in 1927, and in the last of these versions, cut for Victor in December, Ellington restructured the composition, changing the order of the strains and the instrumental solos, a practice that became part of his composing routine. Later on he would bring unfinished, seemingly fragmentary bits of music into the studio, then shift them around on the spot until he arrived at a sequence that satisfied him.

Irving Townsend, who produced several of the albums that Ellington recorded in the fifties, described the latter process, which can also be heard on surviving rehearsal tapes:

> *Duke, to the bewilderment of people who have watched him record, writes and rehearses music in small segments, usually of eight measures and almost always without a written conclusion. His first studio rundowns of new music trail off as his musicians reach the end of a phrase at different moments and come to a limping stop. Then, knowing the length of each segment and how it sounds, Ellington proceeds to move his parts around. A typical example, although fictitious, of Duke's final instructions for a performance might go as follows: "Start at letter C. Then go to A and play it twice, only the second time leave off the last two bars. These bars are the beginning of a sheet you have marked X. After X I'll play until I bring you in at C again and you go out with letter D."*

As always, Ellington's ear made his decisions, and to outsiders they could seem capricious. Even intimates found his jigsaw-puzzle approach to musical form to be arbitrary. After he dismantled and reassembled one of Billy Strayhorn's pieces at a 1953 recording session, Strayhorn broke with his mentor, staying away from the band for two and a half years. But contrast lay at the heart of Ellington's style, so much so that he elevated it to the status of a fundamental ordering principle, one that he went so far as to claim as an attribute of his race: "You know how the negroes are. They pass quickly from the extremes of joy to gloom and back again. There must be the same quality in pure negro music." This, too, can be heard in "East St. Louis Toodle-O," in which the contrast between Miley's minor-key solo and the major-key strain with which it is juxtaposed is the first known example of one of Ellington's stylistic fingerprints.

Not only is "East St. Louis Toodle-O" an epitome of much that was to come in his music, but the 1926 recording is so well played as to indicate that the Washingtonians must have been performing the piece regularly. According to Sonny Greer, it was one of the band's signature numbers: "People heard it and said, 'Here they come!'" Ellington, who always knew a good thing when he heard it, responded by making "East St. Louis Toodle-O" his radio theme, playing it nightly for years to come. While "Birmingham Breakdown," a dance tune cut at the same session, was not nearly so impressive, it also represented a vast improvement over the feeble records that the band had previously been making. But "East St. Louis Toodle-O" is one of the most completely realized jazz recordings of the midtwenties, a performance worthy of comparison with such classics of early ensemble jazz as Jelly Roll Morton's "Black Bottom Stomp" or Fletcher Henderson's "The Stampede," both of which had been cut only a few months earlier. When Jimi Hendrix heard it for the first time, he was so struck by Miley's solo that he sought to duplicate its tonal qualities by using a "wah-wah" pedal to alter the timbre of his electric guitar. In 1973 Steely Dan recorded the same piece in an arrangement that sounds at home alongside such rock songs as "Rikki Don't Lose That Number" and "Monkey in Your Soul."

The artistic success of the Ellington band's first electrical recording session was no fluke. Over the next twelve months, the group recorded a total of ten original compositions and four songs by other writers. Three of the originals, "Black and Tan Fantasy," "Creole Love Call," and "East St. Louis Toodle-O," became permanent parts of Ellington's repertoire. That's a high batting average for anyone, and still more impressive for a young musician whose previous work had shown so few signs of what was to come.

"Black and Tan Fantasy," cowritten with Bubber Miley and first recorded in April of 1927, starts out with a tune that might well have been known to Daisy Ellington. Miley borrowed it from "The Holy City," a sacred song by

Stephen Adams published in 1892, changing the first four bars of Adams's refrain from major to minor and stretching them into a twelve-bar blues chorus. (Miley told a friend that the song was a spiritual that his mother had sung to him when he was a boy.) The blues theme is followed by a slippery-sounding major-key alto-saxophone theme played by Otto Hardwick in his sexiest manner, a contrast that Ellington must have engineered. Then comes a string of major-key blues choruses by Miley, Ellington, and Nanton, with Miley sputtering furiously and Nanton playing the first of his eerie-sounding "talking" solos to be preserved on record. At the end Ellington deals a new card, a four-bar coda in which Miley and the band intone the solemn theme from the slow movement of Chopin's *Funeral March* sonata, a tune to which generation after generation of English-speaking children have sung the mock-serious words *Pray for the dead and the dead will pray for you.*

"Creole Love Call," recorded in October, is even simpler, consisting of six twelve-bar blues choruses in a medium tempo, four of which feature the same theme, a softly rocking riff that is first scored for a clarinet trio, then for the full band. Yet Ellington once again has a card tucked up his sleeve: In the first chorus, a woman's voice is superimposed atop the clarinets, singing a wordless countermelody that sounds almost as though it is being played on a plunger-muted trumpet. The singer, a stage performer named Adelaide Hall who had made her Broadway debut in 1921 in Eubie Blake's *Shuffle Along*, was sharing a theater bill with the Washingtonians when she heard them playing "Creole Love Call" as she stood in the wings. She started humming along with the band, and as soon as Ellington heard her, he left the piano and went backstage. "Adelaide, that's what I've been looking for!" he said, then brought her out to sing the number with the band. They recorded it together a few days later.

The clarinet solo in "Creole Love Call" is by Rudy Jackson, who had previously played with King Oliver. Jackson, who shared composing credit for the song with Ellington and Miley, apparently neglected to inform his collaborators that he had stolen the song from his old boss. Six months later, not long after he left the Washingtonians, Oliver sent a stiffly worded letter to the copyright department of Victor Records:

> *I have recently listened to a recording by your company of "Creole Love Call," played by Duke Ellington's band.*
>
> *Permit me to bring to your attention the fact that this number was written by me and copyrighted Oct. 11, 1923; #570230 under the title of "Camp Meeting Blues."*

The writer also recorded this particular number on the Columbia records and has collected royalties for same.

Will you, therefore, be good enough to forward me a contract covering "Creole Love Call" and should you desire further information, the same will be given, gladly.

It was nothing more than the truth: "Creole Love Call" *is* "Camp Meeting Blues," restructured and rescored à la Ellington for a ten-piece band. Except for Hall's wordless riff, all of the song's thematic material, as well as Jackson's "improvised" clarinet solo, had been lifted from Oliver's 1923 recording. He had Ellington dead to rights, and only a technicality kept him from collecting royalties on "Creole Love Call" for the rest of his life: "Camp Meeting Blues" had been copyrighted under a different title, "Temptation Blues," then renamed at the recording session. The change of title made the registration impossible to trace, leaving Oliver high and dry. It was a costly mistake, for not only did Ellington re-record "Creole Love Song" many times, but it later became part of the medley of hits that his band played at its public performances. But if Ellington (or, more likely, Jackson) plagiarized the material out of which "Creole Love Call" was made, it was what he did with what he stole that made the results his own. Not only did he spot the potential in Adelaide Hall's impromptu backstage vocal, but he deserves full credit for deconstructing the constituent parts of Oliver's 1923 version and turning them into a better-ordered whole. The opening clarinet riff, for instance, is not heard until the fourth chorus of "Camp Meeting Blues," when it is played as a clarinet solo. It was Ellington, not Oliver, who saw the thematic possibilities of the solo, then added the transfiguring touch of Hall's wistful voice.

Neither "Creole Love Call" nor "Black and Tan Fantasy" is as subtle, or as complex, as the compositions that Ellington would be turning out on a regular basis a few years later. But for all their bluesy simplicity, both pieces, like "East St. Louis Toodle-O," also had a near-pictorial quality that bore little resemblance to the extroverted dance music that most other jazz musicians were performing in 1927. It was natural that they should have attracted the attention of commentators who were starting to notice the expressive potential of jazz. The first of these men to comment on Ellington in print was R. D. Darrell, one of the earliest American music critics to take recordings seriously and review them in the same way that other critics reviewed live performances. Though Darrell specialized in classical music, he had an ear for jazz, and in June of 1927 he started reviewing Ellington's recordings for *Phonograph Monthly Review,* a Boston-based magazine founded the preceding October whose cover billed it as "An Independent American Magazine for Amateurs Interested in Recorded Music and Its Development." Darrell, who knew nothing about jazz, started listening to review copies of Ellington's early 78s by chance and came to the conclusion that he was "an orchestrator in the class of Ravel, Respighi and Strauss."

Darrell's reviews of Ellington's records were the first to appear in any magazine—they may have been the first to appear anywhere—and the excitement with which he reported on his first hearing of "Black and Tan Fantasy" is still contagious:

> *Two unusually interesting records lead the Brunswick list, indeed are right in the forefront of the releases from all companies. The* Black and Tan Fantasy *... deserves perhaps the first prize; in it The Washingtonians combine sonority and fine tonal qualities with some amazing eccentric instrumental effects. This record differs from similar ones by avoiding extremes, for while the "stunts" are exceptionally original and striking, they are performed musically, even artistically. A piece no one should miss!*

Darrell continued to write about Ellington for *Phonograph Monthly Review* until 1931, and his reviews were read by a small but vocal audience of aficionados in America and England. While his role in spreading the word about Ellington was soon forgotten and remained so until after his death, he was, so far as is known, the first music critic to recognize that jazz, which until that time had been primarily a soloist's music, had now produced a composer of consequence. But record reviews, however prescient, did little to improve the lot of a working jazz musician in 1927, and one suspects that Ellington was more pleased to read Dave Peyton's column in *The Chicago Defender* that April. Peyton, a bandleader-journalist who took jazz seriously but liked it best when it was polite, assured his readers that Ellington was the "conductor of what leading judges have called the foremost jazz orchestra in America." Peyton also mentioned that he was "a pupil of the famous Henry Grant," a touch that must have pleased Ellington, and included a paragraph that would have given even more pleasure to Irving Mills: "Ellington insists that all his remarkable rhythms and harmonies would not be before so wide a public today were it not for Irving Mills of Jack Mills, Inc., New York music publishers."

Stories like this one (which was picked up by the *New York Amsterdam*

News and *The Pittsburgh Courier,* two other top black weeklies) both fed and reflected the band's growing reputation. So did the fact that Ellington and his sidemen were now recording for several different labels. On Vocalion they were billed as "Duke Ellington and His Kentucky Club Orchestra," on Victor "Duke Ellington and His Orchestra," on Brunswick and Pathé "The Washingtonians." In addition to recording under multiple names, the band recorded multiple versions of Ellington's most popular numbers: four of "East St. Louis Toodle-O," three of "Black and Tan Fantasy," two of "Birmingham Breakdown." Most were basically identical to the originals. Was he re-recording these songs in order to polish them or merely to bring in more money? Either way, he would continue the practice throughout his career, tinkering with and—sometimes—improving the masterpieces of his youth long after he grew old.

All this was made possible by Irving Mills, who must have had a hand in the writing of Peyton's column and was also, so he said, playing an active role in the band's recording sessions:

> *Duke would have a skeleton of something when he came in the studio. I would time the tune and make suggestions and he listened. He had a high respect for what I'd do in the recording room. We never fought over an arrangement in the studio. . . . I created the balances. I cut out the arrangements. Whatever they did, I thinned it out. His music was always too heavy. He overarranged.*

The trumpeter Louis Metcalf, who had joined the band in 1926, angrily recalled Mills's meddling a half-century later: "We got a session down there, and we're gonna play certain numbers. We'd get out there, and this guy Mills would change it all around. Mills was kind of a show-off cat. . . . Man, we had some arrangements, and then this monkey comes in, and that's when everybody began to get down on Duke. They'd say, 'How can you let this man louse up your band?' " But Ellington knew what Mills was doing for him, and Mills knew that he knew. Not only was the band making new records every few weeks and getting written up with steadily increasing regularity, but Mills was also publishing sheet-music versions and stock arrangements of Ellington's compositions, an undertaking made more difficult by the fact that most of them were worked out on the spot in the rehearsal studio and on the bandstand rather than being written down in advance. Ellington, Mills said, "knew how to construct at the piano because the boys knew what he wanted. . . . But he didn't leave anything [written] behind. It didn't make any difference—we knew we could always get it after it was perfected by the whole band by taking it off of the records." Mills would eventually publish simplified piano arrangements of dozens of Ellington compositions, ranging from "East St. Louis Toodle-O" and "Creole Love Call" to such recherché instrumentals as "The Mystery Song" and "Rude Interlude." Transcribed from his records, they remain in print—and continue to sell.

Such services do not come cheap, and Mills was well paid for his labors. The terms of the deal that he struck with Ellington the preceding winter were their secret, but at the end of 1929, Samuel Buzzell, Mills's lawyer, drew up a certificate of incorporation for Duke Ellington, Inc., that divided ownership of the resulting corporation equally between Ellington, Mills, and Buzzell. After Mills and Ellington had come to a parting of the ways, the *Amsterdam News* reported that the two men had agreed to a 45-45 split of the band's profits, with the remaining 10 percent going to Buzzell. In 1933 *Time* reported that "Mr. Mills's 'piece'" of Ellington was 50 percent. Whatever the exact truth of the matter, Mills was in no doubt of what it meant. "I owned the band, you know, he worked for me . . . the band belonged to me and not to him," he said in 1984. As for the publishing rights to Ellington's music, Mills's share was usually larger still, and Louis Metcalf went so far as to claim that "a clause in [the band's] contract" specified that "every composition that Duke or any of the band wrote had to be sold outright for twenty-five dollars to his manager."

Today these terms sound close to indentured servitude, but in 1927 it was common for black performers to sign over large chunks of their take to white managers. When Louis Armstrong signed his first management contract in 1929, he agreed to pay Tommy Rockwell $75 out of the first $250 that he earned each week, plus half of any additional net profits, and they split Armstrong's record royalties evenly. Like Armstrong, Ellington knew that he could not function at the top levels of the music business without a white manager. He also knew that what Mills did for him went beyond mere management. For one thing, Mills relieved him of the day-to-day responsibilities of a businessman, which he would always find tedious. In George Wein's words, "Duke didn't want to know, and didn't want to be bothered. He really did not care about business. He was concerned about music, and the business would take care of itself." Even more important, though, Mills was starting to construct the public image of the jazzman-as-artist that would define

Ellington in the eyes of the media throughout the decade to come. In return he uncomplainingly gave most of his income to Mills.

As his manager-partner explained it:

> *Duke was a good listener. He followed instructions. He's sponsored. He's got nothing to worry about: money, or the job, or the men. Now he can work. All he has to do is write. . . . Duke always knew his position and was always very grateful for everything that was being done, because he knew he was getting all the best of everything. Everything we created [was] "from the pen of Duke Ellington," whether he wrote it or he didn't write it.*

That last remark goes to the heart of the matter. In order to make Ellington a celebrity, Mills shone a pin-spot of publicity on the band, but it was focused on the leader, leaving his sidemen in the dark. Some of them resented the secondary status to which they were now being relegated. What had started out as a cooperative venture was evolving into an enterprise directed by one man alone. In 1969 Fred Guy complained that Mills "wanted Duke to be the star, not the band. The men were just the rank and file." No longer was Duke one of the boys: When it came to musical matters, he was the boss, and though he held the reins with the lightest of touches, everyone knew it. Barry Ulanov, who interviewed many of his sidemen in the forties, wrote that Mills's decision to make him the band's true leader soon led to "serious disillusionment for the men in the band, a deepening sense of personal and collective tragedy which has never left these brilliant musicians."

Not all of them felt that way. Sonny Greer, for one, understood and appreciated what Mills was doing: "He was blue-white diamond. He was the guy. He was *the* guy. . . . Everything first class, every time you look around, he said, 'I better get you guys another set of uniforms.'" Mills poured money into the band without stint, treating it as a long-term investment that would sooner or later pay off in the form of fatter royalties. But in order to make that happen, he first had to make Ellington well-known, and he did so by selling him as an artist:

> *For me, the development of Duke Ellington's career was an over-all operation consisting of much more than merely securing engagements for him or selling his songs. Anyone could have done that. My exploitation campaign was aimed at presenting the public [with] a great musician*

who was making a lasting contribution to American music. I was able to guide Duke Ellington to the top of his field, a field in which he was the first to be accepted as an authentic artist, because I made his importance as an artist the primary consideration.

Still, the engagements had to be secured, and the next step in the selling of Ellington was to find a more suitable showcase for his artistry. That came in December when the band opened at the Cotton Club, the Harlem cabaret where he would perfect the musical style that propelled him, assisted by Mills, to the very top of the tree.

4

"THE UTMOST SIGNIFICANCE"

At the Cotton Club, 1927–1929

I N 1927 HARLEM was a playground for white people who could afford to pay for liquor and sex—and who liked having sex with black people, so long as they didn't have to talk to them afterward. Of the uptown nightclubs that catered to white patrons, the Cotton Club, which billed itself as "the Aristocrat of Harlem" in its newspaper ads, was the best known and most expensive, as well as the one with the dirtiest pedigree. Owney Madden, the owner, was an Englishman of Irish parentage whose family had emigrated to New York's Hell's Kitchen when he was eleven years old. He was slight of stature and spoke in a high-pitched voice that sounded, Sonny Greer said, "like a girl." But appearances were deceiving, for Madden was a vicious street fighter who in his youth had racked up a long list of cold-blooded killings. He now ran one of New York's most successful bootlegging gangs, investing his profits in Broadway shows like Mae West's *Sex* (and, it was whispered, having a backstage affair with West herself). In 1920, while he was serving an eight-year term in Sing Sing for manslaughter, he acquired a failed Harlem supper club called the Café de Luxe that had been "owned" by Jack Johnson, the famous black boxer, who served as the front man for yet another mobster. After Madden was paroled in 1923, he turned it into a cabaret with a stiff cover charge whose scantily dressed dancers and sexually suggestive stage shows became the talk of Manhattan.

Located on Lenox Avenue at West 142nd Street, the Cotton Club was a second-story walk-up that held between six and seven hundred people who sat in two tiers of tables surrounding the dance floor. The walls were covered with what Irving Mills, who was prone to malapropisms, called "muriels." The rest of the décor, as Cab Calloway recalled, was suggestive in a less innocent way:

> *The bandstand was a replica of a southern mansion, with large white columns and a backdrop painted with weeping willows and slave quarters. The band played on the veranda of the mansion. . . . The waiters were dressed in red tuxedos, like butlers in a southern mansion, and the tables were covered with red-and-white-checked gingham table-cloths. . . . I suppose the idea was to make whites who came to the club feel like they were being catered to and entertained by black slaves.*

Spike Hughes, who visited the club a few years later, described it as "expensive and exclusive; it cost you the earth merely to look at the girl who

"Expensive and exclusive": Behind its nondescript façade on Harlem's Lenox Avenue, the Cotton Club was one of New York's toniest nightspots, a mobbed-up mecca for moneyed whites who wanted to be amused by black entertainers—including Duke Ellington and his band

took your hat and coat as you went in." He was stretching it, but not by much. According to Ellington, the cover charge was "$4–$5, depending on what night it was," the equivalent of fifty or sixty dollars today. John Hammond remembered the food as being "bad and expensive," and a menu from 1931 shows that he was at least half right: A sirloin steak cost two dollars. Bootleg champagne (not on the menu) went for $30 a bottle. The prices meant that only well-to-do customers could afford to take the ride that was described in the club's ads as "15 Minutes in a Taxi Through Central Park" to see "The Best Creole Revue Ever Staged in New York with the Greatest Array of Colored Talent Ever Assembled."

Ellington had much to say in *Music Is My Mistress* and elsewhere about the elegance of the club and its clientele:

> *The Cotton Club was a classy spot. Impeccable behavior was demanded in the room while the show was on. . . . The performers were paid high salaries, and the prices for the customers were high too. They had about twelve dancing girls and eight show girls, and they were all beautiful chicks. They used to dress so well! On Sunday nights, when celebrities filled the joint, they would rush out of the dressing room after the show in all their finery. Every time they went by, the stars and the rich people would be saying, "My, who is that?"*

What he took care not to say was that Madden hired only light-skinned women as Cotton Club Girls, and that blacks who sought admission to the club were turned away by the bouncers whom Carl Van Vechten, a white critic and photographer known for his fascination with Harlem and its residents, described as the "brutes at the door." In July of 1927 *The New York Age*, a black newspaper, warned its readers that the club, by order of the New York Police Department, "does not cater to colored patrons and will not admit them when they come in mixed parties." The color bar, Spike Hughes said, was not quite absolute: "If you were very famous, like Ethel Waters or Paul Robeson, then the management would allow you to show your coloured face inside the door; but you had to be tucked away discreetly in an inconspicuous corner of the room." It was, however, strictly enforced whenever racially mixed groups sought admission, so much so that W. C. Handy, the composer of "St. Louis Blues," was once turned away from a show of his own songs. Connie's Inn, which opened in 1923, had been the first Harlem cabaret to exclude blacks, but Madden went further: While the shows at Connie's Inn were written and directed by blacks, the Cotton Club only allowed them to perform onstage.

Ellington's silence about the awkward fact that he made his name playing in a segregated club in the middle of Harlem is understandable. "Harlem Negroes did not like the Cotton Club and never appreciated its Jim Crow policy in the very heart of their dark community," Langston Hughes wrote in 1940. Unlike Ellington, Hughes did not find it "classy" that "thousands of whites came to Harlem night after night, thinking the Negroes loved to have them there, and firmly believing that all Harlemites left their houses at sundown to sing and dance in cabarets, because most of the whites saw nothing but the cabarets, not the houses." But the Cotton Club was a prestigious booking all the same, and Irving Mills, who was never shy about taking credit for other men's achievements, said that he made it happen. Mills also said that it was his idea for the club to start presenting the Broadway-style stage shows for which it is now remembered, and that he talked George "Big Frenchy" DeMange, the manager, into putting on the club's first full-scale revue.

This may or may not be so, but it is true that Mills pulled the string that got Ellington into the Cotton Club. It was attached to Jimmy McHugh, who later composed such blue-chip standards as "I'm in the Mood for Love" and "On the Sunny Side of the Street." McHugh started out writing and plugging songs with Mills, in due course becoming general manager of Jack Mills Inc. Unable to make it on Broadway, he took a shot at Harlem and started writing songs for the Cotton Club. Andy Preer, the leader of the house band, died in 1927, and McHugh saw in his death an opportunity to improve the quality of the club's music: "I heard Duke and I wanted him. For one thing he and his boys could read [music]. The band I had to let go couldn't. I had to sit down at the piano and play every tune for them until they learned it."

All that was needed was to get Ellington out of a conflicting engagement, which was no trouble for a multiple murderer. One of Madden's associates made Clarence Robinson, the producer of the Philadelphia show in which the band was appearing, an offer he couldn't refuse: "Be big or you'll be dead." Two weeks later, on December 4, 1927, Ellington and his men opened at the Cotton Club. "Everybody was betting we wouldn't last a month," he said in 1940. They lasted for three years, and when they left to go on the road, their leader was on the verge of becoming a star.

ᘛᘚ

Nineteen twenty-seven was a phenomenal year for American culture. It was the year of *Show Boat, The General, Elmer Gantry,* Irving Berlin's "Blue Skies," Stuart Davis's *Egg Beater No. 1,* Aaron Copland's jazz-flavored *Piano*

Concerto, and the last volume of H. L. Mencken's *Prejudices.* Charles Lindbergh flew from New York to Paris in May, and Sacco and Vanzetti were executed in August. For those who knew how to make it, there was money to burn: Babe Ruth, who hit sixty home runs for the Yankees that year, was paid a yearly salary of $70,000, the equivalent of $857,000 today. (A laborer at Fisher Body's assembly plant in Flint, Michigan, made $1,783.) You could buy a loaf of bread for nine cents, a copy of *Time* for fifteen cents, a raccoon coat for $40, an Atwater Kent radio for $70, or a Model T for $290. Radio was big, but the phonograph was bigger: One hundred million records were sold in America in 1927, and among them were Louis Armstrong's "Potato Head Blues" and Bix Beiderbecke's "Singin' the Blues."

The entertainment listings in the "Goings On About Town" section of the December 3 issue of *The New Yorker* read like a magic carpet ride. On Broadway Katharine Cornell was starring in Somerset Maugham's *The Letter,* Alfred Lunt and Lynn Fontanne in George Bernard Shaw's *The Doctor's Dilemma,* and Fred and Adele Astaire in George and Ira Gershwin's *Funny Face.* If you felt like taking in a movie, you could check out *The Jazz Singer,* which had opened in October and was still going strong, though the magazine gave it a mixed notice: "Al Jolson superb in the Vitaphone which accompanies this dull movie." Alfred Stieglitz was showing works by John Marin, America's first cubist painter, at Room 303, the photographer's modernism-friendly art gallery. Among the books reviewed in the magazine was Thornton Wilder's *The Bridge of San Luis Rey,* and the list of recommended new titles for Christmas shoppers included Willa Cather's *Death Comes for the Archbishop* and Ernest Hemingway's *Men Without Women.*

"Goings On About Town," however, had yet to come upon the Cotton Club. The only Harlem nightspots mentioned in the December 3 issue, and for many more issues to come, were Barron Wilkins's Exclusive Club, Small's Paradise, and Club Ebony. "The later the better, and do not dress," the magazine advised readers interested in visiting Harlem. A week later Lois Long, the wife of high-society cartoonist Peter Arno ("We're going to the Trans-Lux to hiss Roosevelt") and the cabaret correspondent of *The New Yorker,* whose "Tables for Two" column she wrote under the fey pseudonym of "Lipstick," announced, "I am mad at Harlem. It is getting too refined. All the Harlemites are getting a little ashamed of the Black Bottom, that quaint old native dance handed down by levee-working grandfathers. . . . Give me a Holy Rollers meeting any time. Or Small's. Or, possibly, the Ebony."

The New Yorker had only just started covering "popular records" in 1927, and the unnamed critic who wrote about them seemed not to have heard any black musicians. (He favored Ben Bernie and the Clicquot Club Eskimos.) Indeed, one could read the magazine for month after month without running across a hint that black people of any kind existed, though a couple of weeks later a poetess named Frances Park opined on "Harlem 1927": "A slim brown girl / With a heart of flame / Will never admit / She feels it shame / To be dark of skin / With ink-black hair, / Nor wish she were / As the white folk there." But "Lipstick," unlike her colleagues, knew her way around Harlem, and she also knew that certain of its nightspots were friendlier than others to visitors from downtown. In due course "Goings On About Town" advised its readers to stick to Connie's Inn and Small's unless you have "a friend who'll personally conduct you." Soon the advice was more direct: "Better find a friend who knows his way about; the liveliest places don't welcome unknown whites."

As for the Ellington band, it was already known throughout upper Manhattan. A reviewer for *The New York Age* had written in October that "with the possible exception of Fletcher Henderson's band, Duke Ellington seems to head the greatest existing aggregation of colored musicians." But Ellington had to win the support of white journalists in order to make it big. Fortunately, Abel Green, who had been following the band since its Hollywood Café days, covered its Cotton Club debut for *Variety*. Green devoted most of his column to the "teasin'est torso tossing" of the "almost Caucasian-hued high yaller gals" of the chorus line: "Possessed of the native jazz heritage, their hotsy-totsy performance if working sans wraps could never be parred by a white gal." But he also gave a nod to the musicians who backed them up: "In Duke Ellington's dance band, Harlem has reclaimed its own after Times Square accepted them for several seasons at the Club Kentucky. Ellington's jazzique is just too bad" (i.e., very good).

Some witnesses felt that the Ellington band wasn't at its best that night. One of them was Irving Mills, who said years later that "the first show was kind of weak." That stands to reason. Because the band was brought in at the last minute, Ellington didn't have enough time to rehearse his men, and it wasn't until he opened at the Cotton Club that the ten-piece instrumentation heard on his recordings became permanent. Prior to that time, the size of the group had fluctuated from gig to gig. Adding new players to so unified an ensemble at the last minute would have thrown the old ones off their game—though not for long. Ellington and the band played two floor shows a night, one at midnight and the other at two A.M., and they played for dancing before, between, and after the shows. The long hours that they spent on the bandstand evidently whipped them into shape, for the records that they cut for Victor on December 19 include a well-played version of "Harlem River Quiver," a song written by McHugh and Dorothy Fields, his fresh-faced new lyricist, for the band's first Cotton Club revue.

What else did the band play? This question is difficult to answer with exactitude. Ellington made studio recordings of a half dozen McHugh-Fields songs, most of which were written for Cotton Club shows, but little else is known about the other Ellington-penned numbers that were heard there. Surviving programs of the five shows seen at the club between 1927 and 1929 are insufficiently informative on this point, nor do newspaper reviews offer much more in the way of specific detail. No live recordings of the band were made during this period, and almost no contemporary manuscript material survives.* It has long been taken for granted that many of Ellington's compositions of the late twenties were written to accompany Cotton Club production numbers, and some scholars have suggested that the chance to write music for the club's shows played a pivotal role in his development as a composer, but it wasn't until 1930 that he wrote a score of his own. Prior to that time, McHugh and Fields wrote the songs. All that Ellington did was orchestrate them.

It's possible that some of his instrumental compositions were used to accompany production numbers, but we cannot be sure. *Music Is My Mistress,* as usual, sheds little light on the subject: "The music for the shows was being written by Jimmy McHugh with lyrics by Dorothy Fields. . . . They wrote some wonderful material, but this was show music and mostly popular songs. Sometimes they would use numbers that I wrote, and it would be these we played between shows and on the [radio] broadcasts." Barney Bigard, who joined the band after it opened at the Cotton Club, makes things marginally clearer: "We played two shows each night to accompany the chorus line or acts that they had. . . . We played for dancing in between. Some of the acts brought in their own music, but Duke wrote for a lot of them." While this sounds plausible, Ellington identifies only one composition in *Music Is My Mistress,* "The Mystery Song," that was written specifically to accompany a Cotton Club act. Hence it seems likely that when the band played his music at the club, it was usually for dancing by the customers.

---

* The band recorded a 78 called "A Nite at the Cotton Club" for Victor in April of 1929, but it is a studio re-creation, not the real thing. Irving Mills serves as the master of ceremonies, and his introduction shows that a night at the Cotton Club was widely understood to be an expensive pleasure: "Great to see so many friends here tonight, enjoying themselves in spite of the cover charge!"

"Pace, pace, pace": The frenzied climax of a Cotton Club floor show. Note the skimpy attire and "high yellow" complexions of the Cotton Club Girls, who were paid adequately and treated decently by the white gangsters who ran the club

We know even less about the shows themselves, which were staged by Dan Healy, a vaudevillian turned Broadway performer who had appeared in Irving Berlin's *Yip Yip Yaphank* and the *Ziegfeld Follies of 1927*. Fields recalled that in addition to the songs that she and McHugh wrote for the club, the performers there interpolated other numbers that were among "the most shocking, ribald, bawdy, dirtiest songs anyone had ever heard in the 1920s," though the surviving lyrics now seem tame: "Jelly roll, jelly roll, nice and brown / If you want my jelly roll, you've gotta come to town."* Spike Hughes, however, agreed with Fields: "Every dance routine was too long and too loud, and after an hour of suggestive songs sung without charm or humour the discriminating customer could scream at the reluctance of the singers to say in plain language

---

* Another song known to have been sung at the club was Andy Razaf's "Kitchen Man," recorded in 1929 by Bessie Smith: "His frankfurters are oh, so sweet / How I like his sausage meat."

that fornication was fine, and leave it at that." According to Healy, such songs were a must. "The chief ingredient [in the shows] was pace, pace, pace!" he said. "The show was generally built around types—the band, an eccentric dancer, a comedian . . . And we'd have a special singer who gave the customers the expected adult song in Harlem."

That was all that Healy had to say about what happened onstage. In 1930 a British newsreel cameraman shot a minute-long sequence showing Ellington accompanying the chorus line in fragments of a lively finale-type production number, but contemporary reviews contain only sketchy descriptions of the routines, and the only detailed account that has come down to us is that of Marshall Stearns:

> *I recall one where a light-skinned and magnificently muscled Negro burst through a papier-mâché jungle onto the dance floor, clad only in an aviator's helmet, goggles, and shorts. He had obviously been "forced down in darkest Africa," and in the center of the floor he came upon a "white" goddess clad in long golden tresses and being worshipped by a circle of cringing "blacks." Producing a bull whip from heaven knows where, the aviator rescued the blond and they did an erotic dance. In the background, Bubber Miley, Tricky Sam Nanton, and other members of the Ellington band growled, wheezed, and snorted obscenely.*

This lurid description puts flesh on the memories of Howard "Stretch" Johnson, a high-minded Cotton Club tap dancer who later became a Communist Party organizer. For Johnson, Healy's shows were "top-flight performances designed to appease the appetite for a certain type of black performance, the smiling black, the shuffling black, the black-faced black, the minstrel coon-show atmosphere which existed." It was all part of the image of the club, one of whose programs was bedecked with a caricature of a grinning darky doorman bowing obsequiously to three white patrons in evening dress.

But Ellington and his sidemen were not coon-show clowns, nor did they think it demeaning to perform at a popular nightspot that paid each of them $75 a week, an annual salary of nearly $48,000 in today's dollars, not counting tips, which were often considerable. According to Ellington, "It didn't really matter what the salary was. A big bookmaker . . . would come in late and the first thing he'd do was change $20 into half dollars. Then he'd throw the whole thing at the feet of whoever was singing or playing or dancing. If you've ever heard $20 in halves land on a wooden floor you know what a wonderful sound it makes." That was more than decent money for a man of any color in 1927, and Ellington himself took a pragmatic view of what he and his colleagues had to do to get it: "The girl you saw doing the squirmy dance . . . was not in the throes of passion. She was working to get that salary to take home and feed her baby, who sometimes lived pretty well." Even Johnson saw the bandleader's music as "a creative form of irony which masked the commercial pandering to an upper-class white audience thrilled at the opportunity to hear and witness what it thought was genuine black exotica."

Not only did Ellington make a good living playing at the Cotton Club, but he was being paid to hone his skills on company time. As Freddie Jenkins remembered it, "He used to set us on the stand and pay us union scale, maybe for five hours, just to help him formulate chords. He'd assign different notes to every instrument in the band and say—'Play that, B—a—a—m!' . . . Sometimes he'd do that three or four times before he found just the combination he wanted." Even if he was only writing music for the band to play between shows and on radio broadcasts, though, he still had to turn out more of it than ever before. This meant that he could no longer count on improvising arrangements on the spot in collaboration with his musicians: He had to learn how to write them down. By 1928 Ellington was supplying the band with fully notated charts, though he also continued to create new compositions at rehearsals and to insist that the players memorize their parts so that they would not have to fumble on the bandstand: "He would just start to play at the piano, maybe like a hint of the upcoming song, and then you would go for it." And his style, at once earthy and sophisticated, was well suited to the needs of the club, which sought to persuade its customers that they were getting a taste of the real Harlem without making them feel too uncomfortable in the process.

How did Owney Madden and his associates treat their hirelings? "Stretch" Johnson, who called them "a band of the most vicious thugs and racketeers that had ever been produced in New York," said that Madden's men "recognized [the dancers] as, in their opinion, a more talented group of blacks, but generally they thought of us as niggers, like everybody else . . . they kept their distance and we kept ours." The female members of the chorus line, however, had a different point of view. One of them recalled in 1985 that Madden's men "were very protective of the girls." The job was exhausting—the dancers worked seven nights a week, and once a year they went up to Sing Sing to perform for friends of the management—but the pay, $35 a week, was adequate, and the fact that the owners of the club kept their distance struck most of the women as a relief rather than an insult. Instead of fraternizing with the gangsters, they went out with the musicians (Sonny Greer and Fred Guy both married Cotton Club Girls). Madden, on the other hand, got along well with Ellington, and the two men often stayed up late after the shows to play bridge. "He loved Duke and he loved me," Greer said. "And his influence was so powerful that we was always in the clear. . . . I keep hearing about how bad the gangsters were. All I can say is that I wish I was still working for them. Their word was all you needed. They had been brought up with the code that you either kept your word or you got dead."

Whatever Madden thought of his other black employees, he paid them on time, and he also poured money into the floor shows, which according to one account were budgeted at $4,000 a week ($52,000 in today's dollars). One show followed another: *The Cotton Club Show Boat* in April, *Hot Chocolate* in October, *Springbirds* the following March. By 1929 the club's ads, most of which made mention of "Duke Ellington's Recording Orchestra," sported enthusiastic quotes from such Broadway columnists as Mark Hellinger, Louis Sobol, and Walter Winchell ("The Cotton Club Revue is one of the outstanding diversions in New York"). Winchell, who was a friend of Dorothy Fields's father and had close ties to Madden, was on hand for Ellington's opening night. After that he was seen frequently at the Cotton Club, meaning that the Ellington band appeared no less frequently in the city's most influential entertainment column. Most artists will swallow a fair amount of humiliation in return for free publicity, and Duke Ellington, at least for a time, was no exception. He knew that far worse fates could befall a black musician than playing for big money in a segregated nightclub.

As 1927 gave way to 1928, Ellington continued to tinker with the personnel of his band, seeking out new players whose styles, like those of Bubber Miley and Tricky Sam Nanton, were sufficiently unorthodox to arouse his imagination. He had hired two such men in mid-1927, a Creole bassist from New Orleans named Wellman Braud (pronounced "Bro") and Harry Carney, an alto saxophonist and clarinet player from Boston who started playing baritone saxophone after joining the band. Early the following year he talked another New Orleans musician, Barney Bigard, into signing up, and shortly after that Arthur Whetsel came back to New York and rejoined the trumpet section, bringing the number of players up to eleven. Ellington had long appreciated Whetsel's playing, but the other three men were just as inspiring.

Braud, born in 1891, was the band's senior member, a sober-sided Louisianian of long musical experience who believed himself to have been "the first person to start the walking bass." He was the first string bassist to play in the Ellington band—his predecessors were tuba players—and today he is remembered as an exponent of the now-obsolete "slap-bass" technique, in which the player uses his right hand to slap the strings against the fingerboard, creating a percussive effect. Unlike most early jazz bassists, Braud was also adept with the bow, getting a smooth sound that contrasted nicely with the pop and snap of his two-beat pizzicato style, and his round tone and rhythmic vigor gave the Ellington band a firm foundation. Gene Ramey, a young bassist from Texas, was impressed by how Braud, Guy, and Sonny Greer were "a totally different kind of rhythm section. For the first time you could hear the bass player coming through." Even younger players like George Duvivier, who disdained the slap-bass technique as outdated, admired Braud: "Wellman was playing solos with real notes, without the fol-derol that was associated with bass solos. . . . [He] had an enormous sound." He was also an excellent cook and was later admired by his colleagues for the spicy New Orleans–style dishes that he prepared backstage whenever the band was on the road.

Ellington appreciated Braud's playing, though he seems not to have cared for the older man's bossy personality. In addition to composing a mu-sical portrait of Braud in 1970, he included a revealing pen portrait of the bassist in *Music Is My Mistress:*

> *When Mr. Braud joined us . . . he was already a celebrated veteran of New Orleans jazz, and a clean, neatly dressed coach who knew all the answers. He and Freddy Guy were the two Big Daddies. As a bass player, he believed in crowding the microphone, and when you got ready to blow a chorus Mr. Braud would already have established so compel-ling a beat that you could not miss.*

Though the seventeen-year-old Harry Carney had only a sliver of Braud's musical experience, he was to become the longest-lasting piece in the puzzle that was the Ellington Effect. He started playing with the band in June of 1927, and according to Carney, Ellington became a "sort of guardian" to him. Not only did he spend the rest of his life in the band, but Carney and Elling-ton eventually became the closest of companions. At the time, though, he was teased by his older bandmates, one of whom, Sonny Greer, nicknamed him "Youth." Even then he was, in Ellington's words, "a very well-behaved, well-organized young man," and he took his duties seriously enough to change in-struments upon joining the band, having concluded that it would "give more variety" to the clarinet-dominated reed section if he started doubling on baritone saxophone. Soon the big horn became his primary instrument: "My greatest kick with the instrument, which then seemed so much bigger than me, was that I was able to fill it and make some noise with it. I enjoyed the tone of it and I started to give it some serious study, and I've been carrying it around ever since." Influenced by Coleman Hawkins, Fletcher Henderson's star soloist, and Adrian Rollini, whose bass saxophone graced the small-group records of Bix Beiderbecke, Red Nichols, and Joe Venuti, Carney strived to duplicate Hawkins's facility and Rollini's tone, thereby becoming the first great baritone-sax soloist in jazz. Ellington was fascinated by the massive sound, dark as twice-burnt umber and fine-grained as mahogany, that Carney drew from the cumbersome instrument, and for the next half century it would serve as one of his signature timbres.

One reason why Carney cut back on his clarinet playing was the presence in the reed section of Albany Leon Bigard, born in 1906 and always called "Barney," who was one of the finest jazz clarinet soloists of the twenties and thirties. Bigard, who doubled on tenor saxophone but preferred playing the smaller horn, was a light-skinned middle-class Creole who had recorded with King Oliver and Jelly Roll Morton. Distant and glum, he was, like so many humorless men, a practical joker who liked nothing better than to see a fellow musician put on the spot. But Ellington loved his "woody tone," a peculiarly resonant sound common to New Orleans clarinet players: "He was invaluable for putting the filigree work into an arrangement, and sometimes it could remind you of all that delicate wrought iron you see in his hometown."

Bigard came on board when Ellington grew "kind of tired" of Rudy Jackson's playing. He was struck by the self-assurance with which his new employer spoke of his plans for the future:

> *"I want you to join my band," he says. "I don't know how long we're going to stay here, but we are trying to build up a good band. If we can do it, and the boss likes us, then we can stay at this Cotton Club a long time. We'll have a good job there." I noticed he kept talking in the plural: "Our band," "We can stay there," and liked that from the start about him. . . . Just like he was going to turn the music business upside down and you would be part of it.*

Ellington knew that a good dance band needs showmen as well as soloists, and in 1928 he found one. The diminutive Freddie Jenkins was a left-handed trumpet player—a childhood accident had damaged the fingertips of his right hand—whose antics on the bandstand irked Bubber Miley, who complained about his "posturing and posing." Before long his new colleagues started calling him "Posey," and the nickname stuck. But Ellington knew better than to complain about Jenkins's showboating: "He brought us a new kind of sparkle: his every move was a picture, in the groove, and right on top of the action." Some of his tricks are documented in *Check and Double Check,* a 1930 film that includes a performance by the band in which the ever-smiling Jenkins upstages his poker-faced colleagues by tossing his head, tapping his foot, shaking his hips, and flapping his derby mute like a sail in a high wind. He was also a competent soloist and section man who had no trouble reading Ellington's charts, making his arrival a net gain on all counts.

Unlike Jenkins, Johnny Hodges, who replaced Otto Hardwick as the band's lead alto saxophonist in May of 1928, was incapable of showmanship. His shyness with strangers was often mistaken for hauteur, and he rarely smiled in public, preferring to conceal his anxieties with phlegmatic inscrutability whenever he got up on the bandstand to play. "Everybody said Johnny was gruff," said Cue, his second wife. "They thought he was cold. He was just afraid." But Hodges needed no charm to hold an audience's attention. He was, then and later, Ellington's greatest soloist, the only one (save for Bechet and, later, Ben Webster) who was as impressive on his own as with the full band behind him. "He may look as though he's on his last walk to the gallows," said one of his bandmates, "but he appreciates the applause and he thanks the audience with a million dollars' worth of melody!" At first Hodges was best known for his up-tempo solos, but he quickly emerged as a peerless bluesman, and later on he became the band's principal ballad soloist, the role in which he is best remembered today. The rich yet penetrating tone and well-controlled glissandi with which he adorned such songs as Ellington's "I Got It Bad (And That Ain't Good)" and "Warm Valley" and Billy Strayhorn's "Passion Flower" were appreciated by musicians and fans alike. Lawrence Welk, whose squareness is a universal byword, was "so impressed with Johnny's great ability" that the two men actually recorded an album together. "He plays from the heart rather than the notes," Welk said. "Besides everything else, he plays the prettiest saxophone of anyone I know."

Born John Cornelius Hodges in Boston in 1907, Hodges was usually called "Rab" or "Rabbit," a nickname whose origins are obscure.* He was a

---

* Later on Otto Hardwick dubbed him "Jeep," after the character in the *Popeye* comic strip.

childhood friend of Harry Carney and a protégé of Sidney Bechet ("I had quite a few of his riffs") who played alto, clarinet, and soprano saxophone, Bechet's own instrument, with equal skill. He was working with Chick Webb's band when Ellington and Hardwick came to a four-year parting of the ways that appears to have been brought about by the excessive drinking of the man known to his colleagues as "Professor Booze." Unlike Hardwick, Hodges was a poor sight reader, and he was intimidated by the prospect of mastering Ellington's book of written arrangements. Barney Bigard recalled, "Johnny was scared when he first joined us . . . Harry Carney and I would take him in hand and if Duke had written a new orchestration with a sax ensemble we would go over it with Johnny until he had it down pat." His gifts as a soloist were never in doubt, though, and on his first recording session with the band, he played a pair of self-assured choruses on "Yellow Dog Blues" and "Tishomingo Blues" (the first on soprano saxophone, the second on alto). Though he sat alongside Bubber Miley and Tricky Sam Nanton, the stars of the band, the stone-faced Hodges sounded as if he hadn't a care in the world.

All of these men helped to inspire the stream of compositions that flowed from Ellington's pen in 1928 and 1929, most of which were recorded almost as soon as they were written. He had yet to hit his stride as a composer, but he was well on the way to it. To be sure, many of his latest pieces, especially such swingers like "Hot and Bothered" and "Jubilee Stomp," were largely given over to showy solos by the members of the band. But "Awful Sad," "Black Beauty," and "Misty Mornin'" sound a lyrical note new to Ellington's work, while the atmospheric tone of "Black and Tan Fantasy" and "Creole Love Call" permeates "The Blues with a Feelin'." These latter numbers bear out the truth of Harry Carney's words: "When you look back, you can see that from the late '20s onward, every time there was an addition to the band, the new instrumentalist seemed to give Duke new ideas and something to draw from and add in his writing." It was as if they were all characters in a long-running show of his devising, and it was the theatricality of the musical settings that he devised for them that he surely had in mind when he later proclaimed himself to be "a man of the theater."

The best way to understand the musical course that Ellington was charting is to observe how he singles out specific kinds of musical numbers that he wants to learn how to write, then develops them into genres in which he will thereafter specialize. Just as the Cotton Club's production numbers could be broken down into recognizable types, so did Ellington build his repertoire according to musical formulas, more often than not perfecting each successive formula in a "prototype" work that would serve as the model for later pieces in the same genre. On occasion, though, the prototype was already so fully realized that it became, like "Black and Tan Fantasy" and "Creole Love Call," a permanent part of the repertoire. In one such piece, which Ellington called "The Mooch," he took the squirmy shimmying of the Cotton Club chorus line and made it into art.* A medium-tempo swinger that he later described as "a sex dance," it opens with a slithery minor-key clarinet trio punctuated by foul growling from Miley, immediately followed by a major-key theme so full of big-city joie de vivre that only the closest of listeners will spot it as a twelve-bar "blues." Next come a pair of instrumental solos and a duet, set first in the minor key and then in the major, followed by a reprise of the dark, ominous clarinet trio with which the piece opened. As they move from mood to mood, the six choruses of "The Mooch" paint a picture of urban debauchery that needs no dancers to tell its Hogarthian tale.

Such pieces struck the musicians as disorientingly daring. Bigard, whose tenure with King Oliver had not prepared him for Ellington's off-center harmonies, had trouble adjusting to their demands: "There was always something going on to keep your mind busy . . . my mind was busy figuring out those strange chords that Duke kept putting behind me." Freddie Jenkins was also disconcerted by the band's "third class discords," which he thought "odd." But the bandsmen soon caught on to what their leader had in mind, as did the public. Slickly designed ads in the programs of Broadway shows touted the Cotton Club as offering "A Show That Rivals Broadway's Best," and in December it made its first fleeting appearance in *The New Yorker*'s "Tables for Two" column: "Also, anyone interested in jazz should go up and hear the orchestra at the Cotton Club."† A month later Victor signed Ellington, and though he continued to record for other labels under a variety of pseudonyms, this new relationship with America's most prominent record label was a sign of his growing fame.

---

* The piece is known today as "The Mooche," but Ellington originally spelled the title without a terminal "e," thereby intending to suggest (in his words) "a certain lazy gait peculiar to some of the folk of Harlem." It was copyrighted as "The Mooch," and is still identified as such on sheet music. The title, however, was spelled "The Mooche" on 78 labels when it was first recorded in 1928, and the alternate spelling, like that of "East St. Louis Toodle-O," is now in universal use.

† The premiere of George Gershwin's *An American in Paris* was reviewed in the same issue of the magazine, whose critic called the jazz-influenced work "a charming combination of urbanity and naïveté—really a highly desirable blend in a young composer." The word *jazz* appears nowhere in the review.

In February of 1929 Duke Ellington got the second-biggest break of his life: CBS started broadcasting his Cotton Club performances from coast to coast. The band was initially heard on Wednesdays at eleven P.M., as well as in early-evening studio programs that aired on Mondays and Thursdays. Each thirty-minute broadcast consisted of eight songs, some of them current pop hits and others drawn from the club's stage shows, though Ellington was also allowed to perform two or three of his own pieces on every show.

Ellington had been broadcasting locally since 1923, but his CBS debut marked the first time that his band was heard by a nationwide radio audience. How did a black dance band get onto a national radio network in 1929? Because the Columbia Broadcasting System was a fledgling venture that was still finding its way. William Paley, the new owner, had taken charge in January and was frantically searching for talent to throw up against such popular NBC series as *Amos 'n' Andy*. Enter Ted Husing, who had just gone to work for CBS as a football announcer and was also a jazz buff who spent his off hours at the Cotton Club and other Harlem nightspots. Ellington remembered him as "a beautiful cat with an up-to-the-minute awareness then known as hip," and Bigard called him "a real fan of [the] band." It was at Husing's behest that Paley agreed to put Ellington on CBS, with Husing serving as announcer. So far as can be definitively known, this was the first time that a jazz band made a national broadcast from Harlem, as well as the first time that any black band was heard in a regular network radio slot.

One scholar of American radio has called Ellington's Cotton Club broadcasts "the first important national propagation of black music by a pop group" and "the first encounters most white Americans had with black music." This ignores the effect of the band's recordings, nor are there any ratings figures available to prove how popular the broadcasts were. But the number of radio listeners in America jumped from sixteen million in 1925 to sixty million in 1930, and the effects of the new medium on the entertainment industry were multiplied still further by the coming of the Great Depression. Even if you could no longer spare seventy-five cents for the latest Victor record by Duke Ellington and His Cotton Club Orchestra, you could still hear the band for free on CBS. Anecdotal evidence, including references in newspaper articles, indicates that the broadcasts were helping to make the band more widely known outside New York. Ellington thought so: In *Music Is My Mistress* he says, "The engagement at the Cotton Club was of the utmost significance, because as a result of its radio wire we were heard nationally and internationally."

As Sonny Greer recalled it, the band's suppertime broadcasts were so popular that "the people didn't get anything to eat until we come off [the air]. Cats working all day, starved to death until we got off."

Ellington's style soon acquired a nickname. According to Greer, George Gershwin, a Cotton Club habitué and an admirer of Ellington's compositions, referred to them as "jungle music" in conversation with Paul Whiteman. Whoever came up with the phrase, it stuck: The Ellington band billed itself as "the Jungle Band" on the label of the two-sided "Tiger Rag" that it cut for Brunswick in January of 1929, and soon Husing was using the tag on the air. Not long after that, Daisy and Ruth Ellington tuned in a broadcast at their Washington home. It was, Ruth said, the first time that they had heard Duke's music since his move to New York, and what they heard startled them: "Here we were, my mother and I, sitting in this very respectable Victorian living room, my mother so puritanical she didn't even wear lipstick, and the announcer from New York tells us we are listening to 'Duke Ellington and His Jungle Music'! It sounded very strange and dissonant to us." Whatever she thought of the music, Daisy must have been dismayed to hear the phrase *jungle music* used in connection with her son. In 1929 those were fighting words for middle-class blacks who prided themselves on having put their primitive origins behind them. The days of *Roots* were far in the future. But Ellington embraced the despised word: Between 1929 and 1932 he not only allowed it to be incorporated into his publicity but wrote and recorded three compositions, "Jungle Blues," "Jungle Nights in Harlem," and "Echoes of the Jungle," whose titles make reference to the heritage of which he was so proud. "Oh, we've been African all the way back," he assured a reporter four decades later.

By then, though, Bubber Miley, the co-inventor of jungle music, was no longer around to play it with Ellington. Miley's last recording session with the band was on January 16, 1929, after which Cootie Williams replaced him. He had been missing sessions as early as April of 1927, and the reason for some of his absences was almost certainly that he was too drunk to play. While Miley was not the band's only drinker, he and Otto Hardwick seem to have been the only ones who let it interfere with their duties. "Bubber was temperamental," Ellington said in 1944. "He liked his liquor. He used to get under the piano and go to sleep any time he felt like it." Barney Bigard put it more directly:

> *Their drinking never hurt their music, but what bugged the rest of us was that every time some big-shot who could help the band would come down to the club, either one or two of them would be gone. Duke would*

get so mad that when they came back he would tell them, "Well, you all
did a great job. We had some very important people in here to listen to
you and you weren't here. That's great for the future of the band, isn't
it!" Finally, he got so disgusted with them that he got rid of both of them
by making life so unpleasant that they quit.

Could the fact that the band was now making three coast-to-coast network broadcasts every week have played a role in Ellington's decision to part
ways with Miley? Paul Whiteman eased Bix Beiderbecke out of his band
around the same time for a similar reason: Beiderbecke's alcoholism made it
impossible for him to cope with the unrelenting demands of Whiteman's
broadcast schedule. If Miley had controlled his drinking well enough to function effectively on the bandstand and in the studio, Ellington would have continued to look the other way. He was, after all, an enthusiastic drinker in his
own right, and took a tolerant view of the excesses of his sidemen: "Liquor
drinking among the musicians was done from the gladiator perspective, in just
the same way as when they challenged each other on their instruments . . . all
our horn blowers were lushies." Early on he formulated the managerial credo
to which he hewed throughout his life and which he shared with his musicians
whenever their behavior got out of hand: "Look, fellows. I thought everyone
knew I am *not* a disciplinarian. I hired you because you are superb in your field
and I want you with me because of that fact. Apart from being excellent musicians, you are all *men*, so govern yourselves accordingly." But it was one thing
to have a few too many and another thing altogether to miss gigs or skip recording dates. In the end there was too much at stake: Miley had to go, and
that was that. He died three years later, six weeks after his twenty-ninth birthday, and though Ellington mourned the trumpeter's passing, he never admitted to any second thoughts about firing his friend.

Charles Melvin "Cootie" Williams, Miley's replacement, was born in
Mobile, Alabama, in 1911. Unlike his predecessor, he was a teetotaler: "With
the Ellington band I drank Coca-Cola *only*." A Louis Armstrong disciple,
Williams had a big, burnished tone that he preferred not to cloak with mutes,
and he didn't know how to use a plunger: "I used to laugh when Tricky would
start to blowing, you know. It sounded funny to me." Ellington never asked
Williams to play growl trumpet, but one night it hit him that he'd been hired
to take Miley's place and so had better deliver the goods: "He didn't say nothing. Till he come to me, sitting up there playing, and he come to me and I
said, 'Well, this man hired me to play like that.' So I kept on listening to
Tricky. One night I had the plunger and I said, 'Wah, wah.' And I woke up

everybody, and they said, 'That's it. That's it. Keep on. That's it. That's it.'" Williams became at least as good a growler as Miley had been, and his Armstrong-inflected open-horn solos brought a bright luster to the band. Along with Arthur Whetsel, he also cracked the whip whenever he thought that his colleagues were failing to take care of business. "He didn't want to throw his weight around, but by the time that he'd had enough, then he would explode," Helen Oakley recalled. "And that would pull everybody together."

Ellington would permanently add two more players (and a woman singer) in the next couple of years, but not until the end of 1934 did anyone else leave the band. After a long period of experimentation, he had found the men for the job, the ones who made it possible for him to do his best work, and it was no accident that the rest of the world now started to take note. In April the band shared a bill with the Marx Brothers at the Palace Theatre, America's top vaudeville house, and *The New York Times* commented on his music for the first time: "Then there is a first rate blackamoor band, come down from deepest Harlem to provide a series of jazz specialties that range from tepid to torrid." A month after that, "Lipstick" discovered Ellington and wrote him up breathlessly in *The New Yorker*:

> *Another thing that your most high-hat friends have recently discovered in a body is the Cotton Club in Harlem, which has a perfectly elegant revue that goes on at twelve-thirty and again around two o'clock. . . . I cannot believe that most of them realize that they are listening to probably the greatest jazz orchestra of all time, which is Duke Ellington's—I'll fight anyone who says different. It is barbaric and rhythmic and brassy as jazz ought to be; it is mellow as music ought to be. There are throbbing moans and wah-wahs and outbreaks on the part of the brasses, and it is all too much for an impressionable girl.*

Seven weeks after "Lipstick" doffed her dainty hat to Ellington, Louis Armstrong made his Broadway debut singing Fats Waller's "Ain't Misbehavin'" in *Hot Chocolates,* an all-black revue that moved downtown from Connie's Inn, where it had started life as a floor show. It was followed on July 2 by *Show Girl,* a big-budget backstage comedy produced by Florenz Ziegfeld that starred Ruby Keeler and Jimmy Durante and featured a score by George Gershwin and an appearance by Ellington and his musicians, who performed onstage in a nightclub scene, after which they rushed back to Harlem for the late show at the Cotton Club. Marietta Clinkscales came up from Washington one night to see her star pupil, who spotted her from the stage: "I came on and I could see her up in the balcony, up in the mezzanine, waving a handkerchief."

According to Ellington, it was Will Vodery, Ziegfeld's chief orchestrator, who got the band into the show: "Will Vodery got us the gig in *Show Girl* . . . simply by mentioning my name to Flo Ziegfeld." Unknown to the public at large, Vodery, like Will Marion Cook, was one of the era's most accomplished black musicians, and Ellington claimed to have received "valuable lectures in orchestration" from him during the run of the show. Long after his name had faded from memory, Ellington would continue to praise him, declaring in a 1943 article about arrangers that Vodery's "chromatic tendencies penetrated my ear, and are largely responsible for the way I think [about] music, even today."

This reference to a forgotten artist deserves to be taken seriously, for it answers a question about Ellington's musical development: If he didn't listen to classical music in his youth, how and when did he acquire the knowledge of modern chromatic harmony that is evident in his post-1930 compositions? The answer appears to be that he got it from Will Vodery. In 1946 Barry Ulanov observed that Vodery had

> *assimilated the classical experience and translated it into the terms of the musical comedy pit band. It was more easily assimilable for Duke in those terms and made far more of an impression upon him than it would have in its original form. . . . From Vodery, as he [Ellington] says himself, he drew his chromatic convictions, his uses of the tones ordinarily extraneous to the diatonic scale, with the consequent alteration of the harmonic character of his music, its broadening, the deepening of his resources. It has become customary to ascribe the classical influences upon Duke—Delius, Debussy and Ravel—to direct contact with their music. Actually his serious appreciation of those and other modern composers came after his meeting with Will Vodery.*

Show Girl, unlike *Hot Chocolates*, failed to make the grade, in part because the songs were not up to Gershwin's high standards. (Only one standard, "Liza," came out of the show.) Brooks Atkinson of *The New York Times* called it "the least notable of the recent Ziegfeld productions." Most of the other reviewers agreed, and many of them, like Atkinson, didn't even bother to mention Ellington. But he still wrung a fair amount of acclaim out of the 111-performance run. Flo Ziegfeld took the trouble to publish an article calling the members of his band "the finest exponent[s] of syncopated music in existence. Irving Berlin went mad about them, and some of the best exponents of modern music who have heard them during rehearsal almost jumped out of their seats with excitement over their extraordinary harmonies and exciting rhythms."

It was a great moment for Ellington and his men. "We were the first to play a Ziegfeld show," Sonny Greer said with pride years later. "Never had no colored band play it." Irving Mills knew it, too. Even though he claimed not to be making any money off Ellington, he continued to cover the band's expenses, paying the salaries of the new members who joined when Ellington opened at the Cotton Club. "I was out thousands of dollars before anything ever developed," Mills later said. "I didn't know where the money was coming from." But he knew where it was going to come from: "You know I was a music publisher, I was glad to get my songs plugged and I was glad to have a home for the band to have it together for the records." He also knew that there were many more ways—and places—to sell Duke Ellington.

5

"I BETTER SCRATCH OUT SOMETHING"

Becoming a Genius, 1929–1930

HOLLYWOOD HAS ALWAYS had an equivocal relationship with jazz. Once the presence of a saxophone on the soundtrack of a Hollywood film was an aural signpost pointing to steamy sexuality. Now it indicates world-weary sophistication. But no matter what signals the sound of jazz is intended to send, its making and makers are usually romanticized when they are portrayed in movies, just as the music itself is softened for mass consumption. Nor has the American film industry ever been at ease using black musicians in anything other than the most stereotypical of roles, when it allows them on the screen at all. Louis Armstrong was customarily relegated to such parts—in 1938 he even played a character referred to on-screen as "Uncle Tom"—and though the first feature-length talking picture was called *The Jazz Singer,* it was not until two years later that black jazz musicians of any importance appeared in a commercial movie. Moreover, the film in question was shot in Manhattan, not Hollywood, and it was directed not by an old studio hand but by an experimental filmmaker.

Dudley Murphy, the director who brought jazz to the silver screen, collaborated with Fernand Léger, the French cubist painter, on *Ballet mécanique,* a Dadaist film that was made in 1924. Five years later he persuaded RKO to hire him to direct a pair of short subjects based on black popular music. The first, made early in 1929 and released that fall, was *St. Louis Blues,* starring Bessie Smith and James P. Johnson, which *Variety* described as "pungent with tenseness in action and replete with Aframerican local and other color." *St. Louis Blues* ended up doing poorly at the box office, but by then Duke Ellington and his band had reported to RKO's New York studios in August of 1929 to make their talking-picture debut in Murphy's next film, a nineteen-minute two-reeler called *Black and Tan,* while continuing to appear on Broadway in *Show Girl.* It's possible that Carl Van Vechten introduced Ellington to Murphy—a production still taken on the set shows the three men together— but Murphy, like so many avant-garde artists of the twenties, had long been fascinated by jazz and the culture that spawned it, and he would not have needed Van Vechten, or anyone else, to send him to Harlem.

The plot of *Black and Tan,* concocted by Murphy himself, is exiguously simple. Fredi Washington, a willowy flapper, longs to support Ellington, her impoverished composer-companion, even though she suffers from a heart

Arthur Whetsel, Fredi Washington, and Duke Ellington in a publicity still from *Black and Tan.* While *Black and Tan* shows Washington dancing herself to death in the flimsiest of costumes, it also presents Ellington and the members of his band as serious, committed artists—an uncommon way for black jazzmen to be portrayed on-screen in 1929 and for many years afterward

condition. (Both performers go by their own names.) She has found a night-spot that will hire him, but only if she dances with his band, thus putting her life at risk. When two dimwitted movers come to their apartment to repossess the piano, Washington bribes them with a bottle of gin so that Ellington and Arthur Whetsel can continue rehearsing his latest opus, "Black and Tan Fantasy." The action shifts to the stage of the club, where Washington, attired in a near-nonexistent costume, dances to "Cotton Club Stomp," collapsing at the end of the number. Her performance, together with a pair of dances per-formed by six real-life Cotton Club Girls and the Five Hot Shots, a precision tap team that also appeared at the club, offers a glimpse of what a Cotton Club floor show might have looked like. Murphy then cuts to Washington's deathbed, where she discloses that her last wish is to hear Ellington and the band perform "Black and Tan Fantasy" accompanied by a choir. (The pres-ence of a choir in their Harlem apartment is, to say the least, unexpected.) She dies at film's end, gazing soulfully at the out-of-focus face of her lover.

Today *Black and Tan,* with its chiaroscuro lighting and kaleidoscope-like multiple images of the Ellington band, suggests an uneasy yoking of arty expressionism with minstrel-show comedy. But in 1929 it was revolutionary, not merely because it was the first commercial sound film in which an impor-tant jazz band was seen but because it presented the neatly dressed, nicely spoken Ellington as an *artist.* As the film gets under way, we see him coach-ing Whetsel in the proper way to play "Black and Tan Fantasy," and his musi-cians carry themselves with like poise in the nightclub scene, looking more like a chamber orchestra than a dance band. Moreover, *Black and Tan* got decent reviews and enhanced the reputation of its star. "This short, though billed and exploited as a slice of Harlem nite life[,] should go anywhere," said *Variety,* whose reviewer also praised the film's "fanciful and attractive" cam-era work. Black newspapers agreed. *The Chicago Defender,* whose editors kept a close watch on how blacks were characterized in the media, called *Black and Tan* "excellent entertainment . . . one of the most accurate slices of Harlem night life yet to be shown by any medium." Three years later *The New York Age* praised it as the first film to have steered clear of the "nauseat-ing lowdown niggerisms" that had blighted earlier screen appearances by black performers.

Black and Tan also marked—literally—a transition in Ellington's private life. After 1928 his left cheek bore a prominent crescent-shaped scar that is easily visible in the film's last scene (and in the photograph reproduced on the cover of this book). Though rarely mentioned by journalists, it made fans curious enough that he felt obliged to "explain" its presence in *Music Is My Mistress:*

I have four stories about it, and it depends on which you like the best. One is a taxicab accident; another is that I slipped and fell on a broken bottle; then there is a jealous woman; and last is Old Heidelberg, where they used to stand toe to toe with a saber in each hand, and slash away. The first man to step back lost the contest, no matter how many times he'd sliced the other. Take your pick.

None of Ellington's friends and colleagues was in doubt about which one to pick. In Irving Mills's words, "Women was one of the highlights in his life. He had to have women. . . . He always had a woman, always kept a woman here, kept a woman there, always had somebody." Most men who treat women that way are destined to suffer at their hands sooner or later, if not necessarily in so sensational a fashion as Ellington, whose wife attacked him with a razor when she found out that he was sleeping with another woman.

Who was she? One possible candidate is Fredi Washington. The costar of *Black and Tan* had launched her theatrical career in 1922 as a dancer in the chorus of the original production of Eubie Blake's *Shuffle Along.* Sonny Greer later described her as "the most beautiful woman" he had ever seen. "She had gorgeous skin, perfect features, green eyes, and a great figure. When she smiled, that was it!" Washington was light enough to pass for white but adamantly refused to do so, a decision that made it impossible for her to establish herself in Hollywood, though she appeared with Paul Robeson in Dudley Murphy's 1933 film of Eugene O'Neill's *The Emperor Jones* (for which her skin was darkened with makeup) and starred in *Imitation of Life,* a 1934 tearjerker in which she played, with mortifying predictability, a light-skinned black who passed for white. Ellington never spoke on the record about their romantic involvement, but Washington later admitted to the film historian Donald Bogle that she and Ellington had been lovers: "I just had to accept that he wasn't going to marry me. But I wasn't going to be his mistress." Their relationship was widely known at the time in the entertainment world, enough so that Mercer Ellington could write in his memoir of "a torrid love affair Pop had with a very talented and beautiful woman, an actress. I think this was a genuine romance, that there was love on both sides, and that it amounted to one of the most serious relationships of his life."

Edna, however, was no more forthcoming than Duke, saying only that she was "hurt, bad hurt when the breakup came" and referring to the affair in *Ebony* with an obliqueness worthy of her wayward husband: "Ellington thought I should have been more understanding of him. . . . Any young girl who plans to marry a man in public life—a man who belongs to the public—should try to understand as much about the demands of show business first and not be like I was." In point of fact, though, her lack of "understanding" extended to slashing her husband's face. That she did so is certain, but nothing else is definitely known about the assault, not even its exact date. "Something happened between [Ellington] and his wife and he's been terrible with women ever since," Lawrence Brown said. "I mean, like he's always trying to make somebody's wife, because somebody made his wife and they got in such a fight, that slash he has on the side of his face, she cut him while he was sleeping, with a razor." Brown was a presumptively biased witness, since he later married Fredi, becoming one of a number of Ellington sidemen (five, Mercer claimed) who took up with their boss's ex-girlfriends at one time or another. But Barney Bigard also claimed that the Ellingtons were mutually unfaithful, describing Edna's boyfriend as "quite a figure in the music world." Regarding the act itself, an unnamed "close friend" of Ellington told a biographer that Edna had vowed to "spoil those pretty looks" before cutting him, a secondhand account that is obviously unverifiable but nonetheless sounds believable.

Since the scar can be seen in *Black and Tan,* Edna must have found out about the affair well before the film was shot, which raises the possibility that her wrath was provoked by a different woman. Mercer writes in his memoir that his father had also been seeing "a Park Avenue socialite" whose family "managed to involve the police in discouraging the affair." As for Washington, Mercer also said that the unnamed actress with whom Ellington was involved "was one of those people who do not let their hearts rule them completely, and I believe that what brought the affair to an end was the fact that he never had any intention of divorcing [Edna], so that marriage was out of the question."

After the attack, Ellington fled his Harlem apartment, leaving everything behind, including his clothes—but he steered clear of Fredi Washington. Instead he moved in with Mildred Dixon, a dancer with a heart-shaped face who had made her Cotton Club debut along with Ellington in December of 1927. Their liaison, Mercer recalled, took him by surprise: "I came home from school one day, and there was a strange woman living with my father and taking care of me and Ruth. My mother, it turned out, had moved back into the building up the street, where we had lived before. They had separated without telling us. Nobody in my family liked to be the bearer of bad news." It wasn't quite like that, but it was close enough: Ellington and Mildred lived briefly at her place, then found a five-room flat in a building perched on the high bluff known to Harlemites as Sugar Hill, a sedate neighborhood of handsome row houses and apartment buildings whose population had become predominantly black a few years before Ellington moved there. The neighborhood is now decayed and unsafe, but in the thirties and forties it was the home of W. E. B. DuBois, W. C. Handy, Joe Louis, and Paul Robeson. Advertisements in the *Amsterdam News* touted it as "the Finest and Most Exclusive Section in Harlem," and Ellington agreed: "If you ever sat on a beautiful magenta cloud overlooking New York City, you were on Sugar Hill." Langston Hughes, who cast a colder eye on the pretentions of blacks with money, described it more matter-of-factly as a place full of "nice high-rent houses with elevators and doormen . . . where the plumbing really works and the ceilings are high and airy. For just a few thousands a year one can live very well on Sugar Hill in a house with a white-tiled hall." (In 1930 Ellington told a census taker that he was paying $95 a month in rent, about $1,200 today.)

That Ellington should have chosen to bring his new companion to Sugar Hill says much about his social ambitions. Once they got there, though, he kept Mildred out of sight, so much so that the 1930 census report does not even list her as a resident of the flat that they shared. The infrequent press reports in which mention was made of Mildred always referred to her as his wife, just as Barry Ulanov claims in his biography that "Mildred became Mrs. Ellington." But she never did, and Ellington is not known to have said a word about her for public consumption beyond what he told Ulanov. Only among friends did he admit to his love for the quiet woman whom he called "Sweet Bebe" and who made a favorable impression on all who knew her. Mercer spoke of her "innate class," and Helen Oakley described her as "very nice, extremely nice—she went to Vassar, and she was just a darling gal."

That we know so little about Mildred says even more about her close-mouthed companion. Ellington kept no diaries and almost never wrote personal letters, and the mask of smiling, noncommittal urbanity that he showed to the world was firmly in place by the time he gave his earliest surviving interviews, which date from 1930. Had there ever been a time when he spoke openly of his private life and inner thoughts? If so, it was over by then, and one suspects that it was his violent break with Edna that led him to drop the curtain on such matters. Not only would he have found it embarrassing to admit to having been cut up by his own wife, but to talk about it in public—or about his extramarital relationships with Mildred, Fredi, and the countless women who followed them into his bed—would have compromised the image that meant so much to him. A black artist who sought to "command respect for the race" by presenting himself as a man of distinction could not afford to have such things become generally known, much less to talk about them himself. But Ellington carried his discretion to extremes, and continued to do so until he died. Did it simply become a habit? Or was his silence an outward sign of his determination never again to let a woman get the best of him?

Whatever the reason, Mildred's devotion to him was no secret. According to Barney Bigard, "Duke used to gamble, you know, and sometimes he didn't have enough money to pay off the boys in the band and she'd give him her [Cotton Club] salary to pay off. And he treated her badly." That he did, but at the time Ellington was so much in love with her that when he brought his mother, father, and sister to New York to live with him, he insisted that she join them. Daisy refused at first to go along with so scandalous an arrangement, forcing Mildred to live in another apartment in the same building. J.E. balked as well, but not because he was unwilling to live under the same roof as his son's mistress. He was loath to leave Washington, Ruth said, because he didn't care for the idea of "being put out to pasture at such a tender age of forty-nine!" He must have been even more dubious about the emasculating prospect of being replaced at the head of the table. But in time both parents accepted the ménage, acknowledging their son, however reluctantly, as patriarch and sole breadwinner of the Ellington family. That suited him down to the ground. He wanted to put his mother on a velvet cushion and make his father do his bidding. He wanted to preserve and protect his sister's innocence ("He just thought I should be there, like a doll") and keep his son dependent (Mercer was forced to wear his hair in girlish braids for much of his childhood). Above all, he wanted to be free of the wife of his youth—without having to divorce her.

All he wanted, in other words, was to have everybody in the palm of his hand, and at the age of thirty-one, he got it. Even for a man who knew the value of good looks, a scar on the left cheek might well have seemed a tolerable price to pay.

∽

Such triumphs have their price in money as well as flesh, but Ellington could afford them. According to Freddie Jenkins, "We would be in the recording studio at seven A.M. and record until noon. In the afternoons we were making movie shorts, or doing a matinee at the Ziegfield [*sic*], or rehearsing. Then we'd play a night show at the Ziegfield, be back at the Cotton Club at eleven and play until four A.M." Though it was a stressful life, it was also a profitable one.

Ellington was doing well enough to add more players to his band, and in July of 1929 he hired Juan Tizol, a trombonist from Puerto Rico. Though the band included several light-skinned musicians, Tizol was Ellington's first side-man who was not "officially" black. In Rex Stewart's words, his "pure white countenance made him stand out like a blob of sour cream in the middle of a bowl of black caviar." Not only was Tizol nominally white, but he was, in Tricky Sam Nanton's phrase, "a legit man." A classically trained musician who moved to the United States in 1920 to work in the pit band of Washington's Howard Theatre, Tizol played the valve trombone, an instrument favored in Spanish-speaking countries but rarely encountered in jazz bands. He didn't consider himself to be a jazzman: "I take all my solos straight. Sweet style." He also preferred playing written-out solos to improvising, and his compact, fo-cused tone, warmed by a fast vibrato, was well suited to the lyrical melodies that Ellington loved to hear him play. Some of them were by Tizol himself, for he was a talented tunesmith who contributed several original compositions to the band's book, most of which had a Latin flavor and two of which, "Cara-van" and "Perdido," became jazz standards.

Tizol's compositions were scored by Ellington, since the trombonist had no gift for orchestration. Instead he doubled as the band's copyist, taking El-lington's untidy manuscripts and "extracting" in longhand the parts to be played by each musician. It was an intimidating task, both because Ellington was so prolific and because of his peculiar manner of notating his music. "This thing ain't supposed to work, man," the pianist Jimmy Jones said after looking at an Ellington score for the first time. Instead of writing "full scores" in which each part has its own line, he opted for three- and four-line "short scores" with the saxophones jammed onto a single staff—except for Harry Carney, whose baritone-sax part occupied a line of its own—and the trum-pets and trombones on the other staves. The trombone staff also contained a sketchy bass line, but Ellington never wrote out guitar or drum parts, leaving them to be made up by Fred Guy and Sonny Greer. (He also improvised his own piano parts.)

These methods arose from Ellington's lack of formal training, but even after he mastered the basics of notation, his scores remained unconventional. As Mercer explained it, he

> *wrote in such a cryptic fashion that the average person couldn't figure out what he was doing. He'd put clefs that didn't really belong on that particular staff, and he had a system of not changing the accidental so long as the accidental didn't belong to the particular part that that instrument was playing. . . . As a result, people who had a chance to look at the music, and maybe play it, found it didn't make sense.*

Adding a fifth brass player opened up new compositional vistas for Ellington, who started thinking of his trumpets and trombones as two separate sections instead of a single multivoiced choir. In addition, the fact that Tizol used valves instead of a slide allowed the trombonist to play chromatic passages like the descending line that ends the first strain of "Caravan" with exact intonation, which would become more useful to Ellington as his music grew harmonically richer. According to Mercer, Ellington also appreciated the fact that "he could write for [Tizol] along with the saxophones. On valve trombone he could move more quickly than Tricky Sam could on slide." That, too, mattered to the fast-maturing composer, who was now mixing the colors on his instrumental palette in increasingly unorthodox ways.

What Ellington thought of Tizol as a person is harder to know. In *Music Is My Mistress* his praise was more opaque than usual: "Tizol is a very big man, a very unselfish man, and one of the finest musicians I've ever known." This poker-faced paean gives no hint that the dour, bespectacled Tizol, like Barney Bigard, was also a practical joker who went in for such stunts as smearing Limburger cheese on mouthpieces and setting off stink bombs during performances. "You would never believe it if you met him casually," said Bigard. "He always seemed so far above everything, but he was the ringleader of us pranksters."

It's unlikely, however, that any pranks were played when the Ellington band spent two weeks playing for Maurice Chevalier on Broadway in the spring of 1930. Nowadays Chevalier is known, if at all, for his appearance in *Gigi*, but in the thirties he was an international star who was almost as popular in America as he was in his native France, and it was a colossal coup for Ellington and his men to accompany him at the Fulton Theatre. Chevalier took full credit in his memoirs: "I went to hear him, and my decision was quick and sure: the Duke and nobody else." On another occasion he claimed to have insisted that Ellington be engaged even after he was warned that many New Yorkers would look with disfavor on his being accompanied by a black band: "I am French and I do not know the American racial prejudices! Either Ellington is with me, or I do not sing and I cancel the show, that's all!"

No doubt this is true, but Ellington made a point of mentioning in *Music Is My Mistress* that Irving Mills claimed to have "fought" with the singer's manager "to have us play in concert with Maurice Chevalier." While Mills himself appears to have made no such claim, he did place in *Variety* a full-page ad "signed" by Ellington and the band in which prominent mention was made of Chevalier, *Show Girl*, the Cotton Club, Victor Records, and "MR. IRVING MILLS, the first to recognize our possibilities, and whose judgment and untiring efforts are responsible for our success." A few months later he planted an even more self-celebratory feature story in *The New York Age:*

> *Mills signed Ellington, and after years of work and study he developed this organization into one of the most talked of musical combinations in the world . . . Mills personally supervises every orchestration and arrangement the band plays. He arranges the bookings and directs the exploitation in general. He selects the records made for the various phonograph companies and is master of the destinies of Duke Ellington.*

Mills's efforts on behalf of Ellington, if not tireless, were both masterly and assiduous, and he proved his worth again in August, when he arranged for the band to go to Hollywood to appear in a full-length film, a feature called *Check and Double Check* that starred the most popular radio comedy team in the world. Forty million Americans tuned into NBC every weeknight to hear *Amos 'n' Andy,* a show in which two white men, Freeman Gosden and Charles Correll, played a pair of black sharecroppers who had come north from Georgia to Chicago to seek their fortune. Black listeners had divided opinions about *Amos 'n' Andy,* but everyone else loved it, and the program's success made a film version inevitable. RKO signed up Gosden and Correll, who donned blackface to appear in *Check and Double Check,* a makeshift expedient that fooled no one. (When *Amos 'n' Andy* was adapted for TV two decades later, the characters created by the two men were played by black actors.) So, too, did the lighter-skinned members of the Ellington band, who were ordered by the studio to wear dark makeup for a ballroom scene, a stipulation that was covered as news by the black papers. Juan Tizol recalled it with boiling indignation: "They made me and Barney a lot darker and they gave us the cold cream and so forth, when we were through, to go there and wash it off and take all that stuff off. Oh, it was awful."

Though *Check and Double Check* received indifferent reviews and did only middlingly well at the box office, Ellington and his musicians were paid $27,500, the equivalent of $356,000 today, and their Victor recording of "Three Little Words," a song written for the film by Bert Kalmar and Harry Ruby, was their biggest hit to date. As for the ballroom scene, in which they perform Ellington's "Old Man Blues," it is a priceless souvenir that shows the viewer how the band looked onstage in 1930. Undoubtedly at Mills's insistence, the men were dressed in tuxedos and required to do nothing other than make music, and if Freddie Jenkins's scene-stealing antics now seem obtrusive, they do nothing to lessen the impression that he and his colleagues are craftsmen, not comedians.

The dignity with which the Ellington band is pictured in *Check and Double Check,* as in *Black and Tan* before it, was part of Mills's strategy of "selling Ellington" to whites. It would be maintained in his other film appearances of the thirties, which ranged from band-oriented shorts like *A Bundle of Blues* (1933) to guest spots in such features as *Murder at the Vanities* and Mae West's *Belle of the Nineties* (both 1934). At a time when Hollywood was turning Louis Armstrong into a clownish savage garbed in leopard-skin outfits, Ellington wore sleek evening dress and led a band of polished professionals. He is never treated as a figure of fun—not even when he's having fun, as in the "Rape of the Rhapsody" sequence of *Murder at the Vanities,* in which the band muscles its way in on an overripe orchestral rendition of Liszt's Second Hungarian Rhapsody and sets the room to swinging. (Note the solo by the handsome gent at the piano, who grins sexily as he flings his hands around in his best rent-party style.)

Not long before *Check and Double Check* was filmed, Cab Calloway, who played the Cotton Club while the Ellington band was in Hollywood, met its leader for the first time. His account of their meeting deserves to be quoted at length:

> *Duke was more than suave. He had something special and he carried it with him all the time. He was a handsome, almost shy-looking man, with his hair brushed straight back and a thin mustache. He wore loose-fitting comfortable clothes, and he was almost always smiling. But mostly it was that air of self-assurance that got to me.*

Ellington had every reason to be self-assured. The records that he cut in 1930 are proof of it. But his films tell another part of the same story, one that is almost as important.

∽

"Old Man Blues," which was recorded for Victor in Hollywood that August, just before Ellington returned to New York and the Cotton Club, brought to a close what Gunther Schuller has called the band's "'workshop' period." Unlike the up-tempo showpieces that preceded it, most of which consisted of strings of solos bookended by nondescript theme choruses, "Old Man Blues" (whose underlying harmonies are borrowed from Jerome Kern's "Ol' Man

River," written three years earlier) demonstrates that Ellington now knew how to fuse written ensembles and improvised solos into fully integrated musical structures. While the piece itself, a thirty-two-bar tune cast in standard AABA pop-song form, is in no way elusive, the arrangement is still full of surprises. After an eight-bar vamp-till-ready introduction, it gets under way not with the customary full-band theme statement but with an improvised duet by Tricky Sam Nanton and Barney Bigard, followed by an even more startling change of key. Only then do the trumpets proclaim the fanfarelike theme, which gives way to a sequence of solos by Harry Carney, Johnny Hodges, and Freddie Jenkins superimposed on an instrumental background that changes from phrase to phrase. Observe, for instance, how Ellington plays a thrusting stride-piano obbligato behind the first and last parts of Carney's solo, then lays out on the song's minor-key bridge as Nanton and Juan Tizol move in with a sly "wah-wah" riff.*

Ellington is said to have thought "Old Man Blues" to be his best composition yet, but "Mood Indigo," recorded two months later by a seven-piece combo drawn from the band, is even more inspired, and unlike "Old Man Blues," which was never played in later years, it became a permanent part of the band's repertoire. A nocturne whose "exquisitely tired and four-in-the-morning" quality (in Constant Lambert's phrase) he would evoke time and again, "Mood Indigo" opens with a three-part chorale intoned by muted trumpet, muted trombone, and low-register clarinet, the combination that André Previn had in mind when he marveled at how "Duke merely lifts his finger, three horns make a sound, and I don't know what it is." Then Barney Bigard steps out from the ensemble to play the tune, backed by the ticktock strokes of Fred Guy's banjo and the steady walk of the rest of the rhythm section. Arthur Whetsel plays a delicate solo and Ellington ripples through a four-bar piano interlude, after which the chorale is repeated as the record spins to a close. Two months later the full band re-recorded "Mood Indigo," but Ellington knew better than to tamper with the scoring of the introductory chorale. It is as simple and unforgettable as a proverb.

Ellington's account of how "Mood Indigo" came to be written was one of the tales that he most enjoyed telling in later years:

We had a little six-piece date [not counting Ellington] in 1930 at OKeh. So we went down, and that night when I was waiting for my

---

* In a pop song written in AABA form, the contrasting eight-bar B strain is known to musicians as the "bridge" (or, alternatively, the "release").

mother to cook dinner, why, I said, "Yeah, I need another number, I better scratch out something while I wait." So I did the orchestration in fifteen minutes. . . . We recorded it, and that night at the Cotton Club, when it was almost time for our broadcast, Ted Husing, the announcer, asked, "Duke, what are we going to play tonight?" I told him about the new number, and we played it on the air, six pieces out of the eleven-piece band. The next day, wads of mail came in raving about the new tune, so Irving Mills put a lyric on it, and royalties are still coming in for my evening's work more than forty years later.

Some of his anecdotal set pieces contain more truth than others, and while this one is basically true, there was more to the story of "Mood Indigo" than he cared to admit. It is entirely possible, for instance, that he broadcast the piece from the Cotton Club on the same day that he recorded it. "Mood Indigo" first appears in NBC's logbooks on October 20, 1930, six days after the Harlem Footwarmers (one of the many pseudonyms used by the band when it recorded for labels other than Victor) first cut the song for OKeh. The log for the October 14 Cotton Club broadcast is incomplete, though, so that part of Ellington's story may well be accurate. But Bigard pooh-poohed the rest of it, claiming to have written the second strain of the song by himself: "Duke once said in a piece in one of those magazines that he wrote 'Mood Indigo' while his mother was fixing breakfast or something. Don't know how he did that. . . . Duke figured out a first strain and I gave him some ideas for it too. He wrote out a three-part harmony for the horns, we added my second strain and recorded it." He, too, was telling the truth—up to a point. While the first two recordings of "Mood Indigo," released by OKeh and Brunswick, initially credited the song to Ellington and Irving Mills, Bigard's name was added to the labels when these releases were subsequently re-pressed. Thereafter it appears on all later recordings of the song, as well as on the sheet music, though Bigard received no royalties until he threatened to sue Ellington twenty-eight years later. (Bigard said in 1978 that he had initially accepted a flat fee of $25.)

Compounding the general confusion, the label of the first pressings of the Brunswick recording identifies the song as "Dreamy Blues," not "Mood Indigo." This alternate title is nowhere to be found on OKeh's matrix card for the Harlem Footwarmers recording, which lists the song as "Mood Indigo." Why the discrepancy? Ellington said on at least one occasion that the short-lived alternate title was Mills's idea: "I wanted to call it 'Mood Indigo,' but Irving said that wasn't commercial enough!" Mills, on the other hand, claimed that "Mood Indigo" was his title, while Bigard claimed it for himself, adding that he had no idea how the song came to be called "Dreamy Blues."

Perhaps not, but Al Rose, a jazz buff who lived in New Orleans for much of his life, claimed that the second strain was written by Lorenzo Tio Jr., Bigard's clarinet teacher, and that the song was known in New Orleans as "Dreamy Blues." And Bigard later acknowledged that Tio had had a hand in writing the song:

> *My old teacher Lorenzo Tio had come to New York and he had a little slip of paper with some tunes and parts of tunes that he had written. There was one I liked and I asked him if I could borrow it. . . . It was just the second strain. There was no front part on what Tio gave me. I changed some of it around, for instance the bridge on the second strain, and got something together that mostly was my own but partly Tio's.*

Yet he continued to deny any knowledge of how Brunswick 4952 came to be released, however briefly, as "Dreamy Blues," disingenuously suggesting that "maybe the record company put the wrong label on the record . . . it was always 'Mood Indigo' to me and I ought to know."

Whatever the explanation, the fact remains that as with "Creole Love Call," Ellington may have been misled yet again by one of his own sidemen— and since he not only tried to deprive Bigard of credit for his contribution to "Mood Indigo" but succeeded in mulcting the clarinetist of a quarter-century's worth of royalty payments, turnabout was fair play. In any case, his contribution to "Mood Indigo" was as indispensable as the role that he played in the transformation of "Camp Meeting Blues" into "Creole Love Call." It was his introductory chorale that turned "Mood Indigo" from a song into a composition, one whose veiled, dulcet scoring, once heard, will always be remembered.

The story of "Mood Indigo" was complicated still further when, in 1931, Irving Mills turned it back into a song by adding lyrics: "You ain't been blue / Till you've had that mood indigo." The sheet music jointly credits Ellington, Mills, and Bigard with having written "words and music," and no other collaborator was officially credited when the song was copyrighted on February 21, or at any later time. But Mitchell Parish, a Mills Music staffer who wrote the words to Ellington's "Sophisticated Lady," as well as such other standards as "Deep Purple," "Star Dust," and "Sweet Lorraine," claimed that he did the same for "Mood Indigo": "Ellington recorded it under the title 'Dreamy Blues' before I was asked [by Mills] to write the lyric—which I did without getting credit."

Ellington confirmed that Parish was the lyricist. "At the time he was signed with the company . . . and so they just bought him outright, and he was on a regular stipend, on a salary," he said in 1962.

In one final turn of the screw, the popular crooner Gene Austin, who made the first vocal recording of "Mood Indigo" for Victor in August of 1931, allegedly told his wife years later that it was he, not Parish, who had written the words:

> *Duke was playing that tune one night in one of the [Harlem] clubs. Gene said, "Hey, Duke, I like that tune. Do you have lyrics to it?" The Duke said, "No." Gene says, "I know you're writing with Mitchell Parish. Have Mitch write some lyrics and I'd like to record it." . . . They had delivered the music to his home address on Riverside Drive. There was no lyric. Gene hurried and wrote all the lyrics in the cab going down to the Victor company. I said, "Gene, why didn't you call them on it," and he said, "Oh, Lou, I've written a lot and was getting big royalties so I thought I'd let Mitch have the royalties," letting others think Parish wrote them.*

No matter who wrote "Mood Indigo," it remains an imperishable classic, one of a handful of songs that come to mind whenever Ellington's name is mentioned anywhere in the world. It was, he said, "our first big hit," and he would remain indissolubly identified with it. When the Ellington band broadcast a radio tribute to Franklin Roosevelt after his sudden death in 1945, "Mood Indigo" was one of the songs that was performed. When *Time* put Ellington on its cover in 1956, the title of the story was "Mood Indigo & Beyond." In March of 1931 Cab Calloway recorded one of the first cover versions by an American band, and the arrangement he used was a virtual carbon copy of Ellington's big-band chart. Two years later the Boswell Sisters cut a close-harmony vocal version, one of twenty-eight other covers known to have been made between 1930 and 1939. As late as 1954, the Norman Petty Trio put "Mood Indigo" on the pop charts with a countrified version. Ellington would recycle its characteristic instrumental colors on numerous occasions, most notably in a 1940 composition called "Dusk" that is as poetic as "Mood Indigo" itself, and recorded the song in several dozen customized renderings ranging from a fifteen-minute "uncut concert arrangement" handcrafted by Billy Strayhorn to a down-and-dirty small-group performance in which the composer sat in with Louis Armstrong's All Stars. Sidney Bechet, Tony Bennett, Rosemary Clooney, Nat "King" Cole, Perry Como, Floyd Cramer, Doris Day, the Dukes of Dixieland, John Fahey, Ella Fitzgerald, the Four Freshmen, Erroll Garner, David Grisman, Coleman Hawkins, Woody Herman, Lena Horne, Dr. John, André Kostelanetz, Jimmie Lunceford, Henry Mancini, the Mills Brothers, Charles Mingus, Thelonious Monk, Pérez Prado, the Preservation Hall Jazz Band, Charlie Rich, Paul Robeson, Nina Simone, Frank Sinatra, the Singers Unlimited, even Debby Boone and Joe Jackson: All have sought to put their stamp on a song so redolent of its time and place that Brian De Palma included a performance of the original 1930 arrangement on the soundtrack of *The Untouchables* in order to establish the film's period setting. It will be remembered as long as Ellington himself is remembered, and maybe even after that.

❧

Between them, "Old Man Blues" and "Mood Indigo" sum up what Ellington had achieved by 1930, and point to where he would go from there. It is, one suspects, no coincidence that his oldest surviving musical manuscripts date from that year, for he must have known that he had come decisively into his own as a composer. Yet it is not hard to imagine "Old Man Blues" having been whipped up in the same impromptu manner that was described by a writer for *Metronome* who saw the Ellington band at work three years later:

> *The men take up their instruments, and the arrangement is started. Ellington takes the men by sections, first the reeds, then the trumpets, then the trombones, and gives each man his notes for four bars. The men play them singly, then as a section, with remarkable rapidity. Any necessary changes are made section by section; the men make suggestions and from time to time Ellington turns to the piano to trace out an idea.... Then they play it a sufficient number of times to fix it in their memories.*
>
> *While the other sections are at work, Juan Tizol, the Puerto Rican valve trombonist, will have been busy with a score, taking down the arrangement as it is made for the other sections, sometimes writing down the trombone parts, sometimes indicating them sketchily, for elaboration later....*
>
> *Then Duke takes the score home with him, to see if any further refinements are possible. About noon the day after he went to work on the tune he has polished it to his satisfaction, sometimes entirely rewriting parts of it, and goes to bed.*

On occasion, the article went on to say, Ellington wrote out entire compositions independent of the band, but the author implied that it was not his normal practice to do so. That must have been an exaggeration, since he was turning out too many charts for the Cotton Club shows to have created all of them in the rehearsal studio. One of Mercer's first memories of his father was of hearing him at work in the middle of the night: "This is a man who came in at three or four o'clock in the morning and sat religiously at the piano and composed." Yet there is plenty of circumstantial evidence indicating that in 1930 and for some time afterward, he continued to "write" pieces in face-to-face collaboration with his sidemen. No music stands are visible in the ballroom scene of *Check and Double Check,* and their absence was deliberate. To use music onstage, Ellington felt, was untheatrical, even square: "In the old days, you know, when you played on the stage, you just never brought music on the stage . . . I found out that guys memorize things that they heard much more quickly and much more easily than they did if they read it." Nor are there any passages in "Old Man Blues" or "Mood Indigo" so technically involved that his players would have found them impossible, or even difficult, to pick up by ear.

The time came when it was impractical for Ellington to compose "on" the band (though he would always use it to edit and polish what he wrote in private). As he explained in 1956, "it . . . just got to be too damn much music." But knowing that he wrote many of his best-remembered compositions of the Mills era by working them out on the piano in the presence of his musicians makes it easier to understand certain of their features, above all his informal approach to what classically trained musicians call "voice leading." An untrained musician who harmonizes a melody does so by superimposing it atop a series of chords, in the same way that a singer might accompany himself by strumming casually on a guitar. Every chord is treated as a separate musical event, one of a collection of freestanding bits of musical color that are assembled in aurally logical sequences known as "chord progressions." A musician who has studied counterpoint, by contrast, is trained to think of a chord progression not as a sequence of three- and four-note chords but as a stack of horizontal "voices" that are woven together contrapuntally to produce harmony. It becomes second nature for him to make each individual voice sound like a tune that is being sung out loud, avoiding wide leaps in favor of melodies that move smoothly from note to note in a stepwise manner.

Ellington, by contrast, claimed to have taken only a half dozen lessons in harmony and is not known ever to have studied counterpoint. Ignorant of the rules of classical voice leading, he worked out attractive-sounding chord progressions at the piano, then (at first) taught them to his musicians by rote. This explains why his part-writing is full of unmelodic angularities like the downward plunge in the third bar of the clarinet part of "Mood Indigo." By the same token, his compositions are largely devoid of contrapuntal development, save for the rough-and-ready kind produced when two musicians improvise simultaneously. When he does pit two fully independent sectional voices against one another, as in the opening of *Diminuendo and Crescendo in Blue,* the listener is taken aback. And because he had no training in counterpoint and played the piano, a chordal instrument, instead of a single-line wind instrument, he thought almost exclusively in terms of vertical harmony, not horizontal melody. Though he was able on occasion to squeeze out a well-turned melody, some of his best-known "tunes," like that of the chorale in "Mood Indigo," amount to little more than elaborations on the top notes of the chord progressions that he worked out at the piano, while others, like "I Got It Bad (And That Ain't Good)," are purely instrumental constructs whose wide-ranging patterns, which fit easily under a pianist's fingers, can be challenging for a singer to execute.

Don George, one of Ellington's lyricists, shed light on his melodic deficiencies in this fascinating anecdote:

> *Duke had a strange way of composing. Most tune writers wrote the melody first, then worked out the chord structure behind it, but Duke wrote the chords and that was that. At first I felt as though I were feeling my way through a labyrinth and had forgotten to unwind the string behind me that would return me to the entrance; but gradually, through some form of musical osmosis, the words fell in the right places and lo! . . . we had a song.*

To be a facile melodist is not a prerequisite of musical greatness. No more than Beethoven or Stravinsky was Ellington a natural tunesmith: His genius, like theirs, lay elsewhere. Over time he found a near-infinite number of ways to conceal this deficit, just as (in Gunther Schuller's words) "the parallel blocks of sound he favors so predominantly are handled with such variety that we, as listeners, never notice the lack of occasional contrapuntal relief." But it is impossible to write truly popular songs without also being able to write truly memorable tunes, and so it stands to reason that the charges of plagiarism that were to be leveled against Ellington in years to come would center not on his instrumentals but his hit songs, nearly all of which were collaborations with band members who did not always receive credit—or royalties—when the songs were recorded and published.

The best-known example is "Sophisticated Lady," one of his most popular ballads, recorded in February of 1933. Whenever he was asked about the song, he would trot out a variation on this well-worn anecdote:

> *We were playing in Chicago. In between the shows, in the theater, I used to go up in a room that they had—I think it was the pit-orchestra leader's room and he had a piano—and I was up there and writing something.*
>
> *I said, I have to write a thing to capture a real sophisticated lady, you know, one who is traveled and learned. And I took as an example some friends of mine whom I knew at that time, who were school teachers in Washington. These kids were very, very sophisticated. They used to fly off to their weekends around the country and summer in Europe.*

The part of the tale that he conveniently neglected to tell was that he did not write the song's "sophisticated," elaborately chromatic melody. It was a joint creation of Otto Hardwick and the trombonist Lawrence Brown, who joined the band in 1932. "I had a theme which I played all the time which is the first eight bars," Brown said. "And Otto Hardwick played . . . the release." Ellington turned these melodic fragments into a song by splicing them together, then harmonizing them. The label of the first recording of "Sophisticated Lady" credited all three men, along with Irving Mills. But Ellington offered Brown and Hardwick what the trombonist later described as "the terrific check of $15" ($250 apiece in today's dollars) for all their rights in the song. They took the money, and when "Sophisticated Lady" was copyrighted and published in May, their names had vanished from the credits, never to be seen again.

The way in which "Sophisticated Lady" and "Mood Indigo" were written came to be common practice for Ellington. "I mean, like if anybody stood up and took a solo, you know, and he heard something that [the musician] made playing that [Ellington] liked, he'd tell them, 'Play the solo. Play it again,' until he got it," Bigard explained. "When he got it, then that's it. Then the next thing you know there's a tune coming out of it." According to Freddie Jenkins, Ellington would share credit with the musician whenever "the piece didn't require too much work to fit the band." In other cases, though, he took it for granted that he deserved the lion's share of credit for such "collaborations": "There are many instances where guys have come in with four bars or eight bars and said, 'Hey, this is a good lick!' And I'd say, 'Yeah, it is a good lick, let's make something out of it.' Then you take it home, arrange it up, add what needs to be added to it and it comes up a number." It was exceptional for him to take sole credit for songs whose melodic material, like that of "Sophisticated Lady," was wholly the work of other men.* His usual custom was to write the bridge to a song whose main theme came from a member of the band (as was the case with Juan Tizol's "Caravan" and Johnny Hodges's "Never No Lament," which was later turned into "Don't Get Around Much Anymore") or to expand one of their favorite licks into an instrumental composition, adding material of his own as needed (as he did with "Mood Indigo" and Cootie Williams's "Concerto for Cootie," which became "Do Nothin' Till You Hear from Me").

These magpielike borrowings troubled some of the borrowees more than others. Tizol, for one, affected to find them amusing: "Oh, he'd steal like mad, no questions about it. He'd steal that from his own self." And Williams spoke benignly of the practice:

> *All of us used to sell the songs to him for $25. Some of the fellas, in later years, they sued him. But I didn't do it. No, I believed in if I sold a person something and he paid for it, I didn't believe in going back, you know, and saying I didn't mean it that way. So I let it go. It was fun then. You know, I got a lot of experience doing things like that. And it was a pleasure, you know, to have the band to play your song. To have someone playing your song. That's why we did it.*

But certain of Ellington's musicians, especially Brown and Johnny Hodges, felt cheated when a melodic fragment that they had sold for a pittance was turned by their boss into a hit song. Indeed, Brown saw the practice as a form of musical kleptomania and the Ellington band as a "factory" for the manufacture of collective compositions to which the leader signed his name alone. "Every man in there was a part of the music, the band, and everything

---

* Even when he shared credit for a song instead of buying it outright, though, Ellington extracted the maximum profit from the deal, a lesson that he learned from Irving Mills. In Clark Terry's grudgingly admiring words, "If he liked [a song] he'd explain that, in order to record it, he would have to make himself half-composer. But what you didn't realise was that he was going to publish it too—he had his own publishing company. First of all, publishing-wise, half belongs to the publishing company, so he's already got half of it. Now he's half-writer of it as well, so whack! There goes another bit, and he's got six bits and you got a quarter!"

that happened, and every successful move that the band made," he said—and not just to interviewers, but to Ellington himself. "I don't consider you a composer," the trombonist told his boss early in their relationship. "You are a compiler."

Clark Terry put the process in clearer perspective when he described Ellington as "a compiler of deeds and ideas, with a great facility to make something out of what would possibly have been nothing . . . perhaps even Barney would never have written down 'Mood Indigo.'" And it was true: None of the many Ellington sidemen who went out on their own came remotely near approaching his success, nor did any of them write so much as one hit song. It took the mind of a composer to turn their fragments into full-blown creations. "Immature poets imitate; mature poets steal; bad poets deface what they take, and good poets make it into something better, or at least something different," T. S. Eliot wrote in *The Sacred Wood*. "The good poet welds his theft into a whole of feeling which is unique, utterly different from that from which it was torn; the bad poet throws it into something which has no cohesion." He could have been talking about Duke Ellington.

Billy Strayhorn said it best:

> *So this guy says you and he wrote it, but he thinks he wrote it. He thinks you just put it down on paper. But what you did was put it down on paper, harmonized it, straightened out the bad phrases, and added things to it, so you could hear the finished product. Now, really, who wrote it?*
>
> *It was ever thus.*
>
> *But the proof is that these people don't go somewhere else and write beautiful music. You don't hear anything else from them. You do from Ellington.*

It should be remembered that Ellington's financial sleight of hand was anything but unusual. Most of the top singers and bandleaders of the day insisted on being "cut in" on the royalties from the songs that they performed and recorded. But the difference was that unlike them, he was a great composer. So, too, were many of his sidemen great soloists, and some of the songs for whose melodies they were partly or wholly responsible became standards that are still performed throughout the world. Hence it *matters* who wrote "Mood Indigo" and "Sophisticated Lady," not just because of the money but because Ellington was one of the supreme creative figures of the twentieth century. The nature of his genius is illuminated by knowing that he found it hard to write singable tunes (as opposed to instrumental pieces, which he turned out with unfailing facility) and that his later development as a composer was in part a response to this incapacity.

While this does nothing to diminish Ellington's greatness, his lifelong reluctance to give full credit to his collaborators places his personality in an unflattering light. Whether or not Bigard stole "Mood Indigo" from Lorenzo Tio Jr., he was right to criticize Ellington for his own musical appropriations: "That's the only thing I didn't like about Duke. He never gave the boys in the band the credit they deserved. . . . It wouldn't cost him nothing to credit them—he was a genius." It was true, and those who have spent time around geniuses know that some of them cannot bear to be thought less than perfect.

6

"A HIGHER PLATEAU"

Becoming a Star, 1931–1933

WHAT DUKE ELLINGTON lacked in collegiality, he more than made up for in talent, and he was doing things with his musicians that no other big-band composer had done up to that time. Gunther Schuller did not overstate the case when he said that in pieces like "Mood Indigo" and "Old Man Blues," Ellington had achieved "the perfect balance between composition and improvisation . . . This achievement is, of course, above all else, Ellington's greatest contribution to the development of jazz." Other arrangers of the twenties and thirties, among them Bill Challis and Don Redman, used the dance-band instrumentation with a like degree of coloristic imagination, but unlike them, Ellington was also producing original compositions of permanent interest. It is instructive to listen to his recordings of the period in tandem with those of Fletcher Henderson, the bandleader who had been one of his first professional models ("I tried desperately to try and sound like Fletcher Henderson") when he came to New York in 1923. Despite its lack of discipline, the Henderson band was a first-class group, and in Coleman Hawkins it had one of the most influential jazz soloists of the twentieth century. But after 1926, Ellington's music was so far in advance of anything that Henderson was playing that direct comparisons are pointless, even embarrassing.

In this respect he had only one rival, Jelly Roll Morton, who had grappled with similar compositional problems in his small-group recordings of the midtwenties and solved them with comparable success—and it's interesting to note that Ellington never spoke of Morton other than with icy contempt. "Sure, Jelly Roll Morton has talent . . . talent for talking about Jelly Roll Morton," he told Leonard Feather. "Jelly Roll Morton played piano like one of those high school teachers in Washington; as a matter of fact, high school teachers played better jazz." He should have known better, and very likely did. "Probably he was jealous of [Morton] in those days," Barney Bigard said. It is, however, impossible to prove that Ellington heard any of the Red Hot Peppers' Victor recordings, much less that he was influenced by them in any way, and so one must take his word for it that Morton's music meant nothing to him.

Conversely, he would never have a bad word to say about Paul Whiteman, whom he described to a newspaper columnist in 1932 as his "favorite musician." Long after Whiteman's music fell out of fashion, Ellington remained loyal to the man who had shown him what a jazz orchestra could do: "Paul Whiteman was known as the King of Jazz, and no one as yet has come near carrying that title with more certainty and dignity . . . there is no doubt but that he has carried jazz to the highest position it ever has enjoyed." He made a point of mentioning Whiteman when being interviewed by Howard Taubman of *The New York Times* prior to the Carnegie Hall premiere of *Black, Brown and Beige,* and what he said was notable:

> *Our band came along just when Paul Whiteman and his orchestra had popularized the symphonic style. And don't let them kid you about Whiteman. He has been a big man in our music. He's done a lot for it, especially with his concerts where he gave composers a chance to write new, extended works.*

Today Whiteman's "symphonic jazz" is known only to musical archaeologists, but for the young Duke Ellington it was very much a thing of the present. Working in tandem with Ferde Grofé, Whiteman had organized in 1920 one of the first modern American dance bands to use written arrangements, an innovation that opened the door to the big-band era. While his earliest recordings sound overpolite and rhythmically stiff to modern ears, so does most other recorded "jazz" of the period, and his agenda was in any case quite different from that of the black musicians of New Orleans and Chicago. Whiteman never said that he sought to "make a lady out of jazz," an apocryphal quote that continues to be cited sniffishly, but what he did say was equally to the point: "The modern jazz can be played without so much roughness and made quite attractive. That's what I aim to do." To that end he put together a twenty-eight-piece concert orchestra that performed an unusually wide range of popular music with polish and warmth. For most white Americans in the twenties, Whiteman's music *was* jazz, the very thing that novelists like F. Scott Fitzgerald and John O'Hara had in mind when they wrote about the manners and morals of what came to be known as "the Jazz Age." And some of it was jazz by any definition—Bix Beiderbecke's presence in the trumpet section ensured that—while much of the rest of it, including George Gershwin's *Rhapsody in Blue,* the first of many such essays in "symphonic jazz" that Whiteman commissioned, was deeply informed by the sounds of black jazz.

Ellington had tangled feelings about Gershwin, whom he regarded with a volatile mix of admiration, envy, and resentment. He would be judiciously critical of *Porgy and Bess,* arguing in public that "Gershwin's music, though grand, was not distinctly or definitely negroid in character" and expressing more frankly in private his dislike of the racial attitudes embedded in the opera's libretto: "*Porgy and Bess,* those people in those alleys, waking up, dusting those carpets out the window and beating their brooms in time and all that bullshit." In 1940, though, he told an interviewer who asked him to name the greatest American composer that it was "George Gershwin, without a doubt. He had the broadest scope and wrote in the vein of all America. He occasionally was influenced by the masses, but much of his work was purely original." And for all his reservations about *Porgy,* Ellington knew that Gershwin's concert works were far more ambitious than anything to which he had set his hand, just as he knew that the premiere of *Rhapsody in Blue,* at which Jascha Heifetz, Fritz Kreisler, Sergei Rachmaninoff, John Philip Sousa, and Leopold Stokowski were present, had conferred on its composer the same cultural legitimacy after which the status-conscious Ellington hungered.

Though he continued throughout 1931 to build on the success of "Mood Indigo" and "Old Man Blues" with such three-minute gems as the jaunty "Rockin' in Rhythm" and the darkly nostalgic "Echoes of the Jungle," and despite his insistence that he wasn't interested in "symphony techniques," Ellington was definitely interested in writing pieces that, like Gershwin's *Rhapsody in Blue* and Concerto in F, burst out of the straitjacket of song form. "At present he is at work on a tremendous task, the writing, in music, of 'The History of the Negro,' taking the Negro from Egypt, going with him to savage Africa, and from there to the sorrow and slavery of Dixie, and finally 'home to Harlem,' " a journalist reported in December of 1930. Three months later he published an essay called "The Duke Steps Out" in which he spoke of the racial roots of his musical ambitions:

> *The music of my race is something more than the "American idiom." It is the result of our transplantation to American soil, and was our reaction in the plantation days to the tyranny we endured. What we could not say openly we expressed in music, and what we know as "jazz" is something more than just dance music . . . the characteristic melancholy music of my race has been forged from the very white heat of our sorrows.*

Once again Ellington set forth his plans to chronicle the history of his race in sound, explaining that he was "engaged on a rhapsody unhampered by any musical form in which [he] intend[ed] to portray the experiences of the coloured races in America in the syncopated idiom." The work, he added, would consist of "four or five movements . . . I am putting all I have learned into it in the hope that I shall have achieved something really worth while in the literature of music, and that an authentic record of my race *written by a member of it* shall be placed on record." Many years passed before he got around to delivering on that promise, but by the time that "The Duke Steps Out" was published, Ellington had indeed written a rhapsody of his own, a six-and-a-half-minute piece that took up both sides of a ten-inch 78, and if it was something less than a masterpiece, it was also something more than a cameo.

If Ellington's various accounts of the genesis of *Creole Rhapsody* can be trusted, it came about in the most casual of ways. *Time* reported in its 1956 cover story on Ellington that Irving Mills happened to mention to a reporter that his client was working on a "rhapsody" that was "part of a larger work." Though he was doing no such thing, "Duke Ellington, too proud to let his manager down, and unwilling to let such a whopper stand, produced the music on time—or almost on time." In *Music Is My Mistress* Ellington told the same story somewhat differently:

> *Irving Mills came to me one day with an original idea. He was always reaching toward a higher plateau for our music.*
>
> *"Tomorrow is a big day," he said. "We premiere a new long work—a rhapsody."*

"Really?" I replied. "Okay."

So I went out and wrote Creole Rhapsody, *and I did so much music for it that we had to cut it up and do two versions. One came out on Brunswick and the other, longer one, on Victor. Irving almost blew his connection at both companies for recording a number that was not only more than three minutes long, but took both sides of the record.*

It is, as usual with Ellington, a rattling good tale, but the facts, also as usual, fail to bear all of it out. Ellington said in his autobiography that the band was playing at Chicago's Oriental Theatre when Mills approached him about writing a "new long work," but that was in February. The band recorded the first version of *Creole Rhapsody* in New York on January 20, 1931, toward the end of a long run at the Cotton Club. Nor does Barry Ulanov's biography say anything about Mills's having ordered him to write the piece. What we do know is that NBC's logbooks show that he had recently broadcast three pieces from the Cotton Club whose titles suggest that they *might* have been *Creole Rhapsody*. "Cotton Club Rhapsody" aired on November 20, "California Rhapsody" on December 23, and "Brooklyn Rhapsody" on January 20, the same day that Brunswick recorded *Creole Rhapsody*. Nothing is known about these latter pieces, and it is possible that one or more of them was *Creole Rhapsody* in disguise.

Regardless of how and when it actually got written, the Brunswick version of *Creole Rhapsody* is, as Ellington rightly said in "The Duke Steps Out," "unhampered by any musical form." Its main distinction is its length: Ellington had recorded a two-sided version of "Tiger Rag" in 1929, but it was nothing more than an extra-long showcase for his soloists. *Creole Rhapsody*, by contrast, is a through-composed work in which improvisation takes a backseat, and the entire piece is played at the same medium-brisk tempo, creating an impression of unity that is belied by the piece itself, a potpourri of unrelated themes (the first of which is closely based on the introduction to "Move Over," a little-known Ellington recording from 1928) connected by piano interludes. The obvious model was *Rhapsody in Blue* and the multi-strain concert-style works that were being written by Ferde Grofé and other composers for Paul Whiteman's band in the late twenties, though listeners unfamiliar with these now-obscure pieces will be more likely to find *Creole Rhapsody* reminiscent of a Broadway production number. The opening theme, which returns at frequent intervals throughout the piece, sounds like a life-in-the-big-city music cue of the sort that a stage-savvy composer like Alfred Newman might have written for one of the Hollywood films that

Ellington watched in between playing live stage shows at the movie houses where he and his band would soon be appearing regularly.

Five months later, on June 11, Ellington and the band recorded a revised *Creole Rhapsody* for Victor that was two minutes longer than the original, meaning that it had to be issued on a twelve-inch 78, a format usually reserved for classical releases. As was his custom, he took apart the Brunswick version and put its sections back together in a different order, inserting new material along the way. In the second version, each section is played in a different tempo, a device that Ellington may have borrowed from *Rhapsody in Blue* (he also threw in a near-verbatim quotation from the Gershwin work). *Rhapsody in Blue*, like the other "symphonic jazz" scores performed by the Whiteman band, is as episodic as *Creole Rhapsody*, but because of its greater duration, the episodes are sufficiently long—and tuneful—to endow the piece with a modicum of solidity. The shorter sections and ever-changing tempos of the Victor version of *Creole Rhapsody*, by contrast, give it a hectic, overcrowded air, leaving an impression of incoherence that is at odds with the superior workmanship of the new material, some of which is as good as anything that Ellington ever wrote.

In neither version, however, does he show any understanding of how to organize an extended composition other than in the medleylike manner of Gershwin and Grofé. No underlying logic propels the collagelike sequence of musical events in *Creole Rhapsody*. Ellington simply staples the sections together, reiterating instead of developing them, and both versions straggle to a halt instead of coming to a satisfying conclusion. The effect, as with *Rhapsody in Blue*, is not unlike Donald Tovey's acid description of one of Franz Liszt's less successful tone poems as "an introduction to an introduction to a connecting link to another introduction to a rhapsodic interlude, leading to a free development of the third introduction, leading to a series of still more introductory developments of the previous introduction, leading to a solemn slow theme (which, after these twenty minutes, no mortal power will persuade any listener to regard as a real beginning), and so eventually leading backward to the original mysterious opening by way of conclusion." Given the fact that Ellington had never before tried, so far as we know, to write a large-scale work and had not heard the classical models that could have shown him how to do so, it is a wonder that either version of *Creole Rhapsody* is listenable. In fact the best parts of both recordings are still a joy to hear. But his stubborn unwillingness to learn from the classics (unlike Gershwin, who studied them so carefully that he managed to write a full-length opera just eleven years after *Rhapsody in Blue*) forced him to fumble for wheel-inventing "solutions" to basic problems of musical architecture. This is why so little of the craft on display in "Old Man Blues," whose repeating-chorus form Ellington understood in his bones, can be heard in *Creole Rhapsody*.

None of this prevented Irving Mills from selling *Creole Rhapsody* in a full-page *Variety* ad whose headline, "Duke Ellington: America's New Vogue (A Different Kind of Music)," stressed the piece's novelty. So did the stories that Mills planted in newspapers around the country, often accompanied by a photo of Ellington presenting a copy of the score of *Creole Rhapsody* to Paul Whiteman, who declared himself eager to perform the piece with his own orchestra: "Wild and barbaric as its rhythms may be, 'Creole Rhapsody' is musically correct in form and structure." Touting *Creole Rhapsody* as a step forward for jazz fit into Mills's promotional strategy, and it was true to boot. For all its structural weaknesses, and inferior as it was to Gershwin's efforts in the same line, Ellington really had tried to do something new in jazz. Spike Hughes, who kept an eye on American jazz recordings in his column for *The Melody Maker*, an English magazine for dance-band musicians, saw at once what he was up to: "*Creole Rhapsody* is the latest development of a form which Ellington has made his own. . . . It is, in fact, the first classic of modern dance music. The individual player is, for the first time, completely subservient to the personality of the composer."

So did Percy Grainger, the celebrated Australian pianist-composer, who invited the Ellington band to perform for his students at New York University in October of 1932. Grainger, an authority on English folk song who was far more inclined than most of his classical-music contemporaries to take popular music seriously, was giving a series of lectures at NYU called "A General Study of the Manifold Nature of Music." Already interested in the improvisational elements of jazz, he had recently discovered Ellington's music, apparently by reading about it in R. D. Darrell's record column, and was fascinated by its pastel instrumental colors and lush harmonic language. They reminded Grainger of the music of Frederick Delius, an English composer who had lived on a Florida plantation in his youth and sought in his compositions to evoke his memories of the black spirituals that he heard there, infusing them with the modern harmonies of Grieg and Debussy. Grainger decided to devote an entire class to Ellington, whom he introduced to his students with a flourish: "The three greatest composers who ever lived are Bach, Delius and Duke Ellington. Unfortunately Bach is dead, Delius is very ill, but we are happy to have with us today The Duke." He then went on to praise the "high emotional and technical qualities" and "rhapsodic improvisation" of Ellington's music as the band played musical examples for his bedazzled students.

It's not known whether Grainger and Ellington specifically discussed *Creole Rhapsody*, but it would be surprising if the work was not mentioned, since Whiteman and his band played it three months later at Carnegie Hall as part of their "Fifth Experiment in Modern Music," a series that was inaugurated in 1924 with the Aeolian Hall performance at which *Rhapsody in Blue* was premiered. Ellington's piece shared the bill with Ferde Grofé's *Tabloid*, a forgotten piece of program music about a newspaper city room whose unorthodox instrumentation stole the show ("Four typewriters, a revolver, a machine-gun, an emergency wagon siren, a policeman's whistle and the clack of telegraph keys were used for realism"). Though *Creole Rhapsody* went unmentioned by the critic of *The New York Times,* who probably knew nothing of its composer, an excerpt was heard in a Paramount short released in August of 1933 that featured the bands of Ellington and Cab Calloway and the Mills Blue Rhythm Band, all of them managed by Irving Mills, who praised his most famous client on camera: "When I first heard him, he was conducting a little five-piece orchestra up in Harlem. Today he is acclaimed by music authorities both here and abroad as the creator of a new vogue in music."

That was the next-to-last hurrah for *Creole Rhapsody.* After broadcasting it over the BBC during his first European tour, Ellington appears to have dropped the work from his regular repertoire, though he is known to have performed it on occasion as late as 1940 and made a point of including it in a list of favorite recordings that he compiled for *Down Beat* to commemorate the twenty-fifth anniversary of his Cotton Club debut. In 1960 he and Lawrence Brown taped a wistful duet version of a theme from *Creole Rhapsody* that Ellington titled "Creole Blues," but it languished unheard in Columbia's vaults for years. Reporters rarely bothered to ask him about *Creole Rhapsody,* and Ellington, who liked to pretend that the past had never happened, saw no reason to remind them of the piece. It had served its purpose, and that was that.*

∾

Two weeks after recording the first version of *Creole Rhapsody,* Ellington turned over the bandstand of the Cotton Club to Cab Calloway and went on his first national tour, a yearlong marathon that took him to Baltimore, Boston, Buffalo, Chicago, Cleveland, Denver, Des Moines, Detroit, Indianapolis, Kansas City,

---

* In 1969 Ellington turned some of the themes from *Creole Rhapsody* into a rock-and-roll piece called "Neo-Creole" that he later incorporated into his score for the film *Change of Mind.*

Minneapolis, Omaha, Philadelphia, Pittsburgh, Washington, and other stops on the Paramount-Publix movie-house circuit. A full-page ad in *Variety* hailed his departure, bragging of "continuous sensational, nightly turn-away of crowds" at the Cotton Club. It was Ellington's first taste of the exhausting manner in which he was to spend the rest of his life, and it is doubtful that he would have gotten through the tour in one piece without the help of Richard B. Jones, who had just joined the Ellington organization as band boy and general dogsbody. Rex Stewart described Jones, who was known to the musicians as "Jonesy" and would be immortalized in the title of Ellington's 1934 recording of "Stompy Jones," as "Duke's A number one chargé d'affaires . . . the greatest prop man, valet and light-board operator that any traveling band ever had. Jonesy was untiring, alert and utterly devoted to the band, especially to Duke."

Thanks to the tour, the broadcasts, the records, the film appearances, and the work of Irving Mills, Ellington was about to become a star. Up to then his celebrity, though real, had been substantially regional. Prior to 1930 his name had appeared only fifteen times in stories printed in the national edition of *The Chicago Defender*. From then to the end of 1935, it would appear in 284 different articles. But no amount of acclaim could offset the effects of the Great Depression, which had laid waste to the record business. American record sales plummeted from sixty-five million in 1929 to ten million in 1932. *Variety* announced the news with a story whose double-decker headline sent chills down the spines of musicians from coast to coast: "RCA Victor Unloading Stars/Must Buy Up Fat Contracts." One of the stars who was unceremoniously unloaded was Ellington, who cut a half dozen sides for Victor in June of 1931, then went for eight months without releasing a record.

It was an alarming development, one that called for a decisive response, and Mills, who was nothing if not decisive, responded by hiring Ned Williams to publicize the Ellington and Calloway bands. A mustachioed dandy who wore spats and carried a cane, Williams wrote a pair of advertising manuals that gave promoters the tools they needed to do the job of selling Ellington as a "class attraction" whose music was "accepted seriously by many of the greatest minds in the world of music." They contained punchy catchphrases with which to salt local advertisements ("Primitive rhythms! Weird melodies! Amazing syncopations!") and prewritten feature stories that could be, and often were, reprinted in toto by busy editors:

> *When Duke bends over the piano and his masters of melody begin fondling their instruments, one hears the very quintessence of physical Africa moving in sinuous and suggestive rhythms.*

> *No other band is like Ellington's and it is doubtful if any other band will be like it. Whatever number goes into the Ellington music mill must come out Ellington music. No such weird combinations, such unique and effective cross rhythms and countermelodies with strange and broken tempos are attempted by any other organization.*

The manuals were so useful that phrases from their well-thumbed pages kept popping up in Ellington's clips for years to come. But his fortunes had started to bounce back well before then, so much so that in December of 1931 he was able to present each of his musicians with a Christmas gift of $250 in cash ($3,500 today). In the same month, the readers of *The Pittsburgh Courier* voted for him as their favorite bandleader. *Variety* reported that the band's asking price was $5,000 a week, twice as much as Louis Armstrong. "As fast as he got the money, that's how fast he spent the money," Mills recalled. "If he knew he was going to wear four suits, he had four trunks with forty suits." He was spending money so fast that it sometimes ran short. "When I got to high school, the garage bill was always late being paid, the car notes were far behind, the rent was paid late, and it was always a matter of coming through in the nick of time to continue to have ownership," Mercer said. That would never stop him from buying what he wanted. To Ellington money was nothing more than a means to the end of living as he pleased and providing for his family. A carefree grasshopper in a world of anxious ants, he spent and gave away whatever he made, assuming that his talent would keep the cash flowing for as long as he lived, and in 1932 there seemed no reason for him to think otherwise. It was a nerve-racking year for America, where one out of four people was unemployed, but Ellington, like most successful entertainers of the day, viewed the Great Depression from a safe distance.

Another sign that the financial tide was turning came when Ellington resumed making records in February, this time for Brunswick. They were credited to "Duke Ellington and His Famous Orchestra," not "Duke Ellington and His Cotton Club Orchestra," signaling to the public that he was now a touring artist rather than the mere leader of a house band. Ellington's third session yielded up yet another indication of his increased prestige: He cut a twelve-inch 78 on which the band backed Bing Crosby in a performance of "St. Louis Blues." Crosby, who had quit the Paul Whiteman band two years earlier, was well on the way to becoming America's number-one entertainer. Not only was his nightly CBS radio show immensely popular, but he was about to start shooting his feature-film acting debut, Paramount's *The Big Broadcast*, whose success would make him (in Ellington's words) "the biggest thing, ever," a triple-barreled star whose films and radio broadcasts were as successful as his recordings. Crosby's later reputation as an asexual crooner obscures the fact that in 1932 he was still a bona fide jazz singer and silver-screen heartthrob. He had learned the secret of swing from none other than Louis Armstrong, who proudly called him "the *Boss of All Singers*," and in return Crosby gave Armstrong full credit for showing him the way: "I'm proud to acknowledge my debt to the Reverend Satchelmouth. He is the beginning and the end of music in America." That Brunswick should have paired him with Ellington, and given them the extra elbow room of a twelve-inch 78, shows how seriously the bandleader was taken by his new record label.

The Crosby-Ellington "St. Louis Blues" pits the singer against Barney Bigard, Johnny Hodges, Tricky Sam Nanton, and Cootie Williams, all of whom are in scene-stealing form, though Crosby holds his own without breaking a sweat, nonchalantly scatting his way through a climactic up-tempo chorus. But the flip side, a four-minute instrumental remake of "Creole Love Call," is at least as interesting, for it gives us one of our first glimpses of Ellington's penchant for revisiting and transforming the works of his youth. While he had recorded multiple versions of many of his best-known numbers, the remakes were usually closely similar to the originals. The 1932 "Creole Love Call," by contrast, is a slowed-down version in which Adelaide Hall's wordless vocal is played on trumpet by Arthur Whetsel and the orchestral part is enriched with new countermelodies and glints of dissonance. Is it an improvement on the 1927 version? That is beside the point: Ellington's purpose was not to replace the original but to offer a different perspective on it. As Russell Procope, who joined the band in 1946, said of his later versions of "Mood Indigo," "A new arrangement would freshen it up, like you pour water on a flower, to keep it blooming."

The French jazz critic Hugues Panassié, who devoted an entire chapter to Ellington in *Le jazz hot*, his pioneering study of American jazz, heard several of these alternate versions for the first time when the band played in Paris in 1933. He found it fascinating that Ellington saw no need to prepare definitive texts of his compositions, preferring to leave them (in Clark Terry's phrase) in a state of becoming:

> *What struck me strongly was the discovery that the arrangements themselves sometimes differed from those used on the records. I understood that some had been done over, improved, enriched over the years by new ideas that came to Duke or his men. For others, I realized with astonishment*

*at the second concert, several quite different arrangements existed which
Duke used alternatively—sometimes one, sometimes another. Thus the
"Mood Indigo" of the first concert scarcely resembled that of the second.*

Another way in which Ellington enriched his music was to add musicians
to the band. A year earlier he had hired his first full-time vocalist, Ivie Anderson, who had been singing with Earl Hines's band in Chicago. Anderson had a
low, pointed voice with crystalline diction and a cutting nasal edge. Her first
records were too obviously influenced by the stagey style of Ethel Waters, but
she soon loosened up and proved to have an infallible sense of swing. Though
not conventionally attractive, Anderson had abundant sex appeal, and Ellington enhanced her gamine appearance by instructing her to dress only in white
onstage, which set off her dark brown skin. He also gave her another piece of
advice: "When I joined his band I was just an ordinary singer of popular songs.

Tough yet vulnerable: Ivie Anderson at the London Palladium in 1933. The band's
first female vocalist, Anderson was prominently featured at Duke Ellington's European
debut. Her tart, ironic singing meshed perfectly with his urbane musical style, and after she left the band in 1942, he never found another singer who suited him so well

Duke suggested I find a 'character' and maintain it." The character she assumed, that of a tough yet vulnerable woman who viewed the world with knowing irony, seems not to have been all that different from what she was like in private life. While a surviving radio interview reveals Anderson to have been cultivated and soft-spoken, she was also a card shark who could outplay anyone in the band but Ellington himself, and her toughness, Rex Stewart said, was no pose: "Off stage our Miss Anderson was another person entirely, bossing the poker game, cussing out Ellington, playing practical jokes or giving some girl-advice about love and life." Asthma finally forced her out of the band in 1942, but by then her classic performances of "I Got It Bad (And That Ain't Good)," "Rocks in My Bed," and the anthemic "It Don't Mean a Thing (If It Ain't Got That Swing)," Anderson's 1932 recording debut, had secured her reputation as the best singer ever to work with Duke Ellington.

A few weeks after recording with Crosby, Ellington made an even more consequential hire, that of the trombonist Lawrence Brown, whom Irving Mills had heard playing in the house band at Frank Sebastian's Cotton Club in Los Angeles, which shared its name with the Harlem nightspot. Born in 1907, Brown was a thoroughly schooled musician from Kansas who had moved to California as a child. The son of an African Methodist Episcopal minister, he was a nonsmoking teetotaler who was promptly and permanently dubbed "Deacon" by his new bandmates. Though he loathed the nickname, he earned it many times over: Ellington described his demeanor as "very staid, a little stuffy, really," and no one made him stuffier than Ellington himself. From the outset, the two men found it inordinately difficult to get along. "I never knew you, I never met you, I never heard you," Ellington told Brown at their first meeting. "But Irving says get you, so that's that." The exchange set the tone for a four-decade relationship so contentious that they stopped speaking to one another save at rehearsals, ultimately parting company not with frigid civility but in a shocking burst of violence.

It was understandable that Brown should have disliked Ellington. Not only did the trombonist believe that his new boss had stolen "Sophisticated Lady" from him, but he undoubtedly feared that Ellington would also steal back Fredi Washington, whom he married a year after joining the band. He may well have been right to be afraid. Jean Bach, who knew both Ellington and Washington, later claimed that the bandleader arranged the marriage in order to cover up his continuing romance with the actress: "Duke decided and they plotted. He said, 'There's this young guy coming in from California. He's obviously not married. So you two should get married. And there would be a reason to travel with the band.' Lawrence didn't know what hit him. He just thought this gorgeous woman wants to get married." True or not, he came to regard Ellington not merely with distaste but with a contempt that flowered into full-blown hatred. At the end of his life, Brown dismissed him as "an exploiter of men and a seducer of women," a judgment as summary as a slap in the face. For his part, Ellington spoke distantly of Brown in *Music Is My Mistress,* summing up his playing with a left-handed compliment: "As a soloist, his taste is impeccable, but his greatest role is that of an accompanist."

In fact, he was one of the orchestra's most identifiable solo voices, a masterly technician with a chocolate-smooth, cellolike tone whose section mates marveled at his skill. "I sat next to him in the Ellington band for five years and never heard him make one mistake," said Claude Jones. "I can't say that for any other trombonist I know." Brown's style bore no resemblance to the raucous playing of most jazz trombonists of his generation: "It was my own idea. Why can't you play the melody on the trombone just as sweet as on the cello? I wanted a big, broad tone, not the raspy tone of tailgate. . . . To get the smoothness I wanted, I tried to round the tone too much, instead of keeping it thin. Mine, to my regret, has become too smooth." The self-doubt revealed in that remark encompassed his solo work: "I can't play jazz like the other guys in the band. All the others can improvise good solos without a second thought. I'm not a good improviser." It was true that Brown, like many other jazzmen of the thirties and forties, preferred to map out his solos in advance instead of spinning them off the top of his head, but he was also capable of playing with swaggering abandon, as he does in the devil-take-the-hindmost interlude with which he caps Ellington's 1942 recording of "Main Stem," and except for the nonpareil Tommy Dorsey, no trombone player was better at caressing a tune.

Though Ellington rushed to feature Brown in numbers like "The Sheik of Araby" that highlighted his sure-footed virtuosity, it was the trombonist's lyricism to which he responded most strongly, and "Sophisticated Lady" was the first of the many ballads, including "Solitude" and "In a Sentimental Mood," with whose worldly air the two men (and, later, Johnny Hodges) would long be identified. The band would play "Sophisticated Lady" thousands of times in dozens of different versions, and it evolved at last into a feature for Harry Carney, who invested the melody with a dark-brown richness all his own. The 1933 recording, by contrast, has a brisk, even youthful air, and it opens not with Carney but with Brown, who plays his own tune warmly and sensitively, first "straight," then with graceful ornamentation. The performance, which also contains an elaborate saxophone-section variation on the theme, ends with eight fluttery bars from Hardwick that have a near-Victorian air.

Ellington had worked this vein before, and to him it was as "black" as the blues, but there would always be a small clique of critics who thought otherwise, treating Brown as an alien presence who put his authenticity at risk. The first of them was Spike Hughes, formerly one of Ellington's most unswerving advocates:

> *The one person, to my mind, who is definitely out of place [in the band] is Lawrence Brown. This artist is a grand player of the trombone, and would be a tremendous asset to any other band on account of his original style, but his solo work is altogether too "smart," or "sophisticated," if you will, to be anything but out of place in Duke's essentially direct and simple music.*

John Hammond, who liked nothing more than to offer unsolicited advice to musicians and nothing less than to have it ignored, agreed with Hughes, calling Brown a "brilliant musician [who] is out of place in Duke's band. He is a soloist who doesn't respect the rudiments of orchestral playing. Constantly he pushes himself to the foreground. In any other orchestra no objection would be raised; but Duke's group is very properly the voice of one man, and that gent is not Mr. Brown."

Eight decades later, the lofty condescension of these reviews still grates. You can almost see Hammond and Hughes patting their precocious charge on the head, warning him not to get too big for his britches. For the moment he kept his mouth shut, but he knew what they were writing about him and found it galling, though he also knew that his listeners disagreed. Ellington's "sophisticated" ballads would always rank among the band's most popular numbers, and a time would come when he felt secure enough to strike back in print at the meddlers who prided themselves on knowing what was best for him. As for the notion that Brown was too much the soloist to fit into Ellington's trombone section, one can only laugh at its absurdity, since there has never been a less well-matched trio. No one in his right mind would have dreamed of asking three musicians as dissimilar in sound and style to play ensemble passages together—no one, that is, but Duke Ellington, who gloried in their incongruity. "Your poppa likes to hear the trombones play loud," Tizol told Mercer Ellington, and he never missed an opportunity to turn them loose and let them tear up the joint.

Brown was later to claim that even after Ellington hired him, he did not allow the trombonist to play with the band until he added another musician to the roster. The problem, Brown said, was that he would otherwise have been the thirteenth man on the bandstand, an anomaly that the triskaidekaphobic composer allegedly refused to tolerate. This sounds too good to be true, especially since Ellington had decided that thirteen was his lucky number after opening a successful engagement at Chicago's Oriental Theatre on February 13, 1931 (a Friday, no less). But Brown did not cut his first record with the band until May 16, 1932, the same day that Otto Hardwick, Ellington's wandering prodigal, returned once more to the studio, suggesting that there may be something to the story.

Either way it is a matter of amply attested record that Ellington was superstitious to a fault, and a catalogue raisonné of his phobias would fill a closely packed page or two. He hated the color green because it reminded him of grass: "When I was eight, I decided that grass was unnatural. It always makes me feel sort of creepy. It reminds me of graves." He hated brown even more because he happened to be wearing a brown suit on the day his mother died. "Once someone gave him a sweater flecked with brown," Don George recalled. "He turned away, saying, 'It isn't blue.'" It was his lifelong habit to throw away any garment with a loose button, and Mercer Ellington said that he would not buy socks or shoes for anyone because he was convinced that it would cause them to "walk away from him." He feared sea travel, air travel, drafts, yellow manuscript paper, people who whistled or ate peanuts backstage . . . the list goes on and on.

Many of his superstitions centered on death, of which he was so afraid that it was said that he would walk out of a room whenever the subject was broached, and most of them were both irrational and unproductive. But the day that Brown and Hardwick joined the band was lucky by any stretch of the imagination. For the next eight years, the instrumentation of the Ellington band (save for the number of bass players, which fluctuated between one and two) remained constant, as did nearly all of the faces on the bandstand. After endless trial and error, he had found the lineup that he wanted—three trumpets, three trombones, four saxophones, and four rhythm-section players—and he had also found the men he wanted, all of whom played their instruments in ways so personal that each one was instantly identifiable. Having created the conditions necessary for the proper functioning of the Ellington Effect, he now reaped its rewards. One by one, week by week, the scores piled up, and what had once been a band book now became an oeuvre.

The perfect instrument: Duke Ellington and his band at the Cotton Club, 1933. Top: Sonny Greer. First row: Tricky Sam Nanton, Juan Tizol, Lawrence Brown, Cootie Williams, Arthur Whetsel, Freddie Jenkins. Second row: Otto Hardwick, Harry Carney, Johnny Hodges, Barney Bigard, Fred Guy. Bottom: Wellman Braud, Ellington. With the hiring of Brown and the return of Hardwick, Ellington had finally hit on the ideal combination of players, and for the next eight years he used them with unprecedented imagination and resourcefulness

But every working musician must be as much a businessman as an artist, and Ellington and his sidemen never forgot the necessity of paying the rent. In February of 1932, at the end of their yearlong tour, John Hammond published an item in his *Melody Maker* column that reminded them, and everyone else who read it, of the ruthless realities of their line of work: "Speaking of the Duke, I hear that he will return to New York early in February, his first visit in well over a year. Trouble with local racketeers, I fear, has been one of the causes of his prolonged absence." While there is no proof that racketeers had either run him out of town or stopped him from coming back, it is incontestable that the mob then held sway over his professional fortunes. As Mercer Ellington explained it, "The syndicate that ran [the Cotton Club] gave him a contract with options, so that as his popularity increased he couldn't always take advantage of lucrative outside dates." No sooner did he wrap up the movie-house tour than he hit the road again for a second year of barnstorming, but in March of 1933 he returned to the Cotton Club. The songs were good—Harold Arlen and Ted Koehler had started writing for the floor shows in 1930—and so were Ethel Waters and the other headliners.* Still, it was the same old segregated Cotton Club, and by 1933 Ellington was starting to wonder whether the price of his success was too high.

"At first I was happy," he told a reporter for *The New Yorker* a decade later. "There were lots of pretty women and champagne and nice people and plenty of money." But there was also the grinding responsibility of making music in a commercial environment, one that was hostile to the aspirations of a cultured musician, let alone one who saw himself as an artist with a mission. The Cotton Club was prestigious and profitable, but it was also uncomfortable by definition if you happened to be black, and Irving Mills, though he had worked wonders for Ellington, was a businessman whose eye was ever and always on the main chance. As Ellington recalled it:

> *I'd bring something I thought was good to the music publishers and they'd ask, "Can an eight-year-old child sing it?" I'd bring something new to them and they'd say, "This ain't what we're looking for. We want something like Gazookus wrote last week." I'd see guys writing little pop numbers that were going over big. I didn't see why I should try to do something good. I thought I'd stop writing. . . . I felt it was all a racket. I was on the point of giving up.*

His disillusion was evident to his friends and colleagues, as well as to Mills, who may have been crude but was nobody's fool. The situation called for stronger medicine, and he supplied it: He sent his golden goose to England. The idea of sailing across the Atlantic appalled Ellington, who was unnerved by the prospect of traveling on an ocean liner that could hit an iceberg and sink to the bottom of the sea, but judicious doses of champagne and brandy soothed his nagging fears, and on June 9, the SS *Olympic* docked in Southampton. Ellington and his men spent the next fifty-five days touring Europe, a venture that would help to cement their reputations in America and restore their leader's waning confidence in his own gifts.

---

* Ellington had been allowed to supply a score of his own for his sixth Cotton Club show, "Blackberries of 1930," but none of the songs was successful and the experiment would not soon be repeated.

Ellington was not the first American jazz musician to perform in Europe. Sidney Bechet and the Original Dixieland Jazz Band went there in 1919, and many others followed them, the most famous of whom was Louis Armstrong, who toured England for the first time in 1932. But Armstrong's extroverted demeanor puzzled a considerable number of the people who saw him perform there. Even to those English musicians and fans who cherished his records, the gaudy spectacle of what the poet (and jazz buff) Philip Larkin called "the stageshow Armstrong" was at odds with their finicky sense of propriety. As one dance-band musician put it, "I much regret to have to admit to finding something of the barbaric in his violent stage mannerisms." What they wanted was what Irving Mills was selling, a clubbable artist who wouldn't frighten the horses. Spike Hughes assured the readers of the *Daily Herald* that Ellington and his tuxedoed musicians filled the bill: "It is not a 'show' band; its members do not wear funny hats, nor do they attempt any 'comedy.' It is a band content to play music for its own sake."

No sooner did they arrive in London than they were treated like visiting royalty—once they found places to stay. The best London hotels were disinclined to put up black guests, and though Ellington himself claimed to have had no trouble finding a suite in Mayfair at the recently opened Dorchester, whose staff treated him so respectfully that he returned there for the rest of his life, his sidemen were forced to settle for smaller hotels and rooming houses in Bloomsbury. Three days later they opened at the Palladium, the same 2,300-seat variety house where Armstrong had made his European debut a year earlier (and where Alfred Hitchcock would soon film the climactic scene of *The 39 Steps*). They were presented by the bandleader-impresario Jack Hylton as part of a mixed vaudeville-style program, going on after Max Miller, a "blue" comedian who was a fixture on England's music-hall stages. For added insurance, Ellington brought along Bessie Dudley, a Cotton Club dancer who was billed as the "Original Snake-Hips Girl," and a two-man tap team. Ellington, like Armstrong, was forced to perform there and in similar venues, since the British musicians' union was unalterably opposed to allowing foreign musicians to work in England, and the Ministry of Labour obliged the union by refusing to grant the work permits necessary for the members of American bands to appear in hotels, restaurants, or nightclubs.

Pictures shot on the stage of the Palladium show the musicians dressed in white blazers, white shoes, and medium-dark slacks (Ellington is wearing an all-white outfit and seated at a white piano). Behind them was a backdrop that incoporated grinning-darky caricatures of banjo players. Sonny Greer had brought his full kit to England: timpani, chimes, a vibraphone, even a small gong. Ellington, who relished the drummer's showmanship, said that Greer sat above the band "like a high priest, or a king on a throne." As for the Duke himself, he was terrified by the crowd's full-throated response to the opening-night show: "This was a night that scared the devil out of the whole band, the applause was so terrifying—it was applause *beyond* applause. On our first show there was 10 minutes of continuous applause."

The press was all over the map. Everyone admired the way the band looked onstage, and many reviewers, implicitly comparing Ellington to Armstrong, praised him for his decorous carriage: "Ellington was always composed, always the gentleman." But Ernest Newman, the doyen of English classical-music critics, called him "a Harlem Dionysus drunk on bad bootleg liquor" in his weekly column for *The Times,* a piece of phrasemaking nasty enough to stick (Barry Ulanov cited it a decade and a half later in his Ellington biography). *The Times*'s daily reviewer was no less snooty:

> *He does at once and with an apparently easy show of ingenuity what a jazz band commonly does with difficulty or fails to do. And the excitement and exacerbation of the nerves which are caused by the performances of his orchestra are the more disquieting by reason of his complete control and precision. It is not an orgy, but a scientific application of measured and dangerous stimuli.*

The jazz press was, of course, transported. *The Melody Maker* reported that the sound of the band in person "literally lifts one out of one's seat." Some of the highbrows felt the same way, and a few of them knew enough about jazz to appreciate what they were hearing. Among the latter was Constant Lambert, who in 1927 had written *The Rio Grande,* a work for piano, chorus, and orchestra that was one of the earliest pieces written by a European classical composer to make idiomatic use of the language of jazz-based popular music. Lambert, who doubled as a critic, wrote in *The Sunday Referee* that Ellington was "probably the first composer of real character to come out of America . . . after hearing what [he] can do with fourteen players in pieces like 'Jive Stomp' and 'Mood Indigo,' the average modern composer who splashes about with eighty players in the Respighi manner must feel a little chastened."

Two weeks later Ellington played a matinee concert sponsored by *The Melody Maker.* He performed the same popular program that he had offered at the Palladium, which included songs like "Stormy Weather" and "Three Little Words" in addition to his own compositions, and it failed to pass muster with

Spike Hughes, who showed his priggish side in his review: "Is Duke Ellington losing faith in his own music and turning commercial through lack of appreciation, or does he honestly underestimate the English musical public to such an extent that a concert *for musicians* does not include 'The Mooche,' 'Mood Indigo,' 'Lazy Rhapsody,' 'Blue Ramble,' 'Rockin' in Rhythm,' 'Creole Love Call,' 'Old Man Blues,' 'Baby, When You Ain't There,' or 'Black Beauty'?" Ellington was unamused by Hughes's presumption, thereafter referring to him as "the Hot Dictator," but he paid attention to the review. A second concert met with Hughes's approval, no doubt because Ellington took care to play all the pieces that he had mentioned, as well as one, "Sirocco," by the critic himself. Hughes also wrote program notes that set what he thought to be a proper tone for the occasion: "'Echoes of the Jungle' dates from 1931. This is a direct contrast to 'Old Man Blues.' Where the first composition is definitely *allegro,* this is *andante;* where in the former work the scoring is full and brilliant, the latter is particularly remarkable for the extremely economical use made of the orchestra."*

After finishing its two-week run at the Palladium, the band performed in Birmingham, Blackpool, Glasgow, Harrogate, and Liverpool, as well as cutting a few records and playing on the BBC, which also broadcast an interview with Ellington. In between performances he and his musicians found time to drop by a party that was thrown by Lord Beaverbrook for the Prince of Wales, an amateur drummer who sat in with the band. "Windsor can play good drums—good, hot drums," Ellington said. And he also made a point of meeting with Constant Lambert, whose interest in the composer was not new. Lambert had been writing about Ellington's music as early as 1931: "He gives the same distinction to his *genre* that Strauss gave to the Waltz or Sousa to the March." He may also have played some of Delius's music for Ellington, who claimed in *Music Is My Mistress* and on other occasions that he had never heard any of the English composer's music before coming to England. However it came about, Ellington bought several Delius scores during his stay, and they made a lasting impression on him. "There was one English

---

* It was more than just a sop to Hughes's vanity for the Ellington band to have performed "Sirocco." He was a jazz composer of distinction, the first anywhere to be influenced by Ellington, and he had traveled to the United States earlier in 1933 to record several of his pieces with an all-star band whose members included Henry "Red" Allen, Benny Carter, Sid Catlett, and Coleman Hawkins. "Sirocco," recorded in England the previous year, bears the unmistakable stamp of Ellington's own "Mystery Song." (Hughes's other jazz recordings include the first cover versions of Ellington's "Misty Mornin'" and "The Mooche," both made in 1930.)

"Always the gentleman": Broadcasting on the BBC, June 14, 1933. Ellington was an immediate hit with British audiences, who appreciated his decorous manner, and he in turn was inspired by the enthusiasm with which they responded to his challenging compositions

composer—and that's about the only time I've ever heard him absolutely point out something he liked," Mercer said. "And in fact I heard him say this twice: if it was painting it was Monet and most of the artists around the Renaissance period. And Delius was the one person he liked so much in [classical] music."

Ellington also recorded a two-minute promotional interview with Percy Brooks, the editor of *The Melody Maker* and the man who had dubbed Louis Armstrong "Satchmo" in 1932. "Souvenir of Duke Ellington" is a studied performance in which both men are almost certainly reading from a script. First we hear Ellington tinkling away at "Mood Indigo" on the studio piano, after which Brooks asks him a series of obvious questions to which he makes stilted replies: "Just as soon as possible, we will be back again. If it doesn't turn out to be an annual trip, I will be the most disappointed man in the world. . . . It has been positively embarrassing at times to be asked the most analytical questions about work which I have nearly forgotten by now." Even so, it is touching to listen to their chat, in which Brooks treats Ellington with manifest respect, in much the same way that it is touching to listen to "Ellingtonia," a snappy three-minute medley of "Black and Tan Fantasy," "It Don't Mean a Thing," "Mood Indigo," and "Bugle Call Rag" that Jack Hylton and his all-white dance band recorded in London four months later.

On July 24 Ellington and his men left for a brief tour of the continent, playing one concert in Holland and three in Paris at the Salle Pleyel, the two-thousand-seat hall where Armstrong had made his Paris debut. Hugues Panassié was there, and was impressed: "Duke directed his orchestra in lordly fashion. At the piano, with a quick, elegant gesture, he would lift an arm from time to time to indicate a nuance to his musicians. The ease and nobility of his manner . . . were indescribable." Dick de Pauw, the band's tour manager, set down an equally vivid pen portrait of the offstage Ellington:

> *Duke never shows the slightest sign of life before five o'clock in the evening. Indeed, this business of rousing him and getting dressed in time for the first house was the most bewildering task of the tour. . . . I discovered that Duke suffered from a kind of nervous complex in the matter of time, because, no matter how early he happened to be, he would never commence to dress until the last possible second, and then when everybody around was all worked up and yelling, "The show's on!" he would scramble on his coat while running down the corridor and, with that bland smile of his, stride onto the stage and commence playing—all in one breath as it were. He simply could not face the ordeal of being dressed-up and waiting back-stage all ready for the curtain to rise—he had to run on in a whirl of excitement in order to get the right mood for that opening number.*

Needless to say, there was also time for carousing, including a visit to Le Chabanais, the luxurious Paris brothel whose celebrated patrons included Salvador Dalí, Guy de Maupassant, Henri de Toulouse-Lautrec, and King Edward VII. Ellington and Irving Mills went there together, accompanied by Mills's interpreter and an unnamed companion whom the composer later described as "some society woman, one of those dowagers . . . from America." The visit was the source of an oft-told anecdote that Mercer thought to be apocryphal but to whose accuracy Ellington gleefully attested in an unpublished 1964 interview. The madam, he said, invited him to choose a female companion for the evening. At first he hesitated, but Mills and the dowager cheered him on, and in due course he changed his mind: "I was feeling my champagne . . . so finally I stood up and I waved to the madam and I says, 'Madame? I'll take the three on the end.'"

Ellington and his sidemen returned to New York on August 9, where they learned that they had been written up in *Time* on the same day that they opened at the Palladium. The story, entitled "Hot Ambassador," was the first time that the weekly newsmagazine had mentioned the band other than in passing, and though it was written in *Time*'s condescending, self-parodic house style, it was still good news for Ellington and Mills:

> *Pianist Percy Grainger has likened the texture of Ellington's music to that of British Composer Frederick Delius. Scholarly musicians are looking forward to a Duke Ellington review which is scheduled for New York next season. Such lofty recognition has injected no jarring, self-conscious note into Ellington's performances. . . . Ellington's arrangements, apparently tossed off in the approved hot, spontaneous manner, have been carefully worked out at rehearsals beginning often at 3 A.M. after his theatre and night-club engagements, which gross as much as $250,000 a year. Ellington will sit at the piano, play a theme over, try a dozen different variations. Spidery Freddy [sic] Jenkins may see an ideal spot for a hot double-quick trumpet solo. Big William Brand [sic] may be seized with a desire to slap his double-bass, almost steal the percussion away from Drummer Sonny Greer. Duke Ellington lets all his players have their say but listens particularly to the shrewd advice of pale Cuban [sic] Juan Tizol, his valve trombonist.*

They also read "Introducing Duke Ellington," an article published in the August issue of *Fortune* that described Ellington's rise to fame in such a way as to leave no doubt of his musical achievements: "Ellington has never compromised with the public taste . . . He has played *hot* music, his own music, all the way along." But it also stressed the profitability of Duke Ellington, Inc., making the band sound like nothing so much as a blue-chip stock: "Cleverly managed by Irving Mills, [Ellington] has grossed as much as $250,000 a year, and the band's price for a week's theatre engagement runs as high as $5,500. . . . The top salary in this group is $125 a week—approximately equal to the best symphonic wages."

The combined effects of the tour and the burst of publicity that followed it put an end to Ellington's funk. Even in the sober account that he wrote for *Music Is My Mistress*, he made clear how much it had meant to him to have his music taken seriously in Europe: "The atmosphere in Europe, the friend-ship, and the serious interest in our music shown by critics and musicians of all kinds put new spirit into us, and we sailed home . . . in a glow that was only partly due to cognac and champagne." He had put it more emphatically after returning to America in 1933: "The main thing I got in Europe was *spirit,* it lifted me out of the groove. That kind of thing gives you courage to go on with a lot of things you want to do yourself. . . . If they think I'm *that* important, then maybe I have kinda said something, maybe our music does mean something."

Part of what he meant by "that kind of thing" was that he now had an in-kling of what it would be like to live in a land where the color of his skin mat-tered less than the size of his talent: "Europe is a very different world from this one. You can go anywhere and talk to anybody and do anything you like. . . . When you've eaten hot dogs all your life and you're suddenly offered caviar it's hard to believe it's true." Years later, on a return visit to England, Ellington was staying at a luxury hotel, standing on the veranda and chatting idly with a white acquaintance. "You know, I love this place," he said. "I don't know if you realize this, but I have the utmost difficulty staying in a hotel like this in the United States." The knowledge that there were places in the world where he could check into such hotels without wondering whether his reservation would be honored buoyed him up for some time to come, and its effects on his music were immediate—and audible.

7

"THE WAY THE PRESIDENT TRAVELS"

On the Road, 1933–1936

E LLINGTON AND HIS musicians paused in New York just long enough to cut four sides for Brunswick. Then they went back on the road, not to return until January. This time, though, they played for two months in Dallas, San Antonio, and Oklahoma City before heading north to Chicago. While the band had long been reluctant to tour the South—only a handful of black groups from the north had dared as yet to do so—it was received with enthusiasm everywhere. Moreover, the newspapers that covered the tour did so no less enthusiastically (though most of them refused as a matter of policy to print a photograph of a black man, opting instead to run respectful caricatures, one of them drawn by Al Hirschfeld, that were commissioned and distributed by the Mills office). The *Dallas News* went so far as to call Ellington "something of an African Stravinsky." Prior to 1933 it had been unthinkable for Ellington to be described as a composer of significance other than in a black paper. Soon it would become a cliché.

Ralph Ellison, who saw the band when it came to Oklahoma City in November, never forgot the impression that it made on him:

And then Ellington and the great orchestra came to town; came with their uniforms, their sophistication, their skills; their golden horns, their

Duke Ellington by Al Hirschfeld, c. 1931. Irving Mills commissioned the jazz-loving theatrical cartoonist to draw a sketch that could be published by newspapers whose editors were unwilling to run photos of a black person—even one who, like Ellington, was an international celebrity. This witty (and respectful) art-deco caricature was included in one of the advertising manuals sent out by Mills's office

flights of controlled and disciplined fantasy . . . Where in the white community, in any white community, could there have been found images, examples such as these? Who were so worldly, who so elegant, who so mockingly creative? Who so skilled at their given trade and who treated the social limitations placed in their paths with greater disdain?

Ellington and his men had become a symbol of racial aspiration, one that cut across the dividing lines of region and class. In December *The Pittsburgh Courier,* one of the country's most influential black papers, ran a story about their appearance in Amarillo, proudly reporting that they had been "the talk of the city." To the readers of the *Courier,* it was stop-press news that Ellington had been a hit with southern whites, just as it was news that he made big money at a time when no one else seemed to be making any money at all: "Carrying more than $30,000 worth of musical and uniform equipment and the startling earning power of over $5,500 weekly, the debonair Duke Ellington's brilliant band . . . has earned the unique distinction of being the highest paid and most glamorous musical aggregation in all America." Nowhere does money talk more eloquently than to poor but proud men and women who fight every day to put bread on their tables.

Having successfully dipped his toe into the muddy waters of the South, Ellington now jumped in headfirst. In July of 1934 the band performed in Atlanta. From there it went to Birmingham, Chattanooga, and Nashville. After that its trips below the Mason-Dixon Line became more frequent. Somewhere along the way, Ellington (or, more likely, Mills) learned how to insulate himself and his men from the hostile world around them by traveling not in a rented bus but on two private Pullman sleepers and a seventy-foot baggage car:

> *Everywhere we went in the South, we lived in them. On arrival in a city, the cars were parked on a convenient track, and connections made for water, steam, sanitation, and ice. This was our home away from home. . . . When we wanted taxis, there was no problem. We simply asked the station manager to send us six, seven, or however many we wanted. And when we were rolling, of course, we had dining-car and room service.*

Not only were the private cars safer, but they eliminated the necessity to search for black-owned boardinghouses or local citizens who rented rooms (often at extortionate rates) to traveling musicians. The Pullman, by contrast, cost each musician five dollars a day, which was, Ellington noted, "cheaper than room rent." Though there was nothing luxurious about their narrow berths, they were infinitely more comfortable than sleeping sitting up on a bus. They were more convenient, too, for the Ellington band traveled heavy: Ivie Anderson's clothes filled three trunks, while six were necessary to house Sonny Greer's drums, timpani, vibraphone, and other miscellaneous percussion instruments. As for Ellington, he required no fewer than five personal trunks, plus another custom-made container for his shoes.

Traveling by train suited Ellington in other ways. In addition to setting him apart from his sidemen—he slept not in a berth but in a roomette—it provided him with "mental isolation . . . Folks can't rush you until you get off." For a touring bandleader whose occupation forced him to compose on the road, such privacy was a must. Ruth Ellington remembered seeing her brother "in a [railroad] siding somewhere in Texas, the heat at 110, the sweat pouring off him on to a piece of manuscript paper on his knee, catching up on something he wanted to finish." And he loved the ever-changing sounds of train travel, above all the train whistles: "Especially in the South. There the firemen play blues on the engine whistle—big, smeary things like a goddam woman singing in the night."

It was natural for such homely sounds to find their way into his work, most famously in "Daybreak Express," a jazz counterpart of Arthur Honegger's *Pacific 231* that the Ellington band recorded in 1933, ten years after the Swiss composer produced his own exercise in musical onomatopoeia. Like *Pacific 231,* "Daybreak Express" is an orchestral tour de force that reproduces the sounds of high-speed train travel with uncanny, almost eerie accuracy. Barney Bigard marveled at the way in which Ellington was able to "take an ordinary situation and put it into some music . . . We'd all be up at night gambling and we'd hear the whistle blow as we went over a crossing. Duke would hear all the same things. The only difference was, we were playing poker and he was writing music about that whistling." He would do so on many other occasions. Two years later, for instance, he wrote *Reminiscing in Tempo,* whose rock-steady rhythmic patterns, he explained, were "all caught up in the rhythm and motion of the train dashing through the South."

Ellington also relished the respect that arose from his traveling in a private train car. He spoke of it often: "Many observers would say, 'Why, that's the way the President travels!' It automatically gained us respect from the natives, and removed the threat and anticipation of trouble . . . we've never let ourselves be put into a position of being treated with disrespect." His musicians appreciated it, too. As Sonny Greer noted with amusement, "The average one of them crackers down south, they never been inside a Pullman car . . . Ofays and everybody would come down, we were traveling like kings." Even so, they never forgot that trouble was all around them. "I think it was in Alabama somewhere and we played in this theatre and it was strictly white, you know," Bigard recalled. "So they decided, the manager decided to give one night to the Negroes. But the funny part about it . . . you could see their feet patting on the floor. No applause. They wouldn't—they were afraid to applaud." And on occasion Bigard and his colleagues were brought face-to-face with the realities of life in the Deep South:

It was a real rough town. I can't remember the name, but anyway the cops would parade around the colored section because there was a ten o'clock curfew. You couldn't be downtown after ten or they would take you in and beat the hell out of you. We didn't know any better and we decided to walk back to the railroad station. There was about five of us and these cops stopped us and looked us over. One big cop looked us up

and down and said, "Well. These niggers are different from the nig-
*gers down here." They just let us go on about our business.**

Not that they had to go all the way to Alabama to be mistreated. In
1944 Ellington told a reporter of an encounter with a St. Louis policeman
who came up to him after a performance and said, sure that he was paying
the composer a compliment, "If you'd been a white man, Duke, you would
have been a great musician." Ellington smiled blandly and replied, "I guess
things would have been different if I'd been a white man."

After such slights, the publication in 1934 of Constant Lambert's *Music
Ho!: A Study of Music in Decline* must have seemed to him like a message in a
bottle sent from another, better world. Lambert's survey of the parlous state
of modern music was the first English-language book in which Ellington's
work was discussed at length. No one who read it could doubt that the author had the highest possible regard for the man whom he called "a real
composer . . . the first Negro composer of distinction," exalting him above
Stravinsky and Schoenberg. Not all of Lambert's praise was equally astute,
nor was it indiscriminate, but it is impressive how much he got right—and
how early in Ellington's career that he managed to do so. Among other
things, he recognized that "the real interest of Ellington's records lies not in
their [instrumental] colour, brilliant through it may be, as in the amazingly
skilful proportions in which the colour is used." And though he pointed to
Ellington's inability to compose on a large scale as a fundamental limitation,
he did not dismiss the results for that reason. On the contrary, Lambert suggested that Ellington's gifts might be compromised were he to experiment
with larger forms, arguing that while the first recording of *Creole Rhapsody*
was effective enough in its own loose-jointed way, the longer version was
"nothing more than a potpourri without any of the nervous tension of the
original version. Ellington has shown no sign of expanding his formal con-
ceptions, and perhaps it is as well, for his works might then lose their peculiar concentrated savour."

Ellington was uncharacteristically tickled when a Philadelphia classical-
music critic read him passages from *Music Ho!* "Hot damn!" he said. "I guess

---

* The only member of the band who was unfazed by the Deep South was Ivie Anderson. "Being a woman, naturally, she felt that she could get away with things and that no
one would harm her or hit her," said Herb Jeffries, who joined the band in 1939. "And
of course, when she was in the south, you had to be very careful with her, if you got out
of line with her, she'd tell you off, you know, she'd tell a redneck off in a minute, especially if he used that word [nigger], you know, I mean she didn't care."

that makes me pretty good, doesn't it?" As a rule he was suspicious of analysis of his music, especially when it was flossily written. He responded to one such rhapsody by saying, "May be something to it. But it seems to me such talk stinks up the place." In common with other autodidacts, he distrusted the act of analysis itself, fearing that it might poison the wellsprings of his creativity by making him self-conscious:

> *If you take a beautiful flower and enjoy it, you can just look at it and smell it and whatever there is to it, but when you start pulling the petals off and then you get down to the veins and the stem and all that sort of thing . . . by the time you've gotten through that you say, "Well, gee. This is a beautiful flower!" It was.*

Just as he knew how he wanted to talk about himself and his work, so did he know how he wanted to be written about, and he rarely gave an interview in which he failed to make the desired impression. When *The Chicago Defender* profiled Ellington in the spring of 1934, every sentence hit the target: "Self-taught musically and fairly cultured as the result of planned reading, he considers himself a missionary in his particular effort—the popularization of Race music. This music, he says, 'is 98 per cent emotional and cannot be written down on paper. It observes no conservatory laws, but smacks a little of the barber shop quartet and the mass singing of slaves.'" So, too, did *Symphony in Black: A Rhapsody of Negro Life,* a one-reel short costarring a very young Billie Holiday and directed by Fred Waller (later known as the inventor of Cinerama) that was filmed in New York starting in October of 1934 and released the following September. Though Ellington does not speak in *Symphony in Black* and is seen only briefly on-screen, the film succeeds in presenting him as a race-conscious composer who takes it for granted that the world will accept him on his own self-defined terms.

Symphony in Black opens with a shot of a letter that is being delivered to the "Duke Ellington Studio": "Dear Duke: Just a reminder that the world premiere of your new symphony of Negro Moods takes place two weeks from today." We see Ellington seated at his piano, scribbling away at a manuscript, then performing onstage with his band (which was expanded to twenty-four pieces for the shoot). What follows is an album of semiabstract, artily photographed snapshots of Negro life: First hot, sweaty laborers shoveling coal and toting bales on the wharf, then a love-triangle scene in which Holiday sings a bluesy aria of grief, followed by a dance sequence featuring Bessie Dudley and Earl "Snakehips" Tucker. The film is accompanied by a nine-minute "symphony" whose four movements are titled "The Laborers," "A Triangle," "A Hymn of Sorrow," and "Harlem Rhythm." Gunther Schuller has called the film "a touching, highly atmospheric, ambitious quasi-documentary," describing the score as "major" and comparing "A Hymn of Sorrow" to "Mahler and early Schoenberg." In fact Ellington merely knocked together three older compositions, "Ducky Wucky," "Saddest Tale," and "Merry-Go-Round," into a Broadway-style production number that is, if anything, even less structurally sound than *Creole Rhapsody*.

Considered as a work of art, *Symphony in Black* promises rather more than it delivers. But it was also a triumph of image-making, or would have been had anyone seen it. The film was not screened widely and, so far as is known, went practically unreviewed. Perhaps for this reason, Ellington makes no mention of it in his autobiography and never made a commercial recording of the score, which remains one of his least well-known efforts. Yet *Symphony in Black* shows how he wanted to be seen by the public, and how Irving Mills meant for him to be seen—as a man apart.

In addition to knowing how he wished to be portrayed by the press, Ellington now understood with absolute clarity how he wanted his band to sound, and a decade of backbreaking work had given him the compositional tools that he needed in order to make it happen. To be sure, he was expected from time to time to squander his gifts on standard-issue pop tunes, many of which were published by Mills. It speaks volumes about the music business that Ellington's 1934 recording of "Cocktails for Two," a song written for *Murder at the Vanities* that he arranged in a tongue-in-cheek style reminiscent of a society band, became one of his biggest hits. Yet rarely did the band enter a studio without cutting at least one memorable side.

Among the best of them is "Rude Interlude," recorded a month and a half after the band returned from England. Ellington had told Percy Brooks that he decided to write a "rude song" after hearing Flo Lambert, Constant's wife, mistakenly refer to "Mood Indigo" as "Rude Indigo." What he meant by "rude," it turned out, was a languorous nocturne whose slowly shifting harmonies hover in the air like low-lying clouds on a humid day. The darkly scored ensemble passages are punctuated by staccato piano chords placed as unpredictably as the orchestral explosions that bring *The Rite of Spring* to a shattering close. It was his most unusual piece to date, and some of his fellow musicians found it impenetrable, even offensive. "When I heard the record, I wanted to puke, it was so distasteful to me," one of them said. Not so the open-eared Jelly

Roll Morton, who thought it to be "a beautiful mood piece" and proclaimed that its composer was "on the right track musically because he wasn't afraid to experiment." Spike Hughes, by contrast, condescended to its composer: "Harmonically, like even the best in jazz, 'Rude Interlude' is child's play to a hardened cynic like myself." Ellington himself said that "Rude Interlude" "contained new departures in musical tempo and arrangement—some pretty daring departures . . . I offer it as my first contribution to what I sincerely believe is due to be the new form of 'sophisticated jazz.'"

Yet his experimental turn of mind did not stop him from writing pieces that were as accessible as "Rude Interlude" was elusive. From the unpretentious two-beat swing of "Drop Me Off in Harlem" to the down-to-earth riffing of "Stompy Jones," he made danceable music that was as well wrought as the most far-reaching of his musical experiments. He even contrived to toss off a hit song whose shapely tune was all his own:

> *We had arrived in a Chicago recording studio . . . with three numbers ready and a fourth needed. The band ahead of us went into overtime, which gave me an opportunity to do my fourth number. So, standing up, leaning against the studio's glass enclosure, I wrote the score of "Solitude" in twenty minutes. After we played and recorded it the first time, I noticed that everybody in the studio was moved emotionally. Even the engineer had a tear in his eye.*
>
> *"What's the title?" somebody asked.*
>
> *"'Solitude,'" answered Artie Whetsol [sic], who had played so soulfully on it.*

A "Mood Indigo"–style lament of hushed, almost hymnic solemnity, "Solitude" is also an example of Ellington's unswerving determination to go his own musical way. "Such taboos as that you can't use parallel octaves, you can't use parallel fifths, you can't let a seventh rise—he went to work on those right away, and proved they could sound good," the well-schooled Mercer Ellington said in 1969. "Solitude," whose first phrase ascends to a major seventh (the note on which the word *solitude* is sung in Eddie De Lange's vocal version), then inches upward another half step, demonstrates how the self-taught Ellington had acquired the power to transform such academic solecisms into art.

It was to be expected that the ensemble heard on these now-classic recordings would sooner or later undergo changes, some of which were bound to be jolting. But well into the forties, Ellington almost never failed to use such changes to his advantage. Toward the end of 1934, for instance, Freddie Jenkins was stricken with tuberculosis and forced to leave the band, thus allowing Ellington to move Rex Stewart into the brass section. Stewart, who played the stubbier, mellow-sounding cornet instead of the more brilliant trumpet, was born in Philadelphia in 1907 but grew up in Washington, where he first met his future employer. Sufficiently chubby and round-faced to be dubbed "Fat Stuff," he started out as an imitator of Louis Armstrong, whom he had replaced in Fletcher Henderson's band. But Stewart's curious ear soon led him to assimilate the harmonically oblique playing of Bix Beiderbecke, whom he heard in New York in 1926: "Didn't sound like Louis or anybody else. But just so pretty. And that *tone* he got. Knocked us all out." To their contrasting approaches he added his own "cocked-valve" technique, in which he played certain notes by pushing down the valves of his cornet partway, thus giving them the squeezed, foggy tone heard on "Boy Meets Horn," the 1938 composition that would become his de facto theme song.* The result was a musical approach capable of piquing Ellington's interest, and while it was rare for him to hire a musician who was well-known, it was under his leadership that Stewart united the disparate elements of his playing into a balanced style.

Like Barney Bigard before him, Stewart was skeptical about Ellington's musical innovations: "To be absolutely truthful, I didn't think much of the band when I joined, perhaps due to my receiving what I considered low pay. . . . Then, too, I didn't like their tempos or the music they played." It was Stewart who confessed long afterward to having "wanted to puke" when he first heard "Rude Interlude." Not until he started playing with the band did the two men get on the same musical wavelength. But they saw at once that they were both cut from middle-class cloth, a fact to which Ellington later attested:

> *Rex Stewart had been taught the responsibility of commanding respect for his race and to this end he maintained an offstage image very deliberately. It was a dignified, decent-sort-of-chap image, and he never strayed far away from it, so that he was always posing to some extent and never really relaxed. It is possible that tensions and conflicts came from this and were apparent in his music, but he was an exciting player who made a big contribution during the years he was with us.*

---

* "Boy Meets Horn" was originally called "Stew Burp" and, later, "Twits and Twerps," a pair of titles that drolly suggest the sound of Stewart's half-valved notes.

More important, Stewart was a top-flight soloist, and with his arrival, all of the key voices that graced the band to the end of 1939 were now in place. In addition, he was also a talented writer who published two books, a memoir and a collection of essays called *Jazz Masters of the Thirties*, in which he displayed a sympathetic but keen eye for Ellington's personal peculiarities. No other musician has added more to our understanding of what it was like to play in the Ellington band, as well as of what its leader was like personally.

As well as having lingering doubts about Ellington's music, Stewart felt self-conscious about sharing a bandstand with men who wore handmade shoes and memorized their parts, and he was appalled by the high-stakes card games that they played on the train. Above all, it unnerved him that they habitually showed up late for gigs: "I can see them now, sauntering to the stand; the time is 8:40 and the band was scheduled to start at 8:30. Harry Carney is trimming a reed, Greer is about to finish setting up his paraphernalia. Some others are tuning up while Tricky Sam is heatedly making a point with Toby. Johnny Hodges is contemplating the scene, unsmiling and bored. . . . 8:59, there are a few scattered hand claps and Himself enters."

Stewart soon realized that such one-downsmanship was the norm in the band, and that it could become flagrant enough for the public to take angry note. The bassist George Duvivier saw Ellington and Jimmie Lunceford pitted against one another in a battle of the bands, and could not understand why Ellington put up with the willful misconduct of his men:

> *I remember Ivie Anderson telling Duke, "You better tell your men to get on the stand on time tonight!" Well, Jimmie played his set, and by the time he finished there were only about six or seven of Duke's men on the stand, ready to go. The crowd started drifting away, and there was nothing to hold them—just a clarinet and a trombone! By the time the whole band got on, they'd wasted half an hour, and soon it was time for Lunceford to play again. If you were going up against a band like Lunceford's you had to come on full-force.*

Part of the problem was that the band was riven by petty personal feuds. Stewart promptly found himself in the middle of one of his own, for Ellington favored him with solos as soon as he joined, which threw Cootie Williams into a snit. "We didn't speak to each other for at least two years," Stewart claimed in *Boy Meets Horn,* his posthumously published memoir. "I don't think Cootie Williams ever forgave Duke for hiring Rex," Sonny Greer said. Some of the tensions, however, must have been caused, or at least exacerbated, by Ellington's touring schedule, which was so arduous that the journalist George Frazier claimed at one point that the band was about to break up: "Word is making the rounds that seven of Duke Ellington's boys are soon to leave him—the entire sax section, Wellman Braud, and two others. . . . It'll be a bad bringdown if that band of his splits."

It didn't, but a second bassist, Billy Taylor, joined late in 1934, and Braud quit the following March. The cost-conscious Irving Mills had tried to cut his pay when Taylor joined him on the stand. As Frazier reported, six other men threatened to walk out in protest, and Braud eventually quit in disgust. Five months later Ellington hired yet another bassist, Hayes Alvis, who played alongside Taylor until 1938. It was an unwieldy combination, but he wanted a fuller, more flexible rhythm-section sound, and electronic amplification was still primitive in the thirties, as was jazz string-bass technique itself. Braud was a strong player but not a modern one. It's more than likely that Ellington had tired of his slap-bass style, though it would not be until 1939 that he found a virtuoso who could singlehandedly give him the sound for which he longed.

A few days after Braud's departure, the band recorded "In a Sentimental Mood," whose winding melody was appreciated by listeners and musicians alike, making it the fourth of Ellington's songs (after "Mood Indigo," "Sophisticated Lady," and "Solitude") to become a pop standard. The success of "In a Sentimental Mood" inspired him to spin one of his colorful how-I-did-it tales, in which he claimed to have written the song in a single sitting at a North Carolina dance in order to soothe "two chicks, one on each side of me. . . . That was written very spontaneously. One playing—zhwoop!—just like that." As usual, though, he left out a key piece of information, which was that the first eight bars were written by Otto Hardwick, who can be heard playing them on the first recording of the song (whose working title was "Paradise"). Ellington added a bridge, harmonized the song, and scored it in a high-calorie style that set John Hammond's teeth on edge. Hammond disliked "In a Sentimental Mood" so much that he panned it twice, claiming in *Down Beat* that it contained "hardly any of the old time Ellington sincerity and originality," then upping the ante in his *Brooklyn Eagle* column: "I'm afraid I was too kind . . . I urge you to buy some of his older gems as an antidote."

Even if "In a Sentimental Mood" was, as Rex Stewart said, "a community effort," its doleful air was a direct reflection of Ellington's state of mind.

Daisy, his mother, had been diagnosed with cancer the preceding September. Not long afterward, the band recorded a blues called "Saddest Tale" on which Ellington chants an introductory couplet in a husky voice that sounds close to tears: "Saddest tale told on land and sea / Is the tale they told when they told the truth on me." He must have known that the end was near. In March Daisy entered Detroit's Providence Hospital for treatment, and Ellington rearranged his schedule so that he could spend as much time as possible with her. She died on April 27. Her body was taken back to Washington by train, after which Ellington sent three thousand flowers to her funeral and buried her in a thousand-pound iron casket that cost $3,500.

Daisy's death plunged her son into a depression that Mercer Ellington later described in detail: "His world had been built around his mother, and the days after her death were the saddest and most morbid of his life . . . he just sat around the house and wept for days. Then you could be very sure he was drinking." But after a few days of mourning, Ellington rejoined his band for three months of one-nighters that took them to Arkansas, Georgia, Illinois, Indiana, Iowa, Kentucky, Louisiana, Maine, Massachusetts, Michigan, Minnesota, Missouri, Nebraska, New York, Ohio, Oklahoma, Pennsylvania, Texas, Toronto, Vermont, and Wisconsin. It was as though he were working to stave off despair.

Not long after Ellington and his musicians returned to New York, Benny Goodman's band, which had been performing on the road to meager crowds, arrived at California's Palomar Ballroom, where it reversed its sagging fortunes in a single stroke. "Let's die playing our own thing," Gene Krupa told his frustrated colleagues, and the young dancers at the Palomar exploded with enthusiasm when the band tossed aside the polite fare that it had been playing, tore into its hottest charts, and blew the house down. Historians credit Goodman's stint at the Palomar with lighting the fuse that detonated what was soon to be dubbed the Swing Era. Throughout the decade to come, American popular music was dominated by big bands, most of them white, that played a jazz-informed brand of dance music tailored to the tastes of the teenagers born in the baby boom that followed World War I.

While some of these groups, Goodman's in particular, were true jazz bands, the hard-charging up-tempo riff tunes in which they specialized (Goodman's teenage fans called them "killer-dillers") were simpler and more linear than Ellington's thicker-textured scores. Irving Mills had long warned him of the dangers of getting ahead of his listeners: "I simplified most all the tunes. That's why all of my tunes, you could sing—'Solitude,' 'Sophisticated Lady,' 'Mood Indigo,' 'Sentimental Mood.' But nine tenths of everything he recorded

"Unusual and interesting": A 1935 promotional circular for *Reminiscing in Tempo*. Irving Mills shrewdly promoted Duke Ellington as a man apart from his fellow jazz musicians, a "class attraction" whose music was "accepted seriously by many of the greatest minds in the world of music"

you can throw in the wastebasket. They don't sell . . . he's made no money for anybody." But he ignored Mills and wrote as he pleased, paying no heed to the change in the musical weather, and one month after Goodman played the Palomar, he recorded a piece that was more musically advanced than anything he had yet attempted.

On September 12 the band went into a New York studio to cut *Reminiscing in Tempo,* a thirteen-minute-long instrumental composition that took up all four sides of a pair of ten-inch 78s. Ellington wrote it during the string of one-nighters that followed Daisy's death: "Every page of that particular manuscript was dotted with smears and unshapely marks caused by tears that had fallen." The piece, he said, was a conscious attempt to pull himself out of the slough of "negation" and "destruction" into which he had descended: "Dangling out there somewhere in a wilderness of the unknown, with no desire for adventure, where things and creatures that I neither saw nor heard were moving around . . . My ambition was dribbling away. Soon there would be nothing. I was not sure where I was. After my mother passed, there was really nothing, and my sparkling parade was probably at an end."

It should be recalled, however, that this extravagant recounting of remembered sorrow was written by an old man about an event that took place when he was thirty-six years old. Could he have meant it literally? Or was it retrospective posturing? "He always wrote what he felt," Mercer Ellington said. "I don't think he ever wrote in contrast to his mood. . . . The happy tunes were written during happy days and the sad things were written when he was feeling sad." Yet *Reminiscing in Tempo* is not a Tchaikovskian outpouring of untrammeled grief but a reflective medium-tempo ensemble piece, and the way in which Ellington introduced it at a 1948 concert is at least as informative as what he said in *Music Is My Mistress:* "*Reminiscing in Tempo* was written originally to portray the mood of someone who has reflections. Some of them, of course, are very wonderful, very fine, very pleasant, and some, of course, are not very pleasant. But regardless of whether it's laughter or tears, the tempo continues the same." Moreover, the piece contains no improvisation (every solo is fully notated) and is noteworthy above all for the assurance with which its two simple themes are woven together across an unprecedentedly long time span. Never before had a jazz composer sought to work on so large a scale.

Judging by the fact that so many copies of the original 78 version remain in circulation today, it would seem that *Reminiscing in Tempo* sold well. Several publications ran favorable reviews, most notably *The New Yorker,* whose critic was uncomprehending but enthusiastic: "It isn't, as one might suspect, a medley of Ellington tunes, but a sort of improvisation with virtuoso bits from various instruments popping out. Unusual and interesting." Spike Hughes, on the other hand, called *Reminiscing in Tempo* "a long, rambling monstrosity that is as dull as it is pretentious and meaningless." Brunswick's publicity department put together a four-page circular that acknowledged the critical controversy: "Whatever your musical opinion of this latest work in the modern idiom created by Duke Ellington—trailblazer in the new music—it will not be indifferent!" In later years a new generation of classically trained critics would embrace *Reminiscing in Tempo.* Gunther Schuller called it "one of Ellington's greatest master strokes," praising his "formal control" and comparing his harmonic language to that of "such other heady harmonists as Delius, Ravel, Rachmaninov, and Scriabin." Max Harrison went further, arguing that it was "one of the best pieces he ever wrote" and lamenting Ellington's failure to build on its promise: "*Reminiscing in Tempo* was, at least *in potentia,* the 'great leap forward' in his growth as a composer, and it suggests that he could have developed quite separately from any specific group of performers. That after all is what most composers do."

But *could* he have done as they did? Or was Ellington now tied to his band-based method of composition? More skeptical listeners are likely to hear in *Reminiscing in Tempo* not tightly organized musical discourse but a pronounced tendency to wander from key to key. In addition to lacking the sure sense of harmonic direction that gives classical compositions their feeling of forward movement, Ellington did not understand how to develop the simplistic "themes" (an ascending two-note motif and a two-measure chromatic spiral that turns endlessly on itself) out of which the musical material of *Reminiscing in Tempo* is generated. Instead he repeats them over and over again, altering their harmonization and instrumentation and transposing them into a succession of keys. The piece's apparent "unity," such as it is, arises in large part from the fact that it is played, like the original *Creole Rhapsody,* at a single, unvarying speed.*

What we hear in *Reminiscing in Tempo,* in other words, is something in between true large-scale development and Ellington's now-familiar "mosaic" method of composition, an impression confirmed by examining the manuscript. Though the record labels indicate that the piece is divided into four parts, the last section sounds as if it was tacked on as an afterthought. The manuscript reveals that this section was sketched and scored separately from the rest of the piece, and since it is not heard on any of the three surviving recordings of live performances of *Reminiscing in Tempo* that were given by the band in 1945 and 1948, it's probable that Ellington wrote it in order to fill up the other side of the second of the two 78 discs on which the piece was first released by Brunswick.

None of this means that Ellington was congenitally incapable of teaching himself how to write architecturally sound pieces, merely that he did not do so. For all its formal indecisiveness, *Reminiscing in Tempo* is still a giant step forward from *Creole Rhapsody,* and there can be, as Max Harrison rightly says, little doubt that Ellington could have advanced still further. Was he inhibited by the example of George Gershwin, whose *Porgy and Bess*

---

* It's interesting to consider the possibility that *Reminiscing in Tempo* might have been influenced by the music of Delius, which Ellington had heard for the first time after visiting England in 1933. Given the fact that Delius's rhapsodic scores are not known (to put it mildly) for their architectural rigor, it stands to reason that a jazz composer who, like Ellington, was largely unfamiliar with the classical literature might well have been swayed by Delius's approach to musical form.

opened eighteen days after *Reminiscing in Tempo* was recorded? Perhaps, though it is more likely that his later reluctance to embrace the challenge of extended form arose from the critical response to *Reminiscing in Tempo*, which foreshadowed the similar controversy that erupted after the 1943 premiere of *Black, Brown and Beige*. It is highly suggestive that Ellington, according to Lawrence Brown, played *Reminiscing in Tempo* "practically every night" for a short time after the recording was made, then dropped it from the band's active repertoire, thereafter reviving it only on such special occasions as his 1939 concert at the City College of New York.

When Leonard Feather met Ellington in 1936, the composer downplayed *Reminiscing in Tempo*: "Duke assured me that he attached no enormous importance to the piece, which he said was written entirely on a train during a few hurried days of one-night stands." But it seems more likely that he was so proud of it that he was unwilling to risk being taunted again by critics who failed to appreciate his musical courage. When a radio interviewer asked him

Genius at work: A studio portrait shot in the thirties by advertising photographer Valentino Sarra. Ellington's soigné image may have made John Hammond bristle, but to admirers like Ralph Ellison, it exemplified the racial pride that he endeavored to inspire in his fellow blacks

four years later to name his "masterpiece," his reply was unhesitating: "*Reminiscing in Tempo.* Because after it was completed, it gave me the most satisfaction of having accomplished what I set out to do."

Of the unfavorable reviews of *Reminiscing in Tempo,* John Hammond's was the most venomous. A rich, socially well-connected jazz buff, Hammond had briefly worked for Irving Mills and was now maneuvering to make a place for himself in the record business. Though he was, politically speaking, a man of the left, his main interest was in music, with racial justice coming a close second, and it makes more sense to think of him not as a cultural revolutionary but as an aesthete with political interests. Edmund Wilson, who knew Hammond in the thirties, described him as resembling "somebody who had modeled himself on Proust, then received an injection of Communism." Before long he would be recognized as the producer who helped to make Count Basie, Charlie Christian, Benny Goodman, Billie Holiday, and Teddy Wilson famous. In 1935, though, he was mainly known as an outspoken critic who, like Spike Hughes, believed devoutly in black jazz—so long as it suited his straight-ahead preferences. In truth Hammond was not so much a critic as a bossy know-it-all with good but by no means infallible taste, and he was notorious for being self-confident far past the point of arrogance. *The New Republic*'s Otis Ferguson, a jazz critic of greater discernment and more generous disposition, put it pithily: "John won't compromise on anything because he never learned to and he never learned to because he never had to."

In 1977 Hammond published an autobiography in which he sought to give the impression of being frank about his "problems" with Duke Ellington, whom he called "a supreme jazz arranger and a great although limited composer" whose orchestra was "not all that a jazz band should be, particularly rhythmically . . . My biggest argument with him concerned his failure, certainly his inability, to get people up on a floor to dance." He also suggested that the reason for this alleged inability was that Ellington had "lost contact with his origins," cultivating an ersatz sophistication of manner that was mirrored in his music. That sounded condescending enough in 1977, but in 1935 it bordered on bigotry. At least one of Ellington's sidemen, Rex Stewart, believed Hammond to be a racist: "John likes to play the boss man when it comes to niggers. If you're black and don't kowtow to him, he won't have anything to do with you. As a matter of fact, he'll even try to keep you from getting work."

It was true that Ellington's audiences were growing whiter, and that they continued to do so. As Cootie Williams noted, "Our type of music wasn't really for black people . . . While we were on tour we were playing for white audiences. The rich, upper class of blacks would come but mostly we would be playing for whites." But Hammond, who had already expressed strong reservations about the band's deviations from the narrow path of danceability, made the mistake of supposing that there was only one way to play jazz—or to be black. Piqued by Ellington's refusal to do what he wanted, he now let fly with a vengeance, publishing an article in *Down Beat* called "The Tragedy of Duke Ellington, the 'Black Prince' of Jazz":

> *The real trouble with Duke's music is the fact that he has purposely kept himself from any contact with the troubles of his people or mankind in general. It would probably take a Granville Hicks or Langston Hughes to describe the way he shuts his eyes to the abuses being heaped upon his race and his original class. . . .*
>
> *Consequently Ellington's music has become vapid and without the slightest semblance of guts. His newer stuff bears superficial resemblance to Debussy and Delius without any of the peculiar vitality that used to pervade his work. The Duke is afraid even to think about himself, his struggles and his disappointments, and that is why his* Reminiscing *is so formless and shallow a piece of music.*

To criticize Ellington for remaining aloof from "the troubles of his people" was, of course, ridiculous. Even if he was fortunate enough to be able to ride a private Pullman car, a black musician who toured the Deep South couldn't help but see those troubles up close day after day. But it was even more ridiculous for Hammond to suppose that Ellington's worldly success had any effect on his music, much less to suggest that he would have written better pieces had he exposed himself to "the seamier side of existence." No doubt Hammond would have preferred that he write a twelve-bar blues about the martyrdom of the Scottsboro Boys, not a tone poem inspired by the death of his mother. But Ellington wasn't that kind of musician, any more than Ravel was that kind of composer or Renoir that kind of painter. Like them, he was an impressionist, an artist who dealt not in ideas but images, and the life that he portrayed in sound, related though it was to the world around him, was his *inner* life. As Cézanne put it, his goal was "not to paint the subject but to 'realize' sensations." He looked, listened, and felt, then transformed his feelings into music. That was what he had done in *Reminiscing in Tempo,* whose failings, such as they are, have nothing to do with the quality of his feelings, much less their subject matter.

In addition to being simple-minded, Hammond's review was an unforgivably personal assault, and it brought about a permanent break between the two men—but not before its author revealed himself to be at least as much of a poseur as he thought Ellington to be. In April of 1936 the band spent a month performing in the Urban Room of Chicago's Congress Hotel, playing half-hour-long "rhythm concerts" three times each week. Helen Oakley, one of Ellington's white friends, witnessed at one of these concerts what Barry Ulanov called a "curious encounter between Duke and one of his severest critics." The critic, who was almost certainly Hammond, spoke loftily of "an artiness which pervades all of [Ellington's] writing today." Then the band played a piece that he liked. "That last thing you played," he said. "Exquisite. The real Duke."

Neither Ellington nor Oakley told him that it was *Reminiscing in Tempo*.

8

"SWING IS STAGNANT"

Diminuendo in Blue, 1936–1939

"IF YOU NEVER read anything about yourself, then you'll never read anything bad," Duke Ellington said. Few artists who profess such a credo are high-minded enough to live by it, and Ellington, who read his clippings closely, was no exception. He knew what John Hammond had written about him, though he also knew that the critic's tirade would have little measurable effect on his record sales. It was a different story when *Variety* published an article in January of 1936 that cited his orchestra as one of a number of "bands who fail to impress [college students] noticeably." Four years later *Down Beat* reported that America's top white bandleaders were pulling in twice as much money as their black counterparts. The subtitle of the piece said it all: "Negro Leaders Could Make More Money Running a Rib Joint." Now that whites had their own bands to admire, they had less time for Ellington. So did Hollywood: *Symphony in Black* was the last film of this period in which he received the meet-the-great-artist treatment to which Irving Mills had accustomed him. The spotlight had shifted to Benny Goodman, who appeared in a pair of big-budget feature films, *Hollywood Hotel* and *The Big Broadcast of 1937,* that featured his band prominently. Meanwhile, Ellington made *The Hit Parade,* a flimsy B movie shot in 1937 at Republic, a second-tier studio, in which he shared screen time with the pretty-boy society pianist

Eddy Duchin. Not until the forties would he be employed again by a major studio, or given the chance to host a network radio show.

It didn't help that Mills, preoccupied as he was with his publishing business and the other bands in his growing stable, was paying less attention to his senior client. Nor was it encouraging that Ned Williams, Mills's resident publicity wizard, had left the firm in August of 1935, or that the Cotton Club closed its doors six months later, a victim of the lingering effects of the Great Depression and the Harlem race riot of 1935. Not only were white New Yorkers newly afraid to go slumming uptown, but fewer of them could now afford to drink overpriced champagne, in Harlem or anywhere else. They were more likely to stay home and listen to swing bands on the radio. But Ellington kept up the good work, and his orchestra, if anything, grew even better. "In the late 1930s we had a *great* band," Sonny Greer proudly recalled. Instead of trying to catch the wave of the swing craze, he looked inward, following up *Reminiscing in Tempo* with a quartet of three-minute "concerti" that featured Barney Bigard, Lawrence Brown, Rex Stewart, and Cootie Williams. (This appears to be the first time that the term *concerto* was publicly used by a jazz composer to describe his own work.) "I'm more of a primitive artist in that I only employ the materials at hand," he explained. "I always write for the men in the band. That has sustained us throughout. I'm not so much concerned with what the styles of the times are as I am with the styles and the capabilities of the men in our band." The most successful of these pieces was "Echoes of Harlem," recorded in February of 1936, which opens with a sinister-sounding growl-trumpet solo superimposed over a loping minor-key bass ostinato, followed by a gentler major-key open-horn theme. Though it is credited to Ellington on the record label, "Echoes of Harlem" was a collaboration with Williams, who wrote the first theme: "Duke got his name on the label. I didn't mind."

Ellington found yet another way to employ the materials at hand when his contract with the American Record Corporation expired and Irving Mills started his own record label. The new venture consisted of two lines, Master Records (whose releases cost seventy-five cents each) and the budget-priced Variety line (which sold for thirty-five cents). In order to build up a catalog quickly and cheaply, Mills launched a series of small-group releases played by combos that included groups that were drawn from the Ellington band. Though Ellington had made records that, like "Mood Indigo," featured smaller lineups, he rarely presented such groups as part of his stage act. But Benny Goodman did, and the Goodman Trio, a racially integrated "band-within-the-band" that featured the black pianist Teddy Wilson alongside Goodman and Gene Krupa, became popular soon after it started cutting records for Victor, as did Tommy Dorsey's Clambake Seven, which was launched the following year. It was Helen Oakley, a jazz-loving young publicist whose idea it had been for Goodman and Wilson to appear together, who suggested that Ellington do the same thing after she went to work for Mills (to whom Ellington had recommended her) in 1936.

In December Rex Stewart and His 52nd Street Stompers cut their first records for Variety, followed three days later by Barney Bigard and His Jazzopators. Johnny Hodges and Cootie Williams soon followed suit. "Nothing was ever planned, nor even dreamed up," said Oakley, who produced many of these dates. "Duke would seat himself at the piano, confident and relaxed. . . . These sessions would grow like Topsy till in the early hours, suddenly time was up." Cootie Williams, however, remembered it differently, explaining that "most of the small group recordings were rehearsed beforehand and not made up in the studio." In addition to playing piano at the sessions, Ellington sketched out arrangements and turned some of his sidemen's riffs into "tunes" for which he shared credit.* He also laid claim to a sizable chunk of the royalties, which Oakley thought fair enough:

> *On these small band originals, if it were not for Duke's ability to size up potential and shape sounds, many would have amounted to little. . . . This was understood, and the instrumentalists who were most often able to come up with an original concept for a memorable eight bars accepted as a matter of course a joint credit. It became an issue only in the event a hit was developed, and the primary composer came to consider he was due a greater share of the proceeds.*

One such hit was Juan Tizol's "Caravan," which was recorded at Bigard's first session, then remade by the full band after the small-group version became a surprise success. The original label of Bigard's recording of "Caravan" gave Tizol sole credit for the minor-key tune, but he sold his interest in the song to Irving Mills for $25, after which it was credited to "Mills-Ellington-Tizol." According to the trombonist, he wrote the main strain and Ellington the bridge (which is, like so many of his bridges for other men's melodies,

---

* Over the years Hodges would prove to be Ellington's most fertile source of song-worthy melodic fragments. Oakley described him as "an absolute song factory." Once he caught on to what his employer was up to, though, he insisted on being paid for his contributions. "Come out of the kitchen," he growled when he caught Ellington turning one of his riffs into a tune that was recorded in 1938 as "Hodge Podge." (The song was jointly credited to both men on the resulting small-group recording.)

functional to the point of forgettability). Ellington also wrote the arrange-ment, in which Tizol's sinuous theme is supported by a two-to-the-bar bass line that swings, pendulum-like, between dissonance and consonance. For the full-band version he added strangely tilted treble piano chords and the exotic-sounding tom-tom obbligato by Sonny Greer that helped to make "Caravan" one of the band's most enduringly popular numbers.

Studio-only combo performances were a regular part of Ellington's re-cording program for the next five years. The results were uneven, in part be-cause Mills often required Ellington's men to record "doggy tunes" (Oakley's phrase) that he published, nearly all of which were sung by then-obscure fe-male vocalists about whom little is known today. But the best of these sides are classics of small-group jazz, and they are all the more treasurable for giving Ellington's principal soloists a chance to hold forth at greater-than-usual length in casually structured settings that also allow Greer's drumming to be heard with special clarity. Moreover, some of the later sides were nearly as popular as "Caravan," and one of Hodges's blues tunes, "Jeep's Blues," became a jukebox staple. "Corner after corner there were jukeboxes, and you could go forty blocks up Harlem and never stop hearing Johnny Hodges," Oakley said.

As for Ellington, he used the series as a sketchbook in which he tried out new numbers that would sometimes, like "Caravan," be turned into pieces for the full band. On occasion the transformation was radical: In 1938 Cootie Wil-liams recorded "Have a Heart," a bouncy swinger that was remade two weeks later as "Lost in Meditation," a smooth-as-butter ballad feature for Lawrence Brown. Insofar as possible, Ellington tried never to let a good tune go to waste.

❧

Listenable and profitable as the combo sides were, they were ancillary to El-lington's long-term ambitions, one of which he confided to a reporter for *The Chicago Defender*. He was, he said, working on an all-black musical: "The synopsis revolves around an unknown orchestra playing in a Georgia 'gut-bucket' with the typical hoi polloi. Then it moves with a complete simplicity of progression until this same orchestra ends in a Harlem hot spot sur-rounded by Broadway glamour. . . . Several movie producers are interested in the book." Perhaps they were, but there is no reason to think that the show was (at least as yet) any less a figment of his imagination than the *African Suite* with which he had been teasing reporters since 1930. Of more immedi-ate interest was his upcoming debut at the newly reopened Cotton Club, which had relocated to the Times Square area. Little had changed save for its address. The club still specialized in slick all-black floor shows ("50 SEPIAN

STARS—50 COPPER COLORED GALS") custom-made for the delecta-
tion of white audiences, and though the romance of a late-night voyage to
Harlem was no longer part of the package, the Cotton Club remained a spot
to which rich tourists and visiting celebrities who had heard little or no black
jazz in person were ritualistically taken.

One of the latter was James Agate, the drama critic of the London *Times,*
who was in town to review shows (and, like other gay white tourists who visited Harlem in the twenties and thirties, to indulge his taste for working-
class sexual partners who were prepared to oblige him for a fee). Agate visited
the club in May of 1937, two months after the Ellington band opened there,
informing his readers that dinner and drinks for a party of three had cost
him no less than five pounds, the approximate equivalent of $385 today. He
was impressed, in a manner of speaking, by what he saw and heard:

> *This is the place to hear swing music as the negroes like it. What I person-
> ally think about it doesn't matter; it stirs American audiences to frenzy.
> Duke Ellington conducts, presuming conducting is the word. A first-class
> cabaret follows. This takes place in a purplish penumbra, in which the
> dancers, naked except for diamond girdle and breastplate, are a twilit
> salmon-pink. They are extraordinarily attractive. . . . The waiters share
> the general frenzy; the very plates, as they are put before you, shimmy.*

Paul Hindemith, a far more musically knowledgeable observer, went to
the club around the same time and recorded his reactions in his diary. Hindemith was a devotee of jazz, ragtime, and American dance music but, like
other European classical composers of his generation, knew them only from
records and sheet music. Though he was hard to please, the Cotton Club did
it: "There is not much besides a lot of scantily clad dark people tap dancing
and singing, but it is all done with incredible verve. The orchestra played
continuously for about three hours, the wildest I ever heard. . . . The whole
thing was really a rhythmic and tonal orgy, done with remarkable virtuosity." He went back the next night for more.

We can hear some of what Hindemith and Agate heard, for the Mutual
Broadcasting System started airing live performances from the bandstand of the
downtown Cotton Club early in 1937. An off-the-air recording made on March
18 survives, and many more such "air checks" would be made in the next few
years. While the band played as well in the studio as it did in public, the surging,
unpredictable vitality of its best broadcast recordings is revelatory. Artie Shaw,
another Swing Era bandleader whose live broadcasts, like Ellington's, are often

more exciting than his studio sides, explained the phenomenon this way: "When you're playing in a recording studio and you've got a very good take, the record's three minutes and fifteen seconds, so up to three minutes it's perfect, the last fifteen seconds you're going to be very cautious. You don't want to lose that. . . . You tended to play safe toward the end of a recording. Whereas in radio you didn't care. You played what you wanted to. It was going to disappear anyway." In addition, Ellington's off-the-air recordings document the band's improvisatory approach to his compositions. The 1938 broadcast of "Echoes of Harlem," for instance, is much slower than the 1936 full-band studio version, and also contains a longer trumpet cadenza. The air checks, like the alternate takes of the studio recordings, also provide insights into Ellington's composing process, as in the case of "Serenade to Sweden," a 1939 piece out of which he chopped a full-chorus piano solo before taking it into the studio.

What they cannot show us is how the band *looked* on the stand, a matter over which Ellington fussed endlessly and expensively. He was as sensitive to the colors of the clothes he wore onstage (and the stage lighting that set them off) as he was to the instrumental colors that he drew from the members of his band. Rex Stewart recalled a 1944 show at New York's Roxy Theatre that was disrupted when "dress rehearsal revealed that none of [their] five sets of uniforms fitted the color scheme of this particular presentation . . . a rush order provided [them] with a sixth outfit—and double prices." All known still photos of the Ellington band taken in the thirties and forties were shot in black-and-white, but Stewart's description of the "unforgettable, show-stopping ensemble" that Ellington wore one night at the downtown Cotton Club hints at what we are missing: "Duke made his dramatic entrance attired in a salmon-colored jacket and fawn-gray slacks and shoes. The shirt, I remember, was a tab-collared oyster shade and his tie some indefinable pastel between salmon and apricot. The audience cheered for at least two minutes."

Beneath it all he wore a corset, a useful tool for a performer whose appetite for food was as gargantuan as his appetite for sex. One of Ellington's nicknames was "Dumpy," and Tricky Sam Nanton paid awestruck tribute to his capacity: "He's a genius, all right, but Jesus, how he eats!" Some of his best-remembered quirks had to do with food, such as his practice of wrapping up a leftover chop in a handkerchief or napkin, then tucking it in one of his pockets after a meal. It was a habit he had acquired in his early days, when food, like money, was harder to come by. "After a while, you eat in self-defense," he told Whitney Balliett. "You get so you hoard little pieces of food against the time when there isn't going to be any."

One journalist who watched him eat took careful note of what he ordered:

Fashion plate: Duke Ellington in his dressing room at New York's Paramount Theatre, photographed in May 1946 by William Gottlieb. In the thirties, he traveled with five trunks of clothes plus a separate trunk for his shoes. Ellington's hair, as always, has been meticulously straightened, a look that he never abandoned, even after it became unfashionable among younger blacks

Duke, who is always worrying about keeping his weight down, may announce that he intends to have nothing but Shredded Wheat and black tea. . . . Duke's resolution about not overeating frequently collapses at this point. When it does, he orders a steak, and after finishing it he engages in another moral struggle for about five minutes. Then he really begins to eat. He has another steak, smothered in onions, a double portion of fried potatoes, a salad, a bowl of sliced tomatoes, a giant lobster and melted butter, coffee, and an Ellington dessert—perhaps a combination of pie, cake, ice cream, custard, pastry, jello, fruit, and cheese.

His appetite really whetted, he may order ham and eggs, a half-dozen pancakes, waffles and syrup, and some hot biscuits. Then, determined to get back on his diet, he will finish, as he began, with Shredded Wheat and black tea.

In addition to wearing a corset, Ellington wore his hair in a "conk," a style created with a hair-straightening process that made use of hot lye. Straight hair, or "good hair," was as highly valued by middle-class blacks of his generation as was light skin, and they were willing to endure much for it. Black newspapers were full of ads for products that promised to rid the user of "kinky woolly hair. . . . All hipsters in Harlem are using superior hair straightener." No amount of shame was too much to bear in the quest for good hair. Every jar of Kongolene, one of the most popular hair-processing products of the day, was decorated with a logo on which the initials *KKK* were, fantastic as it may sound, clearly visible. Most of the top black band-leaders of the period, including Ellington and Cab Calloway, wore conks (Louis Armstrong and Lionel Hampton were prominent exceptions) long after the style had been repudiated by a new generation of politically conscious musicians. "We were against kinky hair in those days," recalled the jazz trumpeter Joe Wilder. "We didn't have better sense. . . . You know there was no pride in nappy hair in those days. We all wanted straight hair—we wanted people to think we had good hair."

In time Malcolm X came to see the conk he had worn in his youth as an unnatural act of "self-degradation." He wrote contemptuously of the practice in *The Autobiography of Malcolm X,* taking care not to mention Ellington (whom he admired) by name: "You'll see the conk worn by many, many so-called 'upper class' Negroes, and, as much as I hate to say it about them, on all too many Negro entertainers. . . . I don't see how on earth a black woman with any race pride could walk down the street with any black man wearing a conk—the emblem of his shame that he is black." But Ellington would never stop straightening his hair, oblivious of the impression that it made on younger blacks for whom "good hair" was a badge of dishonor.

❧

By 1937 Ellington's recordings were so central to his career that Irving Mills produced a film short called *Record Making with Duke Ellington and His Orchestra.* A mini-documentary that explained how records were made, it shows the band rehearsing and recording "Daybreak Express" ("This is an express train, this is not a freight train," Ellington tells his musicians). The film was intended to promote Variety Records, but by the time it came out in September, the label had shut down. Unable to strike a distribution deal with any of the existing European record labels, Mills decided that it wouldn't be profitable enough to record the Ellington band on his own, so he relinquished most of the rights to his existing masters to the American Record Corporation, which then resumed recording Ellington for its Brunswick and Vocalion labels.

It was for Master that the band recorded "The New Birmingham Breakdown" and "The New East St. Louis Toodle-O" in March of 1937. Unlike the 1932 remake of "Creole Love Call," these new versions of Ellington's first two mature recordings are thoroughgoing recompositions, not spruced-up revisions, and the same is true of the two-part "New Black and Tan Fantasy" that he cut for Brunswick ten months later. In all three cases he offers a fresh perspective on a work of his youth: "East St. Louis Toodle-O" is slowed down to a near-crawl and augmented with tolling chimes and dissonant brass chords, while "Black and Tan Fantasy" is doubled in length by the addition of clarinet and baritone-sax solos and a Ravel-like background piano obbligato. In years to come these recompositions (some of the most intriguing of which were later to be crafted by Billy Strayhorn) would become more common, a sign not of flagging inspiration on Ellington's part but of his lifelong desire for his music to remain in the "state of becoming" of which Clark Terry admiringly spoke. Even when revisiting the past, he lived in the present tense.

Ellington had more than former glories on his mind in 1937. In September he recorded *Diminuendo and Crescendo in Blue*, a six-minute-long composition that takes up, like the first version of *Creole Rhapsody*, both sides of a ten-inch 78. A few weeks later he wrote an article for *The Chicago Defender* in which he discussed why he wrote the piece: "Like all of our compositions, 'Blues Crescendo' and 'Blues Diminuendo' concern themselves with capturing and revealing the emotional spirit of the race. That is why so many white musicians find them difficult to understand and in several cases, meaningless." Part of what he may have had in mind was that *Diminuendo and Crescendo in Blue*, unlike most of his recent compositions, was based on the twelve-bar blues, the most elemental of jazz structures—but writ spectacularly large. It consists of twenty-two consecutive blues choruses, interrupted only by a single brief modulatory passage. Not only are there no improvised solos in the piece, but there are no real themes, only a kaleidoscopic assemblage of riffs tossed back and forth between the sections of the band. When described as baldly as that, *Diminuendo and Crescendo in Blue* sounds like a recipe for monotony. It is, in fact, Ellington's most inspired large-scale work of the thirties, a piece that plays to all of his musical strengths and demands nothing that he is not capable of supplying in abundance.

Diminuendo and Crescendo in Blue starts in medias res with two jumping choruses in the key of E-flat. Instead of stating a melody, the brass and reeds exchange antiphonal call-and-response figures so closely interwoven that the ear cannot tease them apart. Then Ellington moves smoothly through the keys of G, C, and F minor before settling on D-flat, at which point he starts to gradually lower the volume, introducing brief written-out obbligati by Cootie Williams and Harry Carney, followed by a quiet rhythm-section chorus that wraps up the first side of the record. He then switches back to E-flat and stays there throughout the second side. The four saxophonists pick up their clarinets and play a purring low-register riff that is answered by the trombone section. During the next twelve choruses, the volume stealthily increases as the musicians ascend by stages into their upper registers. The bomb goes off when, one minute before the end, a trumpeter (almost certainly Rex Stewart) tears loose from the section and plants a screaming solo on top of the fiery shout choruses that swing the piece to a close.

Diminuendo and Crescendo in Blue is a choice example of Ellington's mosaic method of composition. Instead of the usual contrasting themes, he gives us a parade of cunningly varied blues riffs, just as the "structure" of the piece amounts to nothing more than a long diminuendo followed by a longer crescendo. Rather than flowing into and out of one another, the successive choruses are conceived as separate musical units that Ellington juxtaposes with an unerring sense of balance, scoring each one in such a way as to keep the listener in a constant state of surprise, nowhere more so than when the clarinets are heard for the first time. No less surprising are the four modulations in the first section, the last three of which are completely unprepared. This creates a sense of tonal instability balanced by Ellington's decision to circle back to E-flat at the midway point and stay there throughout the second half of the piece.

For a time Ellington played *Diminuendo and Crescendo in Blue* regularly, never to better effect than at the "Carnival of Swing" big-band festival held in May of 1938 on New York's Randall's Island, where it stopped the show cold. A correspondent for *The Melody Maker* reported that three thousand members of the twenty-five-thousand-person audience stormed the stage toward the end of the performance: "A call was put in for extra policemen and the session was delayed about ten minutes." The jazz critics who reviewed the recording were, predictably enough, less impressed. *Down Beat* went so far as to dismiss it as "nothing more or less than a series of old El-lington tricks neatly lined up with none too brilliant strategy." But Aaron Copland admired *Diminuendo and Crescendo in Blue* and said so in print, and it is instructive to read what America's greatest classical composer thought of America's greatest jazz composer:

> *The master of them all is still Duke Ellington. The others, by compari-son, are hardly more than composer-arrangers. Ellington is a composer, by which I mean, he comes nearer to knowing how to make a piece hang together than the others. His recent* Diminuendo in Blue—Crescendo in Blue . . . *cannot be placed in the completely successful category with his "Mood Indigo" or the amazing "Clarinet Lament"—but they are far from being dull pieces nevertheless. (The end of the* Diminuendo *is particularly inventive.)*

Ellington would long be troubled by the lack of a logical transition be-tween the two halves of *Diminuendo and Crescendo in Blue*, a structural flaw that he papered over in the forties by sandwiching a contrasting blues compo-sition between the two halves of the original piece, creating what he called a "blues cluster." It was, however, a makeshift expedient. Not until 1951 would he finally figure out how to lock together the first and second parts of *Di-minuendo and Crescendo in Blue* in a way that satisfied his ear—and his fans.

Being a superstitious man, Ellington must have taken it for granted that tri-umphs must always be succeeded by tragedies. If so, then he would not have been surprised by how quickly the writing of *Diminuendo and Crescendo in Blue* was succeeded by the death of his father. The two men had been spend-ing more time together after Daisy's death, and at one point Ellington paid his father $100 a week to accompany the band on the road as "social secre-tary." But J.E. took to serious drinking, and by the time that he finally went to the Catskills to dry out, it was too late. His alcohol-weakened lungs were ravaged by pleurisy, and he died five weeks after his son recorded *Diminu-endo and Crescendo in Blue*. Ellington buried him in Washington in what the papers described as a "$5,000 casket" made of "hermetically sealed . . . ham-mered bronze." He was fifty-eight years old.

Had father and son grown closer? Barry Ulanov claimed as much in his Ellington-vetted biography, but Mercer Ellington thought not. "For the most part, even though he would take him from time to time on the road with him, I think basically he did not like his father because J.E. had embarrassed his mother," he told an interviewer years later. He was probably right. Though Ellington felt no obligation to be faithful to any woman, least of all his wife, he would have found it intolerable that his father felt the same way about his mother. It's no surprise that he got over J.E.'s death far more quickly than that of Daisy: He was back on the road days after the funeral, and there would be no *Reminiscing in Tempo* to commemorate the passing of the man from whom he had learned the ways of the great world.

A month later Irving Mills marked the tenth anniversary of Ellington's Cotton Club debut by placing a full-page ad in the trade papers in which he proclaimed, "The DUKE is still KING!" It was festooned with laudatory quotes from the illustrious likes of Glen Gray, Rudy Vallee, André Kostelanetz, Ferde Grofé, Abe Lyman, Victor Young, Leith Stevens, Xavier Cugat, and Leo Reisman (all of whom were white). Judging by his records, he was still perched on top of the heap, and he would soon commit some of his finest work to wax. In 1938 he recorded, among other things, "The Gal from Joe's," a two-beat shimmy that features Johnny Hodges in the drag role of a young lady of easy virtue; "Prelude to a Kiss," perhaps the most poetic of his many studies in chromatic balladry; "Riding on a Blue Note" and "Stepping into Swing Society," a pair of medium-tempo riff tunes in which he takes the musical formulas of the Swing Era and transfuses them with color and flair; "Battle of Swing," a concerto grosso–style blues in which the full band plays jagged unison lines to which Barney Bigard, Hodges, Rex Stewart, and Juan Tizol respond in close harmony; "Old King Dooji," a driving minor-key stomp that foreshadows "Ko-Ko," the clinching achievement of his middle years; and such small-band gems as Hodges's "Hodge Podge" and "Jeep's Blues," Williams's "Delta Mood" and "Mobile Blues," and Ellington's own "Blue Light," a crystalline musical etching in the manner of "Mood Indigo" whose main theme Lawrence Brown later claimed to have written.

While it is impossible to single out a recording from 1938 that is fully representative of Ellington's late-thirties compositional methods, "I Let a Song Go Out of My Heart" says as much about what he could now do as anything else that he recorded in that year of grace. It opens with a four-bar rhythm-section introduction that sets a medium-slow walking tempo, at the end of which Hodges enters with the main theme, a swooping tune in which an octave-wide leap is balanced by off-beat syncopations. Hodges, Brown, and Harry Carney pass the melodic baton from hand to hand, alternately accompanied by "ooh-wah" brass riffs and choralelike reed harmonies. In the second chorus, the full band enters and restates the theme (one of Ellington's favorite structural devices) in a warmly scored block-chord ensemble variation, with Bigard soloing on the bridge. Then the first half of the opening chorus returns, transformed this time into a "sumptuously velvety" twelve-bar coda (Gunther Schuller's phrase) that fades down and out. Like "Old Man Blues" before it, this dancer-friendly ballad is structured so imaginatively that the casual listener is likely to overlook the resourcefulness with which Ellington has juxtaposed the instrumental colors on his palette.

The label of the original 78 release of "I Let a Song Go Out of My Heart," which was another of Ellington's unacknowledged collaborations—the main theme is based on a Hodges riff—says that it came "from 'Cotton Club Parade of 1938,'" which opened on March 10, a week after the song was recorded. In fact it was dropped from the show, all of whose songs were written by Ellington. It was his first Cotton Club score since "Blackberries of 1930," and even though none of the other tunes caught on with the public, his contribution to "Cotton Club Parade of 1938" was well reviewed and widely noticed, as were the band's regular radio broadcasts from the club. Even *The New York Times*, which had been slow to take note of black jazz, deigned to praise the "skilled tickler of the ivories" who had "written the entire show . . . replete with tunes which will soon be hits."

But appearances were deceiving, both for the Cotton Club and for Ellington himself. *Variety*'s review of the show mentions in passing that the club "has the same $1.50–$2 table d'hote dinner policy and no couvert [cover charge] thereafter," a sign that the once-glamorous night spot was struggling. (It closed permanently two years later.) So was Ellington, though his sidemen were not privy to the extent of his financial difficulties. "We worked clean through the Depression without ever knowing there was one," said Barney Bigard. But Mercer, unlike Bigard, knew that his record sales were sagging and that his parents' medical bills had stretched his credit to the limit: "Now he was not only broke, he was also in hock to many people from whom he had borrowed to keep the band going."

He also lost two musicians in 1938. Freddie Jenkins, who had returned to the band the preceding March, was worn out by what he later called "the 'TOO-sies'—TOO much money, TOO much drinking, TOO many women, while TOO young" and decided to retire from music, and Arthur Whetsel was laid low by a brain tumor that made it impossible for him to continue playing. He quit in February, after which Ellington told a reporter, "Not only am I losing one of my best musicians but one of my closest companions as well. One who has been at hand along with the rain and the sunshine."* Wounded by grief and puzzled by the public's changing tastes, Ellington gave an interview in October in which he said that "swing is stagnant, and without a future," adding that to him it sounded "like the monotonous rhythmical bouncing of a ball. After you hear just so much, you get sick of it because it hasn't enough harmony and there isn't enough to it. . . . I predict that Negro music will be alive years after swing is dead. Negro music has color, harmony, melody and rhythm." He even recorded a tune called "Swing Is Stagnant," which was judiciously retitled "Buffet Flat" before being released.

As always, he tried to put the best possible face on his troubles. It was in 1938 that he started telling journalists, possibly as a diversion, that he had finished writing his first opera. But he knew that he needed a change, and it came in 1939, when he stopped drinking and acquired a new girlfriend.

"I don't drink any more," Ellington wrote in *Music Is My Mistress*. "I retired undefeated champ about thirty years ago, and now I call myself a 'retired juicehead.' I drank more than anybody ever." While it would have been no small feat for him to go toe-to-toe with Sonny Greer or Otto Hardwick, there is no reason to doubt his word. But he had seen what alcohol could do and was doing to many of his colleagues—as well as to his father—and so he called it quits, renouncing the "gladiatorial" boozing that he described with nostalgia in his autobiography. From then on he settled for hot water with lemon peel. On the bandstand he drank endless Coca-Colas, each one sweetened still further with four teaspoons of sugar.

When it came to sex, though, he generally preferred to say yes, and it was around this time that he left Mildred Dixon and moved in with a brand-new companion. Beatrice Ellis, usually known as "Evie," was a long-legged Cotton Club "showgirl" whose job was to stand around and look pretty. She was, in accordance with the club's policy, light-skinned, so much so that Clark Terry, on first meeting her, "didn't know if she was colored or white." Everyone who

---

* Whetsel was replaced by Wallace Jones, who served as the band's lead trumpeter until 1944. Though he rarely soloed, Jones was required to play Whetsel's high-register ensemble part in "Mood Indigo," and Mercer Ellington claimed that doing so "was what drove [him] into becoming a funeral director! . . . He had nightmares and cold sweats about it."

"He didn't want anyone to have permanency": Beatrice "Evie" Ellis and Duke Ellington in the forties. Ellington left Mildred Dixon for Evie, a Cotton Club showgirl, in 1939. He stayed with the temperamental Evie until his death, but never married her. She pulled a gun on the chronically unfaithful Ellington after catching him in bed with another woman, but she never left him

knew her agreed that she was also very, very pretty, though Mercer, who grew close to Evie in later years, described her as "typical of many attractive black women at the Cotton Club; very intelligent but not very well educated. The goal for these women was to snare a handsome black bandleader, because if they fooled around with the white patrons, the best they could hope to become would be mistresses."

Opinions vary on when she met Ellington. According to one report, Joe Glaser, Louis Armstrong's manager, saw her dancing at a Chicago club and brought her to New York at the age of sixteen (Glaser had a penchant for teenage girls) to work at the Cotton Club. In another, less likely version of the story, it was Ellington who saw her in Chicago and persuaded Glaser to bring her to the Cotton Club. Whatever the truth of the matter, it appears that Mildred got wind of their affair soon after it began, as Barry Ulanov indicates:

Mildred had heard about a girl who was crazy about Duke and for whom Duke seemed to have some affection. Bea Ellis, a beautiful show-girl at the downtown Cotton Club, had indeed spent a lot of time at the place with him.

"There's something there," Mildred told Duke one afternoon . . .

"I think there is," Duke said.

"Do you love her?" Mildred asked Duke.

"I think I do," Duke said.

"All right," Mildred said, "you do as you think best."

Early in 1939, Mildred gave Duke his freedom and Bea Ellis became Mrs. Ellington.

Ruth and Mercer stayed behind in the Sugar Hill apartment that Ellington had shared with Mildred, and so, for a time, did Mildred herself. A society-column item indicates that she was still living at 381 Edgecombe with Margaret Whetsel, Arthur Whetsel's widow, in 1941. Moreover, Ellington appears to have kept on paying Mildred's bills, albeit circuitously. In 1945 the trade papers reported that she was managing Tempo Music, the music-publishing firm that Ellington had launched four years earlier, and she was still there as late as 1950. Whether the job was anything more than a tax-deductible sinecure is not known. Throughout his life Ellington would use his business enterprises, including Tempo Music, as a way of subsidizing (and controlling) his family members. But his willingness to support Mildred says something about his continuing loyalty to her—as well as about his guilt at having cut her out of his life so heartlessly.

The black press linked Evie to Ellington early in their relationship, but in later years he kept her, as he had Mildred, out of the public eye. Though she gave frequent dinner parties at home, the two were rarely seen together elsewhere. He was less discreet in private, sometimes introducing her to friends as "Mrs. Ellington," and he even allowed Ulanov to refer to her in that way in his biography—once. But the label on the doorbell to their apartment said "Bea Ellis and Edward K. Ellington," and after 1946 Ellington never spoke of her to reporters, going so far, Mercer claimed, as to pay off gossip columnists and place expensive ads in trade publications to prevent their liaison from being mentioned in print. And though he showered Evie with gifts, he refused to marry her, even after Edna died in 1966.

It was a recipe for trouble, and Evie, whose nickname reportedly stood for "evil," stirred up plenty of it once she realized that she had misjudged her lover. According to Mercer:

She felt very exploited, and worried that she wouldn't be taken care of if he died, because he didn't believe in wills. . . . Evie was very much obsessed with the idea of becoming Mrs. Ellington, but somehow he was able to persuade her that if he were to get a divorce from my mother, it would be a very expensive undertaking. Wouldn't she rather see him have more money? She went along with the idea, and that was where she made her mistake. Instead of saying, "I'd rather have you and be poor," she had said, "I'd rather wait for the money."

Worse yet, Ellington made no pretense of being loyal to her. One night he showed up late for a gig, then charmed the restive audience with this one-liner: "Ladies and gentlemen, if you had seen her you would understand." He believed that he had an absolute right to sleep with any woman at any time, and his sexual appetite was so comprehensive that he even bedded unattractive women to whose charms his friends were blind, explaining that "everyone has to dig a little distortion once in a while, in order to lead a rounded life." Because he spent so much time on the road, there was no way for Evie to stop his flings, and none of his friends was willing to help her do so. So he did as he liked and she stayed home and fumed, waiting impatiently for his infrequent visits.

Ellington's friends never settled on an explanation of his satyriasis, about which he was so unapologetic that in 1952 he wrote a piece for *Ebony* in which he shared with the world his definition of an "exciting woman": "She is a fuzzy piece of fluff gratifying to the touch. . . . She sways seductively through your consciousness with the same subtle power with which a train moves through the night." Mercer, who witnessed many of his most intimate relationships up close, believed him to be a Don Juan who "had a basic contempt for women. He spent so much time celebrating and charming them, but basically he hated them." Don George disagreed: "A lot of men who are womanizers don't like women, but Duke was a womanizer who liked them as well as loved them." Perhaps it would be more accurate to say that he liked women but was wary of them. As he warned the photographer Gordon Parks:

I do not wish to disenchant you, my friend, but fair lady's power lies not in her soft beautiful arms. It's discreetly concealed midway between her upper left thigh and her lower right hip. Love her madly, Friday through Friday if necessary, respect her. But watch her. She has more ways to destroy you than the Soviet Army.

In 1951 Ellington recorded a monologue called "Pretty and the Wolf" in which he tells the tale of a "pretty little girl—a little country, but pretty" who comes to the big city, where she meets a "smooth, handsome, successful, cool" fellow who promises to help her "get somewhere." Though his purpose is to get her into bed, it is the girl who does the bedding, and she ends up leading her hapless victim around by the nose. That, one suspects, was Duke Ellington's notion of love—and marriage. "You grow up, you find out that the girls want to do it [i.e., have sex] more than you do," he said in 1964. "They're the pursuers, they're the huntresses." In *Man with Four Sides,* written around the same time as "Pretty and the Wolf," one of the characters says, "Women who cry and women who laugh, / They all want all, nobody settles for half."

The truth was that like so many other great artists, Ellington was an opportunist who saw other people in terms of what they could do for him. His detachment, George believed, was complete: "Duke's only concern was getting the next eight bars straight in his head. He was totally involved in his craft and used people to their own good as fuel for his music. . . . He didn't want a role that would give him permanency in anyone's life. He didn't want anyone to have permanency in his own life." Least of all did he wish to give his lovers even half of himself, and Evie, who must have thought herself to be the exception, was shocked to learn otherwise.

Having made what he took to be necessary adjustments to his private life, Ellington now endeavored to persuade jazz fans that he was as important as ever. Starting in February of 1939, *Down Beat* published a four-part series of articles in which he held forth on every aspect of the Swing Era. He led with his chin in "Duke Says Swing Is Stagnant," in which he dismissed swing as "adolescent," exempting only Benny Goodman and the xylophonist-bandleader Red Norvo: "It is the repetition and monotony of the present day swing arrangements which bode ill for the future. The mechanics of most of the current 'killer-dillers' are similar and of elementary quality." He then devoted two consecutive pieces to the sins of jazz critics, pointing to John Hammond as the main offender and hinting at the well-known fact that Hammond, who was now working as a record producer, was in the habit of puffing his own releases by writing favorable reviews of them.

Ellington also slipped in a barbed reference to Hammond's alleged ties to the Communist Party, an imprudent sideswipe that he was later forced to retract in print:

He apparently has consistently identified himself with the interests of the minorities, the Negro peoples, to a lesser degree, the Jew, and to the underdog, in the form of the Communist party.

Hammond's judgment may have become slightly warped, and his enthusiasm and prejudices a little bit unwieldy to control. . . . John has identified himself so strongly in certain directions that he no longer enjoys an impartial status which would entitle him to the role of critic.

The series ended with a piece in which Ellington commented on fourteen of his fellow bandleaders, sometimes praising them with the faintest of damns. Bob Crosby's all-white New Orleans–style group, for instance, was described as "[a] band with an amazing amount of color. We feel that here the tan has attained a very luxurious lustre, perhaps through absorption." Sneakiest of all are his backhanded remarks about Benny Goodman, in which close readers will have no trouble detecting a discreet whiff of malice: "His practice of offering his own renditions of all the worthwhile music he encounters during his career of musical activities . . . deserves sincere tribute."

Were these articles, like his decision to leave Mildred and take up with Evie, a sign of restiveness? What happened next suggests as much. In March the Ellington band returned to Europe for a monthlong tour, giving concerts in Paris, Brussels, Antwerp, the Hague, Amsterdam, and several cities in Sweden. The atmosphere was tense, nowhere more so than when the group passed briefly through Germany en route to Sweden, laying over for six hours in Hamburg. The train was surrounded by SS guards whom Rex Stewart described as "frightening to see . . . their attitude, their steely glinted, non-smiling frozen glances said, 'Here's death à la carte.'" The band was acclaimed everywhere else it went, above all in Stockholm, where Ellington's reception was so perfervid that he titled one of his new compositions "Serenade to Sweden." But even before he sailed back to New York, *The Melody Maker* reported that he and Mills had "severed their long business association" and that the band would now be booked by the William Morris Agency. Details of the professional divorce soon found their way into the trade press: Duke Ellington, Inc. was dissolved, Mills exchanged his interest in the company for Ellington's shares in Mills Artists and the bands of Cab Calloway and Ina Ray Hutton, and Jack Robbins replaced Mills as his publisher.

Mills later claimed that he had initiated the break "because [he] sensed that Duke had fallen into a different attitude toward his music, and was taking off in what [Mills] thought was a wrong direction." When Ellington wrote *Reminiscing in Tempo,* he explained, he "lost touch with the huge, loyal following that loved genuine Ellington music." Ellington himself said nothing. His only recorded statement about their separation was made in an unpublished 1964 interview in which he said, "Irving Mills decided in '38 that we should split up, because he wanted to gamble more with his money and so forth, and he knew I didn't want to do it." Other witnesses supplied their own versions, among them Sonny Greer: "Duke started getting disenchanted with Irving Mills in 1938, when we were at the downtown Cotton Club. . . . He began to think that Mills was not giving him the attention he deserved. This was right after Benny Goodman had played in Carnegie Hall. Duke started thinking if Benny Goodman can play in Carnegie Hall, why can't I? And Irving wasn't able to get Duke in there."

Ulanov, who got his version from Ellington himself, agreed with Greer that "lack of attention" was at fault. But he also told of how Ellington paid a surprise visit to Mills's office and asked to look at the books:

> *Duke Ellington sat down at the table and looked through all the books of Duke Ellington Incorporated, the record of his business association with Irving Mills. He looked at almost every page, at some with greater interest than others, at the reports on his best-selling records and those which hadn't sold so well, at the results of this theater booking and that location stand, the Cotton Clubs, East and West, Europe and short stands from coast to American coast.*
>
> *"Thank you very much," Duke said to the secretary, after better than an hour's poring over the books of Duke Ellington Inc. He got up slowly, adjusted his jacket and tie, put on his hat and overcoat and walked out of the office. He never returned.*

Bob Udkoff, one of Ellington's friends, confirmed this account, adding a telling detail. He said that Ellington had asked Mills to buy "the most expensive casket made" for Daisy, to which Mills replied that it would cost him $5,000. When Ellington looked at the books in 1939, he discovered that Mills Music had only paid $3,500. As Udkoff told it, this petty misrepresentation was the straw that broke the camel's back.

What led Ellington to look at Mills's books? It's probable that he was embarrassed by articles in the black press that criticized him for putting his financial affairs in the hands of a white manager whom he allowed to take advantage of him. The ever-helpful John Hammond worked this vein in his 1935 *Down Beat* article about Ellington: "The Duke has been exploited in a way that is absolutely appalling . . . Although he and his orchestra have earned between \$5-and-\$10 thousand a week consistently for the last eight years, he has received disgracefully little himself." In 1936 Adam Clayton Powell Jr. fanned the flames with a column for the *New York Amsterdam News* in which he called the bandleader "a musical sharecropper" who harvested "Massa Mills' cotton." Porter Roberts said much the same thing in *The Pittsburgh Courier,* claiming that Ellington had "EARNED something like \$2,000,000—for somebody else." Ned Williams wrote to a friendlier black paper, *The New York Age,* to refute Powell's column, calling it "an unfounded and unwarranted libel" and adding that the members of the band travel "in a style and comfort to which no other orchestra, white or colored, in the country is accustomed." (He neglected to mention that Ellington's sidemen paid for their own accommodations out of their salaries.) But Hammond, who had worked for Mills, was in a position to know whereof he spoke, and he always insisted that his old boss had taken financial advantage of Ellington. No doubt he did—that was the way Mills operated—and if so, it stood to reason that Ellington would grow restive, especially when his own people started attacking him.

Whatever the cause of the break, the results were clear-cut: Ellington signed with William Morris, while Irving Mills went on to a long and fabulously successful career that was underwritten by his lion's share of Ellington's copyrights. Only one of the thirty-three paragraphs of *Variety*'s 1959 feature story about the fortieth anniversary of Mills's career mentions his relationship with Duke Ellington. Yet his ex-protégé never took his former patron to task. The account of their break published in *Music Is My Mistress,* if characteristically evasive, was true as far as it went: "We dissolved our business relationship agreeably, and in spite of how much he made on me, I respected the way he had operated. He had preserved the dignity of my name. Duke Ellington has an unblemished image, and that is the most anybody can do for anybody."

In private Ellington was more realistic, acknowledging that Mills had swindled him but explaining that there was no way that he could prevail were he ever to say so for the record. He always pointed out that it was Mills who not only made him famous but took great care to shield him from humiliations that would have gnawed at his personal dignity. Ellington was intensely aware that even though he had structured his life in such a way as to steer clear of racist confrontations, he would never become famous enough to be invulnerable to them. Well into the forties, he instructed his publicists and road managers to call ahead in order to ensure that he would be welcome at any Manhattan nightclub or restaurant that he cared to visit. When he went to Yale in the late thirties to dine with Marshall Stearns and his students, one of his hosts was shocked to see another student in the dining hall rise from his seat, say "I don't eat with niggers," and stalk out. "Gentlemen, let us enjoy our repast," Ellington told the party, then sat down and dined with apparent unflappability. He knew that if such things could happen to him at Yale, they could happen anywhere, and he would never forget what Mills had done to insulate him from such ugly encounters.

In addition to seeking a bigger piece of the financial pie, Ellington switched managers to bolster his prestige still further. Though the William Morris Agency was comparatively new to the world of popular music, it was a Hollywood powerhouse whose glittering client list included Jimmy Cagney and Judy Garland. "Duke was very respectful of William Morris," a friend later said. "I think he was a little awed by him." But it would take more than prestige to keep him afloat on the roiling sea of swing. In recent months his recordings had declined in consistency, and it was starting to look as though he had been demoralized by his shrinking popularity. Worse still, he learned upon returning from Europe that his recordings would now be overseen by John Hammond, who had been appointed associate director of popular recording at Columbia, which had recently bought out ARC. In 1943 Leonard Feather published a tale about the only recording session at which Ellington and Hammond are known to have worked together:

> John Hammond . . . was supervising the recording [of "Serenade to Sweden"], and at one point he told Duke that one of the soloists was departing too far from the melody, and that Duke should have him keep it straight.
>
> Duke fixed Hammond with a cool grin and said, "John, you're getting more and more like Irving Mills every day."
>
> According to those who were in the studio at the time, John never quite got over that.

Ellington may have prevailed in this skirmish, but he also knew that Hammond had persuaded Columbia to sign Benny Goodman's band and was about to do the same with Count Basie. Since the producer had close ties to both bandleaders, Ellington had good reason to wonder whether he would get lost in the resulting shuffle, and better reason to assume that Hammond would make sure of it. As Stanley Dance said, "Anybody that John couldn't push around was out of favor with John." So Ellington returned to Victor after five years, and his new label agreed not to sign any other black big bands to its full-priced Victor label, only to the thirty-five-cent Bluebird line, a concession that sealed the deal.

The arrival of Evie Ellis, the European tour, the break with Irving Mills, and the decision to change record labels helped to fill Ellington and his men with new energy. "After our very successful European jaunt, the band started hitting on all cylinders like a wondrous musical juggernaut," Rex Stewart wrote. But America, still in thrall to the King of Swing, did not yet notice. "That Ellington's is the most unappreciated band in existence is no secret among most musicians. . . . High time the Ellington band got the recognition it deserves," *Down Beat* declared in its review of "Serenade to Sweden." Something more was needed to propel him back to the top of the heap—and it had just arrived.

9

"THE EYES IN THE BACK OF MY HEAD"

With Billy Strayhorn, 1938–1939

BILLY STRAYHORN'S FAVORITE time of day was the middle of the night, which he called "halfway to dawn." It was a suitable hour for a man who lived in the shadows. To the public at large Strayhorn's name was nothing more than the answer to a trivia question, and the curious fact that he, not Duke Ellington, had written "Take the 'A' Train," the Ellington band's ubiquitous theme song, was all that most people knew about him. Though Ellington started playing his music in 1939, it was not until four years later that a jazz magazine published the first feature-length story to be written about Strayhorn, and the mainstream media paid him even less heed. His name appeared only once in the *Reader's Guide to Periodical Literature* prior to his death in 1967.

Among musicians, Strayhorn's name came to be as familiar as his bespectacled face, lazily self-mocking voice, and perpetually quizzical expression (Don George said that he looked like "a small, slightly burned, whole-wheat-toast owl"). In addition to "Take the 'A' Train," they were aware that such celebrated Ellington recordings as "Chelsea Bridge," "Day Dream," "Johnny Come Lately," "Midriff," "Passion Flower," "Raincheck," and "Upper Manhattan Medical Group" were also written by the man known to his colleagues as "Swee' Pea," and that he and Ellington had collaborated more and more closely as the years went by.* Yet it was still widely thought that he was a mere appendage to the master, a talented but derivative protégé and "aide-de-camp" (as Stanley Dance put it) who aped Ellington so sedulously that no one but them could tell their music apart. Irving Kolodin asserted in his program notes for the band's 1943 Carnegie Hall concert that Strayhorn's "assimilation of Ellington's mannerisms and the expression of them in ideas of his own has progressed to the point where members of the band can't be sure themselves whether a certain new creation is the work of Ellington or Strayhorn." Barry Ulanov claimed that their work had "so great a similarity that it was more often than not impossible to tell who had written what." More recently Wynton Marsalis has described Strayhorn as "a Duke Jr. of sorts," going on to say that had the two men not been collaborators, "Duke might as well have sued him for plagiarism."

Strayhorn himself spoke with amusement of the "whodunit game indulged in by the band," perhaps because he knew that most of its members were well aware of who wrote what. In time, though, it came to be taken for granted that the question would remain permanently open, as Gunther Schuller contended in *The Swing Era*: "Strayhorn's role in the Ellington canon will perhaps never be completely or precisely defined, especially in respect to the later years, when the two men's talents and style did merge in a truly indistinguishable manner." It was common well into the nineties for Ellington "experts" to credit him with pieces that Strayhorn had written in whole or part. On the rare occasions when critics commented on pieces that Strayhorn was known to have written on his own, their remarks were often studded with loaded adjectives. Schuller spoke of "a certain effeteness which was to mar much of Strayhorn's work," while James Lincoln Collier wrote in his 1987 Ellington biography that the two men's collaboration had a negative effect on Ellington, encouraging his supposed tendency toward "lushness, prettiness, at the expense of the masculine leanness and strength of his best work." Meanwhile, Ellington's enemies used the younger man as a stick with which to beat their *bête noire*, and Lawrence Brown actually claimed that Strayhorn was "the genius, the power behind the throne."

---

* It was Otto Hardwick who dubbed him "Swee' Pea," a nickname that came from the character of the same name in the Popeye comic strip, an adorable baby who was thought by the members of the band to resemble Strayhorn. (He was also called "Strays" and, in his earliest years with the Ellington band, "Weely.")

Only a handful of perceptive outsiders had understood all along that Strayhorn was a major artist in his own right. Some of them, like Gil Evans, the master orchestrator of postwar jazz, were profoundly influenced by his example: "From the moment I first heard 'Chelsea Bridge,' I set out to try to do that. That's all I did—that's all I ever did—try to do what Billy Strayhorn did." "I'd like to really know just what's what in that little lab of theirs," Quincy Jones wrote in 1959. "I'd like to know how much Billy is responsible for in Duke's work these days. . . . I bet he orchestrates a lot of Duke's things." But it was not until researchers examined the two men's manuscripts that the full extent of Strayhorn's contribution to what he dubbed "the Ellington Effect" became a matter of record. Prior to that time he lingered on the near fringes of obscurity, and to this day he sometimes fails to receive his scholarly due.

Up to a point, Strayhorn wanted it that way. He shunned public appearances, and though he gave infrequent interviews in which he diffidently but firmly pointed out that "my playing and writing style is totally different from Ellington's. . . . He is he and I am me," he never bothered to explain the difference, much less insist on its significance. Though he wrote some three hundred compositions and arrangements for the Ellington band, he gave only one solo concert and released only one solo album in his lifetime. His name may have been prominently displayed on many (though by no means all) of the albums that the band released after 1956, but the fact that he and Ellington were jointly credited with such multimovement works as *Such Sweet Thunder*, *Far East Suite*, and the score for *Anatomy of a Murder* led most listeners to assume that Strayhorn was the junior partner in their creation. Ellington rarely failed to praise him from the bandstand and in interviews, describing him in a 1964 TV appearance as "one of the most important people in [the] group—very seldom seen in public appearances, but always heard." Yet Strayhorn's physical absence from the band's performances meant that his soft-spoken assertions were drowned in the cataract of Ellington's gigantic personality. Personally as well as musically, they were the oddest of couples, and their partnership was predestined to be productive— but dissonant.

Ellington publicly spoke of his reliance on Strayhorn as early as 1946: "Billy sits in the control room at all Ellington record sessions to give final okays or turn masters down. Duke respects his taste above all others and lives by it musically." Later on he called Strayhorn his "favorite human being," and in *Music Is My Mistress* his praise was unstinting:

"Very protective but controlling": Billy Strayhorn and Duke Ellington in the forties. The brilliantly gifted, unapologetically gay composer of "Lush Life" and "Take the 'A' Train" shunned the spotlight of publicity but was never able to come to terms with his capricious mentor's reluctance to give him full credit for his work

He was my listener, my most dependable appraiser, and as a critic he would be the most clinical, but his background—both classical and modern—was an accessory to his own good taste and understanding, so what came back to me was in perfect balance. . . . We would talk, and then the whole world would come into focus. The steady hand of his good judgment pointed to the clear way that was most fitting for us. He was not, as he was often referred to by many, my alter ego. Billy Strayhorn was my right arm, my left arm, all the eyes in the back of my head, my brainwaves in his head, and he in mine.

Few, however, noticed that Ellington's compliments were couched in terms of what Strayhorn had done for him. No more than the critics did he try to disentangle their work, which necessarily meant that Strayhorn's musical style was swallowed up in the all-encompassing "we" of Ellington's supercharged prose. It was not until after Strayhorn's death in 1967 that the Ellington band recorded an entire album of his compositions, and only long after Ellington's own death seven years later did musicologists answer the question that had come to be asked with steadily increasing intensity: Who wrote what?

It took nearly as long for anyone to acknowledge in print that Strayhorn was a homosexual, though it had been a wide-open secret among his friends and colleagues. That came in 1981, a decade and a half before the first biography of Strayhorn, David Hajdu's *Lush Life,* saw print. Six more years went by before the first full-length study of his music, Walter van de Leur's *Something to Live For,* was published. By then such noted jazz artists as Joe Henderson, Fred Hersch, and Marian McPartland had recorded albums of his music, and soon afterward a PBS documentary drew further attention to his life and work. But even now, few jazz fans are fully aware of the extent of Strayhorn's contribution to the book of the Ellington band, and while his sexuality is no longer secret, fewer still understand what drove him to stay in the shadows his whole life long, or what it cost him to do so.

William Thomas Strayhorn was born in 1915 in Dayton, Ohio, the third of six surviving children of a working-class couple. James, his father, moved repeatedly in order to find a job, ending up in the suburbs of Pittsburgh, where he worked in the city's steel mills, later becoming a common laborer. In 1926 the Strayhorns moved to a racially mixed neighborhood in the city proper. Frustrated by his inability to make a better living, James started drinking to excess and soon grew violent. Lillian Strayhorn, his mother, responded by drawing closer to the fragile child, who was born with rickets and had to be nursed with care. To shield him from his father's wrath, she sent him away to stay with his paternal grandparents, who lived in North Carolina. The boy's grandmother, a church pianist, gave him informal lessons on the instrument, with which he fell in love. Upon returning to Pittsburgh he went to work at a local drugstore as an errand boy, clerk, and soda jerk, using his salary to buy an upright piano: "I started to study and the more I learnt the more I wanted to learn."

Strayhorn started taking private piano lessons, then studying music at his high school, the integrated Westinghouse High, which had a music program that included not merely an orchestra and a marching band but a swing band—the last of which he disdained. Instead he took classes in traditional harmony and counterpoint, becoming so accomplished that he was later allowed to teach the classes himself. In 1934 he played the Grieg Piano Concerto with the school's senior orchestra. Even though he was black, Strayhorn was determined to make his mark as a classical composer. Later that year he wrote a concerto for piano and percussion, which was premiered at a school concert with Mickey Scrima (who later became Harry James's drummer) playing the percussion part. Some of his friends said that it sounded like *Rhapsody in Blue.* That makes sense, for Strayhorn also hoped to become a Gershwin-style songwriter. His aspirations came into clearer focus when he heard Ellington play "Ebony Rhapsody" at a Pittsburgh stage show: "Something changed when I saw him on stage. . . . He had a chord which I have never discovered, I haven't heard it since, I couldn't figure this chord out. I went home after going to see this show at the Penn Theatre in Pittsburgh, and I couldn't figure out what was in that chord, it was just wonderful." In 1935 he wrote the songs and book for a twenty-minute musical called *Fantastic Rhythm* that he scored for a medium-size pit band, then expanded into a full-length show that was performed in several theaters in Pennsylvania and continued to be revived as late as 1944.

At the age of eighteen, Strayhorn wrote a song called "Lush Life," the lament of a young man who has been dumped by his lover and now expects "to live a lush life in some small dive." Despite certain verbal infelicities (he rhymes "awful" with "troughful") and a world-weary pose, much of the lyric is technically impressive and sounds nothing like the work of a teenager. Strayhorn later described "Lush Life" as "a song most persons have to listen to twice before they understand it, and then lots of them don't know what it's about." This suggests that his use of the word *gay* ("I used to visit all the very gay places") may have been meant to signal that his unorthodox longings were no longer inchoate. Not only was the now-familiar alternate meaning of the word growing more common in homosexual circles, but it can also be found in Strayhorn's second-best song of the thirties, a wistful ballad called "Something to Live For" in which the narrator longs for someone to make his life "gay as they say it ought to be," a neatly turned internal rhyme that underlines its presence. While it is the music of "Lush Life" and "Something to Live For" that impresses present-day listeners more than their self-consciously precocious lyrics, the fact that he aspired to writing both words and music points to an ambition that was soon to serve him well.

In 1936 Strayhorn enrolled in the Pittsburgh Musical Institute, but withdrew in order to concentrate on popular music. It was around this time that he bought his first jazz record, a piano solo by Art Tatum, and was, like every other pianist before and since, stupefied by what he heard: "Everything he did made musical sense—every nothing became a something." He then started a jazz combo of his own, the Mad Hatters, which made demo recordings on which he can be heard playing in a simpler style based on that of Teddy Wilson. After the Mad Hatters folded, he worked with other Pittsburgh bands. Years later he told an interviewer, "I had given no real serious thought to making music my career," but his friends knew that it was time for him to get serious, and one of them arranged in December of 1938 for Strayhorn to meet Ellington backstage at the Stanley Theatre, where his band was playing a weeklong stand.

Strayhorn introduced himself by sitting down at a piano and playing "Sophisticated Lady" and "Solitude," first in Ellington's style and then in his own. After that he played and sang "Lush Life" and "Something to Live For." The older man was impressed by his skill (not to mention his nerve) and charmed by his infectious laugh, of which a reporter later wrote that it "begins softly until it builds to a boiling bubble that leaves Billy, and usually any bystanders, completely bereft of speech." The never-speechless Ellington suggested that Strayhorn try writing a lyric to one of his tunes, and Strayhorn hastened to comply: "Duke was very nice to me and let me stay in the theatre all next day working on the number." Next he arranged a vocal chart for Ivie Anderson that she sang onstage. At the end of the week, Ellington offered him a job. "I would like to have you in my organization, but I have to find some way of injecting you into it," he explained. Then he paid Strayhorn $20 for the chart, told him how to take the A train to his Harlem apartment, and sent him on his way with instructions to stand by and await his call.

Strayhorn occupied himself for the next six weeks by writing arrangements of "Lush Life" and "Something to Live For" for the Ellington band. The manuscripts survive and, according to Walter van de Leur, are indicative of his ability to comprehend what Ellington had been doing: "In an almost instantaneous assimilation of Ellington's writing style, he scored both arrangements for specific voices in the orchestra, naming personnel (Bigard, Hodges, Tizol) on the manuscripts." Then he screwed up his courage and went off to meet Ellington, though not before writing a swinging instrumental that was inspired by the subway directions to Harlem that the older man had given him. "Take the 'A' Train," he later said, "was born without any effort—it was like writing a letter to a friend."

He caught up with the band on January 23 at a theater in Newark and went backstage, where Ellington told him that he was hired: "I'm not going to let you go this time . . . I don't have any position for you. You'll do whatever you feel like doing." He instructed Strayhorn to go to New York, where Mercer would book him a room at the Harlem YMCA. Two days after checking in, Strayhorn knocked on the door of the family penthouse on Edgecombe Avenue. Ruth, who noticed that he spoke French "like a native," took to him immediately: "Billy established instantaneous communication with the family, it was as if he had always been there." Mercer felt the same way, and the two young men talked all night. From then on Strayhorn only stopped by the Y long enough to change his clothes, after which he came back to the Ellington apartment. A few days later Mercer said, "What the hell are we paying all the rent [at the YMCA] for? Go get your shit and move it here."

Not long after Ellington returned from the road, he gave Strayhorn his first assignment: "One day Duke sent me two pieces and he said, 'Arrange these for a recording tomorrow at ten o'clock.' So what could I do? I learned fast! . . . I couldn't really arrange, but that didn't really make any difference to him. That's the only way I can explain how I managed to do those arrangements." He stayed up all night writing charts for a small-group session at which Johnny Hodges cut "Like a Ship in the Night," a forgettable pop song, and a pair of Ellington-Hodges originals, "Savoy Strut" and "Dooji Wooji." Though there was nothing out of the ordinary about his arrangements, they were effective enough. Three weeks later, on March 21, Jean Eldridge, who sang briefly alongside Ivie Anderson during the first part of 1939, recorded "Something to Live For" with the full band. The arrangement was by Ellington, but Strayhorn sat in on piano, weaving a frilly obbligato in and out of Eldridge's vocal. It was his professional recording debut, as well as the first time that his name appeared on a record label. What he felt when he was told that his song would be credited to "Ellington-Strayhorn" and that he would split the royalties with his employer is not known. More than likely the twenty-three-year-old novice was too overjoyed to think twice about it.

Two days after recording "Something to Live For," Ellington and his musicians sailed for Europe, leaving Strayhorn behind. "I left him at my house with my son and my sister," Ellington recalled. "While I was gone for six weeks, [he was] there going through my scores." He was also writing "Day Dream" and "Passion Flower," his first mature instrumental compositions, which would be recorded by Hodges in 1940 and 1941. While both numbers are rooted in Strayhorn's earlier work, they show that his encounter with Ellington had widened his musical horizons—and that he already had a compositional voice of his own. "Passion Flower," whose Ravel-like chromaticism is so extreme as to briefly dissolve the listener's perception of a tonal center, is harmonically advanced in a way that was all but unprecedented in jazz. At the same time, both songs also show that Strayhorn, unlike Ellington, was blessed with the gift of tunefulness, though their opulently wide-ranging melodies ("Day Dream" opens with a bold upward leap of an octave) are conceived not in vocal but in idiomatically instrumental terms.* Indeed, they may well have been written with Hodges's playing in mind, since Strayhorn had now had the opportunity to work with him, and from then on the saxophonist, whose tone was compared by Charlie Parker to the voice of the coloratura soprano Lily Pons, would be his most favored soloist.

The only thing missing from Strayhorn's toolbox was the ability to write fluently for the full band, and the fact that his new employer was temporarily absent from the scene made it possible for him to learn the craft of big-band orchestration by studying Ellington's manuscripts. He modestly claimed that it took "a long time" for him to unravel their mysteries, but Ellington later spoke with wry amusement of his assimilative powers:

> *He had a good musical education but he had never had any writing experience—orchestration. So he looked at my things and decided, I suppose, that it all looked very simple, so when I came back he said, "I've been looking at your things and I think I could do some of that." I said, "Yeah, all right, have a shot."*

Strayhorn started turning out vocal arrangements for Ivie Anderson, and within weeks Ellington "gave [him] charge of all the singers." Around the same time he recorded his first solo, eight light-fingered bars à la Teddy Wilson on Cootie Williams's "Blues A Poppin'," a Williams original that Strayhorn had also arranged. After that he was put in charge of the small-group sides as well: "From then on, Duke did very little of the arranging for the small groups. Oh, he did a little, but he turned almost all of them [over] to me. You could say I inherited a phase of Duke's organization." Strayhorn's

---

* Except for Ella Fitzgerald, even the most talented singers found Strayhorn's songs elusive, and still do. Frank Sinatra, one of his greatest admirers, tried unsuccessfully to record "Lush Life" in 1958. Surviving outtakes from the session show that it was the chromatically twisting melody of the chorus that defeated him.

new colleagues were impressed by his prodigious talent. "He got everything that Duke had and more," Juan Tizol said. "Strayhorn learned. He already knew about it, by looking at the scores he learned a lot and started writing just like Ellington—I'm talking about his chords and so forth. Strayhorn's writing was a little more sweeter, more sweet music than Duke's." They also found the studious young man likable once he started bar-hopping with Otto Hardwick and Sonny Greer, who fondly spoke of him as "a guy that everybody loved. . . . I never saw a man like that, could cabaret all night long and walk the chalk line. He was amazing. He got me so I hated to look at him. I used to say, 'Man, how you do that?' And he would laugh."

Ellington witnessed the aftermath of Strayhorn's first night on the town with the boys in the band, who lurched back to their train barely in time for an early-morning departure:

> *I was down in the station and here comes Strayhorn, this nice little schoolboy whom we had all looked down upon to look up at, and here he was, running drunk, and he's got my hat on. So here comes Strayhorn juiced with my hat on, and Sonny Greer has been priming him for his entrance now because he's got him juiced, and he comes over and he looks at me, Strayhorn looks at me, and he points his finger, and he says, "Hey, man, I don't dig you!"*

Ellington made his own feelings known by recording "Weely," a musical portrait of Strayhorn, in October. While it is hard to see what this uninteresting riff tune has to do with its ostensible subject, the gesture was important in and of itself, since it clued in the listening public to the coming of a new colleague. But on the same day that the band recorded "Weely," Hodges cut "Your Love Has Faded," another of Strayhorn's early ballads, which was remade two days later by Ivie Anderson and the full band. Even though Strayhorn had written the song for the Mad Hatters in 1937, the labels of both records credited it solely to Ellington. For Ellington as for Irving Mills, such credit hoggery was nothing new. For a shy young composer who was still coming out of his shell, however, it was more than just a matter of money. By withholding credit for his work, Ellington struck at Strayhorn's as-yet-unformed sense of identity—and kept on doing so for years to come.

∽

Ellington later assured innocent reporters that he and Strayhorn came to be so close that they finished writing each other's pieces, a charade with which the younger man went along: "Every once in a while, [Ellington] calls me from some place I've never heard of, from some distant part of the world and says, 'Billy, I'm working on a song, but I'm stuck, can't finish it. Now, the first part goes like this: Bah bah bah bee boo bee bee bah bah bah bah bah boo. I want you to finish it for me.'" On rare occasions, always enforced by necessity, they collaborated face-to-face. Gordon Parks saw the two men finish writing a number together in a San Francisco hotel room after watching a late-night horror movie on TV:

> *At about one-thirty Edward switched off the television set. "That flick," he said with a yawn, "was the worst. No other has aroused my imperial displeasure so thoroughly." He picked up some manuscript paper and handed it to Strayhorn. "Gather up the genius, Swee' Pea. The maestro is limp at the heels." He then flopped down on the couch. Turning to me he mumbled wearily, "You are about to witness a remote and covetous collaboration between flower and beast." Five minutes later he was snoring deeply. Strayhorn worked.*
>
> *It was well past three when Strayhorn shook Edward's shoulder. "Wake up, Monster. I stopped on C minor. Take it from there." Edward rose slowly, yawned and stumbled over to the manuscript. Strayhorn took the couch.*
>
> *"C minor. C minor. How indelicate of you, Pea. C minor." Edward was mumbling himself back to consciousness. "Working with you is like tearing one's heart in half. C minor. How dull. How unimaginative to awaken one and assign him to such an ordinary chord. C minor. You are a slaughterer of the innocent." Strayhorn snored peacefully now. Edward worked. In a couple of hours he roused Strayhorn and they worked together. And so it went until the piece was finished at dawn.*

No doubt it sometimes happened just like that, but only fifty-two surviving manuscript scores of pieces written or arranged by Ellington and Strayhorn between 1939 and Strayhorn's death in 1967 are in the handwriting of both men. One of them, an Ivie Anderson–sung blues called "Rocks in My Bed" that was credited to Ellington but actually cowritten by him and Strayhorn, illustrates some of the differences in their compositional styles. As was customary when they worked together on a vocal chart, Ellington scored the purely instrumental portion, with Strayhorn supplying accompaniment for the singer. Johnny Hodges and Barney Bigard split the first two choruses, supported by full-ensemble block chords—but as soon as Anderson makes her entrance, Strayhorn takes over the helm and backs her with a written-out countermelody for the saxophones, followed by a root-and-branch reharmonization of the song. Throughout her two vocal choruses, the various sections of the band support Anderson with an unobtrusive web of contrapuntal lines. Such an approach was alien to Ellington, whose notion of "counterpoint" usually amounted to having one of his soloists improvise an obbligato to a full-band passage (as Bigard does in "Rocks in My Bed").

Not only did Strayhorn think contrapuntally, but his harmonic vocabulary was nothing like that of his mentor. Extensive study of the music of the French impressionists had given him access to a chromaticism far more elaborate than Ellington's homespun species, so much so that he was capable of unconsciously quoting *Valses nobles et sentimentales*, a work by Ravel that he had yet to hear, in the opening bars of "Chelsea Bridge," the most advanced of the pieces that he wrote for the Ellington band in 1941. Having mastered the rules of classical voice-leading in his youth, Strayhorn used widely spaced open-position quartal harmonies, whereas Ellington, like the self-taught pianist-composer that he was, preferred closed-position triadic harmonies that fall naturally under a pianist's hands (though his harmonic language soon grew more adventurous, possibly in response to Strayhorn's example). Conversely, the blues had next to no place in Strayhorn's output, just as his orchestral palette was brighter and more treble-weighted than the bass-dominated sounds favored by his older colleague, who never tired of finding new ways to sneak Harry Carney's baritone saxophone into his voicings.

Above all, Strayhorn shunned Ellington's ad hoc mosaic structures. His pieces develop organically from start to finish, with transitional passages carefully integrated into the flow of musical events—except when Ellington got his hands on a Strayhorn manuscript and reworked it in the studio, as he did with "Chelsea Bridge," from which he excised a minute and a half of music, rearranging what remained in such a way as to undermine its formal coherence. It was not the last time that he would "improve" a Strayhorn chart by dismantling and reassembling it to suit the imperious dictates of his ear, nor would Strayhorn easily accept Ellington's high-handed willingness to alter his compositions. Even after they came to terms with their musical differences and arrived at a mutually acceptable modus vivendi, the two men sometimes let their sensitivities show through their guarded exteriors. In a joint radio appearance from 1962, Ellington jovially described how he went about recording a Strayhorn piece: "There is nothing like taking a Billy Strayhorn orchestration in a recording studio. . . . This is the first time it is to be played and you start to record it, and then take it and turn it all around . . . just destroy the whole orchestration pattern. It doesn't destroy it, but [you] twist it around, turn it upside down, and this and that." Having given the interviewer this glimpse of his working methods, Ellington proceeded to make a startling confession, couching it in the loftily ironic tone that he assumed whenever he wanted to obscure the issue: "Maybe Billy Strayhorn's orchestrations might sound *too good*. . . . And we don't want Strayhorn to sound too good *too young*." To which Strayhorn replied, "You wanted to know about collaboration, and now you know. This is the *real* story." Though his tone was as arch as Ellington's, both men were kidding on the square.

Now that musicologists have definitively established who wrote what in the Ellington-Strayhorn oeuvre, it is hard to see how anyone could ever have confused their styles. Yet many knowledgeable listeners, among them such distinguished scholars as Gunther Schuller, did so time and again. The reason why is clear: Strayhorn's work was being performed and recorded by a band whose members had been handpicked by Ellington himself and whose playing styles created an impression of similarity that was strong enough to throw the smartest of outsiders off the scent. But the impression was deceptive, and both Ellington and Strayhorn, unlike their critics, knew it.

"I feel that his was the only band I could do anything with—the only place where I would fit," Strayhorn told Sinclair Traill in 1959. It made sense that he should have felt at home in Ellington's rowdy crew of iron-willed individualists, for he had always found it hard to fit in. The words that turn up repeatedly in the recollections of his admiring schoolmates tell the tale: *egghead, oddball* . . . and *sissy*. "He had a hard time making friends," Mickey Scrima said. "To tell you the truth, people used to call him a sissy." And Scrima knew Strayhorn well enough to understand that he had poured his otherness into his art:

> *The guy went through a lot of shit in his life, from his father right on through school—the kids calling him a sissy, you know. He kept it all in and put on a big front that everything was fine, nothing bothered him. Then he sat down and wrote all that music with all that emotion. All his feelings came out in the music. That's what made his stuff so incredible and different from Duke's. It was great music, like Duke's was, and it was so full of dark feeling.*

By all accounts Strayhorn was at ease with his sexuality. Though he was disinclined to talk about it other than indirectly and never "came out" in public, he also never pretended to be heterosexual, and expected his friends and colleagues to treat him as they did everyone else. This attitude was unusual in the thirties and forties, not least in the world of jazz, which was (and still is) something of a boys' club with a locker-room feel, a subculture in which open homosexuality, if not unknown, was still uncommon. "There wasn't a lot of guys who was homosexual and acted like that, like there it was and you have to accept it—and if you don't, that's your problem," said the clarinetist Jimmy Hamilton, who joined the band in 1943. While most of Ellington's musicians accepted it, some of them, it appears, did not. Barney Bigard, in a passage that was censored by his wife from the transcript of his oral-history interview, spoke critically of Strayhorn's sexuality, and it is noteworthy that the clarinetist mentioned him only in passing in *With Louis and the Duke,* his posthumously published autobiography, while Rex Stewart said nothing at all about him in *Boy Meets Horn.*

As for his relationship with Ellington, it would always be fraught with tension. According to Mercer Ellington, "Pop never cared one bit that Strayhorn was gay. . . . He knew plenty of gay men and women, so there was no question about, 'Hey, is this person a freak or something?' Pop knew the story. He backed up Strayhorn all the way." But Mercer also reports that Ellington believed in the existence of "a Faggot Mafia. . . . He went on to recount how homosexuals hired their own kind whenever they could, and how, when they had achieved executive status, they maneuvered to keep straight guys out of the influential positions." And while Ellington treated him with the trust and respect that Strayhorn's own father had withheld, there was—as usual with Ellington—more to it than that. According to Lena Horne, who had a fling with Ellington before becoming one of Strayhorn's closest friends, "Duke treated Billy exactly like he treated women, with all that old-fashioned chauvinism. Very loving and very protective, but controlling, very destructive."

Nor was his influence on Strayhorn a one-way street. Derek Jewell cites "someone who knew [Ellington] in the 1930s" as follows: "I think Duke was a much simpler character before he met Strays. You could even say he was sweeter. But he was so much more interesting once Strays happened along." The singer Herb Jeffries, who joined the band in October of 1939, put it less euphemistically:

> *Duke was a magnificent role model. He was brilliant at it. But some of*
> *it was hocus-pocus—grand gestures and particular five-dollar phrases*

that he'd pronounce with dramatic emphasis. Meanwhile, he never really read anything except the Bible . . . and he knew far less about the fine arts, including other composers, than he liked to let on. In Billy, Duke saw that image he considered so important, in flesh and blood.

When it came to high culture, Ellington was a poseur, a strangely incurious man who knew next to nothing about classical music and read not systematically but at random, taking care to display *Remembrance of Things Past* on his shelves for the benefit of journalists who assumed that he had read the whole thing from cover to cover, just as they believed him whenever he said that he had just finished writing his first opera (or symphony, or Broadway show). Not Strayhorn. In addition to being a classical-music connoisseur—he favored Rachmaninoff, Stravinsky, and the French impressionists—he was impressively well read in 1939, and grew more so in years to come. Could the bourgeois from U Street who learned in childhood the importance of keeping up appearances have been unconsciously jealous of his bilingual protégé from Pittsburgh, who turned himself by sheer force of will into that which his patron longed to be? And if he was, might that jealousy someday come between the two men?

Eventually Strayhorn himself would think such dark thoughts—but not yet. For the moment he was deliriously happy, and not just because he had found his calling. In the fall of 1939 Mercer introduced him to a casual acquaintance from the neighborhood, a black pianist named Aaron Bridgers who was working as an elevator operator while studying piano with Art Tatum. By year's end, Strayhorn had moved out of the Ellington apartment to set up housekeeping with Bridgers in Harlem. Though both men were discreet about the nature of their relationship, it was evident to all who knew them that they were lovers. Ulanov later implied as much in his biography of Ellington, and Ruth Ellington never doubted it: "We accepted Aaron as a new member of the family, because he was with Billy. . . . They were together, and that's how it was. They didn't go through the motions of any kind of pretense."

If Strayhorn had wondered how he wanted to live his life, the liaison with Bridgers answered his questions. But it also drove a wedge into the center of that life. Ellington had opened up the world of jazz to him. He played Strayhorn's music, paid him generously, and denied him nothing save for credit, which he gave only on his own capricious terms, though those with ears to hear knew that something was up. When Victor released Strayhorn's vocal arrangement of "Flamingo" a year later, John Lewis heard it and marveled: "It had nothing to do with what had gone on in jazz at all before. It sounded as if Stravinsky were a jazz musician." So did Gerry Mulligan: "When Strayhorn came on the scene, he just blew us away . . . To bring all that complexity to bear and have it be so beautiful was something incredible to everybody who knew anything." Ellington, who knew plenty, felt the same way, praising "Flamingo" as "a turning point in vocal background orchestration, a renaissance in elaborate ornamentation for the accompaniment of singers."

It would have made sense for so gifted an artist to strike out on his own. But Strayhorn needed no Irving Mills to warn him that he could not function as a celebrity bandleader while living more or less openly as a gay man. So he hung back, accepting Ellington's largesse—and capriciousness—in return for being allowed to love whom he pleased. Meanwhile Ellington laid on the praise whenever interviewers asked him about Strayhorn. When they didn't, which was usually, he kept his opinions to himself. This was why most mainstream-media articles about Ellington said nothing about Strayhorn, and why those that did described him in terms that diminished his importance. In Richard O. Boyer's "The Hot Bach," the 1944 *New Yorker* profile that was the most comprehensive journalistic account of Ellington's life and work to appear in his lifetime, Strayhorn is dismissed as Ellington's "staff arranger and a talented composer in his own right."

It was a near-Faustian bargain, one whose very existence Strayhorn denied. "He has never made me feel that I am walking in his shadow," he said of Ellington in 1965. But he knew full well that he had chosen safety and security over fame and fear, and he grew less comfortable with the choice. On the surface, Ruth Ellington said, he gave the impression of being calm and collected: "The one thing that stood out about Billy . . . is that no matter what anyone said or did, he was never sensitive about his own feelings or anyone trying to hurt him, and he was always understanding and sympathetic and seeing every point of view, without any reference to himself whatsoever." His friends knew better, especially after the "cabareting" that Sonny Greer admired degenerated into alcoholism.

Most of the time he brushed off Ellington's half-unintentional, half-calculated slights with an ironic aside or a repetition of his favorite catchphrase, "Ever up and onward." But it says much about their relationship that Strayhorn's nickname for Ellington—which he used to the older man's face—was "Monster," and on one occasion he let his own mask slip. In 1957 Ellington was profiled in *Look,* and the piece, as usual, made no mention of his longtime collaborator. Soon after the issue hit the newsstands, Strayhorn dined with a friend, the dancer Honi Coles, who had read the article and was irate about it.

"You wrote every bit as much of that music they're fussing all over as Ellington and they didn't even mention your name," the friend told him. "Why do you let them get away with that? . . . I think you do care or you wouldn't be drinking like a fucking fish every fucking time I see you."

"I'm better off without all that," Strayhorn replied. "Let him have his articles. I'm better off this way."

Then he burst into tears.

10

"THE SEA OF EXPECTANCY"

The Blanton-Webster Band, 1939–1940

DUKE ELLINGTON SAID in 1964 that he thought of his compositions as "a continuing autobiography": "My music talks about the new people I keep meeting, especially the new men who pass through the band and sometimes stay. I use their particular ways of expressing themselves, and it all becomes part of my own style." While the coming of Billy Strayhorn was a key chapter in that chronicle, Strayhorn did not make his first noteworthy contributions to Ellington's book of arrangements until the fall of 1940, and five years had gone by since a new soloist, Rex Stewart, last joined the band. It was time for a change—though no one, not even Ellington himself, knew how fateful it would be.

Billy Taylor, Ellington's bassist, had now held that chair for five years. While Ellington regarded him as "one of the ace foundation-and-beat men on the instrument," the fact that he had hired Hayes Alvis to play alongside Taylor, just as he had hired Taylor to play alongside Wellman Braud, shows that he sought something more from his rhythm section. Jazz bass technique was still in its infancy in 1939. In the late thirties most bassists were recovering tuba players with catch-as-catch-can techniques who had taught themselves the instrument out of necessity. Many of them, like Count Basie's Walter Page, were solid "foundation-and-beat" men, but Bob Haggart, Milt

Hinton, and Slam Stewart were the only well-known jazz bassists whose technical equipment was sufficiently developed to permit them to function not just as section men but also as soloists, and none of them was looking for a job (Haggart played with Bob Crosby, Hinton with Cab Calloway, while Stewart co-led a popular combo with Slim Gaillard). If Ellington wanted to trade up, he would have to find the new man himself.

On October 20, 1939, the band pulled into St. Louis for a two-week stand at the Hotel Coronado. At some point shortly thereafter, Johnny Hodges went to Club 49, an after-hours spot frequented by traveling musicians, where he heard a twenty-one-year-old bassist named Jimmie Blanton. Impressed by his playing, Hodges went back to the hotel where the band was staying and rousted Ellington out of bed to hear the youngster, who was then working with Fate Marable, the pianist-bandleader in whose riverboat orchestra Louis Armstrong had played two decades earlier. According to Mercer, he "arrived in his pajamas and topcoat." An eyewitness, the trumpeter Ralph Porter, tells what happened next:

> *Duke asked Marable if he could sit in—they knew one another well. Duke and Blanton began playing together and still hadn't exchanged a word. Duke kept changing key and Blanton was on to every move. The tune ended and Marable called out "How do you like my bass player?" Duke coyly said, "I was just going to ask you the same question." Then he laughed and said, "He's my bass player now."*
>
> *Duke already had a bass player but he added Jimmie Blanton to the band, bought him a white suit, and next night stood him out front of the band and featured him.*

Word of the encounter spread quickly. "We wonder if the maestro is planning to add Jimmie Blanton, bass fiddler with Fate Marable's band, to his aggregation," a columnist for *The St. Louis Argus,* a black newspaper, reported a week later. Ellington never forgot his late-night visit to Club 49: "I flipped like everybody else . . . we didn't care about his [lack of] experience. All we wanted was that sound, that beat, and those precision notes in the right places, so that we could float out on the great and adventurous sea of expectancy with his pulse and foundation behind us." Blanton left St. Louis with the band on November 3, and Ellington started featuring him at once. Within weeks jazz-savvy journalists were taking note. An Indianapolis columnist who heard Blanton play "Sophisticated Lady" with Ellington told his readers that "it was really unique and fascinating and spine-chilling." Less than three years later, he was dead.

"All we wanted was that sound": Jimmie Blanton and Johnny Hodges, Detroit, 1940. The outstanding jazz bassist of the forties accompanies the Ellington band's most celebrated soloist. Blanton's hard-swinging, technically advanced playing spurred his colleagues, Hodges included, to new heights of virtuosity

Because he died so young and appears never to have been interviewed, we know little about Blanton's life beyond the barest of details. He was born in Chattanooga in 1918. Gertrude, his mother, was a professional musician who gave him piano lessons as a child, and he is also said to have played violin and alto saxophone in a family band before switching to bass around the time that he went to Tennessee State University to study music. It's not known whether Blanton studied the instrument there, but he later made use of playing techniques with which few jazz bassists were then conversant, indicating that he took lessons from a classically trained teacher prior to meeting Ellington. Barney Bigard said that he was studying with an unnamed "professor" in 1939:

"When he left St. Louis to join us his professor gave him a list of all the symphony bassists in the towns around the country and a letter of introduction to them. . . . Jimmy [*sic*] would go look them up and take his lesson." (The "professor" in question appears to have been Karl Auer, the longtime principal bassist of the St. Louis Symphony.) Blanton started playing with Marable during his summers at TSU, then joined the Jeter-Pillars Orchestra, a St. Louis–based territory band with which he is believed to have cut his first records in 1937. He appears to have been working regularly with Marable when he met Ellington.

While Blanton was not the first classically trained jazz bassist, he was the first one to develop into an improvising soloist of the top rank. "Listen, you're going to hear something you never heard before—a bass player who plays melody, and in tune," Ellington told Leonard Feather in 1941. Blanton was all that and much more. His focused sound was slender but penetrating, his pizzicato playing awesomely fleet, his sense of swing unerring. "He shocked us all . . . he had those tremendously long fingers and he really knew his positions," Milt Hinton said. Best known for his unprecedented ability to play hornlike solos in the upper register of his instrument, Blanton was one of the few jazz bassists of his generation who, like Slam Stewart, was also adept with the bow. Not only did his playing stun jazz musicians and buffs, but it caught the ear of classical musicians who had never heard a bass plucked with such fluency. Rex Stewart claimed that Igor Stravinsky "spent [an] entire evening enjoying Blanton" at a New York club. "Despite his youth, there was a certain calm assurance which vibrated visibly, and you could sense this permeating his public and private life," he added. "When he spoke, which was rarely, people listened, feeling, truthfully, that he was wise beyond his years." Photographs show that he was boyishly handsome, and it amused Ellington's sidemen that he preferred making music to carrying on with the girls who pursued him. "They'd find out the hotel he was staying in and they would call his room," Bigard said. "He'd answer and say, 'Yes. Just a minute. I've just got to finish what I was doing.' Don't you know he would just leave that receiver down and forget that they were on the line. Just go right back to that bass and start in with his practicing again."

They also worried about his health, for the physically fragile Blanton was thought to be taking his life in his hands by frequenting late-night jam sessions with compulsive regularity. "What really struck me when I finally saw him was how slight and frail a young man he was," said George Duvivier. "It kind of frightened me because I knew all about the Ellington orchestra: how they lived and traveled and their after-hours escapades. The thought occurred to me, 'My Lord, this guy just might not make it!' " None of his new compatriots seems to have been surprised when Blanton was diagnosed with tuberculosis (a disease that in the thirties and forties was vastly more common among blacks than whites) two years later. The speed with which it laid him low suggests that he was already ill at the end of 1939, and that he might even have known that his time was short.

Ellington rushed Blanton into a recording studio as soon as he could. On November 22, three weeks after he joined the band, the two men cut a pair of duets in Chicago. "Blues" and "Plucked Again," the first bass-and-piano jazz duets ever to be commercially recorded, are top-of-the-head improvisations remembered today only because they allow us to hear Blanton's playing up close for the first time. A year later he and Ellington recorded four more carefully prepared sides, the best of which is "Pitter Panther Patter," that show off his pizzicato work to much better effect (while also showing that his bowed intonation was iffy). By that time Blanton had been featured on two full-band recordings, "Jack the Bear" and "Sepia Panorama," though his springy ensemble playing is audible on every side that he recorded with Ellington. "He wouldn't interfere with your solo—playing riffs behind your riffs—he would play a good, solid beat for you," Bigard said. Blanton's virtuosity stunned his less facile section mate. In January of 1940 the Ellington band arrived in Boston, and Billy Taylor quit the band there. "Right in the middle of a set, [he] packed up his bass and said, 'I'm not going to stand up here next to that young boy playing all that bass and be embarrassed,'" Ellington wrote in *Music Is My Mistress.* "He left the stand . . . and went on out the front door. I think it takes a big, big man to acknowledge the facts and take low."

It was in Boston that Ellington made an equally consequential addition to the band. A columnist for the *New York Amsterdam News* reported in January, "Ben Webster denies plans to switch from Teddy Wilson to Duke Ellington, but the grapevine has him making the change." (In those far-off days the hiring of a new musician by a top bandleader was thought worthy of note by the entertainment columnists of black newspapers.) Once more the rumor was true, and Ellington's sidemen, who liked to affect a blasé pose, rejoiced at the arrival of a saxophonist who was, after Johnny Hodges and Sidney Bechet, the greatest soloist ever to pass through their ranks.

Born in 1909 in Kansas City, Benjamin Francis Webster was the son of a violent drunk who quit the scene shortly before his birth. His mother and great-aunt, both of them churchgoers, endeavored to raise him in the paths of righteousness. "My mother, she wanted me to be a little Lord Fauntleroy, with that big Buster Brown collar, and take violin lessons," Webster recalled.

He had other ideas. Having inherited his father's temper, the boy smashed his violin to bits at the age of twelve, taught himself how to play stride piano, and started haunting the nightclubs of the ghetto on whose fringes he lived, where he discovered the pleasures of hard drinking and loose women. Webster spent two years at Wilberforce University in Ohio, the oldest private black college in America, but all he cared about was music, and when he heard Fletcher Henderson's band, his fate was sealed. An adequate but undistinguished pianist, he took up the alto saxophone in 1928. A year later he was playing alongside Lester Young in the reed section of Young's father's band. Soon afterward he switched to tenor and started working his way up through the ranks of the best black bands. Henderson, Bennie Moten, Cab Calloway, and Teddy Wilson were all impressed enough by his still-unfinished playing to hire him, though his personality gave some of them second thoughts.

Apprehensive friends soon nicknamed Webster "the Brute," and Rex Stewart, who called him "the hoodlum swingster," seems to have been the first person to compare him to Dr. Jekyll, whose rampaging alter ego, the sadistic Mr. Hyde, terrorized the citizens of London. Alcohol was the potion that unleashed his demons. Webster was, in the words of his friend Jimmy Rowles, "kind of an introvert, always respectful when he was sober." But drinking disabled his inhibitions and made him as violent as his father had been. He never allowed the Lord's name to be taken in vain in his presence, and when anyone broke his rule in a bar, he beat them up. Predictably enough, he treated his lovers like whores. To the saxophonist Garvin Bushell, he was "an unusual character, very humorous, also very tough. He didn't get along with the girls at all because he'd knock them down if they said the wrong thing to him. . . . I think Ben was influenced by the hustlers and pimps—he had their mannerisms."

It was Webster's dream to work with Duke Ellington. "Every time I'd run across some of Duke's men I would ask for a job," he said. In August of 1935 he got his chance, if only for a brief time: "Barney Bigard took a little vacation . . . and I joined Duke when the opportunity popped up." He can be heard playing a thrusting solo on the band's recording of "Truckin'," a song written by Rube Bloom and Ted Koehler for a Cotton Club show, in which Ivie Anderson celebrates a Harlem dance craze. At a time when other Swing Era bands featured tenor-sax solos, none of Ellington's men specialized in the instrument. From then on, he said, "I always had a yen for Ben." But he would not poach a member of a band in which he had a financial interest, and Webster was playing with Cab Calloway at the time, so the flirtation went no further—for the moment.

After Ellington broke with Irving Mills and traded his interest in the Calloway band back to his ex-manager, such niceties became irrelevant. In January of 1940 Webster joined the band of his dreams, and gave as good as he got. Playing Ellington's big-band charts alongside Johnny Hodges, a longtime idol, knocked the rough edges off Webster, whose mature style combined lyricism with pile-driving swing. He described it as "a kind of alto approach to the tenor," influenced by Hodges and Benny Carter, but it was also a manifestation of his own split personality. For a time he had been obsessed with Coleman Hawkins, but when a friend suggested that emulation had become imitation, Webster changed his ways, retaining the older man's voluminous tone while embracing Lester Young's tunefulness, punctuating his solos with pungent growls that were all his own.

Off the bandstand Webster was warm, generous, and a good comrade—when sober. He became close to and protective of Jimmie Blanton, who nicknamed him "Frog." Rex Stewart was touched by his solicitousness: "Ben was a different man as he watched over Blanton like a mother hen . . . he cut way down on his whiskey and would sit by the hour counseling young Jimmy [*sic*] on the facts of life." One night he carried Blanton home on his back through a blizzard, the young man's bass tucked under the saxophonist's arm. The closeness of their mutual understanding can be heard in a version of "Star Dust" recorded at a dance in 1940, in which Webster all but whispers Hoagy Carmichael's melody as Blanton accompanies him with self-effacing simplicity.

A month after he joined the band, Webster played alongside Blanton on Ellington's final sessions for Columbia, which took place in Chicago. Columbia seized the opportunity to cut sensitively sung vocal versions of "Mood Indigo" and "Solitude" by Ivie Anderson, plus Anderson's only commercial recording of "Stormy Weather," which she had sung onstage with the band ever since Ethel Waters premiered the song at the Cotton Club in 1933, and a pleasant but uneventful instrumental remake of "Sophisticated Lady." Webster is heard throughout the date, proclaiming his arrival with relaxed authority. When it was over, Ellington signed a contract with Victor and hit the road to play a string of stage shows in Michigan and Indiana. The next time he set foot in a studio, he would cast off from the past and set eager sail on the sea of expectancy.

Three weeks later, on March 6, Ellington and the band returned to Chicago for their first Victor session. First up was "You, You Darlin'," a dull pop tune sung by Herb Jeffries. Then came "Jack the Bear," a previously unrecorded

Ellington instrumental that Billy Strayhorn had rewritten to feature Jimmie Blanton. As if to proclaim to the world that all bets were off, Blanton launched "Jack the Bear" by stepping out in front of the band and tossing off a lighter-than-air eight-bar solo. Because his style long ago became the lingua franca of jazz bass playing, the impact that this solo had on those who first heard it seven decades ago is no longer possible for contemporary listeners to fully appreciate, but its swinging vitality remains as listenable today as it was in 1940. The mosaic-like structure of "Jack the Bear" is all of a piece with Ellington's recent record-ings, as are the familiar voices of his soloists. (Best of all is Tricky Sam Nanton, who uses his plunger in such a way as to create the impression that we are hear-ing not one but two trombonists, both of whom have sex on their minds.) Yet something has clearly happened, and it goes well beyond the fact that Victor's engineers were now recording the band with a you-are-there immediacy that is missing from its Columbia sides. Was it nothing more than Blanton's galvaniz-ing presence in the rhythm section? Or was Ellington responding in a new way to what he was hearing on the bandstand?

The answer came when the band turned to his latest composition, a seven-chorus minor-key blues called "Ko-Ko." From the curt trombone riff that sets the piece in motion to the spiraling bitonal crescendo that brings it to a charging close, "Ko-Ko" is the greatest of Ellington's three-minute mas-terpieces, an exercise in motivic development as taut as *Reminiscing in Tempo* is shapeless. Except for a dirt-plain two-chorus solo by Nanton and three bass breaks by Blanton, "Ko-Ko" is the composer's show all the way, most spectacularly in the fourth chorus, in which he flings a double handful of dissonant piano chords and arpeggios across a series of call-and-response ex-changes by the band. Though he had experimented with minor-key orches-tral mayhem in 1938 with "Old King Dooji," "Ko-Ko" is something else again, a relentless procession of musical events that contains not a wasted gesture. Every bar surges inexorably toward the final catastrophe, after which no response is possible but awed silence.

When the band played "Ko-Ko" at Carnegie Hall in 1943, Ellington informed the audience that it was "a little descriptive scene of the days that inspired jazz. I think it was in New Orleans, in a place called Congo Square where the slaves used to gather and do native and sensuous dances, religious dances." (It was typical of him to yoke the latter two qualities.) Not long af-terward he told Barry Ulanov that the piece was "an excerpt from the incom-plete score for Duke's opera, *Boola*." The history of *Boola* is one of the many unsolved mysteries of Ellington's life. Having announced in 1938 that he had finished writing his first opera, he started making explicit references to

Boola in 1940: "I felt long ago there was need for expressing more of the American Negro's true feeling. So I wrote *Boola* in operatic form. It's orchestrated and ready for production—probably in New York." By 1941 he was claiming to have spent nine years working on it. But while Ellington did write part of a scenario for *Boola,* no musical manuscript material definitively related to the work has survived, making it impossible to know whether or not this statement was anything more than another of his musical castles in the air. Not that it really matters, for "Ko-Ko" is complete in itself, an unremitting assault on the senses in which he at once sums up and moves beyond all of his compositional achievements to date. Even if he had never written anything else, "Ko-Ko" alone would have earned him a permanent place in the annals of twentieth-century music.

Therein lay the miracle: "Jack the Bear" and "Ko-Ko," far from being isolated events, ushered in a flood tide of new work that continued without crest for week after week. Nine days later came "Concerto for Cootie," a sequel to "Echoes of Harlem." In May the band cut "Bojangles," "Cotton Tail," "Dusk," "Never No Lament," and "A Portrait of Bert Williams," followed by "Harlem Air-Shaft," "All Too Soon," "Rumpus in Richmond," and "Sepia Panorama" in July, "In a Mellotone" in September, and "Across the Track Blues" and "Warm Valley" in October. By now Ellington had become so prolific that he would soon hire a full-time copyist, Tom Whaley, to help Juan Tizol keep up with the job of extracting parts from his scores for the men in the band to play.

Ellington was so busy turning out new pieces that he didn't even take the time to write tenor-saxophone parts for the older numbers in the book. Instead he encouraged Ben Webster to improvise his own parts on the spot. Mercer Ellington found the process fascinating:

> *Every time Ben got up and played by ear, the whole gang jumped on him and said, "Hey, you've got my note!" So Ben decided he would get away from this and find a note nobody had. What was a four-part reed chorus in four-part harmony suddenly had five parts. . . . A semi-dissonant sound resulted from the five parts, because there was no written part for him. Ellington heard it, liked it, and learned how to apply it—another device for the orchestra.*

It took time for the critics to catch up. "Not up to the Ellington standard," *Down Beat* said of "Ko-Ko." But even the dullest of dullards finally figured out that the records he cut in 1940 were setting a new standard, not just for him but for jazz in general, and today the recordings of what has come to be known as "the Blanton-Webster band" are generally thought to mark the summit of his compositional achievement. Long before his death, that view was enough of a commonplace for Ellington to find it oppressive. "I find I have all these other lifetimes to compete with," he said. In time he found the competition so irksome that he relegated the Blanton-Webster years to a single sentence in *Music Is My Mistress:* "During this period— 1940–41—we produced some very good music." He had a point, for the band continued to play on a high level long after Blanton died, just as Ellington continued to write first-rate pieces. But never again would he do so with such consistency, nor would any of his later bands strike so perfect a balance of virtuosity and idiosyncrasy.

Given its deservedly high reputation, it is surprising that the music written by Ellington for the Blanton-Webster band should have been so similar in tone to the pieces he had been turning out since the midthirties. Even the musical genres in which he worked remained unchanged. He was still writing exotic jungle music like "Ko-Ko," "sophisticated" instrumental ballads like "Warm Valley," tender "Mood Indigo"–like night pieces like "Dusk," keenly observed life studies like "Bojangles" and "A Portrait of Bert Williams," miniature jazz "concerti" like "Concerto for Cootie," irresistibly danceable medium-tempo riff tunes like "Never No Lament," and near-themeless string-of-solos numbers like "Across the Track Blues." Yet in all cases these compositions are more colorful and formally supple than their predecessors. The difference was that he now worked with the concentration and self-discipline that are the fruits of maturity alone. Each chart is stripped of superfluities, making its points as succinctly as possible, then driving them home just as the needle reaches the last groove.* It was, in short, the mixture as before—only better.

In only one area was there no perceptible increase of mastery: Ellington still found it hard to write tunes. Only "All Too Soon" has anything like a hummable melody, and it is, as usual with him, so instrumental in quality as to be all but unsingable (though Mildred Bailey and Ella Fitzgerald would prove equal to the challenge). Just one of his 1940 compositions to hit the

---

* Surviving live recordings of Ellington's 1940 pieces demonstrate their musical economy. Whenever he opens up a chart to make additional room for solos, its total effect is diminished (though the solos are always interesting in their own right).

charts was "Concerto for Cootie," which became a standard three years later under the title "Do Nothin' Till You Hear from Me" after Bob Russell added a lyric—and, again as usual, the piece was an unacknowledged collaboration with a sideman. It was Cootie Williams from whom Ellington bought the main theme, a chromatic warm-up exercise that the trumpeter liked to play, a transaction so widely known that it got into Walter Winchell's column. For his part, Williams remembered the deal with rue: "I stood on the bus—got down there on the steps of the bus from Boston to New York, begging him to buy this song for $25 . . . about the time we got to New York, he said, 'Well, okay. I'll buy it.' "*

But it was what Ellington did with the tunes he poached that brought them to lasting life, and the way in which he spun Williams's snippet of melody into "Concerto for Cootie," among the most formally unpredictable of his 1940 compositions, shows how he was freeing up the repeating-chorus and multiple-strain structures that had always dominated his work. He had been experimenting with these forms for years, but now he threw out the rule book altogether, writing pieces that sound straightforward on first hearing but prove on closer inspection to all but defy analysis. In "Harlem Air-Shaft," seemingly unrelated musical episodes are shoved up against one another in the manner of a cubistic collage. "Harlem Air-Shaft" starts cold with three four-bar phrases, each set in a different key, then plunges headlong into a sequence of three thirty-two-bar choruses, each based on one of the four-bar phrases with which the piece opened. The second chorus contains three stop-time passages in which the rhythmic momentum is jerked to a halt, then restored to motion by Sonny Greer's drum breaks. In the fourth and last chorus, the volume drops to a whisper and explodes seconds later into a shouting coda. It sounds almost as if Ellington had flung the pages of the manuscript in the air, then played them in the order that they fluttered to the floor.

While Ellington had always had a knack for weaving together borrowed bits and pieces of melody into tunes as flowing as "Sophisticated Lady," he now applied the same technique on a larger scale. "Sepia Panorama," for example, is a symmetrical four-theme musical arch—ABCDDCBA—whose third section was lifted from an unfinished (and uncredited) Billy Strayhorn

---

* Williams was not the only member of the band to furnish the uncredited melody for a 1940 composition that later became a hit song. The same thing happened with "Never No Lament," whose main theme, a Johnny Hodges riff, was turned by Ellington and Russell into "Don't Get Around Much Anymore."

arrangement of "Tuxedo Junction," a popular riff tune of the day. On paper the combination makes no sense, but Ellington was never afraid to let his ear make his decisions, and what should have been a musical muddle instead sounds impeccably right.

The middle section of "Sepia Panorama," a pair of blues choruses improvised by Jimmie Blanton and Ben Webster, reminds us that the blues was one of Ellington's most valued compositional devices. The word *device*, however, is the clue to understanding his arm's-length approach to the blues. Twelve-bar blues choruses pop up in surprising places throughout his compositions of the forties. The middle section of "Jack the Bear," for instance, consists of three blues choruses by Harry Carney, Tricky Sam Nanton, and the full ensemble, surrounded by a mosaic of disjunct thematic material. Yet it was rare for the band to record straight blues tunes, most of which were reserved for the small groups, above all the ones led by Johnny Hodges, whom Helen Oakley dubbed "Mister Blues." When Ellington used the word *blue* in the title of a composition, it was like as not to be a nostalgic ballad ("Blue Tune," "Blue Mood") or an urbane swinger ("Riding on a Blue Note"). Most of the actual "blues" that he wrote, like "Battle of Swing" and "Subtle Lament," are repeating-chorus pieces that employ the time-honored twelve-bar pattern but are not "bluesy" in the ordinary sense of the word. Of the nineteen new instrumental pieces by Ellington that were recorded by the full band in 1940, only two, "Ko-Ko" and "Across the Track Blues," were twelve-bar blues.

Why was Ellington so reluctant (if that is the word) to embrace the blues? Because, like James P. Johnson, Fats Waller, and the other East Coast stride pianists of his generation, he had only a limited feel for the traditional blues idiom. In *Music Is My Mistress* he declared the blues to be not "a song of sorrow" but "a song of romantic failure," which says much about his sensibility. Though he gradually evolved into a forceful and persuasive bluesman, most of his own "blues" solos of the thirties and forties are lacy, pastel-colored interludes that sound not funky but decorative. Understanding as he did the importance of the blues to jazz, he took care to bring natural blues players like Hodges and Nanton into the band, contrasting their earthiness with his suavity, just as he used the blues idiom as one of the myriad colors on his musical palette. But to listen to a piece like "Across the Track Blues" is to recall what Sergei Diaghilev said when he first heard Maurice Ravel's *La Valse:* "Ravel, it's a masterpiece, but it isn't a ballet. It's a *portrait* of a ballet, a painting of a ballet." So, too, is "Across the Track Blues" (whose working title was "Pastel") a portrait of the blues, one in which the unmediated emotions of the authentic bluesman are transformed into the musical counterpart of a color-field abstraction, then put in a handsome frame and hung in the Ellington Museum for the purpose of quiet contemplation.

It is Ellington's command of instrumental color that sets his work apart from every other big-band composer of the Swing Era. The jungle-style plunger-mute playing that he had formerly used as a show-stopping device was now fully integrated into his brass writing, in which he repeatedly came up with sonic combinations so innovative that they defied accurate transcription by even the keenest of listeners. He treated his sidemen as "found objects" whose one-of-a-kind timbres he used like the painter he had been: "You write just for their abilities and natural tendencies and give them places where they do their best . . . Every musician has his favorite licks and you gotta write to them." Billy Strayhorn spoke of how he had "often seen him exchange parts in the middle of a piece because the man and the part weren't the same character." This explains one of the peculiarities of Ellington's career, which is that he was a major composer but not an influential one. Except for Strayhorn, Spike Hughes, and Charlie Barnet, a longtime Ellington enthusiast whose musical goal (in his words) was "to incorporate Duke Ellington's harmonic approach and tone colors with Count Basie's rhythmic drive," none of Ellington's contemporaries tried to sound like him.* They played his songs and sang his praises, but that was as far as it went. Not only did they steer clear of literal imitation—which would have been impossible in any case—but they hardly ever tried to emulate his unique method of writing big-band music conceived for performance by specific players with highly individual timbres.

No less unique was the way in which Ellington blended those timbres, a method known as "cross-section voicing." Most Swing-Era arrangers kept the sections of the band separate, playing them off against one another in the call-and-response patterns that Fletcher Henderson (and, later, Benny Goodman) turned into a trademark of the period. Not Ellington, who habitually mixed the sections of his band together and voiced each individual section in ways that were no less unorthodox. Russell Procope, who joined the reed section in 1946, explained his voicing techniques as follows:

---

* In 1939 Barnet went so far as to record an "original" composition called "The Duke's Idea" in which he not only evokes Ellington's orchestral style but imitates Johnny Hodges's saxophone playing.

We don't have a first saxophone player, or second saxophone player, or third saxophone player. We have things where anybody might be playing the lead. . . . Sometimes you have clarinet on top. Johnny Hodges plays quite a bit of lead, and there are some arrangements where he plays lead in the first half and I do in the second half. This is just one of the things that give variety. The people sitting there listening can't put their finger on it, don't realize exactly what's going on, but they hear the difference.

All this notwithstanding, purely musical analysis alone cannot explain the Ellington sound, since the inspirations for so many of his compositions were extramusical. What he said about these latter pieces, of course, can never be taken at face value. Many of his best-known song titles, like "Harlem Air-Shaft," were later shown to have been concocted after the fact, just as more than a few of his explanations of what a given piece was "about" were meant to tickle the fancies of musically uneducated listeners. Such was surely the case with the impromptu fable that he spun about "Mood Indigo": "It's just a little story about a little girl and a little boy. They're about eight and the little girl loves the little boy. They never speak of it, of course, but she just likes the way he wears his hat. Every day he comes by her house at a certain time and she sits in her window and waits. . . . Then one day he doesn't come."

At the same time, though, it is wrong to suppose that he was cynical about these exegeses. He resorted to verbal description so often, and his descriptions were so pictorially specific, that it is safe to assume that he responded on a visceral level to such narratives, in much the same way that he converted visual images into music. He claimed, for instance, to have been inspired by the sight of the steel furnaces in Ohio and Indiana: "I think of music sometimes in terms of color, and I like to see the flames licking yellow in the dark and then pulsing down to a kind of red glow."* And the emotions that were triggered in him by his memories of nonmusical sounds were just as likely to find their way into his scores. "The memory of things gone is important to a jazz musician," he said in 1946. "Things like the old folks singing in the moonlight in the back yard on a hot night, or something someone said long ago."

---

* Ellington was, like Olivier Messiaen, Alexander Scriabin, and Jean Sibelius, a synesthete: "I hear a note by one of the fellows in the band and it's one color. I hear the same note played by someone else and it's a different color. . . . If Harry Carney is playing, D is dark blue burlap. If Johnny Hodges is playing, G becomes light blue satin."

In the end, there can be no "explanation" of what happened to Ellington in 1940. The change in his music was a change in the man, and he was always reluctant to talk about such things, even to his closest friends. He was stimulated by Blanton and Webster, just as he was stimulated by his decision to break with Irving Mills and by the arrival in his life of Evie Ellis, but beyond that there is little to be said save for mere description. At the age of forty, he turned the key in the lock of youthful promise and attained true mastery of the composer's art. How he did it was his secret.

ॐ

Throughout 1940 Ellington's sidemen grew in stature alongside their leader, and Johnny Hodges was now universally recognized as one of the greatest of jazz saxophonists, an unquestioned peer of Coleman Hawkins, Benny Carter, and Lester Young. He continued to be featured prominently and regularly with the full band, most notably in "Warm Valley," whose title, according to Rex Stewart, was an allusion to Ellington's chief after-hours interest: "Once, we were riding a train to California and entered a succession of undulating, gently molded hills. When we reached a certain place, Duke remarked, "Look at that! Why, that's a perfect replica of a female reclining in complete relaxation, so unashamedly exposing her warm valley." Hodges also continued to make records with combos drawn from the Ellington band, and the dates that he led in 1940 and 1941, at which he cut Strayhorn's "Day Dream" and "Passion Flower," the ferociously swinging "Squaty Roo," and a down-home blues with the wonderful title of "Things Ain't What They Used to Be," show him at the peak of his powers.

In any other band, Hodges would have been the undisputed star of the show, but the entire Ellington band was a murderer's row of soloists, each of whom was determined to rise to the occasion in 1940, none more than Ben Webster. An enthusiastic and inspirational ensemble player, Webster hit the bull's-eye whenever he stood up to solo, be it on a dreamy ballad like "All Too Soon" or a damn-the-torpedoes swinger like "Cotton Tail," the hurtling variation on "I Got Rhythm" with which he would always be identified.* Underneath it all Blanton, Ellington, Fred Guy, and the consistently underrated Sonny Greer churned away, supplying the propulsive rhythmic impetus that turned every up-tempo tune into a stampede.

---

* "Cotton Tail" is solely credited to Ellington, but Webster is thought to have both composed the tune and arranged the equally celebrated *soli* chorus played by the saxophone section, which he wrote during his tenure with Teddy Wilson's band.

The only members of the Blanton-Webster band whom the public did not view as stars in their own right were Fred Guy, Otto Hardwick, Wallace Jones, and Herb Jeffries, Ellington's new male singer. While Jeffries had worked with Earl Hines, it was his brief film career that was his main claim to fame when he joined Ellington. On tour with Hines in the Deep South, he saw "hundreds of tin-roofed theaters, segregated for blacks only. They played white cowboy pictures because there were no black cowboys in the movies. . . . I felt that we could do better, that we could provide heroes for youngsters." When he came to Los Angeles, he seized the opportunity to star in a series of all-black singing westerns in the style of the "horse operas" of Gene Autry. The first, released in 1938, was *Harlem on the Prairie,* billed as "A Gene Autry Epic Under Cork," followed by three sequels, one of which, *The Bronze Buckaroo,* gave Jeffries his nickname. Today these films, which were shot on the lowest of budgets, look laughably inept, but in the late thirties they were more than popular enough with black audiences to make him a decent catch for Ellington. As yet unformed as a vocalist, he found his niche when Ellington and Strayhorn heard him imitate Bing Crosby one day. "That's it! Don't go any further. Just stay on Bing," they told him, and he developed into a "black Crosby" whose croony singing pleased his boss but sat somewhat uncomfortably alongside Ivie Anderson's tart style.

The Ellington band was now so cohesive a performing unit that it even managed to survive the loss of one of its most illustrious veterans. In November Cootie Williams went to work for Benny Goodman, performing with the Goodman sextet and playing featured solos with the full band. As Williams remembered it, Ellington took the news calmly, telling him, "Well, go ahead on. You've got a chance to make some money. And make a name for yourself." He even negotiated Williams's contract with Goodman, getting the trumpeter $200 a week (a whopping $168,000 a year in today's dollars). It was whispered among Ellington's sidemen, however, that Williams decided to leave the band when he asked for and failed to get a raise. According to Rex Stewart, "All white musicians in name bands earned more than we did and Cootie would move into the white pay schedule with Benny Goodman. Nevertheless, I especially prayed that Coots and Duke would come to terms, especially as we had heard that the amount involved was only 25 dollars a week."*

---

* Stewart also claimed that Ellington refused to pay Johnny Hodges extra for doubling on soprano saxophone, causing Hodges to stop playing the instrument with the band in 1941. Hodges, however, denied it: "I gave it up when Cootie Williams left the band. . . . I started having a lot of alto solos to play, and I figured they were responsibility enough."

Williams remembered it differently. "Duke knew about it, and helped set everything up," he later said. "He got me more money, and I told him I'd be back in one year's time. . . . If Duke didn't want it to be known like it was, it wasn't my place to tell. But that Goodman band—I loved it. It had a beat and there was something there that I wanted to play with." In addition, the orderly Williams had grown tired of his colleagues' lack of discipline. Sonny Greer, he said, would "get drunk and fall off the drums and things like that. That was no good for me." And he admired Goodman for the lack of racial prejudice that led him to hire Lionel Hampton, Teddy Wilson, and (later) Charlie Christian, making him the first white leader of a racially integrated big band: "He's just Goodman, not one way with this man and another way with someone else. The same with everyone. I think I was happier in music the first year I was with him than I ever was."

Whatever his reason, Williams's decision flummoxed jazz fans everywhere. Not only was it still rare in 1940 for black instrumentalists to work with white groups, but Williams, who had been with Ellington for more than a decade, was seen as an indispensable cog in the band's machinery, a supremely versatile artist who played plunger solos and gleaming lead-trumpet parts with interchangeable ease. Raymond Scott, the eccentrically innovative composer of "Powerhouse" and "Dinner Music for a Pack of Hungry Cannibals," marked the occasion by recording a lament called "When Cootie Left the Duke," while *Down Beat* reported that Williams "was almost in tears" on his last night with the band. But Ellington, distressed though he was by losing so valued an old hand, had no intention of being thrown off his stride. No sooner did Williams give his notice than Ellington found a replacement who, if he was not quite equal as a soloist to his predecessor, would bring something to the band that the sober-sided Williams never even tried to supply.

"Raymond? He has perfect taste." That was how Ellington described Ray Nance, a classically trained musician who also sang, danced, and played the violin exceptionally well, having taken up the instrument at the age of nine. Born in Chicago in 1913, he played trumpet for Earl Hines and Horace Henderson before joining Ellington. A short, ebullient extrovert who loved to cut up onstage so much that he acquired the nickname "Floorshow," Nance was something of a cross between Williams and Freddie Jenkins, a fine soloist who also knew the value of showmanship. Like Williams, he was not a growl player, but he soon mastered the skill, and he proved his worth as a soloist on the first recording of "Take the 'A' Train," to which he contributed an incisive two-chorus solo (the first muted, the second open) that became an integral part of Ellington's later performances of the song. The critics turned up their noses at Nance. Harry Lim dismissed him in *Down Beat* as "a kid that [*sic*] has a lot of showmanship . . . but who just doesn't meet the standard required by a band of Duke's calibre." But the public loved him, so much so that his name soon began to be featured in newspaper ads alongside those of Hodges, Stewart, and whoever happened to be singing with the band. In time Nance fell victim to narcotics, and in his later years he was said to subsist on "a diet of heroin and whiskey." But in 1940 he was still young, strong, and dedicated to his new boss, and Ellington used his multiple talents wisely and well, turning what could have been a disaster into an opportunity.

Nance replaced Williams a few days before the band arrived in Fargo, North Dakota, to play a dance at the Crystal Ballroom. Jack Towers and Dick Burris, a pair of talented young engineers, received permission from Ellington to record the event on a portable disc cutter, and the result is the first fully

Part of the Blanton-Webster band, photographed by William Gottlieb. From left: Ray Nance, Wallace Jones, Sonny Greer, Rex Stewart, Harry Carney, Otto Hardwick, Ben Webster, and Barney Bigard. (Not pictured are Ivie Anderson, Lawrence Brown, Fred Guy, Johnny Hodges, Herb Jeffries, Tricky Sam Nanton, and Juan Tizol.) This incomparable ensemble inspired Duke Ellington to compose such miniature masterpieces as "Cotton Tail," "Harlem Air-Shaft," "Jack the Bear," "Ko-Ko," "Never No Lament," and "Warm Valley"

representative document of what the Ellington band sounded like in live performance. Not only is the sheer forcefulness of the playing astonishing—Greer in particular sounds like a different drummer—but the lustrous sound is closely similar in quality to what Victor's engineers were capturing in the studio. Also present was Daniel Halperin, a local fan who left behind this description of how Ellington's men looked while getting ready to play a gig:

> *Slowly they drifted in. Wallace Jones smiling, Lawrence Brown sophisticated and mean, Rex Stewart blowing strange noises on his shining cornet as he walked toward his seat, Otto Hardwick adjusting the support strap round his neck, Fred Guy disdainful in a shy way. Just then Carney stood up, looked around him, began to tap his foot and suddenly, without any warning whatsoever, the orchestra burst into full cry. . . . I felt cheated by the records to which we had been listening for so many months. They were nothing like this.*

Ellington's men were notorious for playing poorly on the bandstand when they were tired or hungover or, as was often the case, simply didn't give a damn on a particular evening. Their harassed leader, who once likened his job to "what the scientists do in a mental institution," resigned himself to the inevitability of bad nights, knowing (as did his musicians) that they soon would be followed by good ones. "I live for the nights that this band is great," he told a member who was mystified by its inconsistency. "I don't worry about the nights like what you're worrying about. If you pay attention to these people they will drive you crazy. They're not going to drive me crazy." Fortunately for posterity, the Blanton-Webster band was at its very best at Fargo, and the proof of its transcendent greatness was preserved for all time.

11

"A MESSAGE FOR THE WORLD"

Jump for Joy, 1941–1942

ALWAYS CONSIDER my problems opportunities to do something," Duke Ellington told Ralph Gleason. "Like Jimmy Valentine or Houdini." At the beginning of 1941, a few weeks after Cootie Williams left the band, Ellington was confronted with another "opportunity," this one of an unusually nerve-racking kind. The American Society of Composers and Publishers, America's largest musical performing-rights organization, was determined to extract more money from the radio networks for the privilege of airing songs written by its members, on whose behalf ASCAP collected and distributed performing-rights fees. The networks responded by setting up a competing organization called Broadcast Music Incorporated (BMI). At BMI's behest, the networks stopped airing ASCAP-registered songs. That amounted to some 1,250,000 songs, including nearly all of the top hits of 1940. The boycott went into effect on January 1, forcing bands that performed on the radio to play either BMI-controlled or public-domain songs during their programs. Soon every bandleader was frantically commissioning arrangements of nineteenth-century ballads (the most frequently aired of which was Stephen Foster's "Jeanie with the Light Brown Hair") and unknown tunes by BMI songwriters.

Two days after the boycott went into effect, Ellington and his men began a seven-week stand at the Casa Mañana, a popular nightclub not far from the MGM studios that had a broadcast wire, and its leader was caught flat-footed. From the time that Irving Mills took over the management of the band in 1927, it had specialized in the music of Duke Ellington—and he had been a member of ASCAP since 1935. That was where Billy Strayhorn came in. "When we opened . . . we had air time every night, but could not play our library," he recalled. "We had to play non-ASCAP material. Duke was in ASCAP, but I wasn't. So we had to write a new library." Strayhorn, however, was still finding his footing: Ellington had only recorded three of his full-band arrangements in 1940, and none was of an original composition. Though his versions of "Chloë," a twenties ballad that he had adapted from a stock arrangement, and "Flamingo," a brand-new pop tune sung by Herb Jeffries, were dazzling, they were mere drops in an empty bucket that had to be filled as quickly as possible.

Ellington thereupon proceeded to pull a rabbit out of his hat, advising the press that his son would be joining the band. "After spending $8,000 for a musical education for my son I will now have a chance to realize the returns," he said. "Mercer will sit at my right hand during 1941 and write compositions under his own name. He'll do much arranging as well as composing." It sounded believable enough, and it was true that Mercer, a classically trained musician who had studied at the Juilliard School with William Vacchiano, the longtime principal trumpeter of the New York Philharmonic, aspired to write for his father's band. Nor did he need to be told twice what had fallen into his and Strayhorn's laps: "Overnight, literally, we got a chance to write a whole new book for the band. It could have taken us twenty years to get the old man to make room for that much of our music, but all of a sudden we had this freak opportunity. He needed us to write music, and it had to be in our names." But Mercer was even less seasoned than Strayhorn. He had written as yet only one piece of music that the old man had been willing to record, a formulaic school-of-Ellington instrumental called "Pigeons and Peppers" that was cut by a Cootie Williams–led small group in 1937, seven months after Mercer's eighteenth birthday. Nevertheless, Ellington had no choice but to rely on his son and his protégé, who holed up together in a hotel room, chugged blackberry wine and chain-smoked, and turned out charts as fast as they could.

A month after the ASCAP boycott went into effect, Ellington took the band into a Hollywood studio and recorded five new compositions by Strayhorn and Mercer. The first one was a brisk, engagingly tuneful swing number that Strayhorn had previously scrapped, believing that it sounded too much like one of Fletcher Henderson's charts to pass muster. Mercer thought otherwise, and "Take the 'A' Train" went straight into the book, together with a puckish riff tune called "John Hardy's Wife" and "After All," a ballad whose melody was intoned by Lawrence Brown's trombone. Mercer's contributions were "Blue Serge," a midnight-black orchestral study to which Ben Webster contributed one of his most impassioned solos, and "Jumpin' Punkins," a carefree medium-tempo feature for Sonny Greer that bore Duke's stamp on every page. Later that year the band cut Mercer's "Moon Mist," a slowly swaying, pastel-colored ballad in which Ray Nance's sweet-toned violin playing was heard to sumptuous effect.

It was no coincidence that all of the pieces that Mercer produced during this time sounded as though his father had composed them, for they were written under Ellington's close supervision: "He'd set problems for me, scratch out what he thought was in poor taste, and preset harmonies for me to write melodies against." Strayhorn, by contrast, needed no hand-holding from Ellington, who promptly made "Take the 'A' Train" the band's new theme song. Over the next few months he continued to write and arrange pieces that were

"Every note of music, every lyric, meant something": A souvenir program for *Jump for Joy,* Ellington's first stage musical, which opened in Los Angeles in 1941. The all-black, socially conscious revue delighted West Coast audiences but never made it to Broadway

recorded as soon as the copyist's ink was dry. Among other things, Hodges cut combo versions of "Day Dream" and "Passion Flower," Barney Bigard recorded a similar tune called "Noir Blue," and the full band weighed in with "Chelsea Bridge," a Ravel-influenced nocturne inspired, Strayhorn said, by James McNeill Whistler's *Nocturne: Blue and Gold—Old Battersea Bridge*. By the time that ASCAP agreed to cut its fees, bringing the boycott to an end, Strayhorn was solidly established as a composer of consequence. Even after Ellington's own music returned to the airwaves, "Take the 'A' Train" remained his theme song, and the band would play it at least once a night for the rest of his life.

∾

While Ellington's two "yearlings," as he liked to call them, were courting writer's cramp by creating a new book of arrangements for him to play on the air, he was otherwise occupied. In February he took to the pulpit of Los Angeles's Scott Methodist Church to deliver a secular sermon in honor of the local black community's annual Lincoln Day services. The title of his remarks was "We, Too, Sing 'America,'" an allusion to Langston Hughes's poem "I, Too, Sing America," and what he had to say was both proud and eloquent:

> *I contend that the Negro is the creative voice of America, is creative America, and it was a happy day in America when the first unhappy slave was landed on its shores. . . . We—this kicking, yelling, touchy, sensitive, scrupulously demanding minority—are the personification of the ideal begun by the Pilgrims almost 350 years ago.*

Five months later he put that pride onstage when *Jump for Joy: A Sun-Tanned Revu-sical,* his first full-length stage show, opened at the Mayan Theatre in Los Angeles. Ellington had often spoken of his longing to write a Broadway musical, and though he had composed the music for two Cotton Club revues, *Jump for Joy* was a show of a different color, an all-black revue whose goal, he said, was "to give an American audience entertainment without compromising the dignity of the Negro people. . . . The American audience has been taught to expect a Negro on the stage to clown and 'Uncle Tom,' that is, to enact the role of a servile, yet lovable, inferior." He had spent too many nights playing for rich whites at the Cotton Club to settle for less, but in 1941 it was daring for a black man even to consider such an undertaking, and it stands to reason that *Jump for Joy* should have been the brainchild of an unusual cast of characters.

The sparkplug for the show was Sid Kuller, a second-string Hollywood gagman and part-time lyricist who had written special material for movies by the Ritz Brothers and was currently at work on *The Big Store,* a Marx Brothers film. A jazz buff, Kuller heard Ellington at the Casa Mañana and invited him to hold weekend jam sessions at his house in Hollywood. One night the writer came home late from the studio. "Hey, this joint sure is jumpin'!" he said. "Jumpin' for joy," Ellington replied. Kuller then suggested that they should collaborate on a stage revue called *Jump for Joy,* and raised twenty thousand dollars on the spot from the Hollywood personages who were present. "Count me in," said John Garfield, a stage actor who in 1941 was turning himself into a well-paid silver-screen tough guy. In due course he became one of the principal investors in and de facto producers of *Jump for Joy.*

It is a lovely tale, one that Kuller would repeat to interviewers for the next half century. But the backstory of *Jump for Joy* was more complicated than he let on. Years later he casually referred to the show's backers as "the leftist Hollywood crowd." He spoke more truly than most jazz historians know. In addition to writing jokes by the bushel, he had worked on *Meet the People,* a revue that had run for 160 performances on Broadway in 1940. *Meet the People* was cut from the same political cloth as Marc Blitzstein's *The Cradle Will Rock* and Harold Rome's *Pins and Needles,* the most successful of the many left-wing musical revues and straight plays that grew out of the WPA's Federal Theatre Project.* Both shows figure prominently in the history of the Popular Front, the "anti-fascist" alliance through which agents of the Soviet Union sought to infiltrate and co-opt liberal groups in America and Europe in order (among other things) to manipulate public opinion by fostering the emergence of a "progressive," Communist-friendly middlebrow culture. To speak of American culture in the thirties and forties is in large part to speak of the Popular Front and its adherents, both witting and unwitting. The plays of Lillian Hellman and Clifford Odets, the novels of John Steinbeck, the Western-themed ballet scores of Aaron Copland, the prolabor shows of Blitzstein and Rome: All were in their varying ways exercises in Popular Front–style cultural populism, and the makers of *Jump for Joy* meant to follow in their footsteps.

The success of *Pins and Needles* on Broadway inspired a group of Hollywood-based writers, among them Dashiell Hammett, Lillian Hellman,

---

* *Pins and Needles,* which ran for 1,108 performances on Broadway, was so beloved of the American left that Michael Straight, a wealthy American student at Cambridge University who later became a Russian spy, taught its best-remembered song to his Communist friends in England: "Sing me a song of social significance / There's nothing else that will do."

Langston Hughes, and Ira Gershwin, to launch the Hollywood Theatre Alliance, whose purpose was to mount similar shows in Los Angeles. The HTA first tried to produce a "Negro Revue" whose book would be cowritten by Hughes and Donald Ogden Stewart, author of the screenplay for *The Philadelphia Story*. When that venture fell through, Kuller approached Ellington, who was involved in preliminary discussions with the group, about writing a similar show. Ellington and the HTA then joined forces to start another group called the American Revue Theatre, under whose auspices *Jump for Joy* was produced. It was no secret that the HTA, like other such organizations in Los Angeles and New York, was full of Communists—including Hammett, Hellman, and Stewart—and the House Un-American Activities Committee would later describe it as a "Communist-front organization." True or not, many of the members of "the leftist Hollywood crowd" who were involved in the creation of *Jump for Joy* were card-carrying Communists and fellow travelers (like John Garfield) whose goal was to advance the agenda of the Popular Front by creating a black counterpart of *Pins and Needles*.

How widely was this understood at the time? The local black press was either ignorant of the Communist tint of the show's creative team or preferred to downplay it. A columnist for the *California Eagle*, for instance, reported in February that "Jno. Garfield, who because he's always been interested in interracialism is dubbed 'radical,' is a frequent Casa Mañana visitor. He likes Ellingtonia." And while the Popular Front had long taken an interest in black jazz, there is no reason to suppose that Ellington was aware of its activities in anything more than the most general way. It is well within the realm of probability that he did not fully grasp the extent to which the HTA was Communist-dominated. In his only known statement on the subject, made in a 1971 interview, he told Stanley Dance that his "social[ly] conscious" friends in Hollywood included "a lot of those intellectuals— some of them were labeled Communists." It's true, too, that Ellington was also peripherally involved in other Popular Front undertakings throughout the thirties and forties. He endorsed, for instance, the reelection of Franklin Roosevelt to a fourth term in a strident full-page ad that was placed in *The New York Times* by the Independent Voters Committee of the Arts and Sciences, a Communist-controlled Popular Front group specifically organized to win the support of high-profile liberals. (His fellow signers included Marian Anderson, Tallulah Bankhead, Thomas Hart Benton, Albert Einstein, Helen Keller, Carl Sandburg, and Orson Welles.)

But all who knew Ellington well agreed that he was never a political animal. He appeared regularly at NAACP benefits, and Irving Mills had long despaired at his open-handed contributions to black charities: "Whatever town he went to, there were people on his back for donations, and he helped everybody. He spent more money than he was making." The civil-rights movement, however, was the only cause in which he took a sustained interest. "I've never been interested in politics in my whole life, and don't pretend to know anything about international affairs," he wrote in 1950. In private, Mercer Ellington said, he was outspoken about his detestation of Communism:

> *When something bad happened on the international level, he often saw the handiwork of people in powerful positions, communists, financiers, or both. While he believed that communists worked ceaselessly to overthrow the power of the United States, he also held that capitalists worked exclusively for personal gain. The impact of their machinations on the society he lived in truly disturbed him.*

It's that his postwar anti-Communist statements were made in order to cover his prewar tracks. Ellington, like many other blacks, appreciated the Communist Party's stance against racism, and his sentiments were widely shared in Harlem. As early as 1933, Adam Clayton Powell Jr. had proclaimed, "I don't mind being called a Communist . . . the day will come when being called a Communist will be the highest honor that can be paid an individual and that day is coming soon." Ellington himself would actively support the candidacy of Benjamin J. Davis Jr., who ran for New York's city council on the Communist ticket in 1943. But like most blacks of his generation, he was also a longtime Republican for whom the party of FDR was also the party of southern segregation, and if he had ever harbored genuine Communist sympathies, it's inconceivable that he would have smeared John Hammond in 1939 for the producer's alleged Communist ties. In any case, Ellington's Federal Bureau of Investigation file shows that the bureau took only a cursory interest in him. The thirty-five-page file, opened in 1953, consists exclusively of responses to background checks by other government agencies, all of which recycle the same list of associations with known and alleged Communist fronts, most of them active promoters of civil rights and, during World War II, Russian war relief. Perhaps J. Edgar Hoover thought otherwise, but nothing in Ellington's file indicates that he was other than what he said he was, a largely apolitical black artist of liberal inclination who, like most liberal artists of the thirties and forties, knew his fair share of fellow travelers.

It's no surprise, then, that Ellington was ready and willing to collaborate with a group of hard-left Hollywood artists and writers "whose sympathies fitted into my scene and scheme" to create a pro-black musical, just as they themselves were happy to collaborate with one of America's most admired jazzmen. For him, the point of the association was that he wholeheartedly approved of the concept of *Jump for Joy*, which he described as "an all-Negro show with a social-significance theme. . . . Everything, every setting, every note of music, every lyric, meant something. All the sketches had a message for the world." He was also drawn to the idea of collaborating with Sid Kuller, who understood (or thought he did) how hard it would be for a team of white writers to turn out comedy sketches about black life and was prepared to work overtime to fill in the gaps in his grasp of black culture. "Traditionally, black humor had been portrayed by blacks for white audiences from a white point of view," Kuller later told an interviewer. "Our material was from the point of view of black people looking at whites." And Ellington himself knew that *Jump for Joy* would need to make its political points with the lightest of touches in order to go over with a mass audience, which explains why he was open to working with a comedy writer: "We included everything we wanted to say without saying it. . . . Just to come out on the stage and take a soap box and stand in the spotlight and say ugly things is not entertainment."

He was no less eager to ensure that *Jump for Joy* would steer clear of the racial stereotypes with which long experience had made him all too familiar. "I am a Negro," he told a black reporter in 1941. "Brag about it every day." The last thing he wanted to do was write a show that was any less prideful, and having spent years playing for the Cotton Club's high-yellow chorus line, he adamantly refused to bow to pressure from the producers to make the performers in the show look uniformly and artificially "black." At one point John Garfield dared to suggest to the light-skinned Herb Jeffries that he should wear makeup to darken his skin. "You don't seem to fit the right shade," Garfield said, and Jeffries complied, blacking up in his dressing room for that night's performance. When he came onstage, Ellington was enraged: "Ellington was looking at me like my zipper was open or something . . . when the first half of the show was over, he came flying backstage and said, 'What the hell are you doing, Al Jolson?'" The makeup was removed at once.

Everyone involved with *Jump for Joy*, in short, was on the same page, and

Ellington and his collaborators had put together an impressive cast and production team. In addition to Ivie Anderson, Herb Jeffries, and the Ellington band, which played in the pit, the sixty-person cast included such black stage performers as Wonderful Smith, a carhop turned comedian who parlayed his appearance in the show into a high-profile job as Red Skelton's radio sidekick, and Marie Bryant, an adorably pug-faced singer-dancer who later became an assistant dance director at MGM and Columbia and is best remembered today for her appearance in Gjon Mili's 1944 jazz short *Jammin' the Blues*. (Asked what she did for a living, Bryant replied, "I teach Betty Grable to shake her buns.") Kuller and Hal Fimberg wrote or cowrote most of the sketches, assisted by a platoon of collaborators—Ellington claimed that *Jump for Joy* was written by fifteen different people—and Nick Castle, who was to make a name for himself as Twentieth Century-Fox's house choreographer, staged the musical numbers. The bill was topped by Dorothy Dandridge, who won brief fame in 1951 as the drop-dead-gorgeous star of *Carmen Jones*. She was still a teenage starlet in 1940, but her looks were already impressive: Jeffries later described Dandridge as "the most beautiful woman I had ever seen in my life. By all standards."

The fly in the ointment was that Ellington had no intention of allowing the writing of the score to interfere with his other professional and personal pursuits. Instead of working face-to-face with Kuller and Paul Francis Webster, the show's principal lyricist, he wrote tunes wherever he happened to be at any given moment, then called his colleagues up and played the results to them over the phone. Not only did he have no taste for the disciplined work that goes into the making of a musical, but his ambitions were in irreconcilable conflict with his schedule. In a pattern of behavior that would become familiar to his future theatrical collaborators, he finessed the issue by putting off serious work until the eleventh hour, at which time Henry Blankfort, the production supervisor of *Jump for Joy*, came to his hotel to beg the great man to get down to business before it was too late:

> *Duke was in the bathtub. Beside him was a stack of manuscript paper, a huge container of chocolate ice cream, a glass of scotch and milk, and Jonesy. Jonesy was his valet, and his job was to keep adding warm water and let out cooling water to maintain a constant temperature in the tub for the Maestro. And Duke was serenely scribbling notes on the paper and then calling to Billy Strayhorn. Billy would take the notes and play them on the beat-up old upright piano in Duke's room. Duke would listen and then write more notes . . . and about four or five hours later, two more songs for the show were finished.*

Somehow the score got written, and when *Jump for Joy* opened, Ellington and the producers were sure that their show was destined for Broadway. "We had a national tour all planned—leading to an open run in New York," Kuller said. Ellington recalled the mostly black first-nighters as enthusiastic, in part because none of them had ever seen a musical that, like *Jump for Joy,* sought to show them as they were and tell the world how they felt: "As the audience screamed and applauded, comedians came off stage smiling, and with tears running down their cheeks. They couldn't believe it."

The critics saw it differently. Nearly everybody praised Ellington and his band, and a few reviews were entirely favorable, including Ed Schallert's notice in the *Los Angeles Times:* "Duke Ellington and his orchestra, heading a group of star singers and dancers, brought zest and class to the musical revue 'Jump for Joy' last night." But most were freighted with qualifications, above all the make-or-break notice in *Variety,* whose unequivocal support would be needed if *Jump for Joy* were to have any chance of transferring to New York: "Main trouble with 'Jump with [*sic*] Joy' is that it doesn't jump. Rather, and more to the point, it lags . . . skits and blackouts are, for the most part, pointless and not too funny. . . . Mebbe the piece can be tightened and whipped into acceptable form, but the chances are against it." Even the black reviewers disliked the sketches. Almena Davis, who wrote about the show for the *Los Angeles Tribune,* believed that "a good part of the trouble" with *Jump for Joy* lay in the fact that Kuller and Fimberg were white: "To paraphrase a line from 'Jesse James,' we will never have a good colored theatre until we take all the 'grey' [i.e., white] writers out and 'shoot 'em down like dogs,' having first developed some good colored writers to fill their places."

The creative team responded by rewriting *Jump for Joy,* not just once but repeatedly. "The show was never the same, because every night after the final curtain we had a meeting up in the office," Ellington remembered. "All fifteen writers would be present whenever possible, and we would discuss, debate, and make decisions as to what should come out of the show the next night." When Dorothy Dandridge dropped out early in the run, he sent for Big Joe Turner, wrote him into the show to enhance its firepower, and gave him "Rocks in My Bed" to sing. Through it all the crowds kept coming, and according to Ellington, they liked what they saw: "The Negroes always left proudly, with their chests sticking out." But even a fan like George T. Simon acknowledged his doubts about the show when he reviewed it for *Metronome:*

Duke Ellington's band was supposed to be the featured attraction, but it spent its time down in the pit, struggling through enticing, but intricate, accompaniments. And no matter how hard you try, you can't make a feature of a pit band . . . the revue, as a whole, lacked the spontaneity that you'll find in vaudeville acts such as those at the Apollo in Harlem.

The box-office grosses kept on sagging, and *Jump for Joy* closed in September after eleven weeks and 101 performances. It reopened in November for a weeklong run, after which Ellington briefly incorporated a vest-pocket version into his traveling stage show, but never made it to New York. The only attempt to revive *Jump for Joy* in his lifetime, a 1959 production in Miami Beach, lost its backers $100,000. After that the show went unseen until the surviving sketches and musical numbers were reconstructed forty years later for a noncommercial Chicago production.

Ellington believed, as did his collaborators, that *Jump for Joy* flopped because it was ahead of its time, and it is now generally regarded as (in Gary Giddins's words) "a milestone in Ellington's career and a benchmark in American theater." Indeed, it has come to be taken as an article of faith that the show was a critical and commercial failure not through any fault of its own but because white audiences were unprepared to embrace a musical that presented blacks as real people, not shiftless louts. That may well be true, but there is also reason to think that the critics were at least partly right. Because so few of the sketches are extant, it is no longer possible to speak authoritatively about their overall quality. Given the fact that none of the show's principal authors are known to have written anything else of lasting interest, though, it seems likely that they were at least as uneven as the reviews indicate.

Fortunately, several of the songs were recorded by the Ellington band, and one of the dance numbers, "Bli-Blip," was commercially filmed after *Jump for Joy* closed, allowing us to see Marie Bryant and Paul White, her dance partner, in action. Their performance is delightful, as are Ivie Anderson's 1941 recordings of "I Got It Bad (And That Ain't Good)" and "Rocks in My Bed," the only two songs from *Jump for Joy* that are still regularly performed today. Both are superior, and "I Got It Bad," a poignant lament for lost love, would become one of Johnny Hodges's best-remembered ballad features. Joe Turner also cut a no-nonsense combo-backed version of "Rocks in My Bed" for Decca that hints at what his stage performance may have been like, while a silent film shot by friends of the cast shows that the versions of some of the other songs that were recorded by Ellington for Victor match the stage action of the show closely.

What else can we learn from this cache of evidence, as well as the lyrics of the songs that went unrecorded? Except for "Bli-Blip," "I Got It Bad," and

"Rocks in My Bed," it appears that most of the vocal numbers were both musically lackluster and lyrically heavy-handed. The latter conclusion will surprise no one familiar with *The Cradle Will Rock* and *Pins and Needles*. For all Ellington's determination to say everything he wanted to say "without saying it," his collaborators were even more determined to pound home their antiracist message. On occasion the results are witty enough, as in "Sun-Tanned Tenth of the Nation," the show's opening number, which began with a rhyming prologue that was spoken from the pit by Ellington himself: "The punch that should be present in a colored show alas is / Disinfected with Magnolia and dripping with Molasses; / In other words: we're shown to you thru Stephen Foster's glasses." Considerably less deft, however, is the title song, whose lyric celebrated the death of Uncle Tom: "All the hounds, I do believe, / Have been killed, ain't you thrilled." Worse still is the ham-fisted "I've Got a Passport from Georgia," in which Paul White sang of his longing to flee the south for a place "where the signs read, 'OUT TO LUNCH,' not, 'OUT TO LYNCH.'"

Such sentiments were very much to the point in 1941. "I've Got a Passport from Georgia" actually had to be cut from the show after White received threatening calls from people claiming to belong to the Ku Klux Klan. But good intentions and good art are not the same thing, and the incongruity in tone between Ellington's swinging score and the sandwich-board oratory of his Popular Front collaborators may well have had something to do with the show's failure to thrive. It didn't help that so many different people were putting in oars. "We had too many chefs," said Herb Jeffries. "I think at that time we had maybe seven different people who were financing the show . . . there was trouble and arguments." Factor in Ellington's reluctance to concentrate on the writing of the score and you have a recipe for turmoil.

Even those who loved the show understood that it was not all that it could have been. Norman Granz, who saw it several times, offered what appears to be the most clear-eyed appraisal of what went wrong with *Jump for Joy:*

> It didn't do very well at the beginning and so they brought Joe Turner in. So before Joe Turner, it was one Jump for Joy, *and after it was another* Jump for Joy. *And I don't know that Joe made all that much difference to the public, because inevitably the show did not work economically. . . . I would not have thought immediately that* Jump for Joy *made a social contribution. If you ask me about it now, I would say that it did. But I'm not so sure that it did have the impact that they had hoped that it might have initially, because the people that went to see the show already felt that way.*

Ellington spoke proudly of *Jump for Joy* for the rest of his life, and he never stopped grieving over its failure to move to Broadway. "That killed me," he told a friend. Five years later he took another run at the Great White Way, but once more he fumbled the ball, sabotaged yet again by his unwillingness to make the sacrifice of time and energy needed to turn a clever idea into a fully realized show. It would not be the last time that Daisy Ellington's pampered son ran afoul of the gods of the copybook headings.

One good thing that Ellington got out of *Jump for Joy* was the friendship of Orson Welles, who came to a performance with Dolores del Rio, his glamorous girlfriend of the moment, in tow. He sent a message backstage inviting Ellington to drop by his office at RKO the next morning to chat about making a film. Curious as to what the creator of *Citizen Kane* might have up his sleeve, Ellington showed up as requested and found himself in the presence of a human whirlwind. After offering to restage *Jump for Joy* and explaining in detail how he would have rewritten it, Welles changed the subject. "I want to do the history of jazz as a picture, and we'll call it *It's All True,*" he said. "I want it to be written by Duke Ellington and Orson Welles, directed by Duke Ellington and Orson Welles, music written by Duke Ellington. . . . You can start work today! You get $1,500 a week. Now there it is and if you don't take it you're a fool."

Ellington succumbed on the spot, and the red carpet was rolled out: "A lot of research people were hired. I had fifteen million assistants, people of great significance in the literary field, and all that sort of thing. And Duke Ellington was the Number One everything in every department." He had no idea that *It's All True* was one of the biggest white elephants ever to charge through the streets of Hollywood, a multipart fictionalized quasidocumentary about whatever happened to interest Welles at the time. Since RKO's executives had yet to figure out that the wonder boy of Hollywood was incapable of staying within a budget, they were willing to do whatever he wanted, and what he wanted at the moment was for Ellington to score a segment of *It's All True* starring Louis Armstrong. Elliot Paul was working on a script based on *Swing That Music,* Armstrong's autobiography. Once the press got wind of the possibility of an Armstrong-Ellington-Welles film, the great engine of publicity began to rumble, hiss, and spew out copy.

The two men soon forged a long-lasting mutual admiration society. Welles, in fact, is reported to have said that Ellington was the only genius he had ever known, save for himself. While this "quote" has the smell of press agentry, it is clear that each man spotted in the other a kindred spirit. Both were spoiled children who in adulthood took for granted that the rest of the world should and would accommodate their needs. Both had unlimited appetites for food and sex. Both knew how to spur their collaborators to unprecedented heights of inspiration—and would, if left to their own devices, take credit for everything those collaborators did. As well as being artists of the first rank, they were natural-born editors who were made to head up the kind of collective enterprise in which it is taken for granted that the job of the man at the top is to fuse the joint efforts of his underlings into a coherent whole, after which he "signs" the results himself. While the word *auteur* is not part of the vocabulary of jazz, it could just as easily have been coined to describe Duke Ellington as Orson Welles.

It's hard to imagine how two such men could have successfully worked together, but their ability to do so was never put to the test. Welles was a man of violent but transient enthusiasms, and after he flew to Brazil in February to hurl himself into one of the other panels of *It's All True*, an account of Rio de Janeiro's annual carnival, "The Story of Jazz" was put on hold. Soon thereafter RKO figured out that Welles couldn't be trusted with a checkbook, and Ellington's employment was terminated: "I think I wrote 28 bars, a trumpet solo by Buddy Bolden which, of course, was to be a symbol of the jazz.* It was very good, but Orson never heard it, and I can't find it. I don't know where it is. It was the only thing I ever wrote for the $12,500 I got."

The demise of *It's All True* and the closing of *Jump for Joy* were not the worst disappointments that Ellington suffered in 1941. Not long after *Jump for Joy* closed, tuberculosis finally felled Jimmie Blanton. Ellington "called doctor after doctor until [he] found out who the top people on TB were in Los Angeles," then checked him into Los Angeles General Hospital. He was moved from there to a sanitarium near Pasadena, where the doctors decided that his case was hopeless. Jimmy Rowles recalled that the only decoration on the white walls of his tiny room was a picture of Ben Webster. The band left Los Angeles in December, leaving Blanton behind to await his fate. He was "replaced" by the talented Alvin "Junior" Raglin, a San Francisco–area bassist, but Blanton, as everyone knew, was irreplaceable.

Blanton died in July of 1942, by which time Herb Jeffries and Barney Bigard had also left the band. Bigard's departure was particularly hard, for he had been with Ellington ever since the band had taken the Cotton Club

---

* Bolden, one of the legendary figures of early New Orleans jazz, would later figure in another of Ellington's extended works, the 1957 TV special *A Drum Is a Woman*.

by storm. The clarinetist still loved playing with Ellington, but he was tired of the demands of the road, which had grown still more demanding after Pearl Harbor:

> *Silly things like sleeping bad, eating bad, traveling in crowded trains, couldn't get cabs when you needed them. . . . We used to have such bad accommodations on account they took the pullmans [i.e., the band's private Pullman cars] away for the war effort. We traveled on the regular trains and it seemed like the whole country was on the move to someplace or another. The trains were always packed and jammed and lots of times we had to sit in the aisles.*

Bigard was struck by the coolness with which his old colleague received his notice. "When I told him I was leaving he just looked at me and didn't say a word," he wrote in his autobiography. Nor did Ellington have much more to say to reporters who asked him how he felt. " 'He's just leaving. That's all,' said Duke irritably, when asked for comment," *Down Beat* reported. And the exodus was not yet complete: Ivie Anderson quit a month after Blanton's death, going back to Los Angeles to run Ivie's Chicken Shack, a restaurant that she had recently opened. The asthma from which Anderson had long suffered is usually given as the reason for her departure, though she said in a radio interview that she, too, was tired of the road, and Lawrence Brown heard that she quit when Ellington declined to give her a raise.

Life went on, just as it had when Cootie Williams defected to Benny Goodman's band. Not even the coming of World War II, in which Ellington was too old to serve, wrought any immediate changes in his routine. But he was already demoralized by the fate of *Jump for Joy*, and he must have known that the near-simultaneous loss of Anderson, Bigard, and Blanton was an unsparing blow to the sonic identity of the ensemble that had spurred him to his greatest musical achievements. It makes sense that he was too upset by the loss of Bigard to want to talk about it. He knew that whatever triumphs the future held in store, Duke Ellington and His Famous Orchestra would never be again as they were.

12

"I DON'T WRITE JAZZ"

Carnegie Hall, 1942–1946

B ARNEY BIGARD MADE his last recordings with the Ellington band on June 26, 1942. He was replaced by Chauncey Haughton, a now-forgotten tenor saxophonist who doubled on clarinet and had worked with Cab Calloway and Chick Webb. It was the first time that Ellington accepted an inferior substitute for one of his prized soloists. Haughton's hiring was a sign of the dilemma that his new boss was facing. If the music of the Blanton-Webster band is best understood as the culmination of Duke Ellington's first twenty years of music-making, then he might have felt compelled to turn his back on its etched perfection. While he could have gone on writing flawless miniatures for as long as his inspiration held out, it was never his way to do the same thing over and over again. The failure of *Jump for Joy*, together with the fact that the instrument that he had so painstakingly assembled was starting to come apart, must have made him even less inclined to stick to his last. He would always crave new challenges, and now he embraced the biggest one of all, the challenge with which he had grappled with varying success for more than a decade: the problem of extended form.

Part of what pushed Ellington toward writing the multimovement piece about the black experience in America that he had been mulling over for more than a decade was his urgent need for publicity. On August 1, four days after

Ivie Anderson cut her last studio sides with the band, the American Federation of Musicians banned its members from making commercial recordings, claiming that they were being cheated by radio stations that played their records without paying royalties. The unreleased sides that Ellington had already made would be issued in dribs and drabs throughout the first part of the ban, but otherwise he and his musicians could only be heard in person, on radio, or on the wartime "V-Discs" that the AFM permitted Ellington and other artists to record for distribution to soldiers, sailors, and marines. Not until the end of 1944 would the band make another record for Victor.

The AFM strike shut off one of Ellington's most powerful engines of publicity, and because he had spent so much of the past two years in California, his East Coast profile was low. Hence, as he recalled it, the need to cause talk in New York: "William Morris says to me, 'What you need is a Carnegie Hall concert.' So I started whipping up material." The "material" was *Black, Brown and Beige,* on which he began work during a theater engagement in Hartford: "The light was not too good for writing music, and the movie they were showing was *The Cat Woman.* It was about a woman who used to change into a cat and do people in. Since I could see what was going on on the screen, it sometimes got pretty scary back there in the dark."

The starting point was a thirty-three-page typescript scenario titled *"Black, Brown and Beige* by Duke Ellington" that is an expanded version of an earlier, incomplete holograph scenario for *Boola,* his long-planned opera about black history. While neither scenario is dated, Ellington claimed as early as 1938 to have "completed" an opera, and in 1940 he began to refer to *Boola* by name in interviews. After *Jump for Joy* closed, he discussed the project with the classical music critic Alfred Frankenstein, who explained to the readers of the *San Francisco Chronicle* that while the opera was not yet done, "you gather that he could finish it if he wanted to in less time than it takes to run through a couple of choruses." Ellington told Frankenstein that "all arrangements of historic American Negro music have been made by conservatory-trained musicians who inevitably handle it with a European technique. It's time a big piece of music was written from the inside by a Negro." He then talked about *Boola* in detail, describing it in much the same way that he had described his unwritten *African Suite:*

> *"Boola," says Ellington, is the name Negro historians use to symbolize their race. "If they want to tell you that Negroes took part in this or that event," said Ellington, "they will say 'Boola was there.' My opera traces Boola's whole history in four scenes. The first scene is laid in Africa. . . .*

The second scene is Negro life in slave times, the third, Negro life in the period after the Civil war, and the fourth, Negro life today. There isn't any continuous plot, but there is one symbolic figure—Boola himself—who appears throughout."

Might he have written the *Boola* scenario around this time? His claims to have finished a piece could not be trusted until it was played in public—and sometimes not even then. Except for "Ko-Ko," which may or may not have come from the score for *Boola*, no part of the opera was ever performed or recorded. All that survives of it is the incomplete scenario. But Ellington also said in an interview published a week prior to the Carnegie Hall concert that he had "taken some of the music from [*Boola*] and turned it into a half-hour tone poem for his band," and he later told Barry Ulanov that *Boola* had "yielded much of the material" for *Black, Brown and Beige*. It's possible, though, that what he meant was that the scenario for *Black, Brown and Beige* was based on the *Boola* scenario, both of which contain indications for musical treatment: "A message . . . shot through the jungle by drums. BOOM! BOOM! BOOM! BOOM! Like a tom-tom in steady precision." The "Work Song" section is described in comparably evocative words as "not a song of great Joy—not a triumphant song—but a song of Burden—a song punctuated by the grunt of Heaving a pick or axe." Likewise "Come Sunday," which he envisioned as a portrait of a plantation church that slaves were not allowed to attend: "And now Come Sunday—that nice quiet little house with the steeple . . . the music was so sweet and tender even from that distance."

In June of 1943 *Variety* reported that Ellington was writing a book about *Black, Brown and Beige* in which "the story will be printed on the upper half of each page in the book, with the music related to each portion below on the same page . . . [He] feels that detailing the thoughts which motivated the work will help toward a better understanding of it." The text of the book would presumably have been based on the scenario, but outside of selected passages that were included in the liner notes for an album of excerpts from *Black, Brown and Beige* that was released by Victor in 1944, no part of it appeared in print during his lifetime. Had the scenario been published in its entirety, it might have been easier for critics to grasp the meaning of the piece, and to see how firmly rooted it was in the historical narrative that he was seeking to depict in music. In 1943 Ellington told an interviewer that he had assembled "a collection of 800 books on Negro history and prehistoric African art which he has read many times." While he liked on occasion to pretend to be better read than he was, the *Boola* and *Black, Brown and*

Beige scenarios demonstrate Ellington's wide knowledge of black history. They also suggest that he had undeveloped but nonetheless genuine talent as a writer:

> *A song eased the lash. The whip fell*
> *Less frequently across his weary back.*
> *Boola sang. His master smiled. His slaves*
> *Were happy. He complimented himself on*
> *His great philanthropy.*

What neither scenario does is shed light on the meaning of the work's ambiguous title. According to Mercer Ellington, it was meant to suggest the intraracial prejudice of which his light-skinned father was well aware: "*Black, Brown and Beige* was his criticism of his own race. And their prejudices within itself. There were these different castes: the black, the brown or tan ones and the ones light enough to pass for white. And yet they wanted, as a whole . . . recognition and equal rights and yet within themselves they restricted each other." But Ellington himself said in 1956 that the title of *Black, Brown and Beige* referred to "the [black] state of mind, not the color of the skin," going on to explain that the collective self-image of blacks in America mirrored their changing social and economic situation: "So gradually it got lighter . . . but it never got quite white." Either way, it says much about Duke Ellington that a status-conscious child of the black middle class should have chosen to draw so direct a parallel between self-image and skin tone in a work that celebrated the history of his race.

Six scant weeks after he started writing *Black, Brown and Beige,* Ellington stepped in front of a capacity crowd at Carnegie Hall and unveiled his grandest composition. The concert, a black-tie affair, was the climax of what the William Morris Agency had been promoting as "National Duke Ellington Week," and the advance publicity paid off. Betty Roché, who had replaced Ivie Anderson in September, was stunned to see so many famous faces in the auditorium: "I [saw] some ordinary people sitting there, and next to them might be Glenn Miller, and next to them Eleanor Roosevelt. Frank Sinatra came backstage and brought me a bouquet of roses. I was introduced to Mrs. Roosevelt and Glenn Miller—just everybody—Leopold Stokowski." As always, Ellington and his men were dressed to kill. *Time* reported that the members of his "flamboyant black band" were wearing "grey coats, each with a jet black carnation in his buttonhole." And while their leader sounded nervous onstage, he later claimed not to have been, even though he had been working on *Black, Brown and Beige* all the way up to the wire. "That first night at Carnegie was the only time in my life that I didn't have stage fright," he recalled in *Music Is My Mistress*. "I just didn't have time—I couldn't afford the luxury of being scared."

What the audience heard that evening was a forty-five-minute work in three movements that defied easy categorization. Howard Taubman had called it a "tone poem," while *Billboard*'s Elliott Grennard, who responded more warmly to the piece than most of his colleagues, opted for a different comparison: "To this reviewer's ears *Black, Brown and Beige* is the first jazz symphony of its time and will point the way to a whole school of jazz literature for the concert stage." Black listeners with longer memories might well have heard in it a latter-day counterpart of the historical pageants like *The Evolution of the Negro in Picture, Song, and Story* that had been so popular in Ellington's youth. Like *Reminiscing in Tempo* and *Diminuendo and Crescendo in Blue* before it, *Black, Brown and Beige* contains little improvisation— the solos are written out—and some of it, like the introduction to "The Blues," barely sounds like jazz at all. Structurally speaking, the piece is an uneasy hybrid of concisely argued musical statements à la "Ko-Ko" and the Whiteman-style symphonic jazz of *Creole Rhapsody*, whose self-contained sections are stitched together with elaborate transitional passages.

"Black," the twenty-two-minute first movement whose subject is life under slavery, is the most fully sustained of the three parts. In it, Ellington said, he sought

> to show the close relationship between work songs and spirituals. "Work Song," used in many forms, recognized that a work song was sung as you worked, so that there was a place for the song and a place where you grunt. "Come Sunday," the spiritual theme, was intended to depict the movement inside and outside the [white] church, as seen by workers who stood outside, watched, listened, but were not admitted. This is developed to the time when the workers have a church of their own. The section ends with promises.

More so than in any other section of *Black, Brown and Beige*, Ellington's music here is explicitly programmatic. From the thundering timpani and "talking" trombone of "Work Song" to the diaphanous orchestral accompaniment to the "sermon" preached by Johnny Hodges in "Come Sunday," he is painting pictures in sound, and doing so with a feel for orchestral color as sure as anything to be heard in the music of Debussy or Ravel. And while the sharp contrasts of tone that he believed to be intrinsic to the black temperament ("They pass quickly from the extremes of joy to gloom and back again") threaten at times to overwhelm the movement's tenuous structural unity, "Black" makes sense to the ear when it is approached not as a systematically developed musical statement but as a sequence of freely related episodes.

"Brown," the second movement, is a tribute to "the contribution made by the Negro to this country in blood." It opens with the Latin-flavored "West Indian Dance," which portrays the free Haitians who fought in the Revolutionary War, connected by an overelaborate transitional passage to a swinging section representing the Civil War and "the lighter attitude prevailing after the Proclamation of Emancipation." Both episodes are attractive but aimless and seem to have no real relationship to one another. Next comes "The Blues," the most carefully wrought episode of *Black, Brown and Beige*. Inez Cavanaugh's notes for the album place this section "at the end of the Spanish-American War, when the many Negro soldiers decorated for their heroism at San Juan Hill returned to their homes." She then quotes from Ellington's scenario: "Many soldiers returned to attract other men's mates. Some returned to find their own women otherwise attracted . . . it was the old story of the love triangle. In all love triangles there is the short side—and he who loves and loses is on the short side—*with* the Blues!"

"The Blues" contains the only vocal passage in *Black, Brown and Beige*, for which Ellington supplied his own lyric, the best he ever wrote: "The Blues ain't nothin' but a cold grey day, / And all night long it stays that way." The opening lines are set as a minor-key recitative accompanied by wailing dissonances that border on atonality. Ben Webster then supplies a fulsome interlude that leads into a contrasting major-key ensemble, followed by a reprise of the bleak harmonies with which the section began. Betty Roché, who sang "The Blues" at Carnegie Hall, was a warm-voiced alto whom Ellington neatly described as having "a soul inflection in a bop state of intrigue" and whose first stint with the band, which lasted for eighteen months, was far too short.

From the tightly organized lamentation of "The Blues," Ellington plunged into "Beige," a potpourri-like portrait of life in Harlem that is even harder to follow than the brief synopsis that Irving Kolodin supplied in his program notes for the Carnegie Hall concert:

The Harlem of the '20s, hotcha, excitement, razz-ma-tazz, is mirrored
in tom-toms and screaming brass. . . . But, as Ellington says, there are
more churches in Harlem than ginmills. As for the Negro of the bands
and the stage, Ellington has the epigram: "All they hear really is a few
people trying to make a living." A waltz shows the striving to sophisti-
cation, but underneath is the clamor of feeling which is yet undisci-
plined according to European standards. It is a panorama of life—a
longer "Harlem Air Shaft," showing the struggles for expression, the
yearning for education which can rarely be used, the true straight line
of the Negro's character which is too often turned aside and deflected by
his surroundings.

"Beige" does indeed recall the structure of "Harlem Air-Shaft," containing
as it does such improbably varied elements as a faux-sophisticated waltz,
an interpolated section by Billy Strayhorn that sounds like a super-suave

"Well, I guess they didn't dig it": Victor's 1944 album of excerpts from *Black, Brown
and Beige*. Ellington believed passionately in the most ambitious of his large-scale compositions but shelved it after Paul Bowles and other critics panned the Carnegie Hall
premiere. After 1943, Ellington never again played the complete work in public

film-music foxtrot, and a Broadway finale that reprises "Come Sunday" to pointless effect, flinging about here-comes-the-coda gestures (including a piano cadenza that bears a suspiciously close resemblance to *Rhapsody in Blue*) for two full minutes. Ellington always found it hard to write convincing finales, and this one sounds as though he ran out of time before figuring out how to weave together the disparate strands of his narrative into a clinching conclusion.

In *Music Is My Mistress* Ellington incorrectly remembered the running time of *Black, Brown and Beige* as fifty-seven minutes. Even allowing for the error, a three-movement work that ran for three-quarters of an hour was still a staggering departure from anything that he, or any other jazz composer, had done in the past. That he managed to finish it in six weeks is no less staggering, and no less indicative of its weaknesses, on which the critics pounced. Right though they were, too many of them failed to praise *Black, Brown and Beige* for what it was, just as later critics would make the equal and opposite mistake of praising it for what it wasn't, claiming for the piece a structural cohesion that it lacks. Eight years after *Reminiscing in Tempo,* Ellington had yet to acquaint himself with the elementary principles of symphonic musical organization known to all classically trained composers, and it showed.

To be sure, he himself insisted that *Black, Brown and Beige* ought not to be judged by the standards of classical music, while simultaneously denying that it was jazz: "We stopped using the word jazz in 1943. That was the point when we didn't believe in categories."* Yet it was Ellington's own decision to premiere the piece in the temple of the American classical-music establishment. By doing so, he exposed himself to the scrutiny of knowledgeable listeners who were naturally inclined to measure his efforts against more traditional yardsticks—some of whom, like Paul Bowles, were also familiar with jazz and thus predisposed to take him seriously, which made their criticisms all the more painful. Had they said what they had to say about *Black, Brown and Beige* in a more encouraging way, he might have learned from the experience and tried again. But they didn't, and neither did he.

Black, Brown and Beige might have made a stronger impression had it been recorded in its entirety after the premiere, thus allowing critics and other

---

* The word *jazz* appears only once in the liner notes to the 78 album of excerpts from *Black, Brown and Beige,* and it is not used to describe Ellington's music: "He opened at a little Broadway spot called the Kentucky Club, and soon the city's jazz enthusiasts were spreading glowing word of his band."

interested parties to listen to it at leisure. But RCA Victor did not reach an agreement with the American Federation of Musicians until November of 1944, and Eli Oberstein, the label's new recording director, refused to record the complete work after the AFM strike was settled. He opted instead for eighteen minutes' worth of excerpts, most of them from "Black" and "Brown," out of which Ellington chose the handful of snippets that he later played in concert. "What I'm trying to do with my band is to win people over to my bigger composing ideas," he explained. "That's why I pared down *B, B and B* . . . maybe they'll say, 'Gee, this guy isn't so bad at all,' and they'll listen to the longer and more ambitious works and maybe even enjoy them." Perhaps—and perhaps, too, he realized that the haste in which he wrote "Beige" compromised its artistic worth so severely as to make the movement unrevivable in its original form.

Whether or not he knew that he had fumbled the ball just short of the goal line, Ellington never admitted to having been shattered by the critics' response to *Black, Brown and Beige.* He kept a stiff upper lip, describing the piece as "the history of the Negro with no cringing and no bitterness" and saying, "I'd love to see [it] staged on Broadway as an opera or pageant." He recorded "Black" for Columbia in 1958, and in 1963 he recycled parts of the complete work into a stage revue called *My People* that was received almost as tepidly as the Carnegie Hall premiere. Two years later he made a private recording of "Black," "Brown," and most of "Beige" that was not released in his lifetime, and shortly thereafter he included "Come Sunday" in the "concert of sacred music" that he presented at San Francisco's Grace Cathedral. But he never again played all of *Black, Brown and Beige* after 1943, a fact that speaks eloquently of his enduring hurt.

∾

What had he been thinking? Was his decision to premiere *Black, Brown and Beige* at Carnegie Hall motivated solely by musical considerations? Or had he also been driven by a different kind of desire? Even though he chose not to lead a conventional middle-class life, Duke Ellington always believed devoutly in preserving the outward appearances of respectability. Trained from childhood onward to "act on behalf of the race," he was so determined not to embarrass his brethren that he would go to no end of trouble to cover up his deviations from the gentleman's code of propriety. It made sense that he should have hated the word *jazz,* whose original gutter connotations were still part of America's collective memory. In 1965 he complained that most

Americans "still take it for granted that European music—classical music, if you will—is the only really respectable kind . . . jazz [is] like the kind of man you wouldn't want your daughter to associate with." He sought the same respect for his own music, in which the seeming contradictions of his background, part bourgeois and part street, were productively embodied. From "Black and Tan Fantasy" to *Black, Brown and Beige*, he had sought to fuse the nostalgic sentimentality of his mother's beloved salon ballads with the blunt sexuality of the blues. He longed to make a lady out of jazz—even though she was already his mistress. That was why he brought her to Carnegie Hall: He had something to prove.

Ellington returned to Carnegie Hall six more times between 1943 and 1948, and each time he premiered another new work. None was as grandiose as *Black, Brown and Beige*, but all were conceived specifically for concert-hall performance, and while he would later claim that the Carnegie Hall appearances were "really a series of social-significance thrusts," they were also meant to solidify his reputation as a composer whose musical significance extended beyond the sphere of jazz. At the first of these concerts, in December of 1943, he grafted musical ambition onto social significance by premiering *New World A-Coming*, a fourteen-minute concerto in one movement for piano and band whose title was borrowed from a newly published book in which the black journalist Roi Ottley called for racial equality in America: "Spiritually aligned with the vast millions of oppressed colored peoples elsewhere in the world, giving American black men strength and numbers, Negroes are no longer in a mood to be placated by pious double-talk—they want some of the gravy of American life."

While Ellington apparently never got around to reading Ottley's book, he had his own ideas about the world to which the title referred, imagining it as "a place in the distant future where there would be no war, no greed, no categorization, no nonbelievers, where love was unconditional, and no pronoun was good enough for God." Accordingly, *New World A-Coming* was subdued and meditative in tone, a spacious work that Barry Ulanov described in *Metronome* as "a series of florid piano passages, in and out of tempo, amplified with great tonal beauty by the orchestra, rich in its chord structure, in its soft, sensuous mood." It was, in other words, a rhapsody—a jazz counterpart of *Rhapsody in Blue*, to be exact. Ellington was fond of the piece and performed it often in later years, but *New World A-Coming* never caught on with the listening public, no doubt because it contained none of the indelible melodies that make it easier to forgive the twenty-five-year-old George Gershwin his own youthful ignorance of how to put together a large-scale musical composition.

After *New World A-Coming* Ellington moved in a different direction, collaborating with Billy Strayhorn on *Perfume Suite,* first performed at Carnegie Hall in December of 1944. The four movements, "Balcony Serenade," "Strange Feeling," "Dancers in Love," and "Coloratura," endeavored (in Ellington's words) "to capture the character usually taken on by a woman who wears . . . different blends of perfume." In fact, such thematic unity as *Perfume Suite* purported to have was factitious. Ellington simply threw together a quartet of unrelated pieces, the first two of which had previously been written by Strayhorn, and premiered them under a portmanteau title confected after the fact.* An attractive but minor effort, *Perfume Suite* is important mainly for what it foreshadowed: After 1944, virtually all of Ellington's "large-scale" pieces would be multimovement suites to which Strayhorn contributed. These works, as Walter van de Leur explains, were usually "a mix of (retitled) old and new compositions by Ellington and Strayhorn, unified by a programmatic title and explanatory remarks." Some of them were striking, like *The Deep South Suite* (1946), whose finale, "Happy-Go-Lucky Local," is a sketch of a rickety train in which Ellington musicalizes the sounds of the bluesy steam whistles that he loved. Others, like *A Tonal Group* (1946), *Liberian Suite* (1947), and *The Symphomaniac* (1948), were less memorable. But even the best of them make no attempt to scale the heights of *Black, Brown and Beige.* They are collections of cameos, no different in scope or style than any of Ellington's other miniature masterpieces.

Only twice more, in *The Tattooed Bride* (1948) and *A Tone Parallel to Harlem* (1951), did he move beyond his self-imposed limitations to write single-movement works that appeared to essay what Gunther Schuller has called "organically larger form." But while both of these pieces break the three-minute barrier (each is fourteen minutes long), neither aspires to the systematic thematic development of *Reminiscing in Tempo* or the longer episodes of *Black, Brown and Beige.* Instead they are extended pieces of programmatic "symphonic jazz" that consist of more or less end-stopped musical episodes played in continuous succession, capped by codas that reprise the main themes in order to create an impression of structural unity. And despite their harmonic resourcefulness and matchlessly colorful scoring, *Harlem* and *The Tattooed Bride* are melodically nondescript, making them sound more aimless than they are.

---

* Far from having anything to do with Ellington's stated conception, the harmonically recherché "Strange Feeling," a vocal movement whose lyrics ("This strange feeling is seeping through my blood / This strange feeling is sleeping somewhere cuddled up inside me") were also written by Strayhorn, seems to refer to his collaborator's homosexuality.

"We didn't like the tone poems much," Johnny Hodges admitted. Neither did most of the critics. Howard Taubman's *New York Times* review of the 1946 Carnegie Hall concert sounded a sharp note of skepticism: "There is, however, the danger of becoming pretentious. The Duke's best friends had better tell him—some of his program last night was arty, and that, in the words of a number Ellington used to do, ain't good." *Time*'s unsigned review was even harsher:

> But for fans of the Duke's "Mood Indigo," "Sophisticated Lady" and "It Don't Mean a Thing" days, the concert had the taste of a stale highball. They had come for ginmill stuff and had been served something more like a bad-year champagne. The Duke once more dragged out such pretentious symphonic items as Black, Brown and Beige . . . Until late in the evening, when the band got back to being itself on easy-riding bounce tunes, the whole thing sounded more like André Kostelanetz than a night in Harlem. Four sessions in Carnegie Hall had had an unmistakably mopey, not to say arty, effect on the Duke.

Yet Ellington kept on writing suites long after the band had stopped making annual visits to Carnegie Hall, and after it was evident to all but the most fanatical of his devotees that they were no substitute for the true large-scale works from which he had steered clear ever since *Black, Brown and Beige.* What was the reason for his persistent devotion to a pseudo-form that so often failed to bring out the best in him? In 1956 Ellington said that he was tired of "having the John Hammonds of the world tell me I should stick to three-minute songs." It seems not to have occurred to him that in writing the suites, he was doing just that.

∽

Despite the lukewarm response to *Black, Brown and Beige,* Ellington's Carnegie Hall debut was still a pivotal moment in his career—and a profitable one. *Variety,* as always, took a hardheaded view of its outcome: "Whether or not the concert was an artistic success, it is agreed that the comment it created was invaluable to Ellington's future. . . . The Duke should cash in plenty henceforth." And so he did. According to *Billboard,* he received "the greatest pre-performance press ever accorded a jazz man, and on the strength of it William Morris Agency has boosted the price of the aggregation $500 a night" ($6,400 in today's dollars). The band's annual gross leaped from

$160,000 in 1939 to $405,000 in 1944. Ellington claimed $394,000 in expenses that year, paying himself a weekly salary of $500, and everyone else in the band was paid commensurately. "I heard musicians made this kind of money, but I'd never made any," said Jimmy Hamilton, who replaced Chauncey Haughton in May of 1943.

Not only did Ellington's price go up, but he landed an important gig as a result of the publicity surrounding the Carnegie Hall concert. The band moved into New York's Hurricane Restaurant in April for a twenty-five-week residency that slashed his traveling expenses and gave him invaluable publicity. Radio was at its listening peak in 1943, and the Mutual Broadcasting System rushed to take advantage of Ellington's long-term engagement at the Hurricane (later renamed the Zanzibar Club). For the next two years he was heard regularly on network radio, making live broadcasts from the Hurricane and, in May, launching a Sunday-evening series called *Pastel Period* that was devoted to ballads and lyrical instrumental pieces. Though he claimed to have lost $18,000 by taking the lower-paying job, the national exposure provided by his broadcasts more than made up for it.

The band itself continued to perform on a high level. "Everyone seemed to think the band was at its best [with Blanton and Webster], but it was still playing well when we were at the Hurricane and Zanzibar," Harry Carney said years later. Surviving air checks of the Mutual broadcasts, as well as the commercial recordings that Victor (now known as RCA Victor) began to make after settling with the AFM in 1944, confirm his recollection. Not only did the musicians play with undiminished authority throughout the midforties, but Ellington was composing as well as he ever had. "Blue Cellophane," "Carnegie Blues," "A Gathering in a Clearing," "Magenta Haze," "Rockabye River": All of these sides, and many others as well, were indistinguishable in quality from the Blanton-Webster classics.

The band was still up to its old tricks. The old reliables were as temperamental as ever, and they continued to make trouble for new players who did not yet understand that merely reading the music on their stands was not enough to make them Ellington men. Harold "Shorty" Baker, who shuttled in and out of the trumpet section at frequent intervals between 1942 and 1962, described his own hazing as follows: "When I first joined that band, they let me sit there playing wrong notes for a week without telling me the parts had been changed! Nobody ever marked changes." Unflappable as always, their leader made the most of whatever they cared to give him. George Avakian, who became Ellington's record producer when the band signed

Recording for Victor in the midforties. Though the Blanton-Webster band of 1940–41 is generally regarded as Duke Ellington's strongest group, he continued to turn out first-rate compositions during the rest of the decade, and the band, despite the loss of several key players, performed them with undiminished authority, both on record and in person

with Columbia in 1947, looked on in amazement as the composer threw together an impromptu gem called "New York City Blues" in the studio:

> *The musicians trickled in very slowly. Duke was not among the first to arrive, and something like two hours after the session was supposed to begin, the engineer and I were still discussing yesterday's baseball scores with the musicians, and Duke said, "All right, let's start." And he began setting up a blues with whoever happened to be there. There was some kind of odd instrumentation—as I recall, there was only one, possibly two, brass players, and about three saxophones.*

Nor had much of anything changed on the road, where black musicians, however famous they might be, were subject at all times to unexpected degradations. Early in his run at the Hurricane, Ellington learned that the restaurant's headwaiter refused to accept reservations from black patrons, telling them that the club was sold out, and had to complain to the owner so that his friends could come and see him play. When he played Ciro's, one of Hollywood's most expensive nightclubs, in 1945, his very presence there was news. According to *Billboard*, "Booking Ellington into Ciro's sets a precedent, in that it is the first time that any of the swank [Hollywood] strip spots have gone in for a high-priced, big-name Negro band." But nothing was said about how the club's manager had warned Ellington, "We don't allow the help to socialize with the guests." George Raft, who was friendly with Sonny Greer, demanded that his own table be set up in the alley outside the club so that he could enjoy the musicians' company, and got his way.

To veteran players accustomed to such slights, what happened at Ciro's was more of the same. But Kay Davis, a middle-class black from Chicago who started singing with the band at the end of 1944, wasn't used to being treated like a second-class citizen and was stunned by what she saw on her first trip to the Deep South: "I remember getting off the train to play in Macon, Georgia. The police chief came up to us threateningly in the station and Duke's manager explained that this was the Duke Ellington band. 'I don't care about Duke Ellington any more than any other nigra,' he said. We ran and got back on the train."

Ellington, too, was up to his own time-honored tricks in the midforties, as the reminiscences of his friends and colleagues make clear. All agree that he was as slick and manipulative as ever. When Ben Webster asked him for a raise, he replied, "I can't afford to pay you what you're worth. Nobody can." His need for privacy also remained strong. "He kids around with us, but if you get too close to him, he'll make a joke or put you on, and edge away," another sideman told Nat Hentoff. Above all, no one, not even his lovers, was permitted to interfere with his composing. "Duke was so involved in himself and what he had to do that other people and other things were like side dishes," a close friend said. "They were just there. He took them for granted."

No matter how he had spent the day, he ended it at the piano. In 1944 Gunther Schuller roomed next door to Ellington and never forgot what he heard there:

He would just play, improvising, more or less fooling around, ruminating, as it were, sometimes for long periods of time, working on some melody or motive, trying out some harmonic progression or a chain of chords, always so beautifully voiced. Then, every once in a while there would be silence, and I would hear the scratching sound of a pencil. Duke had heard something he thought worthy of committing to paper.

Then the keyboard ruminating would commence again. . . . Around four or five in the morning he'd finally lie down to catch a few hours' sleep, then get up around ten thirty to hand out some music to Tom [Whaley]—maybe only twenty or thirty bars.

But no matter how late he stayed up composing a piece, he still waited until the last possible minute to finish it. According to Herb Hendler, who served as his A & R man at Victor during this period, "When Duke was coming in, I used to set up tables in the studio for his copyists. He'd sit at the piano and bang away. Then he'd give a lead sheet to the copyists, and an arrangement would be done there and then, with Duke adding odd phrases as he went along." And he was still womanizing, always on the qui vive for yet another pickup. Young Joya Sherrill, who started singing with the band in 1944, was fascinated by his attitude toward the women who ceaselessly pursued him: "I saw so many women around him and I would say, 'But Duke . . . you were just with this one the other day. You just told this one you loved them.' He said, 'Joya, I love all of my women.' And he really, I think he really meant that." He always had plenty of them to love. Ruth Ellington found it "shocking . . . the way the women kind of fell on their faces in front of him." Yet he was far from picky about his sexual partners. "He never seemed to be interested in the perfect woman," Mercer said. "If she had a scar, or was slightly misproportioned—big-busted, big-hipped, or a little off balance—then he was more interested." To Don George, an up-and-coming lyricist with whom Ellington collaborated on such hit songs as "Everything but You" and "I'm Beginning to See the Light," he explained that his promiscuity "keeps my juices flowing, and that's where I get all my ideas for the music I write."

Seven years after Ellington's death, George published a memoir called *Sweet Man* in which he breached the wall of silence that the composer's intimates had maintained with regard to his sex life. Parts of the book read like a French stage farce, only more explicit: "Duke would check into two, three or four hotels, hand out keys to different ladies, then, later on, pick out the hotel room he wanted to go to." It was the highest priority of his publicists to prevent the press from reporting on such escapades. Not only were they concerned about his reputation, but Ellington was just as determined to keep Evie Ellis in the dark about them, for his short-tempered consort, with whom he had been living since 1939, was ready and willing to resort to violence. According to Mercer, she went after him with a gun at least twice. Having been carved up by a wife, Ellington didn't propose to get shot by a mistress, though he refused to curtail his coupling, explaining to George that "we can't permit anything to interfere with man's inalienable right to have a little pussy on the side."

Ellington's extramarital relationship with Evie was no more conventionally respectable than were his extra-extramarital activities. It didn't help that Ruth Ellington, according to Mercer, "did not allow Evie in her home." Their mutual hostility made his domestic life uncomfortable, especially during holidays: "So when Easter, Christmas came around, or whatever, instead of him taking a grip on it, he ran! So he couldn't demand everyone would be in one room. The only way he could compensate for it was to see each one, one at a time . . . so as a result of this he planned as best as possible to be working on holidays. Christmas, Thanksgiving, whatever." Proverbially unwilling though he was to confront disagreeable matters, Ellington also knew that his refusal to regularize his liaison with Evie by divorcing Edna was not without its advantages. "I think Evie was his protection," said Phoebe Jacobs, a publicist who knew both Ellington and Evie. "In other words, every time he got too involved with another woman, he'd always say, 'Well, I have to go back to Evie.'"

None of these shenanigans made it into "The Hot Bach," a three-part profile of Ellington that appeared in *The New Yorker* in June and July of 1944. Written by Richard O. Boyer, "The Hot Bach" sketched its subject with sympathetic clarity: "Duke Ellington, whose contours have something of the swell and sweep of a large, erect bear and whose color is that of coffee with a strong dash of cream . . . is a calm man of forty-five who laughs easily and hates to hurry."* While the piece says nothing about Ellington's sex life, the other facets of his offstage personality had never before been conveyed so clearly in print. "The Hot Bach" disclosed that his religious belief was not just for show: "I've had three educations—the street corner, going to school, and the Bible. The Bible is most important. It taught me to look at a man's insides instead of the cut of his suit." It showed him battling stoically with racial prejudice: "You have to try not to think about it or you'll knock yourself out." It showed him talking about food, about clothes, about women, and, ever and always, about music: "As Bach says, if you ain't got a left hand, you ain't worth a hoot in hell."

---

* Elsewhere in the piece, Boyer notes that "Duke is six feet tall and weighs two hundred and ten pounds." The former figure was accurate, the latter almost certainly on the low side, though Ellington lost a good deal of weight later in life.

Boyer was also struck by the care that Ellington took to conceal that personality from the public, hiding it behind a mask of charm:

> *Ellington has, like most entertainers, a stage self and a real self. On the stage, at least when he supplies the "flesh"—the trade term for personal appearances in movie houses—he presents himself as a smiling, carefree African, tingling to his fingertips with a gay, syncopated throb that he can scarcely control. As the spotlight picks him out of the gloom, the audience sees a wide, irrepressible grin, but when the light moves away, Ellington's face instantly sags into immobility.*

That *The New Yorker* now thought him worthy of a three-part profile demonstrates the extent of his celebrity in 1944—as well as the wisdom of Irving Mills. Though the two men had parted ways five years earlier, Ellington continued to reap the benefits of Mills's farseeing decision to market him not merely as a glamorous jazzman but as a great artist. But the coming of the Swing Era, which was a white man's game, had shifted attention away from the pioneering black bands. In 1941 *Down Beat* had invited its readers to name the "best swing band" of the year, and Benny Goodman had beaten Ellington 2,130–1,841. It is interesting that *Time* should have treated the poll as news, and even more interesting that the story was one of the few times that Ellington's name appeared in *Time* during the forties. The premiere of *Black, Brown and Beige* had gotten him back into the magazine, but you can only make your Carnegie Hall debut once, and in the world of the media, merely being a genius is not news. Hollywood had turned its back on him as well. The band appeared in Vincente Minnelli's *Cabin in the Sky,* a screen version of the all-black Broadway musical, but Ellington and his men shared the screen with Louis Armstrong, Lena Horne, Rochester, Ethel Waters, and the Hall Johnson Choir, performing briefly at a nightclub full of happy black dancers. William Morris had no more aces in the hole. Print ads show that the agency was still using Mills-coined slogans ("Weird melodies! Amazing syncopation!") to pump up his image. Like the man himself, they were old news.

Nor were wider cultural trends working in Ellington's favor. Though no one knew it yet, the AFM strike had pulled the rug out from under the big-band era. The bands had been decimated by the draft, which sent thousands of musicians marching off to war (among them Lawrence Brown, Chauncey Haughton, and Wallace Jones). Now they were competing with romantic crooners like Frank Sinatra, whose singing appealed to women whose boyfriends and husbands were no longer around to take them out dancing. It was a losing battle: No fewer than six of the foremost bandleaders of the Swing Era, Les Brown, Tommy Dorsey, Benny Goodman, Woody Herman, Harry James, and Jack Teagarden, were forced to disband their groups in the winter of 1946, with Louis Armstrong following suit a year later. World War II, it seemed, had changed the way that Americans felt about popular music. They looked to it for reassurance, not stimulation. The biggest hit records of the war years were wistful ballads like "I'll Be Seeing You," "I'll Walk Alone," "Sentimental Journey," and "White Christmas." Up-tempo swingers, by contrast, seemed increasingly out of place.

Sensing a change in the wind, Ellington had started featuring his vocalists more prominently. At one point in 1944 he had four of them, Kay Davis, Al Hibbler, Marie Ellington (no relation), and Joya Sherrill, on his payroll. Marie Ellington, who later married Nat "King" Cole, had been hired, according to her, "because of my looks," and Davis, a classically trained soprano with a graduate degree from Northwestern University, specialized in the wordless vocal obbligati to such instrumental numbers as "Creole Love Call" and "On a Turquoise Cloud." The smooth-voiced Sherrill scored several jukebox hits, including "Everything but You" and "I Didn't Know About You," while Hibbler was a real find, a blind, virile shouter whose soulfully swoopy vibrato and inexplicably affected diction ("Don't get a-*round* much *en-tie* more") put off the critics but delighted the fans. "Hibbler's no singer, he's a tone-pantomimist," Ellington proclaimed. "What other singer creates such tonal drama?"

Most of the new songs that Ellington wrote for his new singers were undemanding pop ditties, but they were pleasingly performed and well arranged (sometimes by Ellington, more often by Strayhorn). Even the least of them helped to keep the pot boiling. In 1943, for instance, Ellington and Bob Russell turned "Never No Lament" into "Don't Get Around Much Anymore," which became an overnight success when it was covered by the Ink Spots. Ellington loved to tell what happened next. Strapped for cash, he dropped by the William Morris office to borrow $500 ($6,400 in today's dollars). Before he did so, he picked up his mail and found an envelope that contained a royalty check:

> *The figure $2,250 is what I thought I saw as I slid it back in the envelope. To myself I said, "Hey, if this is $2,250, I don't need to make this touch up here, but maybe my eyes deceived me and it's really $22.50." So I pulled the check out again and it said $22,500! By the time I got my*

head back in my collar I was at the elevator exit on the first floor rush-
ing to get a taxi. Man, what a surprise! What a feeling! I could breathe
without inhaling or exhaling for the next three months!

But writing pop songs did not make the best use of Ellington's gifts. Never a natural melodist, he continued to collaborate with Johnny Hodges and some of his other sidemen on many of his midforties hits, including "Don't Get Around Much Anymore" and "I'm Beginning to See the Light." It had always been so. Of the half dozen ballads that figured most promi- nently in the medley of hits that he now played at all of his concerts (it came to be alternatively known among the cognoscenti as the "dreaded medley" and the "ASCAP medley") in order to push his songwriting royalties high enough to keep the band running, "Solitude" was the only one composed by Ellington alone. Hence it irked him that Eli Oberstein was pushing hard for more vocals and fewer instrumentals, and he wasn't shy about complaining to reporters: "For one thing, the return of Eli Oberstein to Victor as record- ing director meant tremendous pressure in choosing material. . . . *Black, Brown and Beige* was distributed but was seriously cut." By 1946 Ellington had had enough of Oberstein, and of RCA Victor. Brad McCuen, who went to work for the label two years later, was told that the last straw was a recording-studio incident in which Oberstein, speaking with his colleagues without realizing that an open mike in the control room allowed Ellington and his musicians to hear what was being said behind their backs, ordered the engineers to get ready to cut "a little Saturday-night nigger music."

Even more stressful was the fact that the Ellington band was losing one after another of its soloists. Ben Webster had already departed in 1943, the victim of his own temperament. Clark Terry, who joined the band a few years later, heard that Webster "slapped Duke one time in the spur of the moment." According to Don George, "He just got drunk, called Duke a motherfucker and quit." Whatever the real reason, Ellington found Webster too hard to handle and started cutting back on his solos, leading the saxophonist to hand in his notice and start a combo. After him, the deluge: Juan Tizol joined Harry James in 1944, Rex Stewart struck out on his own a year later, and in 1946 Otto Hardwick retired from the music business. The cruelest blow of all came soon after that, when Tricky Sam Nanton was found dead in his hotel room, a victim of years and years of excessive drinking.

Gifted players replaced them all, some of whom would stay at least as long as their predecessors. Jimmy Hamilton played in the saxophone section until 1968, and Russell Procope, who replaced Hardwick in 1946, remained with the band until Ellington's death twenty-eight years later. One or two of the new musicians became stars in their own right, above all Cat Anderson, the trumpet section's iron-lipped high-note man, whose shrieking above-the-staff climaxes, like Hibbler's melodramatic singing, were loathed by the critics and loved by the public.* Most of them, however, preferred to keep below the radar of publicity, in particular Hamilton and Procope, a pair of well-behaved professionals whom Ellington could count on to do their jobs without fuss. While he valued them, he also knew their limitations. "He was very important to us throughout the twenty-five years he was in the band," Ellington wrote of Hamilton in *Music Is My Mistress*. His praise of Procope was even fainter: "What is more, he became a conscientious, all-around musician, one always to be depended on." And that was the trouble: He needed more than what they had to offer. "There is no such thing as a 'replacement' in my band," he said in 1951. "A new musician means for us a new sound and the creation of new music, which he, and he alone, can properly express." That was the keystone of the Ellington Effect. He craved new sounds at least as much as he craved new women—and he wasn't getting them.

Just as Ellington looked for more than mere conscientiousness from his sidemen, so did he demand more sympathetic treatment from his record label. After cutting his last sides for Victor in September of 1946, he signed an exclusive contract with Musicraft, an obscure independent label founded in 1937 and best known for having recorded Dizzy Gillespie, Leadbelly, Teddy Wilson, Josh White, and the original-cast album of *The Cradle Will Rock*, Marc Blitzstein's prolabor musical. Musicraft promised him the moon—a three-year contract with a guarantee of $100,000 in royalties per year—and *Variety* described the deal as "probably unequaled by any other Negro band in the business." But it was still a giant step in the wrong direction for Ellington, who had spent the past six years working for America's biggest record label.

He remained beyond category, of course. NBC had proved it yet again when, two days after the death of President Roosevelt, it aired "A Tribute to F.D.R. by the American Negro," the second episode of *Your Saturday Date with the Duke*, Ellington's new weekly radio series. The band performed such pieces as "Come Sunday," "Mood Indigo," *New World A-Coming*, and a vocal

---

* Anderson, who described himself as "highly strung," was despised by many of his fellow musicians, so much so that he actually drove Rex Stewart out of the band. According to Clark Terry, the trumpeter was a kleptomaniac who "had a habit of staying on the bus at rest stops and pretending he was sleeping. Then when everybody got off the bus, he'd ransack [the band's] things."

version by Al Hibbler of "Nobody Knows the Trouble I've Seen," prefaced by the portentous words of a solemn-voiced network announcer: "Duke Ellington—composer, conductor, fine artist—speaks in his way of the deep sorrow of his people . . . Through Duke Ellington's music, the heart of the Negro weeps for Franklin Roosevelt." Ellington and his men are thought to be the only popular musicians who were heard on any of the radio networks, which switched to news, religious, or classical music after FDR's death was reported. *Variety* reported that "no other dance band could have filled the spot without arousing criticism."

But he was no longer commercial, at least not as far as NBC was concerned. His new show was "sponsored" not by a maker of cigarettes or toothpaste but by the US Treasury Department, which used it to sell war bonds. At the ripe age of forty-six, the host of *Your Saturday Date with the Duke* had become the dean of a fast-shrinking field. A year later, Barry Ulanov published *Duke Ellington,* the first full-length book about Ellington, a fancily written but well-informed survey of his life and work that was produced with its subject's grudging cooperation. "You don't build a statue to a man while he's still alive," Ellington told Leonard Feather. "People will think I'm a thing of the past, something to look back on." The press thought so, too, and the headlines of the stories about him that came out in 1946 show how far he had slipped: "Is the Duke Declining? 'Loss of Stars Killing His Band.'" "'I'm Not Slipping'—Duke Ellington: 'My Current Ork Just as Good and Perhaps More Flexible,' He Says." "Ellington Fails to Top Himself: Mix Finds Concert Good, Not Great."

It was time once again for a change, and Ellington knew it better than anyone. But now that World War II was over, would he be able to grapple with postwar cultural shifts? Were his inner resources sufficient to the daunting task of stylistic regeneration? What—if anything—did Harlem's Aristocrat of Jazz have up his sleeve?

13

"MORE A BUSINESS THAN AN ART"

Into the Wilderness, 1946–1955

T HE FAILURE OF *Jump for Joy* to move to Broadway had been and would remain one of Duke Ellington's greatest disappointments. It made him more open than he might have been to a proposal that was made to him in mid-1946. It came from Perry Watkins, the only working black scenic designer in New York City and the first black member of United Scenic Artists, the union of designers and artists for the entertainment industry. Watkins, who had collaborated with Orson Welles and John Houseman on the legendary all-black "Voodoo *Macbeth*" presented in 1936 by the WPA's Negro Theater Unit, now wanted to produce an updated version of *The Beggar's Opera*, John Gay's tale of low life in London, in which the gangsters, pimps, and whores of the 1728 ballad opera would be transplanted to present-day America. Bertolt Brecht and Kurt Weill had done something similar, but their *Threepenny Opera* was not yet well-known outside Europe (a 1933 Broadway production had been a dismal flop, closing after just twelve performances). Watkins's version, by contrast, would be all-American—and racially integrated. As he explained a year later, "*Beggar's Holiday* was conceived from the first—more than a year before it reached Broadway—as a bi-racial musical." Then he spotted Ellington in a restaurant, went to his table, and offered to commission him to write the score. Ellington agreed on the spot.

Watkins promptly discovered that his new partner had never heard of *The Beggar's Opera*. "I realized all of a sudden that Duke never went to the theater very much," he recalled. Ellington spent too much time on the road to do so, much less to have learned how much the musical-comedy idiom had evolved in recent years. In this deficiency lay the fundamental flaw in all of his theatrical projects: He didn't understand what a contemporary musical *was*. Except for *Show Girl,* the failed 1929 George Gershwin musical in which the Ellington band had briefly appeared, the only shows with which he is likely to have been closely familiar were the community pageants of his youth and the Cotton Club revues for which he had played. His experience with *Jump for Joy,* a plotless revue, had taught him nothing about how to write an *Oklahoma!*-style "book show" whose songs drive the action. Yet he still wanted to write a successful Broadway show, and always had. "Ellington wanted the recognition of writing a Broadway show," said his friend Luther Henderson, a classically trained orchestrator who worked on *Beggar's Holiday.* "In fact, he wanted the recognition of writing a Broadway show more than he wanted to write a Broadway show." What he didn't want to do was interrupt his busy schedule in order to learn the craft of book-based musical-comedy writing. It was *Black, Brown and Beige* all over again—only with higher stakes.

Watkins lengthened the odds by picking John Latouche to write the show's book and lyrics. Enormously personable and greatly talented, he scored a modest hit on Broadway in 1940 with the stage version of *Cabin in the Sky,* in whose screen adaptation the Ellington band had appeared. But Latouche, who is now best known for his libretto for Douglas Moore's 1956 opera *The Ballad of Baby Doe* and the lyrics for a handful of show tunes, most notably "Lazy Afternoon" and "Taking a Chance on Love," was a poisoned chalice, a gay alcoholic with a hard-earned reputation for unreliability. Vernon Duke, who worked with him on *Cabin in the Sky,* remembered his colleague as "ever alert, his wit ever sharp and often merciless," but handicapped by his personal shortcomings: "Extremely erratic by nature, Latouche worked spasmodically and swiftly . . . short periods of work to be followed by long days and nights of blissful laziness and idle gallivanting." It was a judgment with which all who knew him concurred. But there was no question of his talent, and he was already at work on a draft of *Twilight Alley* (as *Beggar's Holiday* was initially known).

What Latouche had written so far was promising enough for Watkins to persuade John Houseman, who had cofounded the Mercury Theatre with Welles in 1937, to consider becoming the show's director. While directing would never be Houseman's strong suit—he was first and foremost a uniquely creative producer, both on Broadway and, later, in Hollywood—his pioneering work with the Negro Theatre Unit had made him something of a hero to theatrically minded blacks. But though he liked the sound of *Twilight Alley,* he had good reason to fear that getting the show from the page to the stage would be tricky:

> *Latouche was not only lazy, but he had been working on several other projects during the summer; he had written a number of lyrics but only the roughest draft of our first act and almost nothing of the second. Ellington, teeming with tunes and mood pieces, still had not faced the necessity of composing a complete musical score. Added to these unpleasant discoveries was another of which I only gradually became aware: our producers were desperately short of money. Finally—owing to the Duke's enormous list of future commitments—we had no leeway at all but must start rehearsals within four weeks or not at all.*

What Houseman meant by "a complete musical score" was clearly not what Ellington meant. Having worked on one Broadway musical, a *succès d'estime* called *Lute Song* that closed after four months, he knew that the composer of a successful musical had to supply purpose-written songs conceived and executed in close collaboration with the librettist, and Ellington didn't work that way. His *Twilight Alley* songs were either written on the road or pulled out of his trunk. Still, Watkins had managed to assemble a plausible-looking cast: *Oklahoma!* had made a star out of Alfred Drake, the MacHeath of *Twilight Alley,* while Zero Mostel, who played Peachum, was not yet a star but was well on his way. Libby Holman was cast as Jenny, and though her above-the-title days were long behind her, she was still remembered for such hit revues of the twenties and thirties as *The Little Show* and *Three's a Crowd,* as well as for her scandalous private life. (Openly bisexual, she had been indicted in 1932 for allegedly murdering her husband, Zachary Smith Reynolds, who was heir to the R. J. Reynolds tobacco fortune and whose death made her a millionairess.) *Jump for Joy*'s Marie Bryant and Avon Long, lately of the 1942 revival of *Porgy and Bess,* were cast in supporting roles, and when Watkins's scenic designs proved to be inadequate, Oliver Smith, who had worked for Ballet Theatre and on two Broadway hits, *Billion Dollar Baby* and *On the Town,* was brought in to create what turned out to be a brilliantly stylized big-city set. The prospect of collaborating with these pros induced Houseman to sign on, and *Twilight Alley* went into rehearsal on October 21.

Ellington had miraculously contrived to spend the whole of that month in New York, playing at the Aquarium Restaurant and working on the show in his off hours. Come November, though, at the moment when his presence was needed most, he returned to the road for a month of one-night stands in Baltimore, Buffalo, Chicago, Cincinnati, Cleveland, Indianapolis, Kansas City, Minneapolis, Omaha, Philadelphia, Rochester, Syracuse, and Toronto, pausing in New York just long enough to appear at Carnegie Hall with Django Reinhardt, who was visiting America for the first time and touring with the band.* His absence upset Latouche, who threatened to quit because he expected to collaborate directly with his composer instead of "working" with him over the phone. He was kidding himself. As Luther Henderson put it, "Ellington would never leave his band—never, ever, not for anything. . . . [So he] said, 'I will leave you Strayhorn.'" Not only did Strayhorn write the dance music for *Twilight Alley* and orchestrate the score in tandem with Henderson, but he also composed the best song in the show, "Brown Penny," by himself, and helped out with several others. According to Houseman, he "would run up to the Duke's apartment and fish out of a drawer, crammed with unperformed music, whatever tune seemed to fit the scene." Yet his program credit was the same as the one that he had received for *Jump for Joy:* "Orchestrations under personal supervision of Billy Strayhorn." It was taken for granted that Ellington's name was necessary to sell the show, and Strayhorn, once again, was eased into the shadows.

Latouche found it impossible to come up with a convincing ending. His first attempt was a heavy-handed sermon delivered posthumously by MacHeath, who had just been dispatched in the electric chair: "The deed has been done by all of us—the hates hated by all of us. . . . The one thing we share in this inequal world is guilt." No one found it good enough, so he started tinkering with the book, causing the show to grow longer and longer. By now the producers' checks were bouncing, and rehearsals were getting out of hand. On December 1, two nights before the Boston tryout of *Twilight Alley* opened, Ellington showed up at the Boston Opera House and was so dismayed by what he saw there that he skipped town the next day. Houseman felt the same way, claiming that "the last twenty minutes of the show . . . were virtually improvised by Drake and the cast before an audience that included the usual number of vulturous ill-wishers from New York." *Billboard* summed up the debacle as

---

* The great gypsy guitarist's appearances were less eventful than they should have been. Hired as a guest soloist, he jammed with the band on standards and impromptu riff tunes, and Ellington wrote nothing new for him to play.

gently as possible, calling the show "something of an opera, ballet, operetta, musicomedy and play with music. It's all and none of these. . . . Alley has a lot of everything but not enough of anything in particular to pull it into the hit class."

Houseman quit or was fired—he was never sure which—and George Abbott, Broadway's top show doctor, was brought in to do what he could before *Twilight Alley* reached New York. He fired Holman, hacked away at the dialogue scenes, changed the title to *Beggar's Holiday,* and boggled at the continuing absence of his composer: "I never saw Duke Ellington, never worked with him. Billy took care of whatever I asked for. He sat down and wrote it right there, whatever was needed." What he couldn't do was talk the producers into putting up more cash. "I think I could have made a hit show . . . had I been able to have the proper changes of cast," Abbott said in his memoirs. "But having extravagantly squandered hundreds of thousands of dollars, the management now suddenly became penurious and was unwilling to squander a little more to salvage what they had already wasted." Furious at the consequences of their penury, he refused to let his name be printed in the Broadway program.

Beggar's Holiday opened at the Broadway Theatre the day after Christmas. The reviews were mixed, though some of the critics, like Brooks Atkinson of *The New York Times,* had unexpectedly friendly things to say: "Let appropriate salutes be fired in honor of Duke Ellington and John Latouche. Using John Gay's 'Beggar's Opera' as a ground plan, they have composed a flaring musical play in modern style . . . Mr. Ellington and Mr. Latouche have given Broadway a score and lyrics we can be proud of." *Life* agreed with Atkinson about the songs, praising the "full-blooded musical score" and "biting lyrics," while Barry Ulanov, writing in *Metronome,* did what he could for his friend: "There are so many good tunes in the show it is hard to make a choice." Alas, there weren't. Except for Strayhorn's "Brown Penny," the score was undistinguished, though Lena Horne tried her best to make a hit out of "Tomorrow Mountain," a hope-for-the-future ditty whose lyrics were lifted by Latouche from "The Big Rock Candy Mountain" ("Under cigarette trees, we'll take our ease / While the cops fan off the flies"). Ellington did his bit by recording five of the songs for Columbia, but he rarely performed them outside the studio, and they were soon forgotten. As for Latouche's book, even Ulanov conceded that it was a mess: "It offers no really sympathetic character; such warmth as is stirred in the audience by the talented members of the cast is managed entirely by Marie Bryant's dancing and singing, by Alfred Drake's singing and the excellent music assigned all the other principals." Of the production team, only Oliver Smith got away clean, with Eric Bentley sneering that his "fine settings look like a tombstone over a play that died during rehearsals."

Beggar's Holiday closed on March 29, 1947, after 111 performances. A two-week run in Chicago failed no less completely, and the investors lost all their money. "The thing that was wrong with the show," Ellington later said, "was that it was about twenty years ahead of its time . . . nobody could understand why anybody would have an integrated show." While he was right about that, it is also true that later attempts to revive *Beggar's Holiday* have been no more successful, and he seems never to have figured out that Broadway shows, however fine their intentions, cannot be written on the fly, least of all when one of the authors lacks the necessary stage experience. Ellington stuck around town long enough to attend the cast party, then headed to Chicago to lick his wounds. As for Strayhorn, he ducked out while his boss was holding court for his fans that night. "The party's just starting," Smith told him. "Not for me, it isn't," Strayhorn replied. Not only was he wounded by the show's failure, but he resented Ellington's unwillingness to give him appropriate credit for the hard work he had done. "That show meant a lot to him," Aaron Bridgers said. "He gave it everything he had in him." A seed of doubt had been sown, and soon it would bear fruit.

For Ellington the bad news had only just begun. He canceled his recording contract with Musicraft, having figured out that the label was incapable of delivering on its roseate promises. The William Morris Agency shut down its big-band department around the same time. Meanwhile, the critics started to turn on him. Mike Levin, for one, was politely but firmly dismissive of his 1947 Carnegie Hall concert in the pages of *Down Beat:*

> *No jazz admirer denies Ellington's greatness. But no Ellington fan will likewise deny that his concerts would go far better if the yearly last minute scuffles could be avoided, the music planned, written and rehearsed in time to give the band a decent opportunity to live up to its reputation . . . the Ellington organization showed itself competent as always, brilliant in a few places, but sadly lacking in fire and technical execution at others.*

A month later, Ted Hallock reviewed a Chicago performance even more dismissively for *Down Beat:* "Ellington is not as good as Ellington has been.

The obvious degeneration applies to the leader more than the sidemen because the tremendous incentive and feeling of happiness once instilled by the Duke into every player with whom he came in contact has now vanished." Hallock's review was too much for Marshall Stearns, who fired back in the same magazine, pointing out that "each year, the critics . . . commence the annual burial rites. A month or so later, after the band has ironed out the program on the road, the brighter critics change their minds and hop back on the band-wagon. No wonder Duke says despairingly: 'There are no jazz critics.'"

Stearns had a point—but so did his colleagues. It wasn't just that Ellington refused to change his procrastinatory ways. The band's unevenness also reflected the instability of its personnel roster. In mid-1947 he returned to Columbia, from which John Hammond had since departed, and started making records with George Avakian, who loved Ellington's music so much that he was more than willing to put up with the undisciplined ways of his sidemen. But many of the musicians whom Avakian admired most were no longer there. When the band straggled into Columbia's Hollywood studios in August to cut its first four sides under the new contract, the only horn players left from the prewar lineup were Lawrence Brown, Harry Carney, Johnny Hodges, and Ray Nance.

Ellington paid his first postwar visit to England in the summer of 1948, but he left the band behind, bringing with him only Nance and Kay Davis, appearing with a local rhythm section, and laying off his other musicians for the duration of the two-month tour. It was, to be sure, a matter of necessity—the British musicians' union was as sticky in 1948 about allowing foreign musicians to work in England as it had been in 1933—but the band's absence seemed to symbolize the dire straits in which its leader found himself. Even his body was turning on him: He collapsed in agony after a concert at Washington's Howard Theatre and had to undergo surgery to remove a cyst from his kidney after returning to New York.

In yet another sign of the times, Fred Guy handed in his notice the following January. Ellington did not replace him. "You just grow and grow and grow and it gets more expensive," he explained. "Getting rid of the guitar was a useful economy." True though it was that fewer bandleaders were carrying rhythm guitarists on their rosters, the consummately reliable Guy had served as a stabilizer for Sonny Greer, who was drinking so much that he could no longer be counted on to keep the rest of the band swinging. According to a musician who heard Ellington around that time, "All the booze had gone into Sonny's legs and the tempo was going haywire."

Mike Levin, long one of Ellington's staunchest advocates, now advised the beleaguered bandleader to throw in the towel: "Isn't it about time the Ellington orchestra was disbanded before what was left of a great reputation is completely dragged in the muck? . . . Little is said of the cold cash attitude of many of the sidemen and of the frightful trash the band has been turning out for the last three years." Another controversy erupted, but this time Ellington's defenders betrayed their own doubts. The bandleader Charlie Barnet, a passionate fan who had been playing his compositions for years, responded to Levin in a manner that was almost certainly more revealing than he knew:

> *You're right that Ellington sounds dispirited and tired a lot of the time these days. But who the hell doesn't? Do you have any idea what it's like, night after night, playing to sparse crowds and unenthusiastic ones at that? . . . The things I admit are wrong about Ellington, just as you do, are a reflection of the whole business today, not just Duke.*

Ellington himself weighed in the following month, and his response was no less revealing: "If I didn't like the way this band plays I wouldn't pay so much to listen to it and write for it. Our band is operating at a loss now." Most revealing of all, however, was the fact that no one outside the trade press took note of the Duke-should-quit imbroglio. General-circulation magazines no longer kept up with his doings, though that didn't stop him from continuing to write and record worthwhile music. Columbia released its first "long-playing" albums, which held up to twenty minutes' worth of music on each side, in 1948, and his first LP, a collection of instrumentals called *Mood Ellington*, contained eight tracks recorded the preceding year, "The Clothed Woman," "Golden Cress," "Hy'a Sue," "Lady of the Lavender Mist," "New York City Blues," "On a Turquoise Cloud," "Progressive Gavotte," and "Three Cent Stomp," that were as good as anything he had ever recorded.

"The Clothed Woman," premiered at Carnegie Hall in December of 1947 and recorded by an Ellington-led sextet three days after the concert, is still regarded as one of the most harmonically advanced of jazz compositions. Gunther Schuller would later describe it as "visionary," praising Ellington for having written the piece in "a freely atonal harmonic language and a commensurately free rhythmic/metric structure in the manner of a declamatory recitative." So he did, but there is more to "The Clothed Woman" than Schuller lets on. The first section is a cadenza-like out-of-tempo piano solo full of grace-note tone clusters so dissonant that most listeners (including Schuller) fail to notice that the all-but-atonal harmonies are superimposed on top of a conventional twelve-bar blues in F. A swinging full-band interlude then sweeps us into a four-to-the-bar rent-party stomp in the manner of Willie "the Lion" Smith, after which Ellington briefly returns to the outer-space harmonies with which he began.

Some of the vocal sides recorded around this time, especially Al Hibbler's "Do Nothin' Till You Hear from Me" and "Don't Get Around Much Anymore," are equally fine, and it is interesting to see how Ellington carved these deservedly well-remembered numbers out of "Concerto for Cootie" and "Never No Lament," two of the Blanton-Webster band's best sides. In both cases Ellington and Bob Russell, his lyricist, retained the opening themes of the original versions but substituted more easily singable bridges. The charts (the first by Strayhorn, the second by Ellington) are simple and bluesy sounding, and Hibbler's straight-from-the-shoulder singing is inspired. Both songs entered the band's permanent repertoire, a happy development that had the less happy effect of causing Ellington to shelve the instrumental pieces on which they were based.

If such records had been the norm in 1947, then Ellington's critical reputation would have been as solid as his bank account. But for every "Clothed Woman" or "Don't Get Around Much Anymore," the band was obliged to record a novelty like "Cowboy Rhumba," "I Fell and Broke My Heart," or "You're Just an Old Antidisestablishmentarianismist," and the ratio of quality to dross did not long escape the notice of Ellington's detractors. One of them, Alec Wilder, published in the *Saturday Review* an essay occasioned by *Mood Ellington* that remains one of the most astute appraisals of his limitations to see print. Wilder, a popular songwriter ("I'll Be Around," "While We're Young") who also composed instrumental sonatas and other works in which classical forms are infused with melodic and harmonic elements drawn from jazz and pop music, observed that the eight tracks included on *Mood Ellington*

> *are, on the whole, representative Ellington, showing that the man has the knack, as always, for creating lovely melodic lines, strong unusual rhythms, and unique orchestral effects. . . . But can you call them compositions? And can you call the man who put them together a composer? To me, the works of Ellington in terms of composition extend only as far as the song form extends, that is, the thirty-two-measure convention of Broadway and the radio, with slight extensions and variations. Beyond this, I find little integration or growth of ideas, and nothing that can be called structure.*

Wilder had had problems with *Black, Brown and Beige:* "Ellington was unhappy and unconvincing when he attempted the larger, longer forms. It was, I thought, unsuitable and even pretentious of him to develop his thematic material in terms of so-called 'serious' music." But he also felt that it was necessary for Ellington's own sake that he keep trying to break out of "the confining mold of the eight-measure phrase, the three-minute or the four-minute record. . . . I do not think that it is enough for a man of Duke's talent to be 'as good as ever.'" And he made the thoughtful suggestion that Ellington's "fortunate alliance with Columbia, with its Long Playing record, on which he can go on for six, eight, or eleven minutes (if that is his choice)[,] could be a determinative factor when he starts recording again."

Overstated though it was, Wilder's essay was full of challenging insights. It was also ahead of the curve. Because of a second recording ban by the American Federation of Musicians, the Ellington band stopped recording altogether at the end of 1947 and cut no more commercial sides of any consequence until December of 1950. But George Avakian was determined to do right by Ellington as soon as he could, so much so that he was even willing to record the suites: "I had carte blanche, we were making gigantic profits on the popular albums and anything I wanted to do, I didn't have to ask any questions." Spurred by the coming of the LP, he would not hesitate to commit Columbia Records to the great cause of making it possible for Ellington to do his best work.

Yet the world continued to turn throughout his absence from the recording studio, and by 1949 it was spinning so fast that it looked as if he might not be able to keep up. It was Louis Armstrong, not Duke Ellington, who in that year became the first jazz musician to make the cover of *Time,* an honor that the trumpeter shared with such other notables of the moment as J. Edgar Hoover, Douglas MacArthur, Cole Porter, Albert Schweitzer, Elizabeth Taylor, Mao Tse-tung, and a superannuated vaudeville comedian named Milton Berle who had moved to television the preceding June to host a weekly variety series called *Texaco Star Theater.* Within months Berle was the first full-fledged celebrity of the new electronic medium that was to dominate the postwar entertainment industry. Most Americans could not yet afford a TV set of their own in 1949—a console with a sixteen-inch screen cost $695, half the price of a new car—but they wanted one anyway, even though there was little of interest to see on network TV, least of all Berle's frenetic brand of slapstick comedy. Not that the movies were much more adventurous. The top-grossing film of 1949 was Cecil B. DeMille's *Samson and Delilah* and the most popular stars were Abbott and Costello,

Gary Cooper, Bing Crosby, Bob Hope, and John Wayne. The hottest records of the year included the Andrews Sisters' "I Can Dream, Can't I?," Frankie Laine's "Mule Train," Vaughn Monroe's "Riders in the Sky," and Columbia's original-cast album of *South Pacific,* the new Rodgers and Hammerstein musical, which sold more than a million copies.

It isn't hard to see why Americans were turning to escapist entertainment in 1949. That was the year when China went Red, Russia tested its first atomic bomb, and the United States and its terrified European allies joined together to form NATO, the multinational military alliance whose purpose was to repel a possible Soviet invasion of Western Europe. William Faulkner, who won the 1949 Nobel Prize for literature, described in his acceptance speech the state of collective tension that had replaced the giddy optimism of the postwar moment: "Our tragedy today is a general and universal physical fear . . . There are no longer problems of the spirit. There is only the question: When will I be blown up?" But some American artists were starting to respond to what W. H. Auden had dubbed "the age of anxiety." *Life,* the most trend-conscious of mass magazines, ran a feature in August called "Jackson Pollock: Is He the Greatest Living Painter in the United States?" that described the up-and-coming Pollock as "the shining new phenomenon of American art" while simultaneously making it clear that his abstract-expressionist style was not for everybody ("Still others condemn his pictures as degenerate and find them as unpalatable as yesterday's macaroni"). For all the success of *South Pacific,* 1949 was also the year of Arthur Miller's *Death of a Salesman,* a play that dared to suggest that the American dream had its nightmarish side. So, too, did such bitterly disillusioned film-noir thrillers as *Criss Cross, D.O.A., Gun Crazy,* and *White Heat,* in which Jimmy Cagney, long one of Hollywood's most beloved stars, played a murderous gangster teetering on the edge of madness.

Younger jazz musicians were no less responsive. Now that the swinging sounds of the big-band era had been supplanted by romantic balladry and gimmicky novelty songs, it was progressive-minded beboppers like Charlie Parker, Dizzy Gillespie, and Miles Davis who set the tone of postwar jazz—though their music, like Pollock's drip paintings, would never become truly popular. Most Americans preferred Perry Como, and a growing number of them were embracing other styles of music as well. It was in 1949 that Hank Williams recorded "I'm So Lonesome I Could Cry" and Louis Jordan stormed the charts with "Saturday Night Fish Fry." Black listeners were no more interested in modern jazz than white ones. Jordan's cheery, stripped-down combo jazz spoke more strongly to them, and *Billboard* took note of their tastes by scrapping the now-stilted phrase *race music* and replacing it with *rhythm and blues.*

Could an aging jazzman still make a living by writing and performing adventurous big-band music that was neither blandly popular nor radically experimental? No one, least of all Duke Ellington himself, knew for sure.

A talented new sideman could always stoke Ellington's imagination, and he found one in 1950. The tenor saxophonist Paul Gonsalves, who had been playing with the big bands of Count Basie and Dizzy Gillespie, joined Ellington in November and stayed until his death in 1974. Born in Massachusetts in 1920, Gonsalves was a Hawkins-Webster clone ("Coleman Hawkins was *it* for me") whose Cape Verdean parentage led his new bandmates to dub him "Mex." Ellington admitted to having hired him because he "knew all of Ben's solos note for note," but Gonsalves blossomed into a star instrumentalist whose ability to rouse an audience with up-tempo blues solos would become consequential to the band's future. Sweet-tempered and much loved, he was an uncontrollable drinker who discovered the parallel pleasures of heroin during his tenure with Gillespie, and in time he became the band's most unreliable sideman. According to Ellington,

> *He wants to be liked by everybody, and doesn't want anything from anyone except a kind word and a water chaser. . . . He has respect for respect, but never makes demands for himself. There is never an evil thought in his mind. In fact, his purity of mind suggests to me that he would have made a good priest. His punch line, of course, is "Jack Daniels," but that is just a kind of façade.*

A month after Gonsalves's arrival, Ellington recorded *Masterpieces by Ellington,* his first twelve-inch LP, which contained four long tracks, *The Tattooed Bride* and richly colored "concert arrangements" of "Mood Indigo," "Solitude," and "Sophisticated Lady" on which the saxophonist was prominently featured. These extended versions were arranged by Strayhorn, who went uncredited in the liner notes and whose contribution to the album did not become known until long after his death. As Walter van de Leur remarked in his study of Strayhorn's music, the title might as well have been *Masterpieces by Ellington, Arranged by Strayhorn.* But Ellington, too, was hard at work, and on January 21, 1951, the band made its Metropolitan Opera House debut with an NAACP benefit concert whose centerpiece was the premiere of *A Tone*

Parallel to Harlem. The piece had been commissioned by NBC the preceding year as part of what was meant to be a multimovement group composition called *Portrait of New York* (the other composers were Vernon Duke, Don Gillis, Skitch Henderson, and Sigmund Romberg) designed for performance by Arturo Toscanini's NBC Symphony, and a fully scored version would be premiered in June by the Ellington band and seventy NBC musicians at Lewisohn Stadium, the summer home of the New York Philharmonic.

Harlem opens with a two-note motif, a descending minor third played by Ray Nance in which the trumpeter appears to be "speaking" the word "Harlem," which will recur throughout the work. What follows its initial statement is a kind of musical travelogue, one whose events Ellington summed up as follows:

> *It is Sunday morning. We are strolling from 110th Street up Seventh Avenue, heading north through the Spanish and West Indian neighborhood toward the 125th Street business area. Everybody is nicely dressed, and on their way to or from church. Everybody is in a friendly mood. Greetings are polite and pleasant, and on the opposite side of the street, standing under a street lamp, is a real hip chick. She, too, is in a friendly mood. You may hear a parade go by, or a funeral, or you may recognize the passage of those who are making our Civil Rights demands.*

You may indeed hear all these things, though not necessarily in that order, for *Harlem* is not a conventional piece of first-this-happens-then-that program music. If you listen *very* closely, though, you might also hear a not-too-distant echo of the equally fanciful program concocted by Deems Taylor for the 1928 premiere of George Gershwin's *An American in Paris,* the tone poem after which *A Tone Parallel to Harlem* was almost certainly modeled. While Ellington is not known to have acknowledged any resemblance between the two pieces, he was definitely familiar with *An American in Paris,* which Gershwin had interpolated into *Show Girl* two decades earlier as the score for a production number. *Harlem* is organized in the same manner, all the way from the introductory "strolling" music to the hymnlike major-key theme that Ellington states midway through *Harlem* and weaves throughout the rest of the work, just as *An American in Paris* pivots on the jazzy trumpet theme that will later supply the musical material for its climactic peroration. The main differences between the two pieces are that *Harlem* is jazz, not jazzy, while Gershwin's thematic material, unlike most of Ellington's, is straightforwardly melodic—which is why *Harlem,* musically rewarding though it is, holds together less well than *An American in Paris,* on whose tuneful themes the average listener has no trouble hanging his hat.

Who arranged the full-orchestra version of *Harlem?* By his own admission, Ellington had no wish to learn how to write for a string section. "What on earth would I want with strings?" he told Leonard Feather at the time of the Metropolitan Opera House premiere. "What can anybody do with strings that hasn't been done wonderfully for hundreds of years? It wouldn't be any novelty, anyway: Paul Whiteman used strings 30 years ago. No, we always want to play Ellington music—that's an accepted thing in itself."* So he left the job to Luther Henderson, who knew quite well why Ellington wanted to hear his music performed by symphony orchestras: "He wanted me to legitimize him in this society we call classical music." Henderson's choice of words was perceptive. If Ellington had been seriously interested in the orchestra as a musical medium, he would have learned how to write for it himself. What he really wanted was the "legitimacy" that came from having his works performed by symphony orchestras, and he could get that without learning how to write for strings. It was because he never bothered to do so that his later "symphonic" works, interesting though some of them are, lack the defining touches of orchestral color that could only have been supplied by the man himself.

The critics mostly thought well of *Harlem,* less so of the band that played it. "Something important and vital is missing . . . at no point did the band or the evening really catch fire," Mike Levin wrote, adding that "the Ellington rhythm didn't seem to be booting the men as it should have." That Greer was falling apart was obvious to everyone, including Ellington, who hired a second drummer, Bill Clark, to cover up for his inadequacies. Greer's colleagues had long been troubled by the inconsistency of his playing. "Cootie [Williams] and I always sat near the drums and, whenever Greer wasn't putting the beat down hard enough, we would both whip his flagging rhythm until it moved and swung," Rex Stewart said. Even so, the subtlety with which he responded to the band's playing had always kept Ellington content—but no longer. *Down Beat* reported in February that "Greer's 30-year association with Duke might very soon be at an end."

---

* He put it more earthily in an unpublished 1956 interview: "Writing for the symphony orchestra is a technique, you know. And rather than expose myself completely to all this shit, I mean, I just turn it over . . . I make a six-line score and give it to Luther [Henderson] and let him do it . . . with suggestions, you know."

Ellington hated to fire anyone, and it's hard to imagine him dropping the blade on the band's last surviving charter member. Norman Granz relieved him of the responsibility, doing so in the most jaw-droppingly sensational way imaginable. Shortly after the premiere of *Harlem,* the hard-nosed promoter, whose Jazz at the Philharmonic concert tours had made him rich, announced that Johnny Hodges was leaving the Ellington band to start a Granz-managed combo of his own—and that Greer and Lawrence Brown were going with him.

Granz had tried without success to make Duke Ellington, Inc. a wholly owned subsidiary of JATP. His proposal to Ellington sounded plausible enough on paper: "Why don't you give up the band and I'll pay you a weekly salary . . . and any time we get ready to tour, well, then, you can hire the cats and you can pay them more and be sure to get them, then the rest of the time they'll find other gigs to do. And you can devote your time to writing." But he failed to grasp what was apparent to anyone conversant with Ellington and his ways. "It was obvious when I was smarter about the band," he later said, "that he needed [it] just for his compositions, to hear what they sounded like. . . . I think that the fact of the public recognizing the great Duke Ellington leading a great band—and Duke was obviously the most imposing of bandleaders—I think that was necessary to satisfy his ego." So Granz chose instead to go after Hodges, who was willing to be lured. Ellington and the taciturn saxophonist had long had an abrasive relationship, mainly because Hodges resented having been suckered into accepting flat fees for riffs that his boss spun into big-money songs. "When Pop turned some of their songs into hits, Rab wanted the deal changed, and when he was refused he became unhappy," Mercer recalled. "That explains why he would sometimes turn toward the piano onstage and mime counting money."

By 1951 Hodges's long-brewing spite was starting to boil over. The cornet player Ruby Braff testified to its intensity:

> *Duke and Johnny Hodges had long periods when they didn't speak to each other. At one time they lived in the same apartment block. I was waiting with Johnny Hodges outside the building for a cab one time when Duke came down, also looking for a cab. They didn't speak but Johnny said to me loudly, "What do you think about a guy who has to have a whole band to say what he wants to say? What do you think about a guy like Louis Armstrong, who can speak for himself all on his own and make the whole world listen?"*

Hodges's abrupt departure took Ellington by surprise. "He was incredibly *égoiste* in the French sense," Granz recalled. "It disturbed him equally if the room service didn't work somewhere, or if Johnny Hodges quit the band. Both upset his life, and he hated it. So he was really piqued when I took Johnny away." More than that, he knew that Hodges had become the very essence of the band's sound. Clark Terry later said that "even when he's playing a harmony part in the section you can feel him through the whole band." Not since Tricky Sam Nanton's death had he lost a player whose departure was so devastating, and Hodges added insult to injury by scoring a jukebox hit with "Castle Rock," a jump tune whose R & B–style riffs appealed to the same blacks who were deserting Ellington in droves.

The next man to abandon ship was Billy Strayhorn, though it took him longer to break with the band and his departure was never completely clearcut. Strayhorn had started pulling away from Ellington in the wake of *Beggar's Holiday*, and the process accelerated after an eye-opening chat with Lennie Hayton, a veteran Hollywood arranger who had recently married Lena Horne. Strayhorn mentioned that he had no formal publishing agreement with Ellington, and Hayton replied that he had to negotiate a deal at once. He then had a talk with Leonard Feather about the nuts and bolts of the music-publishing business. "The next time I saw him, a week or so later, I asked him if our conversation had been of any use to him," Feather recalled. "He said, 'Oh yes, thank you very much. I've found the skeletons. They give their regards.'" What he found was that several of his pieces had been copyrighted by Tempo Music in Ellington's name (or, in some cases, the names of both men). The discovery, Mercer said, hit him between the eyes: "That was the first time I saw any conflict between the old man and Strayhorn. . . . They had a talk about it, but Strayhorn wasn't satisfied, and he pulled away."

Feather, who knew both men well, understood that Strayhorn's anger was in part a response to the paternalism with which Ellington treated him:

Money wasn't quite the problem. How could it be, when Billy had everything? The problem was the lack of independence that his business problems represented . . . he was totally dependent upon Ellington for all his needs. The actual source of his frustration was artistic. He hadn't had very much of a chance to do much of his own thing since the whole period of "Chelsea Bridge," during the ASCAP strike. Surely he knew he wasn't being acknowledged for many of the things he was doing. He was obviously frustrated as an artist. He decided it was time to do something about it.

That cut to the heart of the matter. In recent years Ellington had used his protégé more as an arranger than as a composer—at least sixty of his vocal charts were played on *Your Saturday Date with the Duke*—and when he gave Strayhorn credit for his work, it was only when it suited him to do so. Onstage he was careful to acknowledge Strayhorn's contributions, though his habitual use of the royal "we" confused the issue. At the 1944 Carnegie Hall premiere of *Perfume Suite,* for instance, Ellington announced from the stage that the work had been "prepared by Billy Strayhorn and myself," but the *New York Times* review described the work as "his [i.e., Ellington's] 'Perfume Suite.'" On record he was less scrupulous. It had long been common for the two men to share credit on record labels for songs that, like "Brown Penny" and "Something to Live For," were the work of Strayhorn alone, and Ellington sometimes even took credit for Strayhorn-written instrumentals like "The Air Conditioned Jungle" and "Flippant Flurry" (both of which were composed with Jimmy Hamilton, who got the same treatment when he wrote the instrumental accompaniment to "Pretty and the Wolf," Ellington's comic monologue about the shrewd country girl and the slick city man).

For years Strayhorn had looked the other way, presumably out of gratitude for all that Ellington had done for him. But gratitude, like guilt, is a rope that wears thin, and his failure to receive credit for *Masterpieces by Ellington* may have put an end to his patience. Nat Cole's 1949 recording of "Lush Life" had brought his name to the attention of a wider public, and after 1951 Strayhorn started working independently of Ellington on compositional projects of his own. He could easily have set up shop as a freelance composer-arranger had he wished to do so, but his lack of ambition, coupled with the need to stay out of sight so that he could keep his homosexuality out of the spotlight, made it hard for him to sever his ties to his patron. The result was a depression that led him to start drinking to excess. "He drank just constantly," a close friend said. "If he was down, he drank to drown it, and if he was up, he drank to celebrate."

❧

Unlike Strayhorn's break with Ellington, the departure of Hodges, Brown, and Greer took place in full view of the public. It thus demanded a counter-coup, and Ellington's response was appropriately dramatic: He talked Louis Bellson, Willie Smith, and his old colleague Juan Tizol into quitting Harry James's band in March and going to work for him, a masterstroke that some unknown journalistic wag dubbed "the Great James Robbery." The three men left with James's blessing—the trumpeter was an Ellington fan—and their presence made an immediate difference. Tizol's talents were, of course, a well-known quantity, while Smith, best remembered today as the lead saxophonist of Jimmie Lunceford's band, was as capable of filling Hodges's chair as anyone in the business. It was Bellson's hiring that caused the loudest talk. After Buddy Rich, he was jazz's leading drum virtuoso, a powerhouse whose crisp, extroverted playing was different in every way from Greer's more subdued style—and he was white. Ellington had never before hired an unequivocally white sideman, and even in 1951, it was daring for him to do so. Bellson feared that his presence might cause trouble, but Ellington finessed the issue: "During our first 1951 tour, just before we headed south for Birmingham, Alabama, he said, 'We're going down South so we're going to make you a Haitian.' That's how they described me so we wouldn't wind up in trouble. I stayed in hotels where they stayed."

Not only was Bellson, in Ellington's words, "the epitome of perfection," but he was cheerful and modest, with none of the go-to-hell attitude of his

"I stayed where they stayed": At play in a Florida parking lot, 1955. In the thirties, Ellington and his musicians traveled by rail in private Pullman cars. Two decades later, though, they rode a chartered bus from town to town and stayed in segregated motels like this one whenever they ventured south of the Mason-Dixon Line. Ellington passed off the white drummer Louis Bellson as a Haitian after he joined the band in 1951

new colleagues. Moreover, he also composed and arranged, a rarity among drummers, and did so well enough that Ellington added two of his pieces, "The Hawk Talks" and "Skin Deep," to the band's working repertoire. Though Bellson was briefly stymied by the fact that Ellington never wrote out parts for his drummers to play, he had no trouble catching on to the routine: "Duke gave me full credit for knowing what to do in the rhythm section. He said, 'I had Sonny Greer, and now I have Louis Bellson. I want to hear Louis Bellson.'"

The new men jolted the rest of the band into action, and by May, when Ellington opened at Birdland, one of New York's most prestigious jazz clubs, the results were plain to hear. In Willie Smith's words:

For some reason or other, the band decided to wake up and really play. Great as they are, it's very seldom you can get all those guys to want to play together at one time. Some spark got into them and for six months the band was unbelievable. It had so much fire and determination— every set, no lulls, no letdowns. People used to get up in the middle of a number at Birdland and start yelling.

Jack Tracy heard the band in Chicago that month and described it in *Down Beat* as "a powerful, rocking, enthusiastic bunch of musicians who bore absolutely no relationship to the drab band that played a February concert here at the Civic Opera." George Avakian didn't need to be told twice to get them into the studio at the earliest possible opportunity. *Ellington Uptown*, the resulting album, contained high-spirited performances of *Harlem*, "The Mooche," "Perdido," "Skin Deep," and an extended version of "Take the 'A' Train" that featured a barn-burning Paul Gonsalves solo and a hip vocal by the recently returned Betty Roché, all of which showed the world what the arrival of Bellson and his friends had wrought.

Not long after the Great James Robbery, Ellington hired another stalwart individualist, this one poached from Count Basie's trumpet section. Born in St. Louis in 1920, Clark Terry was, unlike most of Ellington's older players, conversant with the new musical language of bebop. As personally disciplined as he was musically inventive, he was a superlative addition to the roster, though Ellington did not always use him to optimum effect, in part because Terry was reluctant to co-compose with him. Understanding as he did the financial implications of splitting his publishing rights with bandleaders or selling tunes to them outright, he had no wish to cut Ellington in on his royalties. But Terry admired the man and his music unreservedly and remained on board until 1959, and throughout that time his witty solos and secure ensemble work were highlights of the band's performances and recordings.

Ellington took another giant step in 1951 by signing with Joe Glaser's Associated Booking Corporation. Glaser had parlayed his friendship with Louis Armstrong, his first and most loyal client, into a multimillion-dollar business that over the years represented such black music stars as Billie Holiday, Lionel Hampton, Dinah Washington, and B.B. King. A famously coarse man, he had the arm-twisting savvy necessary to secure the bookings that the Ellington band needed in order to stay afloat at a time when most of the rest of the surviving Swing Era bands were fighting for their lives. He and Ellington would never be friendly, and while Glaser spoke respectfully of his new client in public, calling him "a fine, high-class genius," he had different things to say about Ellington behind closed doors. On one occasion, George Wein claimed, Glaser referred to him as "that crazy nigger Duke Ellington." But he knew how to do what had to be done, and that was enough for Ellington. In addition to finding steady work for the band, he let Ellington draw frequent cash advances on his Associated Booking account—he even made regular payments to Evie Ellis at one point in the sixties—thus ensuring that the bandleader would stay in debt to the agency, whose close ties to the Chicago mob were universally known in the entertainment world. Ellington understood what it meant to owe money to a man who, like Glaser, had worked for Al Capone, and as long as he did, he would never stray far from Associated Booking.

The collective presence of Bellson, Smith, Terry, and Tizol was so energizing at first that Ellington's fans paid little mind to the departure of Al Hibbler, who left in September of 1951 to go solo. But the gas finally ran out, and by 1952 the critics were once more taking disapproving note. "No one could convince me in a thousand years that any band could have an 'off night' to this extent," Ted Hallock wrote in *Down Beat* after a March concert in Portland, Oregon. Charles Mingus took him to task, firing off a letter to the magazine in which he called the review "vicious and certainly unwarranted . . . Hallock must not realize that there are many factors that can cause even the greatest band to bog down *one* night." In truth the band really was having an off night, as live recordings made before and after the Portland concert reveal. But Hallock was right about its overall condition, as Willie Smith, who was used to the spit-and-polish professionalism of the Lunceford band, would later admit:

After about six months, they went back to their old habits, and I went with them. . . . Cat Anderson would sometimes lean over and tap me on the shoulder when someone got up to take a three-or-four-chorus solo. "Let's go back and have a drink," he'd say. "No, we can't do that," I'd answer, from force of habit and training. "Don't worry, we'll be back in time," he'd say.

The problem was aggravated by the band's grueling schedule, which had become harder to tolerate now that chartered buses replaced the Pullman sleepers that had long spared the musicians some of the rigors of the road. Just as important, though, the postwar heroin epidemic had lately infected Ellington's band, which now contained a contingent of addicts led by Paul Gonsalves and Ray Nance that came to be known to insiders as the "Air Force." Gonsalves took to falling asleep on the bandstand, keeping his mouthpiece in place and puffing out his cheeks in a futile attempt to conceal his condition.

Ellington found their behavior mystifying. Once he stood with Ralph Gleason in the wings of a San Francisco theater and watched as two of his trumpet players nodded off in midsong. "I don't understand it at all," he told Gleason, shaking his head bemusedly. "I'm a cunt man myself." Yet he refused to put his foot down, explaining that "you have certain responsibilities as a human being. You don't help a man by taking away his chance to practice his trade. He'll be better off with the band than on his own somewhere. And besides, why make his family suffer?" His concern was sincere, though his reluctance to fire any of the band's addicts had at least as much to do with his own temperament. "I seldom have the urge or fortitude to be a disciplinarian," he said. "Nor do I have the impudence to be rude, or the gall or brass to demand *order*." The band's playing suffered accordingly, so much so that Willie Smith, fed up with his laxness, quit not long after the Portland concert.

❧

Ellington's reputation had already taken a hard hit from an unexpected quarter. In November of 1951, *The St. Louis Argus* published a story by Otis N. Thompson, a black reporter, which quoted him as saying that blacks in America "ain't ready yet" for desegregation and that efforts to bring it about by way of legal action were a "silly thing . . . It's something that nothing can be done about." According to the story, he questioned "the 'good it's doing us' to get one or two people in a few white schools or certain jobs." His approach to solving the problem of segregation? "Get together one hundred million dollars and then we can do something."

These statements are not so far removed from what Ellington really thought about America's racial problems, but Thompson, whose story was picked up by other black newspapers around the country, had deliberately framed the bandleader's opinions in so contentious a way that the ever-touchy black community blew its collective stack. The response was so heated that Ellington was forced to issue a statement that was reprinted in many of the papers that had carried the original story:

> *What has been published is the exact opposite of what I actually said. . . . I told Thompson that I thought fighting segregation was not a part-time proposition, but a full time one and that little could be accomplished by working spare time. . . . Now, obviously, people can't be expected to work fulltime on race problems without compensation. But if each one of us contributed $1 apiece three times a year, in two years we'd have almost $100,000,000 and then be able to go out and do a real job.*

It was the coolly detached view of a successful man who was worldly enough to know that in America, money talks loudest of all—and when it came to segregation, Ellington believed only in the power of widely shared financial success to ameliorate the sufferings of his people. When it came to other political matters, though, he kept a low profile, and lowered it still further after the *Daily Worker* falsely claimed that he had signed the Stockholm Peace Petition, a Communist-organized undertaking to outlaw nuclear war that was widely supported on the American left (W. E. B. DuBois signed it). He sent a sharply worded telegram to the paper at once and followed it up with an article called "No Red Songs for Me" that was published in *The New Leader,* a prominent liberal anti-Communist journal whose managing editor, Daniel James, was then married to Ruth Ellington. In it he roundly declared, "The only 'Communism' I know is that of Jesus Christ. I don't know of any other."

Preposterous as the controversy seems today, it was no more of a joke than Ellington's having been accused of being an Uncle Tom by a prominent black newspaper. Though he didn't know it, the FBI still kept tabs on his activities—an absurdity in and of itself, since he despised Communism and his Popular Front days were over and done with. "You know why he was anti-Communist?" Mercer told an oral-history interviewer. "Because he was so religious, and anything that downed religion had to be wrong. Aside from that, he liked the idea of one day becoming rich." He also believed that jazz and freedom were consubstantial, so much so that he recorded public-service announcements on behalf of Radio Free Europe and Radio Liberty, the government-sponsored shortwave stations that beamed his music to countries where it was a crime to listen to jazz: "When people behind the Iron Curtain tune to Radio Free Europe for a jazz program, they are getting two things at once: the music they want to hear and a little exercise in individual freedom."*

For all his increasingly frequent skirmishes with the press, Ellington was still a man apart, and in November of 1952 *Down Beat* commemorated the silver jubilee of his Cotton Club debut with an issue containing pieces by Strayhorn, R. D. Darrell, Irving Mills, and Ned Williams, accompanied by shorter tributes from a list of show-business figures that included Milton Berle, Arthur Fiedler, Jackie Gleason, Lionel Hampton, Harry James, Gordon Jenkins, Sammy Kaye, Peggy Lee, Mitch Miller, Cole Porter, and Frank Sinatra. Even Johnnie Ray, the teen idol whose hyperemotional singing style was a precursor of rock and roll, had warm words to say about Ellington. He was grappling with the future, too, filming a series of studio performance films for Snader Telescriptions that are now remembered as among the first "music videos" to be made for TV. But his men remained adrift, and when Louis Bellson quit in mid-1953, Ellington's disappointment was palpable: "It's going to be awfully difficult replacing him . . . He helped hold the band together as a unit with his drive and power."

A few weeks earlier, Ellington had switched labels again and signed with Capitol Records, whose other artists included Nat Cole, Stan Kenton, Peggy Lee, Les Paul, and Frank Sinatra. What possessed him to walk away from Columbia and George Avakian? "I signed with Capitol," he said, "because this firm is doing an excellent job of presenting all of its artists, particularly as it concerns exploitation." In show business, the word *exploitation* means "publicity," and Ellington felt that Columbia's in-house publicists were selling him short. He told Avakian, "They [i.e., Capitol] need me more than Columbia does, and I think I will be better off." While he hated to see Ellington go, Avakian knew he was right. "Ellington's sales were relatively modest," the

---

* Ellington was so adamantly opposed to Soviet Communism that when he toured the Soviet Union in 1971, he insisted for the first and only time that his musicians fly in the first-class section alongside their leader, thus demonstrating the advantages of capitalism, under which anybody with enough money to pay for a ticket could travel first class.

producer said. "They were profitable, we were delighted to keep him on from the dollars-and-cents point of view, but we didn't need him."

Capitol had never had much luck with swinging big bands—it was a singer-oriented company—and Ellington's two-year association with the label produced only two truly noteworthy recordings. "Satin Doll," recorded at the band's first session in April of 1953, was a supple, swaying riff instrumental to which Johnny Mercer, Capitol's co-founder, later appended a lyric ("Cigarette holder, / Which wigs me") that helped to make the tune a standard, the last of Ellington's songs to attain that status and thereby earn a place in the dreaded medley. Even better was *The Duke Plays Ellington,* a small-group album recorded in the same month on which Ellington, accompanied only by Wendell Marshall and Butch Ballard, the band's then-current bassist and drummer, plays a dozen compositions by himself, Strayhorn, and Mercer Ellington, in the process demonstrating the richness of tone and fully developed harmonic originality of his modernized postwar keyboard style, which had grown both simpler and infinitely more compelling since his youthful days as a stride pianist.* It was the first time that he had featured his own playing at such length on record—he had always been reluctant to show off at the piano—and it would not be the last.

Ellington cut several other listenable sides for Capitol, one of which, Strayhorn's "Orson," also recorded in April, is thought by some scholars to be the casus belli that led to a complete break between the two men. As was his custom, Ellington arbitrarily chopped nearly two minutes out of the piece and rearranged its balanced structure on the spot. According to Walter van de Leur, "Though Strayhorn's [immediate] response . . . is not known, these sessions mark the beginning of an unprecedented two-and-a-half year period during which he contributed virtually no new material to the orchestra's repertory." From then on the Capitol sessions grew more desultory, yielding for the most part only remakes, uninteresting vocal sides, and novelties like "Bunny Hop Mambo."

Ellington knew what was happening to the band—and to himself. "It's tough to have to compete with yourself," he told Ralph Gleason in July. "I'm not old enough to be historical, and I'm too young to be biographical. . . . To think that 25 years ago I had the good taste to select Bigard, Tizol, Braud, Carney, and the rest! But today I'm just a young bandleader starting

---

* Films taken in the fifties and afterward show that Ellington (like Vladimir Horowitz, Art Tatum, Thelonious Monk, and Bill Evans) played with flattened fingers, which produces a deeper, warmer sound.

out again." More than ever before, he acknowledged his despair to friendly journalists like Gleason and George T. Simon: "It's getting to be more a business than an art, isn't it? 'Dance music' is now little more than what we have always called the 'business man's bounce.' We're getting instructions on how to play for dances from heads of college prom committees. They like medium dance tempos . . . not too loud." Unable to lift himself out of the doldrums, he settled for one-nighters, mediocre recordings, and sporadic TV appearances. A month after bemoaning his fate to Gleason, he was the mystery guest on *What's My Line?*, a CBS game show whose blindfolded panelists sought to guess the contestants' occupations. With his conk glistening under the hot stage lights, he dodged their questions in a breathy, outrageously phony voice, doing his best to look as though he were having fun. (Arlene Francis: "Would you consider yourself an actor?" Ellington: "I have been mistaken for an actor, yes.")

He sought attention where he could get it, at one point stooping to publish an article in *Ebony* called "Sex Is No Sin" in which he assured his readers that "pure, clean and wholesome sex" was one of God's finest inventions:

> *I want to tell you what I think the sex act is. I think it is like a lovely piece of music, conceived quietly in a background of mutual affection and understanding, made possible by instincts which lean toward each other as naturally as the sunflower slowly turning its lovely face to the sun. I think it is an aria of the sex symphony; an aria which begins beautifully certain of its rightness, moves with that certainty to a distinct tempo of feeling, sings itself happily, steadily, working, working, to a screaming, bursting climax of indescribable beauty and rapture and then throbs, spent and grateful in a re-dedication for the next movement of its perfection.*

To his fellow musicians he remained a giant, and the younger generation held him in the same regard as did his contemporaries. *Thelonious Monk Plays the Music of Duke Ellington*, a 1955 album devoted to the avant-garde pianist's splintery, not-quite-clumsy recastings of such familiar songs as "Mood Indigo" and "Sophisticated Lady," showed how well the boppers appreciated Ellington's innovations, just as his own "New Piano Roll Blues," recorded with Max Roach in 1950, had shown how his angular dissonances prefigured those of Monk. Ray Nance remembered playing a Monk record for him one day in 1948: "Duke was passing by in the corridor, and he stopped and asked, 'Who's that playing?' I told him. 'Sounds like he's stealing some of my stuff,' he said.

So he sat down and listened to my records, and he was very interested. He understood what Monk was doing."*

The public, however, had lost interest in Ellington, and so had the critics. He didn't even place in *Down Beat*'s 1955 critics' poll, whose big-band category was led by Count Basie. The two great survivors of the Swing Era, long the friendliest of rivals, had dealt with changing musical times in totally different ways. Unable to rely on the steady stream of songwriting royalties that made it possible for Ellington to meet his payroll, Basie coped by briefly touring with an eight-piece combo, then launching under Norman Granz's auspices a reorganized "New Testament" band that specialized in blues-based arrangements by Neal Hefti and Ernie Wilkins whose streamlined, danceable simplicity was as suited to the optimism of the Age of Eisenhower as was the devil-may-care insouciance of Frank Sinatra's postwar singing style. Ellington's records, by contrast, were selling worse than ever, and a look at the list of songs that topped the *Billboard* singles chart in 1955 shows that the caravan of mass taste had left him far behind. The pop tunes that Americans favored in 1955 included "The Ballad of Davy Crockett," "Cherry Pink (and Apple Blossom White)," "Mr. Sandman," "Rock Around the Clock," "Sixteen Tons," and "The Yellow Rose of Texas."

Capitol dropped him in May, and in June he was reduced to playing a two-month stint at Elliott Murphy's Aquacade in Flushing Meadows, accompanying an ice show whose tinselly background music required him to add a string section and a harp to his regular lineup. Ellington actually relinquished the piano bench to an anonymous performer hired by the contractor, playing only on his greatest-hits medley. It was, Mercer said, the low point of his career: "It looked like he might not be able to continue to help other people, relatives and friends, as he had throughout his life. He had some glorious moments during these hard times and he was successful artistically, but it wasn't bringing in much coin of the realm."

A year later he was the best-known bandleader in the world.

---

* Ellington later returned the compliment. His 1953 trio recording of "Kinda Dukish" ends with a quote from Monk's "52nd Street Theme."

14

"I WAS BORN IN 1956"

Crescendo in Blue, 1955–1960

UKE ELLINGTON'S SECOND ascent to the pinnacle of fame began when, shortly after the Aquacade gig, Johnny Hodges disbanded his now-struggling combo and returned to the fold. Four years on the road had left the master saxophonist weary of the chicken-today-feathers-tomorrow life of a second-tier bandleader: "I had to scuffle, and when you scuffle you can't play what you like, but when you are famous and popular you can. . . . It was a whole lot of work but it was a whole lot of headache too." So Norman Granz devised a face-saving deal under which Hodges would be allowed to make solo albums for Clef, the promoter's own record label, without first obtaining Ellington's approval. With his usual shrewdness, Granz also stipulated that in return for allowing Hodges to record with Ellington, the band would agree to cut an album for Clef—two if Ella Fitzgerald, another Granz artist, were to take part. The concession, which Ellington probably assumed would turn out to be purely hypothetical, seemed a modest enough price to pay, and Hodges rejoined the band in August, once more becoming its most prominently featured and highly paid member. Not only was his greatness as an improviser undiminished, but his presence in the ensemble restored to Ellington's musical palette a color without which the band had not sounded the same. In addition the reed section became stable again after his return, and it stayed that way: Hodges, Harry Carney, Paul Gonsalves, Jimmy Hamilton, and Russell Procope played alongside one another for the next thirteen years.

Around the time that Hodges resumed his chair, Ellington found a drummer capable of filling Louis Bellson's shoes. Sam Woodyard, born in New Jersey in 1925, was a self-taught player without any big-band experience—he had been working in a trio led by the jazz organist Milt Buckner—and at first glance he seemed an unlikely successor to the impeccably trained Bellson. Woodyard, who could not read music, later admitted to having been "scared" about the prospect of working with a band known for its complicated charts. But Ellington liked rough diamonds, and his playing was forthright in a way that meshed well with the recent arrival of rock and roll. Like Bellson, he had a relaxed and agreeable personality, and Ellington guided him through the repertoire with verbal rhapsodies that made his musical desires explicit: "Play four bars introduction, Sam, sixteen bars of exoticity, and then swing the bridge." Whenever he wanted Woodyard to get funky, he asked the drummer to "get in the alley" or "put the pots and pans on," a reminder of how he looked to his men to supply the down-home feel that had never come naturally to him. While Woodyard emulated his predecessor by playing "Skin Deep" and switching to a double-bass-drum kit, Ellington esteemed him in his own right for his ability to swing hard without swamping the rest of the band: "No crash bang, never overpoweringly loud, volume just where it should be—in there." He also worked well with the bassist Jimmy Woode, who had joined the band early in 1955. The two men became a superb rhythm team whose sympathetic interaction inspired Ellington, who in turn responded with some of the best piano playing of his middle years.

Ellington brought the band into New York's Café Society in January. Nat Hentoff took immediate note in *Down Beat,* proclaiming "the end of the recent slump in the Ellington orchestra," crediting Hodges and Woodyard with the renascence and describing the new ensemble as "the most under-rated band in the country." More important, *Time* covered the drummer's arrival in an unsigned review of the Café Society engagement that declared the band to be "practically reborn," thanks mainly to Woodyard: "When the band appeared bored with a number, he seemed to get under and shove—and the band came alive." The only thing still missing was Billy Strayhorn, and Ellington was determined to lure him back as well.

Strayhorn showed up at Café Society for the band's opening night. "I talked to Edward," he told the friend who accompanied him there. "He would like me to be more engaged again. He asked me what sort of project I would like to do." Later that evening Ellington introduced him to Irving Townsend, a producer at Columbia Records, and proceeded to ladle the syrup of flattery all over his amused protégé: "Mr. Townsend, you're so fortunate to have come tonight because you have the pleasure of meeting the wonderful man I told you so much about, Mr. Strayhorn. Mr. Strayhorn has many wonderful, wonderful ideas for recordings, and if Mr. Strayhorn has an idea, it must be truly wonderful." Prompted by George Avakian, Townsend suggested that the band team up with Rosemary Clooney, then one of America's most successful pop singers, who was far more musically accomplished than was generally realized. In 1955 she was known for her hit records of brainless dialect songs like "Come on-a My House" and "Mambo Italiano," none of which she chose—Mitch Miller, her producer, was the guilty party—and all of which she hated. Avakian longed to make a high-class album with her, and the result was *Blue Rose,* a fabulously well-sung collection of tunes written by Ellington and Strayhorn but arranged by Strayhorn alone (though the two men shared credit for the charts). One instrumental, "Passion Flower," a feature for Hodges, was also included. According to Clooney, "Having 'Passion Flower' on there was sort of a wink, an inside thing to those in the know that this was basically Billy's record."

In February the band, which was still without a recording contract, cut a pair of albums for Bethlehem, a small jazz label, called *Historically Speaking—the Duke* and *Duke Ellington Presents . . .* The first one was devoted in part to new performances of old pieces, some of them indifferent (the French jazz critic André Hodeir dismissed the remake of "Ko-Ko," played much faster than the 1940 studio recording, as "a hideous copy which makes a mockery of [Ellington's] own masterpiece") and others remarkable (Ray Nance's plunger solo on "East St. Louis Toodle-O" is as ear-catching as that of Bubber Miley thirty years earlier). Also included was "Upper Manhattan Medical Group," a harmonically adventurous new piece by Strayhorn that was, once again, credited to Ellington on the record label. Though the second album, which consisted mainly of standards, was less interesting, it helped persuade listeners who had yet to hear the band live that the press was not overstating the effects of the hiring of Woodyard and the return of Hodges and Strayhorn.

What Ellington now needed was a medium-size publicity coup, one that, like the Great James Robbery, was big enough to prove that his expensive gentlemen were earning their salaries again. Instead he got the break of a lifetime—and came heart-stoppingly close to blowing it.

The first Newport Jazz Festival, which took place in 1954, was a two-day-long outdoor jazz festival held in an enclave of inherited wealth, most of whose residents knew roughly as much about jazz as they did about black people, and underwritten by a pair of socialites who knew plenty about jazz and were willing to put their money where their taste was. It was also a rip-roaring success that drew thousands of paying customers, most of them anything but rich, who flocked from far and wide to hear Ella Fitzgerald, Erroll Garner, Dizzy Gillespie, Billie Holiday, Gene Krupa, the Modern Jazz Quartet, Gerry Mulligan, and George Shearing. By the time that George Wein, a Boston nightclub owner whom Elaine and Louis Lorillard had hired to produce the festival, was making ready to return to Rhode Island for the third summer in a row, he was in no mood to waste time on a relic like Duke Ellington.

Wein knew how historically important the Ellington band was, but he felt that its leader was resting on his laurels. He also knew that there was, in his words, "no industry buzz on Ellington . . . to the press and to the jazz world he was on the way down." Enter George Avakian, who had struck a deal with Wein and the Lorillards to record the 1956 festival for Columbia. Learning of Wein's reluctance to book the band, Avakian called Ellington and said, "Look, the festival is making it, and we've given them twenty-five thousand dollars for the right to record. Can you put something together that we can call *The Newport Jazz Festival Suite* or some such thing? It would be a good tie-in. I know there's not much time. Can you do it?" Ellington's reply was as unhesitating as it was typical: "Okay. I'll get Strays to work on it right away."

Strayhorn went to work on a three-part suite whose first two movements were composed entirely by him, with Ellington contributing the finale. The piece had not yet been rehearsed when the band rolled into Newport on the morning of July 7, the day of the premiere. Ellington called Avakian from the road the night before, sounding worried. "Look, we've got to be ready to do something to protect this composition . . . the guys are simply not prepared," he said, urging the producer to stand ready to re-record the new work on the Monday after the Saturday-night concert. Avakian, who had enough experience with the band to know what he might be in for, duly booked Columbia's Studio D in Manhattan for a touch-up session.

Ellington also placed a call to George Wein, who asked him what the band would be playing at Newport's Freebody Park on Saturday. "Oh, nothing special," he replied. "A medley, and a couple of other things." The umpteenth repetition of the ASCAP medley was what Wein had feared most, and he hit the ceiling: "Edward, here I am, working my fingers to the bone to perpetuate the genius that is Ellington—and I'm not getting any co-operation from you whatsoever. . . . You better come in here with something new and swinging or the critics are going to kill you." Ellington may have been pulling Wein's leg, but it seems more likely that he was being cagey about the new piece, since he didn't know whether it would be ready to play the next night. The Saturday-afternoon rehearsal, from which Jimmy Hamilton, Ray Nance, Clark Terry, and Jimmy Woode were inexplicably absent and which Avakian later described as "kind of a disaster," did nothing to assuage Ellington's fears, though the producer calmly assured him that anything that went wrong on the stage could be fixed later on in the studio. And Ellington was cutting it even thinner than that, since not only would Columbia be recording the concert, but it was also being taped for broadcast by the Voice of America. If he failed to deliver the goods, the whole world would know.

The evening concert got off to a scary start, for Hamilton, Nance, Terry, and Woode had not yet returned from wherever they went. Ellington was obliged to start the show without them, playing "The Star-Spangled Banner," "Black and Tan Fantasy," and "Tea for Two" minus two trumpeters and a saxophonist and finagling the bassist Al Lucas, an alumnus of the band who was playing with Teddy Wilson's trio, into subbing for Woode. Ellington was already irritated with Wein, who had asked him to play a short introductory set, then come back on at the end of the night. "What are we—the animal act, the acrobats?" he snapped. He grew more irritated as the night wore on, for Wein had scheduled Wilson, the Jimmy Giuffre Trio, the Chico Hamilton Quintet, Anita O'Day, and the Bud Shank Quartet in between his two sets. Giuffre, Hamilton, and Shank, who played "cool" modern jazz, were all popular in 1956, and their up-to-the-minute sounds threatened to make the Ellington band sound quaint.

Ellington called his men together for a backstage pep talk, reiterating the importance of the occasion and telling them that they would have a chance to re-record the suite on Monday. His four wandering players had just made their belated return, which boosted his confidence. "After we finish [the suite], let's just relax and have a real good time," he said. "Let's play the *Diminuendo and Crescendo*." He meant *Diminuendo and Crescendo in Blue,* the rousing composition with which he had stopped the show at the Randall's Island "Carnival of Swing" outdoor festival in 1938. Throughout the forties he had fussed over the transition between the piece's first and second sections, inserting at various times such contrasting "slow movements" as "I Got It Bad (And That Ain't Good)," "Rocks in My Bed," and "Transblucency" to create a three-part "blues cluster," always to inadequate effect. Then he hit upon a better solution, inviting Paul Gonsalves to play an ad-lib "wailing interval" of blues choruses in the key of D-flat, accompanied only by the rhythm section. Live recordings of two performances, taped in 1951 and 1953, show that Gonsalves took at once to the new routine.

Even though the band is known to have played *Diminuendo and Crescendo in Blue* with the wailing interval in place as recently as three months prior to the festival, Gonsalves jokingly feigned not to know which piece Ellington had in mind. The bandleader, who knew how undependable Gonsalves could be when under the influence, seems to have taken him seriously. "Paul, it's the one where we play the blues and change keys," he replied. "I bring you on, and you blow until I take you off, and we change keys. Enough. It's number 107 and 108 in the book." With that terse reminder, he and his musicians strode onstage, accompanied by a fifth trumpeter, Herbie Jones, whom Ellington had apparently summoned as flop insurance. (Unlike the other players, who were dressed in white tuxes, Jones wore a black suit.) They started out by playing "Take the 'A' Train," then proceeded to what was intended to be the main event of the evening, the world premiere of *Newport Jazz Festival Suite*.

Ellington hinted in his onstage introduction at the behind-the-scenes chaos that had preceded the performance. "We have prepared a new thing, and we haven't even had time to title it yet," he said, going on to identify the first two movements of the "new thing" as "Festival Junction" and "Blues to Be There" but neglecting to mention that Strayhorn had written them. Both were competent but unmemorable riff-based instrumental charts, and the mediocre Ellington-penned finale, "Newport Up," brought the suite to a weak and uncertain close. The playing was sloppy, the audience response tepid. Ellington then made the mistake of following the suite with the overfamiliar "Sophisticated Lady" and a flabbily sung rendition of "Day In, Day Out" by Jimmy Grissom, among the most insipid of the male vocalists who had passed through his ranks. One shudders to imagine what George Wein was thinking.

"He had to change the energy," Clark Terry later said. "Maybe he was bewildered there for a minute, but he knew how to come out of it." So he kicked off *Diminuendo and Crescendo in Blue,* and as the antiphonal riffs of the opening chorus exploded from the bandstand, the energy changed instantly. Then Gonsalves stepped to the microphone and proceeded to play twenty-seven straight choruses of the blues. He was whipped into a mounting frenzy by Sam Woodyard's popping backbeats and the unseen backstage presence of

"You blow, and then I take you off": At the 1956 Newport Jazz Festival, immediately after a showstopping performance of *Diminuendo and Crescendo in Blue*. Paul Gonsalves's twenty-seven-chorus "wailing interval" set the crowd to dancing and helped put Ellington on the cover of *Time*

Jo Jones, who had played drums for Teddy Wilson earlier in the evening and now egged on Gonsalves by shouting words of encouragement and slapping a rolled-up copy of *The Christian Science Monitor* against the lip of the stage. Avakian, who was standing in the wings, was floored. "I'd never heard a rhythm section like that," he recalled. "I'd never heard the Ellington band wailing that way." Heard in cold blood, Gonsalves's solo sounds banal and repetitious, but on the night of July 7, 1956, just six days after Elvis Presley went on *The Tonight Show* to sing "Hound Dog," his uncomplicatedly direct, R & B–influenced playing came across as heartfelt, even to a modern jazzman like Paul Desmond, Dave Brubeck's intellectually inclined alto saxophonist. "What you and the band played was the most honest statement that night," Desmond told Gonsalves after the performance. And Avakian was right about Ellington, Woode, and Woodyard: No other rhythm section, not even Count Basie's crack team of musical arsonists, had ever played with such unquenchable fire.

Not only was Avakian unable to believe what he was hearing, but he was no less floored by what he was seeing:

A platinum-blonde girl in a black dress began dancing in one of the boxes (the last place you'd expect that in Newport!) and a moment later somebody else started in another part of the audience. Large sections of the crowd had already been on their feet; now their cheering was doubled and redoubled . . . Halfway through Paul's solo, it had become an enormous single living organism, reacting in waves like huge ripples to the music played before it.

Fourteen minutes and fifty-nine choruses after *Diminuendo and Crescendo in Blue* got under way, Cat Anderson's incendiary high notes brought the piece to a near-hysterical close, followed by an ovation that was, if possible, louder than the performance. Fearing a full-scale riot, Wein tried to stop the concert, but Ellington forestalled him by bringing on Johnny Hodges, who played two solo numbers, "I Got It Bad" and a down-in-the-alley version of "Jeep's Blues," that revved the audience all the way back up. It took three more songs to calm everyone down, after which Ellington told the audience, "We do love you madly," a catchphrase that was now his standard sign-off. Then he quit the stage in triumph, knowing that he and Gonsalves had saved the day. "Paul Gonsalves, Jimmy Woode and Sam Woodyard lifted that stone-cold audience up to a fiery, frenzied, screeching, dancing climax that was never to be forgotten," he wrote seventeen years later in *Music Is My Mistress*.

"Within an hour, reporters and critics were buzzing about it," Avakian said of the concert. One of the buzzers was Whitney Balliett, who described Ellington's second set as a "magnificent frenzy," singling out the "extraordinary ten-minute solo blues interlude played by Paul Gonsalves as honest, old-time rhythm and blues—a bomb that blew the crowd to its feet, to dancing, to rushing crazily at the bandstand." Irving Townsend offered the band an exclusive three-year contract, and in October Columbia released *Ellington at Newport,* a more-or-less live album that Avakian pieced together out of a combination of actual concert tapes and a studio version of *Newport Jazz Festival Suite* that was recorded in New York two days after the premiere. It became, and remained, the biggest-selling album of Ellington's long career. The critics, predictably enough, had their doubts about *Ellington at Newport,* and about Gonsalves's marathon solo. Some of them also took note of the fact that the ensemble playing on *Diminuendo and Crescendo in Blue* left much to be desired in the way of exactitude. "I am afraid the music that caused the conflagration doesn't wholly hold up," Nat Hentoff wrote in *Down Beat*. But by then nobody cared about such hairsplitting qualifications, for *Time* put Ellington on its cover six weeks after Newport, and from that moment on he was untouchable.

Contrary to popular belief, *Time*'s cover story was not published in response to the band's Newport appearance. As far back as the end of 1955, Joe Morgen, Ellington's publicist, had been nudging Carter Harman, the magazine's music editor, to take note of the band's resurgence. Harman's initial response was to write the story about Sam Woodyard's arrival that appeared in January. "I wrote this article to keep Joe Morgen quiet," he said. "It didn't work and I knew it wouldn't." What Morgen wanted was an Ellington cover, and in May the editors said yes: Harman interviewed Ellington in Las Vegas, after which he sat for Peter Hurd's cover portrait in San Francisco. All that remained was to find a news peg, and with Ellington's triumph at Newport, the editors had what they needed. Harman started drafting the four-thousand-word piece at the beginning of August, and it was published in the August 20 issue of *Time,* which appeared on newsstands a week earlier. "Mood Indigo & Beyond" was everything that Ellington could possibly have wanted. Studiously avoiding such radioactive topics as his relationship with Evie Ellis, Harman instead stuck to the well-trod anecdotal path traveled by Richard O. Boyer twelve years earlier, mentioning his hypochondria, his vanity, his sex appeal, and his resolute detachment from the eccentricities of his sidemen: "I told those guys in 1927 they were never going to drive me to the nuthouse. 'We may all go there,' I said, 'but I'm going to be driving the wagon.'"

The story, however, concentrated on such recent achievements as his performance at Newport. Ellington had pushed for that emphasis in his interview with Harman: "I think it'd be better for you—well, for me, too, of course—if we don't emphasize the history point of view . . . it would do me a helluva lot more good if the reason for the goddamn thing has to do with now." It ended with a quote from the man himself: "We're not worried about writing for posterity. We just want it to sound good right now!" And *Time*'s verdict on whether the band sounded good was unequivocally in the affirmative:

> *The event last month . . . confirmed a turning point in a career. The big news was something that the whole jazz world had long hoped to*

hear: the Ellington band was once again the most exciting thing in the business, Ellington himself had emerged from a long period of quiescence and was once again bursting with ideas and inspiration.

In 1956 a *Time* cover was the coup of coups. With the sole exception of *The Ed Sullivan Show,* on which the Ellington band had yet to appear, no TV program came remotely close to rivaling its impact. Thanks to the combined effect of Newport and *Time,* the travails of the past decade melted away. Three days after the festival, Ellington teamed up with the New Haven Symphony Orchestra to play *Harlem, New World A-Coming,* and a colorful new full-orchestra work called *Night Creature* that would become a staple of his symphonic appearances. On July 10 he entered into his contract with Columbia, signaling the start of a nonstop parade of creativity, his first prolonged period of compositional inspiration since the late forties. Not only was he writing around the clock, but the band was playing with renewed vigor and unanimity—though listeners with long memories noticed that it didn't always look as good as it sounded. When Ellington returned to England in 1958, this time with the full band in tow, his friend Leslie Diamond, who had heard the band on its first European tour, was puzzled by the lackadaisical appearance and behavior of his musicians. "At the Palladium in 1933, they were all in tails—now they come on in crumpled suits, stained and shabby," he told Ellington. "Your instruments used to be all silver or all brass-gold. Now they're mixed up—you take them from whoever gives them to you free. And this habit you've slipped into of letting the musicians drift on one by one—why?"

Part of the difference was that Irving Mills was no longer around to tend to such things, and part of it was Ellington's continuing unwillingness to ride herd on his men, or on himself. No matter how late the musicians were for a recording session, their leader would always be the last to arrive, smilingly saying, "Am I late? Oh, dear. What time is it anyway?" It was his way of reminding the prima donnas in the band who was in charge. "I mean, he made it very clear . . . that there was only one indispensable person in that whole orchestra, and that was Duke," said Norman Granz. "If nobody else showed up, well, that's okay. I'm the one."

Irving Townsend, who had succeeded George Avakian as Ellington's producer at Columbia, was as fascinated by his quirks as any of his previous colleagues and put some of them down on paper. It was Townsend who noticed that he never wore a watch, and that he preferred to see his friends and family individually rather than in groups: "Rarely were even his closest friends gathered with him at the same time. Seldom have I seen his relatives together in one room." He was even more careful to be unavailable after hours to the members of the band, staying when possible in a different hotel. Long experience had taught him that the best way to interact with friends, family, and colleagues was on the phone: "Ellington at ease was Ellington once removed . . . every now and then the phone would ring between six P.M. and six A.M. A dark, sleepy voice would say, 'Good morning. Did I wake you? I'm so sorry. What time is it anyway? What's happening?'" That was why he preferred the anonymity of hotels to the comfortable chokehold of domesticity: "The secret of Duke's security was constant movement. . . . A thousand hotel rooms, a thousand room-service waiters ready to push his breakfast table in on cue, a thousand loyal friends waiting to handle any local problems he might have: these made up the Ellington menage."

Above all, he kept his eye on the future rather than the past. Though he took care to pacify his older fans by trotting out the dreaded medley each night, he preferred to think about the next piece, not the last one, in part because, as he explained to Townsend, "My loot comes from publishing. We have to make new things." But his dislike of the past went further than that, so much so that some thought it close to phobic. A few months before he turned sixty, Townsend and Arthur Logan, Ellington's personal physician and intimate friend, decided to mark the occasion by "gathering up everything ever written by him, making clean copies of it, and presenting to Ellington a complete set of Ellington in bound volumes." They enlisted Billy Strayhorn and the trombonist John Sanders, who doubled, like Tizol before him, as one of the band's regular copyists, to do the dirty work of taking his tattered manuscripts and turning them into fine copies, then assembled the results into a leather-bound presentation set that Logan gave to the great man on the great day. Afterward Logan told Townsend that Ellington "made polite noises and kissed us all . . . but, you know, the son of a bitch didn't even bother to take it home."

Was it that he hated to be reminded that he was on the brink of old age? In later years Ellington answered questions about his age by saying, "I was born in 1956 at the Newport Festival." Strayhorn, however, saw it more as a matter of artistic priorities: "He not only doesn't live in the past. He rejects it, at least so far as his own past accomplishments are concerned. He hates talking about the old bands and the old pieces. He has to play some of the Ellington standards because otherwise the audiences would be disappointed. But he'd much rather play the new things."

Ellington himself explained his attitude in terms of marketing:

My competitors in the band business are not playing across the street. My competitors are the Duke Ellingtons of the 1940s and 1930s. Everybody wants me to play the way I always did. Macy's [has] been in business 50 years, but they're not selling the same stuff they did in 1920.

He knew, too, that he needed help in order to keep the assembly line running smoothly. While he had worked off and on with a number of talented composers and arrangers in the preceding decade, among them Jimmy Hamilton, Luther Henderson, Mary Lou Williams, and Gerald Wilson, Billy Strayhorn was still (as Dizzy Gillespie once described Charlie Parker) the other half of his heartbeat. *Time* had mentioned the younger man only in passing, but its story was accompanied by a photo captioned "The Duke & Family: Mercer Ellington and wife Evelyn, Duke, his sister Ruth, Arranger Strayhorn." That said it all: Strayhorn was part of the family, and Ellington would do whatever was needed in order to get him back. After the cover story came out, the two men sat down to dinner at the Hickory House, Ellington's favorite steak place, to hash out their differences. "He's seeing stars again," Strayhorn told his friends afterward. "He's been seeing stars now since Newport. . . . He wanted to know what I want to do." Ellington agreed to give Strayhorn equal credit for everything that they wrote together. Then he raised his glass of hot water and proposed a toast: "To Duke Ellington and Billy Strayhorn—to their new incorporation."

Ellington already had two big commissions on the horizon, a Shakespearean suite and a TV musical for CBS. Strayhorn was more interested in the first project and started composing music for it, but Ellington had promised Columbia that the band's first album under its new contract would be the soundtrack of the program that the Theatre Guild had commissioned for broadcast on *The United States Steel Hour,* one of the many live-TV anthology series that dominated the Golden Age of Television. With production deadlines looming, the two men put aside Shakespeare and started writing *A Drum Is a Woman,* the latest of Ellington's attempts to create a successful stage work.

A Drum Is a Woman was to be a poetic allegory about the creation myth of jazz, narrated by Ellington himself. It was, he had explained in *Time,* derived from *It's All True,* the abortive jazz-related film project that he and Orson Welles had discussed fifteen years earlier, and it would be as extravagant an affair as could be crammed into a TV studio. The cast included Carmen de Lavallade and Talley Beatty, two of the most admired modern dancers of

"You feel the weight of the joy": Rehearsing *A Drum Is a Woman* at CBS, 1957. El-lington's frequent TV appearances on such popular programs as *The Ed Sullivan Show* kept him famous long after big-band jazz had become unfashionable. Paul Gonsalves is seated immediately behind Ellington

the fifties, and three singers, Ozzie Bailey, Joya Sherrill, and the soprano Mar-garet Tynes, a member of the New York City Opera who was appearing with Harry Belafonte in an off-Broadway show called *Sing, Man, Sing*. Not only were all of the performers black, but they would be given a full hour of prime time to themselves, an unprecedented departure for network TV. Since CBS had commissioned *A Drum Is a Woman* to show off its experimental color-television system, the production budget was more than sufficient to Elling-ton's purposes. "It will be the most ambitious thing we ever attempted artistically," he told *The New York Times*.

Ellington kept his word to Strayhorn, giving his partner full and equal credit for *A Drum Is a Woman*. The result, Strayhorn said, was their "largest hunk of collaboration . . . He wrote lyrics, I wrote lyrics. He wrote music, and I wrote music. He arranged, and I arranged." The surviving manuscript material, however, indicates a more clear-cut division of labor, with Strayhorn writing most of the numbers that were accompanied by the full band. Ellington sketched out the small-group numbers in tandem with his soloists, and he also appears to have written most of the spoken narration, which left something to be desired when it came to clarity. Irving Townsend's synopsis is as good as any:

> *It is an allegory paralleling the history of jazz . . . in which an elaborately fabricated drum is turned into a very sophisticated lady who travels from Africa to the Caribbean to New Orleans to New York City and finally to the moon, meeting in each place a simple man always named Joe, and touching him with her spell before leaving him for the next Joe.*

The "sophisticated lady" in question goes by the semi-anagrammatic name of Madam Zajj. Ellington describes her in his narration as "an exciting, ornately stimulating seductress with patterns of excitement and the power to hypnotize and enervate the will toward total abandonment." She is, in other words, a fantasy figure who embodies his own mixed feelings about women, and the explanation of her relationship to Carribee Joe that Ellington gave to *The New York Times* indicates that whatever else he was, he was no feminist: "A drummer is a skin whipper. And a woman is definitely the most important accessory a man has."

Unusually for Ellington, the music for *A Drum Is a Woman* was written and recorded before the work was staged. Marshall Jamison, the show's producer, armed Paul Felton, Paul Godkin, and Willard Levitas, the director, choreographer, and designer, with advance copies of the album, telling them, "Do whatever the hell you want, because the thing doesn't make any sense." What came out of their joint labors was a mishmash whose "plot" recalls Marshall Stearns's memories of one of the Cotton Club's more lurid floor shows. Though the dancing was lively, the performers had to work in a cramped studio, and Ellington, who read his part from cue cards, sounded more than a little bit silly at times: "For every drum you hear, there's a woman to see. Their gyrations accelerate to a frenzy." Despite savory passages, among them Johnny Hodges's luscious harp-accompanied waltz solo in "Ballet of the Flying Saucers" and Clark Terry's trumpet cadenza in "Hey, Buddy Bolden," an evocation of the legendary New Orleans cornet player, the score is too closely tied to the stage action and narration to be intelligible when heard on its own.*

---

* Except for a number of still photos, the only surviving visual document of the telecast currently in circulation is a fuzzy black-and-white kinescope that fails to show how *A Drum Is a Woman* looked to the handful of viewers who were able to see it in color.

Asked in 1966 which compositions of his had satisfied him the most, Ellington replied, "Of the big things, *A Drum Is a Woman,* and some of my early songs. They're not big pop successes, you know, but in all of them you feel the weight of the joy." Few others agreed. Jack Gould, the TV critic of *The New York Times,* dismissed the work as "shrilly pretentious, lacking in compelling emotional intensity, or merely routine commercial numbers such as might be found in a night-club floor show for visiting tourists" and suggested that the members of the cast "were subjected to regrettably stereotyped roles." Whitney Balliett, who had recently left the *Saturday Review* to become *The New Yorker*'s first full-time jazz critic, called *A Drum Is a Woman* "an almost embarrassingly flimsy affair, which failed both as a piece of light nonsense and as a true indication of Ellington's abilities."

Next came *Such Sweet Thunder,* a thirty-five-minute suite in which Ellington and Strayhorn offered their joint musical reflections on the plays of William Shakespeare. A week and a half after Newport, Ellington had given two concerts at the Stratford Shakespearean Festival. Impressed by the atmosphere there, he agreed to return to Canada the following year to perform a new piece inspired by Shakespeare's writings, with which he was said to be closely familiar. According to Don George, "He had everything by Shakespeare, in many different versions. . . . In all his copies of the Shakespearean plays, he had underlined parts that appealed to him, not only to be set to music but to be performed by him." But nothing that Ellington said about the Bard and his works, then or later, indicated that his knowledge of the canon was other than superficial. Not even Strayhorn could make that far-fetched notion sound believable, though he tried:

> *Ellington has always been intrigued by Shakespeare, 'cause he said Shakespeare certainly knew more about people than anyone he's ever known. Duke also said that the only way Shakespeare could have known as much about people as he did, was by hanging out on the corner, or in the pool room.*

Hence the importance of striking a deal with Strayhorn, who had no need to brush up his Shakespeare. "We used to call him Shakespeare—that was one of his nicknames," Jimmy Hamilton said. Others who knew the plays well backed Hamilton up. According to Thomas Patterson, the founder of the Stratford Shakespearean Festival, "We were with literally the top Shakespeare scholars in the world, and Strayhorn didn't have a thing to apologize for. His knowledge was very deep." Accordingly, it was Strayhorn who devised a plan of action for the proposed suite, scribbling down a list of characters from *A Midsummer Night's Dream* and the instrumentalists who might "play" them: "Clark [Terry] = Puck; alto is Hermia; John [Sanders] = Lysander; violin = Tatania [*sic*]; clarinet = Oberon." Irving Townsend later claimed to have found the title of the eventual work, a phrase spoken by Hippolyta in *A Midsummer Night's Dream*, by flipping through *Bartlett's Familiar Quotations.*

Such Sweet Thunder soon evolved into a much more wide-ranging survey. Eleven of the twelve movements purport to portray characters or situations in *Antony and Cleopatra, Hamlet, Henry V, Julius Caesar, Macbeth, A Midsummer Night's Dream, Othello, Romeo and Juliet,* and *The Taming of the Shrew.* Four are twenty-eight-bar "sonnets" that feature individual soloists, while the finale, "Circle of Fourths," was said by Ellington to be a tribute to the poet himself. "All we did is just little thumbnail sketches, you know, of very short periods, never at any time trying to parallel an entire play or an entire act or an entire character throughout, but just some little short space of time during a character's performance," he added.

Ellington, as always, talked a good game, elucidating his musical portraits so cleverly that few questioned their relationship to the texts of which they were supposed to be illustrative. Why did he portray Lady Macbeth with a scampering jazz waltz called "Lady Mac"? "Though she was a lady of noble birth," he obligingly replied, "we suspect there was a little ragtime in her soul." It sounded great to those who didn't probe too deeply, so much so that *Such Sweet Thunder* can be understood in part as a masterpiece of packaging, a "concept album" that yokes together the names of Ellington and Shakespeare to the former's benefit. The truth, however, was that at least two of the movements, Strayhorn's "Half the Fun" and "The Star-Crossed Lovers," were preexisting compositions that had no more to do with Shakespeare's plays than "Harlem Air-Shaft" had to do with apartment life. Both were retitled and inserted when the composers ran out of time to complete the suite prior to its first public performance, which took place at New York's Town Hall on April 28, 1957. According to Strayhorn, the usual opening-night anarchy prevailed: "We were rushed and that night at the Town Hall concert was the very first time Duke and I had heard the whole suite without a break. We had rehearsed it in pieces, but this was the first time it had been played from beginning to end." Ellington added that the two men had "spent two months talking about [*Such Sweet Thunder*] and then . . . spent three weeks actually writing it." The finale was as yet unwritten, so he announced from the stage that the band would perform in its place an up-tempo swinger called "Cop Out." George Avakian was one of the few people in the hall who got the joke: "It was such a straight crowd that they didn't even know they were being put on."

Such Sweet Thunder was finished and recorded by the time that Ellington presented the work in Stratford on September 5, programming it alongside the score for *A Drum Is a Woman*. It was the last time that he would ever perform either suite complete. Only two movements of *Such Sweet Thunder*, the title piece and "The Star-Crossed Lovers," became regular parts of the band's working repertoire. No one knows why Ellington steered clear of the work in later years, since its critical reception was favorable and has remained so ever since, with John S. Wilson praising it in *The New York Times* as "a long work in the finest Ellington tradition . . . the best work that Mr. Ellington has done in a decade." The only dissent of any consequence came from Whitney Balliett, who called *Such Sweet Thunder* "uncomfortably thin" and dismissed even the strongest of its sections as "casual sketches that depend largely on the soloists involved and not on the ensemble-solo development one expects from Ellington."

Balliett's review was brief but astute. Like virtually all of the suites that preceded and followed it, *Such Sweet Thunder* is a collection of unrelated pieces, some of which, like "Circle of Fourths," are so thin textured as to sound tossed off rather than worked out, and the three most substantial sections, "Half the Fun," "The Star-Crossed Lovers," and "Up and Down, Up and Down (I Will Lead Them Up and Down)," in which Clark Terry "speaks" Puck's signature line "Lord, what fools these mortals be!" on his trumpet, are all by Strayhorn, not Ellington. "The Star-Crossed Lovers," in fact, is one of Strayhorn's most inspired postwar compositions, a fine-spun, seemingly endless arc of melody sustained by off-center harmonies that go yearningly unresolved until the very last bar. That the rest of the suite came off as well as it did was, as Balliett remarked, as much a triumph of performance as of composition, for the band, notwithstanding signs of insufficient rehearsal, sounded "almost as confident, precise, and full-bodied . . . as the great Ellington organization of 1940."

Though Ellington again kept his promise to give Strayhorn equal billing, the younger man's name went largely unmentioned in most of the reviews of *Such Sweet Thunder*. Did he plan it that way, knowing that his worldwide celebrity would swallow up his junior partner's lesser fame? Perhaps, though it is also true that Joe Morgen, the band's publicist, went out of his way to keep Strayhorn out of the public eye. According to Phoebe Jacobs, "Morgen thought that Billy represented competition for Duke's attention, and that Joe Morgen couldn't bear. And Billy was gay, which threw Morgen completely off the deep end." Either way Strayhorn soon figured out that the new arrangement with his patron was, like the old one, a devil's deal. Only by striking out on his own could he hope to make a name for himself, and the reasons for him not to do so were as compelling in 1957 as they had been in 1939.

∿

For all its limitations, *Such Sweet Thunder,* unlike *A Drum Is a Woman,* is a satisfying piece, Ellington's most consistent multimovement composition since *Black, Brown and Beige.* Some of his own contributions, including the eponymous first movement, which sounds as though Shakespeare had walked into a strip joint, and the haunting "Sonnet for Caesar," a dead-slow march in which Jimmy Hamilton's piping clarinet wanders sorrowfully among the trombones, are up to his highest standard, while Strayhorn's three glittering efforts give the suite a core of excellence.

But Ellington's spectacular start at Columbia was followed by a slow fizzle. While his later albums for the label, including *Ellington Indigos,* a 1958 collection of ballad performances, and *Blues in Orbit,* a deceptively offhand-sounding album of smaller-scale compositions, all contained fine things, none had the conceptual unity of *Such Sweet Thunder* or *A Drum Is a Woman,* nor were they nearly so ambitious. In one, *Newport 1958,* he tried without success to make lightning strike twice by returning to the scene of his earlier triumph. Another, falsely billed by Columbia as a complete version of *Black, Brown and Beige,* was actually a revised version of "Black," the work's first movement, augmented by a vocal version of "Come Sunday" performed by the popular gospel singer Mahalia Jackson, who also contributed an impromptu "setting" of the Twenty-Third Psalm. ("He didn't rehearse me nothin'," she later said of the latter performance. "He said, 'Just open the Bible and sing!'") For those who hoped that Ellington would put all of *Black, Brown and Beige* on record, it was a disappointment.

In addition to recording for Columbia, Ellington started in 1956 to make additional private tapes that went into what he called his "stockpile," a cache of unreleased material that accumulated into the seventies. Unlike the scores of his compositions that had been prepared by Strayhorn and John Sanders for his sixtieth birthday, he saw the stockpile as his true legacy, a sonic archive that belonged solely to him—and to posterity. In the words of Brooks Kerr, a blind jazz pianist and Ellington scholar to whom he later became close, "He was the kind of guy that was going to go to his grave with all the secrets in his head. And his legacy would be his unissued recordings that he would will to his family."

Was he writing too much, and did he wait too long to start writing? The answer to the second question is an incontestable yes. "I wouldn't finish anything if I didn't know when I was going to play it," he blithely admitted. Time and again he tarried so much that the musical quality of his work was impaired as a result. When Norman Granz called in his marker and recorded *Ella Fitzgerald Sings the Duke Ellington Song Book* for Verve in 1957, the sessions were, in Fitzgerald's words, "a panic scene, with Duke almost making up the arrangements as we went along." It may have been his bloody-minded way of getting back at Granz for having bested him in the negotiations over Johnny Hodges's contract. The fact that the album mostly failed to come up to snuff didn't seem to bother Ellington, though it troubled Fitzgerald so much that she considered scrapping the project in midsession. "Ella really was very upset, and she didn't want to do it," Granz said. "She wanted to walk out. . . . Strays spent a lot of time holding Ella's hand and saying, 'There, there, it's going to be okay. Don't worry.' "

When he was good, though, nobody was better, and he could still rise to the occasion of a fresh challenge, as he did when Otto Preminger, one of Hollywood's top film directors, invited him to score *Anatomy of a Murder* in 1959. Preminger's latest film was based on the bestselling novel of the same name by John Voelker, a Michigan Supreme Court justice who wrote under the pseudonym "Robert Traver." While jazz-flavored film scores had been popular ever since the release of *The Man with the Golden Arm*, Preminger's 1955 film version of the novel by Nelson Algren about a heroin-using jazz drummer, it is not clear why Preminger deemed such a score suitable for a film that was set in rural Michigan. Though the director was familiar enough with Ellington's music to have initially considered using "Sophisticated Lady" as the theme song for *Laura*, he was at least as interested in the windfall of publicity that would arise from hiring jazz's best-known composer to score his first film. Ellington would also be the first black composer of any kind to write a full-length film score, and that, too, was newsworthy.

Hope Preminger, the director's wife, suggested yet another reason for his decision to approach Ellington:

> *Otto chose Duke because Duke would be a talked-about choice, and Otto valued that. And he liked to use people who really wanted to score a film. Otto was quite unusual because he insisted on having the*

*composer on the set during the production. He felt that they got closer to
the picture that way. Therefore, he said he liked to use composers eager
to prove themselves, because nobody else would sit [still] for spending all
that time on the set.*

Ellington was starting at the top: *Anatomy of a Murder* was a big-budget
screen adaptation of a blockbuster novel, one that was far more candid about
sex than was common in 1959. The cast was led by James Stewart, who played
a "humble country lawyer" (as his character puts it) whose "cornball" manner
(as George C. Scott, his prosecutorial nemesis, puts it) conceals a cold-eyed appreciation of what one of his colleagues describes as "the natural impurities of
the law." Inspired by a passage from the novel in which the first-person narrator goes to a roadhouse to listen to "a new small Negro combo, with a pixi-
lated piano man," Wendell Mayes, the screenwriter, took Stewart's character,
who in the novel was an amateur drummer, and turned him into an amateur
pianist, as Stewart was in real life (though Strayhorn dubbed his on-screen
playing). He also wrote in an on-screen cameo for Ellington, who plays a jazz
pianist named Pie Eye. In addition to playing a duet with Stewart, he was
given a grand total of two lines to speak: "Hey, you're not splittin' the scene,
man? I mean, you're not cuttin' out?"

Ellington later said that Billy Strayhorn acted as his "consultant" on
Anatomy of a Murder. In the event, though, Strayhorn ended up writing very
little of the score, with which Ellington was solely credited, both on-screen
and on the cover of Columbia's soundtrack album. He seems to have composed much of the thematic material prior to watching the first rough cut of
the film, basing it on his initial reading of the script, after which he turned his
themes into lengthy "cues" that may or may not have been meant to be synchronized with the action. Probably for this reason, only a fraction of the
score made it onto the soundtrack, and Ellington is not known to have par-
ticipated in the process of "spotting" the music cues that were used. A lengthy
main-title cue played under a credit sequence animated by the graphic designer Saul Bass, a sprinkling of character-sketching vignettes, a few between-
scenes transitions: These sufficed for Preminger and Richard Carruth, the
film's music editor. No music of any kind is heard during the long courtroom
scenes, nor is it used other than infrequently to underscore dialogue. On the
rare occasions when music is heard in a dialogue scene, it gives the impression
of having little to do with the action that it accompanies.

Since neither collaborator ever discussed the score in detail, it is impossible to know why Preminger used Ellington's music as he did. Assuming

that his motives in hiring Ellington were anything other than publicity-minded, he may have expected the composer to supply an urban-style sub-text to the small-town backgrounds, thereby implying that sexual passion is as likely to be found there as in big cities. One of the most attractive cues, for instance, is a piece called "Flirtibird" that introduces Lee Remick, who plays Laura, a sexually provocative young woman whose husband (Ben Gazzara) shoots and kills the man who has just raped her. But we cannot know whether this was Preminger's intention. All we know is what we hear on the soundtrack, a sparse, fragmentary musical background that is often theatrically naïve. In "Flirtibird," for instance, Ellington echoes one of the oldest of film-music clichés, using Johnny Hodges's glissando-laden alto-saxophone playing to hint at Laura's apparent sexual availability.

Much of the score, especially "Flirtibird" and the main-title theme, a hard-driving blues in six-eight time that Ellington and Peggy Lee later turned into a pop song called "I'm Gonna Go Fishin'," is compellingly listenable when heard in isolation from the film, which may explain why Preminger used so little of it on the soundtrack. "Music in pictures should say something without being obviously music, you know, and this was all new to me," Ellington told Ralph Gleason. It was in any case an experiment that the director did not repeat, with him or any other jazz composer, nor was Ellington given the opportunity to work on another film of comparably high quality. Of the three subsequent feature films that he scored, *Paris Blues* (1961), *Assault on a Queen* (1966), and *Change of Mind* (1969), all are second-rate or worse. The bright promise of his initial venture into film scoring turned out to be a dead end.

By 1959 Ellington's life had settled into an ever-changing yet ever-predictable pattern. He worked the festival circuit, cut two or three albums each year for Columbia, and appeared on TV whenever the opportunity arose. In between these activities, he crisscrossed the United States. Though the movie-house stage shows of the thirties and forties were now a thing of the past, Ellington and the band still played as many one-night stands and club dates as Joe Glaser could line up, and on occasion they sailed for Europe, there to play one of the tours that Norman Granz organized for them.

Granz had taken charge of the overseas bookings in 1958, bringing the band back to Europe after an eight-year hiatus. Notwithstanding their past skirmishes over Hodges and Ella Fitzgerald, Ellington was glad to do business with the promoter. "There was nothing special about it," Granz said. "Duke wanted to tour. 'How much?' was the only question. I gave him the right answer." He sent Ellington to three dozen different cities that fall, including Amsterdam, Berlin, Brussels, Copenhagen, Glasgow, Hamburg, Liverpool, London, Milan, Munich, Paris, Stockholm, and Vienna, and neither then nor later did he charge a commission for his services.* While it was in his interest for the Ellington band to perform throughout Europe under his auspices, Granz was genuinely altruistic about jazz, and his activities had made him rich enough to act on his convictions, though he and Ellington never had a comfortable relationship. "I think my liking for Duke was as a fan probably more than as a human being," Granz said after Ellington's death. "In retrospect, I think I was maybe closer to the music than I was to Duke Ellington as a man."

Between them, Granz and Joe Glaser set a killing pace for Ellington and his men, one of whom summed up their life on the road with terrible brevity in *Time*'s cover story: "You go to the hotel, take a long look at the bed, go play the date, take another look at the bed and get on the bus." The musicians put up with it because Ellington continued to pay them generous salaries—on occasion he even made them "loans" that would never be repaid—and studiously ignored their anarchic offstage behavior. Ellington stayed off the band bus, preferring to ride from gig to gig in Harry Carney's car, but otherwise he pushed himself at least as hard as he did his players. He and Carney, whose good nature made him a boon companion, often traveled for four hundred miles at a stretch, with the saxophonist doing the driving and the composer the navigating. "He's a very good man to have along," Carney said of Ellington. "He sits in the front and he does a lot of thinking. He'll pull out a piece of paper and make notes. We do very little talking, but if he thinks I'm getting weary he'll make conversation so that I don't fall asleep."

Gordon Parks recorded a snippet of their conversation for posterity:

> *The three of us were approaching San Francisco early one morning after an overnight drive from Los Angeles. In the distance, the Golden Gate Bridge floated eerily in the dawn mist rising above the bay. Harry called Edward, who was asleep in the back seat. "Hey, Big Red, wake up and look over yonder. Looks like something you might want to write about." Duke stirred awake, wiped his eyes and looked at the bridge. "Majestic. Majestic. Goddamn those white people are smart," he mumbled and fell back to sleep.*

---

* It was on the 1958 tour that Ellington met Queen Elizabeth II in London. "Struck speechless" by her grace, he responded with one of his most elegant gestures, writing with Strayhorn a piece called *The Queen's Suite*, then recording it and having a single copy of the album pressed for her alone.

Ellington still pretended to have a home life for the benefit of prying reporters. In March of 1957 he appeared on *Person to Person,* Edward R. Murrow's celebrity talk show, to promote the upcoming CBS telecast of *A Drum Is a Woman,* and his portion of the interview was shot in the elaborately decorated Upper West Side apartment that he shared with Evie. We see him exchanging idle chitchat with Murrow while seated at a white piano, showing off oil portraits of his parents, playing a snippet from *A Drum Is a Woman* on the phonograph in his music room, and introducing Mercer and Ruth to the viewers at home. But the impression of domestic stability created by their presence was deceptive, as much so as the fact that Ellington kept Evie out of sight throughout the program. The West End Avenue apartment was hers, not his, and so were the dinner parties that she threw when he was gone. "I just don't have time to be a social cat . . . now all my time goes into music," he told Nat Hentoff.

To that end he kept a vampire's hours, flitting from hotel to hotel and room-service meal to room-service meal, all so that he could carve out of his crowded days and nights the privacy that he needed in order to compose. "You gotta be older to realize that many of the people you meet are mediocrities," he had told Carter Harman. "You have to let them run off you like water off a duck's back. Otherwise, they drag you down." No one was allowed to do that to Ellington, not then and not ever. His refusal to submit to the ordinary demands of love and friendship necessarily made for a solitary life, solitary at times to a degree that bordered on the monastic. Not everybody understood the price that he paid for his single-minded dedication to his art—he seemed, after all, never to be alone—but John Voelker, who met him when *Anatomy of a Murder* was being shot in Michigan, viewed him through the clear eyes of a novelist and a judge and was struck by what he saw: "I gradually felt drawn to him, not because I savor disillusion, but rather because I sensed that, in his case at least, [his disillusion] masked great sensitivity and pride and even, however finely veiled, a vein of melancholy and loneliness."

The melancholy, if that is what it was, is not on display in the many TV appearances by the band that have come down to us. In them one sees only the public Ellington, poised and content. The earliest surviving visual document of a complete concert, videotaped at Amsterdam's Concertgebouw in 1958, lets us turn back the clock and see how Harlem's Aristocrat of Jazz carried himself onstage, his mask securely in place. It's an ordinary night for the band, perhaps a shade better than average: All the chairs on the stand are occupied, every necktie is tied, and though no one does anything all that surprising, the band takes care of business. The program is ordinary, too: Johnny Hodges plays "All of Me" and "Things Ain't What They Used to Be," Paul Gonsalves works out at length on *Diminuendo and Crescendo in Blue*, the ASCAP medley is dished up in two installments, and a pair of Blanton-Webster classics, "Harlem Air-Shaft" and "Jack the Bear," are trotted out for the benefit of local jazz connoisseurs. Ellington hasn't much to say beyond assuring the audience that he loves it madly, preferring to sit in watchful silence at the piano, sprinkling each number with the "strange chords" that Barney Bigard had long ago found so disconcerting.

One thing that the Amsterdam concert dramatizes is the way in which the band's working repertoire evolved over time. Though Ellington claimed not to be interested in the past, he usually took care to offer his fans a cross-section of older pieces. Nor did he simply fob them off with the medley. Except for the improvised solos, the versions of "Harlem Air-Shaft" and "Jack the Bear" that he performed in Amsterdam are note-for-note re-creations of the 1940 charts, played not pro forma but with enlivening enthusiasm (Clark Terry, for instance, steps into Cootie Williams's slot on "Harlem Air-Shaft," tossing off a solo full of twisty bebop triplets). In other cases, though, he played updated versions of his tried-and-true standards, some of which were written for specific occasions, while others had gradually assumed new shapes.

An example of the latter is "Rockin' in Rhythm," which started life in 1931 as a pleasantly raggy two-beat stroll whose "notey" reed-section melody sounds like an orchestrated piano solo. The live version recorded nine years later in Fargo, by contrast, reveals that the song had turned into a hell-raising free-for-all jam tune. In 1953 Ellington and his rhythm section recorded a trio number called "Kinda Dukish" that was based on "Rockin' in Rhythm," and by the time of the Amsterdam concert he was using it as an extended piano prelude to the older song. According to Mercer, Ellington started prefacing "Rockin' in Rhythm" with "Kinda Dukish" in order to give delinquent musicians time to get to the bandstand: "The idea was for the audience to think that the band was waiting for Ellington to make up his mind what tune he wanted to play first. But he was actually waiting for the stragglers to take their chairs."

The concert also shows that after five years of relative stability, Ellington's men were playing extremely well. Not only would the reed section remain intact for another decade, but Quentin Jackson, John Sanders, and Britt Woodman had all been playing trombone together since 1954. Even if the band's soloistic firepower was diminished, it was still a powerful performing unit led by the most individual musician in jazz. Granz was right: Ellington himself was sufficient unto the day thereof, and he continued to draw sustenance from the expensive gentlemen to whom he freely dedicated his life and songwriting royalties. "Watch him some night in the wings," an unnamed sideman told Nat Hentoff. "Those bags under his eyes are huge, and he looks beat and kind of lonely. But then we begin to play, he strides out on the stand, the audience turn their faces to him, and the cat is a new man."

Yet that, too, was a mask, one that Ellington had worn for so long that he could no longer pry it off, not even when the band that he had brought to Newport in 1956 started to come apart at the seams. When Cat Anderson, Quentin Jackson, John Sanders, and Clark Terry quit toward the end of 1959, followed soon after by Jimmy Woode, the accumulated momentum of the preceding three years was dispelled, and so was Ellington's compositional vitality. Once he had found inspiration in new players, but by then few major soloists were willing to go out on the road with a big band. Sam Woodyard was the last incoming member of the Ellington band who succeeded in changing its collective style by the force of his example. A few first-class players came along after that, but never again did a musician as distinctive as Woodyard or Clark Terry join up—and it is not clear that Ellington wished to hire such players. According to the bassist Aaron Bell, who replaced Jimmy Woode in 1960, he would tell his men, "Characterize it for me. Play it the way you want." But since World War II he had mostly been replacing his departing soloists with journeymen who evoked the sounds of days gone by instead of creating brand-new ones of their own. Even the best of them, like Shorty Baker or the trombonist Tyree Glenn, who played with Ellington from 1947 to 1951, were too often expected merely to imitate their predecessors, like replacements in the cast of a long-running Broadway show.

As for the handful of truly original musicians who had joined since the war, some of them, like Terry, felt creatively compromised by their presence in the band:

> *During my last couple of years with the band I began to wonder how much freedom I had to grow. I felt myself slipping away. . . . It suddenly dawned on me that you can sit in the Ellington band so long that you become too much a part of it. For all that seeming looseness of direction, Duke really runs things, and it seems to me that his main goal as a leader is to mold a man so fully into the Ellington way of playing that he finds it hard to pull away.*

That, he added, was what happened to Hodges, as well as Williams and Lawrence Brown. Though all of them left, they all came back, and even Hodges, who had had some success on his own, sounded happiest when in the company of his fellow Ellingtonians. And that was why Terry quit: He feared becoming so fully absorbed into the self-sustaining musical organism that was the Ellington band that he would no longer be able to function without the guiding hand of the master.

And what of Ellington himself? Was advancing age sapping his creativity? Or did he simply spend too much time on the road? The *Time* cover story quoted an unnamed "friend" as follows: "If he retired for a few years and just wrote, he would leave a wealth of music. The record companies should let Duke write tremendous symphonies that would represent America and a style of music. . . . He shouldn't be limited to 14 or 15 men." It was, of course, uncomprehending nonsense, the kind that was echoed by outsiders who failed to understand that he was incapable of doing any such thing. His pianism continued to deepen, as can be heard on *Back to Back* and *Side by Side,* a pair of blues-oriented combo albums featuring Johnny Hodges (who received equal billing with Ellington) that Norman Granz recorded for Verve in 1959. Building on the promise of the 1953 trio sides, he had blossomed at last into a truly great small-group soloist. But the music that he was now writing for the full band was less impressive. He needed the band as much as it needed him, and neither was what it used to be.

What Ellington undoubtedly thought he needed was a new Paul Gonsalves or Sam Woodyard. Instead he found something completely different: a new woman.

15

"FATE'S BEING KIND TO ME"

$\mathcal{A}$potheosis, 1960–1967

T HE ARRIVAL OF middle age did not lessen Duke Ellington's need to keep his personal life away from the public eye. *Time*'s cover story had contained only an evasive reference to "a separation from his wife that became permanent," a sentence even more obscure than the one included in the magazine's earlier story about the premiere of *Black, Brown and Beige* ("His wife, from whom he has been separated for many years, lives in Washington"). He had insisted on it. According to Carter Harman, the terse reference replaced an "unforgivably brusque" description of Ellington's domestic arrangements inserted by a researcher for *Time* who had dared to talk to Edna Ellington. When *Ebony*'s Marc Crawford interviewed her at length in March of 1959, describing her as "the virtually unknown Duchess who has lived a lifetime in Duke's shadow" and allowing Edna to speak for herself about the breakup of their marriage thirty years earlier, he flew into a rage.

A few years later Ellington would specifically acknowledge to Harman, who was considering writing his biography, "the responsibility of not embarrassing the Negro." That responsibility must have weighed on him even more heavily after he won the NAACP's Spingarn Medal, a decoration that singled out "the highest or noblest achievement by an American Negro during the preceding year or years," in September. The winners of the medal included such luminaries as George Washington Carver, Roland Hayes, James Weldon Johnson, Marian Anderson, Richard Wright, Paul Robeson, Thurgood Marshall, Ralph Bunche, and Martin Luther King Jr. No jazz musician had previously won it—nor have any won it since. The decision to single out a jazzman for such high honors was a source of controversy in the black opinion community, which was as self-conscious about middle-class respectability as was Ellington himself. An editorial published in the *Los Angeles Tribune* pushed all of his buttons at once: "Lord knows, we love his music, but its sexy growls and moans have never moved us to go out and register to vote, or bowl over a bastion of prejudice." His own people, it seemed, were no more willing to acknowledge his achievements than were whites—perhaps even less so.

He knew that there would always be somebody looking over his shoulder, and had long ago resolved never to forget his self-imposed duty to act "on behalf of the race." But he was no less determined to lead his life as he pleased, and women still found him toothsome. According to the jazz pianist Marian McPartland, who played throughout the fifties at the Hickory House, one of his New York haunts, he "had so much sex appeal it was almost frightening." It was as evident when, in March of 1960, the band

"I became his slave": Fernanda de Castro Monte with Duke Ellington in Madrid, 1966. An exotic-looking lounge singer who was known as "the Countess," she became Ellington's mistress in 1960 and catered to his every whim. When Evie found out about their affair, she threatened to shoot him on the spot

settled down in Las Vegas to play a three-month run at the Starlight Lounge of the Riviera Hotel. That was where Ellington met Fernanda de Castro Monte, who was working as a lounge singer at the Tropicana. She came to hear Ellington, was smitten at first sight, began an affair with him, and soon grew so obsessed with her new lover that the Tropicana fired her for missing shows. "I became his slave," she told Don George.

Very little is known about Monte, who was never interviewed and rarely photographed, but everyone who met her agreed that she was a strange bird. Ellington introduced her to friends as "the Countess," and that was what the members of the band called her as well, sometimes referring to her as "the Countess from Algeria." According to Derek Jewell, she was around forty at the time of her first meeting with Ellington. George described her as "a tall, strikingly handsome, blond lady who stood bold" and dressed flashily, favoring furs, jewels, and sunglasses. Charles Sam Courtney, a diplomatic official who met the Countess when Ellington and the band came to Turkey in 1963, remembered her as "an aging woman wearing too much make-up but sexy nonetheless" who spoke with a "bizarre" accent that sounded "more like the Bronx than Algeria." While Courtney took it for granted that she "could not have been listed in any peerage," the Countess's exoticity was self-evident, for she carried an Argentinian passport, claimed to have lived in Algeria and Brazil, and is said to have spoken several languages.

She was, in short, a woman uncommon enough to catch Ellington's eye, and she pressed her advantage at once, sending two dozen red roses to the bandleader's dressing room at the Starlight Lounge for several nights in a row, then showing up at a table for one. "She would remain for a set and then disappear mysteriously," Mercer recalled. "This went on for a week, and then Pop knew who was sending the roses." Their affair, he added, progressed to the point where "nobody could see Ellington from the time he left the stand until he came back and sat down at the piano the next evening. Once he got off [the bandstand] he disappeared, as though the night had engulfed him."

What started as a passing fancy grew into one of the longest-lasting involvements of his life. Though the Countess came and went as she pleased, she and Ellington were inseparable whenever they were together, usually during his overseas tours. "She was very much there," the choreographer Alvin Ailey recalled. "I mean, under his armpits. He couldn't walk out onstage and direct the orchestra without her being next to him." She would, he said, follow Ellington into a men's room in order to stay close to him. The Countess went out of her way to take care of her companion, going so far as to pack his suitcases and clean his dressing rooms. Above all, Ellington said, she tended to his stomach: "She makes sure I eat all right, and that's enough for me to give her whatever she wants." Among other things, she introduced him to vodka and caviar, which, so he said, enhanced his virility.

Most of Ellington's friends and colleagues liked the Countess. Even Ruth spoke well of her: "She did a lot for Edward. She interpreted for him. She did research. She was very intellectual. I certainly liked her, as I liked anyone who could make Edward happy." Norman Granz described her as "a very cultured woman. . . . She could introduce you to art dealers and such, and she was certainly very cognizant [of] art." He thought her an improvement on Ellington's previous girlfriends: "Duke did well to have her, I think. It was much better than having some old groupie hanging around." Ellington was careful to keep their relationship secret, partly because the Countess was white, which would have caused a scandal in America, and partly because he was genuinely afraid of Evie, who was as suspicious as ever of her longtime companion's other companions. Inevitably, though, she learned of the affair, and on one occasion she is said to have flown to Tokyo, caught him in bed with the Countess, pulled a gun, and insisted that he choose between them— which he declined to do.

Was Ellington in love with the Countess? Or was he merely thrilled by her obsession with him? He was sixty when they met, an age when the most attractive of men may find themselves beset with self-doubt. It is easy to imagine him falling for her at so discomfiting a moment, but their involvement, far from being transient, was to endure for the rest of his life.

With the arrival of the Countess, Ellington's creative juices started to flow again. In September came *Suite Thursday,* a piece premiered at the Monterey Jazz Festival whose four brief movements were nominally inspired by *Sweet Thursday,* John Steinbeck's 1954 novel about life on the Monterey waterfront. Ellington and Strayhorn had already recorded a colorful jazz version of Tchaikovsky's *Nutcracker Suite,* and *Suite Thursday* was later coupled on LP with a similar treatment of five movements from Grieg's incidental music for *Peer Gynt.* Most of the latter arrangements were by Strayhorn, but *Suite Thursday* appears to have been almost entirely Ellington's work, and despite its slightness, the piece (whose last movement, "Lay-By," displayed Ray Nance's violin playing to highly favorable effect) suggested that he was shaking off the torpor caused by the sudden loss of so many of his players.

A month after recording *Suite Thursday,* Ellington went to France with Strayhorn to work on his second film score, *Paris Blues,* leaving the band behind and spending nearly two months in the city where the film was set. He later described his stay there as "the closest thing to a vacation [he]'d ever been able to think about," though it was of necessity a working holiday: "I've never had a vacation from music in my life. Oh, once in a very great while, I may leave the band for a few weeks, as when I was writing the music for *Paris Blues* in Paris. But I'm never away from music. I may not have been in swimming during the preparation of *Paris Blues,* but at least I was getting a little wet." The score, which includes a splendidly moody title song, received an Academy Award nomination, the first to go to a black composer (it lost to *West Side Story*).* The music, alas, was wasted on Martin Ritt's pretentious film, in which Paul Newman and Sidney Poitier play grimly serious expatriate jazzmen who become entangled with Joanne Woodward and Diahann Carroll. Bosley Crowther dismissed *Paris Blues* in *The New York Times* as "a weak, aimless story," and it is remembered today only for the Ellington-Strayhorn score, which is both more elaborate and more prominently featured than the music for *Anatomy of a Murder.*

Ellington hit another bump in the road when he went from Paris to Las Vegas and, much to his disgust, was promptly forced to make bail for four members of the Air Force. Paul Gonsalves, Ray Nance, and the trumpeters Willie Cook and Fats Ford were all arrested when heroin was found in the apartment that they had been sharing. Asked if there'd been any trouble at the time of the arrest, Ellington replied, "No, there wasn't. The boys, you know, have a profound appreciation of the skulls they were born with." While Cook and Ford got off, Gonsalves and Nance were prosecuted and tried. The saxophonist was put on probation, but because Nance had received a suspended sentence for a 1956 drug charge, he spent two months in jail, after which the band was banned from playing in Las Vegas for two years.

By now Columbia's executives were losing interest in Ellington, whose records no longer sold well. Indeed, his best album of 1961 was made not for Columbia but for Roulette. *Louis Armstrong & Duke Ellington: Together for the First Time* was not nearly so elaborate an affair as the Armstrong-Ellington collaboration originally envisioned by George Avakian, who had wanted to make an album on which Armstrong would be backed by the full Ellington band. The ever-cautious Joe Glaser scuppered that notion, but he let the two men record together with the All Stars, the trumpeter's combo, and the resulting album, which reunited Ellington with Barney Bigard, who

---

* It was not Ellington's first brush with the Oscars. The band had played for dancing at the 1934 Academy Awards banquet in Los Angeles.

was now playing clarinet with the All Stars, was a satisfying set of Ellington-penned songs on which Armstrong sang and played superlatively.*

Six months after taping *Together for the First Time,* the two men appeared together on *The Ed Sullivan Show* to promote it. Sullivan, the most prominent TV variety-show host of the fifties and sixties, had finally brought Ellington onto his program in 1959 as part of a segment occasioned by the release of *Anatomy of a Murder* (which the tongue-tied Sullivan referred to on camera as "Anatomy for Murder"). After that his appearances on the popular and influential series would be frequent, and though he rarely did anything more challenging than heat up one or two of his old chestnuts, Ellington's guest shots with Sullivan, which continued until 1970, gave him national exposure at a time when other big bands were finding it harder to get a hearing on TV.

In 1962 Columbia called it a day, dropping Ellington after six years. The decision was strictly business: Goddard Lieberson, Columbia's president, hated the idea of showing so great an artist the door, but the accountants pulled out their balance sheets and told him that it was no longer cost-effective to record the band, and that was that. Ellington went freelance and took the opportunity to tape three all-star small-group albums. While his collaborations with John Coltrane and Coleman Hawkins were more than worth hearing, it was *Money Jungle* that made the biggest impression. A decidedly modern-sounding trio album, at times almost aggressively so, *Money Jungle* teamed him with Charles Mingus and Max Roach, two of the most revolutionary players of the postwar era. The recording session was stormy—Mingus and Roach, who were as temperamental as they were talented, found it impossible to get along—and Miles Davis, for one, didn't much care for the results: "You see the way they can fuck up music? It's a mismatch. . . . Duke can't play with them, and they can't play with Duke." Most listeners, however, were impressed, above all by the furiously churning title track and "Fleurette Africaine," an astringent minor-key ballad, both of which showed that Ellington could still teach the boppers a thing or two.

Around the time that *Money Jungle* was recorded, Mercer Ellington talked Cootie Williams into rejoining the band, to which Lawrence Brown had returned a year and a half earlier. Even without Columbia, things were

---

* In exchange for Ellington's services, Morris Levy, the owner of Roulette Records, struck a deal that allowed Count Basie, a Roulette artist, to appear on a 1961 Columbia album called *First Time! The Count Meets the Duke* on which the Basie and Ellington bands played together in the studio.

looking up, and the end of the year brought the best news of all: Reprise, Frank Sinatra's new label, signed Ellington to an exclusive contract. Sinatra, who had gone into the record business after growing restive at Capitol, his old label, was having fun at Reprise, where he could record whatever and whomever he wanted. He had signed Al Hibbler and later tried to hire Billy Strayhorn as one of his house arrangers, but Ellington objected, so Sinatra chose instead to take on the entire band. He, Sammy Davis Jr., and Dean Martin announced the deal in November at a Chicago bash described in *Billboard* as "the loudest, swingingest, brassyest, most-sought-after and most-crashed cocktail party of the year." Sinatra informed the reporters that Reprise would not only allow Ellington to record at will but was also creating an "Ellington Wing" that would "showcase new as well as established jazz artists." Ellington, in other words, would function not merely as a recording artist but as an A & R man for Reprise. He liked that idea, just as he liked the idea of working for a man like Sinatra, whom he praised in *Music Is My Mistress* as "a *primo* nonconformist *assoluto*," instead of an executive suite full of drones: "I thought it would be a very good idea to be contracted to some company which is controlled by an artist rather than a businessman. It gives the soul a better opportunity."

Ellington and his men were back in the studio within days of signing, and before long they had taped two albums. *Will Big Bands Ever Come Back?* was a collection of ingenious new arrangements, mostly by Strayhorn, of big-band theme songs recorded by other top leaders of the Swing Era. It stayed in the can until 1965, but the prompt release of Ellington's first "official" album for Reprise, a program of Latin-style compositions in which the band was augmented by an assortment of percussion instruments played by everyone in the studio who wasn't otherwise occupied, boded better for the new association. As was his wont, he sprung the charts on the band at the sessions, wanting them to be played as spontaneously as possible, and Ray Nance, for one, regretted that the musicians had not had more time to work on them, confessing that "after you heard the record, you knew you could have done better." Reprise took advantage of the ongoing bossa nova craze by calling the album *Afro-Bossa,* though the feel of the performances was Caribbean, not Brazilian. Ellington himself described the title track as "a kind of a gut-bucket bolero . . . executed in a pre-primitive manner" (Woodyard played the drum part not with sticks but with his bare hands). Whatever its regional identification, *Afro-Bossa* was an arresting debut. The composer's new muse, it seemed, had done her work well.

Cootie Williams admitted to being pleased to be back in the trumpet section. "My name is still on some of the parts in the arrangements, and that makes me feel specially good," he told Whitney Balliett. Though he and Lawrence Brown were past their prime—their inimitable tones were now afflicted with the musical equivalent of middle-age spread—the playing of both men, along with that of Carney, Johnny Hodges, and Ray Nance, gave the group a direct connection to its prewar triumphs. To hear the live performances that Reprise recorded in France in February of 1963 (they were later released as *The Great Paris Concert*) is to know how much the continuing presence of the old-timers animated their younger colleagues. The band played with such mad abandon that Ellington was transported, whooping with glee all night long. Anyone who supposes that he and his musicians had nothing much of interest to say after 1942 should hear them ripping into the closing pages of *A Tone Parallel to Harlem* at the Theatre de l'Olympia two decades later.

At first Ellington's relationship with Reprise held out much promise. Not only was *Afro-Bossa* his best studio project since *Anatomy of a Murder,* but in 1963 the label allowed him to tape full-orchestra versions of *Harlem* and *Night Creature* in Europe, where union rules governing orchestral recording were less restrictive. He was so energized that in August he premiered a new stage work, a pageantlike revue about black history called *My People* that was performed twice daily (three times on weekends) during a two-week run at Chicago's Century of Negro Progress Exposition, a festival inspired by the same city's Century of Progress International Exposition of 1933 and occasioned by the centennial of the Emancipation Proclamation. In 1961 Ellington had expressed an interest in seeing *Black, Brown and Beige* "staged on Broadway as an opera or pageant." *My People,* which recycled chunks of the earlier work, appears in retrospect to have been more or less what he had in mind, and unlike *Beggar's Holiday,* which was sunk by his inability to assimilate the basics of book-show technique, the oratorio-like structure of *My People* was well within his grasp.

What was most surprising about *My People* was Ellington's interest in engaging with the present-day political climate. In the past he had steered clear of explicit talk about race relations in America, using indirection to say what he had to say. He was skeptical, too, of the efficacy of protest, privately dismissing Martin Luther King Jr.'s March on Washington for Jobs and Freedom, which took place a few days after the opening of *My People,* as an exercise in futility: "The only people who did good out of the goddamn parade was the people who owned businesses in Washington, the hotels, and all that, they had a fucking ball, put all the fucking money in their pockets."

Like Booker T. Washington before him, Ellington had always believed, and would continue to believe, that the way for blacks to overcome the crippling burden of racism was for them to assume individual responsibility for their collective plight and forge a well-heeled, well-educated middle class of their own.

But the world had changed—and so, up to a point, had Ellington himself. Whatever his doubts about the value of marching on Washington, his admiration for King's personal courage was boundless. In 1960 he had actually taken part in a Baltimore lunch-counter sit-in, and his decision to do so won him praise from black newspapers that had criticized his distanced attitude. The following year he added a nonsegregation rider to his contracts, allowing him to cancel any performance held in a segregated hall. Having won the Spingarn Medal, he wanted to be worthy of it, not just in his deeds but in his art, though never at the expense of entertaining his audiences. "I've only got about one minute of social protest written into the script [of *My People*] because while this aspect warrants notice, it unfairly tends to overshadow the continuing contributions of the Negro to American life," he told *Variety*. In fact there was somewhat more "social protest" than that, most notably a number called "King Fit the Battle of Alabam" in which Ellington paid tribute to the "freedom riders" whom the minister led to nonviolent victory over Bull Connor, who had set police dogs on black protesters in Birmingham.

Since the band was committed to play elsewhere throughout the run of *My People*, Strayhorn and the pianist-conductor Jimmy Jones put together a pit orchestra that contained as many alumni as they could find, augmented by Ray Nance and Russell Procope, whose presence helped to give the ensemble a more authentic sound. Joya Sherrill was the top-billed singer, and the dance troupes of Alvin Ailey and Talley Beatty joined her and the other vocalists onstage. Ellington himself put his mark on every aspect of the show, whose two halves were respectively based on "Come Sunday" and "The Blues": "I was the lyricist, the composer, the orchestrator, I directed it, I produced it, I lit the show, I did everything." While Perry Watkins collaborated on the set design, *My People* was for the most part his own show from top to bottom. Unfortunately, his writing ability was still rudimentary by comparison with his musical skills. He had always been an awkward lyricist, and when he paid tribute to his own family in "Heritage (My Mother, My Father and Love)," he stooped to maudlin naïveté: "My mother—the greatest—and the prettiest, / My father—just handsome—but the wittiest." In other numbers he resorted to a hectoring didacticism that was even less convincing for being couched in ill-rhymed doggerel: "What has color got to do with behavior / Or, when under fire, how brave you are?"

The project came together slowly, and according to Ailey, Ellington had trouble deciding on its tone, telling a friend that he "couldn't make up his mind if the show was for Broadway or the Apollo." The reviews were unenthusiastic, the box-office receipts poor, and Reprise chose not to tape an original-cast album. That was the end of *My People*, which went the way of *Jump for Joy* and *Beggar's Holiday*, vanishing into the memory hole that awaits well-intentioned shows that prove in the end not to have been quite good enough.

The road had always been his universal antidote, and he quaffed it now. "If you have the right kind of temperament, traveling can get to you like whiskey and cigarettes," he told a reporter. "Getting into a car or train is like being released. You know there'll be no business problems to talk about while you're moving." To that list he had lately added air travel. For much of his life Ellington was so afraid to fly that his phobia made the trade papers in 1954, with *Billboard* reporting, "Duke Ellington's fear of flying has jeopardized the European tour planned for him by impresario Harold Davison." But he changed his tune in 1960, taking his first overseas flight to work on *Paris Blues* and loving it: "I slept and the whole thing went off very well. It was a smooth flight with just a couple of bumps, like going over a railroad track." Perhaps Norman Granz (or the Countess) talked him into it. Whatever the reason, he was so used to flying by 1963 that he was happy to board a plane in September and fly all the way to Damascus, there to embark on his first State Department–sponsored foreign tour.

The United States government had been sending jazz musicians abroad for years, and even before they traveled under official sponsorship, their overseas performances were viewed in high places as a valuable form of advocacy. "America's secret weapon [in the Cold War] is a blue note in a minor key," *The New York Times* had said of Louis Armstrong's foreign tours. It was taken for granted that Ellington's polished elegance would make him at least as effective a representative as the ever-ingratiating Armstrong, and those who knew him best knew that there was no chance of his making impolitic statements to left-wing foreign journalists. When it came to Communism, his private views were identical to his public ones: "I know damn well sure I wouldn't want to be subsidized by anybody in the government of the United States or anybody else . . . if my drive and so forth is greater than another guy's, then I'm entitled to earn more and spend more." He also felt, though he never said so for the record, that he would be a more suitable ambassador than the genial Satchmo. "He was born poor, died rich, and never hurt anyone on the way," Ellington said when Armstrong died in 1971, and he meant it. But he detested the trumpeter's grinning public persona, finding it closely akin to Tomming: "It's a matter of dignity, it's a matter of embarrassing the race . . . you can't sell your race for your personal gain." He had felt the same way when, in 1955, the State Department sent a touring production of *Porgy and Bess* to the Soviet Union. As far as he was concerned, what black America needed was to be represented abroad by a gentleman who knew which fork to use.

So the Kennedy administration dispatched Ellington, Strayhorn, and the band to Ceylon, India, Iran, Iraq, Jordan, Lebanon, and Pakistan, accompanied by Thomas W. Simons Jr., a State Department escort officer whom the bandleader found sympathetic. As well as giving concerts, Ellington and his musicians listened to local players and gave lecture-demonstrations that went over well. But nobody had warned the State Department about the Air Force, whose senior member, Ray Nance, was sent home from Jordan after getting into a backstage scrap with Cootie Williams that upset him so much that he failed to stand for the playing of "The Star-Spangled Banner." It was suspected that Nance's addiction was the real cause of his misbehavior, but Ellington denied it, and Simons advised the State Department that "the embarrassment and harm which America has suffered as a result of Nance's conduct pales beside the tragedy of a fine American and a fine man." The episode, however, led to a permanent estrangement between Ellington and Nance, who did not rejoin the band until 1965, then left again after a short stay, this time for good.

Ellington himself caused a different sort of trouble for Simons, who informed his superiors that the bandleader's "habitual tardiness was a constant burden . . . the most time-consuming, exhausting, and enervating job the escort had was to try to get the group anyplace on time." And while Simons also reported that Ellington was "a gentleman from head to toe, entirely concentrated on his music, his comfort, and his reputation," he was appalled when the Countess showed up in New Delhi and attached herself to Ellington's entourage, in the process causing "acute embarrassment and apprehension to American officials." Though Simons carefully explained that the bandleader's relationship with his guest could not "under any reasonable definition of the word be described as tawdry," nobody connected with the tour needed to be told that it would cause an international scandal if he were to be photographed enjoying the company of a white woman who was not his wife.

To keep such matters secret for very long is not within the power of even the most determined escort officer. Photos of Ellington and the Countess were duly taken by local paparazzi, but by the time they got into print, President Kennedy had been assassinated in Dallas, and his violent death swallowed up every other story published around the world that weekend. "It's a hit, man," a shocked Ellington told Charles Sam Courtney, who broke the news to him. "He was fingered. . . . John F. Kennedy was the only president since Lincoln who gave a damn about the Negroes." He wanted to continue touring, playing memorial concerts modeled after his 1945 radio tribute to FDR, but the State Department insisted on sending the band home at once, and Ellington later told a reporter that he had been advised that American officials "thought jazz concerts might be considered in bad taste."

Assorted sticky moments notwithstanding, the venture was officially judged a success, and from then on lengthy government-sponsored foreign tours would become a regular part of the itinerary of the Ellington band, which went to Japan in 1964, Africa in 1966, Latin America in 1968, Russia in 1971, East Asia in 1972, and Africa again in 1973. In *Music Is My Mistress* Ellington wrote extensively but not illuminatingly about his travels, during which he was treated like the VIP he was, spending most of his time in concert halls and hotel rooms and uttering orotund platitudes ("Musicians of the past have influenced all musicians of the present") to the local reporters who interviewed him. He saw less and less of the lands that he visited and the people who lived there. By 1971 he was even arranging for the steaks that he ate each day to be shipped directly from New York to Russia via Pan Am airlines, a luxury that was widely reported in American newspapers, one of whose stories bore the headline "Duke Can't Cut It on Russian Steaks."

The State Department tours helped to keep the band afloat during increasingly tight times.* In addition to being financially remunerative, they inspired Ellington to compose several multimovement works, among them *Far East Suite* (1966), *Latin American Suite* (1968), and *The Afro-Eurasian Eclipse* (1971), into which he incorporated snippets of local musical color gleaned from his overseas listening: "You let it roll around, undergo a chemical change, and then seep out on paper in a form that will suit the musicians who are going to play it." By then, though, his energy was slackening, and none of these musical travelogues is more than fitfully inspired. In the later ones, Ellington responded to the mode- and scale-based non-Western music

---

* The band, for instance, was paid $19,000 a week (roughly $100,000 in today's dollars) for performing in Russia.

that he heard on his travels—much of which he privately admitted to finding monotonous—by resorting to one- and two-chord vamps that create a harmonically static feel at odds with his past practice. Unlike his earlier large-scale works, most of which are completely or largely written out, the late suites also contain long improvised solos, few of which are interesting enough to justify their length.

The inconsistency of these works is far from surprising, since Ellington wrote them at a time when he was maintaining a schedule of public appearances that would have crippled a man half his age. It's more surprising that they contain any worthwhile music at all, and that the first of them, *Far East Suite,* should rank among the more listenable efforts of his later years, not least for his own percussive playing, both in the ensemble and, in "Ad Lib on Nippon," as a soloist—though the best movement, a sexy ballad feature for Hodges called "Isfahan," was actually written by Billy Strayhorn. It was no coincidence that the quality of the suites declined after Strayhorn's death. The contrasting style of his contributions, which were more melodic and harmonically richer than the movements written by Ellington, gave to *Far East Suite,* like *Such Sweet Thunder* and *A Drum Is a Woman* before it, a musical variety that is lacking in the post-1966 suites.

Two years after the Far East tour, Mercer Ellington became his father's band manager, simultaneously holding down a chair in the trumpet section (he never took solos). Ellington offered a deadpan explanation of his son's presence: "I knew he'd been off his horn for a long time and he'd lost his chops, but he can get by, and you know I've had so many managers turn left on me. I thought if anyone else is going to steal money off me, I'd keep it in the family." It may have sounded funny, but he meant every word. Al Celley, the road manager since 1944, had been caught embezzling, and Ellington fired him as soon as the band returned from Turkey in 1963, simultaneously giving the boot to William Mittler, his longtime accountant. Unwilling to look after the band's finances himself, he needed the help of someone whom he could trust without reserve, and Mercer, who had tried persistently but without success to establish himself as a bandleader, decided at last to quit "going upstream," as he put it, and accept his familial fate.

In addition to straightening out Ellington's convoluted financial affairs, Mercer rode herd on his musicians, who had so wide a reputation for bad behavior that the band had actually been blacklisted by certain hotel chains. He found it hard at first to give orders to the older men: "Here I was in a position where I had to overlord people who had led me by the hand to the movies, who had taken me out to the circus, who had bought me candy apples or gone swimming with me." But he was determined to get rid of the drug addicts (except for Paul Gonsalves, who was now, after Johnny Hodges, the band's most popular soloist), keep the chronic drinkers like Sam Woodyard on a short leash, and persuade everyone to hit the bandstand on time each night.* The last of these tasks proved to be the hardest: "When I joined the band, it paid to be bad. I had to reverse the system and give them a reason to be good. . . . I started beefing, hollering, and screaming, and in some cases getting into fisticuffs, in order to straighten this situation out." But Johnny Hodges, for years one of the band's prime offenders, decided for reasons of his own to cooperate with Mercer, and over time a modicum of discipline was established.

It was also Mercer's task to figure out how to bring in more money, to which end he and his father hired Cress Courtney, who had worked with the band during its William Morris days and now returned in 1968 as Ellington's personal manager. At first the two men were puzzled by the fact that Ellington was, in Mercer's phrase, a "successful failure" who was world-famous but found it hard to keep the grosses high enough to pay the bills. Eventually, though, they realized that he didn't *want* to operate in a conventional way. In the late forties he had invited Herb Hendler to manage the band. Hendler looked at the books and saw that Ellington was paying his players a total of $4,500 each week, two thousand more than Ralph Flanagan, a popular bandleader of the day and another of Hendler's clients. Upon explaining to Ellington that the payroll had to be trimmed, he received this reply: "I have to stand out in front of that band for five shows a day, sometimes. The band you run has got to please the audience. The band I run has got to please *me.* So that's why I've got to have them, no matter what they cost." Just as he wanted to pay the highest salaries so that he could hang on to his best players, so did he want to get his own money up front so that he could live as he liked and support his family and friends in the grandest possible manner. "Ellington was a great bird-in-the-hand guy," Courtney explained. "You know, he'd see cash, that was it. He didn't want to know about what went on the day after tomorrow."

---

* Ellington's own method for disciplining players who showed up drunk or high was to put them on the spot by making them play lengthy up-tempo solos. Once Gonsalves figured out the system, he would pretend to be drunk whenever he wanted to show off for a friend in the audience.

Ellington and his now-departed business associates played fast and loose with the federal tax code in order to make these things happen, and in the sixties their sins caught up with them. The Internal Revenue Service went after Ellington with a vengeance, disallowing exemptions, personal "loans," undocumented deductions, and write-offs of various family-related expenses, including those that were incurred by Tempo Music, the music-publishing operation that he had long used as a conduit for siphoning cash to Mercer, Ruth, and Mildred Dixon. In time the noose grew so tight that the IRS started garnishing his box-office receipts. By the time of his death, Ellington was thought to owe somewhere between $600,000 and $700,000 in back taxes and penalties.

As well as looking after his father's affairs, Mercer also provided companionship for Ellington, who grew lonely on the road when he had no woman in tow—though he took care, Mercer added, never to ask for his son's company, that being a sign of vulnerability. It was around this time that Rex Stewart remarked that Ellington had "apparently learned to give more of himself in public but less in private." It was a penetrating observation from one who knew him well. His capacity for companionship had been corroded by too many ironic put-ons, too many "friends" who exaggerated their intimacy with him, and too many room-service steaks eaten in solitude. (The Lucullan feasts of Ellington's youth had become as much a thing of the past as the liquor he had once drained by the pint. Now he contented himself with steak, grapefruit, and hot water with lemon peel.)

Even the flock of women who kept on following him from town to town became oppressive. Mercer saw that, too:

> It was no longer a matter of hitting a town, having a fling, and moving on. Women began to cling to him more and more. The world was shrinking because of air travel, and he never knew when and where some of these ladies would show up . . . sometimes he had to run for shelter to get them off his back, and that was where Thunderbird—Evie— was so valuable. He could always go home, close the door, and let her answer the telephone.

Ellington was also uncomfortably aware that his music was no longer in vogue. Frank Sinatra had sold Reprise to Warner Bros. in 1963 in order to rid himself of the daily headaches of running a business, after which the label made itself over into a rock-and-pop imprint, signing Arlo Guthrie, the Kinks, Joni Mitchell, and Neil Young. That left Ellington out in the cold, and instead of continuing to record his own material for Reprise, he resorted to such expedients as putting out a collection of songs from *Mary Poppins,* Walt Disney's hit movie about a nanny with magical powers, and taping a pair of albums called *Ellington '65* and *Ellington '66* that contained not originals but up-to-the-minute pop tunes like "Charade," "Days of Wine and Roses," "Moon River," and "Never on Sunday," interspersed with such unlikely fare as Bob Dylan's "Blowin' in the Wind" and the Beatles' "All My Loving" and "I Want to Hold Your Hand."

He usually left it to Strayhorn to arrange such numbers, though he had spoken tactfully enough to a reporter who asked him about the Beatles in 1964: "I like the Beatles because they're well-behaved young men, and we could use well-behaved men in show business. The most important thing about the Beatles' music is that they're playing in tune. It's what the people like." But he felt hemmed in by the growing ubiquity of rock. In 1965 he shared a bill on *The Ed Sullivan Show* with Herman's Hermits, in 1968 with Vanilla Fudge. Two years after that, the band took part in Sullivan's televised tribute to the Beatles, playing a four-minute medley (the host called it "a jazz concerto") of "All My Loving," "Eleanor Rigby," "Norwegian Wood," "She Loves You," "She's Leaving Home," and "Ticket to Ride," with Ellington's sidemen bedecked in mod Carnaby Street suits with frilly lace cuffs.* The world was changing again, and even though the band was doing its best to keep up, it wasn't enough. A few years later Ellington expressed his frustration to a European TV interviewer, sounding less like a hip jazz musician than a grumpy old man: "The young people are the people who are buying because they are told to buy, and they cannot buy what is not pressed. . . . They tell the little children, they say, 'Now, you buy this million,' and they do it. It has no relationship to music and it has nothing to do with taste."

While the band's pop albums are never less than listenable—Strayhorn actually managed to make something magically droll out of "I Want to Hold Your Hand," and several of his *Mary Poppins* arrangements are little short of poetic—the absence of new compositions is telling, all the more so because Columbia, Ellington's old label, seized the opportunity to release a pair of three-disc albums called *The Ellington Era* that made many of his classic recordings of the twenties and thirties available for the first time in decades. Next to these sets, *Ellington '65* and *Ellington '66,* engaging though they

---

* Ellington was not the only artist of a certain age who embarrassed himself that Sunday night. Peggy Lee sang "Maxwell's Silver Hammer," while Edward Villella danced a solo to "Lucy in the Sky with Diamonds."

were, sounded trivial, and now that Sinatra had left Reprise, it was only a matter of time before Ellington's own relationship with the label petered out, as it did in April of 1965.

❧

Two weeks after taping his last recordings for Reprise, Ellington underwent a public humiliation. When the Pulitzer Prizes for 1965 were announced by Columbia University, no classical-music award was given. Two of the judges on the music panel, Robert Eyer of *Newsday* and Winthrop Sargeant of *The New Yorker*, immediately resigned in protest, explaining to the press that all three judges had recommended to the Pulitzer board that while they did not feel that any new classical piece was worthy of the prize, which in past years had gone to such works as Samuel Barber's Piano Concerto, Aaron Copland's *Appalachian Spring*, and Charles Ives's Third Symphony, it was their unanimous opinion that Ellington should be presented with "a special citation for long-term achievement." The board, they said, dismissed the idea out of hand. A reporter tracked Ellington down in Kentucky and asked if he had any comment. "Fate's being kind to me," he replied. "Fate doesn't want me to be too famous too young."

Sargeant, a longtime admirer who in 1938 had written *Jazz: Hot and Hybrid*, one of the first musically informed books about jazz to be published in America, told the *St. Louis Post-Dispatch*, "We felt a special citation would be appropriate because Ellington, though outside the symphonic form, has created a great deal of music in the past 40 years that is better than a great deal of symphonic music in that it has reached an audience and can be regarded as outstanding in every sense of the word." Aaron Copland agreed. "It's *very* too bad," he told *Newsweek*. "They missed an opportunity to single Mr. Ellington out. He has deserved it for so long." The Pulitzer board, though, chose not to defend itself, and it was not until 1997 that John Hohenberg, a longtime board member, explained that the jury's recommendation had not been taken seriously by the members of the board (according to Hohenberg, it wasn't even brought to a vote) because it did not conform to the rules of the music prize, which then specified that it was to go to a "distinguished musical composition in the larger forms of chamber, orchestral or choral music."

A few thoughtful observers sympathized with the board's dilemma. The classical critic Irving Kolodin, who could not be accused of hostility to jazz in general or Ellington in particular—he had written the program notes for the 1943 Carnegie Hall concert at which *Black, Brown and Beige* was premiered—underlined the irony of the situation when he pointed out in the

"It's *very* too bad": Duke Ellington and Aaron Copland at the 1968 Grammy Awards. America's greatest jazz composer had been passed over for a Pulitzer Prize three years earlier, and America's greatest classical composer, a devoted admirer of Ellington's music, made no secret of his dismay

---

Saturday Review that "larger forms are precisely what [Ellington] is not distinguished for." The general consensus, however, was that Copland was right, and that Ellington had said the last word with his graceful yet pointed retort. It was the board, not the composer, that came off looking small, especially in the wake of its earlier decision to void the vote of another of its juries and withhold a drama prize from *Who's Afraid of Virginia Woolf?* on the grounds that Edward Albee's 1962 masterpiece was insufficiently "uplifting." When *The New York Times Magazine* commissioned from Nat Hentoff a profile of Ellington occasioned by the debacle, it was titled "This Cat Needs No Pulitzer Prize."

He didn't, but the cat himself begged to differ. "I'm hardly surprised that my kind of music is still without, let us say, official honor at home," he told Hentoff. No doubt he was right, but the decision of the Pulitzer board was not just a slap at jazz in general: It was also a concerted assault on the ego of a man whose need for respectability remained so powerful that he continued to insist on publicly denying the existence of the woman who had been his companion for a quarter of a century. And whatever he may have said for quotation, Ellington very definitely took it personally when the Pulitzer board passed him over. In December he got into a quarrel with Mel Tormé, who had been contractually guaranteed top billing for a joint appearance with the Ellington band at Basin Street East, then one of New York's top nightclubs. Tormé showed up for rehearsal and discovered that half of the bandsmen were missing. That night Joe Glaser came backstage and told the singer, "If you don't give Duke top billing in all advertising, promotion, and on the marquee outside, he's not walking on the stage for this entire engagement. That's final, from Duke himself." Tormé begged Ellington, one of his idols, to reconsider but received a chilly reply: "Yeah, baby, well, I'm not mad at you, but, you know, I nearly just won the Pulitzer prize, and this is an insult and I can't help it if you're in the middle."

Tormé went on without Ellington, which was a disastrous choice. "Rarely had my charts been so mangled, played with such astonishing disinterest," he recalled. A few days later, he reluctantly gave in and the billing was changed. It wasn't the first time that Ellington had been so unyielding in a billing dispute: The same thing had happened in 1960 when he shared a bill with the comedian Mort Sahl at a Los Angeles club. Then as now, he was willing to sulk in his dressing room until he got his way. But the fact that he went so far as to cite the Pulitzer debacle to Tormé is an indication of how harshly it had wounded him.

Ellington suffered another humiliation the following March when he made a second full-scale assault on Broadway. *Pousse-Café,* his latest stage project, was a freely adapted musical version of *The Blue Angel* whose setting was transplanted from Berlin to New Orleans. On paper the show looked promising, and his collaborators, who included the director José Quintero and the novelist Jerome Weidman, who had written the book for *I Can Get It for You Wholesale,* the show with which Barbra Streisand made her Broadway debut, were impeccably credentialed. None of them, however, had reckoned on Ellington's unwillingness to commit himself fully to the laborious process of writing a new musical. Theodore Bikel, the star of *Pousse-Café,* wrote in his 1994 memoir of the resulting ordeal:

> *Duke Ellington was nowhere to be found either in the beginning or for*
> *any rehearsals. That was a money decision. He had written a number*

*of songs, which were put into various parts of the script in an attempt to
make them part of a whole, but that is no way to put a musical together.
The songs have to be an integral and organic part of the process, and
the composer needs to be present for it. They did not want to pay the
Duke for being around, and so he stayed away, and all we had were the
songs he had originally done.*

He got what he deserved. *Pousse-Café* opened at the Forty-Sixth Street
Theatre on March 18, 1966, and closed the following night, having received
brutal reviews. It was his most abject failure, one so complete that he said not
a single word about it in *Music Is My Mistress*. But his career, like his music,
had always been full of the sharpest possible contrasts, and in between the
loss of the Pulitzer Prize and the disaster of *Pousse-Café* came a triumph that
was to transform his old age: the premiere of his first concert of sacred music.

Duke Ellington was never ostentatious about his religious observances,
which amounted for the most part to daily Bible study and private prayer in
hotel and dressing rooms, but he was deadly serious about them. Unwilling
though he was to observe the Seventh Commandment, he meant it, more or
less, when he told Richard O. Boyer that "I'd be afraid to sit in a house with
people who don't believe. Afraid the house would fall down." He had believed in God from childhood onward, and he embraced Christianity more
purposefully after his mother's death, wearing a small gold cross around his
neck and reading the Bible three times straight through. "Come Sunday,"
the best-known section of *Black, Brown and Beige,* is a "tone parallel" of a
church service, and when Mahalia Jackson sang it on record in 1958, even
the most skeptical of listeners could not doubt its composer's faith.

It was for this reason that he was hesitant to accept a commission from
the Very Reverend C. Julian Bartlett, dean of San Francisco's Grace Cathedral, and the Reverend John S. Yaryan, the cathedral canon, to compose a
sacred work and perform it in the cathedral. At first he questioned his "eligibility" for the task, which he defined clearly and modestly: "You have to go
out there and make a noise that tells the truth. . . . You can jive with secular
music but you can't jive with the Almighty." In addition, he was unwilling to
water down his music so as to make it acceptable to the church's elders. But
the Rev. Bartlett, who had been impressed by the deep spiritual feeling of
Jackson's version of "Come Sunday," assured him that what he had in mind
was a program "totally in [Ellington's] character, the way [he] wanted to do

it." In the fall of 1964, two years after he first approached the composer, Ellington accepted the commission. The press appears to have been dubious about his musical intentions. "No, we're not going to have a jam session," he said at a press conference held prior to the event. "This is my greatest opportunity to say something." As for the Rev. Bartlett, he described the planned concert with simple sincerity: "The offering of sacred music by Duke Ellington and his musicians will be just that—an offering of his talent to Almighty God. We receive him humbly and with thanksgiving for his tremendous talents."

Ellington's program note for the first performance of the hour-long program, which took place on September 16, 1965, was in part an apologia for what he thought might be understood as his presumption in writing church music: "Every man prays in his own language and there is no language that God does not understand." The language of his "Concert of Sacred Music" was, however, entirely understandable, since most of the music performed at the cathedral consisted of excerpts from *Black, Brown and Beige* and *My People*, augmented by a solo version of *New World A-Coming.* "A lot of it sounded like *Black, Brown and Beige* with more singing and some extra music," said Claire Gordon, a longtime friend who had also been present at the 1943 Carnegie Hall concert. The San Francisco premiere, which played to a packed house, received overwhelmingly favorable reviews, and the work was performed a second time on the day after Christmas at New York's Fifth Avenue Presbyterian Church, where it was recorded for RCA, Ellington's new record label. It was a package deal—he agreed in return to tape a greatest-hits-in-stereo album called *The Popular Duke Ellington*—that paid off handsomely for all parties concerned. Not only did *The Popular Duke Ellington* sell well, but *Duke Ellington's Concert of Sacred Music* won him another Grammy Award.

Ellington used the interval between the San Francisco and New York performances to revise the concert, changing its running order and composing a new instrumental prelude that fused the opening numbers into a single twenty-minute musical sequence called "In the Beginning God." The prelude is one of his most majestic utterances, a six-note theme based on the first four words of the King James Bible that is intoned by Harry Carney as if it had been chiseled out of granite. Unlike most of Ellington's themes, the "In the Beginning God" motif is beautifully suited to symphonic development, and its placement at the very beginning of the piece creates expectations that he fails to fulfill. Instead of spinning out the theme at appropriate length, he follows it with a string of tenuously related, variably inspired musical events. First comes a part-spoken, part-sung bass-baritone solo that describes

"You can't jive with the Almighty": Rehearsing *A Concert of Sacred Music* at Coventry Cathedral, 1966. Ellington's first venture into the field of religious music ranked high among the triumphs of his later years—but some black ministers questioned whether so worldly a musician had any business playing in churches

the primordial chaos ("No symphony, no jive, no *Gemini V*") preceding the moment of creation. Then a choir shouts the names of the books of the Bible, followed by a drum solo from Louis Bellson (who had briefly replaced Sam Woodyard) that is capped with an anticlimactic coda. Not only does this miscellaneous-sounding assemblage fail to gel into a musical whole, but the hipsterisms of Ellington's text sit uneasily alongside the magisterial sound of Carney's saxophone.

The concert continues with an anodyne gospel waltz called "Tell Me It's the Truth," an extended "Come Sunday" sequence, and two dullish vocal numbers from *My People*, "Will You Be There" and "Ain't but the One," after which Ellington plays *New World A-Coming*. The grand finale, also drawn from *My People*, is a long-meter choral version of "Come Sunday" called "David Danced Before the Lord with All His Might" (the reference is to 2 Samuel 6:14) in which Bunny Briggs performs a lengthy tap dance before the altar.

The inspiration for Briggs's inclusion in the program, Ellington explained, was the medieval legend of the juggler of Notre Dame: "It has been said once that a man, who could not play the organ or any of the instruments of the symphony, accompanied his worship by juggling. He was not the world's best juggler but it was the one thing he did best. And so it was accepted by God." The inclusion of the dance was a stroke of theatrical genius, the one moment in which Ellington acknowledged the essentially theatrical nature of the concert without violating its spiritual purpose.

The New York reviews, unlike those of the San Francisco premiere, were all over the map. Alan Rich described the concert as "vintage Ellington . . . properly elemental, sometimes brutal, never less than compelling" in the *New York Herald Tribune*. John S. Wilson of *The New York Times* was a tougher nut to crack: "Mr. Ellington moved carefully in his unfamiliar surroundings. . . . Altogether, there was less of the true Ellington stamp on this concert than one would have hoped for." The truth lies somewhere between these extremes. Over and above its inconsistent musical merits, the First Sacred Concert, as it is now known, comes across today as a period piece, as dated as the jazz, folk, and rock masses that were all the rage in "progressive" churches of the sixties and seventies. Still, Ellington's revisions had significantly strengthened the total effect of the concert, and he would perform it many times in the next few years, usually to great public acclaim.*

For the most part the concert was accepted as a testament of personal faith. Ed Sullivan, whose sense of mass taste was unerring, brought Briggs and the band onto his Sunday-evening program to perform "David Danced Before the Lord," while *Ebony* praised the New York premiere: "A type of music once disdained as being fit only for bars and bordellos was being performed in a sacred concert by a man who had helped earn for it the greatest respect." But the rest of the black community was of two minds, and the black ministers of Ellington's hometown were disinclined to look kindly on the First Sacred Concert when it was presented a year later at Washington's Constitution Hall. The Baptist Ministers Conference, which consisted of the leaders of some one hundred and fifty Washington-area churches, voted not to endorse the concert, and several members refused to allow tickets for the event to be sold in their churches. One of them told *The Washington Post,*

---

* It is interesting to speculate on what would have happened to *Black, Brown and Beige* if the critics who panned the Carnegie Hall premiere had instead encouraged Ellington to revise it as extensively as he did the First Sacred Concert. Had they done so, his subsequent composing career might well have taken a very different shape.

"Duke Ellington represents the type of service that we as Baptist ministers didn't feel represented the Christian impact," while another said that Ellington's own life was "opposed to what the church stands for," mentioning his "nightclub playing and the fact the music is just considered worldly." These views were widely shared among religiously conservative blacks. Even Joya Sherrill, a Jehovah's Witness, preferred not to take part in the San Francisco premiere, telling Ellington that she thought it inappropriate to play jazz in a church.

A month after the First Sacred Concert was performed in Washington, Edna Ellington died of cancer. By then the band was in Italy, where her long-estranged husband issued a tactful statement: "She loved life. She was a woman of virtue and beauty. She would never lie. God bless her." Her passing gave Evie brief hope that Ellington would marry her, but he preferred not to. In Mercer's words:

> *Evie absolutely expected to become Mrs. Ellington, but I think Pop just came right out and said, "No, we're not getting married!" There was no pressure being put on him from any other direction so far as I was aware . . . somehow he didn't want to do it, and I think the main influence against it may have been his sister, Ruth, because she had become as possessive of him as he of her.*

It seems more likely, however, that at the age of sixty-seven, Ellington had no wish to upset his life by altering the status of any of his relationships—not even with the Countess, whom he had previously told that he was legally married to Evie. He still wanted everybody in the palm of his hand, where they had been for the whole of his adult life. Yet one member of his extended family had long been reluctant to cooperate fully with Ellington's wishes, and a few months later he would thwart them once and for all.

By 1964, if not before, Billy Strayhorn was an alcoholic. "He had his good days, but he had his bad days, believe me, the poor thing," a close friend recalled. "He was drinking day and night. Half the time, he wasn't really there." Strayhorn's relationship with Aaron Bridgers had trailed off after Bridgers moved to Paris in 1947 to pursue his own musical career, and since then Strayhorn had been unable to find a suitable romantic partner. Nor was his later work for Ellington gratifying, consisting as it mainly did of arranging the latest pop tunes. Strayhorn put the best possible face on it: "It's more a matter of morality than technique. . . . If I'm working on a tune, I don't want to *think* it's bad. It's just a tune, and I have to work with it. It's not a matter of whether it's good or bad." Mostly, though, the tunes were bad, or at least inappropriate to his talents. He continued to contribute to the suites, but not as frequently, and except for a single solo album released in 1961, he had less and less to say.

Early in 1964 Arthur Logan, Ellington's doctor, noticed that Strayhorn was short of breath and suggested that he undergo a thorough physical examination at once. A few days later he told Strayhorn that he had cancer of the esophagus, the result of a lifetime of drinking and smoking, and that it was terminal. Ellington was appalled by the diagnosis, but Strayhorn appears to have accepted it with a typical mixture of stoicism and irony. During a visit to the Logans' brownstone, he plucked a wax apple out of a lazy Susan and looked at it. "A fruit that only looks like it's alive," he said. "That makes two of us." In 1965 he underwent a tracheostomy, followed by a debilitating course of radiation therapy. Then came a gastrostomy and the removal of his esophagus. Even then he continued to drink, pouring alcohol directly into his feeding tube.

By that time the rest of the world was figuring out what Ellington had always known, which was that Strayhorn, far from being the older man's epigone, was a giant in his own right. In June of 1965, shortly before he went under the knife, he gave his first and only solo concert at New York's New School for Music. John S. Wilson took note of the event by writing a profile for *The New York Times*—the one occasion during his lifetime when he was so honored outside the jazz press—in which he explained, mildly but firmly, that his collaboration with Ellington had endured because the older man didn't tell him "what to write or how to write." But it was too little, too late. Strayhorn turned up at the New York premiere of the First Sacred Concert, accompanying his beloved Lena Horne in a song. It was, so far as is known, his last public appearance.

He began to disintegrate shortly afterward, finishing only two more compositions for the Ellington band. The second of them, which he called "Blood Count," was a feature for Johnny Hodges, his favorite soloist, whose contorted melodic line was the musical equivalent of a howl of pain. "He wrote his epitaph and then had Rabbit play it," said Otto Hardwick when he first heard "Blood Count." After that he waited for death. Ellington called him on the phone each day but never visited, unable to bear the thought of seeing what cancer had done to his friend. The end came early in the morning of May 31, 1967. The band was playing in Reno, and Arthur Logan called Ellington to break the news. "Are you going to be all right?" Logan asked. "Fuck no, I'm not going to be all right!" he replied. "Nothing is all right now." Then he wept. "After I hung up the phone I started sniffling and whimpering, crying, banging my head up against the wall, and talking to myself about the virtues of Billy Strayhorn," he recalled. "Why Billy Strayhorn, I asked? Why? Subconsciously, I sat down and started writing what I was thinking, and as I got deeper and deeper into thinking about my favorite human being, I realized that I was not crying any more."

A week later, the elegy that Ellington wrote that morning was delivered for him at Strayhorn's funeral, which took place at St. Peter's Church in New York. "Duke was sitting by himself, frozen, immobile, staring straight ahead, not seeing, hearing or recognizing anything or anybody," Don George remembered. So heartbroken that he did not trust himself to be able to get through the elegy without breaking down, Ellington sat in stony silence as his heartfelt words were read out loud to the mourners:

> *William Thomas Strayhorn, the biggest human being who ever lived, a man with the greatest courage, the most majestic artistic stature . . . demanded freedom of expression and lived in what we consider the most important and moral of freedoms: freedom from hate, unconditionally; freedom from self-pity (even throughout all the pain and bad news); freedom from fear of possibly doing something that might help another more than it might himself; and freedom from the kind of pride that could make a man feel he was better than his brother or neighbor.*

After twenty-eight years, their stormy voyage together on the sea of expectancy was over.

16

"THAT BIG YAWNING VOID"

Alone in a Crowd, 1967–1974

D UKE ELLINGTON WAS never one to face bad news squarely. He preferred
when he could to ignore it: "I don't have time to get depressed. It
wouldn't help me any. What I don't like doesn't exist." But there would
be no turning away from the death of Billy Strayhorn, which left a hole in his
life that could not be filled. "I'm writing more than ever now," he told a reporter in 1968. "Billy Strayhorn left that big yawning void." In truth, though,
Ellington had stepped up his compositional activity years earlier in order to
compensate for Strayhorn's shrinking output. Nor would he take time off to
recover from his loss. He couldn't afford not to work and wouldn't have
known what to do with himself had he stopped. Instead he kept at it and tried
not to think about the worst news of all, which was that if his musical heir
could die, so could he.

Two months after the funeral, he left the road to play a monthlong engagement at Rockefeller Center's Rainbow Grill, appearing not with the full
band but a five-horn octet. With him were Cat Anderson, Lawrence Brown,
Harry Carney, Paul Gonsalves, and Johnny Hodges, his principal soloists. The
small band made a big impression on the critics. "It has the depth and timbre
and revolving colors of the bigger group, but it is also looser and more intense,
and the soloists have more space and time to roam in," Whitney Balliett wrote

in *The New Yorker*. Surviving air checks of the octet's performances are not nearly so impressive sounding as that, though, and for Ellington the job seems to have been mainly expedient. He claimed to have taken it so that he'd have more time to compose, and the Rainbow Grill, to which he would hence-forth return at least once a year, wasn't big enough to accommodate the entire band, so seven of his men stayed home, thereby lowering the overhead sub-stantially.

All fifteen, however, were on hand when Ellington started taping . . . *And His Mother Called Him Bill* at the end of August. He had decided to pay trib-ute to Strayhorn by recording an entire album of his music for RCA. It was the first time since 1941 that he had featured his protégé's compositions so extensively, and the result was a considerable achievement, the best-played studio album of his old age, in part because the program was chosen from the whole of Strayhorn's output rather than consisting only of new work. In addi-tion to classics of the forties like "Day Dream," "Midriff," and "Raincheck," Ellington dredged up such lesser-known efforts as "Rock Skippin' at the Blue Note" and "Snibor," and he also recorded Strayhorn's last two pieces, "Blood Count" and the slyly swinging "Intimacy of the Blues." The final track was a hushed solo version of "Lotus Blossom" that he tossed off while the musi-cians were putting up their instruments at the end of a recording session. The engineers had the good sense to keep the tape rolling, and you can hear the men in the studio stop packing their horns and fall silent as their leader runs through the song that Strayhorn had loved to hear him play. It is an unutter-ably poignant moment. "When I got a copy the other day of the new album we did of Billy's tunes, I couldn't even look at it, let alone listen to it," he later told a reporter. "I just threw it on the bed."

In October his grief was made visible when NBC's *Bell Telephone Hour* aired "On the Road with Duke Ellington," an hour-long documentary di-rected by Robert Drew, a cinema verité pioneer who had spent part of the preceding year traveling with the bandleader. It is the most illuminating of Ellington's TV appearances, though not because of anything that he said on camera. He had been watching his tongue for too long to let slip anything unexpected, and he sticks to his stock anecdotes throughout the show. What is revealing about "On the Road with Duke Ellington" is the everyday activ-ity that the camera captures. We see Ellington surrounded by middle-aged ladies in an airport, chatting with Louis Armstrong in his dressing room, tinkering with a new composition in his hotel room, saying grace before he tucks into a room-service dinner of steak and grapefruit, and striding from the wings to play the dreaded medley for his adoring fans ("We hope that all of our compositions are among your favorites"). Time and again the camera lingers on the lined face of a man on the verge of extreme old age, one whose features are a map of disillusion. Drew's off-camera narration is insightful: "Being on the road assures Duke Ellington of never really being alone. But it also provides a kind of isolation he needs to compose." And though the women in Ellington's life are never seen or mentioned, we watch as he reads through the funeral oration that he has just written for Strayhorn—and see him sitting alone in a pew at St. Peter's a few days later, staring at his beloved friend's coffin and listening to his own words being read out loud.

Two months after "On the Road with Duke Ellington" aired, Ellington and the band joined Frank Sinatra in the studio to tape *Francis A. and Edward K.,* their first and only joint project. Sinatra had talked about recording with Ellington as early as 1947 but somehow failed to get around to it when the two men were both at Reprise. Now they decided to go ahead. Since Strayhorn was dead and Ellington preferred not to write vocal charts, Billy May, a much-admired pro who had been working with Sinatra since the fifties, supplied the arrangements, which were intended, he said, to evoke the Blanton-Webster band. (Only one of the eight numbers, "I Like the Sunrise," was composed by Ellington.) Though he had a knack for musical mimicry, May did not reckon with the state of Ellington's present-day group. "That's what I tried to write for, to go for [the Blanton-Webster] sound," he later said. "But by 1967 it was completely gone, they had started to go to pot although they still had that distinctive sound." He suspected the worst when he flew to Seattle in November to hear the band run through his arrangements: "We rehearsed them all afternoon and, Jesus, the rehearsal was terrible. They were all terrible sight readers in that band." Ellington promised to play them on the job prior to the sessions, filling in the vocal parts on piano, but May knew as soon as he entered the studio in December that "they [had] never touched the charts again." Even after rehearsing the arrangements, Ellington's musicians could not play them nearly so well as the studio orchestras made up of first-call session men to which Sinatra was accustomed. In order to get the job done as efficiently as possible, May augmented the band with a handful of studio ringers, including Al Porcino, one of Hollywood's top lead trumpeters, and two pianists, Jimmy Jones and Milt Raskin, who played some of Ellington's keyboard parts. While Ellington's men managed in the end to pull themselves together, the album that resulted, Johnny Hodges's contemplative solo on "Indian Summer" excepted, was mostly lackluster, and Ellington made no mention of *Francis A. and Edward K.* in the Sinatra chapter of *Music Is My Mistress.*

May was right about the condition of the band, which had been in decline for the past few years. It was no longer a matter of good and bad nights: Ellington's players, in particular his saxophonists, were now unable to execute his close-voiced block-chord ensembles with secure intonation. The deterioration was apparent on the live recording of the First Sacred Concert, and distressing patches of sour ensemble work can also be heard on *Far East Suite* and . . . *And His Mother Called Him Bill*. One of the reasons for the unsatisfactory playing was that the band's veterans, like their leader, were growing old. A week after finishing *Francis A. and Edward K.*, four key players, Lawrence Brown, Harry Carney, Cootie Williams, and Sam Woodyard, simultaneously fell ill just prior to a three-week engagement in Reno. Benny Carter briefly sat in on lead alto, while Russell Procope covered for Carney by switching to baritone saxophone.

Ellington had other troubles on his mind. Earlier in the year Norman Granz had broken with him. After receiving one too many middle-of-the-night phone calls, the promoter fired off an angry, accusatory letter:

> *I'm really afraid that you're using me not as a manager, but as a servant—and worse than that[,] you are so incredibly, foolishly selfish in the way you do it that I think not even a self-respecting manager would accept it. . . . I'll be glad to give you whatever advice I can on any major issues that come up in your artistic life, but as far as sending your laundry out or wiring money to your friends, I don't think I can do that again.*

What Granz may not have understood was that Ellington was probably making some of those calls not because he needed help but because he longed for companionship and was too proud to ask for it. As the one-nighters grew more frequent and the long hauls longer, he used the telephone to fight off his loneliness. "I know he spent many despondent hours in motels," Mercer said. "This was one reason why he would make long-distance calls at all hours of the night. . . . When I paid his hotel bills, I could always tell what he'd been up to." He may have had himself in mind as much as the human race when he observed in his program notes for the First Sacred Concert that "everyone is so alone—the basic, essential state of humankind."

∽

He could still count on the critics, though. Most of them sang his praises even when he was at less than his best, and one, Gunther Schuller, now wrote of him in a way whose consequences were both significant and lasting.

A classical composer and the longtime principal horn player of the Metropolitan Opera's pit orchestra, Schuller was also a committed devotee of jazz—he played on Miles Davis's *Birth of the Cool* sessions—who had been so "mesmerized" by the Ellington band when he first heard the group live in 1943 that he started transcribing its recordings note for note, thereby becoming one of the first musicians to take down Ellington's arrangements by ear. In 1959 he published a long essay on Ellington's early recordings that eventually became the basis for a full-scale survey history of jazz, the first part of which he brought out in 1968 as *Early Jazz: Its Roots and Musical Development*. The climax of the book was a forty-page chapter called "The Ellington Style: Its Origins and Early Development" in which he analyzed Ellington's pre-1930 music in close and informed detail. Other classically trained critics, Max Harrison and André Hodeir among them, had written penetratingly about Ellington, but never at such length, and the opening of "The Ellington Style" indicated the high seriousness with which Schuller took his music:

> *Duke Ellington is one of America's great composers. At this writing his extraordinary creativity seems undiminished. In looking back over more than forty years of his career, we can only marvel at the consistency with which Ellington and his orchestra have sustained a level of inspiration comparable in its way to that of the major "classical" composers of our century.*

The importance of *Early Jazz* was grasped at once. *The New York Times Book Review*, for instance, called it "clear, thorough, objective, sophisticated and original . . . unparalleled in the literature of jazz." All true—but the review was written not by a musicologist but by Frank Conroy, a novelist and part-time jazz pianist. On the other hand, it is hard to know to whom else the *Times Book Review* could have turned, since there were as yet no scholarly biographies of Ellington, or any other jazz musician. And while Conroy was right to say that *Early Jazz* was "unparalleled" in its field, he failed to point out that the book was the first full-length historical-analytic monograph about jazz to be written by a scholar with extensive performing experience. It was not that jazz had been overlooked by classical-music scholars. Wilfrid Mellers, for instance, had devoted an entire chapter to Ellington in *Music in a New Found Land*, his 1964 survey history of American music, describing him as "pre-eminent, if not unique, in preserving the authenticity of jazz while achieving, too, tenderness and sensitivity." But in 1968 the "literature of jazz" was almost entirely the work of amateur enthusiasts, while academic jazz scholarship was rudimentary at best. This made it still more significant that a writer like Schuller should have chosen to place Ellington alongside Louis Armstrong and Jelly Roll Morton as one of his exemplary figures, the men whom he judged to be the key artists of early jazz.

What Ellington thought of Schuller's book is not known. He probably never read it, since it had always been his view that close critical analysis "stinks up the place." Besides, he was less interested than ever in reflecting on his past triumphs. He continued to write music every day, and to play it as soon as his copyists could put parts on the stands. He even traveled with a portable electric piano, enabling him to experiment with musical ideas at any hour of the day or night: "You know how it is. You go home expecting to go right to bed, but then on the way in you go past the piano and there's a flirtation. It flirts with you. So you sit to try out a couple of chords, and when you look up it's 7 A.M."

Indeed, one of his most important efforts was premiered mere months before the publication of Schuller's book, and he was well pleased with it. Ellington's Second Sacred Concert, which received its first performance in January at New York's Cathedral Church of St. John the Divine, was a considerable advance on its predecessor, for instead of knocking the piece together from existing works, he wrote its thirteen movements from scratch and believed them to be "the most important thing [he had] ever done." Few critics went that far, but some of the Second Sacred Concert exhibits a degree of formal control that he had never before attained. A case in point is "Supreme Being," the twelve-minute second movement, a quasisymphonic structure in which unpitched choral declamation is juxtaposed with sophisticated orchestral writing (though the paucity of memorable themes is, as so often in Ellington's post-1950 music, a major defect).

Alice Babs, the principal vocal soloist, was a classically trained soprano from Sweden whom Ellington had first heard on a 1963 tour. He was so impressed by her singing that he recorded a small-group album with Babs, but it was the Second Sacred Concert that first brought her to the attention of American audiences. According to Ellington, "She sings opera, she sings lieder, she sings what we call jazz and blues, she sings like an instrument, she even yodels, and she can read any and all of it!" Not only did she have a silvery, extraordinarily wide-ranging voice, exact intonation, and near-flawless English diction, but she was also blessed with the unerring rhythmic sense of a natural-born jazz musician. The two solo sections that Ellington wrote for Babs bear out his description of her as "a composer's dream . . . with [Babs] he can forget all the limitations and just write his heart out." In "Heaven," a high-flying vocal meditation with a Latin dance interlude, she manages not to be upstaged by Johnny Hodges at his most romantic. Even lovelier is "T.G.T.T.," a wordless duet for soprano and electric piano whose asymmetrical melody, unusually for Ellington, appears to have been written on its own rather than emerging from its harmonies. As he explained in his program notes, the enigmatic title of the song "means *Too Good to Title,* because it violates conformity in the same way, we like to think, that Jesus Christ did. The phrases never end on the note you think they will. It is a piece even instrumentalists have trouble with, but Alice Babs read it at sight."

Had Ellington worked with a musically experienced poet or librettist instead of writing his own text, the Second Sacred Concert would almost certainly have been taken up more widely. But he wanted, as with the First Sacred Concert and *My People* before it, to make a completely personal statement, and he had written the piece not for finicky aesthetes but true believers: "I think of myself as a messenger boy, one who tries to bring messages to people, not people who have never heard of God, but those who were more or less raised with the guidance of the Church." So he wrote the lyrics himself, thereby saddling the Second Sacred Concert with his childlike, unreflective notions of spirituality, which ran to trite essays in speculative theology ("Heavenly Heaven to be / Is just the ultimate degree to be") and the same wince-making hipsterisms that had marred its predecessor ("Freedom, Freedom must be won, / 'Cause Freedom's even good fun"). Whitney Balliett questioned in *The New Yorker* whether Ellington was putting on his audience with some of the lyrics. He wasn't, but it is regrettably true that one must listen *through* the text to hear the Second Sacred Concert for what it is, a flawed near-masterpiece in which some of his best music is allied to some of his worst lyrics.

∾

The band's shaky playing on the recording of the Second Sacred Concert, taped immediately after the premiere, provides further evidence of its growing decrepitude, which accelerated when Jimmy Hamilton and Sam Woodyard handed in their notices. Their replacements, Harold Ashby and Rufus Jones, were talented players, but the twin departures can be seen in retrospect as the beginning of the band's final decline. While the loss of Ray Nance had been a shock, Cootie Williams's presence helped soften the blow. From now on, by contrast, every departure would be irreparable.

For a time, though, things seemed to continue as before. Ellington toured Latin America for the first time in September, with the *Latin American Suite* following in due course. Yale had already presented him with an honorary degree, the first to be conferred by the university on a jazz musician, and now he was appointed to the National Council on the Arts.* He even hired some interesting new players. One was the pioneering jazz organist Wild Bill Davis, who had arranged Count Basie's hit version of "April in Paris" in 1955 and who now joined the Ellington band as a second keyboard player and sometime orchestrator. An individual stylist who had cut a number of small-group albums with Johnny Hodges, Davis might well have shifted the band's musical direction, like Woodyard before him, had he come along a decade earlier. "Duke could have really incorporated him in the sound, written something *seriously* for him," Norman Granz said. "But he didn't. He just used Bill as a relief soloist most of the time." Neither did he take advantage of Johnny Coles, a Miles Davis–influenced trumpeter who joined the band two years later. Coles had recorded to fine effect a decade earlier with Gil Evans, the greatest big-band arranger of the postwar era and one of the few whose command of orchestral color was comparable to that of Ellington and Strayhorn. But Ellington never got around to writing a feature for Coles, whose tenure became another missed opportunity.

The honors continued to pour in, and the grandest one of all took place on April 29, 1969, when President Nixon celebrated Ellington's seventieth birthday by throwing a White House party at which he presented him with the Medal of Freedom, the highest civilian honor bestowed by the American government. The idea for the party came from Joe Morgen, Ellington's publicist. Willis Conover, the Voice of America disc jockey who had been beaming jazz behind the Iron Curtain since the fifties, planned the event, and Nixon himself decided to give the Medal of Freedom to Ellington. The party was universally recognized as a fitting and long-overdue tribute, not merely to Ellington but to jazz as a whole. As Ralph Ellison put it, "That which our institutions dedicated to the recognition of artistic achievement have been too prejudiced, negligent or concerned with European models and styles to do is finally being done by presidents." If anything more were needed to erase the embarrassment of his having been denied a Pulitzer, this was it.

Conover assembled an all-star band to play for the black-tie affair. Invitations went out to a select list of politicians, musicians, and old friends and

---

* Such official recognition had always been important to a U Streeter like Ellington, who included in *Music Is My Mistress* a fifteen-page list of his "honors and awards." Among other tributes great and small, he noted that he was an honorary deputy sheriff of Lackawanna County, Pennsylvania, and a member of the Poultry and Egg National Board's "National Good Egg Club."

colleagues, among them Harold Arlen, Whitney Balliett, Dave Brubeck, Cab Calloway, Billy Eckstine, Dizzy Gillespie, Benny Goodman, Leonard Feather, Earl Hines, Mahalia Jackson, Marian McPartland, Otto Preminger, Richard Rodgers, Gunther Schuller, Willie "the Lion" Smith, and George Wein. Mercer and Ruth were there, too, along with a handful of Ellington alumni, including Fred Guy and Tom Whaley, who led the band, and Clark Terry and Louis Bellson, who played in it. But except for Harry Carney, who drove Ellington to the White House, none of the current members was present—they were on their way to Oklahoma City to play a concert—and neither, needless to say, were Evie or the Countess.

President Nixon addressed the crowd, describing the proceedings as "a very unusual and special evening." He read the Medal of Freedom citation out loud: "In the royalty of American music, no man swings more or stands higher than the Duke." Then he presented Ellington with the medal, and as everyone applauded, Ellington responded by administering to the president of the United States what Whitney Balliett, who was writing up the proceedings for *The New Yorker*'s "Talk of the Town" department, described as "the classic French greeting of left cheek against left cheek, right against right, left against left, and right against right."* He thanked the president, saying, "There is no place I would rather be tonight except in my mother's arms." Nixon, an amateur pianist, played "Happy Birthday" in the key of G, after which the band went to work and the joint started jumping.

At the end of the set, President Nixon coaxed Ellington back to the platform and asked him to play. "I shall pick a name and see if I can improvise on it . . . something, you know, very gentle, graceful, and something like princess—Pat," he replied. Then he sat down at the piano and improvised a pastel portrait of Pat Nixon, yet another of the on-the-spot musical miracles that he had been shaking out of his sleeve for years. Though he had only played two recitals without the full band, at the Museum of Modern Art in January of 1962 and Columbia University two years later, his rare solo essays were admired by connoisseurs. From "Reflections in D," a study in chromatic ornamentation that he included on *The Duke Plays Ellington*, to "The Single Petal of a Rose," the berceuse-like meditation in the veiled key of D-flat that he tucked into *The Queen's Suite*, his tribute to Queen Elizabeth II, they rank among his most inspired moments on record, and "Pat," which

---

* It was Ellington's long-accustomed salutation, and it puzzled the president. "Four kisses? Why four?" Nixon asked. "One for each cheek, Mr. President," he replied.

"One for each cheek, Mr. President": At the White House, 1969. The elaborate party that Richard Nixon threw in honor of Ellington's seventieth birthday did much to compensate for the embarrassment of his having been denied a Pulitzer Prize

surfaced when the music performed at the White House in 1969 was commercially released on record in 2002, was one of the prettiest.

When it was all over, he and Carney left for Oklahoma City. Medals of Freedom pay no bills, and Ellington was having trouble making ends meet, so much so that Russell Procope had quit the band briefly in 1968 after going unpaid for three weeks. Stanley Dance recalled a nervous morning when Ellington, who never arose before late afternoon for any reason short of a hotel fire, was awake at eight A.M., poring over stacks of papers as he lay in bed. "I'm trying to see where we can get some money from to pay the bus company," he said. Mercer had watched the cash dry up, and he knew where much of it was going, for Ellington continued to play the grand seigneur, spending money that he no longer had on family and friends:

> *During those last horrible days . . . he had so many problems with taxes, also meeting expenses for rent and the number of people in the family he supported, it kept him to a point where basically he had about three possessions. He had a white overcoat, he had an electric piano he used to*

sleep with and a steak sandwich in his pocket. He never had much of anything that was really material. He had three pairs of pants he used on the road, some cashmere sweaters and a hat.

So he stayed on the road, playing wherever Joe Glaser sent him, making new albums for whatever labels cared to release them, and endorsing commercial products like Olivetti typewriters and Hammond organs ("Push a button, and you get rhythm") to help keep the bus rolling. He had outlived virtually all of his Swing Era peers—only Count Basie, Woody Herman, Harry James, and Stan Kenton continued to lead full-time touring bands—but he also knew that his music, like theirs, had outlived its popular appeal. Rock and roll had taken over American pop culture in 1969, the year of *Abbey Road, Easy Rider, Let It Bleed, Tommy,* and the Woodstock festival. Even Miles Davis, the most influential jazzman of the postwar era, embraced the

"It has nothing to do with taste": Onstage with Mercer Ellington, 1971. Intensely aware that the baby boomers preferred rock to jazz, Duke Ellington sought late in life to cater to their tastes by playing arrangements of songs by the Beatles and dressing in gaudily "mod" outfits, sometimes with embarrassing results

new sounds with *In a Silent Way*. To do otherwise was to risk being written off as old-fashioned, and Ellington saw no alternative but to pay homage to the moment. Conscious of the commercial risks of looking his age, he had long worn his conked hair in a grotesque little ponytail that Charles Sam Courtney described as "pomade-shiny, streaked with gray and henna." Now he upped the ante by donning ever more self-consciously trendy outfits and writing a hand-clapping gospel-rock number called "One More Time for the People" that he insisted on playing in the hope of making the people think that he was something other than a seventy-year-old whose tank was nearly out of gas. "If we keep playing that number, then the critics can stop wondering what to pan," he told a friend.

Now, too, came the terrible and crushing losses, the first of which was the departure of Lawrence Brown, who quit in December of 1969, claiming that he had "lost all feeling for music" and had no desire ever again to play the trombone. Brown later said that he was "sick and tired of all of that hypocrisy, exploitation, deceit . . . everything that was going on" in the Ellington band. No doubt he was, since he had been complaining about it for as long as the youngest sidemen had been alive. For years, Joya Sherrill said, he "never got on the bus without saying, 'I'm gonna leave this band.'" But the real reason for his sudden retirement, which he chose not to reveal save to friends, was that after decades of feuding, he and Ellington had finally gotten into a backstage fistfight, and his boss had knocked out his two front teeth.

That was bad enough, but what happened the following May was infinitely worse: Johnny Hodges collapsed and died in the men's room of his dentist's office, cut down by a heart attack at the not-so-august age of sixty-three. Though his health had grown poor, his playing remained secure, and to the end the alto saxophonist offered Ellington's fans the tightest of aural ties to the sounds of days gone by. While Ellington had featured Hodges every night and paid him lavishly, at least by the prevailing standards of jazz, he was tiring of the demands of the road, and he could have led an easier and more financially comfortable life had he wished to do so. According to Norman Granz, Lawrence Welk, who adored Hodges's playing, had made him "a fantastic offer, infinitely more than he was making with Duke" to join Welk's TV group, with time off to do combo dates. But even though he and Welk cut an album of ballads together, Hodges kept on riding the band bus until he died. Once more Ellington penned a tribute in the small hours, this one containing a sentence that was as true as it was uncharacteristically straightforward: "Because of this great loss, our band will never sound the same."

Hodges was "replaced" by Norris Turney, a solid and accomplished saxophonist, but the situation facing him was as impossible as it had been when Harold Ashby and Rufus Jones "replaced" Jimmy Hamilton and Sam Woodyard. The great individualists were vanishing one by one, and the younger men who followed them into the band could not always appreciate the weight of the past that they were being asked to shoulder. Unlike Paul Gonsalves, whom Ellington had initially hired because he could play all of Ben Webster's solos from memory, some of them didn't even know what the band had sounded like in the old days. "When I was with Duke I had never heard of these [older] records," Ashby admitted. "I didn't know anything about it." If Hodges had lived two days longer, he could have shown them exactly what they were missing. Ellington was recording his latest composition, a nine-part work called *New Orleans Suite,* and he had hoped to persuade the old master to pick up his soprano saxophone for the first time in decades to play the seventh movement, "Portrait of Sidney Bechet," on which he was to be featured. Instead Gonsalves filled in on tenor, and though he honored his section mate with an elegiac solo, those who heard the album could think only of what might have been.

The suite itself, however, was a welcome return to past form, both for Ellington as a composer and for the band as a whole. Centered on musical portraits of Bechet, Louis Armstrong, Mahalia Jackson, and Wellman Braud, whose slap-bass playing had long anchored Ellington's rhythm section, *New Orleans Suite* starts off with a surprise, a gospel-tinged organ-piano duet by Wild Bill Davis and Ellington, with Hodges chiming in midway through. "Blues for New Orleans," taped two weeks before the saxophonist's death, is a dirt-simple, heavy-on-the-backbeat blues in which the band struts so soulfully that you'd think Ray Charles had stopped by the studio to sing a couple of choruses. Not only does Hodges wail like a man half his age, but the bright, crisp sound of Davis's electric organ lends to "Blues for New Orleans" the up-to-date feel for which Ellington had been searching in vain. Stanley Dance, present for what turned out to be Hodges's last recording session, recalled how the delighted bandleader "was in the studio—not in the control room—conducting, routining, dancing, clapping his hands, and miming his requirements as the arrangement unfolded."

While not all of *New Orleans Suite* is as inspired as "Blues for New Orleans," the work is still full of aural felicities, among them Norris Turney's flute, an instrument never before used by Ellington. Turney solos on "Bourbon Street Jingling Jollies," a minor-key processional reminiscent of "Sonnet for Caesar" that the composer described for inexplicable reasons of his own as "a rhythmic tone parallel to the excruciating ecstasies one finds oneself suspended in when one is in the throes of the jingling rhythmic jollies of Bourbon Street." The heartening sound of the blues, fundamental and irreducible, is omnipresent throughout *New Orleans Suite,* and despite intermittent moments of uncertain intonation and musical patchiness, even the hard-to-please Max Harrison lauded the album as "jazz without pretense," writing eloquently of the way in which it encapsulated the long-standing traditions that made the band what it was:

> *The strength of the Ellington unit as a self-perpetuating phenomenon is well instanced here. Four years prior to Ellington's death, there were in the orchestra players providing links with the beginnings and the middle period, and new men also who, like many who had come and gone, were borne up in the collective inspiration which had helped to make those veterans what they had become.*

Turney, who made his studio recording debut with the band at the first *New Orleans Suite* session, felt much the same way. "When that band was really together, man, they really played," he said fifteen years later. "Such a sound you never heard before. I was in there. . . . I'd be in that band with all the beautiful sounds floating around you—there was just nothing like it. I can't explain it. It was the greatest experience of my life." But the spokes on the wheel kept on snapping. In January of 1971 Cat Anderson moved to Hollywood to become a full-time studio musician. Those who disdained his crowd-goading squeals and shrieks may have thought his departure no great loss, but Ellington knew what he was losing, and so did some of his friends. "I think the band began to fall apart . . . in the late Sixties," Brooks Kerr said later. "It ambled along. . . . When those four men [Brown, Hodges, Woodyard, Hamilton] left, they created quite a gap which Duke had to work very hard to fill. That's why Duke began to accent the personality aspect of it . . . he had to rely on palaver to get it over 'cause he knew the band wasn't as up to par as it had been."

The onstage "palaver" to which Kerr referred was still amusing, though, and one of Ellington's best bits, in which he taught his listeners how to simulate hipness by snapping their fingers in the correct manner, had recently made it onto record. The version of "Satin Doll" that closes *Duke Ellington's 70th Birthday Concert,* recorded in Manchester a year earlier, shows how he flattered an audience by putting it on:

Thank you very much, ladies and gentlemen. You're very beautiful, very sweet, very gracious, very generous, and this is "Satin Doll." We'll use it now for the purpose of giving background to this finger-snapping bit, and you are all cordially invited to join the finger-snapping. . . . I don't have to tell you, one never snaps one's fingers on the beat—it's considered aggressive. Don't push it, just let it fall. And if you would like to be conservatively hip, then at the same time tilt the left earlobe, establish a state of nonchalance. And if you would like to be respectably cool, then tilt the left earlobe on the beat and snap the finger on the afterbeat. And so by routining one's finger snapping and choreographing one's earlobe-tilting, one discovers that one can become as cool as one wishes to be.

He even had one more musical trick tucked up his now-frayed sleeve. In June of 1970, six weeks after the band finished recording *New Orleans Suite,* Ellington made his debut as a ballet composer when American Ballet Theatre, one of the world's leading dance companies, premiered *The River,* a new ballet by Alvin Ailey set to a score by Ellington, at New York's Lincoln Center. Ailey had choreographed some of Ellington's shorter pieces since working on *My People* in 1963, but *The River* was their first full-scale collaboration, as well as the first time that Ailey, a greatly admired modern-dance choreographer who led his own troupe, had made a ballet for a classical company. Having seen Ellington at work, he knew something of what to expect, but *My People* had not prepared him for what was to come.

After first suggesting a comic ballet to the unresponsive Ailey, who admitted, "I don't have a comic bone in my body," Ellington came back with the idea for a dance that would be "all water music . . . it was to follow the course of this stream through various stages: through a meander, a falls, and then a whirlpool, and then a giggling rapids." In a departure from his usual refusal to look to classical composers for models, he listened to such pieces as Handel's *Water Music,* Debussy's *La mer,* and the four "sea interludes" from Benjamin Britten's *Peter Grimes* "to see what other people have done with water music." Then he started composing, sending Ailey tape-recorded piano versions of bits and pieces of the score. Ailey, who choreographed each section as soon as it arrived, was unnerved when Ellington kept changing his mind, sending new versions as he wrote them. It also bothered him that Ellington insisted on working out of sequence, writing snippet after snippet of music instead of producing self-contained sections for Ailey to stage. Just as he was about to give up, Ellington paid him a visit in person. "I have to have the whole piece . . . so I can see what I'm doing from beginning to end," Ailey complained, and received an emollient but unhelpful reply: "Look, man, if you'd just worry a little bit more about this choreography and stop worrying about the music, you'd be better off."

Furious though he was with Ellington's procrastinatory habits, Ailey was fascinated by his crowded schedule, though he wondered when the hard-working composer found time to sleep, much less write:

> *He would get up about five o'clock in the afternoon and have breakfast until about seven o'clock and get dressed and receive people until about nine o'clock. Then get dressed and go down and do the nine-thirty show or [the] ten o'clock show, come back upstairs at midnight, change clothes, receive more people, go back downstairs, do a one o'clock show until three o'clock in the morning, socialize with people until four o'clock or five o'clock and then come up at five o'clock in the morning and work from five o'clock until ten o'clock.*

Eventually Ellington started knitting his themes into finished movements, which he sent to Ailey "page by page or two pages at a time." Once again, though, he had waited too long to accommodate the iron necessities of the situation, and Ailey had only enough time to finish staging seven of the thirteen movements by the time of the premiere on June 25, from which the composer was absent, having left town to fulfill an engagement in Chicago. The printed program billed the ballet, which was danced to a tape of the score, as "Seven Dances From a Work in Progress Entitled *The River.*" The critics, making due allowance for the fact that the ballet was unfinished, received it with enthusiasm, taking special note of Ellington's musical contribution. Clive Barnes, the dance critic of *The New York Times,* called it "that rare thing among classic scores, something that is contemporary, moving and yet totally unsentimental."

Ailey finished choreographing *The River* the following year, and the complete work became a permanent part of American Ballet Theatre's repertory, though Ellington died before he could see it danced in public. Nor did the band ever perform it live: Ron Collier, a Canadian composer-arranger, scored *The River* for ABT's pit orchestra, and it is in this form that the ballet is danced today. Collier's orchestrations, while more than competent, are impersonal sounding when heard alongside the preliminary versions that Ellington scored for and recorded with the band for Ailey to use in rehearsal, just as Luther Henderson's symphonic arrangement of *A Tone Parallel to*

Harlem, imaginatively realized though it is, lacks the idiosyncratic ensemble colors of Ellington's best music. Even so, *The River,* like *New Orleans Suite,* is a worthy addition to the Ellington catalog, a set of attractively varied character pieces that are as danceable in toto as any of the great nineteenth-century dance scores. Watching a performance suggests how great a loss it was that Ellington never wrote a full-evening ballet. Such a work, in which self-contained musical movements are arranged in a dramatic sequence determined by the choreographer, would have suited his formal limitations, and his ability to write concise musical character studies made him as well suited to the creation of dance scores as were Tchaikovsky or Delibes.

The River is full of such vignettes, including "Spring," a portrait of the origins of a river, and "Vortex," a miniconcerto for percussion and orchestra that made a deep impression on Whitney Balliett when he heard the band record it prior to the premiere:

> *The section passages . . . are brief but dense and booting, there are solo parts by Paul Gonsalves, and there are heavy, dissonant full-band chords. And all this is done against the furious rat-tat-tat-tat of the snare, the glockenspiel, and the timpani. It is exciting, tight crescendo music, and it reminded me of early Stravinsky, except that it is unmistakably a jazz composition.*

At seventy-one, there was still life in the old boy yet.

He remained famous, of course. Television had long ago seen to that, and continued to keep him before the public long after his records were no longer selling. One day in 1970, a couple of months after his final appearance on *The Ed Sullivan Show,* Ellington deigned to walk a block from a Manhattan rehearsal hall to his waiting car. Balliett, who was accompanying him, recorded the ensuing events with obvious amusement:

> *He started west on Fifty-sixth Street, moving in the determined, stiff way of older men with tired feet. He got a lot of double takes, and whenever he passed a garage or a restaurant with its complement of New York early-evening sidewalk loungers, he was greeted with, "Hey, Duke!" or "Mr. Ellington!" Each time, he looked interested and said, "How you been?" or "How's everything?" and shook hands as if he were greeting friends he hadn't seen in twenty-five years.*

But tired he was, and though he remained relentlessly active, barnstorming around America and Canada and touring Australia, Europe, Japan, South America, and the Soviet Union, his capacity for physical regeneration was not unlimited. A recording of his last "solo" concert, which he gave with Joe Benjamin and Rufus Jones at the Whitney Museum of American Art in April of 1972, shows that his piano playing was losing its sureness of touch, and pictures taken around the same time show him looking seedy and weary. Nor was it merely a matter of advancing age: Something was gravely wrong with him.

Like so many superstitious people, Ellington's seemingly nonsensical anxieties pointed to an overweening fear of death. Ever since he lost his mother, it had been the great unmentionable, and it fed his own hypochondria. "If he stubbed his toe, he'd call his doctor," Clark Terry said. "Even if he had to do it from Egypt." The doctor whom he called was Arthur Logan, whom he had met at the Cotton Club in 1937 and on whom he had depended ever since. An extremely light-skinned man who chose in his youth not to pass for white, Logan practiced at Harlem's Upper Manhattan Medical Group (after which Billy Strayhorn's 1956 composition was named) and shared an Upper West Side brownstone with his wife Marian, a former nightclub singer who happily embraced the customs of the black elite after their marriage in 1958. Ellington took constant advantage of his relationship with Logan, calling him in the middle of the night to ask, "Arthur, how am I feeling today?" Logan was happy to oblige his famous friend, presenting Ellington with a monogrammed doctor's bag that he stuffed with innocuous pills of various kinds and giving him "rainbow" multivitamin shots whenever the two men were in the same city. "There's nothing wrong with Edward," he admitted. "It's in his mind. If it makes him happy for me to stick him, I'm going to stick him." Marian was amused by their interdependence: "Of course, Edward needed Arthur. Arthur kept him healthy, so he could make his music. Edward also loved the idea of Arthur. He thought it was magnificent to have his personal physician with him all the time, like some sort of ancient potentate." In time he took on Strayhorn and the rest of the band as patients. It was Logan who told Strayhorn that he was dying of cancer, and in 1972 it became his responsibility to give the same news to Duke Ellington.

Cootie Williams had come down with a respiratory ailment when the band traveled to Houston that May to spend two weeks playing for dancers at the Shamrock Hotel. Local doctors tested the entire band for tuberculosis and emphysema, and advised two of them, Ellington and Harry Carney, to consult their own physicians after returning to New York. Ellington never needed to be told twice to see a doctor, so he paid Arthur Logan a visit as soon as he got home. To their mutual horror, Logan discovered that Ellington, a lifelong smoker, had cancer in both lungs. The two men decided to keep his illness secret for as long as they could, and Ellington returned to the road, determined to beat the disease that had cut Strayhorn down.

Even in his last illness he remained, incredibly enough, attractive to women. The orchestral conductor Maurice Peress, who was working with him on a musical project, testified to his appeal: "Once the word got around that I passed unchallenged in and out of the great man's dressing room, women—old flames and wannabe flames—began pressing notes on me to pass on." And he still had two more good albums in him. Norman Granz, who had lately resumed his professional ties with Ellington, had no interest in recording the full band, having concluded that it no longer played well enough. Ellington, he said, "clung to the band like a crutch, just as old people cling together in marriage because they can't think of anything else to do." But he felt that Ellington the pianist still had something to say, and Granz persuaded him to tape a pair of small-group albums in December and January. On *This One's for Blanton,* a duet album for which Granz paired him with Ray Brown, Ellington tipped his hat to the young bass virtuoso whose playing had helped to inspire his most sustained and distinguished period of compositional activity. *Duke's Big 4,* on which he joined forces with Brown, the guitarist Joe Pass, and Louis Bellson, contained combo versions of "The Hawk Talks" and six Ellington standards, one of them a frisky gallop through "Cotton Tail" that betrays no sign of the dire straits in which he now found himself: Three days after the session, he was admitted to a Los Angeles hospital with what a spokesman described as "chronic exhaustion and a virus infection." Mercer led the band in his absence, and he was back on the road a month later.

Sick or not, Ellington had two additional projects on his plate. One was the Third Sacred Concert, which would be premiered at London's Westminster Abbey in October. The other was his autobiography, for which Doubleday had paid him an advance of $50,000 (about $319,000 in today's dollars). Sam Vaughan, a New York editor who had worked with Dwight Eisenhower on his presidential memoirs, was eager to see the book into print. Ellington, having spent the advance as soon as he got it, had accumulated a huge stack of handwritten notes but needed help to transform them into a finished manuscript. At one time he had considered working on his memoirs with Carter Harman, the author of *Time*'s 1956 cover story, and to that end he talked at length to the journalist in 1964, speaking with unprecedented, often profane candor about a wide variety of subjects, including race and sex. Among other things, he described himself as a "pussy freak" ("I have walked past *money* to get pussy!") and claimed that men who, like him, sought to satisfy women in bed instead of merely satisfying themselves "are the people who get bags under their eyes." But Harman, who wanted to write about "the 'secret' Ellington," realized that what the composer wanted was "to write a book that was a print version of the public Duke Ellington . . . he said, 'No, once you've been in the spotlight, you never dare get out unless it's after midnight and you go into the bathroom, pull down the shade and turn off the light.' " So Harman withdrew from the project, and Ellington chose instead to work with Stanley Dance, a British jazz writer and record producer who had married Helen Oakley, Ellington's old publicist, in 1947. Dance had become one of the bandleader's most trusted associates after moving to the United States in 1959, and eleven years later he published *The World of Duke Ellington,* an invaluable collection of profiles of and interviews with Ellington, Strayhorn, and various members of the band, thus making him a logical candidate to collaborate with Ellington on what eventually became *Music Is My Mistress.*

Ellington's foreword points directly to Dance's limitations as a "journalist": "Stanley is well informed about my activities and those of my associates. . . . However, I am sure he has not revealed more than he ought!" But it was precisely because he trusted Dance's discretion that he asked him to work on his memoirs, and the two men put together a publishable manuscript out of Ellington's pile of scrawled memoranda, which Dance later described as having been written on "hotel stationery, napkins, old sheets of manuscript, and everything like that." Even before they sanitized it, the book was toothless, with only an occasional glint of candor ("Sonny Greer is a big bullshitter, and talks his ass off") shining through the evasions. By the time they were finished, the evasions were all that remained.

In the course of working on *Music Is My Mistress,* Dance saw Ellington's home life with Evie up close:

> *In some ways I used to dread going to the apartment on West End Avenue, because I had to waste so much time. I'd go there and I had to sit for hours watching these terrible movies on TV before we'd get any work done. And Evie by this time could appear a pretty embittered woman. They'd shout at each other sometimes and Duke would press me to eat. I'd be starving, maybe, but I'd say no because I knew Evie didn't want to be bothered.*

Lisa Drew, who edited the manuscript, prodded Ellington to be more frank. But he had no intention of doing so, and the book that Doubleday ended up publishing, according to Sam Vaughan, was "a mixture of the best and the worst of Ellington. All that love-you-madly stuff goes on and on. We spoke to him about it. We said, 'If you say you love everybody all the time, whether it's true or not, you have no credibility.'" Ellington knew well how unforthcoming *Music Is My Mistress* was. "We've written the Good Book, and now we'll write the Bad Book!" he told Dance. But it said what he wanted to say and looked the way he wanted it to look. When he saw that the dust jacket of the twenty-five-thousand-copy first edition was designed in brown, his least favorite color, he insisted that it be withdrawn and reprinted in blue, and Doubleday reluctantly complied with his wishes. And even though he had gone out of his way to avoid giving offense to anyone, the book nevertheless contained a certain number of revealing truths, not least the oft-quoted passage in which Ellington explained its title: "Music is my mistress, and she plays second fiddle to no one. . . . Lovers have come and gone, but only my mistress stays."

He kept on making public appearances in order to stay on the right side of solvency. In February he trotted out the dreaded medley on *Duke Ellington . . . We Love You Madly,* a CBS special produced by Quincy Jones that also featured Ray Charles, Sammy Davis Jr., Billy Eckstine, Roberta Flack, Aretha Franklin, Peggy Lee, Sarah Vaughan, Joe Williams, the jazz-rock group Chicago, and a fifty-three-piece orchestra that was salted with a dozen of his sidemen past and present. "I could feel that he wasn't going to be here forever," Jones recalled. Those who heard how tired he sounded as he addressed the audience must have thought the same thing. He looked and sounded no better when he returned to the Rainbow Grill in August for the next-to-last time, playing poorly and speaking sharply to strangers who approached him. ("You talk too fast," he had told an interviewer in Helsinki a few months earlier. "You don't listen enough.") Stanley Dance visited him in his dressing room and was astonished to hear him say, "I am surrounded by mediocrity, Stanley, and I've never been accustomed to it." To Betty McGettigan, a music-loving Californian who had met Ellington in 1969 and with whom he embarked on a long-distance affair, he was just as blunt. "People always want something of me," he told her.

Two months after closing at the Rainbow Grill, he flew to London for the Third Sacred Concert. Though he refused to admit the gravity of his condition, Mercer started to understand how sick his father was when Ruth, who never traveled with the band, decided to accompany her brother to

England: "I guess I really resented that, figuring that between the two of them they knew he was on his last legs." Ellington's spoken introduction to the premiere performance left no possible doubt of his desperate condition—he sounded sick unto death—though the weakness of the piece itself, a réchauffé of his earlier sacred music that is distinguished only for its gentle solo-piano prelude, said all that needed to be said.

From then on he made no secret of how he felt. "As the days went on, the smile turned into a grimace . . . he knew the game was up; there was no point in going through the finger exercises or trying to preserve his image, by this time he knew he no longer had an image," Mercer said. Yet he continued to keep his engagements, playing dates in Austria, Belgium, Denmark, Ethiopia, France, Holland, Germany, Italy, Portugal, Spain, Sweden, Zambia, and Yugoslavia, then flying back to England for a command performance at the Palladium and another week of touring. Along the way he received a call from Marian Logan, who told him that her husband had died under mysterious and still-unexplained circumstances, with the police finding the doctor's corpse in a Harlem viaduct. The news reduced Ellington to

"He looks beat and kind of lonely": With Jimmy Hamilton, London, 1963. The demoralizing effects of Ellington's unrelentingly brutal touring schedule could be seen by the public long before lung cancer forced him off the road and into the hospital

uncontrollable weeping. "I'll never get over this, I won't last six months," he told her.

At the beginning of December he went to New York for three more weeks at the Rainbow Grill, then returned one last time to the road. The struggles of a lifetime—to command respect for his race, to charm the public, to stay abreast of the times, to keep his family comfortable and his secrets secret—were at an end. Now he struggled merely to get through each show and make his painful way to the next one. It soon became clear that he was no longer up to playing one-nighters, and Mercer started canceling them. On March 21, Mercer took his father to Northern Illinois University Hospital after a performance in DeKalb, Illinois. "Does he know how sick he is?" an intern there asked Mercer. "Do *you* know how sick he is?" Mercer replied. The intern then called Ellington's physicians in New York, who advised him that the bandleader could come home and enter the hospital whenever he wanted. He hung up and asked one last question: "Does he know that when he goes in this time he's not ever coming back out anymore?" The next night Ellington played two shows at Michigan's Sturges-Young Auditorium. Then he flew back to New York, leaving Mercer and the band to carry on. He never again appeared in public.

After spending two days at the apartment with Evie, Ellington checked into the Harkness Pavilion of Columbia Presbyterian Medical Center. On April 4 *The New York Times* reported that he was ill. "It's nothing serious and he'll be out in a few days," said a spokesman. Frank Sinatra sent his private jet to Houston to fly Dr. Michael DeBakey to New York to look his friend over. Once DeBakey confirmed that the situation was hopeless, Sinatra sent thousands of dollars' worth of flowers and fruit to Ellington's hospital room, where he kept on writing music for as long as he could. The electric piano that he had carried with him on the road was at his side, and he toyed with two final projects, a ballet score called *The Three Black Kings* and a comic opera called *Queenie Pie.** His friends, who visited him regularly, were shocked by his appearance. "He had shriveled so much but his hair hadn't; it looked like an oversize wig that had been plopped on," Don George said. Evie came, too, but she was nearly as sick as he was, and when her own doctors concluded in mid-April that she was also suffering from lung cancer, Ellington insisted that she seek treatment at once. Ruth, the Countess, and Betty McGettigan took her place at his bedside, but his feelings for Evie grew stronger as he neared the end: "Even though the intense sedation kept

---

* Both remained incomplete at the time of his death and were finished by other hands.

him alternating between periods of pain and euphoria, to the very end he called her two or three times every day to say to her, 'I love you, doll. Honest, I love you.'" Meanwhile Paul Gonsalves, wasted away by years of addiction, died in London on May 14, and Tyree Glenn followed suit four days later in New Jersey. The news of their deaths was kept from Ellington, who was barely clinging to his own life. On May 23 he developed pneumonia, and at 3:10 the next morning, three weeks after his seventy-fifth birthday, he breathed his last.

Tens of thousands of people filed past his coffin, which lay in state at a funeral home on Manhattan's Upper East Side. He was wearing the Medal of Freedom, France's Legion of Honor, and the Emperor's Star of Ethiopia, his most prized decorations. Gordon Parks viewed the corpse with an artist's detachment: "He appeared to have lost his fear of the inevitable; he seemed fulfilled. But with the energy and the mischief gone, he was a smaller man than I remembered." Count Basie, Dick Gregory, and Johnny Mercer came to see him off. So did the Countess, escorted by Sonny Greer and Russell Procope, who had started a trio with Brooks Kerr and were playing at an East Side club. So, too, did countless strangers and half-remembered colleagues. One of the latter, Frisco Bowman, a septuagenarian musician who had jammed with Ellington in Harlem, assured a reporter that he was "up there now with the Louis Armstrongs and the Jelly Roll Mortons."

John S. Wilson of *The New York Times,* who had covered his career with a combination of critical candor and personal respect, wrote the paper's front-page obituary. Ellington would have appreciated the fact that the word *jazz* did not appear until the eleventh paragraph, when Wilson remarked that it was "a word that he consistently rejected in relation to his work." The appraisal was lengthy and just, describing him as a "master of music" and noting that his music had received "international critical praise and brought listening and dancing pleasure to two generations," though Wilson got some things wrong, claiming that Ellington had divorced Edna and married both Mildred and Evie. (*Time* said only that he was "never lacking for female companionship.") A sidebar of tributes included a few words from President Nixon, who took time out from Watergate to say that "the wit, taste, intelligence and elegance that Duke Ellington brought to his music have made him, in the eyes of millions of people both here and abroad, America's foremost composer." Also cited were Gunther Schuller, who placed him "in the pantheon of musicians along with Bach and Beethoven and Schoenberg," and Bing Crosby, who said that "Duke Ellington and Louis Armstrong were the greatest musicians of all time."

Time, on whose cover he had appeared eighteen years earlier, now declared that his work would be remembered as "the most distinctive single body of composition in all of jazz." And *Jet,* the weekly newsmagazine that specialized in covering the doings of prominent and successful blacks, went all out, publishing a half dozen photos of Ellington lying in state and quoting Mercer as saying, "His absolute faith in God just made him believe that he could go on and on, and he did. . . . If I go through life with half as much valor as he showed in the past year, I would be the strongest man in the world."

That night CBS aired a half-hour special called *A Tribute to Duke Ellington.* Stanley Dance, Ella Fitzgerald, Russell Procope, Billy Taylor, and an ancient-looking Sonny Greer all came to the studio to say a few innocuous words about their friend. Ellington himself was represented by a brief clip from *Duke Ellington . . . We Love You Madly* (in which he looked ashen and drawn) and a lengthy excerpt from the ASCAP medley. "Mood Indigo," "Satin Doll," "Solitude," "Sophisticated Lady": All passed in fleeting review, though none of the soloists was identified, not even Harry Carney, the last of the old-timers, who had stayed with the band all the way to the end.

On May 27 Ellington's funeral was held at the Cathedral Church of St. John the Divine. Ten thousand people were in the pews, with another twenty-five hundred listening on the street via loudspeakers and thousands more listening to a live broadcast of the services carried by WRVR, New York's all-jazz station. Count Basie sat in the front of the church, plainly distraught. Carney, Greer, Procope, and Cootie Williams were present, too, as were Mercer, Ruth, Pearl Bailey, Louis Bellson, and Benny Goodman. Ella Fitzgerald, Earl Hines, Hank Jones, Ray Nance, Joe Williams, and Mary Lou Williams provided the music, and the eulogy was delivered by Stanley Dance, who called Ellington "the greatest innovator in his field, and yet paradoxically a conservative, one who built new things on the best of the old and disdained ephemeral fashion." He went on to say, no less truly, that "his various associates and friends knew different aspects of him, but never, as they readily admit, the whole man." Then he was buried in Woodlawn Cemetery beside his mother and father, whose caskets had been moved to New York when the Washington cemetery in which they were buried was condemned. Carney, Greer, and Don George rode to the cemetery together in a limousine. "I'm not going to live much longer," the saxophonist said. "With Duke dead, I have nothing to live for." Five months later he, too, was dead.

Nat Hentoff, who stood outside the cathedral that day, spoke to an old black man. "I'm just here to bear witness," he said. "A man passed through, and he was a giant."

Mercer and the band flew to Bermuda the next day to play at an IBM convention. They had no choice, for there were bills to be paid. Ellington died intestate—he had preferred to give the members of his extended family everything that he could while he was alive—and in the end the copyrights to his songs were sold off in order to pay his taxes. Mercer led the Ellington "ghost band," as such groups are known to jazz musicians, until his own death in 1996. (It remains in existence, led by Paul Mercer Ellington, Mercer's son, who never knew his famous grandfather.) Evie died in 1976 and was buried in the same grave as her companion, though no mention of her presence is made on Ellington's modest tombstone. Two years later Mercer wrote *Duke Ellington in Person: An Intimate Memoir,* in which he sought with partial success to come to terms with his complicated feelings toward his father.

Unlike many artists who won fame during their lifetimes, Ellington underwent no posthumous decline in his reputation. He is universally acknowledged as the greatest composer in the history of jazz and, increasingly, as one of the greatest of any kind in the history of American music, as well as a peerlessly creative big-band orchestrator, a pianist of formidable originality, and an enduring exemplar of black accomplishment and pride. Untroubled by the radically collaborative nature of his artistic achievement, which led some classical musicians to question how seriously he could be taken as a composer in his own right, the classical-music critic and historian Alex Ross wrote in *The Rest Is Noise: Listening to the Twentieth Century,* his influential 2007 study of musical modernism and postmodernism, that "Ellington carved out his own brand of eminence, redefining composition as a collective art."

His recordings continue to be reissued and his songs continue to be played and sung, though the critics have never stopped wrangling over their comparative importance. While a small but resolute group of commentators, most notably Stanley Crouch, has plumped in recent years for his later work, the vast majority of Ellington's critics agree that he was at his best in the forties. In 1989 Gunther Schuller finally got around to publishing *The Swing Era,* the long-awaited sequel to *Early Jazz,* in which he wrote of the later suites and found them wanting: "Ellington never fully succeeded in his almost lifelong quest to express himself in larger, not just longer, forms . . . he never really understood the nature of the problem he was facing in undertaking to write in larger forms." It is a verdict in which most scholars concur, though it does not diminish his stature in the least: He was, like Chopin,

Paul Klee, Jorge Luis Borges, and Flannery O'Connor, a disciplined lyric miniaturist who knew how to express the grandest of emotions on the smallest of scales, and who needed no more room in which to suggest his immortal longings.

If anyone doubts that he still matters, one need only look at the way in which America's cultural institutions now treat him. In 1987 Jazz at Lincoln Center joined the Metropolitan Opera, the New York City Ballet, New York City Opera, the New York Philharmonic, Lincoln Center Theater, the Juilliard School, and the School of American Ballet as a constituent of America's biggest and most influential performing-arts center, and Wynton Marsalis, the co-founder, placed Ellington's music at the heart of its programming. His musical manuscripts and personal papers were acquired the following year by the Smithsonian Institution. He even scored a Broadway hit at long last with *Sophisticated Ladies*, a glossy 1981 revue based on his songs that ran for 767 performances. And in 1999 he got his Pulitzer, a special award "bestowed posthumously on Edward Kennedy 'Duke' Ellington, commemorating the centennial year of his birth, in recognition of his musical genius, which evoked aesthetically the principles of democracy through the medium of jazz and thus made an indelible contribution to art and culture."

Everyone knows him—yet no one knows him. That was the way he wanted it. "To the very end, he made sure he left nothing behind that would let people know the real Duke Ellington," Norman Granz said. But he had: He left behind his music, the only mistress to whom he told everything and was always true.

AFTERWORD

IKE *POPS,* MY 2009 biography of Louis Armstrong, *Duke: A Life of Duke Ellington* is not so much a work of scholarship as an act of synthesis, a narrative biography that is substantially based on the work of academic scholars and other researchers who in recent years have unearthed a wealth of new information about Duke Ellington and his colleagues. My interpretations of this information are my own, but without these men and women, whose work is fully and appreciatively acknowledged in the source notes and bibliography, no part of *Duke* could have been successfully completed.

In Ellington's case, however, much of the most significant research to be done in the past quarter century and more has come from part-time scholars whose work is as professional—and as consequential—as that of any professor. They labor for love, and I stand on their shoulders. Foremost among them are the superlatively diligent members of the Duke Ellington Music Society, whose invaluable findings have been regularly published since 1979 in *The International DEMS Bulletin,* all of whose issues I have read with the closest attention. I have also profited greatly from the efforts of the Duke Ellington Society UK, which are published in its own quarterly journal, *Blue Light.*

I wish to specifically acknowledge the assistance of Steven Lasker, a longtime contributor to the *DEMS Bulletin* and the world's foremost collector of Ellingtonia, who read every word of the manuscript of *Duke* and commented on it in amazingly painstaking detail. Nobody knows more than Steven about Ellington and his music, and nobody could be more generous to those who seek to profit from his immense knowledge. In addition to graciously allowing me to spend several days sifting through his private collection, he supplied the book's title and cover photograph, as well as several of the other photos reproduced herein. These words of appreciation can be no more than an inadequate substitute for the formal recognition that his scholarship deserves and has yet to receive.

I have also benefited immeasurably from the wise counsel of Brian Priestley and Ken Steiner, two other distinguished Ellington experts who took the trouble to read and comment on the manuscript of *Duke;* John Edward Hasse, the author of *Beyond Category: The Life and Genius of Duke Ellington* and a curator at the Smithsonian Institution's National Museum of American History, who oversees the museum's Duke Ellington Collection and helped me to find my way through its holdings; and the staffs of Rutgers University's Institute of Jazz Studies and Yale University's Oral History of American Music archive and Stanley Dance collection, who opened their doors and files to me. My mistakes, like my interpretations, are mine alone, but there are far fewer of them because of their help.

I cannot begin to list all of the other people who were of direct assistance to me in the writing of *Duke.* I am, however, especially grateful to Bill Shinker and Lauren Marino, my editors at Gotham Books, and Monica Benalcazar, Eileen Chetti, LeeAnn Pemberton, Aja Pollock, Elke Sigal, and Emily Wunderlich, who shepherded *Duke* into print with scrupulous care; Glen Hartley and Lynn Chu, my literary agents, who have watched faithfully over my interests for the better part of a quarter century; Paul Doherty, who furnished me with copies of rare kinescopes and videotapes of Ellington's TV appearances; and Anthony Barnett, Michael Fitzgerald, Tad Hershorn, John Howland, Ethan Iverson, Bill Kirchner, Elizabeth McLeod, Dan Morgenstern, Marc Myers, David J. Smith, Mark Stryker, Steve Voce, and Elijah Wald, all of whom smoothed my path.

I owe particular debts of gratitude to the John Simon Guggenheim Memorial Foundation, which awarded me a Guggenheim Fellowship in 2012 to support the completion of this book; the MacDowell Colony, where I spent five blissful weeks writing about Ellington in the summer of 2012; and the Winter Park Institute of Rollins College, directed by Gail Sinclair, where I spent parts of two terms as a scholar-in-residence working on *Duke* and lecturing about its subject. I also thank Eric Gibson, my editor at *The Wall Street Journal,* who made it possible for me to write *Duke* in the interstices of my day job as the *Journal*'s drama critic; John Podhoretz, the editor of *Commentary,* who published an earlier version of part of the book; and the owners and staff of Mitchell's Sand Castles of Sanibel Island, where I wrote several chapters of *Duke* in perfect comfort.

My greatest debt, as always, is acknowledged in the dedication to this book.

TERRY TEACHOUT

February 6, 2013

APPENDIX

FIFTY KEY RECORDINGS

by Duke Ellington

1. "East St. Louis Toodle-O"
   (Vocalion, 1926, composed with Bubber Miley)

2. "Black and Tan Fantasie"
   (Victor, 1927, composed with Bubber Miley)

3. "Creole Love Call" (Victor, 1927,
   composed with Bubber Miley and Rudy Jackson,
   vocal by Adelaide Hall)

4. "Black Beauty (A Portrait of Florence Mills)"
   (Brunswick, 1928)

5. "The Mooche" (OKeh, 1928,
   composed with Bubber Miley, vocal by Baby Cox)

6. "Old Man Blues" (Victor, 1930)

7. "Mood Indigo" (OKeh, 1930,
   composed with Barney Bigard)

8. "Rockin' in Rhythm" (OKeh, 1931,
   co-credited to Harry Carney)

9. *Creole Rhapsody* (first version, Brunswick, 1931)

10. *Creole Rhapsody* (second version, Victor, 1931)

11. "It Don't Mean a Thing (If It Ain't Got That Swing)"
    (Brunswick, 1932, vocal by Ivie Anderson)

12. "Rude Interlude"
    (Victor, 1933, vocal by Louis Bacon)

13. "Daybreak Express" (Victor, 1933)

14. "Sophisticated Lady" (English Columbia,
    1933, composed with Lawrence Brown and Otto Hardwick)

15. "Solitude" (Victor, 1934)

16. *Reminiscing in Tempo* (Brunswick, 1935)

17. "Caravan" (Variety, 1936, composed with Juan Tizol,
    performed by Barney Bigard and His Jazzopaters)

18. "Riding on a Blue Note" (Brunswick, 1938)

19. "I Let a Song Go Out of My Heart"
    (Brunswick, 1938, composed with Johnny Hodges)

20. "Ko-Ko" (Victor, 1940)

21. "Concerto for Cootie"
    (Victor, 1940, composed with Cootie Williams)

22. "Cotton Tail"
    (Victor, 1940, composed with Ben Webster)

23. "Never No Lament" (Victor, 1940, composed with Johnny Hodges)

24. "Dusk" (Victor, 1940)

25. "Harlem Air-Shaft" (Victor, 1940)

26. "Warm Valley" (Victor, 1940)

27. "Take the 'A' Train"
    (Victor, 1941, composed by Billy Strayhorn)

28. "Blue Serge"
    (Victor, 1941, credited to Mercer Ellington)

29. "Things Ain't What They Used to Be"
    (Bluebird, 1941, credited to Mercer Ellington,
    performed by Johnny Hodges and Orchestra)

30. "Rocks in My Bed" (from *Jump for Joy*, Victor, 1941,
    vocal by Ivie Anderson, composed and arranged with Billy Strayhorn)

31. "Chelsea Bridge"
(Victor, 1941, composed by Billy Strayhorn)

32. *Black, Brown and Beige:*
A Tone Parallel to the History of the American Negro
(privately recorded in concert at Carnegie Hall, 1943, vocal by Betty
Roché, "Sugar Hill Penthouse" section composed by Billy Strayhorn,
commercially released by Prestige in 1977)

33. "Happy-Go-Lucky Local"
(from *Deep South Suite,* Musicraft, 1946)

34. "Do Nothin' till You Hear from Me"
(Columbia, 1947, composed with Cootie Williams,
vocal by Al Hibbler, arranged by Billy Strayhorn)

35. "The Clothed Woman" (Columbia, 1947)

36. *The Tattooed Bride*
(from *Masterpieces by Ellington,* Columbia, 1950)

37. *A Tone Parallel to Harlem*
(from *Ellington Uptown,* Columbia, 1951,
coda composed by Billy Strayhorn)

38. "Satin Doll" (Capitol, 1953)

39. *The Duke Plays Ellington* (Capitol, 1953,
with Wendell Marshall and Butch Ballard)

40. *Diminuendo and Crescendo in Blue*
(from *Ellington at Newport,* Columbia, 1956,
recorded in concert at the Newport Jazz Festival)

41. *Such Sweet Thunder*
(Columbia, 1957, composed with Billy Strayhorn)

42. "Blues in Orbit" (from *Blues in Orbit,* Columbia, 1958,
composed by Billy Strayhorn)

43. "The Single Petal of a Rose" (from *The Queen's Suite,*
privately recorded for Queen Elizabeth II, 1959,
commercially released by Pablo in 1976)

44. *Anatomy of a Murder* (film score, Columbia, 1959)

45. "Fleurette Africaine" (from *Money Jungle,* United Artists, 1962, with Charles Mingus and Max Roach)

46. "Afro-Bossa" (from *Afro-Bossa,* Reprise, 1963)

47. "The Intimacy of the Blues" (from . . . *And His Mother Called Him Bill,* RCA, 1967, composed by Billy Strayhorn)

48. "Blood Count" (from . . . *And His Mother Called Him Bill,* RCA, 1967, composed by Billy Strayhorn)

49. *Second Sacred Concert* (Fantasy, 1968)

50. *The New Orleans Suite* (Atlantic, 1970)

All of these recordings can be downloaded from iTunes

SELECT BIBLIOGRAPHY

ABBOTT, GEORGE. *"Mister Abbott."* New York: Random House, 1963.

AGATE, JAMES. *A Shorter Ego: The Autobiography of James Agate.* Vol. 1. London: George G. Harrap, 1945.

BALLIETT, WHITNEY. *American Musicians II: Seventy-Two Portraits in Jazz.* New York: Oxford, 1996.

———. *Collected Works: A Journal of Jazz, 1954–2000.* New York: St. Martin's, 2000.

BARNET, CHARLIE, WITH STANLEY DANCE. *Those Swinging Years: The Autobiography of Charlie Barnet.* Baton Rouge: Louisiana State University Press, 1984.

BARROS, PAUL DE. *Shall We Play That One Together? The Life and Art of Jazz Piano Legend Marian McPartland.* New York: St. Martins, 2012.

BECHET, SIDNEY. *Treat It Gentle: An Autobiography.* Reissued ed., with a new preface by Rudi Blesh. New York: Da Capo, 1978.

BENAMU, CATHERINE L. *It's All True: Orson Welles's Pan-American Odyssey.* Berkeley: University of California Press, 2007.

BENTLEY, ERIC. *In Search of Theater.* New York: Atheneum, 1975.

BERGER, EDWARD. *Bassically Speaking: An Oral History of George Duvivier.* Musical analysis by David Chevan. Foreword by Benny Carter. Lanham, MD: Scarecrow, 1993.

BERRETT, JOSHUA. *Louis Armstrong and Paul Whiteman: Two Kings of Jazz.* New Haven, CT: Yale, 2004.

BIGARD, BARNEY. *With Louis and the Duke: The Autobiography of a Jazz Clarinetist*. Edited by Barry Martyn. New York: Oxford, 1986.

BIKEL, THEODORE. *Theo: An Autobiography*. New York: HarperCollins, 1994.

BIRD, JOHN. *Percy Grainger*. London: Faber and Faber, 1982.

BOGLE, DONALD. *Bright Boulevards, Bold Dreams: The Story of Black Hollywood*. New York: One World, 2006.

———. *Dorothy Dandridge: A Biography*. New York: Amistad, 1997.

BOYD, HERB, ED. *Autobiography of a People: Three Centuries of African American History Told by Those Who Lived It*. Foreword by Gordon Parks. New York: Anchor, 2000.

BRADBURY, DAVID. *Duke Ellington*. London: Haus, 2005.

BÜCHMANN-MØLLER, FRANK. *Someone to Watch Over Me: The Life and Music of Ben Webster*. Ann Arbor: University of Michigan Press, 2006.

BUCKLEY, GAIL LUMET. *The Hornes: An American Family*. New York: New American Library, 1987.

BUSHELL, GARVIN. *Jazz from the Beginning*. As told to Mark Tucker. Introduction by Lawrence Gushee. Ann Arbor: University of Michigan Press, 1988.

CALLOWAY, CAB, AND BRYANT ROLLINS. *Of Minnie the Moocher and Me*. New York: Thomas F. Crowell, 1976.

CARTER, MARVA. *Swing Along: The Musical Life of Will Marion Cook*. New York: Oxford, 2008.

CARTER, MIRANDA. *Anthony Blunt: His Lives*. New York: Farrar, Straus and Giroux, 2001.

CEPLAIR, LARRY, AND STEVEN ENGLUND. *The Inquisition in Hollywood: Politics in the Film Community, 1930–1960*. Berkeley: University of California Press, 1979.

CHARTERS, SAMUEL. *A Trumpet Around the Corner: The Story of New Orleans Jazz*. Jackson: University Press of Mississippi, 2008.

CHEVALIER, MAURICE. *My Paris.* Photographs by Robert Doisneau. New York: Macmillan, 1972.

CHILTON, JOHN. *Ride, Red, Ride: The Life of Henry "Red" Allen.* London: Cassell, 1999.

———. *Sidney Bechet: The Wizard of Jazz.* New York: Oxford, 1987.

———. *The Song of the Hawk: The Life and Recordings of Coleman Hawkins.* London: Quartet, 1990.

CLAYTON, BUCK. *Buck Clayton's Jazz World.* Assisted by Nancy Miller Elliott. New York: Oxford, 1986.

COHEN, HARVEY G. *Duke Ellington's America.* Chicago: University of Chicago Press, 2010.

COLLIER, JAMES LINCOLN. *Duke Ellington.* New York: Oxford, 1987.

———. *Jazz: The American Theme Song.* New York: Oxford, 1995.

COURTNEY, CHARLES SAM. *Ignorant Armies: Tales and Morals of an Alien Empire.* Victoria, BC: Trafford, 2007.

CROW, BILL. *From Birdland to Broadway.* New York: Oxford, 1992.

———. *Jazz Anecdotes: Second Time Around.* New York: Oxford, 2005.

DAHL, LINDA. *Morning Glory: A Biography of Mary Lou Williams.* Berkeley: University of California Press, 2001.

DANCE, STANLEY. *Duke Ellington.* Notes on the music by Dan Morgenstern. Alexandria, VA: Time-Life Records, 1978.

———. *Johnny Hodges.* Notes on the music by Gary Giddins. Alexandria, VA: Time-Life Records, 1981.

———. *The World of Count Basie.* New York: Scribner, 1980.

———. *The World of Duke Ellington.* New York: Da Capo, 2000.

———. *The World of Swing.* New York: Da Capo, 1974.

DAVIS, FRANCIS. *Outcats: Jazz Composers, Instrumentalists, and Singers.* New York: Oxford, 1990.

DELAUNAY, CHARLES. *Django Reinhardt.* London: Cassell, 1961.

DELSON, SUSAN. *Dudley Murphy: Hollywood Wild Card*. Minneapolis: University of Minnesota Press, 2006.

DENNING, MICHAEL. *The Cultural Front: The Laboring of American Culture in the Twentieth Century*. London: Verso, 1997.

DETERMEYER, EDDY. *Rhythm Is Our Business: Jimmie Lunceford and the Harlem Express*. Ann Arbor: University of Michigan Press, 2009.

DIETRICH, KURT. *Duke's 'Bones: Ellington's Great Trombonists*. Rottenburg am Neckar, Germany: Advance Music, 1995.

DODGE, ROGER PRYOR. *Hot Jazz and Jazz Dance: Collected Writings, 1929–1964*. Selected and edited by Pryor Dodge. New York: Oxford, 1995.

DREGNI, MICHAEL. *Django: The Life and Music of a Gypsy Legend*. New York: Oxford, 2004.

DRIGGS, FRANK, AND HARRIS LEWINE. *Black Beauty, White Heat: A Pictorial History of Classic Jazz, 1920–1950*. New York: Da Capo, 1996.

DUKE, VERNON. *Passport to Paris*. Boston: Little, Brown, 1955.

DUNNING, JENNIFER. *Alvin Ailey: A Life in Dance*. Reading, MA: Addison-Wesley, 1996.

EBERLY, PHILIP K. *Music in the Air: America's Changing Tastes in Popular Music, 1920–1980*. New York: Hastings House, 1982.

ELLINGTON, DUKE. *Music Is My Mistress*. Garden City, NY: Doubleday, 1973.

ELLINGTON, MERCER, WITH STANLEY DANCE. *Duke Ellington in Person: An Intimate Memoir*. New York: Da Capo, 1979.

ELLISON, RALPH. *Living with Music: Ralph Ellison's Jazz Writings*. Edited and with an introduction by Robert G. O'Meally. New York: Modern Library, 2001.

ENSTICE, WAYNE, AND PAUL RUBIN. *Jazz Spoken Here: Conversations with Twenty-Two Musicians*. Baton Rouge: Louisiana State University Press, 1992.

FAINE, EDWARD ALLEN. *Ellington at the White House 1969*. Takoma Park, MD: IM Press, 2013.

FEATHER, LEONARD. *The Encyclopedia of Jazz*. New York: Horizon, 1955.

———. *From Satchmo to Miles*. With a new introduction by the author. New York: Da Capo, 1984.

———. *The Jazz Years: Earwitness to an Era*. New York: Da Capo, 1987.

FERGUSON, OTIS. *The Otis Ferguson Reader*. Edited by Dorothy Chamberlain and Robert Wilson. Highland Park, IL: December Press, 1982.

FIRESTONE, ROSS. *Swing, Swing, Swing: The Life and Times of Benny Goodman*. New York: Norton, 1993.

FOSTER, POPS. *The Autobiography of Pops Foster, New Orleans Jazzman*. Reissued edition with a new foreword by Ron Carter. As told to Tom Stoddard. Interchapters by Ross Russell. San Francisco: Backbeat, 2005.

FRANCESCHINA, JOHN. *Duke Ellington's Music for the Theatre*. Jefferson, NC: McFarland, 2001.

FRAZIER, E. FRANKLIN. *Black Bourgeoisie*. New York: Free Press, 1957.

FRIEDWALD, WILL. *Sinatra! The Song Is You: A Singer's Art*. New York: Scribner, 1995.

GAMMOND, PETER, ED. *Duke Ellington: His Life and Music*. New York: Roy, 1958.

GEORGE, DON. *Sweet Man: The Real Duke Ellington*. New York: G.P. Putnam's Sons, 1981.

GIDDINS, GARY. *Bing Crosby: A Pocketful of Dreams—The Early Years, 1903–1940*. Boston: Little, Brown, 2001.

———. *Visions of Jazz: The First Century*. New York: Oxford, 1998.

GILLESPIE, DIZZY, WITH AL FRASER. *To Be or Not to Bop*. Garden City, NY: Doubleday, 1979.

GLEASON, RALPH J. *Celebrating the Duke, and Louis, Bessie, Billie, Bird, Carmen, Miles, Dizzy and Other Heroes*. Foreword by Studs Terkel. New introduction by Ira Gitler. New York: Da Capo, 1995.

————, ED. *Jam Session: An Anthology of Jazz*. New York: G.P. Putnam's Sons, 1958.

GODDARD, CHRIS. *Jazz Away from Home*. New York: Paddington, 1979.

GOLDBERG, ISAAC. *Tin Pan Alley: A Chronicle of the American Popular Music Racket*. Introduction by George Gershwin. New York: John Day, 1930.

GOLDSBY, JOHN. *The Jazz Bass Book: Technique and Tradition*. San Francisco: Backbeat, 2002.

GORDON, CLAIRE P. *My Unforgettable Jazz Friends: Duke, Benny, Nat, Rex* . . . Arroyo Grande, CA: Phase V, 2004.

GRANATA, CHARLES L. *Sessions with Sinatra: Frank Sinatra and the Art of Recording*. Foreword by Phil Ramone. Chicago: A Cappella, 2004.

GREEN, CONSTANCE MCLAUGHLIN. *The Secret City: A History of Race Relations in the Nation's Capital*. Princeton, NJ: Princeton University Press, 1967.

HADLOCK, RICHARD. *Jazz Masters of the Twenties*. New York: Collier, 1974.

HAJDU, DAVID. *Lush Life: A Biography of Billy Strayhorn*. New York: Farrar, Straus and Giroux, 1996.

HALL, FRED. *More Dialogues in Swing*. Ventura, CA: Pathfinder, 1991.

HAMMOND, JOHN, WITH IRVING TOWNSEND. *John Hammond on Record: An Autobiography*. New York: Ridge, 1977.

HARRISON, MAX, CHARLES FOX, AND ERIC THACKER. *The Essential Jazz Records*. Vol. 1, *Ragtime to Swing*. London: Mansell, 1984.

HARWOOD, ROBERT W. *I Went Down to St. James Infirmary: Investigations in the Shadowy World of Early Jazz-Blues in the Company of Blind Willie McTell, Louis Armstrong, Don Redman, Irving Mills, and a Host of Others, and Where Did This Dang Song Come from Anyway?* Kitchener, Ontario: Harland, 2008.

HASKINS, JIM. *The Cotton Club.* New York: Random House, 1977.

HASSE, JOHN EDWARD. *Beyond Category: The Life and Genius of Duke Ellington.* Foreword by Wynton Marsalis. New York: Simon & Schuster, 1993.

HEATH, JIMMY, AND JOSEPH MCLAREN. *I Walked with Giants: The Autobiography of Jimmy Heath.* Philadelphia: Temple University Press, 2010.

HENTOFF, NAT. *Jazz Is.* New York: Limelight Editions, 1976.

———. *The Jazz Life.* New York: Dial, 1961.

HERSHORN, TAD. *Norman Granz: The Man Who Used Jazz for Justice.* Foreword by Oscar Peterson. Berkeley: University of California Press, 2011.

HINTON, MILT, AND DAVID G. BERGER. *Bass Line: The Stories and Photographs of Milt Hinton.* Philadelphia: Temple University Press, 1988.

HOFFMANN, FRANZ. *Jazz Advertised in the Negro Press, 1910–1967.* Vol. 1, *Out of the New England Negro Press, 1910–1934.* Berlin: privately published, 1989. Vol. 4, *Out of the Chicago Defender, 1910–1934.* Berlin: privately published, 1980. Vol. 7, *Out of The New York Times, 1922–1950.* Berlin: privately published, 1989.

HOHENBERG, JOHN. *The Pulitzer Diaries: Inside America's Greatest Prize.* Syracuse, NY: Syracuse University Press, 1997.

HORAK, JAN-CHRISTOPHER, ED. *Lovers of Cinema: The First American Film Avant-Garde, 1919–1945.* Madison: University of Wisconsin Press, 1996.

HOUSEMAN, JOHN. *Front and Center.* New York: Simon & Schuster, 1979.

———. *Unfinished Business: Memoirs: 1902–1988.* New York: Applause, 1989.

HOWLAND, JOHN. *Ellington Uptown: Duke Ellington, James P. Johnson, and the Birth of Concert Jazz.* Ann Arbor: University of Michigan Press, 2009.

HUGHES, LANGSTON. *Autobiography: I Wonder as I Wander.* Edited and with an introduction by Joseph McLaren. Columbia: University of Missouri Press, 2003.

———. *The Big Sea: An Autobiography.* Introduction by Arnold Rampersad. New York: Hill and Wang, 1993.

HUGHES, SPIKE. *Second Movement: Continuing the Autobiography of Spike Hughes.* London: Museum Press Limited, 1951.

JABLONSKI, EDWARD. *Harold Arlen: Happy with the Blues.* New York: Da Capo, 1985.

JEWELL, DEREK. *Duke: A Portrait of Duke Ellington.* London: Elm Tree, 1977.

JONES, MAX. *Jazz Talking: Profiles, Interviews, and Other Riffs on Jazz Musicians.* New York: Macmillan, 1987.

KELLEY, ROBIN. *Thelonious Monk: The Life and Times of an American Original.* New York: Free Press, 2009.

KISSELOFF, JEFF. *You Must Remember This: An Oral History of Manhattan from the 1890s to World War II.* New York: Harcourt Brace Jovanovich, 1989.

LAMBERT, CONSTANT. *Music Ho! A Study of Music in Decline.* London: Hogarth, 1933.

LANDIS, KENESAW M. *Segregation in Washington: A Report of the National Committee on Segregation in the Nation's Capital.* Chicago: National Committee on Segregation in the Nation's Capital, 1948.

LARKIN, PHILIP. *All What Jazz: A Record Diary, 1961–1971.* Revised ed. New York: Farrar, Straus and Giroux, 1985.

LASKER, STEVEN. *A Cotton Club Miscellany.* Venice, CA: privately published, 2002.

LAVEZZOLI, PETER. *The King of All, Sir Duke: Ellington and the Artistic Revolution.* London: Continuum, 2001.

LAWRENCE, A.H. *Duke Ellington and His World: A Biography.* New York: Routledge, 2001.

LEES, GENE. *Meet Me at Jim & Andy's: Jazz Musicians and Their World.* New York: Oxford, 1988.

LEVINSON, PETER J. *Trumpet Blues: The Life of Harry James.* New York: Oxford, 1999.

LEWIS, JOHN. *Radio Master: The Life and Times of Sports Broadcasting Great Ted Husing.* Minneapolis: Langdon Street, 2010.

MAGEE, JEFFREY. *The Uncrowned King of Swing: Fletcher Henderson and Big Band Jazz.* New York: Oxford, 2005.

MALCOLM X. *The Autobiography of Malcolm X.* As told to Alex Haley. New York: Ballantine, 1999.

MASON, JEFFREY DANIEL. *Stone Tower: The Political Theater of Arthur Miller.* Ann Arbor: University of Michigan Press, 2008.

MCLEOD, ELIZABETH. *The Original Amos 'n' Andy: Freeman Gosden, Charles Correll, and the 1928–1943 Radio Serial.* Jefferson, NC: McFarland, 2005.

MELLERS, WILFRID. *Music in a New Found Land: Themes and Developments in the History of American Music.* New York: Knopf, 1965.

MINGUS, CHARLES. *Beneath the Underdog: His World as Composed by Mingus.* Edited by Nel King. New York: Knopf, 1971.

MORGENSTERN, DAN. *Living with Jazz: A Reader.* Edited by Sheldon Meyer. New York: Pantheon, 2004.

MORTON, JOHN FASS. *Backstory in Blue: Ellington at Newport '56.* Foreword by Jonathan Yardley. New Brunswick, NJ: Rutgers University Press, 2008.

NEWKIRK, PAMELA, ED. *Letters from Black America.* New York: Farrar, Straus and Giroux, 2009.

NICHOLSON, STUART. *Reminiscing in Tempo: A Portrait of Duke Ellington.* Boston: Northeastern University Press, 1999.

NOLAN, TOM. *Three Chords for Beauty's Sake: The Life of Artie Shaw.* New York: W.W. Norton, 2010.

NOSS, LUTHER. *Paul Hindemith in the United States*. Urbana: University of Illinois Press, 1989.

OKRENT, DANIEL. *Last Call: The Rise and Fall of Prohibition*. New York: Scribner, 2010.

OTTLEY, ROI. *New World A-Coming: Inside Black America*. Boston: Houghton Mifflin, 1943.

PALEY, WILLIAM S. *As It Happened: A Memoir*. Garden City, NY: Doubleday, 1979.

PANASSIÉ, HUGUES. *Hot Jazz: The Guide to Swing Music*. Translated from the French by Lyle and Eleanor Dowling. New York: M. Witmark, 1936.

PARSONAGE, CATHERINE. *The Evolution of Jazz in Britain, 1800–1935*. Burlington, VT: Ashgate, 2005.

PERESS, MAURICE. *Dvořák to Duke Ellington: A Conductor Explores America's Music and Its African American Roots*. New York: Oxford, 2004.

PRIAL, DUNCAN. *The Producer: John Hammond and the Soul of American Music*. New York: Picador, 2006.

RICHMOND, PETER. *Fever: The Life and Music of Miss Peggy Lee*. New York: Henry Holt, 2006.

ROSE, AL. *I Remember Jazz: Six Decades Among the Great Jazzmen*. Baton Rouge: Louisiana State University Press, 1987.

ROSS, ALEX. *The Rest Is Noise: Listening to the Twentieth Century*. New York: Picador, 2007.

RUBLE, BLAIR A. *Washington's U Street: A Biography*. Washington, DC: Woodrow Wilson Center, 2010.

RUSSELL, BILL. *New Orleans Style*. New Orleans: Jazzology, 1994.

SCHIFF, DAVID. *The Ellington Century*. Berkeley: University of California Press, 2012.

SCHULLER, GUNTHER. *Early Jazz: Its Roots and Musical Development*. New York: Oxford, 1968.

———. *Gunther Schuller: A Life in Pursuit of Music and Beauty*. Rochester: University of Rochester Press, 2011.

———. *The Swing Era: The Development of Jazz, 1930–1945*. New York: Oxford, 1989.

SERRANO, BASILIO. *Juan Tizol: His Caravan Through American Life and Culture*. Privately published, 2012.

SHAPIRO, NAT, AND NAT HENTOFF. *Hear Me Talkin' to Ya: The Story of Jazz as Told by the Men Who Made It*. New York: Rinehart, 1955.

SHAW, ARNOLD. *Let's Dance: Popular Music in the 1930s*. Edited by Bill Willard. New York: Oxford, 1998.

SHIPTON, ALYN. *Hi-De-Ho: The Life of Cab Calloway*. New York: Oxford, 2010.

———. *I Feel a Song Coming On: The Life of Jimmy McHugh*. Champaign: University of Illinois Press, 2009.

———. *A New History of Jazz*. Revised and updated edition. New York: Continuum, 2007.

SIMON, GEORGE T. *Simon Says: The Sights and Sounds of the Swing Era*. New Rochelle, NY: Arlington House, 1971.

SMITH, WILLIE THE LION, WITH GEORGE HOEFER. *Music on My Mind: The Memoirs of an American Pianist*. Foreword by Duke Ellington. New York: Da Capo, 1978.

STEARNS, MARSHALL. *The Story of Jazz*. New York: Oxford, 1956.

———, AND JEAN STEARNS. *Jazz Dance: The Story of American Vernacular Dance*. New York: Macmillan, 1968.

STEINER, KEN. *Wild Throng Dances Madly in Cellar Club: Duke Ellington and the Washingtonians, 1923–27*. Seattle: privately published, 2008.

STEWART, REX. *Boy Meets Horn*. Edited by Claire P. Morgan. Ann Arbor: University of Michigan Press, 1991.

———. *Jazz Masters of the Thirties*. New York: Macmillan, 1972.

STRATEMANN, KLAUS. *Duke Ellington Day by Day and Film by Film.* Copenhagen: JazzMedia ApS, 1992.

SUDHALTER, RICHARD M., AND PHILIP R. EVANS, WITH WILLIAM DEAN-MYATT. *Bix: Man and Legend.* New Rochelle, NY: Arlington, 1974.

SWEET, BRIAN. *Steely Dan: Reelin' in the Years.* London: Omnibus, 1994.

SYLVESTER, ROBERT. *No Cover Charge: A Backward Look at the Night Clubs.* New York: Dial, 1956.

TEACHOUT, TERRY. *Pops: A Life of Louis Armstrong.* New York: Houghton Mifflin Harcourt, 2009.

TERRY, CLARK, WITH GWEN TERRY. *Clark: The Autobiography of Clark Terry.* Berkeley: University of California Press, 2011.

THIELE, BOB. *What a Wonderful World: A Lifetime of Recordings.* As told to Bob Golden, with a foreword by Steve Allen. New York: Oxford, 2005.

TORMÉ, MEL. *It Wasn't* All *Velvet: An Autobiography.* New York: Viking, 1988.

TRAILL, SINCLAIR, AND GERALD LASCELLES, EDS. *Just Jazz 3.* London: Four Square Books, 1959.

———. *Just Jazz 4.* London: Souvenir, 1960.

TUCKER, MARK, ED. *The Duke Ellington Reader.* New York: Oxford, 1993.

———. *Ellington: The Early Years.* Champaign: University of Illinois Press, 1991.

ULANOV, BARRY. *Duke Ellington.* New York: Creative Age, 1946.

VAIL, KEN. *Duke's Diary, Part One: The Life of Duke Ellington, 1927–1950.* Lanham, MD: Scarecrow, 2002.

———. *Duke's Diary, Part Two: The Life of Duke Ellington, 1950–1974.* Lanham, MD: Scarecrow, 2002.

VAN DE LEUR, WALTER. *Something to Live For: The Music of Billy Strayhorn.* New York: Oxford, 2000.

VON ESCHEN, PENNY M. *Satchmo Blows Up the World: Jazz Ambassadors Play the Cold War.* Cambridge, MA: Harvard University Press, 2004.

WASHINGTON, BOOKER T. *The Booker T. Washington Papers.* Vol. 12, *1912–14.* Edited by Louis R. Harlan and Raymond W. Smock. Champaign: University of Illinois Press, 1983.

———. *Up from Slavery: An Autobiography.* Edited by William L. Andrews. New York: W.W. Norton, 1995.

WEIN, GEORGE, WITH NATE CHINEN. *Myself Among Others: A Life in Music.* New York: Da Capo, 2003.

WELK, LAWRENCE, WITH BERNICE MCGEEHAN. *My America, Your America.* Boston: G.K. Hall, 1977.

WILDER, ALEC. *American Popular Song: The Great Innovators, 1900–1950.* Edited and with an introduction by James T. Maher. New York: Oxford, 1972.

WILK, MAX. *They're Playing Our Song: Conversations with America's Classic Songwriters.* New York: Da Capo, 1997.

WILLIAMS, MARTIN, ED. *Jazz Panorama: From the Pages of* The Jazz Review. New York: Crowell-Collier, 1962.

WILLIAMSON, KEN, ED. *This Is Jazz.* London: Newnes, 1960.

WILSON, EDMUND. *Classics and Commercials: A Literary Chronicle of the Forties.* New York: Macmillan, 1950.

———. *The Thirties.* New York: Farrar, Straus and Giroux, 1980.

WILSON, SONDRA K. *Meet Me at the Theresa: The Story of Harlem's Most Famous Hotel.* New York: Simon & Schuster, 2004.

WILSON, TEDDY, WITH ARIE LIGTHART AND HUMPHREY VAN LOO. *Teddy Wilson Talks Jazz.* London: Cassell, 1996.

WINER, DEBORAH GRACE. *On the Sunny Side of the Street: The Life and Lyrics of Dorothy Fields.* New York: Schirmer, 1997.

WRIGHT, LAURIE. *"King" Oliver.* Chigwell, Essex, UK: Storyville Publications, 1987.

WYATT, ROBERT, AND JOHN ANDREW JOHNSON, EDS. *The George Gershwin Reader.* New York: Oxford, 2004.

ZOLOTOW, MAURICE. *Never Whistle in a Dressing Room; or, Breakfast in Bedlam.* New York: E.P. Dutton, 1944.

SOURCE NOTES

ABBREVIATIONS

BS	Billy Strayhorn
DE	Duke Ellington
DEMS	Duke Ellington Music Society
EC	Duke Ellington Collection (Smithsonian Institution)
IJS	Institute of Jazz Studies (Rutgers University)
MM	*Music Is My Mistress*
OHAM	Oral History American Archive (Yale University)
Reader	*The Duke Ellington Reader*
RIT	*Reminiscing in Tempo: A Portrait of Duke Ellington*

All quotations from these sources are by DE unless otherwise indicated

PROLOGUE
"I WANT TO TELL AMERICA"

SOURCES

Documents
Edmund Anderson, oral-history interview, OHAM; Lawrence Brown, oral-history interview, IJS; *The Duke Ellington Carnegie Hall Concerts: January 1943*, sound recording (Prestige); DE, "*Black, Brown and Beige* by Duke Ellington" (typescript, n.d., EC); DE, unpublished interview with Carter Harman, 1964, EC; Ruth Ellington, oral-history interview, EC; Nat Hentoff, oral-history interview conducted by researchers for Ken Burns's *Jazz* (transcript available online at www.pbs.org /jazz/about/pdfs/Hentoff.pdf); Juan Tizol, oral-history interview, IJS.

Books
Bentley, *In Search of Theater;* Bigard, *With Louis and the Duke;* Büchmann-Møller, *Someone to Watch over Me;* Collier, *Duke Ellington;* Dance, *Duke Ellington;* Dance,

The World of Duke Ellington; Mercer Ellington, *Duke Ellington in Person;* Ellison, *Living with Music;* Enstice, *Jazz Spoken Here;* Feather, *The Jazz Years;* Firestone, *Swing, Swing, Swing;* George, *Sweet Man;* Gleason, *Celebrating the Duke;* Hadlock, *Jazz Masters of the Twenties;* Hasse, *Beyond Category;* Houseman, *Front and Center;* Jewell, *Duke;* Lambert, *Music Ho!;* Mingus, *Beneath the Underdog;* Serrano, *Juan Tizol;* Stewart, *Boy Meets Horn;* Stewart, *Jazz Masters of the Thirties;* Terry, *Clark;* Ulanov, *Duke Ellington;* Vail, *Duke's Diary, Part Two;* van de Leur, *Something to Live For;* Williamson, *This Is Jazz.*

NOTES

DE left watches unworn: "He never wore a watch" (Irving Townsend, "Ellington in Private," *The Atlantic Monthly,* May 1975). **"I don't need time":** Dance, *The World of Duke Ellington,* 257. **Some seventeen hundred–odd compositions:** According to Jørgen Mathiasen, DE is known to have written at least 1,694 identifiable "works and pieces." For a preliminary discussion of the complex problem of calculating the number of DE's compositions, see Mathiasen, "Duke Ellington's Production as a Composer," *DEMS Bulletin,* Dec. 2004–Mar. 2005. DE told Brooks Kerr that he had written roughly five thousand compositions, but he did not keep a catalog of his works and it is impossible to know how he arrived at this number (Steven Lasker, "How Many Compositions Did Ellington Actually Write?," *DEMS Bulletin,* Apr.–July 2005). **"As long as something is unfinished":** George, 133. **"He wants life and music to be in a state of becoming":** Nat Hentoff, "This Cat Needs No Pulitzer Prize," *The New York Times Magazine,* Sept. 12, 1965, in *Reader,* 367.

"Duke drew people to him": Richard O. Boyer, "The Hot Bach," *The New Yorker,* June 24, July 1, and July 8, 1944, in *Reader,* 240 (hereafter cited as Boyer, "The Hot Bach," followed by the page number in *Reader*).

As early as 1930: For a discussion of early interviews with DE in which he speaks of writing such a work, see Mark Tucker, "The Genesis of *Black, Brown and Beige,*" *Black Music Research Journal* (Fall 1993). **"My *African Suite*":** Barry Ulanov, "The Ellington Programme," in Williamson, 131. **"I am expressing in sound":** Quoted in Collier, 216. **Swaffer compared Louis Armstrong to a gorilla:** Hannen Swaffer, "I Heard Yesterday," *Daily Herald,* July 25, 1932.

"A suite in five parts": "Introducing Duke Ellington," *Fortune,* Aug. 1933. **"The history of the American Negro":** "Ellington Completes Negro Opera at Bedside," *Down Beat,* Oct. 2, 1938. **DE completed only three extended works of any kind prior to 1943:** *Creole Rhapsody* was recorded in two different versions in 1931, *Reminiscing in Tempo* in 1935, and *Diminuendo and Crescendo in Blue* in 1937. He also arranged a two-sided "Tiger Rag" in 1929 and a two-part version of "Black and Tan Fantasy" in 1938, but these are not "extended" works in the usual sense of the word. Similarly, *Symphony in Black,* the score for a 1934 short subject subtitled "A Rhapsody of Negro Life," was not a "symphony of Negro moods," as it was described in the film, but a nine-minute suite based on three existing compositions by DE. **"The first jazz composer of distinction":** Lambert, 187–88.

DE **"definitely wasn't direct":** Ruth Ellington, oral-history interview. **"You hear fights, you smell dinner":** Boyer, "The Hot Bach," 235. **"Once Over Lightly":** The first page of the MS. score of "Harlem Air-Shaft" (as the title appears on the original 78 label) is titled "Once Over Lightly" in DE's hand, with "Harlem Air Shaft" added by Tom Whaley, the copyist. The piece was recorded for Victor as "Harlem Air-Shaft" on July 22, 1940, and Whaley began working for Ellington in 1941. (The actual date of composition is not known.) When the piece was played on a July 29 radio broadcast, the announcer referred to it as "Harlem Air-Shaft" and described it as "Duke Ellington's own rhythmic impression of the themes and sounds heard in an apartment courthouse in Harlem." Recording logs for the July 22 session use the title "Rumpus in Richmond" in place of "Harlem Air-Shaft." A second piece recorded at the same session, originally titled "Brassiere," was renamed "Rumpus in Richmond" prior to its 78 release. See Edward Green, " 'Harlem Air Shaft': A True Programmatic Composition?" *Journal of Jazz Studies* (Spring 2011), and Brad McCune, "A Rose by Any Other Name," *Down Beat,* June 7, 1962. **"Crotch warmers":** George, 109. **"I knew you were here":** Dance, *Duke Ellington,* 5.

"He was furious": Anderson, oral-history interview.

"Sell Ellington as a great artist": "Irving Mills Presents Duke Ellington and His Famous Orchestra," 1933 publicity manual (EC).

"You know, Stan Kenton can stand in front of a thousand fiddles": Ralph J. Gleason, "Duke Excites, Mystifies Without Any Pretension," *Down Beat,* Nov. 5, 1952. **Previn compared him to Stravinsky and Prokofiev:** Gleason, 175. **"I just watch people":** Aaron Bell, quoted in *Jazz Journal,* Mar. 1991, in *RIT,* 323.

Mills passed up an opportunity to book DE into Carnegie Hall: Anderson, oral-history interview. It was Anderson who claimed to have tried to persuade Mills to book DE there. See also Firestone, 213. **The band had since given full-evening concerts:** The most interesting of these performances took place at the City College of New York on Jan. 3, 1939. The ambitious program included *Diminuendo and Crescendo in Blue, Reminiscing in Tempo,* and the five three-minute "concerti" that DE had written for Barney Bigard, Lawrence Brown, Rex Stewart, and Cootie Williams. (A copy of the program is part of the collection of the New York Public Library's Schomburg Center for Research in Black Culture.) **"I want you to write":** *MM,* 180–81.

DE began writing *Black, Brown and Beige* in Hartford: *MM,* 181. **"On the day of my visit to his apartment":** Howard Taubman, "The 'Duke' Invades Carnegie Hall," *The New York Times Magazine,* Jan. 17, 1943, in *Reader,* 159.

"Practically before the ink . . . was dry": Edmund Anderson, "Some Personal Recollections of Duke Ellington," *Jazz Journal,* July 1974. **"Choppy":** Ulanov, 251.

"Twenty years of laudable contribution": "R.P.," "Duke Ellington at Carnegie Hall," *The New York Times,* Jan. 24, 1943. **A recording of the concert:** *The Duke Ellington Carnegie Hall Concerts: January 1943.*

"Our aim has always been the development": DE, "Duke Says Swing Is Stagnant," *Down Beat,* Feb. 1939, in *Reader,* 135. **"The Negro is not merely a singing and dancing wizard":** Taubman, "The 'Duke' Invades Carnegie Hall," in *Reader,* 160.

"Buried in the dark, uneasy conscience of Man": DE, *"Black, Brown and Beige by Duke Ellington."*

A 1942 composition by BS called "Symphonette-Rhythmique": van de Leur, 88. It was not until the publication in 2002 of van de Leur's book, which was based on analysis of the surviving manuscripts of BS and DE, that BS's role in the composition of "Beige" was revealed.

The most favorable notice: "The Duke of Jazz," *Time,* Feb. 1, 1943. **"It had many exciting passages":** "R.P.," "Duke Ellington at Carnegie Hall." **"It hardly ever succeeds":** Douglas Watt, "The Duke Has Hot Concert at Carnegie," *New York Daily News,* Jan. 25, 1943. **"An in toto symphonic creation":** Robert Bagar, "Duke Marks 20th Year as Musician," *New York World-Telegram,* Jan. 25, 1943. **"It all but falls apart into so many separate pieces":** Henry Simon, "The Duke Shows Carnegie How," *PM,* Jan. 25, 1943.

"It was formless and meaningless": Paul Bowles, "Duke Ellington in Recital for Russian Relief," *New York Herald-Tribune,* Jan. 25, 1943, in *Reader,* 166.

"Duke Kills Carnegie Cats!": *Metronome,* Feb. 1943. **"Condescending":** "Reactionary Reviewers," *Metronome,* Feb. 1943. **"Duke Fuses Classical and Jazz!":** Mike Levin, *Down Beat,* Feb. 15, 1943, in *Reader,* 166–70. **DE "alienated a good part of his dancing public":** John Hammond, "Is the Duke Deserting Jazz?" *Jazz Record,* Feb. 15, 1943, in *Reader,* 172–173. **"Formless and shallow":** John Hammond, "The Tragedy of Duke Ellington, the 'Black Prince of Jazz,'" *Down Beat,* Nov. 1935, in *Reader,* 120.

"Well, I guess they didn't dig it": "Duke Fuses Classical and Jazz!," in *Reader,* 168. **An "overwhelming success":** *MM,* 181. **"What [he was] attempting to do":** Helen M. Oakley, "Ellington to Offer 'Tone Parallel,'" *Down Beat,* Jan. 15, 1943, in *Reader,* 155–156.

The last time that DE performed *Black, Brown and Beige* **in its entirety:** See Andrew Homzy, *"Black, Brown and Beige* in Duke Ellington's Repertoire, 1943–1973," and Sjef Hoefsmit, "Chronology of Ellington's Recordings and

Performances of *Black, Brown and Beige,* 1943–1973," *Black Music Research Journal,* edited by Andrew Homzy (Fall 1993). According to Homzy, it is "not clear" whether the entire work was performed in Cleveland, but contemporary newspaper reviews of the concert, notwithstanding their ambiguous wording, indicate that DE repeated the Carnegie Hall program in its entirety and that all of *Black, Brown and Beige* was played. See "S.M.," "Record 7,200 Turn Out for Ellington Rhythm," *Cleveland Plain Dealer,* Feb. 21, 1943, and Ardelia Bradley, "7000 Hear the Duke in Brilliant Concert," *Cleveland Call and Post,* Feb. 27, 1943.

"We planned far in advance, but in the end Duke failed to do a single arrangement": John McDonough, "Pablo Patriarch: The Norman Granz Story Part II," *Down Beat,* Nov. 1979. (DE did in fact complete one arrangement, for Juan Tizol's "Caravan.") **"Duke would ask Ella":** Quoted in *RIT,* 315.

Only to pick up his mail: "New York is just where I keep my mailbox" (*Jet,* May 15, 1969).

"I work and I write": Hentoff, "This Cat Needs No Pulitzer Prize," in *Reader,* 363. **"You couldn't give him a piano part":** Tizol, oral-history interview. **"There's no attitude":** Jewell, 111.

"Accumulation of personalities": DE, interview with Jack Cullen, CKNW, Vancouver, Canada, Oct. 30, 1962, in *Reader,* 339. **"With a musician who plays the full compass":** *MM,* 470. **"I never did like anything Ellington ever did":** Quoted in Hadlock, 188. The valve trombonist–composer Bob Brookmeyer had the same reaction to DE in his youth: "I thought the [band] was sloppy and out of tune. That's how much I knew when I was in my late teens" (Enstice, 62). **"My ear makes my decision":** DE, holograph note for *MM,* n.d. (EC).

"Ellington plays the piano": BS, "Billy Strayhorn: 'The Ellington Effect,'" *Down Beat,* Nov. 5, 1952, in *Reader,* 270. **"To mold the music around the man":** Quoted in Gary Giddins, "The Long-Playing Duke," *The Village Voice,* Apr. 27, 1999.

"I recall one occasion when he'd jotted some notes for the saxophones": Stewart, *Jazz Masters of the Thirties,* 97–98.

"He could hear a guy": Büchmann-Møller, 71. **"More than once":** Stewart, *Jazz Masters of the Thirties,* 98. **"It wasn't *our* thing any longer":** Dance, *The World of Duke Ellington,* 60.

"To attempt to elevate the status": "Certainly It's Music!" *Listen,* Oct. 1944, in *Reader,* 246. **"Ninety-nine per cent of the jazz people":** "Why Duke Ellington Avoided Music Schools," *PM,* Dec. 9, 1945, in *Reader,* 253.

"We wanted Duke to be recognized": Irving Mills, unpublished film interview, in *RIT,* 118. **"He is as genial as he is intelligent":** "Irving Mills Presents Duke

Ellington and His Famous Orchestra," 1933 publicity manual (EC). **"Every time you walk out [on] the street"**: DE, Harman interview, 1964.

"At the time I worked with him": Houseman, 194.

"What you need to do": Mercer Ellington, *Duke Ellington in Person,* 187. **"No problem"**: Ibid., 210. (This handwritten note is reproduced in Vail, 452.)

"Ellington is the most complex and paradoxical individual": Stewart, *Boy Meets Horn,* 158. **"A romping, stomping alley cat"**: George, 138.

"That night I saw him": Hentoff, oral-history interview.

"I think all the musicians should get together": Leonard Feather, "Blindfold Test: Miles and Miles of Trumpet Players," *Down Beat,* Sept. 21, 1955.

" 'Now, Charles,' he says, looking amused": Mingus, 323–24. For Tizol's side of the story, see Serrano, 131–40. For another version, see Terry, 149.

"You can't stay in the European conservatory": Fred M. White, "Negro Music as Individual Unit Aim of Duke Ellington," *Morning Oregonian,* May 14, 1934. **"I don't write jazz"**: Boyer, "The Hot Bach," 218. **"Q. Can you keep from writing music?"**: *MM,* 458.

CHAPTER ONE
"I JUST COULDN'T BE SHACKLED"

SOURCES

Documents
DE, unpublished interview with Carter Harman, 1956, EC; Mercer Ellington, oral-history interview, EC; Ruth Ellington, oral-history interview, EC; Doug Seroff, liner notes for *There Breathes a Hope: The Legacy of John Work II and His Fisk Jubilee Quartet, 1909–1916,* sound recording (Archeophone); Mark Tucker, "The Early Years of Edward Kennedy 'Duke' Ellington, 1899–1927," Ph.D. diss., University of Michigan, 1986; Bernice Wiggins and Juanita Middleton, oral-history interview, OHAM.

Books
Mercer Ellington, *Duke Ellington in Person;* Foster, *Autobiography;* Frazier, *Black Bourgeoisie;* Green, *The Secret City;* Hughes, *Autobiography;* Hughes, *The Big Sea;* Jewell, *Duke;* Landis, *Segregation in Washington;* Malcolm X, *Autobiography;* Ruble, *Washington's U Street;* Stewart, *Boy Meets Horn;* Tucker, *Ellington;* Ulanov, *Duke Ellington;* Washington, *Booker T. Washington Papers;* Washington, *Up from Slavery;* Zolotow, *Never Whistle in a Dressing Room.*

NOTES

Born in a neighborhood: For a detailed history of Shaw, see Ruble.

"She spent as much time": Hollie I. West, "Duke at 70: Honor from the President," *The Washington Post,* Apr. 27, 1969.

The poorest blacks: According to Rex Stewart, U Street was home to "the lighter-complexioned people with better-type jobs," while "the working class, the coal men, the fishmongers, the gamblers, pimps and sporting females" lived in "the southwest area" (Stewart, 34).

"During the time I was a student": Washington, *Up from Slavery,* 43–44.

"I have recently spent several days": Booker T. Washington, letter to Oswald Garrison Villard, Aug. 10, 1913; Washington, *Papers,* 248.

"A secret city all but unknown": Green, viii, vii.

"The newest and hottest place": Alicia Ault, "U Street: The Corridor Is Cool Again," *The New York Times,* Apr. 14, 2006. **"A level of living":** www .ellingtonapartments.com. **"He assumed the dogs would not object":** Landis, 19.

"I could play the dances": Tucker, *Ellington,* 6. **"So many pompous gentlemen":** Langston Hughes, "Our Wonderful Society: Washington," *Opportunity,* Aug. 1927. **"The usually darker (although not always poorer) people":** Hughes, *Autobiography,* 59. **"The worst Jim Crow around New Orleans":** Foster, 73.

"The ordinary Negroes": Hughes, *The Big Sea,* 208–9.

The group "interpreted [spirituals] as the slaves did": Jerome I. Wright, quoted in Seroff, liner notes for *There Breathes a Hope: The Legacy of John Work II and His Fisk Jubilee Quartet, 1909–1916.*

"Castes": *MM,* 17.

J.E. Ellington was born in North Carolina in 1879: Census records and Washington city directory listings relating to DE and his family are summarized in *RIT,* 1–2, and Tucker, *Ellington,* 17. **"Rather prominent socially":** *MM,* 10. **"His confidant and very close friend":** Ulanov, 2. **"The way [J.E.'s] table was set":** Mercer Ellington, *Duke Ellington in Person,* 8.

"A Chesterfieldian gentleman": Ruth Ellington, oral-history interview. **"I have always wanted":** *MM,* 12.

"Stiff-lipped": Ulanov, 3. **"The Rosary" made DE weep:** Boyer, "The Hot Bach," 238.

"The violently crossed influences": Ulanov, 5–6. **"They slept apart"**: Mercer Ellington, oral-history interview. **"No one else but my sister Ruth"**: *MM*, 6. **"He spent and lived like a man who had money"**: Ibid., 10.

"The world of make-believe": Frazier, 25. **"I'd guess that eight out of ten"**: Malcolm X, 43.

"My mother, as I said before, was beautiful": *MM*, 12.

"Once upon a time": Ibid., x.

"Spoiled rotten": Ibid., 6. **"Edward, you are blessed"**: Ibid., 15. **"This is the great, the grand, the magnificent Duke Ellington"**: Ulanov, 1. **DE supplied multiple explanations**: See, for instance, Ulanov, 7. (For a significantly different version, see *MM*, 20.) **"Proper speech and good manners"**: *MM*, 17.

J.E.'s father was a mulatto: *RIT*, 1. **"Coffee with a strong dash of cream"**: Boyer, "The Hot Bach," 214. **"Any talk about red people"**: *MM*, 12. See also Ruth Ellington: "In our house, you didn't talk about color" (Ruth Ellington, oral-history interview). **Louis Armstrong wrote a piece for *Ebony***: Louis Armstrong, "Why I Like Dark Women," *Ebony*, Aug. 1954.

"The wonderful feeling of security": *MM*, 15. **DE was overprotected as a boy**: Mercer Ellington, *Duke Ellington in Person*, 7. **"Hostile incidents"**: Tucker, *Ellington*, 24.

Marietta Clinkscales: Unlikely as it may sound, Mrs. Clinkscales's name is not apocryphal. See Tucker, "The Early Years," 52. **"Slipped away"**: Ulanov, 6. **"All through grade school"**: *MM*, 17.

"To get out and try my wings": Ruby Berkley Goodwin, "Meet the Duke," *The Bronzeman*, Aug. 1932. See also Zolotow, 297. In old age DE told the story differently, saying that his mother had accompanied him to Asbury Park that summer and that he first heard Harvey Brooks's playing during a stopover in Philadelphia on his way back to Washington (*MM*, 17–20). No piano rolls by Brooks are known to survive, but he can be heard playing a vigorous sixteen-bar solo on "Quality Shout," cut in 1929 by Paul Howard's Quality Serenaders and reissued on *Jazz in California 1923–1930* (Timeless).

"I hadn't been able to get off the ground": *MM*, 20. **"It wasn't very long"**: Goodwin, "Meet the Duke."

"There was no connection between me and music": DE, Harman interview, 1956.

In the spring of 1914: *MM*, 20. **"Soda Fountain Rag"**: On occasion DE also referred to the piece as "Poodle Dog Rag."

"A pretty good 'hug-and-rubbin'' crawl": *MM*, 20. For more information on the song, which DE never recorded commercially, see Tucker, *Ellington*, 41–43. **A few**

performances of "Soda Fountain Rag" were recorded: The earliest known recording of any portion of the piece is DE's sixteen-bar solo on "Oklahoma Stomp," recorded by the Six Jolly Jesters, a pseudonym for the Ellington band, in 1929 (Vocalion 1449). He also played part of "Soda Fountain Rag" on a 1937 radio broadcast, calling it "Swing Session." This performance was recorded off the air and has been reissued several times, most recently as part of *Duke Ellington at the Cotton Club* (Storyville). The most widely circulated version is the incomplete one played by DE at a concert he gave in 1972 at New York's Whitney Museum of American Art, which was released as part of *Live at the Whitney* (Impulse). The 1937 broadcast probably comes closest to the lost original version of the piece.

"My father said something": Henry Whiston, "Reminiscing in Tempo," *Jazz Journal*, Feb. 1967. Ruth Ellington recalled in her oral-history interview that her mother sometimes played ragtime as well, but Ruth was born in 1915, meaning that her memories would have postdated by several years the time when DE started to play piano in earnest.

"Practically regarded": Mercer Ellington, *Duke Ellington in Person*, 9. **"What I was getting out of music":** *MM*, 32.

"I never will forget": Wiggins and Middleton, oral-history interview.

"The schooled musicians": *MM*, 26. **"Harlem has always had more churches than cabarets":** Ibid., 189. **"Once I asked him what he considered a typical Negro piece":** Edmund Anderson, quoted in Jewell, 52.

CHAPTER TWO
"SOFT AND GUT-BUCKET"

SOURCES

Documents
Helen Oakley Dance, oral-history interview, OHAM; DE, unpublished interviews with Carter Harman, 1956 and 1964, EC; Tom Whaley, oral-history interview, IJS.

Books
Bigard, *With Louis and the Duke;* Bushell, *Jazz from the Beginning;* Calloway, *Of Minnie the Moocher and Me;* Carter, *Swing Along;* Charters, *A Trumpet Around the Corner;* Chilton, *Sidney Bechet;* Stanley Dance, *The World of Duke Ellington;* Stanley Dance, *The World of Swing;* Davis, *Outcats;* Dietrich, *Duke's 'Bones;* Ellington, *Duke Ellington in Person;* Lees, *Meet Me at Jim & Andy's;* Nolan, *Three*

Chords for Beauty's Sake; Schuller, *Early Jazz;* Shapiro, *Hear Me Talkin' to Ya;* Smith, *Music on My Mind;* Steiner, *Wild Throng Dances Madly in Cellar Club;* Tucker, *Ellington;* Ulanov, *Duke Ellington.*

NOTES

"Being at the right place": Gunnar Askland, "Interpretations in Jazz: A Conversation with Duke Ellington," *Etude,* Mar. 1947, in *Reader,* 256. **"Positively the greatest dance record":** Charters, 146.

"IRRESISTIBLE JASS": Reproduced in Tucker, 55.

"Under-conversation music": *MM,* 31. **"All the embassies and big shots":** Tucker, 53. **"I went down to the telephone office":** *MM,* 31.

$10,000 a year: Tucker, 63. **"Well, he picked up the piano by ear":** Henry Whiston, "Reminiscing in Tempo," *Jazz Journal,* Feb. 1967. **"When customers came for posters":** *MM,* 32.

"He had just learned the difference": Marc Crawford, "A Visit with Mrs. Duke Ellington," *Ebony,* Mar. 1959. **"My mother's folks were from a higher station":** Davis, 6. **Mercer was born eight months later:** A second child died in infancy. **"Hard days":** Crawford, "A Visit with Mrs. Duke Ellington." **"Tremendous responsibilities":** DE, Harman interview, 1964.

"I'm still hooked on Ellington": Crawford, "A Visit with Mrs. Duke Ellington." **DE claimed to have lost his virginity:** "I finally got it in when I was around about twelve years old, I guess . . . I don't know who it was" (DE, Harman interview, 1964). **"I think that what put him into show business":** Ellington, 19. **"I started out playing for pussy":** DE, Harman interview, 1964. **"Proper-type stiltedness":** DE, "Man with Four Sides" (typescript, Stanley Dance collection, Yale University).

Arthur Whetsel: Whetsel's last name is misspelled "Whetsol" in *MM* and numerous other sources. See Steven Lasker, "Whetsel vs. Whetsol Plus Sundry Whetseliana," *DEMS Bulletin,* Aug.–Nov. 2002. **"Sharp as a Gillette blade":** Whitney Balliett, "New York Drummers," *The New Yorker,* Nov. 5, 1979, in *Reader,* 489. **"I've never seen another man like him":** Stanley Dance, *The World of Duke Ellington,* 62. **"Brilliant":** Ibid., 60–61 (emphasis in the original).

The gentle muted trumpet tone: "The devices that enabled Whetsel to obtain his haunting, ethereal sound when muted were a pair of wooden 'Solotone' conical mutes, one glued inside the other" (Lasker, "Whetsel vs. Whetsol Plus Sundry Whetseliana"). **"Aural charisma":** *MM,* 54. **"When he played the funeral march":** Boyer, "The Hot Bach," 230. **"His tonal character":** DE, Harman interview, 1964.

"I really thought of him as a member of the family": Ellington, 26. "Duke Ellington was like my brother": Balliett, "New York Drummers," in *Reader,* 489. "Anybody who had been to New York": *MM,* 35.

"I always strove for delicacy": Balliett, "New York Drummers," in *Reader,* 488. "Slushy": Lees, 54. "We used to say": Ibid. "Greer was not the world's best reader of music": *MM,* 53. "He used timpani and tomtoms a lot": Balliett, "New York Drummers," in *Reader,* 487.

"I built up so much of a reputation": *MM,* 33. "I marvelled at his natural technique": H.G. [Henry Grant], *"Shuffle Along* a Great Success," *Negro Musician,* June 1921, quoted in Tucker, 62.

"Half a dozen": DE, Harman interview, 1964. Grant's daughters later said that DE took lessons twice a week (Tucker, 61). "Duke had little direct contact": Ulanov, 195. "If *serious* means European music": DE, "Why Duke Ellington Avoided Music Schools," *PM,* Dec. 9, 1945, in *Reader,* 253. "I am not writing classical music": DE, "Certainly It's Music!" *Listen,* Oct. 1944, in *Reader,* 246. "He lighted the direction to more highly developed composition": *MM,* 28.

"What I absorbed on that occasion": Ibid., 34. "He was playing like James P.": Bushell, 21. "I also tried to copy the spectacular manner": *MM,* 417.

Bechet appeared at the Howard Theatre in January of 1923: Chilton, 56. "My first real encounter": *MM,* 417. DE remembered first hearing Bechet in 1921, but Chilton's account is based on contemporary documents. "Bechet to me": DE, "The Most Essential Instrument," *Jazz Journal,* Dec. 1965, in *Reader,* 369.

"They had caught a Negro": Peter Perl, "Washington Race Riot of 1919 Gave Glimpse of Future Struggles," *The Washington Post,* Mar. 1, 1999. "Harlem, to our minds": *MM,* 36, 35.

"THE MUCH IMITATED RAGTIME AND JAZZ CLARIONETIST": Tucker, 81. DE's first trip to New York: Late in life Sonny Greer told an interviewer that he and DE paid a short visit to New York in 1921 and shared a nightclub bill with the Original Dixieland Jazz Band, but there is no other evidence to substantiate this claim (Tim Weiner, "Keeping Time with Sonny Greer," *Soho Weekly News,* June 15, 1979). "It was another world to us": *MM,* 36.

"A kind of nice, almost arrogant manner": Nolan, 35. "A good-looking, well-mannered fellow": Smith, 149–50. "My strongest influence": DE, Harman interview, 1964.

"The two worlds": Calloway, 105–6. For a nuanced discussion of the response of the Harlem Renaissance writers to jazz, see Alwyn Williams, "Jazz and the New Negro: Harlem's Intellectuals Wrestle with the Art of the Age," *Australasian Journal of American Studies,* July 2002.

Thirty dollars a week: Shapiro, 230. **"Sweet and straight":** *MM,* 70. **"We had arrangements for everything":** DE, "Jazz as I Have Seen It," *Swing,* June 1940. Helen Oakley Dance later acknowledged in her oral-history interview that she ghosted this article, as well as the other pieces that were published in the same series in February, March, May, July, August, and September of 1940, parts of which were recycled in *MM.*

"We had been playing": Stanley Dance, *The World of Swing,* 53. No copies of this unique test recording are known to have survived (Steven Lasker, "Research on *Home,*" *DEMS Bulletin,* Dec. 1996–Feb. 1997).

"We were different in several ways": *MM,* 70.

"I had never made a lead sheet before": Ibid. **"He couldn't really read then":** Stanley Dance, *The World of Swing,* 52.

The Hollywood: For contemporary press reports about the Hollywood, see Steiner. **The owners resorted to arson:** Suspicious fires took place at the club in April and December of 1924 (Steiner, 16, 20). **"This colored band is plenty tor-rid":** Abel Green, *New York Clipper,* Nov. 23, 1923, in *Reader,* 22. Green is cred-ited with having written the oft-misquoted *Variety* headline "STICKS NIX HICK PIX" ("Show Business: King James to the End," *Time,* May 21, 1973).

Whetsel had gone back to Washington: Sources dating back to the thirties claim that Whetsel returned to Washington to study medicine at Howard University, but to date no proof of his enrollment there has been found (Tucker, 293).

"Bubber and I sat there with our mouths open": Bushell, 25. For a detailed explanation of how Miley and DE's other brass players used the plunger, see Diet-rich, 23–25.

"Our band changed its character": DE, "Jazz as I Have Seen It." **"A sort of cooperative organization":** Max Jones and Humphrey Lyttelton, BBC radio in-terview with DE, 1964, in *RIT,* 47. **"A great, big, fat sound":** Stanley Dance, *The World of Duke Ellington,* 7.

Elmer Snowden's departure from the band was involuntary: "So Sonny . . . says, man, when you going to give us a raise. And the man said I just raised you. He had raised Elmer, give Elmer the raise and Elmer didn't give it to the guys, so they fired Elmer and Sonny was supposed to take the job, Sonny said no, I don't want the job. Give it to Duke" (Tom Whaley, oral-history interview). **"It didn't take long":** Burt Korall, "The Roots of the Duchy: Duke Ellington's Drummer," *Down Beat,* July 13, 1967.

"He was rather a serious type": *MM,* 109.

"There were no small bands": Stanley Dance, *The World of Duke Ellington,* 65–66. **"We worked as one man":** Korall, "The Roots of the Duchy."

"Duke worked largely from head arrangements": John McDonough, "Reminiscing in Tempo: Guitarist Freddy Guy's Ellington Memories," *Down Beat*, Apr. 17, 1969, in *Reader*, 483. **"We would just sit down at the piano":** Jones and Lyttelton, BBC radio interview with DE, in *RIT*, 33.

"New colors and characteristics": *MM*, 71.

DE studied informally with Will Marion Cook: It has been speculated that DE may also have studied in Washington with Cook, who at one point was a neighbor to the Ellington family, but DE never claimed to have done so. **He studied violin:** Cook apparently claimed to have studied with Joachim, Brahms's friend and colleague, but his biographer has found "no documentation" of his having done so (Carter, 19). **"A bit of composition":** Ibid., 31.

"Developed Negro music": Cary B. Lewis, "Will Marion Cook," *The Chicago Defender*, May 1, 1915. **Cook served as mentor to many younger musicians:** See Mercer Cook, "Will Marion Cook: He Helped Them All," *Crisis*, Oct. 1944. **"I got most of my instruction riding around Central Park":** *MM*, 337. **"He and I would get in a taxi":** Boyer, "The Hot Bach," 241. This gnomic passage contains the only piece of specifically technical advice on composition that DE is known to have received from Cook. For a discussion of what Cook may have meant when he told DE to "reverse your figures," see Edward Green, " 'It Don't Mean a Thing if It Ain't Got That Grundgestalt!'—Ellington from a Motivic Perspective," *Jazz Perspectives*, July 2008. (DE paid tribute to his mentor by quoting from Cook's 1907 song "Bon Bon Buddy" in the introduction to his 1926 recording of "Li'l Farina.")

"Dad, I don't want to go to the conservatory": Hollie I. West, "Duke at 70: Honor from the President," *The Washington Post*, Apr. 27, 1969. **"You know you should go":** *MM*, 97.

"Jig Walk": DE's band occasionally played "Jig Walk" in the thirties and forties, and it was recorded in 1944 by Pee Wee Russell, Joe Sullivan, and Zutty Singleton.

"A glorified interior": "John and the Missus," "Wild Throng Dances Madly in Cellar Club," *New York Mirror*, Apr. 15, 1925. **"The 'hottest' band this side of the equator":** *Variety*, Apr. 1, 1925, in *Reader*, 23. **"Possessing a sense of rhythm that is almost uncanny":** *Billboard*, Dec. 5, 1925; Ibid. **"The Paul Whiteman of Colored Orchestras":** *Boston Post*, July 9, 1926, quoted in Tucker, 186.

"Where the hell have you been?": Bigard, 72. Bechet would later claim on various occasions to have recorded with the band, but DE denied it: "There was no recording session in 1924 (or any other year) with Sidney Bechet" (Chilton, 70).

The first recordings by the Ellington band to be released commercially: DE also made a handful of recordings during the same period on which he can be heard playing piano for various singers, but they are, like the early band sides, of limited musical interest. **"If one searches for embryonic Ellington elements":** Schuller, 321.

"If the Washingtonians had been better readers": Tucker, 170.

CHAPTER THREE
"ONLY MY OWN MUSIC"

SOURCES

Documents

A Duke Named Ellington, TV documentary (WNET); Sonny Greer, oral-history interview, IJS; John Hammond, oral-history interview, Schomburg Center, New York Public Library; Louis Metcalf, oral-history interview, OHAM; Bob Mills, "Irving Mills," www.redhotjazz.com/irvingmills.html; Irving Mills, oral-history interview, OHAM; George Wein, oral-history interview, EC.

Books

Bigard, *With Louis and the Duke;* Chilton, *Ride, Red, Ride;* Cohen, *Duke Ellington's America;* Collier, *Jazz;* Dance, *The World of Count Basie;* Dance, *The World of Duke Ellington;* Dietrich, *Duke's 'Bones;* Dodge, *Hot Jazz and Jazz Dance;* Ellington, *Duke Ellington in Person;* Goldberg, *Tin Pan Alley;* Hammond, *John Hammond on Record;* Harwood, *I Went Down to St. James Infirmary;* Hughes, *Second Movement;* Lavezzoli, *The King of All, Sir Duke;* Okrent, *Last Call;* Stewart, *Jazz Masters of the Thirties;* Sweet, *Steely Dan;* Teachout, *Pops;* Traill, *Just Jazz 4;* Tucker, *Ellington;* Ulanov, *Duke Ellington;* Wilson, *Classics and Commercials;* Wright, *"King" Oliver.*

NOTES

Not only were men drinking, but so were women: For a discussion of the effect of Prohibition on women, see Okrent, 211–12. **"In the twenties [people] could love":** Wilson, 168.

Irving Mills: No biography of Mills has been written. The best short treatment of his life and work is in Harwood.

"Small, squat, hard-headed": Hughes, 251. **"The arts of persuasion":** Goldberg, 213.

They "looked down on me": Mills, "Irving Mills."

"He could feel a song": *MM,* 77. **I "title[d] all the tunes":** Mills, "Irving Mills." **He claimed to have come up with the title of "It Don't Mean a Thing":** Eliot Tiegel, "Duke and Irving Mills: They Helped Each Other Grow in the Early Years," *Billboard,* Feb. 10, 1973. DE said in 1965 that "Bubber [Miley] was the first man I heard use the expression, 'it don't mean a thing if it ain't got that swing'" (DE, "The Most Essential Instrument," *Jazz Journal,* Dec. 1965). **His staffers supplied lyrics:** "Here's what happens: when you're making thirty, forty, fifty numbers a month, you don't have the time to write all the lyrics. So once you get the idea, the story, you turn it over to somebody to write. . . . That's why we always had three writers on most of the songs" (Mills, "Irving Mills"). **"A guy would record his own tune":** Chilton, 81–82.

"An assortment of incompatible period styles": Hughes, 247–48. **"Have a good cigar, Spike":** Ibid. **The accent of the big-city hustler:** Mills's speaking voice can be heard on "A Nite at the Cotton Club," a two-sided 78 recorded by DE's band for Victor in 1929 but not issued until 1966, and "Irving Mills Presents," a 1933 promotional film short that is available for online viewing at www. youtube.com/watch?v=kEoTwTYnc6g. He also made dozens of commercial recordings as a singer in the twenties and thirties, including several with DE. **"Limited vocabulary":** Bob Mills, "Irving Mills." **"How tremendously Duke was being exploited":** Hammond, oral-history interview. **"As ingenious as it [was] unfair":** "Henry Johnson," "Sold—for Less than a Song," *New Masses,* July 1936. ("Henry Johnson" was Hammond's pseudonym.) **"A man who saved black talent":** Hammond, *John Hammond on Record,* 132.

It is unclear when Mills and DE first crossed paths: For a discussion of various contradictory reports of their first meeting, see Steven Lasker, "Duke Ellington, Jo. Trent, Blu-Disc, Up-to-Date and Various Topics of Related Interest," *DEMS Bulletin,* Dec. 2004–Mar. 2005. **"During [his] first six months in New York":** *MM,* 72. **"The band had been at the Kentucky Club":** DE, "Jazz as I Have Seen It," *Swing,* June 1940. **Mills recalled the song as "Black and Tan Fantasy":** Irving Mills and Charles Emge, "I Split with Duke When Music Began Sidetracking," *Down Beat,* Nov. 5, 1952, in *Reader,* 274. **"He signed the Negro pianist":** "Mills' Music," *Time,* Mar. 22, 1937.

A reference to a black dance step: For more on the todalo and its relationship to "East St. Louis Toodle-O," see Chadwick Hansen's "Jenny's Toe Revisited: White Responses to Afro-American Shaking Dances," *American Music,* Spring 1987, and Mark Tucker's "On *Toodle-oo, Todalo,* and Jenny's Toe," *American Music,* Spring 1988.

"He never had the same men twice": Mills, "Irving Mills."

"Every now and then": Ibid. **"Make and record only [his] own music":** *MM,* 77.

"A great creative artist": Mills and Emge, "I Split with Duke When Music Began Sidetracking," in *Reader,* 274. **Mills reaped the lion's share:** Publishers and songwriters normally split all royalties 50-50. If, however, the publisher supplies lyrics to a given song, then he also receives half of the songwriter's share, or more if multiple writers collaborate on or are credited with the lyrics, as was frequently the case at Mills Music. **"We gave every man in the band":** Mills, "Irving Mills."

"A thinking, knowledgeable man": Stewart, 104, 107. The only extended account of Nanton's life and work is Dietrich, 19–49.

"The inspiration for the 'East St. Louis Toodle-O'": Roger Pryor Dodge, "Bubber," *H.R.S. Rag*, Oct. 15, 1940, in Dodge, 86. Lewandos (spelled without an apostrophe) was a laundry chain that in the twenties had stores throughout the greater Boston area.

"He always had a story for his music": *MM*, 106. DE took credit for this story (and, implicitly, for "East St. Louis Toodle-O" itself) in Ruby Berkley Goodwin, "Meet the Duke," *The Bronzeman*, Aug. 1932. See also DE, "My Hunt for Song Titles," *Rhythm*, Aug. 1933, in *Reader*, 88. **"An idea man"**: Inez M. Cavanaugh, "Reminiscing in Tempo: Tricky Sam Goes Over the Great Times He Had with Duke, Bubber, Freddie Jenkins," *Metronome*, Feb. 1945, in *Reader*, 466–67.

"When I get off": Roger Pryor Dodge, "Harpsichords and Jazz Trumpets," *Hound & Horn*, July–Sept. 1934, in Dodge, 25.

DE would bring unfinished, seemingly fragmentary bits of music into the studio, then shift them around: Typical of the way that DE worked in his maturity is "Warm Valley," a 1940 recording of which three different takes survive. The original take contains three strains. On the second take, the second strain is dropped and replaced with two new ones. The issued third take drops one of the new strains and rearranges the others in a different sequence. BS, who worked with DE on the song, recalled that "we wrote reams and reams of music on that, and he threw it all out except what you hear [on the issued take]. He didn't use any of mine. Now, that's arranging. The tune was written, but we had to find a way to present it" (Bill Coss, "Ellington & Strayhorn, Inc.," *Down Beat*, June 7, 1962, in *Reader*, 501).

"Duke, to the bewilderment of people": Irving Townsend, "When Duke Records," in Traill, 19. The tenor saxophonist Al Sears, who joined the band in 1944, described how confusing DE's composing methods could be to a new member: "You start at letter 'A' and go to 'B' and then suddenly, for no reason at all, when *you* go to 'C' the rest of the band's playing something else which you find out later on isn't what's written at 'C' but what's written at 'J' instead. And then on the next number, instead of starting at the top, the entire band starts at 'H'—that is, everybody except me. See, I'm the newest man in the band and I just haven't caught on to the system yet!" (George T. Simon, "It's Like Nothing Else!," *Metronome*, July 1944, in *Reader*, 461).

"You know how the negroes are": Fred M. White, "Negro Music as Individual Unit Aim of Duke Ellington," *Morning Oregonian*, May 14, 1934.

"People heard it": Tim Weiner, "Keeping Time with Sonny Greer," *Soho Weekly News*, June 15, 1979. **Jimi Hendrix heard it as a child:** Lavezzoli, 37. **Steely Dan recorded the same piece:** The performance can be heard on *Pretzel Logic*, released in 1974. Donald Fagen, Steely Dan's coleader, sent DE a copy of the record that

April in honor of his seventy-fifth birthday, a month before his death: "I would have been very flattered if he heard it, but I don't know if he did" (Sweet, 70–71).

Miley told a friend that the song was a spiritual: Dodge, "Harpsichords and Jazz Trumpets," in Dodge, 23.

"Adelaide, that's what I've been looking for": *A Duke Named Ellington.*

Jackson shared composing credit with Ellington and Miley: The three men were jointly credited on the label of the 1927 Victor recording of "Creole Love Call." When the song was copyrighted by DE the following year, he received sole credit. Barney Bigard claimed that Jackson was fired by DE for having plagiarized "Creole Love Call" (Bigard, 44). In fact, Jackson left the band in January, three months before Joe Oliver sent his letter of complaint to Victor Records. Contrary to popular belief, Oliver does not appear to have sued DE, or anyone else, to recover rights to the song. For a detailed discussion of this matter, see Steven Lasker, "Stack O'Lee Blues," *DEMS Bulletin,* Apr.–July 2008. **"I have recently listened":** Wright, 26.

The opening clarinet riff of "Creole Love Call" is played as a clarinet solo on "Camp Meeting Blues": The clarinetist on Oliver's recording is thought to be either Jimmie Noone or Buster Bailey. Rudy Jackson can be heard playing the same solo on Sippie Wallace's 1925 recording of "Being Down Don't Worry Me."

R.D. Darrell: For a discussion of Darrell, see Collier, 228–31. *Phonograph Monthly Review:* For a short history of the magazine, see Tim Gracyk, *"Phonograph Monthly Review: A Forgotten Publication?,"* *Tim's Phonographs and Old Records,* www.gracyk.com/pmr.shtml. **"An orchestrator in the class of Ravel, Respighi and Strauss":** Quoted in Collier, 229.

"Two unusually interesting records": R.D. Darrell, *Phonograph Monthly Review,* July 1927, in *Reader,* 33–34.

"Conductor of what leading judges have called": Dave Peyton, "The Musical Scene," *The Chicago Defender,* Apr. 16, 1927.

The story was picked up: "Duke Ellington Holds Prominent Place in Broadway's Spotlight," *New York Amsterdam News,* Apr. 20, 1927, and "Duke Ellington, Brunswick Artist, Holds Unique Place in Broadway's Spotlight," *The Pittsburgh Courier,* Apr. 23, 1927.

"Duke would have a skeleton of something": Tiegel, "Duke and Irving Mills." **"I created the balances":** Mills, "Irving Mills."

"We got a session down there": Metcalf, oral-history interview. **"He knew how to construct at the piano":** Mills, "Irving Mills."

Duke Ellington, Inc., was owned by DE, Mills, and Samuel Buzzell: "Certificate of Incorporation of Duke Ellington, Inc.," Dec. 23, 1929 (Steven Lasker collection). According to this certificate, the corporation was divided into three shares, and each man owned a single share. **A 45-45 split of the band's profits:** "Duke Ellington Breaks with Irving Mills, Famed Maestro Under Wm. Morris Banner," *New York Amsterdam News,* Apr. 22, 1939. **"Mr. Mills's 'piece' ":** "Mills' Music," *Time,* Mar. 22, 1937. **"I owned the band":** Irving Mills, unpublished film interview, in *RIT,* 160. **"A clause in [the band's] contract":** "Louis Metcalf," *Jazz Journal,* Dec. 1966, in *RIT,* 80. (No evidence exists to substantiate the accuracy of Metcalf's claim.)

Armstrong agreed to pay Rockwell $75: Teachout, 134. **"Duke didn't want to know":** Wein, oral-history interview.

"Duke was a good listener": Mills, "Irving Mills."

"He wanted Duke to be the star": John McDonough, "Reminiscing in Tempo: Guitarist Freddy Guy's Ellington Memories," *Down Beat,* Apr. 17, 1969, in *Reader,* 484. **"Serious disillusionment for the men":** Ulanov, 56.

"He was blue-white diamond": Greer, oral-history interview. **"For me, the development of Duke Ellington's career":** Mills and Emge, "I Split with Duke When Music Began Sidetracking," in *Reader,* 275.

CHAPTER FOUR
"THE UTMOST SIGNIFICANCE"

SOURCES

Documents

Helen Oakley Dance, oral-history interview, OHAM; Stanley Dance, liner notes for *The Ellington Era 1927–1940,* vol. 1, sound recording (Columbia); DE, unpublished interviews with Carter Harman, 1956 and 1964, EC; Sonny Greer, oral-history interview, IJS; Steven Lasker, liner notes for *Duke Ellington: The Complete 1936–1940 Variety, Vocalion and OKeh Small Group Sessions,* sound recording (Mosaic), OHAM; Irving Mills, oral-history interview, OHAM; Cootie Williams, oral-history interview, IJS.

Books

Balliett, *American Musicians II;* Berger, *Basically Speaking;* Bigard, *With Louis and the Duke;* Boyd, *Autobiography of a People;* Calloway, *Of Minnie the Moocher and Me;* Cohen, *Duke Ellington's America;* Collier, *Jazz;* Stanley Dance, *The World of Count Basie;* Stanley Dance, *The World of Duke Ellington;* Eberly, *Music in the Air;* Feather, *From Satchmo to Miles;* Hajdu, *Lush Life;* Hammond, *John Hammond on*

Record; Harrison, *The Essential Jazz Records;* Haskins, *The Cotton Club;* Howland, *Ellington Uptown;* Langston Hughes, *The Big Sea;* Spike Hughes, *Second Movement;* Jablonski, *Harold Arlen;* Kisseloff, *You Must Remember This;* Lambert, *Music Ho!;* Lasker, *A Cotton Club Miscellany;* Lewis, *Radio Master;* Russell, *New Orleans Style;* Schuller, *Early Jazz;* Shapiro, *Hear Me Talkin' to Ya;* Shipton, *I Feel a Song Coming On;* Stearns, *Jazz Dance;* Stearns, *The Story of Jazz;* Steiner, *Wild Throng Dances Madly in Cellar Club;* Stewart, *Jazz Masters of the Thirties;* Stratemann, *Duke Ellington Day by Day and Film by Film;* Sylvester, *No Cover Charge;* Tucker, *Ellington;* Ulanov, *Duke Ellington;* Welk, *My America, Your America;* Wilk, *They're Playing Our Song;* Winer, *On the Sunny Side of the Street.*

NOTES

The Cotton Club: Jim Haskins's *The Cotton Club,* the only full-length history of the club, is mostly unsourced and must be consulted with caution. **"The Aristocrat of Harlem":** The club's slogan is said to have been coined by Edwina, Lady Mountbatten, a sexual adventuress who slept with many men of many colors (Jablonski, 40). **"Like a girl":** Greer, oral-history interview.

"Muriels": Hammond, 126. **"The bandstand was a replica":** Calloway, 88.

"Expensive and exclusive": Spike Hughes, *Second Movement,* 230. **"$4–$5":** DE, Harman interview, 1964. In his review of DE's 1927 opening at the Cotton Club, *Variety*'s Abel Green reported that the cover charge was $2. Dan Healy, who staged the floor shows, remembered it as being $3 (Jablonski, 55). **"Bad and expensive":** Hammond, 55. **A menu from 1931:** Lasker, *A Cotton Club Miscellany,* 31–32. **$30 a bottle:** Shipton, 74. **"15 Minutes in a Taxi":** Lasker, *A Cotton Club Miscellany,* 28.

"The Cotton Club was a classy spot": *MM,* 80–81.

Madden hired only light-skinned women: It was not until 1932 that Lucille Wilson, who later married Louis Armstrong, became the club's first dark-skinned female dancer. **"Brutes at the door":** Quoted in Jablonski, 53. **"It does not cater to colored patrons":** "Cotton Club, Harlem, Bars Colored Couple Accompanied by White Friends Giving Police Orders as the Reason," *The New York Age,* July 9, 1927. **"If you were very famous":** Spike Hughes, *Second Movement,* 230. Mercer Ellington claimed that anyone with enough money to pay the cover charge was admitted, but virtually all contemporary witnesses agree that except for black celebrities, a strict color bar was enforced by the club's bouncers (Mark Gifford, "Mercer Ellington: An Interview with Duke's Successor," *Jazz Journal,* June 1990). **W.C. Handy was turned away from a show of his own songs:** "Cotton Club Takes Round in Ban Fight," *New York Amsterdam News,* Feb. 13, 1937.

"Harlem Negroes did not like the Cotton Club": Langston Hughes, *The Big Sea*, 224–25. **Irving Mills said that he made it happen:** Irving Mills, unpublished film interview, in *RIT,* 67.

"I heard Duke and I wanted him": Jimmy McHugh, "McHugh's View," *Down Beat*, Apr. 14, 1960.

"Be big or you'll be dead": Ulanov, 57. **Two weeks later:** Many versions of this story have circulated over the years. It is known, however, that *Dancemania*, the show in which DE was playing, opened on Nov. 21, 1927, twelve days before the band opened at the Cotton Club in New York. According to Fred Guy, who claimed to be present when DE signed the Cotton Club contract, "The next day we had to leave for a date in Philadelphia for a week, which gave us no time between our return and our opening. When we got back, we had to rehearse the entire show routines all afternoon and night—literally right up until showtime" (John McDonough, "Reminiscing in Tempo: Guitarist Freddy Guy's Ellington Memories," *Down Beat*, Apr. 17, 1969, in *Reader*, 484). **"Everybody was betting we wouldn't last a month":** DE, "Jazz as I Have Seen It," *Swing*, June 1940. Henry Allen's widely reported claim that King Oliver, not DE, was the original choice of the Cotton Club's management (see Balliett, 35) appears not to be true.

"I am mad at Harlem": "Lipstick" (Lois Long), "Tables for Two," *The New Yorker*, Dec. 10, 1927.

"A slim brown girl": Frances Park, "Harlem 1927," *The New Yorker*, Dec. 31, 1927. **"Better find a friend":** "Goings On About Town," *The New Yorker*, June 9, 1928.

"With the possible exception of Fletcher Henderson's band": *The New York Age*, Oct. 15, 1927, quoted in Tucker, 208. **"Teasin'est torso tossing":** Abel Green, *Variety*, Dec. 7, 1927, in *Reader*, 31–32.

"The first show was kind of weak": Irving Mills, unpublished film interview, in *RIT,* 72. **It wasn't until he opened at the Cotton Club:** According to Barney Bigard, Wellman Braud, the band's bassist, told him that "Duke has had this six-piece outfit on Broadway, but he has just landed this deal at the Cotton Club. The man there wants him to expand the band to ten pieces" (Bigard, 44). Bigard joined the band shortly after it opened at the Cotton Club, making his first recordings with DE on Jan. 9, 1928.

Surviving programs of the five shows: All surviving programs are reproduced in Stratemann, 687–93. Most of them do not identify the musical numbers by title. **No live recordings were made:** The earliest known live recordings by DE date from 1932. For a discussion of the only surviving manuscripts by DE from the early Cotton Club years, see Howland, 127–28. **Some scholars have suggested:** See, for example, Gunther Schuller, who claims in *Early Jazz* that Ellington's musical development "was precisely due to the fortuitous circumstance of working five years at the Cotton Club. There, by writing and experimenting with all manner of descriptive production and dance numbers, Ellington's inherent talent and imagination could develop properly" (339).

"The music for the shows": *MM*, 81. **"We played two shows each night":** Bigard, 47. **DE identifies only one composition:** "I wrote 'The Mystery Song' for the Step Brothers in rehearsal. It was part of their act, not part of the show" (*MM*, 81). The Four Step Brothers were a dance team organized in 1925 that made numerous film and TV appearances and remained active well into the sixties. DE recorded "The Mystery Song" for Victor in 1931.

"The most shocking, ribald, bawdy, dirtiest songs": Winer, 28. **"Jelly roll, jelly roll":** Quoted in Shipton, 80. **"Every dance routine was too long and too loud":** Spike Hughes, *Second Movement*, 230. **"The chief ingredient":** Jablonski, 55.

A minute-long sequence: A silent version of this British Pathé clip can be viewed at www.britishpathe.com/record.php?id=50945. (The soundtrack has not been located.) See "A Short and Silent Ellington Movie," *DEMS Bulletin*, Apr.–July 2001. **"I recall one":** Stearns, *The Story of Jazz*, 183–84.

"Top-flight performances": Kisseloff, 309. **A caricature:** Lasker, *A Cotton Club Miscellany*, 1.

$75 a week: This was Louis Metcalf's recollection (Shapiro, 234). See also "Jazz as I Have Seen It," in which DE gives the same figure. **"It didn't really matter":** Sylvester, 50. **"The girl you saw doing the squirmy dance":** DE, Harman interview, 1964. **"A creative form of irony":** Boyd (unpaginated Kindle edition).

"He used to set us on the stand": Roger Ringo, "Reminiscing in Tempo with Freddie Jenkins," *Storyville*, Apr.–May 1973. **"He would just start to play":** Bigard, 48.

"A band of the most vicious thugs": Boyd (unpaginated Kindle edition). **"They recognized [the dancers] as, in their opinion":** Howard Johnson, quoted in Cohen, 55. **One of them:** Hyacinth Curtis, quoted in A. Peter Bailey, "The Cotton Club Girls," *Ebony*, Dec. 1985. **To play bridge:** Gifford, "Mercer Ellington." **"He loved Duke and he loved me":** Greer, oral-history interview. **"I keep hearing about how bad":** Sylvester, 45.

$4,000 a week: Wilk, 50. **"Duke Ellington's Recording Orchestra":** Lasker, *A Cotton Club Miscellany*, 28–29. **Winchell came to the opening:** Wilk, 55.

"The first person to start the walking bass": Russell, 111. **"A totally different kind of rhythm section":** Stanley Dance, *The World of Count Basie*, 276. **"Wellman was playing solos":** Berger, 134. **He cooked New Orleans–style dishes:** Stewart, 87.

"When Mr. Braud joined us": *MM*, 115.

"A sort of guardian": Cohen, 630. "A very well-behaved, well-organized young man": *MM*, 111. "Give more variety": Stanley Dance, *The World of Duke Ellington*, 73.

"Woody tone": *MM*, 115.

"Kind of tired": Bigard, 44–46.

"Posturing and posing": Cavanaugh, "Reminiscing in Tempo," in *Reader*, 468. "He brought us a new kind of sparkle": *MM*, 121.

"Everybody said Johnny was gruff": Hajdu, 178. "He may look as though he's on his last walk to the gallows": Shorty Baker, quoted in Stanley Dance, *The World of Duke Ellington*, 93. "So impressed with Johnny's great ability": Welk, 57. "He plays from the heart": Stanley Dance, *The World of Duke Ellington*, 91.

A nickname whose origins are obscure: For a discussion of the varying explanations of how Hodges came to be called "Rabbit," see Lasker, liner notes for *Duke Ellington: The Complete 1936–1940 Variety, Vocalion and OKeh Small Group Sessions*, 13. "I had quite a few of his riffs": Don DeMichael, "Double Play: Carney to Hodges to Ellington," *Down Beat*, June 7, 1962, in *Reader*, 474. "Professor Booze": *RIT*, 86. Hardwick claimed that he left the band voluntarily in order to "see the world" (Stanley Dance, *The World of Duke Ellington*, 59). Hodges said that he "had an accident, went through the windshield of a taxicab. Had his face all cut up and I had to go to work for him" (DeMichael, "Double Play," in *Reader*, 473). "Johnny was scared when he first joined us": Bigard, 53–54.

"When you look back": Stanley Dance, *The World of Duke Ellington*, 77. "A man of the theater": Harrison, 191.

"A certain lazy gait": DE, "My Hunt for Song Titles," *Rhythm*, Aug. 1933, in *Reader*, 88. (The correct spelling of the title is used in this article.) According to Marshall and Jean Stearns, Bert Williams is said to have performed a shuffle-like dance called "the Mooche" at the turn of the century (Stearns, *Jazz Dance*, 197–99). "A sex dance": Stanley Dance, liner notes for *The Ellington Era 1927–1940*, vol. 1.

"There was always something going on": Bigard, 48, 47. "Third class discords": Roger Ringo, "Reminiscing in Tempo with Freddie Jenkins," *Storyville*, Apr.–May 1973. "A Show That Rivals Broadway's Best": Lasker, *A Cotton Club Miscellany*, 28. "Also, anyone interested in jazz": "Lipstick" (Lois Long), "Tables for Two," *The New Yorker*, Dec. 22, 1928. "A charming combination": "R.A.S.," "Musical Events," *The New Yorker*, Dec. 22, 1928.

The band was initially heard on Wednesdays at eleven P.M.: The late-night time slot shifted from week to week. In the band's first appearance in the radio section of the *The New York Times*, for instance, "Duke Ellington's Orchestra" is listed as airing over WABC, CBS's New York flagship station, at eleven thirty. Subsequent programs started at different times between eleven P.M. and midnight. Contemporary newspaper program guides confirm that the band was also making early-evening broadcasts in 1929 (see, for example, "To-Day's Radio Programs," *Geneva* [NY] *Daily Times,* Mar. 25, 1929). The latter broadcasts ended in 1930. **Each thirty-minute broadcast:** In 1930 the broadcasts moved to NBC, whose network logbooks have been preserved, making it possible to identify the songs that were performed on the air. See Ken Steiner, "Cotton Club Broadcasts on NBC," *DEMS Bulletin,* Dec. 2008–Mar. 2009.

DE had been broadcasting locally since 1923: For information on these broadcasts, see Steiner, 5, 7. **Ted Husing:** Lewis, 88–90. Some sources credit Paley with having been a Cotton Club regular, but he mentions DE only in passing in *As It Happened,* his 1979 memoir, and Husing appears to have been instrumental in bringing the band to his attention. **"A beautiful cat":** *MM,* 79–80. **"A real fan of [the] band":** Bigard, 48. **The first time that a jazz band made a national broadcast from Harlem:** According to radio historian Elizabeth McLeod, "There were few dance band remotes of any kind on the networks in 1927–28—most such broadcasts were purely local, and were not heard outside New York. Very few New York hotels had network wires. The Cotton Club was by all indications the first Harlem spot to get a network wire, though it had hosted New York–only remotes for several years. The first African-American performers of any kind to have a network series were the Southernaires, a vocal quartet that was a regular NBC feature from the very start of the network in 1926" (personal communication).

"The first important national propagation": Eberly, 47, 49. **"The engagement at the Cotton Club":** *MM,* 77. For a discussion of the significance of DE's Cotton Club broadcasts, see Cohen, 57–58. **"The people didn't get anything to eat":** Greer, oral-history interview.

"Jungle music": Ibid. **"The Jungle Band":** This was the first time that the word "jungle" appeared on the label of a recording by DE. **"Here we were, my mother and I":** Feather, 52. **"Oh, we've been African all the way back":** "Words of Wisdom from Edward Kennedy (Duke) Ellington," *Jet,* May 15, 1969.

"Bubber was temperamental": Boyer, "The Hot Bach," 240. (This quote is all but identical to a parallel passage in DE's "Jazz as I Have Seen It.") **"Their drinking never hurt their music":** Bigard, 51–52. Cootie Williams confirmed Bigard's account: "The reason why he fired Bubber Miley was every time some big shot come up to listen to the band, there wasn't no Bubber Miley. And the whole band had been built around Bubber Miley. And maybe he decided, he says, 'Well, this man has got to go. I have to let him go and get somebody' " (Williams, oral-history interview).

"Liquor drinking among the musicians": *MM,* 73–74. **"All our horn blowers were lushies":** Boyer, "The Hot Bach," 240. **"Look, fellows":** Clark Terry, quoted in Stanley Dance, *The World of Duke Ellington,* 187–88.

"**With the Ellington band I drank Coca-Cola**": Stanley Dance, *The World of Duke Ellington*, 112. "**I used to laugh when Tricky would start to blowing**": Williams, oral-history interview. "**He didn't want to throw his weight around**": Helen Oakley Dance, oral-history interview.

"**Then there is a first rate blackamoor band**": "Leatrice Joy Sings Pleasingly at Palace," *The New York Times*, Apr. 22, 1929. This was the first review of DE to appear in the *Times*. "**Another thing that your most high-hat friends have recently discovered**": "Lipstick" (Lois Long), "Tables for Two," *The New Yorker*, May 4, 1929. Except for a Brunswick Records advertisement that had appeared on Jan. 5, this column is the first mention of DE by name in *The New Yorker*.

"**I came on and I could see her**": DE, Harman interview, 1956. In *MM* DE says that it was his mother who "came up to New York from Washington, and brought my sister Ruth with her. . . . It was the first time she had ever seen me on stage, and I can see her now, waving her handkerchief the whole time we were out there" (98).

"**Will Vodery got us the gig**": *MM*, 98. "**Valuable lessons in orchestration**": Ibid. "**His chromatic tendencies**": DE, "Duke Ellington on Arrangers," *Metronome*, Oct. 1943.

"**He had assimilated**": Ulanov, 196.

"**The least notable**": J. Brooks Atkinson, "The Play: Behind the Scenes with Ziegfeld," *The New York Times*, July 3, 1929. **Many of them didn't bother to mention Ellington:** DE also went unmentioned, for instance, in *Time*'s review ("Theatre: New Plays in Manhattan," July 15, 1929). "**The finest exponent[s] of syncopated music**": Florenz Ziegfeld, "Ziegfeld Rushes to Defense of 'Show Girl' as Likable Offering," *New York Morning Telegram*, July 12, 1929.

"**We were the first**": Greer, oral-history interview. "**I was out thousands of dollars**": Irving Mills, unpublished film interview, in *RIT*, 90–91.

CHAPTER FIVE
"I BETTER SCRATCH OUT SOMETHING"

SOURCES

Documents
Barney Bigard, oral-history interview, IJS; Lawrence Brown, oral-history interview, IJS; Helen Oakley Dance, oral-history interview, OHAM; *A Duke Named Ellington*, TV documentary (WNET); DE, unpublished interviews with Carter Harman, 1956 and 1964, EC; Ruth Ellington, oral-history interview, EC; Jimmy Jones,

oral-history interview, IJS; *Memories of Duke,* film documentary (Time Life); Irving Mills, oral-history interview, OHAM; Juan Tizol, oral-history interview, IJS; Cootie Williams, oral-history interview, IJS.

Books
Bigard, *With Louis and the Duke;* Bogle, *Bright Boulevards, Bold Dreams;* Bradbury, *Duke Ellington;* Calloway, *Of Minnie the Moocher and Me;* Chevalier, *My Paris;* Davis, *Outcats;* Delson, *Dudley Murphy;* Dietrich, *Duke's 'Bones;* Ellington, *Duke Ellington in Person;* George, *Sweet Man;* Horak, *Lovers of Cinema;* Jewell, *Duke;* Jones, *Jazz Talking;* Lambert, *Music Ho!;* Lawrence, *Duke Ellington and His World;* McLeod, *The Original Amos 'n' Andy;* Newkirk, *Letters from Black America;* Rose, *I Remember Jazz;* Schuller, *Early Jazz;* Serrano, *Juan Tizol;* Shaw, *Let's Dance;* Stewart, *Boy Meets Horn;* Stratemann, *Duke Ellington Day by Day and Film by Film;* Ulanov, *Duke Ellington;* van de Leur, *Something to Live For.*

NOTES

Dudley Murphy: For more on Murphy, see Delson. **DE's talking-picture debut:** The Ellington band made a previous uncredited on-screen appearance in *Headlines,* a 1925 silent film directed by Edward H. Griffith. (A print of *Headlines* is at the Library of Congress.) **Black and Tan:** The film was retitled *Black and Tan Fantasy* when it was re-released in the forties. **Carl Van Vechten:** Horak, 132.

"This short, though billed": Review of *Black and Tan, Variety,* Nov. 6, 1929. **"Excellent entertainment":** "'Black and Tan' Is All-Race Talkie," *The Chicago Defender,* Nov. 16, 1929. **"Nauseating lowdown niggerisms":** Vere E. Johns, "radio :-: drama," *The New York Age,* Aug. 13, 1932.

After 1928: The earliest known photograph to show the scar was taken in December of 1928. (It is reproduced in Bradbury, 25.) DE may have acquired it as early as 1927. See Steven Lasker, "Dating Duke and Edna's Breakup—and the Infamous Scar Incident," *Blue Light: The DESUK Newsletter,* Autumn 2013. **"I have four stories about it":** *MM,* 471.

"Women was one of the highlights": Mills, oral-history interview.

"The most beautiful woman": Michael P. Zirpolo, "In Duke's Head," *IAJRC Journal* (Summer 2000). **"I just had to accept":** Bogle, 131. **"A torrid love affair":** Ellington, 47–48.

"Hurt, bad hurt": Marc Crawford, "A Visit with Mrs. Duke Ellington," *Ebony,* Mar. 1959. **"Something happened between [Ellington] and his wife":** Brown, oral-history interview. **Brown married Fredi:** They were married in 1933 and divorced in 1948. Some of their surviving correspondence is reprinted in Newkirk, 74–76, but it sheds no light on her relationship with DE. Washington died in

1994. **Five, Mercer claimed:** Ellington, 127. **"Quite a figure in the music world":** Bigard, oral-history interview. Contemporary Harlem gossip identified Edna's lover as Benny Carter (Steven Lasker, personal communication). **"A close friend":** Jewell, 31. Rex Stewart mistakenly believed that Ivie Anderson had been involved with DE, found him in flagrante delicto, and slashed him (Ibid., 31–32). While it is not impossible that Anderson had a later liaison with DE, she did not meet him until several years after he was scarred.

"A Park Avenue socialite": Ellington, 48.

DE left everything behind, including his clothes: Mercer recalls that when DE left Mildred Dixon for Evie Ellis in 1939, "He never came back . . . and *once again* he left all his clothes behind" (Ellington, 77, emphasis added). *Duke Ellington in Person* contains no prior reference to DE's having done such a thing, which suggests that he also did so when he left Edna but that Mercer's reference to the earlier event was dropped from the book for unknown reasons. **"I came home from school one day":** Davis, 58. **A five-room flat:** The building, at 381 Edgecombe Avenue, still exists. **"The Finest and Most Exclusive Section":** *New York Amsterdam News,* Apr. 25, 1922. **"If you ever sat on a beautiful magenta cloud":** *MM,* 182. **"Nice high-rent houses":** Langston Hughes, "Down Under in Harlem," *New Republic,* Mar. 27, 1944.

Press reports always referred to Mildred as DE's wife: See, for example, "Duke Ellington's Wife in Hospital," *The Chicago Defender,* Jan. 6, 1934. **"Mildred became Mrs. Ellington":** Ulanov, 114. **"Sweet Bebe":** Ellington, 49. **"Innate class":** Ellington, 48. **"Very nice, extremely nice":** Helen Oakley Dance, oral-history interview.

DE's earliest surviving interviews: The first known interview with DE is Janet Mabie's "Ellington's 'Mood in Indigo': Harlem's 'Duke' Seeks to Express His Race," *Christian Science Monitor,* Dec. 13, 1930, in *Reader,* 41–43.

"Duke used to gamble": Bigard, oral-history interview. **Mildred lived in another apartment:** "What he tried to do, he roomed Mildred upstairs, but she just kept appearing, you know? Until finally she was kind of there" (Ruth Ellington, oral-history interview). This may explain why she is not listed as a resident of the apartment in the 1930 census. **"Being put out to pasture":** Ibid. **"He just thought I should be there":** Ibid. **Mercer was forced to wear his hair in braids:** Ellington, 18.

"We would be in the recording studio": Roger Ringo, "Reminiscing in Tempo with Freddie Jenkins," *Storyville,* Apr.–May 1973.

"His pure white countenance": Stewart, 152. **"A legit man":** Quoted in *RIT,* 98. **A classically trained musician:** Serrano, 25–26. See also Dietrich, 51–67. **"I take all my solos straight":** Boyer, "The Hot Bach," 231.

"This thing ain't supposed to work, man": Jimmy Jones, oral-history interview.

DE "wrote in such a cryptic fashion": Ellington, 43. (Mercer unconvincingly claimed that this was to prevent other people from copying his music.) It should also be noted that DE's autograph scores were untransposed, with all instrumental parts written at their sounding pitch. Except for Sergei Prokofiev, no other first-rank composer has written untransposed orchestral scores. This suggests that DE either did not learn the correct transpositions for brass and wind instruments or, more likely, never became fully comfortable with the arcane mechanics of transposition.

"He could write for [Tizol] along with the saxophones": Ibid., 51.

"Tizol is a very big man": *MM*, 56. **"You would never believe it":** Bigard, *With Louis and the Duke*, 56.

"I went to hear him": Chevalier, 128. **"I am French":** Daniel Ringold and Philippe Guilboust, *Maurice Chevalier, le sourire de Paris*, quoted in Bernard Dupuis, "Maurice Chevalier," *DEMS Bulletin*, Dec. 2002–Mar. 2003.

"He fought to have us play in concert with Maurice Chevalier": *MM*, 77. **"MR. IRVING MILLS":** *Variety*, Apr. 2, 1930. The ad is reproduced in Stratemann, 28. **"Mills signed Ellington":** "Duke Ellington and Orchestra to Play for Amos 'n' Andy Picture," *The New York Age*, July 12, 1930.

Mills arranged for DE to appear in *Check and Double Check*: So, at any rate, he claimed. For his version of the story, see *RIT*, 108. **The most popular radio comedy team in the world:** For the show's popularity and significance, see McLeod. **It was covered as news:** See, for example, "Duke Ellington Asked to 'Black Up,'" *The Pittsburgh Courier*, Aug. 30, 1930. **"They made me and Barney a lot darker":** Tizol, oral-history interview.

DE and his musicians were paid $27,500: Stratemann, 38.

"Duke was more than suave": Calloway, 91.

"'Workshop' period": Schuller, 348. These comments refer to the originally issued Victor version of "Old Man Blues," recorded in Hollywood on Aug. 26, 1930, not the later, slightly less effective version credited to the Harlem Footwarmers that was recorded by DE for OKeh in New York on Oct. 30. (The introduction and opening chorus are cut from the abridged version of "Old Man Blues" performed in *Check and Double Check*.)

DE thought that "Old Man Blues" was his best composition yet: Cootie Williams, cited in Lawrence, 138. This statement is unsourced and must be treated, like the rest of *Duke Ellington and His World*, with extreme caution. (For a lengthy list of errata and plagiarisms in Lawrence's book, see Steven Lasker, "An Open Letter to Mrs. Sylvia Miller," *DEMS Bulletin*, Aug.–Nov. 2001.) **"Old Man Blues" was never played in later years:** DE is not known to have played the piece after 1933, though he included it in a 1952 list of his favorite recordings (*Down Beat*, Nov. 5, 1952, in *Reader*, 268). Sidney Bechet, who recorded "Old

Man Blues" in 1940, appears to be the only other major jazz musician to have performed it. **"Exquisitely tired"**: Lambert, 188.

"We had a little six-piece date": DE, interview with Jack Cullen, CKNW, Vancouver, Canada, Oct. 30, 1962; *Reader*, 340. **"We recorded it"**: *MM*, 79.

"Mood Indigo" first appears in NBC's logbooks: Ken Steiner, "Cotton Club Broadcasts on NBC," *DEMS Bulletin*, Dec. 2008–Mar. 2009. **"Duke once said in a piece"**: Jones, *Jazz Talking*, 11. **"Duke figured out a first strain"**: Bigard, *With Louis and the Duke*, 64. **The first two recordings**: DE recorded a near-identical small-group version of "Mood Indigo" (credited to "The Jungle Band") for Brunswick on Oct. 17, 1930. Bigard's name appeared for the first time on the label of the full-band recording made for Victor on Dec. 10, 1930. **Bigard received no royalties**: Bigard, oral-history interview.

"Dreamy Blues": Later pressings of the Oct. 17 recording bear the title "Mood Indigo." The title "Dreamy Blues" does not appear on OKeh's matrix card for the Oct. 14 version, which is reproduced in Steven Lasker, "The Harlem Footwarmers," *DEMS Bulletin*, Aug.–Nov. 2001. **"I wanted to call it 'Mood Indigo'"**: DE, Harman interview, 1964. **Bigard claimed the title for himself**: Bigard, *With Louis and the Duke*, 65.

Al Rose claimed that the second strain was written by Lorenzo Tio, Jr.: Rose, 109. This claim is unsourced and should be treated with caution. **"My old teacher Lorenzo Tio"**: Bigard, *With Louis and the Duke*, 64. **"Maybe the record company put the wrong label on the record"**: Ibid., 65.

"Ellington recorded it under the title 'Dreamy Blues'": Quoted in Shaw, 189. **"At the time he was signed with the company"**: DE, Cullen interview, in *Reader*, 340.

"Duke was playing that tune": Don Peak and Tor Magnusson, "Mood Indigo: Some Thoughts Concerning the Lyricist(s)," *IAJRC Journal* (Winter 2001). LouCeil Austin married Gene Austin in 1949 and Peak interviewed her in 1996 (Gene Austin died in 1972). The fact that Parish was known to his friends as "Mike," not "Mitch," may cast doubt on her story.

"Our first big hit": DE, Harman interview, 1964.

DE's oldest surviving manuscripts date from 1930: van de Leur, 187. **"The men take up their instruments"**: H.A. Overstreet, "Touching Tomorrow's Frontiers Is Duke Ellington's Music," *Metronome*, Oct. 1933, in *Reader*, 100–101.

"This is a man": *Jazz Journal*, June 1990, in *RIT*, 103. **"In the old days"**: DE, Harman interview, 1956.

"It . . . just got to be too damn much music": Ibid.

"Duke had a strange way of composing": George, 29.

"The parallel blocks of sound": Schuller, 343.

"We were playing in Chicago": DE, Cullen interview, in *Reader*, 340.

"I had a theme": Brown, oral-history interview. Barney Bigard confirmed this story (Jones, *Jazz Talking*, 11). "The terrific check of $15": Brown, oral-history interview. Their names had vanished: The label of the first instrumental version of "Sophisticated Lady" (English Columbia CB 591), recorded in February 1933, credits DE, Hardwick, Brown, and Mills. The label of the second version (Brunswick 6600), recorded three months later, credits DE alone. Brown and Hardwick would never again receive official credit for the song. When Mitchell Parish wrote a lyric for the song, his and Mills's names were added to the credits.

"I mean, like if anybody": Bigard, oral-history interview. "The piece didn't require too much work": Roger Ringo, "Reminiscing in Tempo with Freddie Jenkins," *Storyville*, Apr.–May 1973. "There are many instances": DE, Harman interview, 1964. "If he liked [a song]": Steve Voce, "Clark Terry Talks to Steve Voce," *Jazz Journal*, Dec. 1986–Jan. 1987.

"Oh, he'd steal like mad": Tizol, oral-history interview. "All of us used to sell the songs": Williams, oral-history interview. A "factory": Brown, oral-history interview. "I don't consider you a composer": Ibid.

"A compiler of deeds and ideas": *A Duke Named Ellington*. "Perhaps even Barney would never have written down 'Mood Indigo'": Voce, "Clark Terry Talks to Steve Voce."

"So this guy says you and he wrote it": Bill Coss, "Ellington & Strayhorn, Inc.," *Down Beat*, June 7, 1962, in *Reader*, 503.

"That's the only thing I didn't like": Jones, *Jazz Talking*, 11.

CHAPTER SIX
"A HIGHER PLATEAU"

SOURCES

Documents
Lawrence Brown, oral-history interview, IJS; DE, unpublished interview with Carter Harman, 1964, EC; Steven Lasker, liner notes for *The Complete 1932–1940 Brunswick, Columbia and Master Recordings of Duke Ellington and His Famous Orchestra*, sound recording (Mosaic); *Memories of Duke*, film documentary (Time

Life); Irving Mills, oral-history interview, OHAM; *Radio Newsreel,* radio program, June 12, 1940 (Mutual); "Souvenir of Duke Ellington," sound recording (Oriole); Mark Tucker, liner notes for *Slide Trombone Featuring Lawrence Brown,* sound recording (Clef); *The World at Large: Paramount Pictorial No. 837,* film short (Paramount).

Books

Berrett, *Louis Armstrong and Paul Whiteman;* Bird, *Percy Grainger;* Bogle, *Bright Boulevards, Bold Dreams;* Cohen, *Duke Ellington's America;* Dance, *The World of Duke Ellington;* Dietrich, *Duke's 'Bones;* Ellington, *Duke Ellington in Person;* Enstice, *Jazz Spoken Here;* Feather, *The Encyclopedia of Jazz;* George, *Sweet Man;* Giddins, *A Pocketful of Dreams;* Howland, *Ellington Uptown;* Jewell, *Duke;* Jones, *Jazz Talking;* Parsonage, *The Evolution of Jazz in Britain;* Schuller, *Early Jazz;* Stewart, *Boy Meets Horn;* Stewart, *Jazz Masters of the Thirties;* Stratemann, *Duke Ellington Day by Day and Film by Film;* Ulanov, *Duke Ellington;* Vail, *Duke's Diary, Part One.*

NOTES

"The perfect balance": Schuller, 350. **"I tried desperately to try and sound like Fletcher Henderson":** *RIT,* 80.

"Sure, Jelly Roll Morton has talent": Feather, 233, 12. **"Probably he was jealous":** Jones, 7.

DE's "favorite musician": Jerry Wald, "Not on the Air: Radio Reminiscing with Duke Ellington," *New York Evening Graphic,* June 18, 1932. **"Paul Whiteman was known":** *MM,* 103. **"There is no doubt":** DE, "Duke Becomes a Critic!!," *Down Beat,* July 1939, in *Reader,* 139. **"Our band came along":** Howard Taubman, "The 'Duke' Invades Carnegie Hall," *The New York Times Magazine,* Jan. 17, 1943, in *Reader,* 159.

Whiteman's "symphonic jazz": For a concise summary of Whiteman's work and its influence, see my "King of the Jazz Age," *Commentary,* Dec. 2003. **Whiteman never said that he sought to "make a lady out of jazz":** Berrett, 217. The phrase nevertheless became permanently attached to Whiteman, and DE and BS alluded to it without irony in their libretto for *A Drum Is a Woman.*

"Gershwin's music, though grand": Richard Mack, "Duke Ellington—In Person," *Orchestra World,* May 1936, in *Reader,* 118. **"*Porgy and Bess,* those people":** DE, Harman interview, 1964. **"George Gershwin, without a doubt":** *Radio Newsreel.*

"At present he is at work": Florence Zunser, "'Opera Must Die,' Says Galli-Curci! Long Live the Blues!" *New York Evening Graphic Magazine,* Dec. 27,

1930, in *Reader,* 45. (This appears to be the first reference in print to what ultimately became *Black, Brown and Beige.*) **"The music of my race":** DE, "The Duke Steps Out," *Rhythm,* Mar. 1931, in *Reader,* 49–50 (emphasis by DE).

"Part of a larger work": "Music: Mood Indigo & Beyond," *Time,* Aug. 20, 1956. **"Irving Mills came to me one day":** *MM,* 82.

NBC's logbooks show that DE had recently broadcast three pieces: Ken Steiner, "Cotton Club Broadcasts on NBC," *DEMS Bulletin,* Dec. 2008–Mar. 2009.

The obvious model was *Rhapsody in Blue:* For a detailed discussion of Whiteman's "symphonic jazz" and its influence on DE, see Howland, 150–67. **A life-in-the-big-city music cue:** Though they bear no literal resemblance to *Creole Rhapsody,* Newman's main-title cue for the 1931 film version of Elmer Rice's *Street Scene* and Richard Rodgers's "Slaughter on Tenth Avenue" dance sequence from *On Your Toes* (1936) are very much in the same vein. **One of the Hollywood films that DE watched:** DE is known to have been impressed by certain early film scores (see, for instance, Frank Marshall Davis, "Duke Ellington, Who Goes to the Movies Between Shows, Wrote Song Hit 'Solitude,' Three Years Ago," *The Pittsburgh Courier,* Jan. 26, 1935). The extent to which his own music may have been influenced by these scores merits closer study.

DE showed no understanding of how to organize an extended composition: For a contrasting view, see Howland, 167–71.

"Duke Ellington: America's New Vogue": *Variety,* June 2, 1931. **"Wild and barbaric":** "Duke Ellington's 'Creole Rhapsody,'" *The Oklahoma Eagle,* Aug. 15, 1931. **Something new in jazz:** The only known precedent for *Creole Rhapsody* is James P. Johnson's *Yamekraw: A Negro Rhapsody,* a Gershwin-influenced twelve-minute-long piano solo that was published in 1927 and premiered by W.C. Handy at Carnegie Hall the following year in a version orchestrated by William Grant Still. It is not known whether Ellington attended that concert or was familiar with the published version of *Yamekraw,* though it seems likely that he would at least have been aware of it. A Vitaphone short based on *Yamekraw* was released in 1930, but after that the piece sank into obscurity and was not publicly performed again until 1962. **"*Creole Rhapsody* is the latest development":** *The Melody Maker,* July 1931.

"A General Study of the Manifold Nature of Music": Grainger's handwritten lecture notes for this series are part of the collection of Melbourne's Grainger Museum. He spoke on Ellington on Oct. 25, 1932. See Brian Allison, "Grainger Meets Duke Ellington," *Hoard House: News from the Grainger Museum,* July 2009. **"The three greatest composers":** Bird, 204. **"High emotional and technical qualities":** Allison, "Grainger Meets Duke Ellington."

"Four typewriters": "Tabloid's Furor Is Set to Music," *The New York Times,* Jan. 26, 1933. Also on the program were Johnny Green's *Night Club* and "Land of

Superstition," a movement from William Grant Still's *Africa* (Berrett, 175). **"When I first heard him":** *The World at Large.*

DE performed *Creole Rhapsody* as late as 1940: See "Ellington Concert Climaxes Home Coming Program Here," *Macon* (GA) *Telegraph and News,* July 7, 1940. **A list of favorite recordings:** *Down Beat,* Nov. 5, 1952, in *Reader,* 268.

A full-page ad: *Variety,* Jan. 28, 1932. The ad is reproduced in Stratemann, 46. **"Duke's A number one chargé d'affaires":** Stewart, *Boy Meets Horn,* 149, 148.

American record sales: "Phonograph Records," *Fortune,* Sept. 1939. **"RCA Victor Unloading Stars":** *Variety,* Mar. 25, 1931. **DE cut a half dozen sides for Victor in June:** He recorded as a freelancer for Victor the following February with a pair of New York sessions at which he cut two extended medleys of his compositions that were simultaneously recorded with two different microphone setups, thus making it possible for Brad Kay and Steven Lasker to synchronize the performances in 1984 and release both sides in "accidental stereo." (The medleys include "Mood Indigo," "Hot and Bothered," "Creole Love Call," "East St. Louis Toodle-Oo," "Lot o' Fingers," and "Black and Tan Fantasy.") These recordings, in which the 1932 Ellington band can be heard with unprecedented sonic clarity, were officially released for the first time in 1999 as part of *The Duke Ellington Centennial Edition: The Complete RCA Victor Recordings (1927–1973),* a limited-edition twenty-four-CD box set.

A mustachioed dandy: Ulanov, 169. **A "class attraction":** "Irving Mills Presents Duke Ellington and His Famous Orchestra," 1933 publicity manual (EC). **"Primitive rhythms!":** Ibid. **"When Duke bends over the piano":** Ibid.

A Christmas gift of $250: Ulanov, 125. **The readers of *The Pittsburgh Courier:*** Floyd G. Snelson, "Story of Duke Ellington's Rise to Kingship of Jazz Reads Like Fiction," *The Pittsburgh Courier,* Dec. 19, 1931. **$5,000 a week:** "Desperation Salaries: 80 'Name Acts,' $2K or More," *Variety,* Mar. 8, 1932. **"As fast as he got the money":** Mills, oral-history interview. **"When I got to high school":** Ellington, 51.

DE started making records for Brunswick: He did not, however, sign an exclusive contract with the label, for which he appears to have recorded strictly on a freelance basis until 1934 (Lasker, liner notes for *The Complete 1932–1940 Brunswick, Columbia and Master Recordings of Duke Ellington and His Famous Orchestra,* 4). **The band backed Bing Crosby:** Crosby and the Rhythm Boys, the trio with which he performed during his tenure with Whiteman, had previously been heard on Ellington's 1930 recording of "Three Little Words," and their singing can also be heard on the soundtrack of the performance of the song that is included in *Check and Double Check.* (Their vocal parts are "sung" on-screen by the members of the trumpet section.) **"The biggest thing, ever":** Giddins, 267. **"The *Boss of All Singers*":** Louis Armstrong, letter to unknown recipient, c. 1967 (Louis Armstrong Archive, Queens College). **"I'm proud to acknowledge my**

debt": Ken Murray, "Louis, Bix Had Most Influence on Der Bingle," *Down Beat,* July 14, 1950.

One of our first glimpses: A shorter version of this new arrangement was recorded eight days earlier, on Feb. 3, 1932, as part of Victor L-16006, the "accidental stereo" recording officially issued by RCA in 1999. **"A new arrangement":** *Memories of Duke.*

"What struck me": Hugues Panassié, *"Duke Ellington at the Salle Pleyel,"* in *Reader,* 84.

"When I joined his band": Paul Eduard Miller, "Ivie Joined the Duke for Twelve Weeks, Stays with Band for Twelve Years," *Down Beat,* July 15, 1942, in *Reader,* 459. **"Off stage our Miss Anderson was another person entirely":** Stewart, *Boy Meets Horn,* 177.

"Very staid": DE, Harman interview, 1964. **"I never knew you":** Brown, oral-history interview.

"Duke decided and they plotted": Bogle, 133. **"An exploiter of men":** Tucker, liner notes for *Slide Trombone Featuring Lawrence Brown.* The quote comes from an unpublished interview that Tucker conducted in 1985. **"As a soloist, his taste is impeccable":** *MM,* 122.

"I sat next to him": Quoted in Dietrich, 89. **"It was my own idea":** Dance, 119, 120. **"I can't play jazz":** Brown, oral-history interview.

"The one person": Spike Hughes, "Day by Day in New York," *The Melody Maker,* May 1933. **"A brilliant musician":** John Hammond, "Benny Moten Makes His Mark," *The Melody Maker,* May 1933.

"Your poppa likes": Ellington, 28.

DE did not allow Brown to play with the band: Brown, oral-history interview. **DE decided that thirteen was his lucky number:** Ned E. Williams, "Reminiscing in Tempo—Ned on Early Ellingtonia," *Down Beat,* Nov. 5, 1952. **DE opened a successful engagement at Chicago's Oriental Theatre on Feb. 13, 1931:** He returned to the Oriental a month later, on Mar. 13, 1931, which also fell on a Friday (Ken Steiner, personal communication).

"When I was eight": Boyer, "The Hot Bach," 237. **He happened to be wearing a brown suit:** Ellington, 154. **"Once someone gave him a sweater":** George, 68. **He threw away any garment with a loose button:** Stewart, *Jazz Masters of the Thirties,* 85–86. **"Walk away from him":** Ellington, 154. **People who whistled or ate peanuts backstage:** Ellington, 153.

DE would walk out of a room whenever the subject of death came up: George, 68.

"Speaking of the Duke": John Hammond, "Meet John Hammond! Our New American Correspondent," *The Melody Maker,* Feb. 1932. **"The syndicate that ran [the Cotton Club]":** Ellington, 41.

"At first I was happy": Boyer, "The Hot Bach," 242.

Sailing across the Atlantic appalled DE: Ibid., 243. **Judicious doses of champagne and brandy:** DE, "Jazz as I Have Seen It," *Swing,* Sept. 1940.

"I much regret": Joe Crossman, "What I Think of Armstrong," *The Melody Maker,* Oct. 1932; Parsonage, 239. **"It is not a 'show' band":** Spike Hughes, "Meet the Duke!" *Daily Herald,* June 13, 1933.

DE's sidemen were forced to settle: Ulanov, 134. **"Original Snake-Hips Girl":** Dudley's billing is given on the poster for the concert, reproduced in Vail, 81.

Pictures shot on the stage of the Palladium: They are reproduced in Stratemann, 67. **"Like a high priest":** Ellington, 66. **"This was a night that scared the devil":** DE, "Duke Tells Of 10 Top Thrills In 25 Years," *Down Beat,* Nov. 5, 1952.

"Ellington was always composed": *Rhythm,* July 1933; George, 125. **"A Harlem Dionysus":** Quoted in Ulanov, 142. **"He does at once":** "The Palladium: Mr. Duke Ellington and His Orchestra," *The Times* (London), n.d.; clipping, EC.

"It literally lifts one out of one's seat": "The Duke at the Palladium," *The Melody Maker,* June 17, 1933. (This review, credited to a "special correspondent," may have been written by Spike Hughes.) **"Probably the first composer of real character":** Constant Lambert, "Matter Musical: The Art of Duke Ellington," *Sunday Referee,* June 25, 1933.

"Is Duke Ellington losing faith": "Mike's Report," *The Melody Maker,* July 1, 1933. ("Mike" was Hughes's pseudonym.) **"The Hot Dictator":** DE, "Jazz as I Have Seen It." **DE played all the pieces Hughes mentioned:** A program of the second concert, given on July 23, is reproduced in *DEMS Bulletin,* Oct.–Nov. 1997. It lists fifty pieces, all but eleven of them by DE, from which the numbers performed that day were chosen. The originals were a representative cross section of DE's work up to that time, ranging from "Black and Tan Fantasy" to "Sophisticated Lady" and including *Creole Rhapsody.* The other numbers were all identified with jazz, including "Bugle Call Rag," "St. Louis Blues," "Tiger Rag," Lawrence Brown's features on "Rose Room" and "The Sheik of Araby," and Hughes's "Sirocco." **Program notes:** Ibid.

"Windsor can play good drums": DE, "Jazz as I Have Seen It." **DE made a point of meeting with Constant Lambert:** A relic of their meeting survives, a page torn out of an autograph album on which the two men's signatures are preceded by the motto "Don't mean thing / Ain't got Swing" in Ellington's handwriting. This item was offered for sale by James Pepper Rare Books, Inc., of Santa Barbara, California, in 2012. (It is now in private hands.) **"He gives the same distinction":** Constant Lambert, "Gramophone Notes," *New Statesman and Nation,* Aug. 1, 1931. **DE had**

never heard any of Delius's music: *MM,* 470. "When Ellington and his orchestra played before Percy Grainger's music classes at New York University, Mr. Grainger drew some casual comparisons with the music of Bach and Delius. 'I'll have to find out about this Delius,' said Mr. Ellington" ("Introducing Duke Ellington," *Fortune,* Aug. 1933). DE's friend Edmund Anderson claimed to have introduced him to the music of Delius, Debussy, and Ravel in a series of listening sessions that took place around 1936: "He laughed at the idea that he was supposed to be like Delius, but he *loved* that music" (Jewell, 52). **"There was one English composer":** Enstice, 188.

"Just as soon as possible": "Souvenir of Duke Ellington."

"Duke directed his orchestra": Hughes Panassié, "Duke Ellington at the Salle Pleyel," in *Reader,* 84. **"Duke never shows the slightest sign of life":** *The Melody Maker,* Aug. 12 and 19, 1933, in *RIT,* 146, 147–48.

"Some society woman": DE, Harman interview, 1964. **Mercer thought it to be apocryphal:** Ellington, 61.

"Pianist Percy Grainger": "Hot Ambassador," *Time,* June 12, 1933.

"Ellington has never compromised": "Introducing Duke Ellington," *Fortune,* Aug. 1933.

"The atmosphere in Europe": *MM,* 85. **"The main thing I got":** DE, "Jazz as I Have Seen It." **"If they think I'm *that* important":** Ulanov, 151. In Ulanov's book, this remark is presented as part of a single quotation attributed to DE that begins with a slightly different version of the preceding two sentences from DE's 1940 article for *Swing,* thus indicating that some of Ulanov's "quotations" derived from previously published sources. (Ulanov had access to DE's scrapbooks.)

"Europe is a very different world": Ibid., 217. A slightly different version of this quotation also appears in "The Hot Bach" (244), attributed to Rex Stewart, not DE. I thank Brian Priestley for pointing out the discrepancy. **"You know, I love this place":** Max Jones, quoted in Cohen, 247.

CHAPTER SEVEN
"THE WAY THE PRESIDENT TRAVELS"

SOURCES

Documents
Barney Bigard, oral-history interview, IJS; Lawrence Brown, oral-history interview, IJS; Helen Oakley Dance, oral-history interview, OHAM; DE, *The Great Concerts: Cornell University 1948,* sound recording (Nimbus); DE, unpublished interviews

with Carter Harman, 1956, EC; Sonny Greer, oral-history interview, IJS; Herb Jeffries, oral-history interview, EC; Steven Lasker, liner notes for *The Complete 1932– 1940 Brunswick, Columbia and Master Recordings of Duke Ellington and His Famous Orchestra,* sound recording (Mosaic); Irving Mills, oral-history interview, OHAM; *Radio Newsreel,* radio program, June 12, 1940 (Mutual); "Souvenir of Duke Ellington," sound recording (Oriole).

Books

Berger, *Bassically Speaking;* Bigard, *With Louis and the Duke;* Stanley Dance, *The World of Duke Ellington;* Ellington, *Duke Ellington in Person;* Ellison, *Living with Music;* Feather, *The Jazz Years;* Ferguson, *The Otis Ferguson Reader;* Hammond, *John Hammond on Record;* Howland, *Ellington Uptown;* Jewell, *Duke;* Kelley, *Thelonious Monk;* Lambert, *Music Ho!;* Lawrence, *Duke Ellington and His World;* Prial, *The Producer;* Schuller, *The Swing Era;* Stewart, *Boy Meets Horn;* Sudhalter, *Bix;* Ulanov, *Duke Ellington;* Wilson, *The Thirties.*

NOTES

Most newspapers would not print a photo of a black man: Ulanov, 153–54. **"Something of an African Stravinsky:** "Higher Development of Jazz Expounded by Duke Ellington," *Dallas News,* Oct. 1, 1933.

"And then Ellington and the great orchestra came to town": Ellison, 81.

"The talk of the city": Omar La Grange, "Texas Town Still Raves Over Duke Ellington," *The Pittsburgh Courier,* Dec. 2, 1933. **"Carrying more than $30,000":** "America's Highest Paid and Most Glamorous Band, Led by the Inimitable 'Duke,' Coming Here for Monster Coronation," *The Pittsburgh Courier,* Jan. 7, 1933.

"Everywhere we went in the South": *MM,* 85–86.

"Cheaper than room rent": DE, Harman interview, 1956. **The band traveled heavy:** Stewart, 149.

"Mental isolation": Boyer, "The Hot Bach," 228. **"Seeing him in a [railroad] siding":** Jewell, 57. **"Especially in the South":** Boyer, "The Hot Bach," 218.

"He would take an ordinary situation": Bigard, *With Louis and the Duke,* 62–63. **"All caught up in the rhythm":** Jewell, 56.

"Many observers would say": *MM,* 86. **"We've never let ourselves be put":** Nat Hentoff, "This Cat Needs No Pulitzer Prize," *The New York Times Magazine,* Sept. 12, 1965, in *Reader,* 367. **"The average one of them crackers":** Greer, oral-history interview. **"I think it was in Alabama":** Bigard, oral-history interview. **"It was a**

real rough town": Bigard, *With Louis and the Duke,* 69. **"Being a woman, naturally"**: Jeffries, oral-history interview.

"If you'd been a white man": Boyer, "The Hot Bach," 232.

The first English-language book: Hugues Panassié's *Le jazz hot,* in which DE also figures prominently, was published in France around the same time as *Music Ho!* It was not translated into English, however, until 1936. **"A real composer"**: Lambert, 187–88.

"Hot damn!": Gama Gilbert, " 'Hot Damn!' Says Ellington When Ranked with Bach," *The Philadelphia Inquirer,* May 17, 1935, in *Reader,* 113. **"May be something to it"**: Boyer, "The Hot Bach," 236. **"If you take a beautiful flower"**: Humphrey Lyttleton, "Critic v. Musician," *Just Jazz 3,* 36.

"Self-taught musically": "Hollywood Calls the Duke Ellington Rehearsals Hot," *The Chicago Defender,* May 12, 1934.

"A touching, highly atmospheric, ambitious quasi-documentary": Schuller, 72, 73.

DE told Percy Brooks: "Souvenir of Duke Ellington." Late in life DE recalled the incident inaccurately, claiming that Flo had called the song "Rude Interlude" and adding that "I guess that had something to do with my American accent!" (*MM,* 84). This version is correct. **"When I heard the record"**: Stewart, 146. **"A beautiful mood piece"**: Ibid. **"Harmonically, like even the best"**: "Mike," "The Record with a Story," *The Melody Maker,* Jan. 27, 1934. **"Contained new departures"**: Doron Antrim, "After Jazz—What? Is American Music Stymied or Are We Going Somewhere?," *Metronome,* Dec. 1933.

"We had arrived in a Chicago recording studio": *MM,* 87. Helen Oakley, who was present in the studio, confirmed the accuracy of this account (Helen Oakley Dance, oral-history interview).

"Such taboos as that you can't use parallel octaves": Stanley Dance, *The World of Duke Ellington,* 37.

"Didn't sound like Louis": Sudhalter, 185.

"To be absolutely truthful": Stewart, 146. **"Rex Stewart had been taught"**: *MM,* 125.

"I can see them now": Stewart, 171.

"I remember Ivie Anderson": Berger, 75.

"We didn't speak to each other": Stewart, 193. **"I don't think Cootie Williams ever forgave Duke"**: Michael P. Zirpolo, "In Duke's Head," *IAJRC Journal* (Summer 2000). **"Word is making the rounds"**: Quoted in Ulanov, 163.

Mills tried to cut Braud's pay: "Inside Stuff—Music," *Variety,* Feb. 12, 1935. For another version of this widely reported story, see Charles Isaac Bowen, "On the Air," *The Baltimore Afro-American,* Feb. 23, 1935. (Braud's name is misspelled "Welden Graud" in this article.) **Hayes Alvis played alongside Taylor until 1938:** He was briefly followed by another bassist, Adolphus Alsbrook, who never recorded with DE. For more about Alsbrook, see "Another Little Known Ellingtonian," *DEMS Bulletin,* Apr.–July 2003, and Kelley, 433–34.

"Two chicks, one on each side of me": DE, radio interview with Jack Cullen, CKNW, Vancouver, Canada, Oct. 30, 1962, in *Reader,* 341. For a discussion of the provenance of "In a Sentimental Mood," see Lasker, liner notes for *The Complete 1932–1940 Brunswick, Columbia and Master Recordings of Duke Ellington and His Famous Orchestra,* 18, 33. **"Hardly any of the old time Ellington sincerity":** Quoted in Prial, 76.

"A community effort": Lasker, *The Complete 1932–1940 Brunswick, Columbia and Master Recordings of Duke Ellington and His Famous Orchestra,* 33.

"Saddest tale told on land and sea": Billie Holiday sings the couplet in the version of "Saddest Tale" heard on the soundtrack of *Symphony in Black.* The song appears to have been dropped from the band's repertoire shortly thereafter, perhaps because it reminded DE of Daisy's final illness. **DE sent three thousand flowers to Daisy's funeral:** "Mother of Ellington Is Buried Here," *Washington Tribune,* June 1, 1935.

"His world had been built": Ellington, 68–69.

"I simplified most all the tunes": Mills, oral-history interview.

"Every page of that particular manuscript": *MM,* 86 (ellipses in the original).

"He always wrote what he felt": Ellington, 164. **"*Reminiscing in Tempo* was written originally":** DE, *The Great Concerts: Cornell University 1948.*

"It isn't, as one might suspect": *The New Yorker,* undated clipping (IJS). **"A long, rambling monstrosity":** Spike Hughes (as "Mike"), "Ellington on the Spot," *The Melody Maker,* Dec. 14, 1935. **"Whatever your musical opinion":** *RIT,* 177. **"One of Ellington's greatest master strokes":** Schuller, 83. **"Formal control":** Ibid., 76. **"Such other heady harmonists":** Ibid., 82. **"One of the best pieces he ever wrote":** Max Harrison, "Some Reflections on Ellington's Longer Works," in *Reader,* 389. **"*Reminiscing in Tempo* was, at least *in potentia*":** Ibid., 391.

The manuscript reveals: For a detailed description and analysis of the surviving manuscript material for *Reminiscing in Tempo,* which is on deposit in EC, see Howland, 171–72. **DE wrote it to fill up the other side:** Ralph Burns did the same thing when Woody Herman recorded his four-part *Summer Sequence* in

1946, writing an extra "movement" (which he then used as the basis for a popular ballad called "Early Autumn") to fill out the last side of the original two-disc set.

"Practically every night": Lawrence, 249. According to Lawrence, Sonny Greer and Cootie Williams confirmed Brown's recollection.

"Duke assured me": Feather, 62. **DE's reply was unhesitating:** *Radio Newsreel.*

"Somebody who had modeled himself on Proust": Wilson, 163. **"John won't compromise":** Ferguson, 99.

"Problems": Hammond, 133. **DE "lost contact with his origins":** Ibid., 137. **"John likes to play the boss man":** Chris Albertson, personal communication.

"Our type of music": Eric Townley, "Reminiscing with Cootie," *Storyville,* June–July 1977. **"The real trouble with Duke's music":** John Hammond, "The Tragedy of Duke Ellington, the 'Black Prince' of Jazz," *Down Beat,* Nov. 1, 1935, in *Reader,* 120.

"The seamier side of existence": Ibid., 119.

"An artiness which pervades all of [Ellington's] writing today": Ulanov, 171–72.

CHAPTER EIGHT
"SWING IS STAGNANT"

SOURCES

Documents
Edmund Anderson, oral-history interview, OHAM; *Artie Shaw: The Centennial Collection,* sound recording (RCA); Barney Bigard, oral-history interview, IJS; Lawrence Brown, oral-history interview, IJS; Helen Oakley Dance, liner notes for *The Duke's Men: Small Groups,* vol. 1, sound recording (Columbia); Helen Oakley Dance, liner notes for *The Duke's Men: Small Groups,* vol. 2, sound recording (Columbia); Helen Oakley Dance, oral-history interview, OHAM; DE, unpublished interviews with Carter Harman, 1956 and 1964, EC; Mercer Ellington, oral-history interview, EC; Phoebe Jacobs, oral-history interview conducted by researchers for Ken Burns's *Jazz* (transcript available online at www.pbs.org /jazz/about/pdfs/Jacobs.pdf); Steven Lasker, liner notes for *The Complete 1932– 1940 Brunswick, Columbia and Master Recordings of Duke Ellington and His Famous Orchestra,* sound recording (Mosaic); Steven Lasker, liner notes for *Duke Ellington: The Complete 1936–1940 Variety, Vocalion and OKeh Small Group Sessions* (Mosaic); *Record Making with Duke Ellington and His Orchestra,* film short

(Paramount); Joya Sherrill, oral-history interview, OHAM; "Souvenir of Duke Ellington," sound recording (Oriole); Juan Tizol, oral-history interview, IJS.

Books

Agate, *A Shorter Ego;* Balliett, *Collected Works;* Bigard, *With Louis and the Duke;* Cohen, *Duke Ellington's America;* Stanley Dance, *Johnny Hodges;* Stanley Dance, *The World of Duke Ellington;* Davis, *Outcats;* Ellington, *Duke Ellington in Person;* George, *Sweet Man;* Malcolm X, *Autobiography;* Noss, *Paul Hindemith in the United States;* Schuller, *The Swing Era;* Simon, *Simon Says;* Stewart, *Boy Meets Horn;* Stewart, *Jazz Masters of the Thirties;* Stratemann, *Duke Ellington Day by Day and Film by Film;* Terry, *Terry;* Ulanov, *Duke Ellington;* Vail, *Duke's Diary, Part One;* Wilson, *Meet Me at the Theresa.*

NOTES

"If you never read anything": George, 150. **"Bands who fail to impress [college students] noticeably"**: "College Rhythm," *Variety,* Jan. 29, 1936, quoted in Stratemann, 132. **The top white bands made twice as much money:** R.L. Larkin, "Are Colored Bands Doomed as Big Money Makers?," *Down Beat,* Dec. 1, 1940.

"In the late 1930s": Michael P. Zirpolo, "In Duke's Head," *IARJC Journal* (Summer 2000). **The first time that the term** *concerto* **was publicly used by a jazz composer:** James P. Johnson's *Jazz-a-Mine* concerto dates from 1934, but it was not premiered until years later, and there is no reason to suppose that DE knew of it. **"I'm more of a primitive artist"**: Simon, 36. **"Duke got his name on the label"**: Eric Townley, "Reminiscing with Cootie," *Storyville,* June–July 1977. (DE may have had another unacknowledged collaborator on "Echoes of Harlem," whose second strain is identical to the main theme of "Blue Mood," a 1932 composition jointly credited to him and Johnny Hodges.)

DE recommended Helen Oakley to Irving Mills: Stanley Dance, *Johnny Hodges,* 41.

"Nothing was ever planned": Helen Oakley Dance, liner notes for *The Duke's Men: Small Groups,* vol. 1. **"Most of the small group recordings were rehearsed"**: Townley, "Reminiscing with Cootie," **"An absolute song factory"**: Helen Oakley Dance, oral-history interview. **"Come out of the kitchen"**: Stanley Dance, *Johnny Hodges,* 44. **"On these small band originals"**: Helen Oakley Dance, liner notes for *The Duke's Men: Small Groups,* vol. 2.

Tizol sold his interest in "Caravan" to Irving Mills: Tizol, oral-history interview.

"Doggy tunes": Helen Oakley Dance, oral-history interview. **"Corner after corner"**: Helen Oakley Dance, oral-history interview.

"The synopsis revolves around an unknown orchestra": *The Chicago Defender*, Nov. 28, 1936; clipping, EC. "50 SEPIAN STARS": Variations on this slogan were used in newspaper ads and can also be seen on contemporary photographs of the club's marquee (Vail, 131).

"This is the place to hear swing music": Agate, 163–64.

"There is not much": Paul Hindemith, journal entry, Apr. 17, 1937, in Noss, 25.

Many more such "air checks" would be made: Many of DE's surviving air checks from the thirties have been collected on *Duke Ellington at the Cotton Club* (Storyville). "When you're playing in a recording studio": Interview with Artie Shaw, released on *Artie Shaw: The Centennial Collection*.

The stage lighting that set them off: Jack Boyd, the band's longtime road manager, also designed its onstage lighting plots. For more about him, see Boyer, "The Hot Bach," and "Boyd Has Traveled a Million Miles with Duke," *Orchestra World*, Jan. 1943. "Dress rehearsal revealed": Stewart, *Jazz Masters*, 91. "The unforgettable, show-stopping ensemble": Ibid., 84–85.

DE wore a corset: Ibid., 52. "He's a genius, all right": Boyer, "The Hot Bach," 215. Some of his best-remembered quirks: See Boyer, "The Hot Bach," 215, and George, 24–25. "After a while": Balliett, 429.

"Duke, who is always worrying": Boyer, "The Hot Bach," 224.

"Kinky woolly hair": Wilson, 89. "We were against kinky hair": Ibid., 88.

"Self-degradation": Malcolm X, 57.

"This is an express train": *Record Making with Duke Ellington and His Orchestra*.

Diminuendo and Crescendo in Blue: For a discussion of the history of this piece, see Eddie Lambert, "Duke's *Diminuendo and Crescendo in Blue*," *DEMS Bulletin*, Dec. 2004–Mar. 2005. Both sides of a ten-inch 78: Although *Diminuendo and Crescendo in Blue* is a single two-part composition, the original 78 release did not make this fact clear, separately identifying the two sides of the record as "Diminuendo in Blue" and "Crescendo in Blue," and Ellington did not always take care in early interviews to explain his intentions. Only the consecutive matrix numbers, M 648 and 649, indicated that the two parts of the piece were meant to be played in sequence. Some commentators, most notably Max Harrison and Brian Priestley, have speculated that DE may have originally meant for the two sections to be played in the opposite order, with "Crescendo in Blue" coming first, but there is no evidence that he had such a thing in mind, nor is he known ever to have performed the work in that way. "Like all of our compositions": DE, "Duke Ellington Tells the Secrets of His Success," *The Chicago Defender*, Oct. 2, 1937.

"A call was put in for extra policemen": Al Brackman, "25,000 American Swing Fans Go Crazy to Music of Duke and Other Jazz Aces," *The Melody Maker*,

June 11, 1938. **"Nothing more or less"**: Paul Edward Miller, "Idolized Composers Find It Hard Not to 'Kid' The Public: The Duke's Latest Opus Is Inferior Stuff with a Fancy Title," *Down Beat,* Dec. 1937. **"The master of them all"**: Aaron Copland, "Scores and Records," *Modern Music,* Jan.–Feb. 1938, in *Reader,* 130.

"Social secretary": DE, Harman interview, 1956. **"A $5,000 casket"**: "Duke Buries Father in $5,000 Coffin," *The Baltimore Afro-American,* Nov. 6, 1937.

Barry Ulanov claimed as much: Ulanov, 201. **"For the most part"**: Mercer Ellington, oral-history interview.

"The DUKE is still KING!": Unidentified clipping, n.d., in Vail, 143. **Lawrence Brown claimed to have written "Blue Light"**: Lasker, liner notes for *Duke Ellington: The Complete 1936–1940 Variety, Vocalion and OKeh Small Group Sessions.* "Transblucency (A Blue Fog You Can Almost See Through)," recorded in 1946 and jointly credited to both men, is based in part on Brown's trombone solo on "Blue Light."

"Sumptuously velvety": Schuller, 94.

The main theme of "I Let a Song Go Out of My Heart" is based on a Hodges riff: According to Rex Stewart, Hodges played this riff over the harmonies of "Once in a While" (*Boy Meets Horn,* 190). Henry Nemo wrote the lyric to the vocal version. DE later reused the song's chord changes in "Never No Lament," recorded in 1940, which became a popular hit under the title "Don't Get Around Much Anymore" when a new lyric by Bob Russell was added two years later. **"Skilled tickler of the ivories"**: Jack Gould, "Night Club Notes," *The New York Times,* Mar. 13, 1938.

"Spot has the same $1.50–$2 table d'hote dinner policy": *Variety,* n.d., in Vail, 149. **"We worked clean through the Depression without ever knowing there was one"**: Bigard, *With Louis and the Duke,* 52. **DE's record sales were sagging**: Ulanov, 197. **"Now he was not only broke"**: Ellington, 70.

"The 'TOO-sies'": Roger Ringo, "Reminiscing in Tempo with Freddie Jenkins," *Storyville,* Apr.–May 1973. **"Not only am I losing one of my best musicians"**: Billy Howe, "Whetsol [*sic*] Is Forced to Leave Duke," *The Pittsburgh Courier,* Mar. 3, 1938. (Whetsel died in 1940.) **"That was what drove him into becoming a funeral director"**: Ellington, 23. **"Swing is stagnant"**: Peter Bellamy, "Duke Ellington Says 'Swing Has No Future,'" *Cleveland News,* Oct. 8, 1938.

DE started telling journalists that he had finished writing an opera: See, for example, "Ellington Completes Negro Opera at Bedside," *Down Beat,* Oct. 2, 1938.

"I don't drink any more": *MM,* 75. **DE would drink endless Coca-Colas**: Sherrill, oral-history interview. This habit continued to the end of his life. When

DE went to the Soviet Union in 1971, the US embassy in Moscow agreed to supply him with fifteen cases of Coca-Cola for his exclusive use during the tour (Harvey G. Cohen, "Visions of Freedom: Duke Ellington in the Soviet Union," *Popular Music,* Sept. 2011).

It was around this time that DE left Mildred Dixon: Sources vary widely as to the date of the breakup, but it cannot have been earlier than Jan. 23, 1939, the date when DE is known to have brought BS to his New York apartment to live with Mercer and Ruth Ellington, since he never returned to 381 Edgecombe after he moved out. **"I didn't know if she was colored or white":** Terry, 122. **"Typical of many attractive black women":** Davis, 58.

Opinions vary on when she met DE: See Jacobs, oral-history interview, and George, 137. **"Mildred had heard about a girl":** Ulanov, 208.

Mildred was still living at 381 Edgecombe: Floyd G. Snelson, "Harlem," *The New York Age,* Jan. 25, 1941. **She was still there as late as 1950:** "Ellington's Tempo Music Reactivated," *Billboard,* Aug. 12, 1950.

Evie was linked to DE in the black press: "The oomph girl, Bea Ellis, is quietly lolling in her 'Sugar Hill' love-nest and will join her heartbeat, Duke Ellington, next week, when he opens his engagement at the Hotel Sherman, in Chicago" (Floyd G. Snelson, "Harlem," *The New York Age,* Aug. 24, 1940). **DE introduced Evie to friends as "Mrs. Ellington":** "He called her Evie, and often introduced her in my presence as Mrs. Ellington" (Irving Townsend, "Ellington in Private," *The Atlantic Monthly,* May 1975). **"Bea Ellis and Edward K. Ellington":** Ellington, 77. **DE paid off gossip columnists:** Ibid.

"She felt very exploited": Davis, 59. **"Evie was very much obsessed":** Ellington, 78.

"Ladies and gentlemen": George, 59. **"Everyone has to dig a little distortion":** Ibid., 51.

"An exciting woman": DE, "The Most Exciting Women I've Known," *Ebony,* Apr. 1952. **"He had a basic contempt for women":** Ellington, 128. **"A lot of men who are womanizers":** George, 109. **"I do not wish to disenchant you":** Gordon Parks, "Jazz," *Esquire,* Dec. 1975.

"You grow up, you find": DE, Harman interview, 1964. **"Women who cry and women who laugh":** DE, *Man with Four Sides* (typescript, Stanley Dance collection, Yale University).

"Duke's only concern": George, 94. **"He didn't want a role":** Ibid., 147–48.

A four-part series: Although these pieces accurately represented Ellington's sentiments, they were, like most of the other articles that he published in the thirties and forties, ghosted by Helen Oakley, who later recalled that "I was so used to him and the way he talked and everything that when I'd write up his little pieces, they sounded like Duke" (Helen Oakley Dance, oral-history interview). **"Adolescent"**: DE, "Duke Says Swing Is Stagnant," *Down Beat*, Feb. 1939, in *Reader*, 133–34.

A sideswipe that DE was forced to retract in print: "It was my intention to merely infer that the political affiliations of Mr. Hammond bordered on the 'left wing.' The impression conveyed that he is in any way associated with the Communist party was both accidental and erroneous" (DE, "Ellington Corrects a Statement Re Hammond," *Down Beat*, May 1939). The text of DE's letter suggests that it was written under the threat of litigation. Hammond wrote for and had close ties to the Communist-controlled *New Masses*, but a 1935 visit to the Soviet Union had disabused him of any lingering illusions about Stalin and Stalinism, and the FBI, which opened a file on Hammond six years later, eventually concluded that "there is no information indicating that he is a member of the Communist Party." **"He apparently has consistently identified himself"**: DE, "Situation Between the Critics and Musicians Is Laughable—Ellington," *Down Beat*, Apr. 1939, in *Reader*, 137. **"He has identified himself"**: DE, "Duke Concludes Criticism of the Critics," *Down Beat*, May 1939, in *Reader*, 137.

"[A] band with an amazing amount of color": DE, "Duke Becomes a Critic!!," *Down Beat*, July 1939, in *Reader*, 139. **"His practice of offering his own renditions"**: Ibid.

"Frightening to see": Stewart, *Boy Meets Horn*, 187. **"Severed their long business association"**: "Irving Mills and Duke Ellington Sever Association," *The Melody Maker*, May 6, 1939, in *Reader*, 141. **Details of the professional divorce**: For a discussion of the break and its aftermath, see Lasker, liner notes for *Duke Ellington: The Complete 1936–1940 Variety, Vocalion and OKeh Small Group Sessions*, 16.

"Because [he] sensed": Irving Mills, "Irving Mills: 'I Split with Duke When Music Began Sidetracking,'" *Down Beat*, Nov. 5, 1952, in *Reader*, 275. **"Irving Mills decided in '38"**: DE, Harman interview, 1964. **"Duke started getting disenchanted"**: Michael P. Zirpolo, "In Duke's Head," *IAJRC Journal* (Summer 2000).

"Lack of attention": Ulanov, 206. **"Duke Ellington sat down at the table"**: Ibid., 207. **"The most expensive casket made"**: *RIT*, 207–8. Udkoff may have been confusing J.E.'s casket with that of Daisy, which was reported as having cost $3,500.

"The Duke has been exploited": John Hammond, "The Tragedy of Duke Ellington, the 'Black Prince' of Jazz," *Down Beat*, Nov. 1, 1935, in *Reader*, 119. **"A musical sharecropper"**: Adam Clayton Powell, Jr., "Soap Box: My Grandfather's Branded, Our Musicians Are Slaves, Owned Body and Soul, Work for Massa Mills," *New York Amsterdam News*, Nov. 21, 1936. **"He has EARNED**

something like $2,000,000": Quoted in Ulanov, 206. **"An unfounded and unwarranted libel"**: "Ned E. Williams Replies to Criticism of Irving Mills by Rev. A.C. Powell, Jr.," *The New York Age*, Dec. 5, 1936.

Only one of the thirty-three paragraphs: Abel Green, "Mills Music's 40-Year Success Story; From 5G & 3 Songs to $5,000,000 Empire," *Variety*, Oct. 28, 1959. **"We dissolved our business relationship agreeably"**: *MM*, 89.

He instructed his publicists and road managers: Helen Oakley Dance and Al Celley both testified to this precaution (Cohen, 168). **"I don't eat with niggers"**: Ibid., 161. (This story was told to Cohen by George Avakian.)

DE switched managers to bolster his prestige: For a detailed account of the switch, see Cohen, 168–71. **"Duke was very respectful"**: Anderson, oral-history interview. **"John Hammond . . . was supervising"**: "Leonard Feather Rebuts Hammond," *Jazz*, May 1943, in *Reader*, 174.

"Anybody that John couldn't push around": Helen Oakley Dance, oral-history interview. (Stanley Dance, Helen's husband, was present at and took part in the interview, and it was he, not Helen, who made this statement.) **DE returned to Victor**: For a discussion of the switch, see Lasker, liner notes for *Duke Ellington: The Complete 1936–1940 Variety, Vocalion and OKeh Small Group Sessions*, 20. As was his wont, Hammond neither forgave nor forgot. In addition to writing a vicious review of *Black, Brown and Beige*, he tried in 1942 to persuade Johnny Hodges to leave Ellington and become a member of a racially integrated house band that Hammond was putting together for CBS (Leonard G. Feather, "Hodges Refuses Scott Offer; He's Accused of Sabotage!" *Orchestra World*, Sept. 1942).

"After our very successful European jaunt": Stewart, *Boy Meets Horn*, 189. **"That Ellington's is the most unappreciated band"**: Review of "Serenade to Sweden" and "The Sergeant Was Shy," *Down Beat*, Dec. 1, 1939.

CHAPTER NINE
"THE EYES IN THE BACK OF MY HEAD"

SOURCES

Documents
Lawrence Brown, oral-history interview, IJS; DE, unpublished interview with Carter Harman, 1964, EC; Mercer Ellington, oral-history interview, EC; Ruth Ellington, oral-history interview, EC; Sonny Greer, oral-history interview, IJS; *Jazz 625*, TV program, Feb. 20, 1964 (BBC); Steven Lasker, liner notes for *The Complete 1932–1940 Brunswick, Columbia and Master Recordings of Duke*

Ellington and His Famous Orchestra, sound recording (Mosaic); Steven Lasker, liner notes for *Duke Ellington: The Complete 1936–1940 Variety, Vocalion and OKeh Small Group Sessions* (Mosaic); BS, public interview, Duke Ellington Society, New York, Mar. 1962; Juan Tizol, oral-history interview, IJS.

Books

Bigard, *With Louis and the Duke;* Cohen, *Duke Ellington's America;* Collier, *Duke Ellington;* Dance, *The World of Duke Ellington;* Ellington, *Duke Ellington in Person;* George, *Sweet Man;* Hajdu, *Lush Life;* Jewell, *Duke;* Schuller, *The Swing Era;* Stewart, *Boy Meets Horn;* Traill, *Just Jazz 3;* Ulanov, *Duke Ellington;* van de Leur, *Something to Live For.*

NOTES

The first feature-length story about BS: Leonard Feather, "Billy Strayhorn—The Young Duke," *Jazz,* Jan. 1943. **BS's name appeared only once in the *Reader's Guide:*** Hajdu, xi.

"A small, slightly burned, whole-wheat-toast owl": George, 80. **"Swee' Pea":** Dance, 61. **He was also referred to as "Weely":** "Weely" is the title of the chapter in Ulanov that is devoted to BS. **"Aide-de-camp":** Dance, 27. **BS's "assimilation of Ellington's mannerisms":** The program for the Carnegie Hall concert is reproduced in *The Duke Ellington Reader* (163). **"So great a similarity":** Ulanov, 223. **"A Duke Jr. of sorts":** Quoted in van de Leur, xvii.

"The whodunit game": BS, "Billy Strayhorn: 'The Ellington Effect,' " *Down Beat,* Nov. 5, 1952, in *Reader,* 270. **"Strayhorn's role in the Ellington canon":** Schuller, 136. **It was common for "experts" to credit DE with pieces that BS had written:** Eddie Lambert's *Duke Ellington: A Listener's Guide* makes this mistake regularly. **"A certain effeteness":** Schuller, 136. **"Lushness, prettiness":** Collier, 272–73. **"The genius, the power behind the throne":** Brown, oral-history interview.

"From the moment I first heard 'Chelsea Bridge' ": Hajdu, 87. **"I'd like to really know":** Quincy Jones, review of *Newport 1958, Jazz Review,* May 1959, in *Reader,* 312. **To this day he fails to receive his scholarly due:** BS is not mentioned at all, for example, in the Ellington chapter of Alyn Shipton's *New History of Jazz.*

"My playing and writing style": BS, "Billy Strayhorn: 'The Ellington Effect' "; *Reader,* 270. **"He is he and I am me":** John S. Wilson, "Billy Strayhorn: Alter Ego for the Duke," *The New York Times,* June 6, 1965. **"One of the most important people":** *Jazz 625.*

"**Billy sits in the control room**": Ulanov, 235. **DE's "favorite human being"**: *MM*, 159. **"He was my listener"**: Ibid., 156.

That came in 1981: George, 78–80. This is the first time that BS's homosexuality was explicitly mentioned in print.

"I started to study": Traill, 43.

"Something changed when I saw him on stage": BS, 1962 interview. **"He had a chord"**: Quoted in van de Leur, 19. *Fantastic Rhythm:* One of the songs from the show, "My Little Brown Book," became part of DE's working repertoire, while another one, "Let Nature Take Its Course," was later adapted for inclusion in the Ellington-Strayhorn musical *Beggar's Holiday* (1946).

"It's a song most persons have to listen to twice": "New Hit, 'Lush Life,' Is Not New," *Down Beat*, Aug. 12, 1949.

"Everything he did made musical sense": Traill, 43. **"I had given no real serious thought"**: Ibid.

BS played and sang "Lush Life" and "Something to Live For": Accounts vary on this point. Ulanov says that BS played only "Lush Life" and that it was not until later that he showed "Something to Live For" to DE (Ulanov, 220, 222). George Greenlee, who arranged the meeting, told Hajdu that he played both songs (Hajdu, 51). **"It begins softly"**: Sinclair Traill, "Billy Strayhorn—An Interview," in Traill, 41. **"Duke was very nice to me"**: Feather, "Billy Strayhorn—The Young Duke." **"I would like to have you"**: BS, 1962 interview.

"In an almost instantaneous assimilation": van de Leur, 25. **"It was born without any effort"**: Quoted in Hajdu, 55–56.

"I'm not going to let you go": DE, TV interview, *The Parkinson Show*, BBC, 1973, in *RIT,* 201. **"I don't have any position for you"**: Wilson, "Billy Strayhorn: Alter Ego for the Duke." **"Like a native"**: Ruth Ellington, oral-history interview. **"What the hell are we paying all the rent for?"**: Hajdu, 58.

"One day Duke sent me two pieces: BS, 1962 interview. **"I couldn't really arrange"**: Bill Coss, "Ellington & Strayhorn, Inc.," *Down Beat,* June 7, 1962, in *Reader,* 499.

"I left him at my house": DE, Harman interview, 1964. **BS wrote "Day Dream" and "Passion Flower"**: Ulanov, 222–23, and van de Leur, 27.

"A long time": BS, 1962 interview. **"He had a good musical education"**: DE, *Parkinson Show* interview.

"He gave [him] charge": BS, 1962 interview. **"From then on, Duke did very little"**: Coss, "Ellington & Strayhorn, Inc.," in *Reader,* 499. **"He got everything**

that Duke had": Tizol, oral-history interview. The trombonist's admiration, however, stopped short of being willing to extract parts from BS's manuscripts, for the young man's unformed handwriting was hard to read. It was "like hen-scratching," he admitted in 1962 (BS, 1962 interview). **"A guy that everybody loved":** Greer, oral-history interview.

"I was down in the station": DE, Harman interview, 1964.

DE took sole credit for "Your Love Has Faded": A 1999 Warner Bros. Publications folio gives DE and BS joint credit for the song. For a detailed discussion of the provenance of "Your Love Has Faded," see Lasker, liner notes for *Duke Ellington: The Complete 1936–1940 Variety, Vocalion and OKeh Small Group Sessions,* 17.

"Every once in a while": Hajdu, 239. **"At about one-thirty":** Gordon Parks, "Jazz," *Esquire,* Dec. 1975.

Only fifty-two surviving manuscript scores are in the handwriting of both DE and BS: van de Leur, 89.

BS had not yet heard Ravel's *Valses nobles et sentimentales:* Ulanov, 225.

DE cut "Chelsea Bridge": For a detailed discussion of the cuts, see van de Leur, 50–54. **"There is nothing like taking a Billy Strayhorn orchestration":** Paul Worth, radio interview with DE and BS, 1962, quoted in van de Leur, 109.

BS's work was being performed by DE's band: In 1998 the Dutch Jazz Orchestra recorded the original, uncut version of "Chelsea Bridge." In addition to showing how Ellington altered the piece, this recording offers a dramatic demonstration of how the Ellington band played Strayhorn's scores in such a way as to give them an unmistakably Ellingtonian coloration. (The performance is included on *Something to Live For.*)

"I feel that his was the only band": Traill, 45. **"He had a hard time making friends":** Hajdu, 18. **"The guy went through a lot of shit":** Ibid., 88.

"There wasn't a lot of guys": Ibid., 70. **Bigard spoke critically of BS's sexuality in his oral-history interview:** Dan Morgenstern, personal communication.

"Pop never cared one bit": Hajdu, 79. **"A Faggot Mafia":** Ellington, 157–58. **"Duke treated Billy exactly like he treated women":** David Hajdu, "Something to Live For," *The Village Voice Jazz Special,* June 23, 1992.

"I think Duke was a much simpler character": Jewell, 63. **"Duke was a magnificent role model":** Hajdu, 78.

DE took care to display *Remembrance of Things Past:* "In a bedroom hall stands a small table with six books on it. Four of them are the elegantly bound 'Remembrance of Things Past' series by Marcel Proust. The fifth is Emily Post's

'*Etiquette,*' and the sixth is Emily Post's '*Etiquette Revised*'" (H. Allen Smith, "Hot and Sweet: Duke Ellington as a Composer Is in Class Alone," *New York World-Telegram,* Sept. 15, 1938). **BS favored Rachmaninoff, Stravinsky, and the French impressionists:** Ulanov, 236.

BS and Bridgers were discreet about the nature of their relationship: "Billy and I both felt that you don't have to talk about such things. You communicate them better in other ways. . . . You shouldn't have to ask" (Hajdu, 66). **Ulanov later implied as much:** Ulanov, 226–28. This appears to be the first published reference to Bridgers, who is described as "Billy's roommate." In 1946 knowledgeable readers would have understood Ulanov to be suggesting that BS and Bridgers were lovers. **"We accepted Aaron as a new member of the family":** Hajdu, 69–70.

"It had nothing to do": Ibid., 86. **"When Strayhorn came on the scene":** Ibid., 86–87. **"A turning point":** *MM,* 153.

DE's "staff arranger": Boyer, "The Hot Bach," 220.

"He has never made me feel": Wilson, "Billy Strayhorn: Alter Ego for the Duke." **"The one thing that stood out":** Hajdu, 78.

BS's nickname for DE was "Monster": See, for instance, Gordon Parks, "Jazz," *Esquire,* Dec. 1975. **"You wrote every bit as much of that music":** Ibid., 171–72. In addition to making no mention of BS, the article credited DE with writing "A Drum Is a Woman" and "Such Sweet Thunder," both of which were jointly written by the two men ("Duke Ellington: A Living Legend Swings On," *Look,* Aug. 20, 1957).

CHAPTER TEN
"THE SEA OF EXPECTANCY"

SOURCES

Documents

Lawrence Brown, oral-history interview, IJS; Helen Oakley Dance, oral-history interview, OHAM; DE, *The Duke Ellington Carnegie Hall Concerts: January 1943,* sound recording (Prestige); DE, unpublished interview with Carter Harman, 1964, EC; Sonny Greer, oral-history interview, IJS; Lawrence Gushee, liner notes for *Duke Ellington 1940,* sound recording (Smithsonian Collection); Milt Hinton, oral-history interview, OHAM; BS, public interview, Duke Ellington Society, New York, Mar. 1962; Juan Tizol, oral-history interview, IJS; Cootie Williams, oral-history interview, IJS.

Books

Barnet, *Those Swinging Years;* Berger, *Bassically Speaking;* Bigard, *With Louis and the Duke;* Büchmann-Møller, *Someone to Watch Over Me;* Bushell, *Jazz from the Beginning;* Cohen, *Duke Ellington's America;* Collier, *Duke Ellington;* Crow, *Jazz Anecdotes;* Dance, *The World of Duke Ellington;* Ellington, *Duke Ellington in Person;* Gammond, *Duke Ellington;* George, *Sweet Man;* Gleason, *Celebrating the Duke;* Goldsby, *The Jazz Bass Book;* Hajdu, *Lush Life;* Stewart, *Boy Meets Horn;* Stewart, *Jazz Masters of the Thirties;* Ulanov, *Duke Ellington;* Vail, *Duke's Diary, Part One;* van de Leur, *Something to Live For.*

NOTES

"A continuing autobiography": Nat Hentoff, "The Incompleat Duke Ellington," *Show,* Aug. 1964.

"One of the ace foundation-and-beat men": *MM,* 164.

The band pulled into St. Louis: Ken Steiner is the first DE scholar to have done extensive primary-source research on Blanton's childhood and youth, and this account is based in large part on his findings, many of them as yet unpublished. **Johnny Hodges went to Club 49:** It is impossible to establish with certainty which members of the band were at the club. Club 49 announced the band's expected presence that night in a newspaper ad that ran the same day: "THE HOME OF ALL CELEBRITIES WILL ENTERTAIN DUKE ELLINGTON AND HIS ENTIRE BAND" (*St. Louis Argus,* Oct. 20, 1939). Wendell Marshall, Blanton's cousin, told Mercer Ellington that it was Hodges who discovered Blanton (Ellington, 85). DE claimed that BS and Ben Webster were there, but Webster had not yet joined the band (*MM,* 164). Rex Stewart gave sole credit to Webster (Stewart, *Boy Meets Horn,* 197). Barney Bigard said that he, Webster, and Johnny Hodges made the discovery (Bigard, 73). According to Lawrence Brown, he and Hodges were the first to draw Blanton to DE's attention (Brown, oral-history interview). Sonny Greer claimed to have discovered Blanton himself (Greer, oral-history interview). The fact that Webster and Blanton later became close companions may explain why Bigard, DE, and Stewart all misremembered his presence that night. For a discussion of the sequence of events, see Ken Steiner, *On the Road and On the Air with Duke Ellington: The Blanton/Webster Era, Part One* (privately published, 2004). **A bassist named Jimmie Blanton:** Blanton's first name is often spelled "Jimmy," but he signed it "Jimmie" in all of his surviving autographs, and it is also printed that way on his letterhead. **DE "arrived in his pajamas and topcoat":** Ellington, 85. **"Duke asked Marable if he could sit in":** John Chilton, "Blanton's Early Days," *Blue Light: The DESUK Newsletter,* Oct.–Dec. 1996.

"We wonder if the maestro": J. Von Chapman, "Town Chatter," *St. Louis Argus,* Oct. 27, 1939. **"I flipped like everybody else":** *MM,* 164. **Blanton:** A telegram sent by Blanton to his family on November 2, the last night of the Hotel Coronado gig, said that he was "joining Duke Ellington's band tomorrow" (Ken Steiner, personal communication). **"It was really unique":** "Ye Scribe," "In the Groove," *Indianapolis Recorder,* Dec. 9, 1939.

Blanton was born in 1918: Blanton's death certificate says that he was born on Oct. 5, 1919, but the date of birth carved on his Chattanooga tombstone is Oct. 5, 1918, the same one that he entered on his application for a Social Security number (Ken Steiner, personal communication). **He took lessons from a classically trained teacher:** According to John Goldsby, Blanton "utilized the instrument's full range—up to the B♭ in thumb position above the octave G" (Goldsby, 49). Self-taught bassists rarely learn thumb position, a technique developed by classical bassists to facilitate the playing of high notes. **"When he left St. Louis":** Bigard, 74.

"Listen, you're going to hear": Quoted in Hajdu, 89. **"He shocked us all":** Hinton, oral-history interview. **Stravinsky "spent [an] entire evening":** Stewart, *Boy Meets Horn,* 196. **"Despite his youth":** Ibid. **"They'd find out the hotel":** Bigard, 74.

"What really struck me": Berger, 100.

"He wouldn't interfere with your solo": Anne Judd, "Barney Goin' Easy," *Jazz Journal,* Sept. 1967. **"Right in the middle of a set":** *MM,* 164. The timing of this event is confirmed by a contemporary report (*Jazz Information,* Jan. 26, 1940).

"Ben Webster denies plans": Nell Dodson, "This Is Harlem," *New York Amsterdam News,* Jan. 20, 1940; Ibid., 4.

"My mother, she wanted me": Büchmann-Møller, 5.

"The hoodlum swingster": Stewart, *Boy Meets Horn,* 197. **A Jekyll-and-Hyde personality:** Stewart, *Jazz Masters,* 121. **"Kind of an introvert":** Büchmann-Møller, 4. **"An unusual character":** Bushell, 89.

"Every time I'd run across some of Duke's men": Büchmann-Møller, 57. **"Barney Bigard took a little vacation":** Ibid., 38. (In fact Bigard had not yet left on vacation. He plays on the session at which "Truckin'" was recorded.) **"I always had a yen for Ben":** *MM,* 163.

Webster's flirtation with DE went no further: He did, however, sit in on one more recording session, a 1936 date on which he can be heard soloing on a DE original called "In a Jam."

"A kind of alto approach": Ibid., 59.

"Ben was a different man": Stewart, *Jazz Masters,* 124.

BS reworked "Jack the Bear": BS, 1962 interview. The manuscript of "Take It Away," the piece that BS claimed to have reworked for Blanton, is in DE's hand (EC). For a discussion of its authorship, see van de Leur, 34.

The greatest of DE's three-minute masterpieces: For an analysis of "Ko-Ko," see Edward Green, "'It Don't Mean a Thing if It Ain't Got That Grundgestalt!'—Ellington from a Motivic Perspective," *Jazz Perspectives,* July 2008.

"A little descriptive scene": DE, *The Duke Ellington Carnegie Hall Concerts: January 1943.* **"An excerpt from the incomplete score":** Ulanov, 253. Only one piece of DE's holograph manuscript for "Ko-Ko" survives, a "2nd Tenor" part for Ben Webster (EC). It was almost certainly added to the piece after Webster joined the band. **"I felt long ago":** "Ellington Composes New Number," *Detroit Evening Times,* July 30, 1940. **DE claimed to have spent nine years working on** *Boola:* Alfred Frankenstein, "'Hot Is Something About a Tree,' Says the Duke," *San Francisco Chronicle,* Nov. 9, 1941.

"Every time Ben got up": Dance, *The World of Duke Ellington,* 39. DE had done the same thing when Lawrence Brown joined the band in 1933: "There were no third trombone parts, so I had to sort of compose my own parts. Then as the new numbers came out they started arranging for third trombone" (Brown, oral-history interview).

"Not up to the Ellington standard": Review of "Ko-Ko" and "Conga Brava," *Down Beat,* May 1940. **"I find I have all these other lifetimes":** Max Jones and Humphrey Lyttelton, BBC radio interview with DE, 1964; *RIT,* 372. **"During this period":** *MM,* 154.

It got into Walter Winchell's column: Walter Winchell, "Lint from a Blue Serge Suit," *The Philadelphia Inquirer,* July 6, 1944. **"I stood on the bus":** Williams, oral-history interview. **The main theme of "Never No Lament" was a Johnny Hodges riff:** It was an obbligato to "I Let a Song Go Out of My Heart," which was itself a Hodges-penned melody (Brown, oral-history interview; Stewart, *Boy Meets Horn,* 190).

Among the most formally unpredictable of his 1940 compositions: "Concerto for Cootie" is the subject of one of the first extended formal analyses of a composition by DE, André Hodeir's "A Masterpiece: *Concerto for Cootie,*" originally published in 1954 (in *Reader,* 276–88).

"Mister Blues": Helen Oakley Dance, oral-history interview.

"A song of sorrow": *MM,* 469.

"You write just for their abilities": Boyer, "The Hot Bach," 228. **"I have often seen him":** BS, "Billy Strayhorn: 'The Ellington Effect,'" *Down Beat,* Nov. 5, 1952, in *Reader,* 270. **"To incorporate Duke Ellington's harmonic approach":** Barnet, 77.

"We don't have a first saxophone player": Dance, *The World of Duke Ellington*, 163.

"It's just a little story": Boyer, "The Hot Bach," 230.

"I think of music sometimes": Ibid., 218. "I hear a note by one of the fellows in the band": George, 226. (This remark was reported to George by Brooks Kerr.) "The memory of things gone": Boyer, "The Hot Bach," 218.

"Once, we were riding a train": Stewart, *Jazz Masters*, 99. A down-home blues: "Things Ain't What They Used to Be" is officially credited to Mercer Ellington, but Hodges is rumored to have gambled away the rights to the song in a poker game ("Mercer Ellington," *Blue Light: The DESUK Newsletter*, Apr. 1996). In later life Hodges spoke of the number in such a way as to indicate that it was one of his own compositions (see, for instance, Dance, *The World of Duke Ellington*, 92). It was later arranged for the full band, whose members supplied a bawdy lyric of their own for the rocking triplet figure that kicks off "Things Ain't What They Used to Be": "All the boys in the band eat puss-eeeeeeeeeeey!" (Gleason, 243).

Webster is known to have written "Cotton Tail": Stewart, *Jazz Masters*, 129. According to Milt Hinton, he also wrote "In a Mellotone" (Büchmann-Møller, 70).

"Hundreds of tin-roofed theaters": David Davis, "Golden Buckaroo," *L.A. Times Magazine*, Apr. 6, 2003. "That's it! Don't go any further": *MM*, 166.

"Well, go ahead on": Williams, oral-history interview. "All white musicians in name bands": Stewart, *Boy Meets Horn*, 193. Jimmy Maxwell, one of Benny Goodman's trumpeters, told David Berger years later that Williams, who had been making $75 a week with DE, was offered $250, not $200 (Berger, personal communication). All other sources, including Williams in his oral-history interview, agree on the lower figure. Stewart claimed that DE refused to pay Johnny Hodges for doubling on soprano saxophone: Stewart, *Boy Meets Horn*, 192. "I gave it up": Dance, *The World of Duke Ellington*, 96.

"Duke knew about it": Williams, oral-history interview. "He's just Goodman": Dance, *The World of Duke Ellington*, 108. Another possible explanation of this remark is that Williams believed that DE played favorites with his musicians, suggesting that the trumpeter continued to resent DE for having given Rex Stewart extra solos when he joined the band in 1934.

"He was almost in tears": Jimmy Gentry, "Nance Takes Cootie Spot with Duke," *Down Beat*, Nov. 15, 1940.

"Raymond? He has perfect taste": Dance, *The World of Duke Ellington*, 138. "Floorshow": Ibid., 61. "A kid that [sic] has a lot of showmanship": *Down Beat*, Sept. 1, 1942, quoted in Collier, 241. His name began to be featured in newspaper ads: See Vail, 232 and elsewhere. **"A diet of heroin and whiskey":** George, 216. (Nance is not specifically identified, but the context leaves no doubt that he was the musician in question.)

"Slowly they drifted in": Gammond, 176–77. All of the recordings made by Towers and Burris that night are available on a two-CD set called *At Fargo 1940: Special 60th Anniversary Edition* (Storyville).

"What the scientists do": DE, TV interview, *The Parkinson Show*, BBC, 1973, in *RIT,* 323. **"I live for the nights that this band is great":** Grover Mitchell, quoted in Crow, 282.

CHAPTER ELEVEN
"A MESSAGE FOR THE WORLD"

SOURCES

Documents
Lawrence Brown, oral-history interview, IJS; Dutch Jazz Orchestra, *Something to Live For: The Dutch Jazz Orchestra Plays the Music of Billy Strayhorn*, sound recording (Challenge); DE, unpublished interview with Carter Harman, 1964, EC; Norman Granz, oral-history interview, EC; Irving Mills, oral-history interview, OHAM; Brian Priestley, "The Early Forties Recordings (1940–1942)," liner notes for discs 8–13 of *The Duke Ellington Centennial Edition*, sound recording (RCA Victor); Patricia Willard, liner notes for *Jump for Joy*, sound recording (Smithsonian Collection).

Books
Benamu, *It's All True;* Bigard, *With Louis and the Duke;* Bogle, *Dorothy Dandridge;* Büchmann-Møller, *Someone to Watch Over Me;* Buckley, *The Hornes;* Carter, *Anthony Blunt;* Cohen, *Duke Ellington's America;* Dance, *The World of Duke Ellington;* Denning, *The Cultural Front;* Ellington, *Duke Ellington in Person;* Gammond, *Duke Ellington;* Giddins, *Visions of Jazz;* Gleason, *Celebrating the Duke;* Hall, *More Dialogues in Swing;* Hajdu, *Lush Life;* Mason, *Stone Tower;* Stratemann, *Duke Ellington Day by Day and Film by Film;* Ulanov, *Duke Ellington;* Vail, *Duke's Diary, Part One;* van de Leur, *Something to Live For.*

NOTES

"I always consider my problems opportunities": Gleason, 167.

"When we opened": Dance, 33.

BS's version of "Chloë" was adapted from a stock arrangement: The band's recording of "Chloë," made on Oct. 28, is clearly based on a version of the song that had been recorded by Tracy-Brown's Orchestra, a Chicago dance band, in 1928 (Priestley, "The Early Forties Recordings").

"After spending $8,000": "Mercer Ellington Joins Dad," unsourced and undated clipping, c. 1940, in Vail, 193. **"Overnight, literally":** Hajdu, 83–84.

"He'd set problems for me": Ellington, 93. The scores of "Blue Serge" and "Jumpin' Punkins" are in DE's handwriting, which suggests that the role played by him in their creation was greater than Mercer cared to admit. According to Leonard Feather, who worked with the Ellington band as a press agent starting in Nov. 1942, Mercer "has seldom done any of the arranging [of his compositions] except on parts of 'Jumpin' Punkins' and 'Moon Mist'" (Leonard G. Feather, "Billy Strayhorn—The Young Duke," *Jazz*, Jan. 1943). For a discussion of the provenance of these compositions, see Cohen, 177–78, 603. **"Chelsea Bridge" was inspired by Whistler's *Nocturne: Blue and Gold—Old Battersea Bridge*:** Ulanov, 226. Even though there is an actual Chelsea Bridge in London, Aaron Bridgers confirmed that this was the specific painting that BS had in mind. According to Bridgers, BS "thought that 'Chelsea Bridge' sounded better: he did know the difference" (van de Leur, 292).

DE's "yearlings": DE, Harman interview, 1964. **"I contend that the Negro":** "Speech of the Week," *California Eagle*, Feb. 13, 1941, in *Reader*, 147.

"To give an American audience": John Pittman, "The Duke Will Stay on Top!," unidentified clipping, in *Reader*, 149.

"Hey, this joint sure is jumpin'!": Willard, *Jump for Joy*. **"Count me in":** Howard Reich, "50 Years Later, Pegasus Puts Ellington's Fiery Musical Back Together," *Chicago Tribune*, Oct. 6, 1991. **One of the principal investors in *Jump for Joy*:** The other investors included W.R. Burnett, the pulp novelist who collaborated on the screenplays for *Scarface*, *Little Caesar*, and *High Sierra*, and Joe Pasternak, who is best remembered for producing Deanna Durbin's film musicals.

"The leftist Hollywood crowd": *RIT*, 233. **The history of the Popular Front:** For a discussion of the Popular Front and its various theatrical ventures, see Denning, 283–319. ***Pins and Needles* was so beloved of the American left:** Carter, 187.

A "Negro Revue": Ibid., 312. **"Mad Scene from Woolworth's,"** one of the sketches that Hughes wrote for this project, would later be recycled for use in *Jump for Joy*. **A "Communist-front organization":** Mason, 18.

"Jno. Garfield": Bill Smallwood, "On the Beam," *California Eagle*, Feb. 6, 1941. **"Social[ly] conscious" friends:** DE, radio interview with Stanley Dance, BBC, 1971, in *RIT*, 230. **A full-page *New York Times* ad:** Advertisement, *The New York Times*, Nov. 3, 1944.

"Whatever town he went to": Mills, oral-history interview. "I've never been interested in politics": DE, "No Red Songs for Me," *The New Leader,* Sept. 30, 1950. "When something bad happened": Ellington, 157.

A longtime Republican: Tom Simon, the US State Department officer who escorted DE and the band on their 1963 tour of the Middle East, told Arne Neegaard that DE confirmed this fact to him in conversation (Arne Neegaard, personal communication). DE's FBI file: The file is headed "Subject: Edward Kennedy (Duke) Ellington. File: 100-HQ-434443." It can be viewed at the FBI's website, vault.fbi.gov.

"Whose sympathies fitted into my scene and scheme": *MM,* 155. "An all-Negro show": DE, Harman interview, 1964. "Everything, every setting": *MM,* 176. "Traditionally, black humor had been portrayed": Willard, *Jump for Joy.* "We included everything we wanted to say": Henry Whiston, "Reminiscing in Tempo," *Jazz Journal,* Feb. 1967.

"I am a Negro": "Ellington Denies Charges of Ingratitude, 'Uncle Tom-ing,'" *California Eagle,* Jan. 30, 1941. "You don't seem to fit the right shade": Emory Holmes II, "When the 'A' Train Hit L.A.," *Los Angeles Times,* Apr. 25, 1999.

"I teach Betty Grable": Buckley, 151. DE claimed that *Jump for Joy* was written by fifteen different people: *MM,* 175. "The most beautiful woman": Bogle, 89.

"Duke was in the bathtub": Willard, *Jump for Joy.* The exact role of BS in the writing of the score of *Jump for Joy* is unclear, but everyone close to the show agreed that he worked hand in hand with DE. While the program credits him only with "musical arrangements," Blankfort and Kuller both thought that he deserved coequal billing with DE. "We should have listed Billy, too: 'By Duke Ellington and Billy Strayhorn,'" Blankfort said. "But Ellington had the name. He was the big draw." Kuller put it more directly: "The thing is, see, Duke was the front man. . . . Listen, the world wasn't ready to accept a show by Duke Ellington. It certainly wasn't ready to accept Duke Ellington *and* some other guy nobody ever heard of" (Hajdu, 92). The opening-night program of *Jump for Joy,* which shows BS's billing, is reproduced in *MM,* 177–79.

"We had a national tour all planned": Reich, "50 Years Later." "As the audience screamed and applauded": *MM,* 180.

"Duke Ellington and his orchestra": Quoted in Reich, "50 Years Later." "Main trouble with 'Jump for Joy'": Review of *Jump for Joy, Variety,* July 16, 1941. "A good part of the trouble": Almena Davis, "Ellington Opus Gets Once-Over," *The Pittsburgh Courier,* undated clipping (EC). (This review was reprinted from *The Los Angeles Tribune.*)

"The show was never the same": *MM,* 175. "The Negroes always left proudly": Ibid. "Duke Ellington's band was supposed to be": "G.T.S." (George T. Simon), "Joe Turner Star of Duke's Revue!," *Metronome,* Oct. 1941.

DE incorporated a vest-pocket version of the revue into his stage show: See the advertisements reproduced in Vail (204, 205, 211). **The only attempt to revive _Jump for Joy_ lost its backers $100,000:** _Variety,_ Mar. 11, 1959, quoted in Stratemann, 399.

"A milestone in Ellington's career": Giddins, 245. **Few of the sketches are extant:** After _Jump for Joy_ closed, the finished sketches were returned to their respective authors and thus were not preserved in DE's papers (Reich, "50 Years Later"). "A Colored Musical Review in Two Acts, entitled: 'JUMP FOR JOY,'" a typescript of a preliminary draft of the book, has survived and is now in the hands of a private collector. While the show was extensively revised after the writing of this draft, it appears to give a reasonably clear sense of how _Jump for Joy_ played on stage.

A silent film shot by friends of the cast: Stratemann, 171. The sole surviving print of this film, which was shot by Andy and Mary MacKay, is now in the possession of the jazz film collector Mark Cantor.

"Sun-Tanned Tenth of the Nation": The title of this number alludes to _One-Third of a Nation,_ the "Living Newspaper" stage documentary about poverty in America that was one of the Federal Theatre Project's most widely discussed productions.

Paul White received threatening calls: Willard, _Jump for Joy._ **"We had too many chefs":** Hall, 110.

"It didn't do very well": Granz, oral-history interview.

"That killed me": Quoted in Cohen, 194. (The friend was Brooks Kerr.)

"I want to do the history of jazz": _MM,_ 240. **"You can start work today!":** Henry Whiston, "Reminiscing in Tempo," _Jazz Journal,_ Feb. 1967. (In _MM,_ DE recalled his proposed salary as $1,000 a week.)

Elliot Paul was working on a script: Benamu, 29.

DE was the only genius he had ever known: This remark is "quoted" without attribution in Maurice Zolotow, "The Duke of Hot," _The Saturday Evening Post,_ Aug. 7, 1943.

"I think I wrote 28 bars": Whiston, "Reminiscing in Tempo."

DE "called doctor after doctor": _MM,_ 165. **A picture of Ben Webster:** Büchmann-Møller, 89.

"Silly things like sleeping bad": Bigard, 77.

"When I told him I was leaving": Ibid. **"He's just leaving":** "Barney Bigard Is Leaving Duke," _Down Beat,_ July 15, 1942. **Ivie Anderson said in a radio**

interview that she was tired of the road: Undated aircheck (Steven Lasker collection). **Anderson quit when DE refused to give her a raise:** Brown, oral-history interview.

CHAPTER TWELVE
"I DON'T WRITE JAZZ"

SOURCES

Documents

George Avakian, oral-history interview, OHAM; *A Duke Named Ellington*, TV documentary (WNET); *Duke Ellington and His Orchestra: The Treasury Shows,* vol. 1, sound recording (Storyville); *The Duke Ellington Carnegie Hall Concerts: December 1944,* sound recording (Prestige); DE, *"Black, Brown and Beige* by Duke Ellington" (typescript, n.d., EC); DE, unpublished interviews with Carter Harman, 1956 and 1964, EC; DE, untitled scenario of *Boola* (holograph MS., n.d., EC); DE and Inez Cavanaugh, liner notes, *Black, Brown and Beige: A Duke Ellington Tone Parallel to the American Negro,* sound recording (RCA Victor); Mercer Ellington, oral-history interview, EC; Ruth Ellington, oral-history interview, EC; Sonny Greer, oral-history interview, IJS; Phoebe Jacobs, oral-history interview conducted by researchers for Ken Burns's *Jazz* (transcript available online at http://www.pbs.org /jazz/about/pdfs/jacobs.pdf); Max Jones, oral-history interview, OHAM; Brad McCuen, oral-history interview, EC; Betty Roché, oral-history interview, OHAM; Joya Sherrill, oral-history interview conducted by researchers for Ken Burns's *Jazz* (transcript available online at www.pbs.org/jazz/about/pdfs/Sherrill.pdf).

Books

Büchmann-Møller, *Someone to Watch Over Me;* Cohen, *Duke Ellington's America;* Crow, *From Birdland to Broadway;* Dance, *The World of Duke Ellington;* Ellington, *Duke Ellington in Person;* Enstice, *Jazz Spoken Here;* George, *Sweet Man;* Gleason, *Celebrating the Duke;* Hajdu, *Lush Life;* Hasse, *Beyond Category;* Jewell, *Duke;* Ottley, *New World A-Coming;* Schuller, *Gunther Schuller;* Schuller, *The Swing Era;* Stewart, *Boy Meets Horn;* Stewart, *Jazz Masters of the Thirties;* Stratemann, *Duke Ellington Day by Day and Film by Film;* Terry, *Clark;* Tucker, *Ellington;* Ulanov, *Duke Ellington;* Vail, *Duke's Diary, Part One;* van de Leur, *Something to Live For.*

NOTES

"William Morris says to me": DE, Harman interview, 1964. The fullest account of the creation of *Black, Brown and Beige* is Mark Tucker's "The Genesis of

Black, Brown and Beige," *Black Music Research Journal* (Fall 1993). **"The light was not too good":** *MM,* 181. (The actual title of the film, directed by Jacques Tourneur, was *Cat People.*)

DE's starting point was a typescript scenario: He confirmed in 1956 that the music of *Black, Brown and Beige* was based on the scenario (DE, Harman interview, 1956). **DE claimed in 1938 to have "completed" an opera:** "Ellington Completes Negro Opera at Bedside," *Down Beat,* Oct. 2, 1938. **He started referring to it by name:** "Ellington Composes New Number," *Detroit Evening Times,* July 30, 1940. **"You gather that he could finish it":** Alfred Frankenstein, " 'Hot Is Something About a Tree,' Says the Duke," *San Francisco Chronicle,* Nov. 9, 1941.

No part of *Boola* was ever performed or recorded: The printed program for a concert given by the band at the City College of New York on Jan. 3, 1939, included "An Aria from the Opera by Duke Ellington depicting the History of the Negro." The program was changed prior to the concert, however, and the "aria" was not performed. (A copy of the program is part of the collection of the New York Public Library's Schomburg Center for Research in Black Culture.) **DE had "taken some of the music":** Howard Taubman, "The 'Duke' Invades Carnegie Hall," *The New York Times Magazine,* Jan. 17, 1943, in *Reader,* 160. *Boola* **"yielded much of the material":** Ulanov, 253. **"A message . . . shot through the jungle":** DE, "*Black, Brown and Beige* by Duke Ellington." **"Not a song of great Joy":** DE, untitled scenario of *Boola.* **"And now Come Sunday":** Ibid.

DE was writing a book about *Black, Brown and Beige:* "Duke's Book Will Explain His Carnegie Hall Symph," *Variety,* June 9, 1943. **Selected passages:** Inez Cavanaugh, a black journalist who wrote the liner notes, described the passages as "the Duke's own interpretation of the music, as reported by Inez Cavanaugh" (DE and Inez Cavanaugh, *Black, Brown and Beige*). **"A collection of 800 books":** Maurice Zolotow, "The Duke of Hot," *The Saturday Evening Post,* Aug. 7, 1943. **"A song eased the lash":** DE, "*Black, Brown and Beige* by Duke Ellington."

"*Black, Brown and Beige* was his criticism of his own race": Enstice, 121. **"The [black] state of mind":** DE, Harman interview, 1956.

DE stepped in front of a capacity crowd at Carnegie Hall: Numerous sources report that the concert was a benefit for "Russian war relief." (See, for instance, Hasse, 263.) In fact it was a benefit for Russian War Relief, Inc., a Popular Front organization later identified as a Communist front, albeit one so carefully camouflaged that it was long regarded, by DE among many others, as a legitimate operation. **"National Duke Ellington Week":** Stratemann, 239. **"I [saw] some ordinary people":** Roché, oral-history interview. **"His flamboyant black band":** "The Duke of Jazz," *Time,* Feb. 1, 1943. **"That first night at Carnegie":** *MM,* 266.

"To this reviewer's ears": Elliott Grennard, "Ellington Preems Tone Poem at Carnegie Hall; 3,300 Pay Way," *Billboard,* Jan. 30, 1943. **A latter-day**

counterpart of the historical pageants: It is not known whether DE saw any of these productions, but Henry Grant, with whom he briefly studied harmony as a boy, directed the chorus in *The Evolution of the Negro in Picture, Song, and Story,* which was performed at Washington's Howard Theatre in 1911. Mark Tucker reports that this pageant was divided into four parts that are reminiscent of the sections of *Black, Brown and Beige,* "Overture," "Night of Slavery—Sorrow Songs," "Dawn of Freedom," and "Day of Opportunity" (Tucker, 12). **The solos are written out:** For a discussion of this aspect of the work, see Wolfram Knauer, "Simulated Improvisation in *Black, Brown and Beige,*" *The Black Perspective in Music,* Jan. 1990.

"To show the close relationship": *MM,* 181.

"The contribution made by the Negro": Ibid. **"The lighter attitude":** Ibid., 182. **"At the end of the Spanish-American War":** DE and Inez Cavanaugh, *Black, Brown and Beige.*

"A soul inflection": *MM,* 167.

"The Harlem of the '20s": *Reader,* 163. (The program for the Carnegie Hall concert is reproduced here.)

DE incorrectly remembered the running time: *MM,* 181.

"We stopped using the word jazz": DE, TV interview, *The Parkinson Show,* BBC, 1973, in *RIT,* 247.

"What I'm trying to do": Ulanov, 275.

"The history of the Negro": Donald Freeman, " 'Asphalt Jungle' Theme by Duke Ellington," *The State Journal* (Springfield, IL), Feb. 25, 1961.

Most Americans "still take it for granted": Nat Hentoff, "This Cat Needs No Pulitzer Prize," *The New York Times Magazine,* Sept. 12, 1965, in *Reader,* 363.

"Really a series of social-significance thrusts": *MM,* 183. **"Spiritually aligned":** Ottley, 183. Ottley spelled out the word "A-Coming" in full in the title of his book, and the program of the 1943 Carnegie Hall premiere follows that usage. On other occasions, however, DE sometimes spelled it in full and sometimes with a terminal apostrophe. For a discussion of this matter, see Ken Steiner's note on *Duke Ellington at Carnegie Hall, Dec. 11, 1943* (Storyville), *DEMS Bulletin,* Apr.–July 2002.

DE never read Ottley's book: DE, Harman interview, 1956. **"A place in the distant future":** Ibid. **"A series of florid piano passages":** Barry Ulanov, "Ellington's Carnegie Hall Concert a Glorified Stage Show," *Metronome,* Jan. 1944.

"To capture the character": *The Duke Ellington Carnegie Hall Concerts: December 1944.* **"A mix of (retitled) old and new compositions":** van de Leur, 94.

"Organically larger form": Schuller, *The Swing Era*, 150.

"We didn't like the tone poems much": Jewell, 115. "There is, however, the danger": Howard Taubman, "Ellington's Band in Annual Concert," *The New York Times*, Jan. 5, 1946. "But for fans of the Duke's 'Mood Indigo' ": "Music: Highbrow Blues," *Time*, Jan. 14, 1946.

"Having the John Hammonds of the world": Cohen, 322. (DE said this to George Avakian.)

"Whether or not the concert": Abel Green, "Ellington, at B.O. and Musically, Niftily in Groove at Carnegie Hall Concert," *Variety*, Jan. 27, 1943. "The greatest pre-performance press": Grennard, "Ellington Preems Tone Poem at Carnegie Hall." The band's annual gross: EC. For a detailed discussion of DE's financial status during this period, see Hasse, 272–74. "I heard musicians made this kind of money": *A Duke Named Ellington*.

DE claimed to have lost $18,000: Boyer, "The Hot Bach," 245.

"Everyone seemed to think": Dance, 77.

"When I first joined that band": Crow, 142. "The musicians trickled in very slowly": Avakian, oral-history interview.

Early in DE's run at the Hurricane: DE, Harman interview, 1964. "Booking Ellington into Ciro's": "Ciro's, Hollyw'd, Books Ellington," *Billboard*, Feb. 3, 1945. "We don't allow the help": Greer, oral-history interview.

"I remember getting off the train": Steve Voce, "Kay Davis: Singer Who Worked with Duke Ellington," *Independent*, Feb. 28, 2012.

"I can't afford to pay you": Büchmann-Møller, 98. DE pulled the same trick on Dizzy Gillespie, failing to pay him for a 1959 recording session, then telling the trumpeter that "I can't pay you what you're really worth." Gillespie was amused by his feint: "Whee, was that a cunning, elegant man! So I smile and I say, 'Don't give it no mind, Duke. Just so long as you *pay* me!' And maybe a year later, he did" (Jewell, 74). "He kids around with us": Hentoff, "This Cat Needs No Pulitzer Prize." "Duke was so involved with himself": George, 147.

"He would just play": Schuller, *Gunther Schuller*, 185.

"When Duke was coming in": Jewell, 81.

"I saw so many women": Sherrill, oral-history interview. "Shocking . . . the way the women kind of fell on their faces": Ruth Ellington, oral-history interview. "He never seemed to be interested": Ellington, 127. "It keeps my juices flowing": George, 155.

"Duke would check into two, three or four hotels": Ibid., 109. The authenticity of George's anecdotes about DE's sexual exploits obviously cannot be verified and has been widely questioned, but they are consistent in tone, subject matter, and language with the unpublished interviews that DE gave to Carter Harman in 1964. **Evie went after DE with a gun**: Ellington, 205. (See also George, 139.) **"We can't permit anything"**: George, 28.

"She did not allow Evie": Mercer Ellington, oral-history interview. **"I think Evie was his protection"**: Jacobs, oral-history interview.

"Duke Ellington, whose contours": Boyer, "The Hot Bach," 214–15. **"Duke is six feet tall"**: Ibid., 222. **"I've had three educations"**: Ibid., 237. **"You have to try"**: Ibid., 218. **"As Bach says"**: Ibid., 226.

"Ellington has, like most entertainers": Ibid., 217.

Time **treated the poll as news**: "Music: Down Beat Poll," *Time*, Jan. 13, 1941. **"Weird melodies"**: Undated advertisement, c. 1944, in Vail, 260.

"Because of my looks": Hajdu, 98. **"Hibbler's no singer"**: Ulanov, 273.

"The figure $2,250": *MM*, 88–89. According to Claire Gordon, who was working for DE in 1943, it is possible that this additional royalty income had another source: "In the office, it seemed to be a good idea for me to get acquainted with Duke's lesser-known, early compositions. There were several lists around the office. I compiled them into one super file and then started crosschecking with the ASCAP list. To my surprise, ASCAP did not credit eight or ten of Ellington's songs. I typed a letter giving all the pertinent information: the name, date, publisher and recordings, if any, and sent them to the head office. Subsequently Duke received an ASCAP rating raise. This meant a check for several thousand more dollars a year for him. I don't think he ever knew how that happened" (Gordon, 104).

The "dreaded medley": Max Jones claimed to have coined this phrase (Max Jones, oral-history interview). **"For one thing, the return of Eli Oberstein"**: "RCA Still Won't Release the Duke," *Variety*, Mar. 27, 1946. **"A little Saturday-night nigger music"**: McCuen, oral-history interview.

"Webster slapped Duke": Büchmann-Møller, 98. **"He just got drunk"**: George, 100.

"Highly strung": Jewell, 82. **"He had a habit"**: Terry, 139. **"He was very important to us"**: *MM*, 221. **"What is more, he became"**: Ibid., 222. **"There is no such thing"**: "New Musicians Mean a New Sound in My Band: Ellington," *Down Beat*, Apr. 6, 1951.

"Probably unequaled by any other Negro band": "Duke Ellington Sealed to Musicraft 100G Deal While Still with RCA," *Variety*, May 22, 1946.

"Duke Ellington—composer, conductor": *Duke Ellington and His Orchestra: The Treasury Shows*, vol. 1. "No other dance band": *Variety*, Apr. 18, 1945, quoted in Stratemann, 262.

"You don't build a statue": *Metronome*, undated clipping, c. Dec. 1946, in Vail, 287. The headlines: Paul Eduard Miller, "Is the Duke Declining? 'Loss of Stars Killing His Band,'" *Hollywood Note*, July 1946; Bill Gottlieb, "'I'm Not Slipping'—Duke Ellington: 'My Current Ork Just as Good and Perhaps More Flexible,' He Says," *Down Beat*, June 17, 1946; Mike Levin, "Ellington Fails to Top Himself: Mix Finds Concert Good, Not Great," *Down Beat*, Dec. 16, 1946.

CHAPTER THIRTEEN
"MORE A BUSINESS THAN AN ART"

SOURCES

Documents
DE, unpublished interviews with Carter Harman, 1956 and 1964, EC; Mercer Ellington, oral-history interview, OHAM; Norman Granz, oral-history interview, EC; Jimmy Jones, oral-history interview, EC; *Person to Person*, TV program, Mar. 15, 1957 (CBS); Gunther Schuller, liner notes for *Mirage: Avant-Garde and Third-Stream Jazz*, sound recording (New World); *What's My Line?*, TV program, July 12, 1953 (CBS).

Books
Abbott, *"Mister Abbott"*; Cohen, *Duke Ellington's America*; Dance, *Johnny Hodges*; Dance, *The World of Duke Ellington*; Dance, *The World of Jazz*; Duke, *Passport to Paris*; Ellington, *Duke Ellington in Person*; Franceschina, *Duke Ellington's Music for the Theatre*; Gleason, *Celebrating the Duke*; Hajdu, *Lush Life*; Heath, *I Walked with Giants*; Houseman, *Front and Center*; Jewell, *Duke*; Schuller, *The Swing Era*; Simon, *Simon Says*; Stewart, *Boy Meets Horn*; van de Leur, *Something to Live For*; Wein, *Myself Among Others*.

NOTES

An updated version of *The Beggar's Opera:* The most detailed accounts of the making of *Beggar's Holiday* are Daniel C. Caine, "A Crooked Thing: A Chronicle of *Beggar's Holiday*," *New Renaissance*, Fall 1986, and Franceschina, 59–75. "*Beggar's Holiday* was conceived": Perry Watkins, "Holiday Is Bi-Racial Production," *Chicago Sun*, Apr. 6, 1947.

"I realized all of a sudden": Hajdu, 101. "In fact, he wanted the recognition": Ibid.

John Latouche: Latouche's name is variously spelled "Latouche," "La Touche," and "LaTouche" in numerous primary sources, but the first version is accurate. "Ever alert": Duke, 314.

"Latouche was not only lazy": Houseman, 191.

"Ellington would never leave his band": Hajdu, 101–2. BS composed "Brown Penny": van de Leur, 98. Not only did he write the music, but the song's lyrics were adapted (presumably by Latouche) from a poem by W.B. Yeats. "Strayhorn would run up to the Duke's apartment": Houseman, 192.

"The deed has been done": Caine, "A Crooked Thing." "The last twenty minutes": Houseman, 194. Some press accounts suggest that the last scene of the show was improvised throughout the run. See, for instance, Richard Harrington, "Duke Ellington's Long-Lost 'Holiday': Smithsonian Revives Broadway Musical," *The Washington Post,* Feb. 1, 1992. "Something of an opera": "Twilight Alley," *Billboard,* Dec. 14, 1946.

"I never saw Duke Ellington": Hajdu, 101–2. "I think I could have made": Abbott, 217.

"Let appropriate salutes be fired": Brooks Atkinson, "The Play in Review: Beggar's Holiday," *The New York Times,* Dec. 27, 1946. "The full-blooded musical score": "Three Musical Hits," *Life,* Feb. 24, 1947. "There are so many good tunes": Barry Ulanov, *Metronome,* undated clipping; reproduced in *DEMS Bulletin,* Sept.–Nov. 1992. "It offers no really sympathetic character": Ibid. "His fine settings look like a tombstone": Bentley, 7.

"The thing that was wrong": Henry Whiston, "Reminiscing in Tempo," *Jazz Journal,* Feb. 1967. "Nobody could understand": DE, Harman interview, 1964. "The party's just starting": Hajdu, 104–5. "That show meant a lot to him": Ibid., 101.

"No jazz admirer denies Ellington's greatness": Mike Levin, "Ellington Pleases Concert Crowd," *Down Beat,* Jan. 14, 1948. "Ellington is not as good": Ted Hallock, "Duke's Chicago Date Lacks Flair," *Down Beat,* Jan. 28, 1948. "Each year, the critics . . . commence": M.W. [Marshall] Stearns and Patricia A. Samson, "Critic Rapped; Crowds Pleased," *Down Beat,* Feb. 25, 1948.

"You just grow and grow and grow": DE, Harman interview, 1964. "All the booze had gone": Jimmy Jones, oral-history interview.

"Isn't it about time": Michael Levin, "Reputation Shredded, Duke Should Disband, Mix Claims," *Down Beat,* June 17, 1949. "You're right that Ellington

sounds dispirited": Charlie Barnet, "You Made a Bad Error, Mix—Barnet," *Down Beat,* July 15, 1949.

"If I didn't like the way": Pat Harris, "I Like Way Band Sounds—Duke," *Down Beat,* Aug. 12, 1949.

"Visionary": Schuller, *The Swing Era,* 154. **"A freely atonal harmonic language"**: Schuller, liner notes for *Mirage: Avant-Garde and Third-Stream Jazz.* **Most listeners fail to notice that "The Clothed Woman" is a blues**: See, for example, the liner notes to *Mirage: Avant-Garde and Third-Stream Jazz,* in which Gunther Schuller makes no mention of the underlying blues structure of the piece's opening section. For a more comprehending analysis, see Scott Healy, "Revealing Ellington's 'The Clothed Woman,'" *Professorscosco,* professorscosco.wordpress.com, Sept. 9, 2011. (Healy's posting also contains a transcription of the piece.)

"They are, on the whole": Alec Wilder, "A Look at the Duke," *Saturday Review,* Aug. 28, 1948, in *Reader,* 259–61.

"I had carte blanche": Cohen, 292.

"Coleman Hawkins was *it* for me": Dance, *The World of Duke Ellington,* 169. **"He knew all of Ben's solos"**: *MM,* 163. **Gonsalves discovered heroin during his tenure with Gillespie**: Heath, 64. **"He wants to be liked by everybody"**: *MM,* 221.

BS's contribution did not become known until long after his death: van de Leur, 117. *Harlem* **was commissioned by NBC**: "Six Composers to Collaborate on NYC Portrait," *Down Beat,* Oct. 20, 1950. **A fully scored version of *Harlem* was premiered**: "C.H.," "Ellington Group in Benefit Concert," *The New York Times,* June 21, 1951. Contrary to countless incorrect statements published in later years, Arturo Toscanini never conducted *Harlem,* nor is he known to have had anything to do with the work's commissioning.

Harlem **opens with a two-note motif**: It is more than likely that this motif was borrowed, consciously or not, from Max Steiner's musical score for the 1932 film version of *The Most Dangerous Game,* in which it figures prominently. The similarity between the opening measures of the two pieces is palpable. DE said in a 1935 newspaper interview that Steiner's score for the film, which he saw in a theater where the band was playing a week-long stage show, was "the best he has ever seen and heard. . . . Everyday during the entire week, he sat in the audience to see it over and over" (Frank Marshall Davis, "Duke Ellington, Who Goes to the Movies Between Shows, Wrote Song Hit 'Solitude,' Three Years Ago," *The Pittsburgh Courier,* Jan. 26, 1935). I thank Steven Lasker for bringing this hitherto unknown interview to my attention. **"It is Sunday morning"**: *MM,* 189.

The program concocted by Deems Taylor for *An American in Paris*: Compare, for instance, this passage from Taylor's *American in Paris* program: "And now the orchestra introduces an unhallowed episode. Suffice it to say that a solo violin approaches our hero (in the soprano register) and addresses him in the most charming broken English; and, his response being inaudible—or at least unintelligible—repeats the remark. This one-sided conversation continues for some little time."

"What on earth would I want": "Duke Readies New Works for Met Opera House Bow," *Down Beat,* Jan. 26, 1951. **"He wanted me to legitimize him"**: Barry Singer, "Bridging the Worlds of Broadway and Jazz, Outside the Limelight," *The New York Times,* Sept. 24, 2000. **"Writing for the symphony orchestra"**: DE, Harman interview, 1956.

"Something important and vital": Mike Levin, "Duke's Concert 'Best in Years,'" *Down Beat,* Feb. 24, 1951. **"Cootie [Williams] and I always sat near the drums"**: Stewart, 193. **"Greer's 30-year association"**: "New Drummer Joins Ellington," *Down Beat,* Feb. 23, 1951.

"Why don't you give up the band": Granz, oral-history interview. **"When Pop turned some of their songs into hits"**: Ellington, *Duke Ellington in Person,* 110.

"Duke and Johnny Hodges had long periods": Steve Voce, "Rabbit," *Jazz Journal,* Jan. 1997.

"He was incredibly *égoiste*": Jewell, 90. **"Even when he's playing a harmony part"**: Dance, *Johnny Hodges,* 3.

"The next time I saw him": Hajdu, 120. **"That was the first time"**: Ellington, *Duke Ellington in Person,* 121.

"Money wasn't quite the problem": Hajdu, 122.

At least sixty of his vocal charts: van de Leur, 96. **The *New York Times* review**: "M.A.S." (Mark Schubart), "Ellington Concert at Carnegie Hall," *The New York Times,* Dec. 20, 1944.

"He drank just constantly": The friend was Marion Logan (Hajdu, 187).

"During our first 1951 tour": Marc Myers, "Interview: Louie Bellson (Part 2)," *JazzWax,* www.jazzwax.com, Sept. 11, 2007.

"The epitome of perfection": *MM,* 226. **"Duke gave me full credit"**: Don Heckman, "Louis Bellson: The Go-To Guy," *JazzTimes,* Nov. 2007.

"For some reason or other": Dance, *The World of Jazz,* 105.

"A powerful, rocking, enthusiastic bunch": Jack Tracy, "Ellington Crew 'Powerful, Thrilling,'" *Down Beat,* May 18, 1951.

"A fine, high-class genius": "Joe Glaser Praises Duke, Satchmo as 'Geniuses,'" *Jet,* Jan. 19, 1967. **"That crazy nigger Duke Ellington"**: Wein, 168. **DE was in**

debt to the agency: For a discussion of DE's financial relationship with Associated Booking, see Cohen, 357–58.

"No one could convince me": Ted Hallock, "Things Ain't What They Used to Be with Ellington's Band," *Down Beat,* May 21, 1952. **"Vicious and certainly unwarranted":** Charles Mingus, letter, *Down Beat,* June 18, 1952. **"After about six months":** Dance, *The World of Jazz,* 105–6.

Gonsalves took to falling asleep: Steve Voce, "Perchance to Steam," *Jazz Journal,* Dec. 1981.

"I don't understand it at all": Gleason, 160. **"You have certain responsibilities":** Nat Hentoff, "The Incompleat Duke Ellington," *Show,* Aug. 1964. **"I seldom have the urge":** *MM,* 454.

DE was quoted as saying that blacks "ain't ready yet": Otis N. Thompson, " 'We Ain't Ready,' Duke Declares," *St. Louis Argus,* Nov. 16, 1951.

"What has been published": DE, "Duke Ellington Says He Didn't Say It: The Duke Says . . . ," *The Baltimore Afro-American,* Dec. 15, 1951.

"The only 'Communism' I know": DE, "No Red Songs for Me," *The New Leader,* Sept. 30, 1950.

"You know why he was anti-Communist?": Mercer Ellington, oral-history interview. **"When people behind the Iron Curtain":** Quoted in Cohen, 261. **DE insisted that his musicians fly first class on his Russian tour:** Harvey G. Cohen, "Visions of Freedom: Duke Ellington in the Soviet Union," *Popular Music,* Sept. 2011.

An issue containing pieces: "Ellington's Silver Jubilee," *Down Beat,* Nov. 5, 1952. **"It's going to be awfully difficult":** Don Freeman, " 'Only One Bellson,' Sighs Wistful Duke," *Down Beat,* June 17, 1953.

"I signed with Capitol": "Duke Switches Record Labels," *Down Beat,* May 6, 1953. **"They need me more than Columbia does":** Cohen, 295.

"Satin Doll": Evie claimed to have been the mystery woman of the song's title (Ellington, *Duke Ellington in Person,* 97). DE liked to call her "Dearest Doll" and "Darling Doll" and painted a canvas called "Satin Doll" that hung in the music room of the Upper West Side apartment that they shared. DE pointed out the painting to Edward R. Murrow when he appeared on *Person to Person,* Murrow's televised celebrity talk show, in 1957. (Its present whereabouts are unknown.)

"Though Strayhorn's [immediate] response . . . is not known": van de Leur, 116.

"It's tough to have to compete": Ralph J. Gleason, " 'It's Tough to Compete with Yourself': Duke," *Down Beat,* July 15, 1953. **"It's getting to be more a**

business": Simon, 36. **"Would you consider yourself an actor?":** *What's My Line?*

"I want to tell you": DE, "Sex Is No Sin," *Ebony,* May 1954.

"Duke was passing by": Dance, *The World of Duke Ellington,* 139. **DE's "Kinda Dukish" ends with a quote from Monk's "52nd Street Theme":** This was pointed out to me by Ethan Iverson (personal communication).

DE didn't even place: "The Critics' Choice: The World's Top Jazz Critics Name the Musicians Who Excite Them," *Down Beat,* Aug. 24, 1955.

"It looked like he might not be able": Ellington, *Duke Ellington in Person,* 111.

CHAPTER FOURTEEN
"I WAS BORN IN 1956"

SOURCES

Documents

George Avakian, liner notes for *Ellington at Newport,* sound recording (Columbia); "Duke Ellington's *A Drum Is a Woman,*" *United States Steel Hour,* TV program, May 8, 1957 (CBS); DE, unpublished interviews with Carter Harman, 1956 and 1964, EC; Norman Granz, oral-history interview, EC; Brooks Kerr, oral-history interview, OHAM; *Person to Person,* TV program, Mar. 15, 1957 (CBS); Clark Terry, oral-history interview, OHAM; Irving Townsend, liner notes for *Such Sweet Thunder,* sound recording (Columbia).

Books

Balliett, *Collected Works;* Cohen, *Duke Ellington's America;* Dance, *Johnny Hodges;* Dance, *The World of Duke Ellington;* Davis, *Outcats;* Mercer Ellington, *Duke Ellington in Person;* George, *Sweet Man;* Gleason, *Celebrating the Duke;* Hajdu, *Lush Life;* Jewell, *Duke;* Jones, *Jazz Talking;* Morton, *Backstory in Blue;* Traill, *Just Jazz 3;* Traill, *Just Jazz 4;* van de Leur, *Something to Live For;* Wein, *Myself Among Others.*

NOTES

"I had to scuffle": Dance, *Johnny Hodges,* 22. **Norman Granz devised a face-saving deal:** Granz, oral-history interview. **The band would cut an album for Granz:** John McDonough, "Pablo Patriarch: The Norman Granz Story Part II," *Down Beat,* Nov. 1979.

Around the time that Hodges resumed his chair: Researchers have established that Sam Woodyard joined the band three weeks before Hodges, but both Woodyard and Mercer Ellington recalled in later years that he and Hodges reported for work on the same day, and it is tempting to prefer the legend to the fact (see Dance, *The World of Duke Ellington*, 191, and Ellington, 109). **"Scared":** Dance, *The World of Duke Ellington*, 190. **"Play four bars introduction":** Ibid., 197. **"Get in the alley":** Ibid., 198. **"No crash bang":** *MM*, 227.

"The end of the recent slump": Nat Hentoff, "Duke Ellington: Café Society, New York," *Down Beat*, Mar. 7, 1956. **"Practically reborn":** "Music: The Duke Rides Again," *Time*, Jan. 23, 1956.

"I talked to Edward": Hajdu, 146. **"Mr. Townsend, you're so fortunate":** Ibid. **Prompted by George Avakian:** Morton, 42. **"Having 'Passion Flower' on there":** Hajdu, 149.

"A hideous copy": André Hodeir, "Why Did Ellington 'Remake' His Masterpiece?," in *Reader*, 299.

"No industry buzz on Ellington": Morton, 5–6. **"Look, the festival is making it":** Hajdu, 151.

"Look, we've got to be ready": Cohen, 322.

"Oh, nothing special": Wein, 152. **"You better come in here with something new":** *RIT*, 305. Other sources suggest that this conversation actually took place between DE's two sets on Saturday (see, for instance, Morton, 123). **"Kind of a disaster":** Ibid., 114.

"What are we—the animal act, the acrobats?": Nat Hentoff, "The Duke," *Down Beat*, Jan. 7, 1957.

"After we finish [the suite]": George Avakian, quoted in Morton, 126. **An ad-lib "wailing interval":** For a discussion of the evolution of the wailing interval, see Charles H. Waters, Jr., "Anatomy of a Cover: The Story of Duke Ellington's Appearance on the Cover of *Time* Magazine," *Annual Review of Jazz Studies* (1993).

"Paul, it's the one": Avakian, quoted in Morton, 126.

"He had to change the energy": Ibid., 129. **Gonsalves stepped to the microphone:** In fact he stepped to the wrong microphone, the one with which the Voice of America was taping the performance. As a result his solo was off mike (though clearly audible) on the version of *Diminuendo and Crescendo in Blue* that was later released on *Ellington at Newport* (Morton, 154–55). It was not until Columbia's master tape was synchronized with the VOA recording for the digitally remastered version of *Ellington at Newport* released by Columbia in 1999, resulting in a two-channel stereo recording, that the resulting sonic imbalance was rectified. **"I'd**

never heard a rhythm section like that": Ibid., 190. **"What you and the band played":** Dance, *The World of Duke Ellington*, 173.

"A platinum-blonde girl in a black dress": Avakian, liner notes for *Ellington at Newport*.

"Paul Gonsalves, Jimmy Woode and Sam Woodyard": *MM*, 227.

"Within an hour": Avakian, liner notes for *Ellington at Newport*. **"Magnificent frenzy":** Whitney Balliett, "Jazz at Newport: 1956," *Saturday Review*, July 28, 1956. **An exclusive three-year contract:** According to Townsend, DE's new agreement with Columbia was "a three-year contract at regular royalties with a thousand-dollar advance for each recorded side" (Irving Townsend, "Ellington in Private," *The Atlantic Monthly*, May 1975). It was renewed in 1959. **"I am afraid the music":** Quoted in Morton, 209.

"I wrote this article": Charles H. Waters, Jr., "Anatomy of a Cover." **"I told those guys in 1927":** "Music: Mood Indigo & Beyond," *Time*, Aug. 20, 1956.

"I think it'd be better for you": DE, Harman interview, 1956. **"The event last month":** "Music: Mood Indigo & Beyond."

"At the Palladium in 1933": Jewell, 87.

"Am I late?": Irving Townsend, "Ellington in Private," *The Atlantic Monthly*, May 1975. **"I mean, he made it very clear":** Granz, oral-history interview.

"Rarely were even his closest friends": Townsend, "Ellington in Private." (Except as indicated, "Ellington in Private" is the source for all subsequent quotes from Townsend in this chapter.)

They enlisted BS and John Sanders: Presumably Tom Whaley also took part in the creation of the presentation scores, but Townsend does not mention him.

"I was born in 1956": Jewell, 87. **"He not only doesn't live in the past":** Nat Hentoff, "This Cat Needs No Pulitzer Prize," *The New York Times Magazine*, Sept. 12, 1965, in *Reader*, 367.

"My competitors in the band business": Art Buchwald, "A Chat with the Duke," *Paris Herald Tribune*, n.d. (clipping, EC).

"He's seeing stars again": Hajdu, 153–54.

"It will be the most ambitious thing": Quoted in Hajdu, 158.

DE kept his word to BS: Starting with *A Drum Is a Woman*, all of the Ellington-Strayhorn suites were jointly credited. **"Our largest hunk of collaboration":** Paul Worth, radio interview with DE and BS, 1962; Hajdu, 158. **"It is an allegory":** Townsend, "Ellington in Private."

"A drummer is a skin whipper": Quoted in Hajdu, 158.

"Do whatever the hell you want": Ibid., 161. A black-and-white kinescope: A copy of this kinescope can be viewed at New York's Paley Center for Media.

"Of the big things": Jewell, 96. "Shrilly pretentious": Jack Gould, "TV Review: Jazz Fantasy, 'A Drum Is a Woman,' Staged," *The New York Times*, May 9, 1957. "An almost embarrassingly flimsy affair": Balliett, 17.

"He had everything by Shakespeare": George, 136. "Ellington has always been intrigued": Traill, *Just Jazz 3*, 46.

"We used to call him Shakespeare": Ibid. "We were with literally the top Shakespeare scholars": Ibid., 163. "Clark [Terry] = Puck": van de Leur, 134. Irving Townsend claimed to have found the title: Traill, *Just Jazz 4*, 18.

"All we did is just little thumbnail sketches": Quoted in Jack Chambers, "Bardland: Shakespeare in Ellington's World," *DEMS Bulletin*, Apr.–July 2005.

"Though she was a lady": Townsend, liner notes for *Such Sweet Thunder*. "Half the Fun" and "The Star-Crossed Lovers" were preexisting compositions: "Half the Fun" was previously known as "Lately," while "The Star-Crossed Lovers," whose original title was "Pretty Little Girl," had already been recorded for Verve in 1955 by Johnny Hodges and a small band of Ellington sidemen. (None of the critics who later wrote about *Such Sweet Thunder* seems to have noticed that the song was recycled.) "We were rushed": Traill, *Just Jazz 3*, 46. "We spent two months talking about [*Such Sweet Thunder*]": Chambers, "Bardland." "It was such a straight crowd": Hajdu, 161.

"A long work in the finest Ellington tradition": John S. Wilson, "Jazz: Ellington," *The New York Times*, Oct. 15, 1957. "Uncomfortably thin": Balliett, 43, 44.

Clark Terry "speaks" Puck's line: All currently available compact disc transfers of the complete *Such Sweet Thunder* incorrectly contain an alternate take of "Up and Down, Up and Down" in which this passage is not included. The originally issued take can be heard on *Ralph Ellison: Living with Music*, a companion CD to Ellison's essay collection of the same name (Columbia/Legacy). "Almost as confident": Balliett, 44.

BS went unmentioned in the reviews: His name, for instance, is nowhere to be found in John S. Wilson's *New York Times* review of the Town Hall premiere. DE would not always be so scrupulous in years to come about crediting BS. DE sometimes received full or partial credit for individual pieces that, like the title track of *Blues in Orbit*, were written by BS alone. In addition, BS was often not always properly credited for his work as an arranger of other people's songs (as was the case with the version of "Where or When" included on *Ellington Indigos*). Walter van de Leur's *Something to Live For* documents numerous post-1957 compositions and arrangements for which he did not receive proper credit, a situation that in some cases persists to this day. (It also remains rare for BS to be identified in liner notes as the sole composer of the specific movements that he contributed to the suites on which he and DE "collaborated.") **"Morgen thought that Billy represented competition"**: Hajdu, 167.

"He didn't rehearse me nothin' ": Dance, *The World of Duke Ellington*, 286.

"He was the kind of guy": Kerr, oral-history interview.

"I wouldn't finish anything": *RIT,* 406. **"A panic scene"**: Leonard Feather, "Ella Today (and Yesterday Too)," *Down Beat,* Nov. 18, 1965. **"Ella really was very upset"**: Hajdu, 168.

"Otto chose Duke": Ibid., 188.

BS dubbed James Stewart's on-screen playing: Hajdu, 189.

DE's "consultant": *MM,* 193.

"Music in pictures should say something": Gleason, 185–86.

"There was nothing special": Jewell, 105. **"Struck speechless"**: Ellington, 118. **A single copy of the album was pressed for the queen alone**: In fact, four or five additional "author's copies" of *The Queen's Suite,* one of which is now at the Library of Congress, are believed to have been pressed at the same time. **"I think my liking for Duke"**: Granz, oral-history interview.

"You go to the hotel": "Music: Mood Indigo & Beyond." **"He's a very good man to have along"**: Dance, *The World of Duke Ellington,* 80.

"The three of us were approaching San Francisco": Gordon Parks, "Jazz," *Esquire,* Dec. 1975.

"I just don't have time": Hentoff, "This Cat Needs No Pulitzer Prize," in *Reader,* 365.

"You gotta be older": "Music: Mood Indigo & Beyond." **"I gradually felt drawn to him"**: "Robert Traver" [John Voelker], "Dukie," *Detroit News Sunday Magazine,* Aug. 6, 1967.

The earliest surviving visual document: This important document is available on DVD as *Duke Ellington Live in '58* (Jazz Icons).

"Rockin' in Rhythm": This piece is officially co-credited to Harry Carney, who claimed to have written the minor-key strain, but there is no definitive evidence that he composed any part of it. Barney Bigard later told Max Jones that he and Johnny Hodges wrote "Rockin' in Rhythm." Asked by Jones about Carney's involvement, Bigard replied, "Carney never wrote nothin' in his life" (Jones, 9). **"The idea was for the audience"**: Davis, 9.

"Watch him some night": Hentoff, "This Cat Needs No Pulitzer Prize," in *Reader*, 368.

"Characterize it for me": Martin Richards, "Aaron Bell," *Blue Light: The Newsletter of the Duke Ellington Society (UK)*, Jan.–Mar. 2004.

"During my last couple of years": Nat Hentoff, "The Incompleat Duke Ellington," *Show*, Aug. 1964.

"If he retired for a few years": "Music: Mood Indigo & Beyond."

CHAPTER FIFTEEN
"FATE'S BEING KIND TO ME"

SOURCES

Documents
Cress Courtney, oral-history interview, OHAM; *A Duke Named Ellington*, TV documentary (WNET); "Duke Ellington: A Concert of Sacred Music," *NET Playhouse*, TV program, June 16, 1967 (NET); *The Ed Sullivan Show*, TV program, June 18, 1959 (CBS); *The Ed Sullivan Show*, TV program, June 9, 1968 (CBS); *The Ed Sullivan Show*, TV program, Mar. 1, 1970 (CBS); DE, unpublished interview with Carter Harman, 1964, EC; Betty McGettigan, oral-history interview, OHAM; Joya Sherrill, oral-history interview, EC.

Books
Balliett, *Collected Works;* Barros, *Shall We Play That One Together?;* Bikel, *Theo;* Bradbury, *Duke Ellington;* Cohen, *Duke Ellington's America;* Charles Sam Courtney, *Ignorant Armies;* Dance, *The World of Duke Ellington;* Dunning, *Alvin Ailey;* Ellington, *Duke Ellington in Person;* George, *Sweet Man;* Gordon, *My Unforgettable Jazz Friends;* Hajdu, *Lush Life;* Hohenberg, *The Pulitzer Diaries;* Jewell, *Duke;* Stewart, *Jazz Masters of the Thirties;* Stratemann, *Duke Ellington Day by Day and Film by Film;* Tormé, *It Wasn't All Velvet;* Vail, *Duke's Diary, Part Two;* von Eschen, *Satchmo Blows Up the World.*

NOTES

"A separation from his wife": "Music: Mood Indigo & Beyond," *Time*, Aug. 20, 1956. "His wife, from whom he has been separated": "The Duke of Jazz," *Time*, Feb. 1, 1943. "Unforgivably brusque": Charles H. Waters, Jr., "Anatomy of a Cover: The Story of Duke Ellington's Appearance on the Cover of *Time*

Magazine," *Annual Review of Jazz Studies* (1993). **"The virtually unknown Duchess":** Marc Crawford, "A Visit with Mrs. Duke Ellington," *Ebony,* Mar. 1959.

"The responsibility": DE, Harman interview, 1964. **"Lord knows, we love his music":** "Ellington and the Spingarn," *Los Angeles Tribune,* Sept. 11, 1959.

DE "had so much sex appeal": Barros, 141. **"I became his slave":** George, 141.

"The Countess from Algeria": Charles Sam Courtney, 100. **She was around forty:** Jewell, 105. **"Tall, strikingly handsome":** George, 142. **"An aging woman wearing too much make-up":** Charles Sam Courtney, 100–101.

"She would remain for a set": Ellington, 125.

"She was very much there": George, 193. **"She makes sure I eat all right":** Ibid., 142.

"She did a lot for Edward": Jewell, 105. **"A very cultured woman":** Ibid., 106. **Evie flew to Tokyo:** George, 140.

"The closest thing to a vacation": Stratemann, 441. **"I've never had a vacation":** Nat Hentoff, "The Incompleat Duke Ellington," *Show,* Aug. 1964. **DE had played at the 1934 Academy Awards banquet:** "Academy Acting Awards Go to Hepburn and Laughton," *The Hollywood Reporter,* Mar. 17, 1934. **"A weak, aimless story":** Bosley Crowther, "Screen: A Story of American Jazzmen in France," *The New York Times,* Nov. 8, 1961.

Paul Gonsalves, Ray Nance, Willie Cook, and Fats Ford: "Nab 4 Duke Ellington Bandsmen on Dope Counts," *Jet,* Feb. 23, 1961. **"No, there wasn't":** "Words of the Week," *Jet,* Mar. 2, 1961. **Nance spent two months in jail:** Stratemann, 442. **The band was banned:** Ellington, 132.

"Anatomy for Murder": *The Ed Sullivan Show,* June 18, 1959.

The accountants pulled out their balance sheets: Miles Kreuger, personal communication. (Kreuger was present at the meeting in question.) **"You see the way they can fuck up music?":** Leonard Feather, "Blindfold Test: Miles Davis," *Down Beat,* June 1964.

Sinatra had tried to hire Billy Strayhorn: Hajdu, 218. **"The loudest, swingingest, brassyest":** "Free-Loaders Mill as Frank Sign Ellington," *Billboard,* Dec. 8, 1962. **"New as well as established jazz artists":** DE followed through on this plan for a time, producing albums by Alice Babs, Dollar Brand (now Abdullah Ibrahim), and Bud Powell. **"A *primo* noncomformist *assoluto*":** MM, 249.

"After you heard the record": Dance, 138. **"A kind of a gut-bucket bolero":** DE, interview with Hugh Downs, *The Today Show,* May 26, 1964 (NBC); Vail, 244.

"My name is still on some of the parts": Balliett, 207.

"Staged on Broadway": Donald Freeman, " 'Asphalt Jungle' Theme by Duke Ellington," *The State Journal* (Springfield, IL), Feb. 25, 1961.

"The only people who did good": DE, Harman interview, 1964.

The sit-in won DE praise from black newspapers: See, for example, "Across the Board," *New York Amsterdam News,* Feb. 27, 1960. "I've only got about one minute": "Ellington Plays Down Social Protest in His Musical for Chi's Negro Expo," *Variety,* July 7, 1963.

"I was the lyricist": DE, Harman interview, 1964.

DE "couldn't make up his mind": Dunning, 175. Reprise chose not to tape an original-cast album: *My People* was recorded and released by Contact, an imprint of ABC-Paramount.

"If you have the right kind": Nat Hentoff, "The Durable Duke," *The Reporter,* May 7, 1964. "Duke Ellington's fear of flying": "Flight Fear May Cancel Ellington's Europe Trip," *Billboard,* May 1, 1954. "I slept": "Airborne Duke," *Jet,* Dec. 8, 1960.

"America's secret weapon": Felix Belair, "United States Has Secret Sonic Weapon—Jazz," *The New York Times,* Nov. 6, 1955. "I know damn well sure": DE, Harman interview, 1964. "He was born poor": *MM,* 236. "It's a matter of dignity": DE, Harman interview, 1964.

Ray Nance was sent home: "Nance Leaves Duke's Band Over Tiff with Cootie," *Jet,* Oct. 24, 1963. "The embarrassment and harm": Thomas W. Simons, Jr., memo to US State Department Office of Cultural Presentations, Sept. 17, 1963, quoted in von Eschen, 128. For Nance's side of the story, see Steve Voce, "Ray Nance: Let's Face the Music and . . . ," *Jazz Journal,* Feb. 1998.

DE's "habitual tardiness": Simons, "General Report on the Ellington Tour," US State Department memo, quoted in von Eschen, 140, 142–43.

"It's a hit, man": Charles Sam Courtney, 109. "Jazz concerts might be considered in bad taste": Sally Hammond, "Duke Ellington's Wish: To Play in Honor of JFK," *New York Post,* Dec. 6, 1963.

"Musicians of the past": Dance, 267. DE arranged for steaks to be shipped by air from New York to Russia: Joe Alex Morris, Jr., "Duke Can't Cut It on Russian Steaks," *Los Angeles Times,* Sept. 20, 1971.

The band was paid $19,000 a week in Russia: Harvey G. Cohen, "Visions of Freedom: Duke Ellington in the Soviet Union," *Popular Music,* Sept. 2011. "You let it roll around": Dance, 18. DE privately admitted to finding mode-based non-Western music monotonous: Jewell, 118.

"I knew he'd been off his horn": Jewell, 111. Al Celley had been caught embezzling: Cohen, 366–69. "Going upstream": Ibid.

The band had been blacklisted: McGettigan, oral-history interview. "Here I was in a position": Ellington, 136. DE's own method: Ibid., 168–69. Gonsalves would pretend to be drunk: Ibid. "When I joined the band": Ibid., 139, 137.

A "successful failure": Ibid., 167. "I have to stand out": Jewell, 91. "Ellington was a great bird-in-the-hand guy": Cress Courtney, oral-history interview.

DE played fast and loose with the tax code: For a detailed discussion of his difficulties with the IRS, see Cohen, 372–75, 569–570.

"He has apparently learned to give": Stewart, 88.

"It was no longer a matter": Ellington, 180.

"I like the Beatles": "Duke Ellington Defends Talent of the Beatles," *The Philadelphia Inquirer*, July 26, 1964. "A jazz concerto": *The Ed Sullivan Show*, Mar. 1, 1970. "The young people": Finnish National Broadcasting Company, undated TV clip, c. Oct. 1973, http://www.youtube.com/watch?v=Q9F_hRpwL4M.

"A special citation": Howard Klein, "Ellington Denied Pulitzer Citation," *The New York Times*, May 5, 1965. "Fate's being kind to me": Ibid. This remark was later misquoted by Nat Hentoff as "Fate is being kind to me. Fate doesn't want me to be famous too young" ("This Cat Needs No Pulitzer Prize," *The New York Times Magazine*, Sept. 12, 1965, in *Reader*, 367). It is Hentoff's incorrect version that is more commonly cited today.

"We felt a special citation would be appropriate": William F. Woo, "Another Pulitzer Prize Hassle," *St. Louis Post-Dispatch*, May 13, 1964. "It's *very* too bad": "Very Too Bad," *Newsweek*, May 17, 1965. The recommendation was not taken seriously: Hohenberg, 147.

"Larger forms": Irving Kolodin, "No Duke for 'Duke,'" *Saturday Review*, May 29, 1965.

"I'm hardly surprised": Nat Hentoff, "This Cat Needs No Pulitzer Prize," *The New York Times Magazine*, Sept. 12, 1965, in *Reader*, 363. "If you don't give Duke": Tormé, 230–36.

The same thing happened when DE shared a bill with Mort Sahl: For details of this dispute, see Bradbury, 102.

"Duke Ellington was nowhere to be found": Bikel, 314.

"I'd be afraid": Boyer, "The Hot Bach," 217. He embraced Christianity more purposefully: Ibid., 244.

DE questioned his "eligibility": Quoted in Cohen, 461. **"You can jive with secular music":** M. Cordell Thompson, "Thousands Bid Farewell to Duke," *Jet*, June 13, 1974. **"Totally in [Ellington's] character":** DE, Harman interview, 1964. **"No, we're not going to have a jam session":** "Duke to Do Sacred Music Concert, Sept. 16," *Jet*, Sept. 9, 1965.

"Every man prays in his own language": Quoted in *MM*, 262. **"A lot of it sounded like *Black, Brown and Beige*":** Gordon, 165. This impression was heightened by the "overture" played by the band at the Grace Catherdral premiere, a prelude based on themes from *Black, Brown and Beige* that was cut from later performances.

DE revised the concert: The Grace Cathedral premiere was filmed for TV and subsequently telecast as "Duke Ellington: A Concert of Sacred Music." It is currently available on home video as *Ralph Gleason Celebrates Duke Ellington: Love You Madly / A Concert of Sacred Music at Grace Cathedral* (Eagle Rock). The commercial recording of the concert issued by RCA in 1966, by contrast, incorporates all of DE's revisions.

"It has been said once": *MM*, 262.

"Vintage Ellington": Alan Rich, "Duke Ellington's Music as Prayer," *New York Herald Tribune*, Dec. 27, 1965. **"Mr. Ellington moved carefully":** John S. Wilson, "Duke Ellington Gives Popular Sacred Music Concert," *The New York Times*, Dec. 27, 1965.

Ed Sullivan brought Bunny Briggs and the band onto his program: *The Ed Sullivan Show*, June 9, 1968. **"A type of music":** "Jazz Goes to Church," *Ebony*, Apr. 1966. **"Duke Ellington represents":** John Carmody, "Baptist Ministers Refuse to Endorse the 'Worldly' Music of Duke Ellington," *The Washington Post*, Dec. 1, 1966. **She thought it inappropriate:** Sherrill, oral-history interview.

"She loved life": "Duke Ellington's Duchess," *Jet*, Feb. 2, 1967. **"Evie absolutely expected":** Ellington, 78. **DE told the countess that he was legally married to Evie:** Ibid., 205–6.

"He had his good days": Marian Logan, quoted in Hajdu, 196. **"It's more a matter of morality":** Dance, 30.

"A fruit that only looks like it's alive": Hajdu, 242.

"What to write or how to write": John S. Wilson, "Billy Strayhorn: Alter Ego for the Duke," *The New York Times*, June 6, 1965.

"He wrote his epitaph": Dance, 62. **"After I hung up the phone":** *MM*, 159.

"Duke was sitting by himself": George, 178. **"William Thomas Strayhorn":** *MM*, 159, 161.

CHAPTER SIXTEEN
"THAT BIG YAWNING VOID"

SOURCES

Documents

Alvin Ailey, oral-history interview, OHAM; Harold Ashby, oral-history interview, OHAM; Lawrence Brown, oral-history interview, IJS; Stanley Dance, liner notes for *New Orleans Suite*, sound recording (Atlantic); Stanley Dance, oral-history interview, OHAM; *Duke Ellington 1969: All-Star White House Tribute*, sound recording (Blue Note); *Duke Ellington's 70th Birthday Concert*, sound recording (Solid State); *Duke Ellington—We Love You Madly*, TV program, Feb. 11, 1973 (CBS); DE, unpublished interview with Carter Harman, 1964, EC; Mercer Ellington, oral-history interview, EC; Norman Granz, oral-history interview (EC); Jimmy Jones, oral-history interview, IJS; Quincy Jones, oral-history interview, Archive of American Television, Nov. 13, 2002; Brooks Kerr, oral-history interview, OHAM; Betty McGettigan, oral-history interview, OHAM; "On the Road with Duke Ellington," *The Bell Telephone Hour,* TV program, Oct. 13, 1967 (NBC); Joya Sherrill, oral-history interview, OHAM; *A Tribute to Duke Ellington,* TV program, May 25, 1974 (CBS).

Books

Balliett, *Collected Works;* Cohen, *Duke Ellington's America;* Courtney, *Ignorant Armies;* Dance, *The World of Duke Ellington;* Dietrich, *Duke's 'Bones;* Ellington, *Duke Ellington in Person;* Faine, *Ellington at the White House 1969;* Friedwald, *Sinatra!;* George, *Sweet Man;* Gleason, *Celebrating the Duke;* Granata, *Sessions with Sinatra;* Hajdu, *Lush Life;* Harrison, *The Essential Jazz Records;* Hentoff, *Jazz Is;* Hershorn, *Norman Granz;* Jewell, *Duke;* Mellers, *Music in a New Found Land;* Peress, *Dvořák to Duke Ellington;* Ross, *The Rest Is Noise;* Schuller, *Early Jazz;* Schuller, *Gunther Schuller;* Schuller, *The Swing Era;* Wein, *Myself Among Others.*

NOTES

"I don't have time": George Frazier, "The Sophistication of Duke Ellington," *Esquire,* Dec. 1969. **"I'm writing more than ever now":** Mary Campbell, "Ellington's Newest Album Tribute to Billy Strayhorn," AP wire dispatch, c. June 1968; undated clipping, IJS.

"It has the depth and timbre": Balliett, 281.

"When I got a copy": Ibid., 289.

"We hope that all of our compositions": "On the Road with Duke Ellington."

Sinatra had talked about recording with DE: Friedwald, 302. "That's what I tried to write for": Ibid., 306. "We rehearsed them all afternoon": Ibid., 304. A handful of studio ringers: See Ibid., 306; Jimmy Jones, oral-history interview; and Granata, 189. Surviving union contracts show that Al Porcino and Bill Miller, Sinatra's pianist, were the only other players who were paid for the sessions (Steven Lasker collection).

"I'm really afraid": Hershorn, 318–19.

"I know he spent many despondent hours": Ellington, *Duke Ellington in Person*, 164. "Everyone is so alone": *MM*, 261.

"Mesmerized": Schuller, *Gunther Schuller*, 178. A long essay: Gunther Schuller, "Early Duke," *Jazz Review*, Dec. 1959. "Duke Ellington is one of America's great composers": Schuller, *Early Jazz*, 319.

"Clear, thorough, objective, sophisticated and original": Frank Conroy, "Birth of the Blues," *The New York Times Book Review*, May 12, 1968. "Pre-eminent, if not unique": Mellers, 315.

"You know how it is": Allen Hughes, "Dr. Ellington Sounds Like Same Old Duke," *The New York Times*, Aug. 3, 1967.

"The most important thing": *MM*, 269.

"She sings opera": Ibid., 288. "A composer's dream": Jewell, 136. "Too Good to Title": Dance, *The World of Duke Ellington*, 260.

"I think of myself as a messenger boy": *MM*, 267–68. "Heavenly Heaven to be": Alice Babs appears to sing this line on record as "Heavenly Heaven to me," which makes more sense, but "to be" is the official version (see, for instance, *MM*, 274). Balliett questioned whether DE was putting on his audience: Balliett, 292.

"Duke could have really incorporated him": Granz, oral-history interview.

The idea for the party came from Joe Morgen: Ellington, 186. For a detailed account of the party, see Faine. Nixon decided to give the Medal of Freedom to DE: Leonard Garment, "A New Revelation from the Nixon White House," *The New York Times*, Aug. 25, 2002. "That which our institutions dedicated": Ibid.

"The classic French greeting": Balliett, 306. "Four kisses?": *MM*, 427. "There is no place I would rather be": Dance, *The World of Duke Ellington*, 287.

"I shall pick a name": Faine, 131. (The musical performances were released in 2002 on *Duke Ellington 1969*.)

Russell Procope quit the band briefly: Jimmy Jones, oral-history interview. **"I'm trying to see":** Stanley Dance, oral-history interview. **"During those last horrible days":** Mercer Ellington, oral-history interview.

"Pomade-shiny": Courtney, 101. **"If we keep playing that number":** Jewell, 156. (Jewell incorrectly identifies the number as "One More Once," a different song.)

"Lost all feeling for music": Brown, oral-history interview. **"Never got on the bus":** Sherrill, oral-history interview. **DE knocked out his two front teeth:** Dietrich, 181–82.

Hodges collapsed and died in the men's room: Gleason, 241. **"A fantastic offer":** Granz, oral-history interview. **"Because of this great loss":** *MM*, 119.

"When I was with Duke": Ashby, oral-history interview.

DE "was in the studio": Dance, liner notes for *New Orleans Suite.*

"A rhythmic tone parallel": Ibid. **"Jazz without pretence":** Harrison, 494.

"When that band was really together": Mark Stryker, "Saxophenomenal," *Dayton Daily News,* June 25, 1995. **"I think the band began to fall apart":** Kerr, oral-history interview.

"Thank you very much, ladies and gentlemen": *Duke Ellington's 70th Birthday Concert.*

"I don't have a comic bone in my body": Ailey, oral-history interview. (All quotes from Ailey are from this interview.)

"That rare thing among classic scores": Clive Barnes, "Dance: Unfinished 'River'; Ballet Theater Presents Ellington Work," *The New York Times,* June 26, 1970.

DE died before he could see it danced: Ailey, oral-history interview.

"The section passages . . . are brief but dense": Balliett, 331. (Balliett identifies this piece as "The Falls," the next movement of *The River,* but the description makes it clear that he was in fact listening to "Vortex.")

"He started west on Fifty-sixth Street": Ibid., 332.

"If he stubbed his toe": Nat Hentoff, "The Incompleat Duke Ellington," *Show,* Aug. 1964. **"Arthur, how am I feeling today?":** George, 240. **"There's nothing wrong with Edward":** Ibid., 241. **"Of course, Edward needed Arthur":** Hajdu, 193.

DE had cancer in both lungs: Ellington, *Duke Ellington in Person,* 191–92. (He was ultimately diagnosed with metastatic lymphoma.) **Logan and DE decided to keep his illness secret:** Marian Logan, quoted in Cohen, 562.

"Once the word got around": Peress, 162. **"Clung to the band like a crutch":** Granz, oral-history interview.

An advance of $50,000: Stanley Dance, oral-history interview. **"Pussy freak":** DE, Harman interview, 1964. **"The 'secret' Ellington":** Stanley Slome, "Duke Pulled Punches in His Autobiography, Confidante Stanley Dance Revealed at Ellington '91," http://ellingtonweb.ca/Slome-HowDukePulledPunchesInAutobiography.htm.

"Stanley is well informed": Dance, *The World of Duke Ellington*, ix. **"Hotel stationery, napkins, old sheets of manuscript":** Stanley Dance, oral-history interview. **"Sonny Greer is a big bullshitter":** DE, "Rex Stewart etc.," unpublished note for *MM* (Stanley Dance collection, Yale University).

"In some ways I used to dread": Jewell, 162.

Lisa Drew prodded DE to be more frank: Ibid. **"A mixture of the best and the worst":** George, 237–38. **"We've written the Good Book":** Ellington, *Duke Ellington in Person*, 172. **Doubleday complied with his wishes:** George, 237. The incorrectly printed jackets were used after his death (Ellington, *Duke Ellington in Person*, 172). **"Music is my mistress":** *MM*, 447.

"I could feel that he wasn't going to be here forever": Quincy Jones, oral-history interview. **"You talk too fast":** Finnish National Broadcasting Company, undated TV clip, c. Oct. 1973, http://www.youtube.com/watch?v=Q9F_hRpwL4M. **"I am surrounded by mediocrity":** Ellington, *Duke Ellington in Person*, 170. **"People always want something of me":** McGettigan, oral-history interview.

"I guess I really resented that": Ellington, *Duke Ellington in Person*, 192.

"As the days went on": Mercer Ellington, oral-history interview. **Uncontrollable weeping:** Ellington, *Duke Ellington in Person*, 198. **"I'll never get over this":** Jewell, 224.

"Does he know how sick he is?": Ellington, *Duke Ellington in Person*, 200.

"It's nothing serious": Albin Krebs, "Wilson Sues Two London Papers for Libel; Notes on People," *The New York Times*, Apr. 4, 1974. **Frank Sinatra flew Michael DeBakey to New York:** Bob Udkoff, quoted in *RIT*, 408. **"He had shriveled so much":** George, 253. **"Even though the intense sedation kept him alternating":** Ibid. 141. **DE breathed his last:** Betty McGettigan claimed to have been with him when he died (McGettigan, oral-history interview).

"He appeared to have lost": Gordon Parks, "Jazz," *Esquire*, Dec. 1975. **"He's up there now":** "Duke Ellington's Friends, Great and Small, Pay Their Respects," *The New York Times*, May 26, 1974.

"A word that he consistently rejected": John S. Wilson, "Duke Ellington, a Master of Music, Dies at 75," *The New York Times*, May 25, 1974. **"Never lacking for**

female companionship": "Undefeated Champ," *Time*, June 3, 1974. **A sidebar of tributes:** "Colleagues and Admirers Pay Tribute," *The New York Times*, May 25, 1974.

"The most distinctive single body": "Undefeated Champ." **"His absolute faith in God":** M. Cordell Thompson, "Thousands Bid Farewell to Duke," *Jet*, June 13, 1974.

A half-hour special: *A Tribute to Duke Ellington*.

DE's funeral: Tom Buckley, "Fellow Musicians Among 12,500 at Services for Duke Ellington," *The New York Times*, May 28, 1974. **"I'm not going to live much longer":** George, 258–59.

"I'm just here to bear witness": Hentoff, 38.

"Ellington carved out his own brand": Ross, 169.

"Ellington never fully succeeded": Schuller, *The Swing Era*, 149.

"To the very end": Granz, oral-history interview.

PERMISSIONS

INDEX

Page numbers in *italics* indicate photographs, illustrations, and captions

ABOUT THE AUTHOR

Terry Teachout is the drama critic of *The Wall Street Journal*, the critic-at-large of *Commentary*, and the author of "Sightings," a biweekly column for the Friday *Journal* about the arts each weekday in America. He blogs about the arts at www.terry teachout.com.

Satchmo at the Waldorf, Teachout's first play, was produced in 2012 by Shakespeare & Company of Lenox, Massachusetts; Long Wharf Theatre of New Haven, Connecticut; and Philadelphia's Wilma Theater. He has also written the libretti for three operas by Paul Moravec, *The Letter* (premiered by the Santa Fe Opera), *Danse Russe* (premiered by Philadelphia's Center City Opera Theater), and *The King's Man* (premiered by the Kentucky Opera). His previous books include *Pops: A Life of Louis Armstrong, All in the Dances: A Brief Life of George Balanchine, A Terry Teachout Reader,* and *The Skeptic: A Life of H.L. Mencken.* In 1992, he rediscovered the manuscript of *A Second Mencken Chrestomathy* among Mencken's private papers and edited it for publication. He served on the National Council on the Arts from 2004 to 2010 and was a Guggenheim Fellow for 2012.

Born in Cape Girardeau, Missouri, in 1956, Teachout attended St. John's College, William Jewell College, and the University of Illinois at Urbana-Champaign. From 1975 to 1983 he lived in Kansas City, where he worked as a jazz bassist. He now lives with his wife, Hilary, in New York City and Connecticut.